This guide to the coast path from Bude to Plymouth (288¼ miles) covers the Cornwall section of the 630-mile South-West Coast Path (SWCP) and is the second book in this three-part series. It was based on *Cornwall Coast Path – Bude to Falmouth* originally written by **EDITH SCHOFIELD** and expanded by **HENRY STEDMAN** (right) and **JOEL NEWTON** (far right) who also researched and wrote the two other books in this SWCP series, plus several other Trailblazer guides.

DANIEL MCCROHAN (far right), who updated the 5th edition of this book, returned to Cornwall for this 7th edition. He's a widely published travel writer who has written articles, television scripts, travel apps, and more than 40 guidebooks for both Trailblazer and Lonely Planet to destinations ranging from Chittagong to Chengdu. He lived

in China for more than a decade and specialises in writing about Asia, but he is from the UK, and relishes any opportunity he is given to explore his homeland, particularly if it means another chance to go camping.

Once again Daniel hiked and camped his way along the entire route, accompanied for much of it by his wife, Taotao (above left), and their 11-year-old daughter Yoyo (above centre and on the cover), who has now joined Daniel on more than half a dozen of his Trailblazer trips. Over the years, Daniel has trekked to Everest Base Camp, cycled solo across the Gobi Desert, hiked numerous sections of the Great Wall of China, and travelled by train across Siberia. To keep up with his adventures, track him down on Twitter (@danielmccrohan) or visit 🖥 danielmccrohan.com.

Authors

Cornwall Coast Path (SWCP Part 2)

First edition: 2003, this seventh edition 2022, reprinted with amendments 2023

Publisher Trailblazer Publications
The Old Manse, Tower Rd, Hindhead, Surrey, GU26 6SU, UK ⌨ trailblazer-guides.com

British Library Cataloguing in Publication Data
A catalogue record for this book is available from the British Library

ISBN 978-1-912716-26-5

© **Trailblazer** 2003, 2006, 2009, 2012, 2016, 2019, 2022: Text and maps

Series Editor: Anna Jacomb-Hood   **Editor & layout**: Nicky Slade
Cartography: Nick Hill   **Proof-reading**: Anna Jacomb-Hood   **Index**: Jane Thomas
Photographs (flora): C5 Row 1 right, © Jane Thomas; all others © Bryn Thomas
Photographs (p114): © Philip Thomas   **Additional material**: Patricia Major
All other photographs: © Daniel McCrohan unless otherwise indicated

The maps in this guide were prepared from out-of-Crown-copyright Ordnance Survey maps amended and updated by Trailblazer.

Acknowledgements

Big thanks, and all my love, to Taotao and Yoyo for being not only so supportive but also crazy enough to don their own rucksacks and follow me across Cornwall. I hope the cream teas and ice creams made up for the sore shoulders and aching backs! Huge thanks, too, to my Mum, to Sam and Heidi, and to Dudu, for helping out at home while I was away. I couldn't do these trips without you. A big shout out, too, to all the hikers I met along the way for great company and for being such inspirations, especially India Hicks whose walk raised more than £2000 for Women's Aid Federation, Mike, who was wild camping the entire length of the path at the ripe of old age of 72, and Bibi, who after Cornwall was planning to continue walking... to John o' Groats! Huge thanks also to all the wonderful campsite managers who make coast path walkers feel so welcome by finding space for us even when their campsites are full. Back at Trailblazer HQ, much appreciation to Nicky Slade for editing, to Nick Hill for maps, to Anna Jacomb-Hood for proofreading, and of course to Bryn Thomas for sending me on yet another smashing Trailblazer hike. Last but not least, thank you to all the readers who contacted us with their own coast path tales and tips, including Louise Connell, Christine Evans, Joen Hermans, Chris Horn, Chris Layton, Tim Lewis, David Mallinson, Lena Meyer, Andreas Niedermair, Richard Oliver, Guy De Pauw, Iain Russell, Verena & Thomas Rhyner, Philip Scriver, Stephen Smith, Frances Trenouth, Duncan Whitehead and Jon Wills.

A request

The author and publisher have tried to ensure that this guide is as accurate and up to date as possible. Nevertheless, things change. If you notice any changes or omissions that should be included in the next edition, please contact us at ⌨ info@trailblazer-guides.com. A free copy of the next edition will be sent to persons making a significant contribution.

Warning: coastal and long-distance walking can be dangerous

Please read the notes on when to go (pp13-16) and outdoor safety (pp74-7). Every effort has been made by the author and publisher to ensure that the information contained herein is as accurate and up to date as possible. However, they are unable to accept responsibility for any inconvenience, loss or injury sustained by anyone as a result of the advice and information given in this guide.

Photos – Cover & this page: Trebarwith Strand (Map 12)
Previous page: Hayle Towans (Map 46)   **Overleaf**: Upton Towans (Map 45)

Updated information will be available on: ⌨ **trailblazer-guides.com**

Printed in China; print production by D'Print (☎ +65-6581 3832), Singapore

Cornwall
COAST PATH

SW COAST PATH PART 2 – BUDE TO PLYMOUTH

142 large-scale maps & guides to 81 towns and villages

PLANNING – PLACES TO STAY – PLACES TO EAT

HENRY STEDMAN, JOEL NEWTON &
DANIEL McCROHAN

TRAILBLAZER PUBLICATIONS

Contents

PART 4: ROUTE GUIDE & MAPS

Using this guide 78

APPENDICES

INDEX 339 OVERVIEW MAPS, PROFILES 343

Contents

ABOUT THIS BOOK

This guidebook contains all the information you need. The hard work has been done for you so you can plan your trip without having to consult numerous websites and other books and maps. When you're packed and ready to go, there's comprehensive public transport information to get you to and from the trail and detailed maps (1:20,000) to help you find your way along it. It includes:

● All standards of accommodation with reviews of campsites, camping barns, hostels, B&Bs, pubs/inns, guesthouses and hotels
● Walking companies if you want an organised tour, and baggage-transfer services if you just want your luggage carried
● Suggested itineraries for all types of walkers
● Answers to all your questions: when to go, degree of difficulty, what to pack, and how much the whole walking holiday will cost
● Walking times in both directions and GPS waypoints
● Cafés, pubs, tearooms, takeaways, restaurants and food shops
● Rail, bus & taxi information for all villages and towns on the path
● Street plans of the main towns and villages both on and off the path
● Historical, cultural and geographical background information

---

❏ THIS EDITION AND THE COVID PANDEMIC

This particular edition of the guide was researched at a time when the entire country was just emerging from some pretty tight restrictions. Most of the hotels, cafés, pubs, restaurants, and tourist attractions have now reopened, but some are still offering a more limited service than they were pre-pandemic.

Most **accommodation** is back open, albeit with some changes such as later check-ins and earlier check-outs to allow for extra cleaning.

The majority of **pubs, restaurants and cafés** are open – though some are still operating reduced opening hours or have a limited menu. You may need to book a table in advance.

Most **train** and **bus services** were operating to reduced timetables but should now be back to normal. However, face coverings may still be required on all forms of public transport.

Museums and galleries may require booking (especially for tours) and may also restrict the number of people inside at any one time.

In this book all we can do is record the opening times as they currently stand, or as the owners of the various establishments are predicting they will be by the time this is published. Do forgive us where your experience on the ground contradicts what is written in the book; please email us – **info@trailblazer-guides.com** – so we can add your information to our updates page on the website.

Hopefully, by the time you read this, coronavirus, lockdowns and other ubiquitous words from the last two years will be nothing but a bad memory of a surreal time. And if that's the case, the operating hours of the establishments en route will be back to 'normal'.

For the latest information visit 🖳 gov.uk/coronavirus.

INTRODUCTION

Synonymous with the sea and the sea's wild storms that created its dramatic coastline, Cornwall is a land of magic, myth and legend, of poetic writing and art. Its known history stretches back 5500 years and has witnessed Phoenician traders, pirates, smugglers and shipwrecks, the rise and

This book covers the second section (288¼ miles) of the 630-mile South-West Coast Path

fall of the tin-mining and fishing industries and a growing market in tourism which dates back to the days of Victorian villas built for long summer holidays.

The origins of the coast path lie in Cornwall's smuggling history. By the early 19th century smuggling had become so rife that in 1822 HM Coastguard was formed to patrol the entire British coastline. A coast-hugging footpath was created to enable the coastguards to see into every cove, inlet and creek and slowly but surely law and order prevailed and the smuggling decreased. By the beginning of the 20th century the foot patrols had been abandoned.

Walking the coast path is one of the best ways to experience fully the sights and sounds that make Cornwall unique and special. As well as the sheer physical pleasure of walking, the sea breeze in your hair, the taste of the salt spray on your lips, you are treated to the most beautiful and spectacular views of this beguiling and some-

The harbour at St Ives. The town became popular with artists in the 1920s and is now the home of Tate St Ives.

times hazardous coastline. The sky and the light change with the movement of even the smallest cloud over the sea that lies ultramarine and translucent on long hot summer days but becomes leaden and silver with mountainous white-crested waves in sudden storms. Watch for the seals that fool you by swimming under water for long periods, then bob up just when you'd thought they'd gone. You might see dolphins, too, or even a basking shark.

The Cornish coast is a holiday paradise that's easily accessible, where you'll enjoy some of the finest coastal walking Britain has to offer

Walking allows you flexibility over the distances you want to cover, your speed depending on your level of fitness. You can be completely independent, carrying all the basics of life – food, shelter and clothes – on your back, or book B&Bs ahead and walk with the knowledge that your creature comforts, hot baths and comfortable beds, will be waiting for you at the end of the day.

As for rest stops, you'll be tempted time and time again. Explore quintessentially Cornish fishing villages or take a quick break on the Isles of Scilly. Try to identify some of Cornwall's profusion of wildflowers. Look into the little rock pools that are so full of life. Immerse yourself in contemporary art in St Ives. Investigate tin-mining history in a landscape so important that it has been

(Below): There are several ferries, some just little boats, which you can use to get across rivers blocking the route. This is the Fern Pit ferry which crosses the Gannel (see p137).

declared a World Heritage Site. Try surfing or simply take a swim to cool off on a hot day.

For food, feast on Cornish pasties and crab sandwiches as you picnic on a clifftop or beach; in picturesque cottage tearooms gorge on scones piled high with strawberry jam and clotted cream. Above all eat fish fresh from the sea, superb shellfish, lobster, crab and scallops. As well as ubiquitous fish and chip shops and beach cafés there are several top-class seafood restaurants in Cornwall, some run by celebrity chefs; Rick Stein has been in Padstow for many years and more recently Paul Ainsworth, Nathan Outlaw and Michael Caines have opened restaurants in Cornwall.

The Cornish coast is a holiday paradise that's easily accessible, where you'll enjoy some of the finest coastal walking Britain has to offer.

There will be numerous chances every day to indulge in a cream tea. It's said that Cornish people will put the jam on first and the clotted cream on top of it whereas in Devon they do it the other way around. We say whatever floats your boat is fine.

❏ THE SOUTH-WEST COAST PATH

Typing 'Minehead to Poole Harbour, Dorset' into Google Maps reveals that travelling between the two can be completed in a matter of 2½ hours by car, along a distance of 98.1 miles. Even walking, along the most direct route, takes only around 28 hours, so Google Maps says, with the path an even shorter one at just 88.2 miles.

It is these two points that are connected by the South-West Coast Path (SWCP). This most famous – and infamous – of national trails is, however, a good deal longer than 88.2 miles. Though estimates as to its exact length vary – and to a large part are determined by which of the alternative paths one takes at various stages along the trail – the most widely accepted estimate of the path is that it is about 630 miles long (1014km). That figure, however, often changes due to necessary changes in the path caused by erosion and other factors.

So why, when you could walk from Minehead to South Haven Point in just 28 hours, do most people choose to take 6-8 weeks? The answer is simple: the SWCP is one of the most beautiful trails in the UK. Around 70% of those 630 miles are spent either in national parks, or regions designated as Areas of Outstanding Natural Beauty. The variety of places crossed by the SWCP is extraordinary too: from sun-kissed beaches to sandy burrows, holiday parks to fishing harbours, esplanade to estuary, on top of windswept cliffs and under woodland canopy, the scenery that one travels through along the length of the SWCP has to be the most diverse of any of the national trails.

(cont'd overleaf)

INTRODUCTION

❏ THE SOUTH-WEST COAST PATH (cont'd from p9)

Of course, maintaining such a monumental route is no easy task. A survey in 2000 stated that the trail boasted 2473 signposts and waymarks, 302 bridges, 921 stiles, and 26,719 steps. Although out of date now, these figures do still give an idea of both how long the trail is, and how much is involved in building and maintaining it to such a high standard. The task of looking after the trail falls to a dedicated team from the official body, Natural England. Another particularly important organisation and one that looks after the rights of walkers is the South West Coast Path Association (see p46), a charity that fights for improvements to the path and offers advice, information and support to walkers. They also campaign against many of the proposed changes to the path, and help to ensure that England's right-of-way laws which ensure that the footpath is open to the public – even though it does, on occasion, pass through private property – are fully observed.

History of the path

In 1948 a government report recommended the creation of a footpath around the entire South-West peninsula to improve public access to the coast which, at that time, was pretty dire. It took until 1973 for the Cornwall Coast Path to be declared officially open and another five years for the rest of the South-West Coast Path to be completed. The last section to be completed, the North Devon and Exmoor stretch, is the first part that most coastal walkers tackle, though it was actually the last section to be opened to the public, in 1978.

   The origins of the path, however, are much older than its official designation. Originally, the paths were established – or at least adopted, there presumably being coastal paths from time immemorial that connected the coastal villages – by the local coastguard in the nineteenth century, who needed a path that hugged the shoreline closely to aid them in their attempts to spot and prevent smugglers from bringing contraband into the country. The coastguards were unpopular in the area as they prevented the locals from exploiting a lucrative if illegal activity, to the extent that it was considered too dangerous for them to stay in the villages; as a result, the authorities were obliged to build special cottages for the coastguards that stood (and, often, still stand) in splendid isolation near the path – but well away from the villages.

   The lifeboat patrols also used the path to look out for craft in distress (and on one famous occasion used the path to drag their boat to a safe launch to rescue a floundering ship). When the coastguards' work ended in 1856, the Admiralty took over the task of protecting England's shoreline and thus the paths continued to be used.

The route – Minehead (Somerset) to Poole Harbour (Dorset)

The SWCP officially begins at Minehead in Somerset (its exact starting point marked by a sculpture that celebrates the trail), heads west right round the bottom south-west corner of Britain then shuffles back along the south coast to South Haven Point, overlooking Poole Harbour in Dorset. On its lengthy journey around Britain's south-western corner the SWCP crosses national parks such as Exmoor as well as regions that have been designated as Areas of Outstanding Natural Beauty (including North, South and East Devon AONB and the Cornwall and Dorset AONBs), or Sites of Special Scientific Interest (Braunton Burrows being just one example – an area that also enjoys a privileged status as a UNESCO Biosphere Reserve), and even a couple of UNESCO World Heritage sites, too, including the Jurassic Coast of East Devon and Dorset and the old mining landscape of Cornwall and West Devon. Other features passed on the way include the highest cliffs on mainland

How difficult is the path?

The South-West Coast Path (SWCP) is just a (very, very) long walk, so there's no need for crampons, ropes, ice axes, oxygen bottles or any other climbing paraphernalia. All you need to complete the walk is some suitable clothing, a bit of money, a rucksack full of determination and a half-decent pair of calf muscles.

No great level of experience is needed to walk the Cornwall section of the coast path as the walking is generally easy and you are never far from help. Villages and accommodation are reasonably close together so it is simple to adapt itineraries to suit all needs and levels of fitness.

Amongst the most challenging sections of the coast path in Cornwall are the stretches between Widemouth Bay and Crackington Haven, and between Port Isaac and Port Quin where the path never seems to be level, the difficult terrain from St Ives to Sennen Cove and the relentlessly steep undulations that immediately precede Polperro. However, as long as you plan ahead and are reasonably fit you should not experience difficulties on any of these stretches.

Britain (at Great Hangman – also the highest point on the coast path at 318m/1043ft, with a cliff-face of 244m), the largest sand-dune system in England (at Braunton Burrows), England's most westerly point (at Land's End) and Britain's most southerly (at the Lizard), the 18-mile barrier beach of Chesil Bank, one of the world's largest natural harbours at Poole, and even the National Trust's only official nudist beach at Studland! The path then ends at South Haven Point, its exact finish marked by a second SWCP sculpture. The path also takes in four counties – Somerset, Devon, Cornwall and Dorset – and connects with over fifteen other long-distance trails; the southern section from Plymouth to Poole also forms part of the 3125-mile long European E9 Coastal Path that runs on a convoluted route from Portugal to Estonia.

Walking the South-West Coast Path

In terms of difficulty, there are those people who, having never undertaken such a trail before, are under the illusion that coastal walking is a cinch; that all it involves is a simple stroll along mile after mile of golden, level beach, the walker needing to pause only to kick the sand out from his or her flipflop or buy another ice cream.

The truth, of course, is somewhat different, for coastal paths tend to stick to the cliffs above the beaches rather than the beaches themselves (which is actually something of a relief, given how hard it is to walk across sand or shingle). These cliffs make for some spectacular walking but – given the undulating nature of Britain's coastline, and the fact the course of the SWCP inevitably crosses innumerable river valleys, each of which forces the walker to descend rapidly before climbing back up again almost immediately afterwards – some exhausting walking too. Indeed, it has been estimated that anybody who completes the entire SWCP will have climbed more than four times the height of Everest (35,031m to be precise, or 114,931ft) by the time they finish!

Given these figures, it is perhaps hardly surprising that most people take around eight weeks to complete the whole route, and few do so in one go; indeed, it is not unusual for people to take years or even decades to complete the whole path, taking a week or two here and there to tackle various sections until the whole trail is completed.

There are glorious views from many of the campsites, such as this one at Trewethett Farm (Map 10).

Other points to bear in mind are basically common sense: don't wander too close to either the top or bottom of cliffs; take care when swimming; be aware of the tides; and listen to weather forecasts. Your greatest danger on the walk is likely to be from the weather, which can be so unpredictable in this corner of the world, so it is vital that you dress for inclement conditions and always carry a set of dry clothes with you.

How long do you need?

If you're a fit walker who isn't carrying too much and who loves to spend all day on the trail you could manage Bude to Plymouth, or vice versa, a distance of around 288¼ miles (464km) depending on your exact route, in about 20 days. There's nothing wrong with this approach, of course. However, **what you mustn't do is try to push yourself too fast, or too far**. That road leads only to exhaustion, injury or, at the absolute least, an unpleasant time.

A fit walker could manage Bude to Plymouth in about 20 days ... but most walkers take roughly three and a half weeks

If you like your walking holiday to be a bit more relaxed with time to sit on the cliff tops, explore towns and villages, laze in the sun on the beaches, scoff scones in tearooms, visit an attraction or two, or sup local beers under the shade of a pub parasol – as well as have a few rest days – then you'll need to set aside at least one month. Most walkers will fit somewhere between these two extremes, taking roughly three and a half weeks which still allows time for exploring and one or two rest days.

When deciding how long to allow for the walk, those intending to **camp** and carry their own luggage shouldn't underestimate just how much a heavy pack can slow them down. For walkers with less time on their hands there are some superb day and weekend walks (see pp39-40) along parts of the coast path.

See pp36-8 for some suggested itineraries covering different walking speeds

The practical information in this section will help you plan an excellent walk, covering every detail from what you need to do before you leave home to designing an itinerary to meet your particular preferences. More detailed information about the day-to-day walking and towns and villages along the trail can be found in **Part 4**.

When to go

SEASONS

'My shoes are clean from walking in the rain.' **Jack Kerouac**

The decision of when to go may be out of your hands. However, if you are in a position to choose which time of the year to go, make your plans carefully. Do you prefer the vibrant colours of springtime wildflowers, or the rich tones of autumnal foliage and heather? Do you want weather warm enough for swimming? Do you like the buzz of big crowds, or do you prefer to walk in solitude? The following information should help you decide when is best for you.

Spring and early summer
April, **May** and **June** are possibly the best months to go walking in Cornwall. The weather is warm enough without being too hot, the days are getting longer, the holiday crowds have yet to arrive and this is usually the driest time of the year. Perhaps the most beautiful advantage is the abundance of wildflowers which reach their peak in May. Cornwall starts to get busier in June as by now the sun is making an average appearance of seven hours a day.

April, May and June are possibly the best months to go walking in Cornwall

Summer
July and **August** are the hottest months and also the busiest. This is the time of the school summer holidays when families and holidaymakers flock in their thousands to Cornwall. Demand for accommodation is high, particularly in August, and many B&B owners and some campsites will only take bookings of at least two nights if not a full week. Surprisingly most of the coast path itself is not that busy, but you'll encounter the crowds at

(**Right**): The ruined engine house of Wheal Coates, an old tin mine (Map 37). You'll see evidence of the once great Cornish tin mining industry (see p180) in several places along the coast.

You'll pass numerous old harbours, some still quite busy such as here at Mevagissey.

beaches, car parks and in towns, especially if the sun is out. The weather is generally good in July, although during particularly settled periods it can be very hot for walking. August can be wetter and overcast.

Autumn

September is often a wonderful month for walking. The days are still long, the temperature has not dropped noticeably and the summer crowds have long disappeared. The first signs of winter will be felt in **October** but there's nothing really to deter the walker. In fact there's still much to entice you, such as the colours of the heathland, which come into their own in autumn; a magnificent blaze of brilliant purples and pinks, splashed with the yellow flowers of gorse.

Winter

November can bring crisp clear days which are ideal for walking, although you'll definitely feel the chill when you stop on the cliff tops for a break. Winter temperatures rarely fall below freezing but the incidence of gales and storms definitely increases. You need to be fairly hardy to walk in **December** and **January** and you may have to alter your plans because of the weather. By **February** the daffodils and primroses are already appearing but even into **March** it can still be decidedly chilly if the sun is not out.

While winter is definitely the low season with many places closed, this can be more of an advantage than a disadvantage. Very few people walk at this time of year, giving you long stretches of the trail to yourself. When you do stumble across other walkers they are as happy as you to stop and chat. Finding B&B accommodation is easier as you will rarely have to book more than a night ahead (though it is still worth checking in advance as some B&Bs close out of season), but if you are camping, or on a small budget, you will find places to stay much more limited. Few campsites bother to stay open all year and many hostels will be closed.

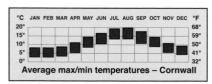

Average max/min temperatures – Cornwall

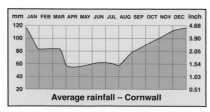

Average rainfall – Cornwall

WEATHER

The Cornish climate is considerably milder than that of the rest of

Britain because of its southerly location and the influence of the Gulf Stream. Winter **temperatures** rarely fall below freezing and the mean maximum in summer is around 19°C. Sea temperatures range from about 9°C in February to about 17°C in August.

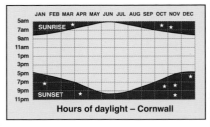

Hours of daylight – Cornwall

Rainfall is highest in the winter due to the regular procession of weather fronts moving east across the Atlantic. In the summer these fronts are weaker, less frequent and take a more northerly track.

Mean **wind speeds** are force 3-4 in summer and 4-5 in winter. Gales can be expected around ten days per month between December and February and less than one day per month from May to August.

DAYLIGHT HOURS

If you are walking in autumn, winter or early spring you must take into account how far you can walk in the available light. It may not be possible to cover as many miles as you would in the summer.

The sunrise and sunset times in the table are based on information for the town of Penzance on the 15th of each month. This gives a rough picture for the rest of Cornwall. Please also bear in mind that you will get a further 30-45 minutes of usable light before sunrise and after sunset depending on the weather.

❏ FESTIVALS AND ANNUAL EVENTS

Passing through a town or village in the middle of a festival or major event can provide a great atmosphere and give you an opportunity to join in the fun. However, if you unknowingly walk into a town heaving with people you may find it more of a headache when searching for accommodation. The events and festivities listed normally take place every year, though the dates may vary slightly, but do double check before you arrive to see if the festival you're trying to visit (or avoid) is still going ahead when you're here. You can visit the festival's website or Facebook page (indicated by **fb**), or see 🖥 visitcornwall.com/whats-on.

In addition to the events listed below, you are also likely to come across bands or groups of singers performing in pubs or in the open air in the main season in Cornwall. Be prepared to join in the Floral Dance if you are lucky enough to be in a village on the right evening.

March to May
- **St Piran's Day (5 March)** Festivities held throughout Cornwall (see box p144).
- **Giant Bolster Festival (May Day Bank Holiday)**, **St Agnes** Re-enactment of the legend of the Giant Bolster culminating in a torchlight procession of giant puppets to the cliff top (above Chapel Porth beach) where the wicked giant was tricked into killing himself whilst proving his love for Agnes.
- **'Obby 'Oss Day (May Day Bank Holiday)**, **Padstow** Festivities and procession as the hobby horse (see box p120) dances through the town. *(cont'd overleaf)*

❏ FESTIVALS AND ANNUAL EVENTS   *(cont'd from p15)*

June to August

● **Polperro Festival (mid June)** Nine days of events including comedy, live music and a fun-run for any walkers tempted by a jog! (**fb**)

● **Golowan (mid to late June), Penzance** Celebration of the midsummer Feast of St John and of west Cornwall's ancient Celtic traditions. Film, theatre, dance, music and a colourful, lively street procession (🖳 golowanfestival.org, **fb**).

● **Mevagissey Feast Week (late June)** Mevagissey adopted St Peter as its patron saint in 1752 and since then has always held a festival to celebrate the saint's day of 29 June. Considered the longest-running festival in Cornwall, it is a volunteer-run blend of traditional and modern events (🖳 mevagisseyfeastweek.org.uk, **fb**).

● **Lafrowda Festival (mid July), St Just** A week-long culture and music festival with all kinds of music. (🖳 lafrowda.co.uk, **fb**).

● **St Ives Biathlon (June/July)** An annual event that involves running along the coast path from St Ives to Carbis Bay then swimming back.

● **Padstow Carnival Week (end July)** Various events throughout the town and a carnival parade at the end of the week.

● **Hayle Heritage Festival (late July to early August)** Events include a summer art show, horticultural show, Old Cornwall Society exhibition, traditional music and dancing, and Cornish wrestling.

● **Camel Sailing Week (early August)** Major regatta on the Camel Estuary.

● **Falmouth Classics and Regatta Week (first two weeks in August)** The highlight of Falmouth's sailing season catering for every class of boat including traditional classic yachts (🖳 www.falmouthweek.co.uk, **fb**).

● **Ocean City Blues N Jazz Festival, Plymouth (early August)** Free, weekend-long, live-music festival that see dozens of local jazz bands and blues singers perform on a stage set up on The Parade, the cobbled area behind The Ship pub in The Barbican.

● **The British Firework Championships (mid August), The Hoe, Plymouth** Two-night contest between professional fireworks companies (🖳 britishfireworks.co.uk).

● **Bude Jazz Festival (last week of August), Bude** Eight days of jazz in 20 venues around the town (🖳 jazzfestivalbude.co.uk).

● **Newlyn Fish Festival (August bank holiday weekend)** The harbour is crammed with boats and the market filled with stalls, cookery demonstrations and entertainment.

September to December

● **St Ives September Festival of Music and Art (mid September)** 15-day extravaganza of music and arts, from classical music to jazz and folk, plus comedy, theatre and poetry (🖳 stivesseptemberfestival.co.uk, **fb**).

● **Looe Live (mid September)** A three-day music festival that is held in various venues in the fishing town of Looe over a weekend in September (🖳 looelive.co.uk, **fb**).

.● **Falmouth Oyster Festival and Fresh Seafood Week (mid October)** Celebrates one of the only remaining oyster fisheries still dredging under sail and oar. A must for lovers of the exquisite bivalve (see 🖳 falmouthoysterfestival.co.uk, **fb**).

● **Lowender Peran Celtic Festival (mid to late October), Hotel Bristol, Newquay** Celtic singing and dancing for all to join in with, held in various function rooms in the hotel on Narrow Cliff, above Tolcarne Beach (🖳 lowenderperan.co.uk, **fb**).

● **Tom Bawcock's Eve (23 December), Mousehole** In memory of a fisherman who put out to sea in a storm so that the starving population would not have a hungry Christmas. The event is celebrated with a carol concert, a torchlit procession and the consumption of an enormous stargazy pie (see p23).

(Opposite): Watergate Bay (Map 28)

Top, **left**: An impressive suspension bridge linking the two sections of King Arthur's Castle at Tintagel (p98) was opened in 2019. **Top**, **right**: Some of those climbs are tough with a heavy pack. **Above**, **left**: Tintagel's YHA (p100) is in an enviable location at Dunderhole Point. **Above**, **right**: Quirky Cornish architecture in Boscastle. **Left**: Crossing Harbour Cove (Map 21), near Padstow. **Below**: The Black Tor Ferry (p117), between Padstow (seen in the background) and Rock.

Right, top: Padstow lifeboat station was moved to its current location near Trevose Head (Map 24), in 1967. **Bottom**: Holywell Bay (Map 33).

Above: Looking south over
Bedruthan Steps (Map 26).

Right: Cape Cornwall
(Map 58, p182).

Left, **top**: The 19th century daymark,
known as the Pepperpot, overlooking
Portreath Beach (Map 40).
Centre: Wild poppies above the
sweeping beach at Fistral Sands,
Newquay (Map 30).
Bottom: The Mermaid's Chair in
Zennor's Church of St Senara (p172).

Left: The tiny settlement at Penberth Cove (Map 64). **Far left**: Red hot poker display below St Michael's Mount (Map 72; © H Stedman). **Left**, **bottom**: Soaking up the view over Parc Bean Cove (Map 83).

This page, **above**: St Mawes Castle (Map 101a). **Right**: Falmouth to St Mawes ferry (p254). **Below**: Strolling round Rame Head (Map 128). **Bottom left**: The 15th century chapel (p308) at Rame Head. **Bottom right**: The Cremyll Ferry (p310); Plymouth in the background.

PLANNING YOUR WALK

1

Practical information for the walker

ROUTE FINDING

For most of its length the coast path is well signposted. At confusing junctions the route is usually indicated by a finger-post sign with 'coast path' written on it. At other points, where there could be some confusion, there are wooden waymark posts with an acorn symbol and a yellow arrow to indicate in which direction you should head. The waymarking is the responsibility of the local authorities along the trail who have a duty to maintain the path. Generally they do a good job although occasionally you'll come across sections of the trail where waymarking is ambiguous, or even non-existent, but with the detailed route maps and directions in this book and the fact that you always have the sea to one side it would be hard to get really lost.

Using GPS with this book

If you have a handheld **GPS receiver**, or GPS on your **smartphone**, you can take advantage of the waypoints marked on the maps and listed on pp330-5 of this book. Essentially a GPS (Global Positioning System) will calculate your position on the earth using a number of satellites and this will be accurate to a few metres. Some units may come with inbuilt mapping, but while it's possible to buy **digital mapping** (see p47) to import into a regular GPS unit or smartphone, it might be considered about as practical as having internet on a mobile phone – you still end up scrolling and zooming across a tiny screen.

Having said this, it is **by no means necessary** that you use a GPS in conjunction with this guide and you should be able to get by with simply the signposts on the trail and the maps in this book. However, a GPS can be useful if for some reason you do get lost, or if you decide to explore off the trail and can't find your way back. It can also prove handy if you find yourself on the trail after dark when you can't see further than your torch beam. If you do decide to use a GPS unit in conjunction with this book don't feel you need to be ticking off every waypoint as you reach it; you'll soon get bored. You should easily get by without turning on your GPS.

Opposite: Mawgan Porth beach (Map 27) from the coast path.

You can either manually key the nearest presumed waypoint from the list in this book into your unit as and when the need arises or, much less laboriously and with less margin for keystroke error, download the complete list (but not the descriptions) for free as a GPS-readable file from the Trailblazer website. You'll need the right cable and adequate memory in your unit (typically the ability to store 500 waypoints or more). This file, as well as instructions on how to interpret an OS grid reference, can be found on the Trailblazer website (🖳 trailblazer-guides.com). See p47 for more on digital mapping.

ACCOMMODATION

There are plenty of places to stay all along the Cornwall Coast Path. It is always a good idea to book your accommodation in advance (see box p22), or at least phone ahead. National holidays and any major festivals and events (see pp15-16) are likely to fill up the available accommodation quite quickly so make sure you are aware of what is taking place in the region.

Camping

Camping can be good fun; modern tents are easy to erect and light, so carrying everything on your back need not be burdensome and will enable you to experience a greater sense of independence.

Most **campsites** are only open from Easter to October so camping in winter is not really practical (unless you're wild camping). You'll find an enormous range of sites from a simple field on a farm with a toilet, shower and little else, to huge caravan and camping parks with restaurants, shops and swimming pools.

Prices range from £5 to about £15 per person and reach their peak in July and August when they can increase to as much as £20-25 per person. Note, prices are sometimes per pitch, which assumes two sharing a tent, so single hikers can end up paying more than normal. It's not generally necessary to book camping pitches in advance (in fact at some campsites it's not even possible), and you will sometimes find that the cheaper walker/backpacker rate is not available online anyway. Many campsites try to find space for coast path walkers even if the campsite is officially full so always call ahead in the morning to tell a campsite that you're planning to arrive that evening, and always tell them that you're a walker, hiking the coast path, and they'll normally find a space for you.

Officially, the coast path is not really suited to **wild camping**. If you want to camp wild you should, in theory, ask permission from the landowner, but it isn't always easy finding out who that is; you may find yourself trudging along miles of country lanes only to be told 'no'. Also, much of the coastline is owned by the National Trust who do not allow wild camping on their land. However, there will always be independent-minded souls who put up their tent as the spirit moves them. By pitching late in the day and leaving before anyone else is up, it is unlikely that you will be noticed.

Hostels

There is a reasonable scattering of hostels along the coast path providing budget accommodation for £15-25 per person per night (less for under 18s), usually in dormitories, although many now have private rooms available too. There are two types of hostels: **YHA hostels**, which are part of the Youth Hostel Association/Hostelling International (YHA/HI; see box below), and **independent hostels**, also referred to as backpacker hostels, which are independently owned. If you are planning to stay in hostels as often as possible you will have to make use of both types. Note, in almost all cases, **hostels require guests to show some form of photo ID when they check in**. A photocopy will suffice.

Hostels are not just for young travellers, the young at heart will be more than welcome at most places. In fact the YHA positively encourage conservation-minded older people who are an important market sector for them. If you find large groups of young people intimidating, you can always check if the hostel has any private rooms (this may be advisable in party towns such as Newquay, for example). Note, many independent hostels' dorms are mixed-sex, although some have single-sex dorms too. YHA dorms are always single-sex and adults only.

One of the big advantages of staying in a hostel, aside from a cheap bed, is the option to cook your own food. Most hostels provide **well-equipped kitchens** and all they ask is that you clean up after yourself. There's also no need to carry a sleeping bag. All hostels recommended in this guide provide linen and may not even allow you to use your own sleeping bag. The YHA hostels are particularly clean and well equipped. Note that hostels very rarely provide towels (sometimes these can be bought or rented at reception).

In some cases **camping** is available at YHA hostels for around £15 per tent per night, and campers can use the hostel's facilities.

Unfortunately, hostels aren't numerous enough or sufficiently well spaced to provide accommodation for every night of your walk so you will have to stay in B&Bs or use campsites on several nights, too. The long stretch between Falmouth and Plymouth is particularly barren with only one hostel (at Boswinger, near Gorran Haven).

Most YHA hostels (but not independent hostels) are open only for group bookings between November and March; however, check the YHA website for the latest details.

❏ YOUTH HOSTEL ASSOCIATION (YHA)

You can join the YHA (☎ 0800-019 1700, ☎ 01629-592700, 💻 yha.org.uk) direct or at any hostel. However, you don't need to be a youth to stay in a YHA hostel. Nor do you need to be a member.

The annual membership fee is £20 (£15 if you pay by direct debit). If you are a member you get 10% off your entire booking (including food). Furthermore, a member can book for a group of up to 16 people, and the whole group will get the discount as long as the member is part of that group (they check ID). Should at least one person be under-26 you will get a further 5% off the entire booking. As part of your membership you get a digital version of the YHA handbook.

If you are from a country other than Britain the equivalent organisation is Hostelling International; their website (💻 www.hihostels.com) has lists of each country's contact details. HI cards are accepted at all YHA hostels in Britain.

Bed and breakfast (B&B) accommodation

B&Bs are a great British institution: for anyone unfamiliar with the concept you get a bedroom in someone's home along with a cooked breakfast the following morning; in many ways it is like being a guest of the family. However, the term B&B can apply equally to a night in someone's back bedroom in a suburban bungalow to one in a cliff-top farmhouse where every need is catered for, from a choice of herbal teas to free shampoos in the bathroom. It is an ideal way to walk in Cornwall as you can travel without too much clobber and relax in the evening in pleasant surroundings with the benefit of conversation with the proprietor. If you are struggling to find a room you could try **Airbnb** (🖳 airbnb .co.uk) but check carefully what you will be getting – standards can vary widely as these informal accommodation providers are unregulated.

Putting up at an **inn** (or pub) is a British tradition that goes back centuries and still appeals to many walkers. However, just because it's called an inn there's no guarantee of old oak beams and a roaring log fire. Although there are some delightful traditional pubs, many places have been refurbished and have lost some of their character and charm. The biggest advantage of staying at an inn is convenience. Accommodation, meals and a bar are all provided under the same roof. If you've had a few too many pints of wonderful Cornish ale you don't have far to stagger home at closing time. On the other hand if you want an early night you may find the noise from the bar keeps you awake.

Guesthouses are often larger Victorian or Edwardian houses with rooms made en suite, filling the gap between B&Bs and hotels, although they may still be referred to as B&Bs. They are sometimes less personal and more expensive (£40-50 per person) but do offer more space and a lounge for guests. They are usually more geared to coping with holiday-makers and their owners are experienced in the hospitality trade, employing staff – if only young locals – to come in to do the bedrooms. They often take payment by credit and debit card without quibble.

Most **hotels** along the coast are classier and more expensive than the above and therefore put many walkers off. The other problem for the walker is having suitably smart clothes to wear in the evening, unless of course, you have the panache to carry off designer fleece and walking boots in the restaurant. Once in a while you may feel you deserve a treat and at the end of a long day that Jacuzzi could be well worth paying extra for!

In general, hotels do not pay walkers any particular attention. They are simply one more guest who, if anything, requires rather more than the average guest when they arrive with pack, heavy boots and sometimes wet gear.

What to expect For the long-distance walker tourist-board recommendations and star-rating systems may be a starting point although by no means all the places on or near the Coast Path are registered. Many walkers rely on the tourist information centres to book their next night's lodging for them. There are numerous guides listing Best Places to Stay and it can be difficult to choose especially in places like St Ives and Penzance which are practically wall-to-wall with guesthouses. Bear in mind that walkers are only one of the many types of people on holiday and B&Bs are not there purely for our benefit. At the end of a long day you will simply be glad of a hot bath or shower and clean bed to lie down on. If they have somewhere to hang your wet and muddy clothes so much the better. It is these criteria that have been used for places included in this guide – televisions and tea- and coffee-making facilities are more or less standard these days.

Wi-fi is now generally the norm, although rural broadband speeds may be slow, and some older properties run by elderly hosts may not have it at all.

Bed and breakfast owners may proclaim that all rooms are **en suite** but this could be just a small shower and loo cubicle in the corner of the bedroom. Establishments without en suite rooms can be just as satisfactory as you may get sole use of a larger bathroom across the corridor and a hot bath is just what you need after a hard day on the trail, so accommodation descriptions indicate where a bath is available. Rooms without en suite facilities are generally cheaper.

Single rooms are sometimes rather cramped 'box' rooms with barely enough room for the bed which can be restricting if you are travelling with quite a big pack. **Twin** rooms have two single beds, while a **double** is supposed to have one double bed, although just to confuse things, twins are sometimes called doubles because the beds can be moved together to make a 'double' bed. This can lead to awkward moments so it is best to specify if you prefer two single beds. Some establishments have **family** rooms, which sleep three or more, although to confuse matters even further, others call these **triple** rooms and may also have a family room sleeping four people (**quad**) or more.

Some B&Bs provide an **evening meal**, particularly if there is no pub or restaurant nearby. Others may offer you a lift to a local eatery, while some will expect you to make your own arrangements. Check the situation when you book.

All accommodation listed should be open year-round (unless stated otherwise). Remember, however, that B&B owners can, and do, change their minds at a moment's notice, deciding to redecorate when it's quiet, or closing the business when they want to go away on holiday.

Smoking in enclosed public spaces is now banned so in effect every B&B is a non-smoking house. A tiny minority may set aside a room for smokers but few do.

Rates Proprietors quote their **tariffs** either on a **per person** (pp) basis or **per room**, assuming two people are sharing; rates are also sometimes given for single occupancy of a room where there are no single rooms. Accommodation **prices in this guide are quoted on a per person basis** and start at around £25pp for the most basic B&B-style accommodation rising to around £80pp for the most luxurious places. Most charge around £35-45pp. Guesthouses charge around £45-50pp and pubs around £30-40pp with breakfast included. Prices in hotels start at around the same but can rise to as much as £100pp or more; sometimes rates are for the room only and breakfast is additional. Solo walkers should take note: single rooms are not so easy to find so you will often end up occupying a double/twin room and are likely to have to pay a single occupancy supplement (£10-25) on top of the per person rate. And in high season you will sometimes have to pay the full room rate.

> ### ❏ BOOKING ACCOMMODATION IN ADVANCE
>
> Booking ahead is a good idea for all types of accommodation (though generally not necessary for camping) as it guarantees you a bed for the night. If you are walking alone it also means someone is expecting you. During the high season (July and August) you may need to book a few weeks ahead, whereas in the winter a few days, or even the night before, should suffice. If you are walking in the low season check if the owner will provide an evening meal or that a local pub serves food. In high season, be aware that many B&Bs require a stay of at least two nights, or else charge a single-night supplement.
>
> Many places have their own website and some offer online/email booking but for some places you will need to phone. Most places ask for a deposit (about 50%) if you book online, which is generally non-refundable if you cancel at short notice. Some places may ask for a 100% deposit if the booking is for one night only. Always let the owner know as soon as possible if you have to cancel your booking so they can offer the bed to someone else.
>
> If the idea of booking all your accommodation fills you with dread, you may want to consider booking up with one of the self-guided walking holiday companies listed on pp28-30. They will happily do all the work for you, saving you a considerable amount of trouble and can also arrange for your baggage to be forwarded to the next night's accommodation.

Larger places take credit or debit cards, as do an increasing number of smaller B&Bs nowadays. If not, they may ask for a deposit payment by bank transfer with the balance to be settled in cash, so it's best to check when you book.

Self-catering holiday cottages
It is possible to walk a considerable part of the coast path from a fixed base using the excellent public transport to get to and from the trail each day; see box on p40 for more information and ideas.

Renting a self-catering cottage makes sense for a group of walkers as it will work out a lot cheaper and simpler than staying in B&Bs. Holiday cottages are normally let on a weekly basis but short breaks are often possible outside peak times. Cottages haven't been listed in this book, but they are numerous (more numerous than B&Bs these days it seems); search on the internet or contact the tourist information centre in the area where you want to stay for further details (see box on p46). Alternatively, contact the Landmark Trust (information ☎ 01628-825920, booking ☎ 01628-825925, 🖳 www.landmarktrust.org.uk) or the National Trust (☎ 0344-800 2070, 🖳 nationaltrustcottages.co.uk), both of which have several properties in Cornwall.

FOOD AND DRINK

Breakfast, lunch and evening meals
The traditional B&B **breakfast** is the celebrated 'full English' breakfast, or in Cornwall, the 'full Cornish': this consists of a choice of cereals and/or fruit juice followed by a plate of eggs, bacon, sausages, mushrooms, beans, fried bread and tomatoes, with toast and marmalade or jams to end and all washed

down with tea or coffee. This is good for a day's walking, but after a week not so good for your cholesterol level. Sometimes B&B owners offer a continental breakfast option or will charge you less if all you want is a bowl of muesli or some toast. Alternatively, and also if you want an early start, it is worth asking if they would substitute the breakfast for a packed lunch. Most B&Bs will fill your flask with tea or coffee for the day, often without charge.

For **lunch** there are several options. The cheapest and easiest is to buy a picnic lunch or pasty at one of the many shops or bakeries you'll pass. Many B&Bs and hostels are happy to make a packed lunch for you for between £5 and £7. Otherwise you could eat out but you need to plan ahead to make sure the pub or restaurant or beach café is open and that you'll reach it in time for lunch. In

---

❏ TRADITIONAL CORNISH FOOD

● **The Cornish pasty** Visitors to Cornwall, whether walkers or not, cannot go home without having tried the ubiquitous pasty at least once. For some, once is enough whilst for others it becomes a lifetime's favourite. The pasty, for those who thought it was just a glorified meat pie, is shaped like a letter 'D', the pastry crimped on the curved side, with a filling of sliced beef with turnip (swede), potato and onion with a light peppery seasoning. The pastry is slow-cooked to a golden colour and is glazed with milk or egg.

Originally Cornish tin miners were sent off to work by their wives with their lunch in the form of a hot pasty containing a savoury filling at one end and fruit at the other – a complete meal that could be eaten without cutlery. Today they are mainly savoury. Pasties are eaten widely and available everywhere providing a meal on the run. Such is the iconic status of the pasty that the Cornish Pasty Association was granted Protected Geographical Indication Status in February 2011, so that pasties are recognised as unique to Cornwall. Try one – you might get hooked.

● **Cornish cream tea** This is another walkers' favourite and you'll never be far from places offering this afternoon treat of scones, jam and clotted cream (thick, spreadable cream made by heating milk to evaporate the liquid) accompanied by a pot of tea; surely the cheapest decadent food available. Choose carefully and check that the scones are made on the premises or you may be disappointed. Prices start at around £5 and usually include two scones, a pot of tea, and plenty of jam and cream. Don't forget, unlike in Devon, here in Cornwall it's **jam first**!

● **Fish** The fishing industry has been one of the biggest influences on the culinary traditions of Cornwall, and local favourites such as stargazy pie, sometimes referred to as 'starry gazey' pie, made with fish heads sticking out of the crust looking towards the sky, are on some menus. Fish pie is widely served, usually a good option washed down with a pint of the local ale. Even if you're on a tight budget the ubiquitous fish and chips can be satisfying if cooked with fresh fish. At the other end of the scale there are plenty of restaurants around the coast offering mouth-watering dishes concocted from locally caught fish. Species found in Cornwall's inshore waters include Dover sole, plaice, turbot, brill, gurnard, pollock, lemon sole, ray, cod, whiting, red mullet, John Dory, mackerel, sea bass and many more. There's also shellfish: lobsters, crabs, scallops, langoustines, clams and mussels, which are often fished for from the smaller coastal villages.

For further information about Cornish food and farmers' markets in Cornwall visit: 🖵 foodfromcornwall.co.uk.

recent times it has become quite the norm for walkers to travel light, taking only water and possibly a fruit bar or piece of fruit, confining their eating to the evening meal. Another option is to have a light lunch and then indulge in a **cream tea**.

During the summer you will also come across **seasonal snack shacks** by popular beaches and car parks serving light snacks such as filled sandwiches or baguettes, cakes, ice creams and soft drinks; the only trouble is not knowing exactly when they will be open. They tend to set up from around 10am to 4pm, but sometimes they won't turn up if it's pouring with rain, so you can't rely on them being there every day, even in mid-summer.

For your **evening meal** the local pub is often the best place to head if your B&B does not provide a meal (most don't), or if you have not pre-booked one. Most pubs have a relatively standard 'pub-grub' menu featuring such regulars as fish and chips, steak and ale pie, and bangers (sausages) and mash, supplemented by one or two 'specials' such as fresh fish probably from a local source. Some pubs also have an attached à la carte restaurant with more elaborate meals. Most pub menus include at least two vegetarian options.

Most of the towns along the coast have Indian and Chinese takeaways/restaurants as well as fish and chip shops. If you want to splash out on fine-dining there are lots of nice restaurants along the coast path and local seafood is invariably on the menu. If they can't serve freshly caught fish in Cornwall they are just not trying.

Self-catering

The coast-path walker doesn't need to carry much food. Almost every village you pass through has a small shop or convenience store with plenty of food for snacks and picnic lunches and often cut sandwiches and pasties plus a limited choice for cooking in the evening. Larger stores are well stocked with a range of groceries including lightweight campers' food such as instant rice meals, mashed potato or pasta and sauce mixes and they'll usually have a selection of wine and beer too. **Fuel for camp stoves** requires a little more planning. Gas canisters are the easiest to come by with most general stores and campsite shops stocking them. Methylated spirit and Coleman fuel is sold in many outdoor shops and hardware stores and can occasionally be found in other shops too. Fuel canisters for stoves are now universally available.

Drinking water

We wouldn't recommend filling your water bottle or pouch from any stream or river on the coast path. Most streams run through farmland before reaching the coast. It may also have run off roads, housing or agricultural fields picking up heavy metals, pesticides and other chemical contaminants that we humans use liberally.

Tap water is safe to drink unless a sign specifies otherwise. Carry a two- or three-litre bottle or pouch and fill it up wherever you stay the night. During the day you could refill it in public toilets although not all meet reasonable standards of cleanliness and the taps are often awkward. As our use of endless plastic bottles becomes more of a problem and they continue to pollute the planet, many shops and cafés are now far more committed than they used to be to filling walkers' bottles up for them. A 3-litre 'platypus' style bag should be sufficient for all but the hottest days.

Real ales and cider

The process of brewing beer is believed to have been in Britain since the Neolithic period and is an art local brewers have been perfecting ever since. Real ale is beer that has been brewed using traditional methods. **Real ales** are not filtered or pasteurised, a process which removes and kills all the yeast cells, but instead undergo a secondary fermentation at the pub which enhances the natural flavours and brings out the individual characteristics of the beer. It's served at cellar temperature with no artificial fizz added, unlike keg beer which is pasteurised and has the fizz added by injecting nitrogen dioxide.

There are plenty of pubs along the coast path serving an excellent range of real ales from around the country. The strength of beer is denoted by the initials ABV which means alcohol by volume followed by a percentage starting with the lowest at about 3.7%.

Distinctive Cornish beers worth watching out for include Betty Stoggs Bitter (4%), a strong hoppy beer, and Cornish Knocker Ale (4.5%) with its beautiful golden colour, both of which are brewed by **Skinner's** (🖳 skinnersbrewery .com) who have won a number of awards. **Sharp's** Brewery (🖳 sharpsbrewery .co.uk) also produces some fine ales, in particular Doom Bar Bitter (4%) named after the Doom Bar (see box on p116) near Padstow, and the citrusy Atlantic Pale Ale (4.2%). **St Austell** Brewery (🖳 staustellbrewery.co.uk) was first established in 1851 and several of their beers have won awards. The most popular brews are Tribute (4.2%) and Proper Job (4.5%), a powerful IPA. The most common of all these ales are St Austell's Tribute and Sharp's Doom Bar, both widely available.

Scrumpy (rough cider) is another Cornish favourite and well worth trying if you come across it on draught. You will immediately notice the difference from keg cider as it will be cloudy, with 'bits' floating in it and no fizz. You may also notice the difference afterwards; scrumpy is notorious for inducing wild nights out with subsequent periods of memory loss, sweating, dizziness, prolonged headaches, shaking, nausea and hot flushes. Another pint, anyone?

MONEY

A few campsites, hostels, B&Bs and small shops still require you to pay with cash as they won't have credit/debit card facilities. You don't need to carry large amounts of money with you as all towns have banks with cash machines (ATMs) which are also found in convenience stores and supermarkets. Some ATMs charge (£1.50-1.95) for withdrawals though there are clear signs warning you of this before you actually withdraw the money.

Alternatively, many supermarkets, some pubs, and a few smaller convenience stores will advance cash against a card (cashback). Cashback is free of charge, although sometimes a minimum purchase of £5 or £10 is required.

Use the table of village and town facilities (see pp32-5) to plan how much money you'll need to withdraw at any one time.

Using the Post Office for banking

Most UK banks have an agreement with the Post Office allowing customers to withdraw cash from branches using their debit card and PIN number. As many towns and villages have post offices, this is an extremely useful facility although be aware that some have had their opening hours reduced considerably, so if you're planning on using this facility check availability in advance.

❏ **INFORMATION FOR FOREIGN VISITORS**

● **Currency** The British pound (£) comes in notes of £50, £20, £10 and £5, and coins of £2 and £1. The pound is divided into 100 pence (usually referred to as 'p', pronounced 'pee') which comes in silver coins of 50p, 20p, 10p and 5p, and copper coins of 2p and 1p.

● **Money** Up-to-date **rates of exchange** can be found on 🖳 xe.com/ucc, at some post offices, or at any bank or travel agent. A charge is applied to use some **ATMs (cash machines)**, particularly those operated by Link (🖳 link.co.uk/consumers/locator); also these may not accept foreign-issued cards.

● **Business hours** Most shops and main post offices are open at least from Monday to Friday 9am-5pm and Saturday 9am-12.30pm but many shops open earlier and close later, some open on Sunday as well. Occasionally, especially in rural areas, you'll come across a local shop that closes at midday during the week, usually a Wednesday or Thursday, a throwback to the days when all towns and villages had an 'early closing day'. Many supermarkets remain open 12 hours a day; the Co-op tends to have the longest hours, often open daily from 7am to 11pm. Banks typically open at 9.30am Monday to Friday and close at 3.30pm or 4pm, but of course ATM machines are open all the time (if they are outside). Pub hours are less predictable; although many open daily 11am-11pm, often in rural areas, and particularly in winter months, opening hours are 11am-3pm and 6-11pm Mon-Sat, 11am/noon-3pm and 7-11pm on Sunday.

Last entry to most **museums** is usually an hour before the official closing time.

● **National holidays** Most businesses in the South-West are shut on 1 January, Good Friday (March/April), Easter Monday (March/April), first and last Monday in May, last Monday in August, 25 and 26 December.

● **School holidays** State-school holidays in England are generally as follows: a one-week break late October, two weeks over Christmas and the New Year, a week mid February, two weeks around Easter, one week at the end of May/early June (incorporating the last Monday in May) and five to six weeks from late July to early September. Private-school holidays fall at the same time, but are slightly longer.

● **Documents** If you are a member of a National Trust organisation in your country bring your membership card as you should be entitled to free entry to National Trust properties and sites in the UK. If you're staying in hostels, you will need to show some form of photo ID when you check in, although a photocopy will suffice.

● **Travel/medical insurance** All visitors to Britain should be properly insured, including comprehensive health coverage. Before Brexit on 1st January 2021, the **European Health Insurance Card** (EHIC) entitled EU nationals (on production of the card) to necessary medical treatment under the National Health Service (NHS) while on a temporary visit here. Since Brexit this system is still valid for the time being but check the

OTHER SERVICES

In addition to a **grocery store** most small towns have a **launderette**, **chemist/pharmacy**, **public toilets** and a **phone box**. Smaller villages may have a grocery store and public toilets, but are unlikely to have much else.

Where they exist, special mention has also been made in Part 4 of other services that may be of use to walkers such as **banks**, **cash machines (ATMs)**, **hiking/camping shops**, **internet access**, **medical centres** and **tourist information centres**.

current situation (⌨ nhs.uk/nhs-services, then click on Visiting or moving to England) before travelling. In any case, not all treatment will be covered and it is not a substitute for proper medical cover on your travel insurance for unforeseen bills and for getting you home should that be necessary. Also consider getting cover for loss and theft of personal belongings, especially if you are camping or staying in hostels, as there will be times when you'll have to leave your luggage unattended.

● **Weights and measures** In Britain, milk can still be sold in pints (1 pint = 568ml), as can beer in pubs, though most other liquid including petrol (gasoline) and diesel is sold in litres. Distances on road and path signs are given in miles (1 mile = 1.61km) rather than kilometres, and yards (1yd = 0.9m) rather than metres. The population remains divided between those who still use inches (1 inch = 2.5cm), feet (1ft = 0.3m) and yards and those who are happy with millimetres, centimetres and metres; you'll often be told that 'it's only a hundred yards or so' to somewhere, rather than a hundred metres or so.

Most food is sold in metric weights (g and kg) but the imperial weights of pounds (lb: 1lb = 453g) and ounces (oz: 1oz = 28g) are frequently displayed too. The weather – a frequent topic of conversation – is also an issue: while most forecasts predict temperatures in Celsius (C), many people continue to think in terms of Fahrenheit (F); see the temperature chart on p14 for conversions.

● **Smoking** The ban on smoking in public places relates not only to pubs and restaurants, but also to B&Bs, hostels and hotels. These latter have the right to designate one or more bedrooms where the occupants can smoke, but the ban is in force in all enclosed areas open to the public – even if they are in a private home such as a B&B. Should you be foolhardy enough to light up in a no-smoking area, which includes pretty much any indoor public place, you could be fined £50, but it's the owners of the premises who carry the can if they fail to stop you, with a potential fine of £2500.

● **Time** During the winter, the whole of Britain is on Greenwich Mean Time (GMT). The clocks move one hour forward on the last Sunday in March, remaining on British Summer Time (BST) until the last Sunday in October.

● **Telephone** From outside Britain the international country access code for Britain is ☎ 44 followed by the area code minus the first 0, and then the number you require. Within Britain, to call a landline number with the same code as the landline phone you are calling from, the code can be omitted: dial the number only. If you're using a mobile phone that is registered overseas, consider buying a local SIM card to keep costs down.

● **Emergency services** For police, ambulance, fire or coastguard dial either ☎ 999 or ☎ 112.

PLANNING YOUR WALK

Phones and wi-fi

The **mobile phone** reception along much of the coast path has improved in recent years; although it's still not unusual to walk for half a day without a signal, and in some small coastal villages you will have to climb up a nearby hill in order to make a phone call. Consequently **public telephone boxes** are marked on the maps wherever one is available. The minimum cost for making a call from a public telephone box is 60p.

Wi-fi is everywhere these days – in most pubs, cafés, restaurants, B&Bs, hotels, and even on many campsites – and it's almost always provided free of charge to customers. Having said that, those of you carrying smartphones may find you're able to get online more often through your mobile phone network in some areas.

WALKING COMPANIES

For walkers wanting to make their holiday as easy and trouble free as possible there are several specialist companies offering a range of services from baggage transfers to accommodation booking and fully guided group tours.

Baggage carriers

The thought of carrying a large pack puts many people off walking long-distance trails. The main baggage company on the SWCP is the aptly named **Luggage Transfers** (☎ 01326-567247, 🖳 luggagetransfers.co.uk; Helston), who cover the whole of the path, charging from £15 per day.

Alternatively, some of the **taxi firms** listed in this guide can provide a similar service within a local area if you want a break from carrying your bags for a day or so. Also, don't rule out the possibility of your **B&B/guesthouse owner** taking your bags ahead for you; plenty of them are glad to do so since it supplements their income and adds to the service they offer. Depending on the distance they may make no charge at all, or charge £10-15; this may be less than a taxi would charge.

Self-guided holidays

The following companies provide customised packages for walkers which usually include detailed advice and notes on itineraries and routes, maps, accommodation booking, daily baggage transfer and transport arrangements at the start and end of your walk. If you don't want the whole all-in package some of the companies may be able to arrange just accommodation booking or baggage carrying.

● **Absolute Escapes** (☎ 0131-610 1210, 🖳 absoluteescapes.com; Edinburgh) Offer walking holidays along the whole path as well as in sections.

● **Celtic Trails** (☎ 01291-689774, 🖳 celtictrailswalkingholidays.co.uk; Chepstow) Organise walking holidays along particular sections of the footpath; length-of-time options are from four days to a week or more.

● **Compass Holidays** (☎ 01242-250642, 🖳 compass-holidays.com; Cheltenham) Organise walks of between three and eight days around the Lizard Peninsula (Helston to Mullion) and the entire Cornwall Coast Path.

● **Contours Holidays Ltd** (☎ 01629-821900, 🖳 contours.co.uk; Derbyshire) Holidays include Westward Ho! to Padstow, Padstow to St Ives, St Ives to Penzance, Penzance to Falmouth and Falmouth to Plymouth in various combinations of three to ten days' walking plus tailor-made tours. Some dog-friendly itineraries.

● **Encounter Walking Holidays** (☎ 01208-871066, 🖳 encounterwalkingholi days.com; Lostwithiel, Cornwall) Organise everything for the walker operating on every section of the path. Short breaks and week-long holidays through to two-month treks. Will help everyone from individual walkers to large groups and specialise in assisting overseas walkers along the route.

● **Explore Britain** (☎ 01740-650900, 🖳 explorebritain.com; Co Durham) Operate a variety of holidays including one based at Land's End, five to six days St Ives to Land's End, three days Bude to Tintagel, fourteen days Padstow to Frenchman's Creek, six days Newquay to Land's End.

● **Footpath Holidays** (☎ 01985-840049, 🖳 footpath-holidays.com; Wilts) Operate a range of walking holidays including inn-to-inn holidays for the whole path and single-centre holidays from Boscastle, Penzance and the Lizard. They also offer short breaks or one-week holidays plus tailor-made tours. Baggage transfer is included as part of inn-to-inn holidays.

● **Great British Walks** (☎ 01600-713008, 🖳 www.great-british-walks.com; Monmouth) Offer a variety of itineraries which can be adapted to suit the customer.

● **Let's Go Walking** (☎ 01837-880075 or ☎ 020-7193 1252, 🖳 letsgowalking .com; Devon) Offer holidays covering the entire coast path with the length of stay to suit the distance walked.

● **Macs Adventure** (☎ 0141-530 8886, 🖳 macsadventure.com; Glasgow) Have walks covering the whole SWCP including Minehead to Westward Ho!, Westward Ho! to Padstow and Padstow to Poole.

● **Mickledore** (☎ 017687 72335, 🖳 mickledore.co.uk; Keswick, Cumbria) Offer a range of holidays along the entire length of the South West Coast Path.

● **Nearwater Walking Holidays** (☎ 01326-279278, 🖳 nearwaterwalkinghol idays.co.uk; Truro) Offer walks covering the whole path as well as sections from 5 days upwards.

● **Responsible Travel** (☎ 01273-823700; 🖳 responsibletravel.com; Brighton) Offer fully supported itineraries for 7 nights'/8 days' walking along sections of the path and can tailor-make according to requirements.

● **The Discerning Traveller** (☎ 01865-511330, 🖳 discerningtraveller.co.uk; Oxford) Offer three different week-long holidays along the path: 'Land's End and St Ives', 'Polperro to Mevagissey', and 'Padstow & Tintagel Coast' which can all be extended to include Bodmin Moor if desired.

● **Walk the Trail** (☎ 01326-567252, 🖳 walkthetrail.co.uk; Helston) Offers walking holidays of any itinerary from short breaks to the entire SWCP and anything in between.

● **Walkers' Britain** (☎ 020-8875 5070, or freephone ☎ 0800-008 7741, 🖳 www.walkersbritain.co.uk; London) Offer eight-day holidays from Marazion

PLANNING YOUR WALK

to Mevagissey including the Lizard & Roseland peninsulas, Padstow to St Ives and St Ives to Penzance.

● **Way2go4 Walking Holidays** (☎ 01288-353647, 🖳 way2go4.com; Cornwall/N Devon border) Offer walks at multiple locations on the coast path.

Group/guided walking tours

Fully guided tours are ideal for individuals wanting to travel in the company of others and for groups of friends wanting to be guided. The packages usually include meals, accommodation, transport arrangements, minibus back-up, baggage transfer, as well as a qualified guide and are often for sections of the trail such as Padstow to St Ives, a popular route for a week's walking. The companies differ in terms of the size of the groups they take, the standards of accommodation, the age range of clients, the distances walked and the professionalism of the guides, so it's worth checking them all before making a booking.

● **Adventureline** (☎ 01209-820847, 🖳 adventureline.co.uk; Cornwall) Has a base in St Agnes and offers a variety of walks along different stretches of the coast path in most areas of Cornwall; one week.

● **Footpath Holidays** (see p29) Fully guided tours (short breaks or one week) are offered from their base in Boscastle.

● **HF Holidays** (☎ 020-8732 1250, 🖳 hfholidays.co.uk; Herts) Two itineraries (seven nights) based in St Ives: north and south Cornwall coast path.

● **Meadow View Guided Hikes** (☎ 07736-066319, 🖳 meadowviewguided hikes.co.uk; Fowey, Cornwall) Leads public scheduled walks and private ones. Well-behaved dogs welcome. Children by arrangement (to ensure their comfort, safety and enjoyment).

● **Walkitcornwall** (☎ 0771-408 4644, 🖳 walkitcornwall.co.uk; Cornwall) Offer guided walking holidays of mainly circular walks focusing on the Cornwall Coast Path.

● **Way2go4 Walking Holidays** (see above) Tours designed to be flexible, along the path on Cornwall/N Devon border, group size typically 6-12 people, short breaks & week holidays.

Budgeting

If you **wild camp**, you can survive on as little as £5-10 per person (pp) per day, but assuming you camp use official **campsites**, you can still get by on less than £15-20pp per day so long as you don't visit pubs, avoid ticketed tourist attractions, and cook all your own food on your camping stove. Even then, unforeseen expenses will probably nudge your daily budget up. Include the occasional pint, and perhaps a pub meal every now and then, and the figure will be nearer £25pp or even £30pp per day. Remember that the time of year you're walking will have a significant impact on your budget; during the height of the season campground charges can sometimes escalate dramatically.

As noted on pp18-19, it isn't possible to stay in **hostels** every night. However, for the nights you do stay in one expect to pay £17-25pp. If you cook your own meals you will need about £30-35pp per day. If you eat the meals provided in some YHA hostels expect to pay around £6.50 for breakfast, about the same for a packed lunch, and approximately £10 for an evening meal.

On the nights when you have to stay in a **B&B** there won't be the facilities to cook for yourself, so you will have to eat out. For these days budget in the vicinity of £60-70pp if you can make do with a simple packed lunch and fish & chips for dinner, or £80-plus if you intend eating lunches and dinners at cafés, pubs and restaurants. (See also p21).

Don't forget to set some money aside for the **inevitable extras**: souvenirs, washing and drying clothes, entrance fees for various attractions, cream teas, beer, buses, boats and taxis, any changes of plan.

Itineraries

All walkers are individuals. Some like to cover large distances as quickly as possible, others are happy to stroll along, stopping whenever the fancy takes them. You may want to walk the coast path all in one go, tackle it over a series of weekends or use the trail for linear day walks; the choice is yours.

To accommodate these differences this book is not divided into rigid daily stages but is designed to make it easy for you to plan your own perfect itinerary.

The **planning map** (opposite the inside back cover) and **table of village and town facilities** (pp32-5) summarise the essential information and make it straightforward to devise a plan of your own. Alternatively, have a look at the **suggested itineraries** (pp36-8) and simply choose your preferred type of accommodation and speed of walking. There are also suggestions for those who want to experience the best of the trail over a day (see p39) or a weekend (see p40), or who want to plan a series of day walks from a fixed base (see box p40).

The **public transport maps** on pp52-3 and **bus service table** (pp54-5) may also be useful at this stage. Having made a rough plan, turn to Part 4 where you will find: summaries of the route, full descriptions of accommodation, places to eat and other services in each village and town; as well as detailed trail maps.

WHICH DIRECTION?

Although the route in this book has been described from Bude to Plymouth, it doesn't make much difference whether you walk the coast path in a clockwise or anti-clockwise direction. There is virtually the same amount of ascent and descent either way and the prevailing south-westerly wind will be in your face for one half of the walk and behind you for the other whichever way you go. Most people choose to walk the path anti-clockwise (starting in Bude), so this way you'll be more likely to enjoy coast-path camaraderie with fellow walkers.

VILLAGE & TOWN FACILITIES & DISTANCES
Bude to Plymouth

PLACE* & DISTANCE* APPROX MILES / *KM*	BANK (ATM)	POST OFFICE	INFO	EATING PLACE	FOOD SHOP	CAMP-SITE	HOSTEL BARN	B&B HOTEL
Bude & Upton	✔	✔	TIC	✔✔✔	✔✔	✔✔✔		✔✔✔
Widemouth Bay 3 / *5*				✔✔✔	✔	✔✔		✔✔✔
Crackington Haven 7 / *11.5*				✔✔		✔		✔✔✔
Boscastle 7 / *11.5*	(✔)	✔		✔✔✔	✔	✔	(YHA)	✔✔✔
Bossiney 4 / *6.5*					✔	✔		
Tintagel 1 / *1.5*	(✔)	(✔)	VC	✔✔✔	✔✔	✔	(YHA & H)	✔✔✔
Trebarwith Strand 2 / *3*	(✔)			✔✔				✔
Port Gaverne 6 / *9.5*				✔✔		✔		✔
Port Isaac 1 / *1.5*	(✔)			✔✔✔	✔			✔✔✔
Polzeath 9 / *14.5*	(✔)			✔✔✔	✔	✔(¾)		
Rock t/o 3 / *5* (Rock+½)	(✔)§			✔✔✔	✔			✔✔
Padstow (ferry)	✔	✔	TIC	✔✔✔	✔✔	✔		✔✔✔
Trevone 5 / *8*				✔✔	✔			✔
Harlyn Bay 1½ / *2.5*				✔				
Mother Ivey's Bay 1½ / *2.5*						✔		
Constantine Bay & Treyarnon 2½ / *4*				✔✔	✔	✔✔	YHA	
Porthcothan 2 / *3*					✔			
Bedruthan Steps 2¾ / *4.4*				(✔✔)		✔		
Mawgan Porth 1½ / *2.5*	(✔)§			✔✔✔	✔	✔✔		✔✔✔
Watergate Bay 2 / *3*				✔✔✔		✔		✔
Porth 2 / *3*	(✔)			✔✔✔		✔		✔
Newquay 4 / *6.5*	✔	✔	TIC	✔✔✔	✔✔✔	✔	H	✔✔✔
Crantock 2 / *3* (or **6**/*9.5* on main road)		✔		✔✔✔	✔	✔✔		
Porth Joke 2 / *3*						✔		
Holywell 2 / *3*				✔✔		✔		✔
Perranporth 4½ / *7*	(✔)	✔		✔✔✔	✔✔✔	✔✔	(YHA)	✔✔
Trevaunance Cove 3½ / *5.5*				✔✔✔				✔
(St Agnes+½)	(✔)	✔		✔✔✔	✔✔	✔✔		✔✔✔
Porthtowan 4½ / *7*		✔		✔✔(✔)	✔	✔		
Portreath 3 / *5*	(✔)§	✔		✔✔✔	✔		YHA(1½)	✔✔
Gwithian 8 / *13*				✔✔✔		✔		
Hayle 4 / *6.5*	(✔)	✔	TIC	✔✔✔	✔✔	✔		✔✔✔
St Ives 6 / *9.5*	✔	✔	TIC	✔✔✔	✔✔✔	✔	H	✔✔✔
Zennor Head 6 / *9.5* (Zennor +¾)				✔✔				✔✔
Lean Point 1 / *1.5* (Gurnard's Hd/Treen+½)				✔				✔
Morvah Cliff 3½ / *5* (Morvah+½)				(✔)		(✔)		
Pendeen Watch 1½ / *2.6* (Pendeen/Trewellard+¾)				✔✔✔	✔	✔		✔✔
Botallack Mine 2 / *3* (Botallack+½)				✔		✔		
Cape Cornwall 1¾ / *2.7*				✔(✔)		(✔)		✔✔
(St Just +1½)	(✔)	✔	TIP	✔✔✔	✔✔			✔✔✔

cont'd on p34

NOTES *PLACE & DISTANCE Places in **bold** are on the path; places in brackets and not in bold – eg (St Agnes) – are a short walk off the path. DISTANCE is given from the place above. Distances are between **places on the route** or to the **main turnoff (t/o)** to places in brackets. For example the distance from Polzeath to the turnoff for Rock is 3 miles. Bracketed distances eg (+½) show the additional distance in miles off the route – eg Rock village is ½ mile from the Coast Path.

VILLAGE & TOWN FACILITIES & DISTANCES
Plymouth to Bude

PLACE* & DISTANCE* APPROX MILES / KM	BANK (ATM)	POST OFFICE	INFO	EATING PLACE	FOOD SHOP	CAMP-SITE	HOSTEL BARN	B&B HOTEL
Plymouth (Mayflower Steps)	(✔)	✔	TIC	✔✔✔	✔✔✔		H	✔✔✔
Cremyll 2¾ / 4.5 (+ferry)				✔✔				✔
Cawsand/Kingsand 3 / 5				✔✔✔	✔✔	✔(Maker Heights)		✔✔✔
Portwrinkle 10 / 16				✔✔				✔
Downderry 3 / 5		(✔)		✔(✔)	✔			✔
Seaton 1¼ / 2				✔(✔✔)				
Looe 4 / 6.5	(✔)		TIC	✔✔✔	✔✔	✔(Bay View Fm)		✔✔✔
Polperro 5 / 8	(✔)§	✔		✔✔✔	✔	✔		✔✔✔
Polruan ferry	(✔)§	✔		✔✔✔	✔	✔		✔
Fowey 7¼ / 11.75	(✔)	✔		✔✔✔	✔			✔✔✔
Polkerris 4¾ / 7.5				✔✔✔(✔)				
Par 2¼ / 3.5	(✔)	✔		✔✔	✔✔			
Charlestown 4½ / 6.75	(✔)+(✔)§			✔✔✔	✔	✔		✔✔
Pentewan 5 / 8		✔		✔✔✔	✔	✔		✔✔
Mevagissey 2¼ / 3.5		✔	TIP	✔✔✔	✔			✔✔✔
Gorran Haven 3½ / 5.5		✔		✔✔✔	✔(bakery)	✔✔		✔
East Portholland 6½ / 10.5				(✔)			YHA (Boswinger)	
Portloe 2½ / 4				✔✔				✔✔
Portscatho/Gerrans 7½ / 12		✔		✔✔✔	✔	✔		✔✔✔
Place ferry								
St Mawes ferry	✔	✔	VC	✔✔✔	✔			✔✔✔
Falmouth 6¼ / 10 (from P'scatho)	✔	✔	VC	✔✔✔	✔✔✔		H	✔✔✔
Maenporth 5 / 8				✔(✔)		✔✔		
Durgan 4 / 6.5 (Mawnan Smith +1)				✔(✔)	✔			✔
Helford Passage ¾ / 1				✔				
(Gweek & Mawgan 5 / 8 to Helford)	✔	✔		(✔✔)	✔✔		✔	
Helford 0/0 by ferry; 5½ /9 from Gweek				✔(✔)	✔			
Porthallow 7¼ / 11.75				✔(✔✔)		✔		✔
Coverack 5 / 8		(✔)		✔✔✔	✔	✔✔	(YHA)	✔✔✔
Cadgwith 7 / 11.5				✔✔	✔(snacks)	✔(Kennack Sands)		✔
Lizard Point 4 / 6.5 (Lizard+½)		✔		✔✔✔	✔(limited)	✔✔	(YHA)	✔✔✔
Mullion Cove 6 / 9.5		✔		✔✔✔(✔)			✔(Teneriffe Fm¾)	✔
(Mullion+½)	(✔)	✔		✔✔✔	✔✔			✔✔✔
Porthleven 6 / 9.5	(✔)	(✔)		✔✔✔	✔	✔		✔✔✔
Praa Sands 4½ / 7		(✔)		✔	✔✔	✔		
Marazion 6¼ / 10	(✔)	✔		✔✔✔	✔	✔		✔✔✔
Penzance 3 / 5	✔	✔	TIC	✔✔✔	✔✔✔	✔✔	YHA	✔✔✔
Newlyn 1½ / 2.5	(✔)			✔✔✔	✔			✔✔
Mousehole (& Paul) 2½ / 4	(✔)§	✔		✔✔✔	✔	✔(+½)		✔✔
Lamorna 2 / 3				✔				✔(1½)

cont'd on p35

B&B/HOTEL ✔ = one place   ₩ = two   ₩₩ = three or more
EATING PLACE (✔) = seasonal or open daytime only
HOSTEL/BARN YHA = YHA hostel (YHA) = seasonal   H = independent hostel
CAMPSITE Bracketed distance eg (½) shows mileage from Coast Path (✔) = basic
INFO TIC/P = Tourist Info Centre/Point NPC = National Park Centre VC = Visitor Centre
BANK/ATM (✔) = ATM only: no bank (✔)§ = ATM with charges for withdrawal

PLANNING YOUR WALK

VILLAGE & TOWN FACILITIES & DISTANCES
Bude to Plymouth

PLACE* & DISTANCE* APPROX MILES / KM	BANK (ATM)	POST OFFICE	INFO	EATING PLACE	FOOD SHOP	CAMP-SITE	HOSTEL BARN	B&B HOTEL
(cont'd from p32)								
Kelynack 2 / 3						✔	YHA	
Sennen Cove/Mayon 5 / 8	(✔)	✔		✔✔	✔	✔(+1)		✔
Land's End 1 / 1.5	(✔)§		VC	✔(✔)		✔	H	✔✔
Porthcurno 5 / 8				(✔)				✔
Treen ½ / 1				✔		✔		
Lamorna 4½ / 7				✔				✔(1½)
Mousehole (& Paul) 2 / 3	(✔)§	✔		✔✔	✔	✔(+½)		✔
Newlyn 2½ / 4	(✔)			✔✔	✔			✔
Penzance 1½ / 2.5	✔	✔	TIC	✔✔	✔	✔	YHA	✔✔
Marazion 3 / 5	(✔)	✔		✔✔	✔	✔		✔✔
Praa Sands 6¼ / 10		(✔)		✔	✔	✔		
Porthleven 4½ / 7	(✔)	(✔)		✔✔	✔	✔		✔✔
Mullion Cove 6 / 9.5		✔		✔✔(✔)		✔(Teneriffe Fm¾)		✔
(Mullion+½)	(✔)	✔		✔✔	✔✔			✔✔
Lizard Point 6 / 9.5 (Lizard+½)		✔		✔✔	✔(limited)	✔	(YHA)	✔✔
Cadgwith 4 / 6.5				✔✔	✔(snacks)	✔(Kennack Sands)		✔
Coverack 7 / 11.5		(✔)		✔✔	✔	✔	(YHA)	✔✔
Porthallow 5 / 8				✔(✔)		✔		✔
Helford 7¼ / 11.75				✔(✔)	✔			
(Mawgan & Gweek 5 / 8 from Helford)	✔			✔	(✔✔)	✔		✔
Helford Passage 0/0 by ferry; 5½ /9 from Gweek	✔							
Durgan ¾ / 1 (Mawnan Smith +1)				✔(✔)	✔			✔
Maenporth 4 / 6.5				✔(✔)		✔		
Falmouth 5 / 8	✔	✔	VC	✔✔	✔✔		H	✔✔
St Mawes ferry	✔	✔	VC	✔✔	✔			✔✔
Place ferry								
Portscatho/Gerrans 6¼ / 10 (from Falmth)	✔			✔✔	✔	✔		✔✔
Portloe 7½ / 12				✔				✔
East Portholland 2½ / 4				(✔)			YHA (Boswinger)	
Gorran Haven 6½ / 10.5		✔		✔✔	✔(bakery)	✔		✔
Mevagissey 3½ / 5.5		✔	TIP	✔✔	✔			✔✔
Pentewan 2¼ / 3.5				✔✔	✔	✔		✔
Charlestown 5 / 8	(✔)+(✔)§		✔✔	✔	✔	✔		✔
Par 4½ / 6.75	(✔)	✔		✔	✔✔			
Polkerris 2¼ / 3.5				✔✔(✔)				
Fowey 4¾ / 7.5	(✔)	✔		✔✔	✔			✔✔
Polruan ferry	(✔)§	✔		✔✔	✔	✔		✔
Polperro 7¼ / 11.75	(✔)§	✔		✔✔	✔	✔		✔✔
Looe 5 / 8	(✔)		TIC	✔✔	✔	✔(Bay View Fm)		✔✔
Seaton 4 / 6.5				✔(✔)				
Downderry 1¼ / 2		(✔)		✔(✔)	✔			✔
Portwrinkle 3 / 5				✔				✔
Cawsand/Kingsand 10 / 16				✔✔	✔	✔(Maker Heights)		✔✔
Cremyll 3 / 5 (+ferry)				✔				✔
Plymouth 2¾ / 4.5	(✔)	✔	TIC	✔✔	✔✔		H	✔✔
(Mayflower Steps)								

(for key and notes see previous page)

VILLAGE & TOWN FACILITIES & DISTANCES
Plymouth to Bude

PLACE* & DISTANCE* APPROX MILES / *KM*	BANK (ATM)	POST OFFICE	INFO	EATING PLACE	FOOD SHOP	CAMP-SITE	HOSTEL BARN	B&B HOTEL
(cont'd from p33)								
Treen 4½ / *7*				✓		✓✓		✓✓
Porthcurno ½ / *1*				(✓)				✓
Land's End 5 / *8*	(✓)§		VC	✓(✓✓)		✓✓	H	✓✓✓
Sennen Cove/Mayon 1 / *1.5*	(✓)	✓		✓✓✓	✓✓	✓(+1)		✓✓
Kelynack 5 / *8*						✓✓	YHA	
Cape Cornwall 2 / *3*				✓(✓)		(✓)		✓✓
(St Just +1½)	(✓)	✓	TIP	✓✓✓	✓✓			✓✓✓
Botallack Mine 1¾ / *2.7* (Botallack+½)				✓		✓		
Pendeen Watch 2 / *3* (Pendeen/Trewellard+¾)				✓✓✓	✓	✓		✓✓
Morvah Cliff 1½ / *2.6* (Morvah+½)				(✓)		(✓)		
Lean Point 3½ / *5* (Gurnard's Hd/Treen+½)				✓				✓
Zennor Head 1 / *1.5* (Zennor +¾)				✓✓				✓✓
St Ives 6 / *9.5*	✓	✓	TIC	✓✓✓	✓✓✓	✓	H	✓✓✓
Hayle 6 / *9.5*	(✓)	✓	TIC	✓✓✓	✓✓	✓		✓✓✓
Gwithian 4 / *6.5*				✓✓✓		✓		
Portreath 8 / *13*	(✓)§	✓		✓✓✓	✓		YHA(1½)	✓✓
Porthtowan 3 / *5*		✓		✓✓(✓)	✓	✓		
Trevaunance Cove 4½ / *7*				✓✓✓				✓
(St Agnes+½)	(✓)	✓		✓✓✓	✓✓	✓✓		✓✓✓
Perranporth 3½ / *5.5*	(✓)	✓		✓✓✓	✓✓✓	✓✓	(YHA)	✓✓
Holywell 4½ / *7*				✓✓		✓		✓
Porth Joke 2 / *3*						✓		
Crantock 2 / *3* (or **6**/*9.5* on main road)		✓		✓✓✓	✓	✓✓		
Newquay 2 / *3*	✓	✓	TIC	✓✓✓	✓✓✓	✓	H	✓✓✓
Porth 4 / *6.5*	(✓)			✓✓✓		✓		✓
Watergate Bay 2 / *3*				✓✓✓		✓		✓
Mawgan Porth 2 / *3*	(✓)§			✓✓✓	✓	✓✓		✓✓✓
Bedruthan Steps 1½ / *2.5*				(✓✓)		✓		
Porthcothan 2¾ / *4.4*					✓			
Constantine Bay & Treyarnon 2 / *3*				✓✓	✓	✓✓	YHA	
Mother Ivey's Bay 2½ / *4*						✓		
Harlyn Bay 1½ / *2.5*				✓				
Trevone 1½ / *2.5*				✓✓	✓			✓
Padstow (ferry)	✓	✓	TIC	✓✓✓	✓✓	✓		✓✓✓
Rock t/o 5 / *8* (Rock+½)	(✓)§			✓✓✓	✓			✓✓
Polzeath 3 / *5*	(✓)			✓✓✓	✓	✓(¾)		
Port Isaac 9 / *14.5*	(✓)			✓✓✓	✓			✓✓✓
Port Gaverne 1 / *1.5*				✓✓		✓		✓
Trebarwith Strand 6 / *9.5*	(✓)			✓✓				✓
Tintagel 2 / *3*	(✓)	(✓)	VC	✓✓✓	✓✓	✓	(YHA & H)	✓✓✓
Bossiney 1 / *1.5*					✓	✓		
Boscastle 4 / *6.5*	(✓)	✓		✓✓✓	✓	✓	(YHA)	✓✓✓
Crackington Haven 7 / *11.5*				✓✓		✓		✓✓✓
Widemouth Bay 7 / *11.5*				✓✓✓	✓	✓✓		✓✓✓
Bude & Upton 3 / *5*	✓	✓	TIC	✓✓✓	✓✓	✓✓✓		✓✓✓

(for key and notes see previous page)

SUGGESTED ITINERARIES

The itineraries that follow are suggestions only; feel free to adapt them to your needs. They have been divided into different accommodation types and each table has different itineraries to encompass different walking paces. **Remember to add your travelling time before and after the walk**.

Note that most campsites are open from Easter to October only; also there are not enough hostels along the coast path to stay in one every night.

STAYING IN HOSTELS (YHA AND INDEPENDENT)

Night	Place	Hostel	Approx Distance miles *km*		Place	Hostel	Approx Distance miles *km*	
		Medium pace				Fast pace		
0	Bude				Bude			
1	Crack'ton Haven		10	*16*	Boscastle	YHA	17	*27*
2	Tintagel	YHA & H	12	*19.5*	Port Isaac		14	*22.5*
3	Port Isaac		9	*14.5*	Padstow		12	*19.5*
4	Padstow		12	*19.5*	Treyarnon	YHA	10	*16*
5	Treyarnon	YHA	10	*16*	Newquay	H	13	*21*
6	Newquay	H	13	*21*	Perranporth	YHA	10*	*16**
7	Perranporth	YHA	10*	*16**	Portreath	YHA	11	*18*
8	Portreath	YHA	11	*18*	St Ives	H	17	*27*
9	Hayle		12	*19.5*	Pendeen		13	*21*
10	St Ives	H	5	*8*	Land's End	H	10	*16*
11	Zennor		6	*9.5*	Penzance	YHA & H	17	*27*
12	St Just	YHA	12	*19.5*	Porthleven		13	*21*
13	Land's End	H	4	*6.5*	Lizard	YHA	12	*19.5*
14	Porthcurno		6	*9.5*	Coverack	YHA	11	*18*
15	Penzance	YHA	11	*18*	Falmouth	H	20†	*32†*
16	Porthleven		13	*21*	Boswinger	YHA	20	*32*
17	Lizard	YHA	12	*19.5*	Charlestown		11	*18*
18	Coverack	YHA	12	*19.5*	Polperro		19	*30.5*
19	Mawnan Smith		14†	*22.5†*	Portwrinkle		13	*21*
20	Falmouth	H	9	*14.5*	Plymouth	H	16	*26*
21	Portloe		13	*21*	(Barbican)			
22	Boswinger	YHA	7	*11.5*				
23	Charlestown		11	*18*				
24	Fowey		10¼	*16.5*	*Note: where there is no hostel it*			
25	Looe		12	*19.5*	*will be necessary to camp or*			
26	Portwrinkle		9	*14.5*	*stay in a B&B. Not all hostels*			
27	Plymouth (Barbican)	H	16	*26*	*are open all year.*			

YHA = YHA hostel; H = independent hostel

* Perhaps longer, depending on route across The Gannel (see pp137-8)

† Using ferry from Helford to Helford Passage (see p241)

CAMPING (EASTER TO OCTOBER ONLY)

	Relaxed pace			Medium pace			Fast pace		
Night	**Place**	**Approx Distance** miles *km*		**Place**	**Approx Distance** miles *km*		**Place**	**Approx Distance** miles *km*	
0	Bude			Bude			Bude		
1	Widem'th Bay	3	5	Crack'tn Hvn	10	16	Boscastle	17	27
2	Crack'ton Hvn	7	11.5	Tintagel	12	19.5	Port Gav	12½	20
3	Boscastle	7	11.5	Port Gaverne	8½	13.5	Padstow	12½	20
4	Tintagel	5	8	Padstow	12½	20	B'than Stps	16	26
5	Port Gaverne	8½	13.5	Treyarnon	10	16	Perranporth	17*	27*
6	Padstow	12½	20	Newquay	13	21	Gwithian	19	30.5
7	Treyarnon	10	16	Perranporth	10*	16*	St Ives	11	18
8	Bedruthan Stps	6	9.5	Porthtowan	8	13	Cape C'wall	17	27
9	Newquay	7	11.5	Gwithian	11	18	Treen	11½	18.5
10	Porth Joke	5*	8*	St Ives	11	18	Penzance	10	16
11	Perranporth	5	8	Pendeen	13	21	Porthleven	16	26
12	Porthtowan	8	13	Land's End	10	16	Lizard	12	19.5
13	Gwithian	11	18	Penzance	15½	25	Porthallow	17	27
14	St Ives	11	18	Praa Sands	11	18	Maenporth	12½†20†	
15	Pendeen	13	21	Mullion Cove	11	18	Portscatho	11	18
16	Cape Cornwall	4	6.5	Lizard	6	9.5	Gorran Hn	16½	26.5
17	Land's End	6	9.5	Coverack	12	19.5	Charlestown	11	18
18	Treen	5½	9	Porthallow	5	8	Polruan	10	16
19	Penzance	10	16	Maenporth	12½†	20†	Looe	12	19.5
20	Praa Sands	11	18	Portscatho	11	18	Cawsand	17½	28
21	Porthleven	5	8	Gorran Haven	16½	26.5	Plymouth	6	9.5
22	Mullion Cove	6	9.5	Charlestown	11	18	(Barbican)		
23	Lizard	6	9.5	Polruan	10	16			
24	Coverack	12	19.5	Looe	12	19.5			
25	Porthallow	5	8	Cawsand	17½	28			
26	Maenporth	12½†20†		Plymouth	6	9.5			
27	Portscatho	11	18	(Barbican)					
28	Gorran Haven	16½	26.5						
29	Charlestown	11	18						
30	Polruan	10	16						
31	Lansallos	5	8						
32	Looe	7	11						
33	Cawsand	17½	28						
34	Plymouth	6	9.5						
	(Barbican)								

Note: distances do not include getting from the coastpath to the campsite

* Perhaps longer, depending on route across The Gannel (see pp137-8)

† Using ferry from Helford to Helford Passage (see p241)

PLANNING YOUR WALK

STAYING IN B&Bs

Night	Relaxed pace Place	Approx Distance miles	km	Medium pace Place	Approx Distance miles	km	Fast pace Place	Approx Distance miles	km
0	Bude			Bude			Bude		
1	C'ton Haven	10	16	C'ton Haven	10	16	Boscastle	17	27
2	Boscastle	7	11.5	Boscastle	7	11.5	Port Isaac	14	22.5
3	Tintagel	5	8	Port Isaac	14	22.5	Padstow	12	19.5
4	Port Isaac	9	14.5	Padstow	12	19.5	M'gan Pth	17	27
5	Padstow	12	19.5	Mawgan Pth	17	27	Perranporth	16*	26*
6	Trevone	5	8	Newquay	6	9.5	Portreath	11	18
7	Mawgan Porth	12	19.5	Perranporth	10*	16*	St Ives	17	27
8	Newquay	6	9.5	Portreath	11	18	Pendeen	13	21
9	Perranporth	10*	16*	Hayle	12	19.5	Porthcurno	15	24
10	Portreath	11	18	St Ives	5	8	Marazion	14	22.5
11	Hayle	12	19.5	Zennor	6	9.5	Mullion	16	26
12	St Ives	5	8	St Just	11	18	Coverack	17	27
13	Zennor	6	9.5	Porthcurno	11	18	Falmouth	20†	32†
14	Pendeen	7	11.5	Penzance	11	18	Portloe	13¾	22.25
15	Sennen Cove	9	14.5	Porthleven	13	21	Mevagissey	12½	20
16	Porthcurno	6	9.5	Lizard	12	19.5	Fowey	17½	28
17	Mousehole	7	11.5	Coverack	11	18	Looe	12	19.5
18	Marazion	7	11.5	Mawnan Smith	11†	18†	Cawsand	18	29
19	Porthleven	10	16	Falmouth	9	14.5	Plymouth	6	9.5
20	Mullion	6	9.5	Portloe	13¾	22.25	(Barbican)		
21	Lizard	6	9.5	Mevagissey	12½	20			
22	Coverack	11	18	Charlestown	7¼	11.75			
23	Porthallow	5	8	Fowey	10¼	16.5			
24	Mawnan Smith	9†	14.5†	Looe	12	19.5			
25	Falmouth	9	14.5	Portwrinkle	9	14.5			
26	Portscatho	6¼	10	Cawsand	9	14.5			
27	Portloe	7½	12	Plymouth	6	9.5			
28	Mevagissey	12½	20	(Barbican)					
29	Charlestown	7¼	11.75						
30	Fowey	10¼	16.5						
31	Polperro	7	11.5						
32	Looe	5	8						
33	Portwrinkle	9	14.5						
34	Cawsand	9	14.5						
35	Plymouth	6	9.5						
	(Barbican)								

* Perhaps longer, depending on route across The Gannel (see pp137-8)

† Using ferry from Helford to Helford Passage (see p241)

PLANNING YOUR WALK

THE BEST DAY AND WEEKEND WALKS

There's nothing quite like walking along a long-distance footpath for several days or even weeks but some people just don't have the time. The following highlights offer outstanding walking and scenery coupled with good public transport (see pp52-5) at the start and finish.

Day walks

● **Crackington Haven to Boscastle**   **7 miles/11.5km (see pp86-90)**
A tough, but exhilarating day's walk along the top of beautiful green cliffs; some of the highest in Cornwall. Begin at the tiny hamlet of Crackington Haven and finish in the enchanting village of Boscastle with its pretty pubs, stone houses and witch museum!

● **Tintagel to Port Isaac**   **9 miles/14.5km (see pp102-9)**
Another tough section, but despite the unforgiving ups and downs it is also one of the most enjoyable. Beginning at historic Tintagel with its castle and Arthurian legend, the path continues past historic mine workings and past the beautiful beaches of Trebarwith Strand and Tregardock before a roller-coaster cliff-top path leads eventually to the pretty white-washed buildings of Port Isaac.

● **Crantock to Perranporth**   **8 miles/13km (see pp140-7)**
An excellent day's walk starting from the picturesque village of Crantock and finishing along the expansive sands of Perran Beach. Take a picnic to have at secluded Porth Joke, or stop for lunch in Holywell at the thatched Treguth Inn.

● **St Ives to Zennor**   **6 miles/9.5km (see pp170-2)**
This walk offers a combination of wild Atlantic coastline, exquisite light and a feeling of remoteness that can't be matched by many other places on the coast path. It's also one of the trickiest parts of the whole trail with many rocky, uneven, boggy sections and some relentless ascents and descents. However, there is a good bus service so you can walk one way and take the bus back.

● **Porthcurno to Mousehole**   **7 miles/11.5km (see pp192-8)**
A charming walk with lots of coves and headlands to explore.

● **Mullion Cove to the Lizard**   **7 miles/11.5km (see pp224-9)**
A cliff-top walk from a classic Cornish fishing village to the southernmost point in mainland Britain, taking in long stretches of windswept heath and beautiful Kynance Cove. This route can be very exposed in bad weather.

● **Mevagissey to Fowey**   **18¼ miles/29.5km (see pp273-85)**
You would need to leave early if contemplating this long but fulfilling day's walk. Featuring plenty of cliff-top walking, the beaches at Par, Pentewan & Polkerris, and the wonderful harbour village of Charlestown, such a hike would constitute a thorough introduction to what walking in Cornwall is all about.

● **Fowey/Polruan to Looe**   **12¼ miles/19.75km (see pp286-99)**
Either starting in Polruan or with a short ferry journey across the River Fowey, this predominantly cliff-top route allows for a lunch-stop in Polperro – a small harbour village, full of character – before ending up in one of Cornwall's most bustling towns: Looe.

PLANNING YOUR WALK

Weekend walks

● **Crackington Haven to Port Isaac**   **21 miles/34km (see pp86-109)**
This challenging walk combines the first two day walks as detailed on p39, with
the addition of the easy cliff-top section between Boscastle and Tintagel which
takes in some wonderful coves, inlets and the lovely beach at Bossiney Haven.

● **Padstow to Mawgan Porth**   **17 miles/27km (see pp121-30)**
The highlights of this section include Pepper and Round Holes, Trevose Head
lighthouse, Park Head, Bedruthan Steps and a long section of coastline as wonderfully indented and eroded as the crooked man's crooked stile.

● **St Ives to Land's End**   **23 miles/37km (see pp170-89)**
Pass through tough granite villages, head out onto Cape Cornwall and enjoy the
rugged atmosphere of this walk.

● **Sennen Cove to Mousehole**   **13 miles/21km (see pp187-99)**
Start and end in tiny fishing villages, walk to Land's End, the furthest point west
in England, and enjoy picnics in beautiful coves crying out to be explored.

● **Praa Sands to the Lizard**   **17½ miles/28km (see pp214-29)**
Pack your camera for the scenic highlights of Mullion and Kynance coves and
enjoy striding out across the windswept heath and turf of the Lizard Peninsula.

● **Falmouth/Place to Mevagissey**   **26 miles/42km (see pp259-73)**
Beginning in Place (see p259), this slightly tougher two-day wandering allows
for a night in Portloe as well as visits to such typical Cornish villages as
Portscatho and Portholland, rounded off with lunch of fish 'n' chips at Gorran
Haven. There are particularly good views from Nare Head and Dodman Point.

● **Mevagissey to Polperro**   **26 miles/42km (see pp273-93)**
Providing the hiker with opportunities to stop overnight in Charlestown and
enjoy a lunch-stop in Fowey, this two-day stroll really does take in some of the
best Cornish towns. Parts of the path can be quite testing but a cream tea in
Pentewan and the views from Gribbin Head should easily divert your mind
away from any aching limbs.

● **Looe to Plymouth**   **21¼ miles/34km (see pp299-320)**
With the option of stopping in Portwrinkle, this relatively undemanding two-day
hike visits the small communities of Seaton and Downderry, before rounding
Rame Head and taking in the twin villages of Kingsand and Cawsand as well as

---

❏ WALKING FROM A FIXED BASE

An option to consider when making your plans is to stay at one place and use public
transport to access different stretches of the coast path. This would particularly suit
those on a short break, or groups who wanted to rent a self-catering cottage (see p22).

When choosing a place to base yourself you need somewhere with good public
transport (see pp52-5), a variety of coast-path walks nearby and preferably somewhere with a bit of atmosphere so that you can enjoy yourself when you are not walking. Consider Boscastle (p90), Tintagel (p98), Port Isaac (p105), Padstow (p117), St
Ives (p165), St Just (p183), Mousehole (p196), Newlyn (p200), Penzance (p202),
Marazion (p208), Lizard Village (p224), Mevagissey (p270), Fowey (p283), Polperro
(p290) and Looe (p296).

the picturesque Mt Edgcumbe Country Park. There is plenty of cliff-top walking and a Napoleonic fort. In fact the particularly sturdy could achieve this in a single day – especially with the option of a ferry from Cawsand direct to Plymouth.

What to take

What and how much to take are very personal choices that take experience to get right. For those who are new to long-distance walking the suggestions below will help you reach a balance of comfort, safety and minimal weight.

KEEP IT LIGHT

When packing your rucksack it cannot be emphasised enough that the less weight you are carrying the more you will enjoy your walk. If you pack a lot of unnecessary items you will undoubtedly find yourself wanting to discard them as you go. If you are in any doubt about taking something, leave it at home.

RUCKSACK

If you are staying in B&Bs or hostels you will need a medium-sized pack of about 40-60 litres' capacity; just big enough to hold a change of clothes, a waterproof jacket, a few toiletries, a water bottle/pouch and a packed lunch. Hostellers may require a few extras such as a towel and food for cooking.

Campers will need a rucksack big enough to carry a tent, sleeping bag, towel, cooking equipment and food. A pack of about 60-80 litres should be ample.

Pack everything inside a large plastic bag (or inside a number of smaller plastic bags for easier retrieval); there is nothing worse than discovering that all your clothes and sleeping bag have got wet, and even though most backpacks come with their own elasticated rain cover, they are, in reality, barely shower proof. Most outdoor shops stock large bags made from tough plastic, or you can use heavy-duty garden bin bags.

If you are walking with an organised tour or using a baggage-carrying service (see p28) you will be able to pack the bulk of your gear into a suitcase or holdall. While walking you need only a lightweight daypack for a spare jumper, waterproof jacket, water bottle/pouch and lunch but don't forget the camera, map and guide book – and some may also wish to bring walking poles, binoculars and a first-aid kit.

FOOTWEAR

Most hikers choose to wear a decent pair of strong, durable **trekking boots**, but it is perfectly possible, particularly in summer, to hike the coast path in **running shoes** or cross-trainers, which are usually much more comfortable. The downside is that they are much less waterproof, if waterproof at all, so you will find you spend many an evening trying to dry them out in preparation for your next day's walk. Many hikers prefer boots with a good ankle support; the ground can occasionally be rough and stony and twisted ankles can happen. Whatever footwear you choose, it is essential that your shoes or boots are thoroughly 'broken in' so they're comfortable and not likely to cause blisters. Never, under any circumstances, attempt to start a hike like this one in new boots!

In addition, some people bring an extra pair of shoes or trainers (or sandals or **flip-flops** – particularly handy for beaches, or for camping) to wear off the trail. This is not essential but if you've got room in your luggage, why not?

If you are walking in the winter you'll be much more comfortable if your boots are waterproof; wet feet equals cold feet. To waterproof leather boots cover them in a layer of wax and take the wax with you so you can redo them a couple of times during your walk.

Gaiters are not really necessary but if you have a pair you may find them useful when it's wet and muddy, or to keep the sand out when walking across dunes and beaches.

CLOTHING

Even if you are setting out in good weather on just a day walk you should always have suitable clothing to keep you warm and dry should the weather change. Most walkers choose their clothes according to the versatile layering system, which consists of an outer layer or 'shell' to protect you from the wind and rain, a mid layer or two to keep you warm, and a base layer to transport sweat away from your skin.

The most important item is a **waterproof/windproof jacket**. Even in summer it can rain for a week and if the sun isn't out the sea breeze can make it feel distinctly chilly. The most comfortable jackets are those made from breathable fabrics that let moisture (your sweat) out, but don't let moisture (the rain) in.

A polyester **fleece**, or woollen jumper, makes a good middle layer as they remain warm even when wet. The advantage of fleece is that it is lightweight and dries relatively quickly. In winter you may want to carry an extra jumper to put on when you stop as you can get cold very quickly.

In summer cotton T-shirts are fine for a **base layer**, but at other times of the year you will be more comfortable wearing a thin thermal layer. Cotton absorbs sweat, trapping it next to the skin which will chill you rapidly when you stop exercising. Modern synthetic fabrics on the other hand, 'wick' sweat away from the body and dry rapidly although they can also quickly start to smell bad. More expensive but with far better odour control is Merino wool, which is lightweight, high-wicking, quick-drying and washable.

Shorts are great to walk in during the summer, although you'll probably want to bring a pair of **long trousers** for cooler days. Also, some sections of the path can become overgrown with stinging nettles and you may appreciate having your legs covered. Don't wear jeans; if they get wet they become incredibly heavy and stick uncomfortably to your skin. They also take forever to dry.

It is worth investing in good **socks**. There are many on the market that are designed with walkers in mind – check out the Thousand-Mile sock range. You will notice the difference particularly when they don't become hard and stiff after the first day of walking. How many pairs you take is a personal preference; if you're happy to hand wash them at the end of each day, three pairs will suffice. If you'd rather wait until you can use a laundry service for your clothes' washing, then you may need four or five pairs.

Underwear goes without saying and how many pairs to take is a personal preference (see above re socks). Women may find a sports bra more comfortable because pack straps can cause bra straps to dig into your shoulders.

A **hat** with a brim is pretty much essential during the summer, keeping you cool and preventing sunburn (which can be a real danger in Cornwall in the summer months). In the cooler months you'll need a woolly hat and some **gloves**.

Don't forget your **swimming gear** and a **towel**; the white-sand beaches and crystal-clear aquamarine seas are extremely inviting.

You will also need a **change of clothing** for the evening. If you're staying in B&Bs and eating out you may feel more comfortable with something tidy. If you're camping, early spring and late autumn nights can be decidedly chilly, so pack something warm, both to sleep in and to walk around the campsite in.

❏ HIKING WITH KIDS

Being able to bring my kids along with me on trips is always a joy but, when it's a hiking trip, the main challenge is to keep them from dying of boredom! My five-year-old daughter Yoyo tagged along with me for part of my Cornwall Coast Path research for the 5th edition of this book. She's since grown into an experienced long-distance walker, and joined me again for this 7th edition, but here's how on that first trip I managed to keep her excited about hiking along the same track for 10 days in a row:

● **Short walks** We aimed for 7km or 8km a day (more if not too hilly); so just a couple of hours in the morning, and a couple of hours in the afternoon.

● **Visible targets** 'We'll have a picnic when we get to the top of that hill' sounds much more encouraging to a five year old than 'We'll stop for lunch at 1 o'clock'.

● **Plenty of breaks** As well as stopping frequently for rests, we took a few mornings or afternoons off – mostly for beach time – and sometimes the whole day if it was wet.

● **Aiming for the beach** I found it helped to target something fun each day, like a beach or a swimming pool or a playground. When Yoyo knew there was going to be some play time up ahead, she was much more excited about getting to our destination.

● **Games** To make the walk more engaging Yoyo and I played games as we went along. Sometimes just something as simple as 'I spy', but she also enjoyed animal- and plant-spotting games – first person to spot 10 snails, for example.

● **Camping** We camped almost every day, and Yoyo absolutely loved it. There's nothing more exciting for a four- or five-year-old than sleeping in a tent!

● **Rucksack** It was great to have the option of my child-carrier rucksack although Yoyo hardly used it in the end. Mostly it carried our tent rather than my daughter.

● **Scrapbook** It may sound strange, but having a plan to make a scrapbook together when you get back home makes the walk itself more fun. Yoyo loved collecting things for her scrapbook along the way (seashells, flowers, tickets, postcards etc).

● **Ice creams** If all else fails **Daniel McCrohan**

PLANNING YOUR WALK

❏ CANINE COMPANIONS

The South-West Coast Path is a dog-friendly path and many are the rewards that await those prepared to make the extra effort required to bring their best friend along the trail. However, you shouldn't underestimate the amount of work involved in bringing your pooch to the path. Indeed, just about every decision you make will be influenced by the fact that you've got a dog: how you plan to travel to the start of the trail, where you're going to stay, how far you're going to walk each day, where you're going to rest and where you're going to eat in the evening etc etc.

The decision-making begins well before you've set foot on the trail. For starters, you have to ask – and be honest with – yourself: can your dog really cope with walking ten-plus miles (16+km) a day, day after day, week after week? And just as importantly, will he or she actually enjoy it?!?

If you think the answer is yes to both, you need to start preparing accordingly. You'll certainly have to put extra thought into your itinerary. The best starting point is to study the advice on pp336-8 and the Village & town facilities tables (pp32-5) to plan where you can stay and eat, and where to buy food for your mutt.

Henry Stedman

TOILETRIES

Only take the minimum. Essentials are **soap**, **shampoo**, **toothbrush**, **toothpaste**, any **medication** and, for women, **sanitary towels** and **tampons**. **Loo paper** is generally provided in public toilets, but bring a roll just in case and carry a small lightweight **trowel** for burying excrement if you get caught out far from a toilet (see pp70-1 for the code of the outdoor loo). **Sunscreen is essential** and lip-salve is also a good idea. Deodorants, hair brushes, razors and so forth are up to you. If you are hostelling or camping you will also need a **towel**.

FIRST-AID KIT

Medical facilities in Britain are good so you only need to take a first-aid kit to deal with basic injuries. In a waterproof bag or container you should have: **scissors** for cutting tape and cutting away clothing; **aspirin** or **paracetamol** for treating mild to moderate pain; one or two **stretch bandages** for holding dressings or splints in place and for sprained ankles or sore knees; if you think your knees will give you trouble **elastic supports** are invaluable; a **triangular bandage** for broken/sprained arms; a small selection of **sterile dressings** for wounds; **porous adhesive tape** to hold them in place; **plasters/Band Aids** for minor cuts; a sturdier, preferably waterproof **adhesive tape** for blister prevention; **Compeed**, **Second Skin** or **Moleskin** for treating blisters; **safety pins**; **antiseptic cream** or liquid; **tweezers**; and treatment such as **Imodium** for acute diarrhoea – you never know when it might come in handy.

GENERAL ITEMS

Other essential items you should carry are: a **torch** (flashlight) in case you end up walking in the dark; a **whistle** to attract attention if you get lost or find yourself in trouble (see box p77); a **water bottle** or pouch (two litres is the best size); a **watch**; a current **tide chart** (available for £1.75 from newsagents or TICs in coastal areas); and a **plastic bag** for carrying any rubbish you accumulate.

You should also carry some **emergency food** with you such as chocolate, dried fruit and biscuits.

Walking poles are now widely used (although opinions are divided on how much they really help). Using them requires some practice.

Useful items to carry are: a **pen-knife**; a **camera**; a **notebook** to record your impressions in a different way; **sunglasses** to protect your eyes from the glare off water and beaches on sunny days; **binoculars**; something to read; and a **vacuum flask** for hot drinks (worth the investment if you're on a budget as buying all those cups of tea or coffee can get expensive).

A **map-case** can be a useful extra for protecting your map and guidebook in the rain, which can very quickly reduce both to pulp.

CAMPING GEAR

Campers will need a decent **tent** able to withstand wind and rain; a **sleeping mat**; a two- or three-season **sleeping bag** (you can always wear clothes inside your sleeping bag if you are cold); a **camping stove** and fuel; **cooking equipment** (a pot with a pot-grabber and a lid that can double as a frying pan is enough for two people); a **bowl**, **mug**, **cutlery** (don't forget a can-opener), **pen-knife** and a **scrubber** for washing up.

MONEY AND DOCUMENTS

It is most convenient to carry your money as **cash**. A debit **card** (with a PIN) is the easiest way to withdraw money either from banks, cash machines or post offices and, along with credit cards, can be used to pay in most shops, restaurants and hotels. Remember to stock up on cash whenever you can, though, as there are numerous villages along the path that don't have facilities for withdrawing money.

Always keep your money and documents in a safe place and in a waterproof container. In particular, those camping or staying in hostels should take care not to leave them lying around; it's much safer to carry them on you at all times.

MAPS

The hand-drawn maps in this book cover the trail at a scale of 1:20,000; plenty of detail and information to keep you on the right track. If you wish to explore inland, Ordnance Survey (☎ 0345-605 0505, 🖥 ordnancesurvey.co.uk) produce eight excellent maps covering the Cornish coast in their Explorer series; the ones with the orange cover. The numbers you'll require are: 111 Bude, Boscastle and Tintagel; 106 Newquay and Padstow; 104 Redruth and St Agnes; 102 Land's End, Penzance and St Ives; 103 The Lizard, Falmouth and Helston; 105 Falmouth and Mevagissey; 107 St Austell and Liskeard; and 108 Lower Tamar Valley and Plymouth. These maps are also good for those with a particular interest in Cornwall's ancient sites as all sites, however minor, are shown.

❏ SOURCES OF FURTHER INFORMATION

Trail information

● **South West Coast Path Association** (SWCPA; 💻 southwestcoastpath.org.uk) The SWCPA promotes the interests of users of the South-West Coast Path by, amongst other things, lobbying the numerous bodies responsible for the path in order to ensure it is maintained to a high standard. There are several places where the Association is actively seeking for the path to be re-routed so that it can genuinely be called a coast path. They publish an annual guide to the entire South West Coast Path (£18 to non-members) and are happy to provide advice and information to assist your coast-path walk. Membership, which includes a copy of the annual guide, costs £27.50 per year (£35.50 for non-UK residents).

Tourist information

● **Tourist information centres (TICs)** TICs provide locally specific information for visitors and may also provide an accommodation-booking service (for which there is usually a charge). Unfortunately many of the local council-run TICs in Cornwall have lost their funding. Some have managed to diversify or are now staffed by volunteers so remain open, while others have simply had to shut. There are TICs in: Bude (see p80), Padstow (p117), Newquay (p132), Hayle (p160), St Ives (p165), Penzance (p203), Looe (p296) and Plymouth (p316).

● **Tourist information points (TIPs)** TIPs have leaflets about local attractions but they are unstaffed. There are TIPs at St Just (p183) and Mevagissey (p270). Many village shops, libraries or post offices also have local tourist information.

● **Visitor centres (VCs)** These generally provide information about their particular attraction, though they sometimes have general leaflets for other places of interest in the area but the staff will probably not be able to help with accommodation or similar queries. There are visitor centres at Tintagel (p98), Land's End (p188), Falmouth (p250), and St Mawes (p253).

● **Tourist boards** For general information about the whole of Cornwall contact Cornwall Tourist Board (💻 visitcornwall.com).

Organisations for walkers

● **Backpackers' Club** (💻 backpackersclub.co.uk) A club for people who are involved or interested in lightweight camping through walking, cycling, skiing and canoeing. They produce a quarterly magazine, provide members with a comprehensive advisory and information service on all aspects of backpacking, organise weekend trips and also publish a farm-pitch directory. Membership costs £20 per year.

● **Long Distance Walkers' Association** (💻 ldwa.org.uk) An association of people with the common interest of long-distance walking. Membership includes a journal three times per year giving details of challenge events and local group walks as well as articles on the subject. Information on over 500 Long Distance Paths is presented in the LDWA's Long Distance Walkers' Handbook. Membership costs £18 per year, £25.50 for a family. International membership is £15/26 without/with the journal.

● **Ramblers** (💻 ramblers.org.uk) Looks after the interests of walkers. Members receive their quarterly *Walk* magazine, have access to both the Ramblers Routes online library (short routes only for non members) and an app as well as group walks. Members also receive discounts at various stores. Individual/joint membership costs £36.60/49.

● **Walking World** (💻 walkingworld.com) Online organisation. Membership fee of £18 allows access to pdf downloads of hundreds of walks throughout the UK including many in Cornwall, with a Find a walk feature.

AZ from Collins (⌨ collins.co.uk/pages/a-z) produce an adventure series of OS map booklets (No 2: North Cornwall & 3: South Cornwall) to the SWCP.

Harvey Maps (☎ 01786-841202, ⌨ harveymaps.co.uk) produce a three-map series that covers the entire South West Coast Path: Map 1 and Map 2 cover the Cornwall sections.

Enthusiastic map buyers can reduce the often-considerable expense of purchasing them: Ramblers (see box opposite) has the complete range of OS Explorer and Landranger maps and members can borrow up to 10 maps for four weeks; all you have to pay for is return postage. Members of Backpackers' Club can purchase maps at a significant discount through the club.

❏ DIGITAL MAPPING

Most smartphones have a GPS chip so you can see your position overlaid onto a digital map on your phone. There are numerous software packages that provide Ordnance Survey (OS) maps for a smartphone, tablet, PC or GPS unit. Maps are downloaded over the internet, then loaded into an app, also available by download, from where you can view them, print them and create routes on them.

It is important to ensure any digital mapping software on your smartphone uses pre-downloaded maps stored on your device, and doesn't need to download them on-the-fly, as this may be expensive and will be impossible without a signal. Note that battery life will be significantly reduced, compared to normal usage, when you are using the built-in GPS and running the screen for long periods.

Many websites have **free routes** you can download for the more popular digital mapping products; anything from day walks to complete Long Distance Paths.

Memory Map (⌨ memory-map.co.uk) currently sell OS 1:25,000 mapping covering the whole of the UK for £166. They also have annual subscriptions from £25.

For a subscription of £2.99 for one month, or £23.99 for a year (on their current offer) **Ordnance Survey** (see p45) will let you download and then use their UK maps (1:25,000 scale) on a mobile or tablet without a data connection for a specific period.

PLANNING YOUR WALK

RECOMMENDED READING

Field guides

The following books are likely to be of interest to the enthusiast but may be too heavy to carry around.

● *Wildflowers of Britain and Europe* by W Lippert and D Podlech (HarperCollins) is a good compact book for beginners. It is organised by flower colour making it easy to flip immediately to the right section.

● *The Wild Flower Key* by Francis Rose and Clare O'Reilly (Warne) is an excellent book for more serious botanists. It is very comprehensive and enables identification of plants whether in flower or not.

● *Birds of Cornwall* by Trevor and Endymion Beer (Tor Mark Press, £2.99) is an extremely lightweight book. Useful but only available secondhand.

● The RSPB's *Pocket Guide to British Birds* by Simon Harrap identifies birds by their plumage and song.

● *Where to watch birds – Devon & Cornwall* by David Norman & Vic Tucker (Bloomsbury, 5th ed).

● *Collins Bird Guide* by Mullarney, Svensson, Zetterström & Grant (Harper Collins, 2nd ed).
● *Green Guide to Seashore Life of Britain and Europe* by Bob Gibbons, Denys Ovenden and Melanie Perkins (Bloomsbury) is a conveniently sized guide to 150 species of seaweeds, molluscs, crustaceans and insects likely to be found along Britain's coastline.
● The Field Studies Council (🖳 www.field-studies-council.org) publishes a series of *Identification Guides* (fold-out charts) which are also practical.
　　There are also several field guide apps for smartphones, including those that can aid in identifying birds from their song as well as by their appearance.

General reading

Good **non-fiction** reads include: *A History of Cornwall* by Ian Soulsby (Phillimore and Co, 1986); *King Arthur: The Dream of a Golden Age* by Geoffrey Ashe (Thames & Hudson, 1990); *The Lost Gardens of Heligan* by Tim Smit (Orion, 2010) and *Poldark's Cornwall* by Winston Graham (Macmillan, 2015).

　　The much-lauded best-selling coast-path **memoir** *The Salt Path* by Raynor Winn (2018) is an inspirational account of the author and her husband's last-minute decision to camp and hike their way along the entire South West Coast Path having been made homeless after losing a financial court case. Her follow-up book, *The Wild Silence* (2020), is largely based in and around Fowey and Polruan on Cornwall's south coast.

　　The Minack Chronicles by Derek Tangye describe the attempts of the author and his wife to set up a flower farm on the wild Cornish coast (originally published 1961-96, reissued 2014).

　　Lamorna Ash's *Dark, Salt, Clear* (2020), meanwhile, is an evocative account of Ash's time spent with a fishing boat crew in Newlyn.

　　Dog-owning hikers will warm to Mark Wallington's coast-path classic *Travels with Boogie: 500 Mile Walkies* (originally published in 1996, reissued in 2006 with *Boogie Up the River* in one volume), a humorous account of his time spent on the trail, accompanied by the more-loathed-than-loved Boogie the dog, in which man and beast survive all that the path can throw at them on a diet of tinned soup and Kennomeat.

　　For something more poetic, *Walking Away: Further Travels with a Troubadour on the South West Coast Path* (2015) is an often-hilarious travelogue by Poet Laureate Simon Armitage, recounting his time walking and reciting odes along the SWCP between Minehead and Land's End.

Fiction

Recommendations include *To the Lighthouse* by Virginia Woolf (first published 1932); *Rebecca* (1938), *Jamaica Inn* (1936) and *Frenchman's Creek* (1941) by Daphne du Maurier; the *Poldark* novels by Winston Graham (12 volumes originally published 1945-2002, reissued in 2015); *Zennor in Darkness* by Helen Dunmore (1993); *The Mousehole Cat* by Antonia Barber (1990).

Getting to and from the Cornwall Coast Path

All the major towns along the coast path are reasonably well served by rail and/or coach services from the rest of Britain. Travelling by train or coach is the most convenient way to get to the trail as you do not need to worry about where to leave your car, how safe it will be while you're walking, or how to get back to it at the end of your holiday. Choosing to travel by public transport is choosing to help the environment and is a creative step in minimising your impact on the countryside.

❏ GETTING TO BRITAIN

By air
The best international gateway to Britain for the Cornwall Coast Path is London with its six airports: Heathrow (the main airport; 🖳 heathrowairport.com), Gatwick (🖳 gatwickairport.com), Stansted (🖳 stanstedairport.com), Luton (🖳 london-luton.co.uk) London City (🖳 londoncityairport.com) and Southend (🖳 southendairport.com). However, some charter and budget airlines also have flights to Newquay (🖳 cornwall airportnewquay.com), Exeter (🖳 exeter-airport.co.uk) and Bristol (🖳 bristolairport.co.uk) airports.

From Europe by train
Eurostar (🖳 eurostar.com) operates a high-speed passenger service via the Channel Tunnel between Paris, Brussels, Amsterdam, Lille and London. The Eurostar terminal in London is at St Pancras International station with connections to the London Underground and to all other main railway stations in London. Trains to Cornwall (and Plymouth) leave from Paddington station; see p50 for details.

For more information about rail services from your country contact your national rail company or Rail Europe (🖳 raileurope.com).

From Europe by coach
Eurolines (🖳 eurolines.com) have a wide network of long-distance bus services connecting over 500 destinations in 25 European countries to London (Victoria Coach Station). Visit the Eurolines website for details of services from your country.

From Europe by car
P&O (🖳 poferries.com) runs frequent passenger ferries from Calais to Dover; and from Rotterdam and Zeebrugge to Hull. Brittany Ferries (🖳 brittanyferries.com) has services from Santander and Roscoff to Plymouth; from Bilbao, St Malo, Cherbourg, Caen and Le Havre to Portsmouth; and from Cherbourg to Poole. There are also several other ferries plying routes between mainland Europe and ports on Britain's eastern coast. Look at 🖳 ferrysavers.com or 🖳 directferries.com for a full list of companies and services.

Eurotunnel (🖳 eurotunnel.com) operates a shuttle train service (Le Shuttle) for vehicles via the Channel Tunnel between Calais and Folkestone taking one hour between the motorway in France and the motorway in Britain.

PLANNING YOUR WALK

NATIONAL TRANSPORT

By rail

The main Cornwall line, operated by Great Western Railway (see box below), runs from London Paddington through Exeter and Plymouth to finish at Penzance, with branch lines connecting major towns on the coast path. There are several services every day as well as a night train (the Night Riviera, Sun-Fri). Cross Country (☎ 0844-811 0124, 🖳 crosscountrytrains.co.uk) operates services from Scotland, the North-East and the Midlands to Penzance.

To get to Bude it's best to take a train to Exeter St David's and then get a bus (see pp52-5). However, the last train from London may arrive too late for the last bus to Bude so check in advance. Barnstaple, 35 miles to the north of Bude, and Okehampton, 30 miles to the east, are other possibilities. The rail service from Exeter to Okehampton (the Dartmoor Line) is now more regular with up to eight trains per day. In the summer GWR runs connecting buses regularly and daily from Okehampton to Bude. In contrast, from Barnstaple there are just one or two buses a day to Bude.

For Padstow get off the train at Bodmin Parkway station and catch Go Cornwall Bus service No 11A (see box p54). For Newquay change at Par, for Falmouth change at Truro and for St Ives change at St Erth.

National rail enquiries (☎ 03457-484950, 24hrs, 🖳 nationalrail.co.uk) is the only number you need to find out all timetable, ticket and fare information. Rail tickets are generally cheaper if you buy them online well in advance. Most discounted tickets carry some restrictions so check these carefully first. Buy tickets through the national rail enquiries website, direct from the relevant train company's website or in person at any railway station. You can also get them online at 🖳 thetrainline.com and 🖳 www.qjump.co.uk.

If you want to book a **taxi** when you arrive visit 🖳 traintaxi.co.uk for details of taxi companies operating at rail stations throughout England.

It is sometimes possible to buy a train ticket that includes **bus travel** at your destination: for further information visit the Plusbus website (🖳 plusbus.info).

By coach

National Express (see box opposite) is the main coach (long-distance bus) operator in Britain. Travel by coach is usually cheaper than by rail but does take longer. To get the cheapest fares you need to book seven days ahead. You can

---

❏ **LOCAL TRAIN SERVICES**

GWR – Great Western Railway (☎ 0345-7000 125, 🖳 www.gwr.com)

● St Erth to **St Ives** via Lelant Saltings, **Lelant** & **Carbis Bay**, Mon-Sat 2/hr in summer, Sun 1/hr, pm only in winter
● **Newquay** to **Par**, Mon-Sat 6/day, Sun 6/day in summer
● Truro to **Falmouth Docks**, Mon-Sat 2/hr, Sun 10/day
● Liskeard to **Looe** (Looe Valley Line), Mon-Sat 10/day, Sun 8/day
● **Plymouth** to **Penzance** via Liskeard, Bodmin Parkway, **Par**, St Austell, Truro, **Hayle** & St Erth, daily 1/hr

❏ NATIONAL EXPRESS COACH SERVICES

National Express (☎ 0871-781 8181, lines open 24 hours; 💻 nationalexpress.com)
Note: the services listed below operate daily but not all stops are included. Places in bold are on or very near the coast path.

101 Birmingham to **Plymouth** via Bristol, Taunton & **Exeter**, 3/day
102 Birmingham to **Plymouth** via Cheltenham, **Exeter**, Torquay & Paignton, 2/day
104 Birmingham to **Penzance** via Bristol, **Exeter**, **Plymouth**, **Newquay**, **Hayle** & St Erth, 1/day
404 London to **Plymouth** via Heathrow Airport, Chippenham, Bath, **Exeter**, Torquay & Paignton, 1/day
406 London Victoria to **Penzance** via Heathrow Airport, Weston-super-Mare, Taunton, **Exeter**, **Plymouth**, **Newquay**, Truro, **Falmouth**, & Helston, 1/day
502 London to Ilfracombe via Bristol, Taunton & **Barnstaple**, 2/day
504 London to **Penzance** via Heathrow Airport, **Exeter**, **Plymouth**, Bodmin, **Newquay**, Truro & **Falmouth**, 2/day plus London to **Plymouth** 1/day

buy tickets from coach and bus station ticket offices, National Express agents, directly from the driver (though not always, so do check in advance), by telephone or online. You need to allow at least four working days for posted tickets.

However, it is not easy to reach **Bude** by coach. Your best bet is to travel to Exeter, Okehampton or Plymouth and from there take the local bus service to Bude (see box pp54-5). Alternatively take a coach to **Barnstaple** and get Stagecoach's service from there to Bude. There are several coach services to other towns on the coast path and also services from **Falmouth** and **Plymouth** to London and elsewhere.

You could also try Megabus (💻 uk.megabus.com) which runs services to Falmouth, Plymouth and Newquay.

By car

The easiest way to drive into Cornwall is to join the M5 to Exeter and then take either the A30 or A38 depending on your final destination. Even if you're using a Sat Nav, a good road atlas is useful for navigating Cornwall's country lanes.

Parking your car can be a problem as you'll need to find long-term parking in a suitable location, then get back to it at the end of your walk.

By air

Although there is the option of taking a domestic flight into **Newquay airport** (see box p49), Newquay is 70 miles from Bude, and buses between the two take at least three hours. Bear in mind that air travel is by far the least environmentally sound option (see 💻 chooseclimate.org for the true costs of flying).

LOCAL TRANSPORT

Bus services

Cornwall has a comprehensive public transport network linking almost all the coastal villages with at least one bus per day in the summer. This is useful for the walker as there's the possibility of linear day and weekend walks *(cont'd on p56)*

PLANNING YOUR WALK

PLANNING YOUR WALK

Public Transport Map 1

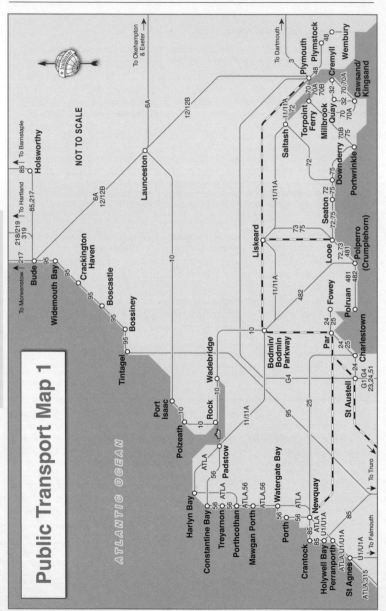

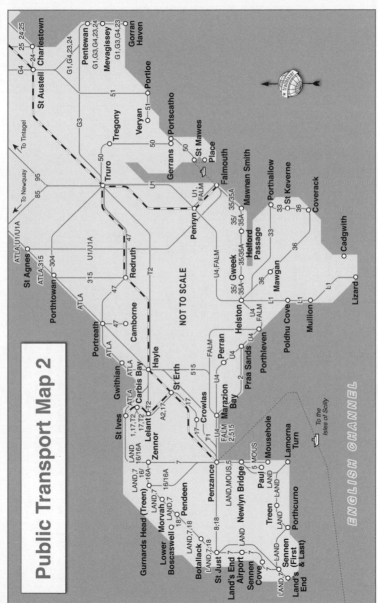

Public Transport Map 2

PLANNING YOUR WALK

□ BUS SERVICES [See public transport maps on pp52-3]

ATLA	First Kernow	Atlantic Coaster St Ives to Padstow via Hayle, Gwithian, Portreath, Porthtowan, St Agnes, Perranporth, Newquay, Watergate Bay, Mawgan Porth, Bedruthan Steps, Porthcothan & Harlyn, May-Sep daily 1/hr
FALM	First Kernow	Falmouth Coaster Falmouth to Penzance via Penryn, Helston, Porthleven & Marazion, daily 1/hr
LAND	First Kernow	Land's End Coaster Penzance to Penzance via Newlyn, Lamorna Turn, Treen, Porthcurno, Sennen, Land's End, St Just, Botallack, Pendeen, Morvah, Gurnard's Head, Zennor, St Ives, Carbis Bay, Lelant & Marazion, May-Sep daily 1/hr (Oct-Apr daily 2-6/day)
MOUS	First Kernow	Penzance to Mousehole via Newlyn, daily 2/hr
G1	GorranBus	Gorran Haven to St Austell via Mevagissey & Pentewan, Wed & Fri 1/day
G3	GorranBus	Gorran Haven to Truro via Mevagissey & Pentewan, Tue 2/day & Thur 1/day
G4	GorranBus	Gorran Haven to Plymouth via Mevagissey, Pentewan & St Austell, 3rd Mon of month 1/day
L1	First Kernow	(open-topped bus) Lizard to Helston via Mullion & Poldhu Cove, summer daily 1/hr, winter Mon-Sat 5/day
T1	First Kernow	Penzance to Truro via Long Rock & Hayle, daily 2/hr
T2	First Kernow	St Ives to Truro via Carbis Bay, Lelant & Hayle, daily 2/hr
U1/U1A	First Kernow	Falmouth to Newquay via St Agnes, Perranporth, Perran Sands & Goonhavern, daily 1-2/hr
U4	First Kernow	Falmouth to Penzance via Penryn, Helston, Porthleven, Praa Sands, Perran & Marazion, daily 1-2/hr
1	St Ives Bus Co	St Ives to Carbis Bay, Mon-Sat approx 1/hr
2	Go Cornwall Bus	Penzance to Praa Sands via Marazion, Mon-Sat 1/hr
5	Go Cornwall Bus	Penzance to Paul via Newlyn, daily 1/hr
6A	Stagecoach	Bude to Exeter via Launceston & Okehampton, Mon-Sat 7/day, Sun 3/day
7	Go Cornwall Bus	Penzance to Land's End via Zennor, Gurnard's Head, Morvah, Pendeen, Botallack, St Just, Land's End Airport, Sennen Cove & Sennen, Mon-Sat 2/day
8	Go Cornwall Bus	St Just to Penzance, Mon-Sat 6/day
10	Go Cornwall Bus	Launceston to Bodmin Parkway via Port Isaac, Polzeath, Rock & Wadebridge, Mon-Sat 1/hr
11/11A	Go Cornwall Bus	Plymouth to Padstow via Bodmin Parkway, Mon-Sat 2/hr, Sun 4/day
12/12B	Go Cornwall Bus	Bude to Plymouth via Launceston, Mon-Sat 6/day, Bude to Launceston, Sun 6/day
16/16A	Go Cornwall Bus	Penzance to St Ives via Gurnard's Head (3/day) & Zennor (3/day) & Carbis Bay, Mon-Sat 1/hr
17	First Kernow	Penzance to St Ives via St Erth, Lelant & Carbis Bay, daily 1-2/hr
18	First Kernow	Penzance to Lower Boscaswell via St Just, Botallack & Pendeen, Mon-Sat 1/hr
23	Go Cornwall Bus	Gorran Haven to St Austell via Mevagissey & Pentewan, Mon-Sat 3/day

24	First Kernow	**Fowey** to Mevagissey via Par, **Charlestown**, St Austell & **Pentewan**, Mon–Sat 2/hr
25	Go Cornwall Bus	St Austell to **Fowey** via **Charlestown** & Par, Mon–Sat 1/hr
33	OTS Falmouth	St Keverne to Helston via **Porthallow**, Mon–Fri 1–2/day
34	Go Cornwall Bus	**Lizard** to Redruth via Ruan Minor (for **Cadgwith**), **Mullion & Poldhu Cove**, Mon–Sat 1/hr, Sun 4/day
35/35A	OTS Falmouth	Helston to **Falmouth** via **Gweek**, **Helford Passage & Mawnan Smith**, Mon–Sat 6/day plus 1/hr Helford Passage to Falmouth
36	Go Cornwall Bus	Helston to **St Keverne** via **Mawgan & Coverack**, Mon–Sat 6/day, Sun 3/day
47	Go Cornwall Bus	Camborne to Truro via **Portreath** & Redruth, Mon–Sat 1/hr, Sun 5–6/day
50	Go Cornwall Bus	Truro to **St Mawes** via Tregony, **Gerrans & Portscatho**, Mon–Sat 6–7/day, Sun 3/day
51	Go Cornwall Bus	Veryan to St Austell via **Portloe**, Mon–Fri 5/day, Sat 4/day
56	Go Cornwall Bus	**Newquay** to **Padstow** via **Watergate Bay**, **Mawgan Porth**, **Porthcothan**, **Treyarnon** & **Constantine Bay Stores**, Mon–Sat 1/hr, Sun 4/day
70/70A	Go Cornwall Bus	**Plymouth** to Cremyll Ferry via **Cawsand & Kingsand**, daily 1/hr
70B	Go Cornwall Bus	**Plymouth** to **Portwrinkle**, daily 1/hr
72	Go Cornwall Bus	**Plymouth** to Polperro via Saltash, **Downderry**, **Seaton & Looe**, Mon–Sat 7/day, Sun 5/day
73	Go Cornwall Bus	Liskeard to **Polperro** via **Looe**, Mon–Sat 1/hr, Sun 5/day
75	Go Cornwall Bus	Torpoint to Liskeard via **Portwrinkle**, **Downderry & Seaton**, Mon–Sat 5/day
85	Go Cornwall Bus	Truro to **Newquay** via **Holywell Bay & Crantock**, Mon–Sat 8/day
85	Stagecoach	Barnstaple to **Bude** via Holsworthy, Mon–Sat 1–2/day
95	Go Cornwall Bus	Truro to **Bude** via **Tintagel**, **Bossiney**, **Boscastle**, **Crackington Haven & Widemouth Bay**, Mon–Sat 6/day
217	Go Cornwall Bus	**Morwenstow** to **Bude**, Mon–Sat 3/day inc 1/day extends to/from Holsworthy
218/219	Go Cornwall Bus	**Hartland** to Bude, Mon–Sat 5/day inc 1/day extends to/from **Clovelly**
304	Hopley's Coaches	Truro to **Porthtowan**, Mon–Fri 1/hr, Sat every 2 hrs
315	Hopley's Coaches	Redruth to **St Agnes** via **Porthtowan**, Mon–Fri 5–6/day
319	Stagecoach	**Hartland** to Barnstaple via Clovelly, Mon–Sat 5/day inc 1/day extends to/from **Bude**
481/482	Travel Cornwall	**Looe** to Polruan via **Polperro & Lansallos**, Mon–Fri 6/day
515	Go Cornwall Bus	**Hayle** to Penzance via **Marazion**, Mon–Sat 3/day

First Kernow (🖥 firstbus.co.uk/cornwall) • **Go Cornwall Bus** (🖥 gocornwallbus.co.uk) • **GorranBus** (Gorran & District Community Bus; 🖥 gorranbus.org • **Hopley's Coaches** (🖥 hopleyscoaches.com) • **OTS Falmouth** (🖥 otsfalmouth.zo.uk) • **Stagecoach** (🖥 stagecoachbus.com) • **St Ives Bus Company** (🖥 stivesbuses.co.uk) • **Travel Cornwall** (Summercourt Travel; see 🖥 gocornwallbus.co.uk for timetables) (cont'd from p51) or a series of walks from a fixed base (see box p40 for more ideas) without having to organise two cars: instead, you can just sit back and enjoy the ride along some of Britain's most scenic bus routes.

Note that between Falmouth and Plymouth the public transport system is not as kind to the walker as it is in the far west; however, with careful planning the buses can still be utilised to your advantage; just be aware that with coastal buses, it is common to have to make changes (and so inevitably wait) inland.

The most useful bus services for coast path walkers are also the most expensive: First Kernow's 'Coasters' are open-topped double-decker tourist buses that travel hourly, up and down the coast between Falmouth and Padstow. The **Atlantic Coaster** goes between Padstow and St Ives. The **Land's End Coaster** does a loop starting and finishing in Penzance, via Land's End and St Ives. The less useful **Falmouth Coaster** goes to Penzance, but misses much of the coast (see the table on pp54-5 for details). Tickets are hop-on-hop-off day tickets that cost a flat-rate £15 (the Falmouth Coaster is £8), so they're expensive if you're just using them for a single trip, but handy if you're in a fix.

Timetables Cornwall Council provides information on all of Cornwall's public transport (bus, rail and ferry) at 🖳 cornwall.gov.uk. The service numbers of the most useful buses are given in the table on pp54-5 so you can go straight to the page you need on the website.

Alternatively contact Traveline (☎ 0871-200 2233, 7am-10pm; 🖳 traveline.info) which has public transport information for the whole of the UK. A very useful **app** is 'Traveline SW'.

Tickets If you are going to be using the bus frequently over several days Explorer tickets are good value. They are valid for one, three or seven days and allow you unlimited travel within the county on the relevant company's services. Contact the bus operators for further details.

Older UK residents can apply for an older person's bus pass allowing them to travel free on any local buses (except before 9.30am on weekdays). What age you can apply depends on when you were born and where you live. In some places it's once you reach the age of 60; in others it's once you reach state pension age (currently 66).

Public transport at a glance The maps on pp52-3 and the table on pp54-5 are designed to make it easy for you to plan your day using public transport. Use the **public transport maps** to see which towns each service covers then turn to the **tables** to check the frequency of that service. Read the tables carefully; some services only run one day a week, or not on Saturdays or Sundays. The definition of a summer service depends on the company and the route; it may be Easter to October or May/July to September so do check.

Note, **bus services do change** from year to year. Use this information as a rough guide and confirm up-to-date details with bus operators before travelling.

Details about the various **ferry** services on the route are given in the relevant place in the text.

THE ENVIRONMENT AND NATURE

2

The Cornish coastline provides a diverse range of habitats – ocean, beaches, sand dunes, steep cliffs, cliff-top grasslands and heathland – resulting in a rich variety of wildlife. For the walker interested in the natural environment it is a feast for the senses.

It would take a book several times the size of this one to list the thousands of species which you could come across on your walk. What follows is a brief description of the more common species you may encounter as well as some of the more special plants and animals which are found in Cornwall. If you want to know more refer to the field guides listed on pp47-8.

Nature conservation arose tentatively in the middle of the 19th century out of concern for wild birds which were being slaughtered to provide feathers for the fashion industry. As commercial exploitation of land has increased over the intervening century, so too has the conservation movement. It now has a wide sphere of influence throughout the world and its ethos is upheld by international legislation, government agencies and voluntary organisations.

Conservation schemes (see box on pp66-7) are outlined on the premise that to really learn about a landscape you need to know more than the names of all the plants and animals in it. It is just as important to understand the interactions going on between them and man's relationship with this ecological balance.

Flora and fauna

FAUNA

In and around the fishing villages

The wild laugh of the **herring gull** (*Larus argentatus*) is the wake-up call of the coast path. Perched on the rooftops of the stone villages, they are a reminder of the link between people and wildlife, the rocky coast and our stone and concrete towns and cities. Shoreline scavengers, they've adapted to the increasing waste thrown out by human society. Despite their bad reputation it's worth taking a closer look at these fascinating, ubiquitous birds. How do they keep their pale grey and white plumage so beautiful feeding on rubbish?

❏ **BIRDING AND BIRDERS**

Along with the Isles of Scilly, Cornwall is England's rare-bird capital. These rarities come from North America, Siberia and southern Europe and it takes an expert to tell them from more common species. The best way to find them is to look for a sea of telescopes. Birders are generally pretty friendly people and may well show you the bird, but they can be grumpy if they haven't seen the rarity – 'dipped out' in birder parlance!

Birdline South West (☎ 0906-870 0241) is the premium-rate phone line for up-to-the-minute rare bird news. Alternatively take a look at the regional birding website 🖥 cornwall-birding.co.uk.

Nobel-prize-winning animal behaviourist Nikko Tinbergen showed how the young pecking at the red dot on their bright yellow bills triggers the adult to regurgitate food. In August the newly fledged brown young follow their parents, begging for food. Over the next three years they'll go through a motley range of plumages, more grey and less brown each year till they reach adulthood. But please don't feed them and do watch your sandwiches and fish and chips – they are quite capable of grabbing food from your hand, especially in St Ives.

The village harbours are a good place for lunch or an evening drink after a hard day on the cliffs. Look out for the birds who are equally at home on a rocky shore or in villages, such as the beautiful little black-and-white **pied wagtail** (*Motacilla alba*) with its long, bobbing tail.

Also looking black from a distance as they strut the beach are **jackdaws** (*Corvus monedula*). Close up, however, they are beautiful with a grey nape giving them a hooded look and shining blue eyes. They are very sociable: you will often see them high up in the air in pairs or flocks playing tag or performing acrobatic tricks.

Small, dark brown and easy to miss, the **rock pipit** (*Anthus petrosus*) is one of our toughest birds, as it feeds whilst walking on the rocks between the land and the sea. They nest in crevices and caves along the rocky coastline.

Seen on or from the sea cliffs

Walking on the coastal path leads you into a world of rock and sea, high cliffs with bracken-clad slopes, exposed green pasture, dramatic drops and headlands, sweeping sandy beaches and softer country around the estuaries.

Stunning **stonechats** (*Saxicola torquata*) with black, white and orange colouring are common on heath and grassy plains where you may hear their distinctive song, which is not dissimilar to two stones being clacked together.

Twittering **linnets** (*Carduelis cannabina*) with their bright red breasts and grey heads fly ahead and perch on gorse and fences.

Green hairstreak butterflies (*Callophrys rubi*) emerge on gorse in May.

The vertiginous swoops of the path mean it's often possible to be at eye level or even look down on birds and mammals. Watch for **kestrels** (*Falco tinnunculus*), hovering on sharp brown wings before plummeting onto their prey – **field voles** (*Microtus arvalis*).

At eye level the black 'moustache' of the powerful slate-grey-backed **peregrine** (*Falco peregrinus*) is sometimes visible. At a glance it can be mistaken for a pigeon, its main prey. But the power and speed of this, the world's fastest bird, soon sets it apart. In the late summer whole families fly over the cliffs. In mid winter look for them over estuaries where they hunt ducks and waders. Despite the remote fastness of the cliffs, peregrines have suffered terribly. Accidental poisoning by the pesticide DDT succeeded where WWII persecution for fear they would kill carrier pigeons failed, and they were almost extinct in Cornwall by the end of the 1960s. Their triumphant return means not only a thriving population on their traditional sea cliffs, but more and more nesting in our cities on man-made cliffs, such as tower blocks and cathedrals.

Cliff ledges, a kind of multi-storey block of flats for birds, provide nesting places safe from marauding land predators such as **foxes** (*Vulpes vulpes*) and rats. It's surprising just how close it's possible to get to **fulmars** (*Fulmarus glacialis*), which return to their nesting ledges in February for the start of the long breeding season that goes on into the autumn. Only in the depths of winter are the cliffs quiet. The Cornish nature reserve at Ropehaven near Black Head is one of the main breeding grounds for fulmars in the UK. Fulmars are related to albatrosses and like them are masters of the air. You can distinguish them from gulls by their ridged, flat wings as they sail the wind close to the waves with the occasional burst of fast flapping. Fulmars are incredibly tenacious at holding their nesting sites and vomit a stinking oily secretion over any intruders, including rock-climbers!

The elegant **kittiwake** (*Rissa tridactyla*), the one true seagull that never feeds on land, is another cliff nester, identified by its 'dipped in ink' black wingtips.

Black above, white below, **manx shearwaters** (*Puffinus puffinus*) make globe-encircling journeys as they sail effortlessly just above even the wildest sea. Small and fast on hard-beating wings, black and white **guillemots** (*Uria troile*) and **razorbills** (*Alca torda*) shoot out from their nesting ledges hidden in the cliffs. There are large colonies around the Godrevy–St Austell area. Guillemots have a long thin bill, razorbill a heavy half circle.

With their unmistakable parrot-shaped bills, **puffins** (*Fratercula arctica*) are a rare prize round these coasts.

Big, rapacious **great black-backed gulls** (*Larus marinus*) cruise the nesting colonies for prey. The second largest breeding colony in Cornwall nests on St George's Island just out to sea from Looe.

Stars of the sea show, however, must be the big, sharp-winged, Persil-white **gannets** (*Morus bassanus*) cruising slowly for fish, then suddenly plunging with folded wings into the sea. Their strengthened skulls protect them from the huge force of the impact with the water.

Two birds more familiar from the artificial cliffs of our cities can be seen here in their natural habitat – **house martins** (*Delichon urbica*), steely-blue backed like a **swallow** (*Hirundo rustica*), but with more V-shaped wings and a distinctive white rump, and **rock doves** (*Columba livia*). These are so mixed

THE ENVIRONMENT AND NATURE

with town **pigeons** (*Columba livia domestica*) it's hard to say if any 'pure' wild birds remain, but many individuals with the characteristic grey back, small white rump and two black wing bars can be seen.

Where the path drops steeply to a rocky bay, **oystercatchers** (*Haematopus ostralegus*), with their black and white plumage and spectacular carrot-coloured bill, pipe in panic as they fly off.

This is also a good spot to get close to **shags** (*Phalacrocorax aristotelis*) and **cormorants** (*Phalacrocorax pygmeus*), common all round the coast, swimming low and black in the water. Shags are smaller and are always seen on the sea – cormorants are also on rivers and estuaries – and in the summer have a crest whilst cormorants have a white patch near their tail and white face. Close up, these oily birds shine iridescently; shags are green, cormorants are purple. They are a primitive species and as their feathers are not completely waterproof both must dry themselves after getting wet; their heraldic pose, standing upright with half-spread wings on drying rocks, is one of the special sights of the coast path.

On or in the sea

The high cliffs are also a great place from which to look out over the sea. Searching for seals is an enjoyable and essential part of cliff walking. You'll spot lots of grey lobster-pot buoys before your first seal, but it's worth the effort. **Atlantic grey seals** (*Halichoerus grypus*) relax in the water, looking over their big Roman noses with doggy eyes, as interested in you as you are in them. Twice the weight of a red deer, a big bull can be over 200kg. On calm sunny days it's possible to follow them down through the clear water as they dive, as elegant in their element as they are clumsy on land.

Seals generally come ashore only to rest, moult their fur, or to breed. Seals 'haul out' – come up on the rocks – on Godrevy Island (Map 44, p158), the Carracks (Map 51, p171), near Zennor Head, and around Land's End (Map 61, p189) as well as on St George's Island near Looe and your walk to the town's harbour will introduce you to Nelson the seal, so named, unsurprisingly, as he only had one eye. The seal died in 2003, but was such a popular visitor to the harbour that in 2008 a sculpture of him was unveiled (see Map 122, p295).

Seal breeding takes place between September and December and the caves below Navax Point (Map 43, p157) are a popular breeding site. It is also possible to see them at the Cornish Seal Sanctuary (see p241) in Gweek.

A cliff-top sighting of Britain's largest fish is also a real possibility, but is more chilling than endearing! **Basking sharks** (*Cetorhinus maximus*) can grow to a massive eleven metres and weigh seven tonnes, and their two fins, a large shark-like dorsal fin followed by a notched tail fin, are so far apart it takes a second look to be convinced it's one fish. But these are gentle giants, cruising slowly with open jaws, filtering microscopic plankton from the sea. You are most likely to see one during late spring and summer when they feed at the surface during calm, warm weather. Look out for coloured or numbered tags, put on for research into this sadly declining species and report them to the address given in the box on p70. Ironically, the Shark Angling Club of Great

❏ **CONSERVATION AND THE FISHING INDUSTRY**

Small boats crowding sheltered harbours and the sea dotted with crab pot buoys are constant reminders of this coast's fishing tradition. However, few people now work full time in fishing. The great pilchard shoals are long gone, probably victims of changing ocean currents rather than over fishing, but it is over fishing combined with increasingly sophisticated catching methods that have left Newlyn as the only major deep sea port.

Controversy between different fishing methods focuses on the damage done by bottom trawling, whilst the accidental catching of seabirds in the miles-long gill nets catching sea bass has led to restrictions on their use in St Ives Bay. Post-Brexit there is still considerable resentment in Cornwall over licences granted to EU fishing boats, especially the French and the Spanish, to fish in British waters. Now, for the small-er ports, crab fishing may be the main business with many exported to, ironically, the seafood-hungry Spanish and French!

Day boats fish inshore under the regulation of the Sea Fisheries' Committees which make bye-laws within the six-mile limit and tourist boats take visitors fishing for the summer shoals of mackerel.

Britain (💻 sharkanglingclubofgreatbritain.org.uk) is also based in Cornwall, in Looe on the south coast.

Taking a longer view and with some good luck, watch the sea for dolphins, porpoises or even a whale. **Harbour porpoises** (*Phocoena phocoena*) and **bot-tlenose dolphins** (*Tursiops truncatus*) are the most likely to be seen, in places like St Ives Bay, Mount's Bay and Falmouth Bay.

Other cetaceans you may catch a glimpse of are **Risso's dolphins** (*Grampus griseus*), **common dolphins** (*Delphinus delphis*), **striped dolphins** (*Stenella coeruleoalba*), orcas or **killer whales** (*Orcinus orca*) and **pilot whales** (*Globicephala melaena*) but, be warned, they are fiendishly difficult to tell apart: a brief glimpse of a fin is nothing like the 'whole animal' pictures shown in field guides. Cetacean-spotting boat-trips are ubiquitous on the Cornish coast and available from most harbour-based settlements.

In pastures, combes and woods

The path rises up onto rich green pasture. **Skylark** (*Alauda arvensis*) soar tune-fully – almost disappearing into the spring sky, while in winter small green-brown **meadow pipits** (*Anthus pratensis*) flit weakly, giving a small high-pitched call. Spring also brings migrant **wheatears** (*Oenanthe oenanthe*): they are beautiful with their grey and black feathers above, buff and white below, and unmistakable when they fly and show their distinctive white rump. **Meadow brown** (*Maniola jurtina*) butterflies flap weakly amongst the long grass. **Buzzard** (*Buteo buteo*) soar up with their tilted, broad round wings, giving their high, wild ke-oow cry. They are probably the most common bird of prey found in Cornwall.

Rabbits (*Oryctolagus cuniculus*) are one of the few mammals you are like-ly to see. Prey for buzzard and foxes, they also play a vital role maintaining the short turf habitat of a range of cliff-top species, including **small copper**

(*Lycaena phlaeas*) butterflies in September and **common blue** (*Polyommatus icarus*) and **small heath** (*Coenonympha pamphilus*) in May and August.

Ravens (*Corvus corax*) cronk-cronk over the cliffs and are distinguished from more common **carrion crows** (*Corvus corone*) by their huge size and wedge-shaped tail. One of the most exciting birds around the Cornish coast is the newly returned **chough** (see box opposite). The **corn bunting** (*Emberiza calandra*) is also a rare sight in Cornwall.

Rain and sun, cold and warmth are normal weather for most of us, but on the coast path the walker soon learns the overwhelming importance of the wind. Dip round a corner into a sheltered combe and suddenly the climate changes. Here are warm bracken slopes and small woodlands. Look out for the big holes and dug-out earth of **badger** (*Meles meles*) setts. Sadly the best chance of seeing a badger is dead on the roadside as they are so shy, and mostly nocturnal like foxes which are equally common, but much shyer than their urban cousins.

In spring familiar birds such as **robins** (*Erithacus rubecula*), **blackbirds** (*Turdus merula*), **blue** and **great tits** (*Parus major & caeruleus*), **chaffinches** (*Fringila coelebs*) and **dunnocks** (*Prunella modularis*) are joined by the small green **chiffchaff** (*Phylloscopus collybita*); it's not much to look at but is one of the earliest returning migrants and unmistakably calls its own name in two repeated notes. **Grey squirrels** (*Sciurus carolinensis*), introduced from North America in the late 19th century, are the other mammal you're most likely to see.

Butterflies such as the **small pearl-bordered fritillary** (*Boloria selene*) come out in May and August in brackeny combes rich in violets. Look out for the spectacular migrants **clouded yellow** (*Colias croceus*), **red admiral** (*Vanessa atalanta*) and **painted lady** (*Vanessa cardui*) in August and September, and the **wall brown** (*Lasiommata megera*) which has declined steeply and is now found almost exclusively near the coast.

In and around estuaries

Descending to the long walk round the estuaries is moving into a different, softer world of shelter and rich farmland. Best for birds in winter, they are a welcome refuge from the ferocity of the worst weather for wildlife and people. There are large flocks of ducks – whistling **wigeon** (*Anas penelope*), a combination of grey and pinky brown, with big white wing patches in flight – and waders like the brown **curlew** (*Numenius arquata*) with its impossibly long, down-curved beak and beautiful sad fluting call, evocative of summer moors.

The **redshank** (*Tringa totanus*), **greenshank** (*Tringa nebularia*), **golden** and **grey plover** (*Pluvialis sp.*) and **black-tailed** and **bar-tailed godwit** (*Limosa sp.*) can also be seen in winter. Look out for the big black, white and chestnut **shelduck** (*Tadorna tadorna*), and for the tall **grey heron** (*Ardea cinerea*), hunched at rest or extended to its full 175cm as it slowly, patiently stalks fish in the shallows. A real rarity 20 years ago, another species of heron, the stunning white **little egret** (*Egretta garzetta*) is now unmissable on Cornish estuaries. Here the more common gull is the nimble **black-headed gull** (*Larus ridibundus*), with its elegant cap, dark in summer but pale in winter. In summer, terns come: the big

❏ CHOUGHS

There is one very special and exciting thrill for walkers on The Lizard and West Penwith – against all the odds, Cornwall's emblem bird, the chough (*Pyrrhocorax pyrrhocorax*), has returned to nest! This stunning little crow, jet black with a bright red beak and legs, is packed with charisma; it's superbly agile in the air and charming on the ground as it pecks, in small flocks, for insects. The chough needs tight, low-grazed turf on the cliff edges. Over the years, flatter pastures were improved with fertiliser and the grass grew too long for choughs, and grazing was abandoned on the steep, rough slopes. Now, as you walk the cliff paths there's a good chance of seeing hardy Dartmoor ponies and Dexter cattle grazing the cliff edge. Pioneered by the National Trust, the improved habitat has allowed choughs to return.

From April to June there's a chough watchpoint most afternoons at the southerly point on the Lizard, from which choughs can be seen near the crevice in the cliff where they nest. All year round they can be seen between Mullion and this southerly point.

For updates on choughs visit Cornwall Bird Watching & Preservation Society's website (🖥 cbwps.org.uk).

sandwich tern (*Sterna sandvicensis*) with its shaggy black cap and loud rasping call, and the smaller sleeker aerobatic **common tern** (*Sterna hirundo*). The Tamar, Looe River, Fal and Hayle estuaries are all good hunting grounds for numerous waders, including the curlew, redshank and dunlin.

After near extinction, owing to pollution, **otters** (*Lutra lutra*) are returning to the rivers in Cornwall, though they are still very hard to see – look out for a slithering, lithe shape, or a dog-like head poking out from the water as they swim.

On sand dunes and heath and around mines

Sand dunes swarm with butterflies in high summer and the scarce **silver studded blue** (*Plebeius argus*) can be seen at Holywell Dunes west of Newquay in July and August. Dry heathland provides the warmth needed for reptiles such as **adders** (*Vipera berus*), **slow worms** (*Anguis fragilis*), a type of legless lizard that is commonly mistaken for a snake, and the **common lizard** (*Lacerta vivipara*) seen on the heath vegetation of cliff tops. They sun themselves on rocks or old mining spoil heaps. With their distinctive and beautiful brown, diamond-patterned backs, **adders** are our only poisonous snake, but they pose little risk to people in walking boots. Except in spring when the cold can make them sluggish, they quickly move off the path when they feel the vibration of feet.

You are very unlikely to see another beneficiary of mining, the **greater horseshoe bat** (*Rhinolophus ferrumequinum*). Old mine shafts where bats live have been covered with bat-friendly metal grilles rather than capped with concrete so they can still come and go. The most common bat is the smaller **pipistrelle** (*Pipistrellus pipistrellus*), but all bats are hard to tell apart in the dusk light.

FLORA

Cornwall is best known for its springtime flora when the cliff tops have spectacular displays of wildflowers. Being the most southerly county, flowers tend to come out in Cornwall earlier than in the rest of Britain; **daffodils** (*Narcissus sp*.)

THE ENVIRONMENT AND NATURE

and **wild primroses** (*Primula vulgaris*) start to appear as early as January. Trees struggle to grow on the coast except in sheltered valleys. **Blackthorn** (*Prunus spinosa*), **gorse** (*Ulex sp.*) and **elder** (*Sambucus nigra*) provide some windbreak.

When identifying wild plants it is best to identify the habitat first as this should considerably narrow your search.

Dunes

Dunes are formed by wind action creating a fragile, unstable environment. Among the first colonisers is **marram grass** (*Ammophila arenaria*; see **photo opposite**) which is able to withstand drought, exposure to wind and salt spray and has an ability to grow up through new layers of sand that cover it. Other specialist plants are **sea holly** (*Eryngium maritimum*), **sea spurge** (*Euphorbia paralias*) and **sea bindweed** (*Calystegia soldanella*). The one thing that these seemingly indomitable plants can't tolerate is trampling by human feet; stay on the path which is nearly always well marked through dunes.

Cropped turf

Traditionally farmed land is an important habitat for many wildflowers in Britain because the low-intensity grazing controls scrub and trees while allowing less aggressive plants to flourish. Unfortunately, traditional methods are being eroded by intensive farming practices such as heavy grazing and the widespread use of herbicides leading to a reduction, and even loss of, many species. However, in a few places low-intensity grazing has been reintroduced.

Short cropped turf is brilliant with flowers from early spring. The most common ones are **thrift**, or **sea pink** (*Armeria maritima*), **spring squill** (*Scilla verna*), **kidney vetch** (*Anthyllis vulneraria*) and **sea campion** (*Silene maritima*). Other wild flowers to look out for are **dyer's greenweed** (*Genista tinctoria*), **sheep's bit** (*Jasione montana*) and **bird's foot trefoil** (*Lotus corniculatus*). Rather unusually you may also come across swathes of **bluebells** (*Endymion non-scriptus*) on the cliff tops. Bluebells are more commonly associated with woodland, but can also be indicators of ancient woods.

Heathland

Heathland once used to stretch right across Cornwall from the Lizard to St Agnes and from Bodmin Moor in the east of the county to the Atlantic coast, covering an area of 80,000ha. Now just 7000ha remain of this internationally

---

❏ LIZARD FLORA

There are several rare plants found on the Lizard Peninsula growing in rough grassland and cropped turf. They include thyme broomrape (*Orobanche alba*), fringed rupturewort (*Herniaria ciliolata*), hairy greenweed (*Genista pilosa*), and green-winged orchid (*Orchis morio*). Cornish heath (*Erica vagans*) is a very special plant as it is unique to the area.

(Opposite) Top: Herring gull (see pp57-8) in Falmouth. This one has been ringed as part of a study: its number (019) indicates that it was ringed in Falmouth in 2013 so it hasn't strayed far. If you see a ringed bird and note both the colour of the ring and the number you can get more information at ▣ cr-birding.org. **Bottom**: Marram grass above Perran Beach.

Above, clockwise from top left: **1**. Grey heron. **2**. Curlew. **3**. Shelduck. **4**. Chaffinch. **5**. Pied wagtail. **6**. Reed bunting. **7**. Redshank. (All ©BT).

Above, clockwise from top left : **1**. Herring gull. **2**. Oystercatchers. **3**. Puffin. **4**. Razorbill. **5**. Atlantic grey seal (© Joel Newton). **6**. Black headed gull. **7**. Great black-backed gull. (All ©BT).

Peacock
Inachis io

Small Tortoiseshell
Aglais urticae

Brimstone
Gonepteryx rhamni

Small Pearl-Bordered Fritillary
Boloria selene

Common Blue
Polyommatus icarus

Painted Lady
Vanessa cadui

Small Copper
Lycaena phlaeas

Meadow
Brown
Maniola jurtina

Red Admiral
Vanessa atalanta

Large Garden/
Cabbage White
Pieris brassicae

Clouded Yellow
Colias croceus

Mesembryanthemum

Tree Echium
Echium (species)

Sea Holly
Eryngium maritimum

Bell Heather
Erica cinerea

Heather (Ling)
Calluna vulgaris

Thrift (Sea Pink)
Armeria maritima

Rosebay Willowherb
Epilobium angustifolium

Common Vetch
Vicia sativa

Forget-me-not
Myosotis arvensis

Rowan (tree)
Sorbus aucuparia

Hottentot Fig
Carpobrutus edulis

Red Campion
Silene dioica

Common Dog Violet
Viola riviniana

Common Centaury
Centaurium erythraea

Common/Spear Thistle
Cirsium vulgare

Ramsons (Wild Garlic)
Allium ursinum

Germander Speedwell
Veronica chamaedrys

Herb-Robert
Geranium robertianum

Lousewort
Pedicularis sylvatica

Self-heal
Prunella vulgaris

Scarlet Pimpernel
Anagallis arvensis

Sea Campion
Silene maritima

Bluebell
Hyacinthoides non-scripta

Hogweed
Heracleum sphondylium

Dog Rose
Rosa canina

Meadow Buttercup
Ranunculus acris

Gorse
Ulex europaeus

Tormentil
Potentilla erecta

Birdsfoot-trefoil
Lotus corniculatus

Ox-eye Daisy
Leucanthemum vulgare

Common Ragwort
Senecio jacobaea

Primrose
Primula vulgaris

Cowslip
Primula veris

Yarrow
Achillea millefolium

Wall Pennywort
Umbilicus rupestris

Honeysuckle
Lonicera periclymemum

important habitat. Much of it has been destroyed by farming but there are still significant tracts around both St Agnes and the Lizard, as well as smaller coastal patches between St Ives and Land's End. Surprisingly, much of this has survived because of the mining industry (see box on p180).

Heather and associated species thrive on land contaminated by mine waste, preferring an acidic, nutrient-poor environment where there is little competition from other plants as few can tolerate such inhospitable territory. The unique nature of the Lizard is also a consequence of poor soil, caused by the underlying serpentine rock, which has similarly saved much of the area from the plough.

Heathland is at its best in August and September when it is ablaze with pinks, purples and yellow. Among the different types of heather found are **common heather** (*Calluna vulgaris*), **bell heather** (*Erica cinerea*), **cross-leaved heather** (*E. tetralix*) and **Dorset heather** (*E. ciliaris*), as well as **Cornish heath** (*E. vagans*), the Lizard being the only place in the world where it is found. **Common gorse** (*Ulex europaeus*) and **western gorse** (*U. gallii*) often grow amongst the heather. Other plants to look out for are **dyer's greenweed** (*Genista tinctoria*), **dwarf burnet** (*Rosa pimpinellifolia pumila*), **burnet rose** (*Rosa pimpinellifolia*), **betony** (*Betonica officinalis*), **bloody cranesbill** (*Geranium sanguineum*), **milkwort** (*Polygala sp.*), **dropwort** (*Filipendula vulgaris*), **heath-spotted orchid** (*Dactylorhiza maculata*) as well as **yellow bartsia** (*Parentucellia viscosa*) and **red bartsia** (*Odontites verna*).

Lime-rich grasslands

Soils in Cornwall are generally acidic, although in some areas coastal grasslands are 'limed' by windblown sand consisting of tiny shell fragments. Kelsey Head (Map 32, p141) is a good example of this type of habitat. **Cowslips** (*Primula veris*) grow in abundance and other lime-lovers are **salad burnet** (*Poterium sanguisorba*), **pyramidal orchids** (*Anacamptis pyramidalis*), **autumn lady's tresses orchids** (*Spiranthes spiralis*), **wild clary** (*Salvia horminoides*), **carline thistle** (*Carlina vulgaris*), **pale flax** (*Linum bienne*), **Cornish gentian** (*Gentianella anglica ssp. Cornubiensis*), and **hairy greenweed** (*Genista pilosa*).

Hedges and field margins

Cornish hedges are not your stereotypical neat row of planted trees and shrubs. They are more like a wall than a hedge as they are constructed from stones and earth. In time, they provide a habitat for all types of vegetation ranging from simple mosses and grasses to fully fledged trees which are allowed to grow along the top of the hedges. Along with rough grassland at field edges these habitats provide a wildlife corridor and refuge for many species of wildflowers and small mammals such as voles and shrews.

Some flowers that you may see are **violets** (*Viola riviniana*), **lesser celandine** (*Ranunculus ficaria*), **red campion** (*Silene dioica*), **Alexanders** (*Smyrnium olusatrum*), **hogweed** (*Heracleum sphondylium*), **yarrow** (*Achillea millefolium*) and **foxgloves** (*Digitalis purpurea*).

THE ENVIRONMENT AND NATURE

(**Opposite**): Flowering heather in late summer on the cliffs above Porthtowan beach (**top**; Map 38) and all around the path to Jacket's Point (**bottom**; Map 13).

Gardens

The warm climate in Cornwall means that some plants not normally found in the British Isles thrive both in gardens and in sheltered areas in the wild as garden

---

❑ CONSERVATION SCHEMES – WHAT'S AN AONB?

It is perhaps the chief joy of this walk that much of it is spent in an Area of Outstanding Natural Beauty (AONB). But what exactly is this, and other, designations and what protection do they actually confer?

National Parks

The highest level of landscape protection is the designation of land as a **National Park** (🖳 nationalparks.uk). This designation recognises the national importance of an area in terms of landscape, biodiversity and as a recreational resource. However, it does not signify national ownership and they are not uninhabited wildernesses, making conservation a knife-edged balance between protecting the environment and the rights and livelihoods of those living in the park. There are 15 in Britain of which nine are in England but there are no national parks in Cornwall.

Areas of Outstanding Natural Beauty

The second level of protection is **Area of Outstanding Natural Beauty** (AONB; 🖳 landscapesforlife.org.uk); there are 46 AONBs in the UK; 33 wholly in England. Much of the South West Coast Path crosses land covered by either this designation or its close relative **Heritage Coasts**, of which there are currently 32 in England. The primary objective of AONBs is conservation of the natural beauty of a landscape. As there is no statutory administrative framework for their management, this is the responsibility of the local authority within whose boundaries they fall.

Cornwall AONB (🖳 cornwall-aonb.gov.uk) covers 958 sq km in 12 different areas including 10 stretches of the Cornish Coastline, the Camel Estuary and Bodmin Moor. One of the coastal areas, Hartland, is covered in the first guide (*Exmoor and North Devon Coast Path*) in this series. The others are in this guide: Pentire Point to Widemouth; Trevose Head to Stepper Point; St Agnes; Godrevy to Portreath; West Penwith; South Coast Western (Lizard to Marazion & Helford River); South Coast Central (Mylor and Roseland to Porthpean); South Coast Eastern (Par Sands to Looe); and Rame Head which is from east of Whitesand Bay to east of Penlee Point.

National Nature Reserves and Sites of Special Scientific Interest

The next level of protection includes **National Nature Reserves** (NNRs) and **Sites of Special Scientific Interest** (SSSIs).

There are 225 **NNRs** in England of which three are in Cornwall (the Lizard; Golitha Falls on the southern edge of Bodmin, and Goss Moor at the headwaters of the River Fal). The coast path passes through the Lizard NNR, an area of 1662 hectares, which was established to protect a rich collection of rare plant species.

There are over 4100 **SSSIs** in England ranging in size from little pockets protecting wild flower meadows, important nesting sites (such as Loe Pool), or special geological features, to vast swathes of upland, moorland and wetland. SSSIs are a particularly important designation as they have some legal standing. They are managed in partnership with the owners and occupiers of the land who must give written notice before initiating any operations likely to damage the site and who cannot proceed without consent from **Natural England** (🖳 gov.uk/government/organisations/natural-england), the single body responsible for identifying, establishing and managing National Parks, Areas of Outstanding Natural Beauty, National Nature Reserves, Sites of Special Scientific Interest, and Special Areas of Conservation.

escapees. These include the **tree echium** (from the Canary Islands), succulents such as the **aeonium** (Canary Islands) and **mesembryanthemum** (South Africa) species and purple **agapanthus** lilies, also from South Africa.

Special Area of Conservation (SAC) is an international designation which came into being as a result of the 1992 Earth Summit in Rio de Janeiro, Brazil. This European-wide network of sites is designed to promote the conservation of habitats, wild animals and plants, both on land and at sea. At the time of writing 256 land sites in England had been designated as SACs.

National Trails
The Cornwall coast path is a section of the South West Coast Path, one of 15* National Trails in England and Wales. These are Britain's flagship long-distance paths which grew out of the post-war desire to protect the country's special places, a movement which also gave birth to National Parks and AONBs.

National Trails in England are largely funded by Natural England and are managed on the ground by a National Trail Officer. They coordinate the maintenance work undertaken by either the local highway authority, or the National Trust, where it crosses their land, and ensure that the trail is kept up to nationally agreed standards.

Conservation and campaigning organisations
These voluntary organisations started the conservation movement in the mid 19th century and are still at the forefront of developments. Independent of government and reliant on public support, they can concentrate their resources either on acquiring land which can then be managed purely for conservation purposes, or on influencing political decision-makers by lobbying and campaigning. Managers and owners of land include well-known bodies such as:
● **National Trust** (⌨ nationaltrust.org.uk) A charity with over 5 million members which aims to protect, through ownership, threatened coastline, countryside, historic houses, castles and gardens, and archaeological remains for everyone to enjoy. The trust owns over 40% of the Cornish coastline, as well as sites such as the Old Post Office (see p98) in Tintagel and Godrevy Point (see Map 44, p158).
● **English Heritage** (⌨ www.english-heritage.org.uk) Previously a statutory organisation, in 2015 English Heritage became a charity that looks after and conserves the National Heritage collection of over 400 historic buildings, including Tintagel Castle (see p98) and Pendennis Castle (see p250).
● **Royal Society for the Protection of Birds** (RSPB; ⌨ rspb.org.uk) The largest voluntary conservation body in Europe focusing on providing a healthy environment for birds and wildlife and with over a million members, and 150 reserves in the UK including two on the coast path: Hayle Estuary (p160) and Marazion Marsh (p208).
● The umbrella organisation for the 46 wildlife trusts in the UK is **The Wildlife Trusts** (⌨ wildlifetrusts.org). **Cornwall Wildlife Trust** (⌨ cornwallwildlifetrust .org.uk) is the largest voluntary organisation (17,000 members) in the county concerned with all aspects of nature conservation. They manage 55 nature reserves.
● **Marine Conservation Society** (⌨ mcsuk.org) A national charity dedicated solely to protecting the marine environment and its wildlife.
● **Butterfly Conservation** (⌨ butterfly-conservation.org) was formed in 1968 by some naturalists who were alarmed at the decline in the number of butterflies, and moths, and who aimed to reverse the situation. They have more than 30 branches throughout the British Isles and operate 33 nature reserves and also sites where butterflies are likely to be found.

*(16 with the completion of the England Coast Path in 2022-3)

MINIMUM IMPACT & OUTDOOR SAFETY

Minimum impact walking

By visiting Cornwall you are having a positive impact, not just on your own well-being, but on local communities as well. Your presence brings money and jobs into the local economy (tourism supports one in five jobs) and also pride in and awareness of Cornwall's environment and culture. Cornwall receives over four million visitors annually, with the coast path attracting at least a quarter of those.

However, the environment should not be considered only in terms of its value as a tourist asset. Its long-term survival and enjoyment by future generations will only be possible if both visitors and local communities protect it now. The following points are made to help you reduce your impact on the environment, encourage conservation and promote sustainable tourism in the area.

ECONOMIC IMPACT

Support local businesses
Rural businesses and communities in Britain have been hit hard in recent years by a seemingly endless series of crises, not least, of course, the financial fallout following the onset of the Covid-19 pandemic. Most people are aware of the Countryside Code – not dropping litter and closing the gate behind you are still as pertinent as ever – but in light of recent economic pressures there is something else you can do: **buy local**.

Look and ask for local produce to buy and eat; not only does this cut down on the amount of pollution and congestion that the transportation of food creates (the so-called 'food miles'), but also ensures that you are supporting local farmers and producers; the very people who have moulded the countryside you have come to see and who are in the best position to protect it. If you can find local food which is also organic so much the better.

It's a fact of life that money spent at local level – perhaps in a market, or at the greengrocer, or in an independent pub – has a far greater impact for good on that community than the equivalent spent in a branch of a national chain store or restaurant. While no-one would advocate that walkers should boycott the larger supermarkets, which after all do provide local employment, it's worth remembering that businesses in rural communities rely heavily on visitors for their very existence. If we want to keep these shops and post offices, we need to use them.

The website ⌨ foodfromcornwall.co.uk provides a list of Cornish food producers and is good for sourcing local produce in Cornwall.

ENVIRONMENTAL IMPACT

A walking holiday in itself is an environmentally friendly approach to tourism. The following are some ideas on how you can go a few steps further in helping to minimise your impact on the environment while walking the South West Coast Path.

Use public transport whenever possible
More use of public transport encourages the provision of better services which benefits visitors, local people and the global environment. During peak periods traffic congestion in Cornwall is a major headache and you're doing yourself (and everyone else in the vehicle with you) a big favour by avoiding it. There's detailed information in this book on public transport services; turn to pp52-5 to make good use of it.

Never leave litter
Litter is a worldwide problem that is unsightly, pollutes the environment and kills wildlife. **Please** carry a rubbish bag with you so you can dispose of rubbish in a bin at the next town rather than dropping it. You can even help by picking up a few pieces of litter that other people leave behind.
● **The lasting impact of litter** You may think a small piece of rubbish has little effect but consider the following: silver foil lasts 18 months; textiles hang around for 15 years; a plastic bag lasts for 10 to 12 years and an aluminium drinks can will last for 85 years on the ground, or 75 years in the sea. An estimated one million seabirds and 100,000 marine mammals and sea turtles die every year from entanglement in, or ingestion of, plastics.
● **Is it OK if it's biodegradable?** Not really. Even a bit of orange peel takes six months to decompose. Apple cores, banana skins and the like are not only unsightly but they encourage flies, ants and wasps and can ruin a picnic spot for others.

Consider walking out of season
By walking the coast path at less busy times of the year you help to reduce overuse of the path at peak periods. Many fragile habitats, such as dunes, are unable to withstand the heavy use and consequent trampling. You also help to generate year-round income for local services and may find your holiday a more relaxing experience; there'll be less stress involved in finding accommodation and fewer people on the trail.

Erosion
Erosion is a natural process on any coastline, but it's accelerated by thousands of pairs of feet. Do your best to **stay on the main trail** and use managed footpaths wherever possible. If you are walking during the winter, or a particularly

MINIMUM IMPACT & OUTDOOR SAFETY

❏ **REPORTING WILDLIFE SIGHTINGS**

Report jellyfish or marine turtle sightings to the **Marine Conservation Society** (💻 mcsuk.org/what-you-can-do/sightings). The website includes a guide to identifying UK jellyfish. Reports are greatly appreciated, as trends in jellyfish distribution can help researchers understand marine turtle behaviour and also relate to climate change.

If you see any of the other larger marine creatures such as dolphins, whales and seals you can report them online through **Seaquest South West Cornwall** (part of Cornwall Wildlife Trust) at **ORKS** (Online Recording Kernow & Scilly; 💻 erciss .org.uk/sharesightings). There is also a free ORKS app.

If you come across a stranded marine animal like a dolphin or porpoise, don't approach it but contact either **British Divers Marine Life Rescue** (Rescue Hotline available 24 hrs, all year ☎ 01825-765546; 💻 bdmlr.org.uk) or the RSPCA hotline (☎ 0300-123 4999, 💻 rspca.org.uk).

wet period, be aware that braiding (the creation of more than one path) usually occurs when the path is muddy. Come prepared with good walking boots that don't mind a little dirt.

Respect all wildlife

Remember that all wildlife you come across on the coast path has just as much right to be there as you. Tempting as it may be to pick wild flowers you should leave all flora alone so the next people who pass can enjoy the sight as well. You never know if you may be inadvertently picking a rare flower, destroying its chances of future survival.

If you come across young animals or birds leave them alone. Every year hundreds of well-meaning but misguided people hand in supposedly abandoned young to the RSPCA, when in fact the only thing keeping the mother away was them.

The code of the outdoor loo

As more and more people discover the joys of walking in the natural environment issues such as how to go to the loo outdoors rapidly gain importance. How many of us have shaken our heads at the sight of toilet paper strewn beside the path, or even worse, someone's dump left in full view? Human excrement is not only offensive to our senses but, more importantly, can infect water sources.

Where to go The coast path is a high-use area and many habitats will not benefit from your fertilisation. As far as 'number twos' are concerned try whenever possible to **use public toilets**. There is no shortage of public toilets along the coast path and they are all marked on the trail maps in this book. However, there are those times when the only time is now. If you have to go outdoors help the environment to deal with your deposit in the best possible way by following a few simple guidelines:

● **Choose your site carefully** It should be at least 30 metres away from running water, beyond the high tide mark and not on any site of historical or archaeological interest. Carry a small trowel or use a sturdy stick to **dig a small hole** about 15cm (6") deep to bury your faeces in. Faeces decompose quicker when in contact with the top layer of soil or leaf mould; by using a stick to stir loose soil into your deposit you will speed decomposition up even more. Do not squash it under rocks as this slows down the decomposition process. If you have to use rocks as a cover make sure they are not in contact with your faeces.

● **Pack out toilet paper and tampons** Toilet paper takes a long time to decompose whether buried or not. It is easily dug up by animals and may then blow into water sources or onto the trail. The best method for dealing with used toilet paper is to pack it out. Put it in a paper bag placed inside a plastic bag and then dispose of it at the next toilet. Tampons and sanitary towels also need to be packed out in a similar way. They take years to decompose and may be dug up and scattered about by animals.

ACCESS

Access to the countryside has always been a hot topic in Britain. In the 1940s soldiers coming back from World War II were horrified and disgruntled to find that landowners were denying them the right to walk across the moors; ironically the very country that they had been fighting to protect. After a long campaign to allow greater public access to areas of countryside in England and Wales, the Countryside & Rights of Way Act 2000 (CRoW), or 'Right to Roam' as dubbed by walkers, came into effect in 2005.

All those who enjoy access to the countryside must respect the land, its wildlife, the interests of those who live and work there and other users; we all share a common interest in the countryside. Knowing your rights and responsibilities gives you the information you need to act with minimal impact.

Rights of way

As a designated **National Trail** the coast path is a **public right of way**. A public right of way is either a footpath, a bridleway or a byway. The Cornwall coast path is a footpath for almost all its length which means that anyone has the legal right to use it on foot only.

Rights of way are theoretically established because the owner has dedicated them to public use. However, very few paths are formally dedicated in this way. If members of the public have been using a path without interference for 20 years or more the law assumes the owner has intended to dedicate it as a right of way. If a path has been unused for 20 years it does not cease to exist; the guiding principle is 'once a highway, always a highway'.

On a public right of way you have the right to 'pass and repass along the way' which includes stopping to rest or admire the view, or to consume refreshments. You can also take with you a 'natural accompaniment' (!) which includes a dog, but it must be kept under close control (see pp336-8).

Farmers and land managers must ensure that paths are not blocked by crops or other vegetation, or otherwise obstructed, that the route is identifiable and the surface is restored soon after cultivation. If crops are growing over the path you have every right to walk through them, following the line of the right of way as closely as possible. If you find a path blocked or impassable you should report it to the appropriate **highway authority**. Highway authorities are responsible

MINIMUM IMPACT & OUTDOOR SAFETY

for maintaining footpaths. In Cornwall the highway authority is **Cornwall Council**. The council is also the surveying authority with responsibility for maintaining the official definitive map of public rights of way.

Wider access

The access situation to land around the coast path is a little more complicated. Trying to unravel and understand the seemingly thousands of different laws and acts is never easy in any legal system. Parliamentary Acts give a right to walk

---

❏ THE COUNTRYSIDE CODE

The Countryside Code, originally described in the 1950s as the Country Code, was revised and relaunched in 2004, in part because of the changes brought about by the CRoW Act (see p71); it has been updated several times since then. The Code seems like common sense but sadly some people still appear to have no understanding of how to treat the countryside they walk in. An adapted version of the 2021 Code, launched under the logo 'Respect. Protect. Enjoy.', is given below:

Respect other people

● **Consider the local community and other people enjoying the outdoors** Be sensitive to the needs and wishes of those who live and work there. If, for example, farm animals are being moved or gathered keep out of the way and follow the farmer's directions. Being courteous and friendly to those you meet will ensure a healthy future for all based on partnership and co-operation.

● **Leave gates and property as you find them and follow paths unless wider access is available** A farmer normally closes gates to keep farm animals in, but may sometimes leave them open so the animals can reach food and water. Leave machinery and farm animals alone – if you think an animal is in distress try to alert the farmer instead. Use gates, stiles or gaps in field boundaries if you can – climbing over walls, hedges and fences can damage them and increase the risk of farm animals escaping.

Protect the natural environment

● **Leave no trace of your visit and take your litter home** Take special care not to damage, destroy or remove features such as rocks, plants and trees. Take your litter with you. Litter and leftover food doesn't just spoil the beauty of the countryside, it can be dangerous to wildlife and farm animals. Fires can be as devastating to wildlife and habitats as they are to people and property – so be careful with naked flames and cigarettes at any time of the year.

● **Keep dogs under effective control** This means that you should keep your dog on a lead or keep it in sight at all times, be aware of what it's doing and be confident it will return to you promptly on command. Across farmland dogs should always be kept on a short lead. During lambing time they should not be taken with you at all (see pp336-8). Always clean up after your dog and get rid of the mess responsibly – 'bag it and bin it'. Use any public waste bin if there is no dedicated bin nearby.

Enjoy the outdoors

● **Plan ahead and be prepared** You're responsible for your own safety: be prepared for natural hazards, changes in weather and other events. Wild animals, farm animals and horses can behave unpredictably if you get too close, especially if they're with their young – so give them plenty of space.

● **Follow advice and local signs** In some areas there may be temporary diversions in place. Take notice of these and other local trail advice.

over certain areas of land such as some, but by no means all, common land and some specific places such as Dartmoor and the New Forest. However, in other places, such as Bodmin Moor and many British beaches, right of access is not written in law. It is merely tolerated by the landowner and could be terminated at any time.

Some landowners, such as the Forestry Commission, water companies and the National Trust, are obliged by law to allow some degree of access to their land. Land covered by schemes such as the Environmental Stewardship Scheme gives landowners a financial incentive to manage their land for conservation and to provide limited public access. There are also a few truly altruistic landowners who have allowed access over their land and these include organisations such as the RSPB, the Woodland Trust, and some local authorities. Overall, however, access to most of Britain's countryside is forbidden to the public, in marked contrast to the general rights of access that prevail in other European countries.

Right to roam

For many years groups such as **Ramblers** (see box p46) and **The British Mountaineering Council** (⌨ thebmc.co.uk) campaigned for new and wider access legislation. This finally bore fruit in the form of the Countryside and Rights of Way Act of November 2000, colloquially known as the CRoW Act, which granted access for 'recreation on foot' to mountain, moor, heath, down and registered common land in England and Wales. In essence it allows walkers the freedom to roam responsibly away from footpaths, without being accused of trespass, on about four million acres of open, uncultivated land.

On 28 August 2005 the South-West became the sixth region in England/Wales to be opened up under this act; however, restrictions may still be in place from time to time – check the situation on ⌨ openaccess.gov.uk.

Natural England (see p66) has mapped the new agreed areas of open access and they are also clearly marked on all the latest Ordnance Survey Explorer (1:25,000) maps. In the future it is hoped that the legislation can be extended to include other types of land such as cliff, foreshore, woodland, riverside and canal side.

❏ CORNISH WORDS AND PLACE NAMES ˙

Along the coast path you will come across many place names which are easily translated once you've become familiar with a few Cornish words. To get you started here are some of the most common words used in place names.

Boel/Voel – cliff	*Kellys* lost, hidden or	*Ros* – heath or moor
Bos/Bud – dwelling	grove	*Tol* – holed
Carrack – rock	*Men/Maen* – stone	*Towan* – sandhill
Chy – house	*Mor* – sea	*Tre* – hamlet or homestead
Cornovii – cliff castles	*oggy* – pasty	*Treath* – beach
Dinas – hill fort	*Penn/Pen/Pedn* – headland	*Wheal* – mine
Dhu/Du – black	*Pol* – pool	*Zawn* – cleft
Enys – island	*Porth* – harbour or cove	

MINIMUM IMPACT & OUTDOOR SAFETY

Health and outdoor safety

AVOIDANCE OF HAZARDS

Swimming

If you are not an experienced swimmer or familiar with the sea, plan ahead and swim at beaches where there is a lifeguard service; these beaches have all been marked on the trail maps. On such beaches you should swim between the red and yellow flags as this is the patrolled area. Don't swim between black-and-white chequered flags as these areas are only for surfboards. If there is a red flag flying this indicates that it is dangerous to enter the water. If you are not sure about anything ask one of the lifeguards; after all they are there to help you.

If you are going to swim at unsupervised beaches never do so alone and always take care. Some beaches are prone to strong rips. Never swim off headlands or near river mouths as there may be strong currents running. Always be aware of changing weather conditions and tidal movement. Cornwall has a huge tidal range and it can be very easy to get cut off by the tide.

If you see someone in difficulty do not attempt a rescue until you have contacted the coastguard (see box on p77). Once you know help is on the way try to assist the person by throwing something to help them stay afloat. Many beaches have rescue equipment located in red boxes; these are marked on the trail maps.

❏ BEWARE OF THE COW!

Most people are aware of the dangers of bulls – indeed, there are restrictions placed upon farmers who mustn't allow adult bulls to graze in fields that are crossed by a public right of way – but few people realise that cows can also be dangerous. Each year there are reports of people who have been attacked, or even trampled to death by cows. Between 2015-16 and 2019-20 the Health & Safety Executive investigated 142 incidents, 22 of which resulted in the death of a person. However, only four of these were walkers or other members of the public, the rest being farm workers.

Cows are particularly protective if there are young calves in the herd, but even without any calves around, a herd of cows can suddenly be spooked, either by a walker or, more likely, by a walker's dog. If you find yourself in a field of worryingly aggressive cattle, move away as carefully and quietly as possible, and if you feel threatened by them let go of your dog's lead and let it run free rather than try to protect it and risk endangering yourself. Your dog will outrun the cows. You might not be able to.

Those without canine companions should follow similar advice; move away calmly, do not panic and make no sudden noises. Chances are the cows will leave you alone once they establish that you pose no threat.

If you come to a field of cows with calves in the herd, think twice about crossing the field; if you can, go another way.

You can report incidents involving dangerous cattle at 🖥 killercows.co.uk.

Walking alone

If you are walking alone you must appreciate and be prepared for the increased risk. Take particular note of the safety guidelines below.

Safety on the Coast Path

Sadly every year people are injured walking along the trail, though usually it's nothing more than a badly twisted ankle. Parts of Cornwall can be pretty remote, however, and it certainly pays to take precautions when walking. Abiding by the following rules should minimise the risks:

● Avoid walking on your own if possible.
● Make sure that someone knows your plans for every day you are on the trail. This could be the place you plan to stay in at the end of each day's walk or a friend or relative whom you have promised to call every night. That way, if you fail to turn up or call, they can raise the alarm.
● Before you go, download and get to know the app **What3words** (⌨ what3words.com). This app reduces the world to three-metre square areas, each with a unique three-word geocode so it makes it easy to tell people precisely where you are.
● If the weather closes in suddenly and fog or mist descends and you become uncertain of the correct trail, do not be tempted to continue. Just wait where you are and you'll find that mist often clears, at least for long enough to allow you to get your bearings. If you are still uncertain and the weather doesn't look like improving, return the way you came to the nearest point of civilisation and try again another time when conditions have improved.
● Always fill your water bottle or pouch at every available opportunity (don't empty it until you are certain you can fill it again) and ensure you have some food such as high-energy snacks.
● Always carry a torch, compass, map, whistle and wet-weather gear with you; a mobile phone can be useful though you cannot always rely on getting good reception, if any reception at all.
● Wear strong sturdy boots with good ankle support, or trainers with good grips.
● Be extra vigilant with children.

Fitness

You will enjoy your walk more if you have a reasonable level of fitness. Carrying a pack for five to seven hours a day is demanding and any preparation you have done beforehand will pay off.

Water

You need to drink lots of water while you're walking; 3-5 litres per day depending on the weather. If you start to feel tired, lethargic or get a headache it may be that you are not drinking enough. Thirst is not a good indicator of when to drink; stop and have a drink every hour or two. A good indication of whether you are drinking enough is the colour of your urine, the lighter the better. If you are not needing to urinate much and your urine is dark yellow you need to increase your fluid intake.

Hypothermia

Hypothermia, or exposure, occurs when the body can't generate enough heat to maintain its core temperature. It's usually as a result of being wet, cold, unprotected from the wind, tired and hungry. It is easily avoided by wearing suitable clothing (see pp42-3), carrying and consuming enough food and drink and being aware of the weather conditions. Check the morale of your companions. Early signs to watch for are feeling cold and tired with involuntary shivering. Find some shelter as soon as possible and warm the person up with a hot drink and some chocolate or other high-energy food. If possible give them another warm layer of clothing and allow them to rest until feeling better.

If allowed to worsen, strange behaviour, slurring of speech and poor co-ordination will become apparent and the victim can quickly progress into unconsciousness, followed by coma and death. Quickly get the victim out of wind and rain, improvising a shelter if necessary. Rapid restoration of bodily warmth is essential and best achieved by bare-skin contact: someone should get into the same sleeping bag as the patient, both having stripped to their underwear, any spare clothing under or over them to build up heat. Send urgently for help.

Hyperthermia

Heat exhaustion is often caused by water depletion and is a serious condition that could eventually lead to death. Symptoms include thirst, fatigue, giddiness, a rapid pulse, raised body temperature, low urine output and later on, delirium and coma. The only remedy is to re-establish water balance. If the victim is suffering severe muscle cramps it may be due to salt depletion.

Heatstroke is caused by failure of the body's temperature-regulating system and is extremely serious. It is associated with a very high body temperature and an absence of sweating. Early symptoms can be similar to those of hypothermia, such as aggressive behaviour, lack of co-ordination and so on. Later the victim goes into a coma or convulsions and death will follow if effective treatment is not given. To treat heatstroke sponge the victim down or cover with wet towels and vigorously fan them. Get help immediately.

Sunburn

The sun in Cornwall can be very strong. The best way to avoid sunburn – and the extra risk of developing skin cancers that sunburn brings – is to keep your skin covered at all times in light, loose-fitting clothing, and to cover any exposed areas of skin in sunscreen (with a minimum factor of 30). Sunscreen should be applied regularly throughout the day. Don't forget your lips, nose, ears and the back of your neck, and even under your chin to protect you against rays reflected from the ground. Most importantly of all, always wear a hat!

Footcare

Caring for your feet is vital; you're not going to get far if they are out of action. Wash and dry them properly at the end of the day, change your socks frequently and if it is warm enough take your boots and socks off when you stop for lunch to allow your feet to dry out in the sun.

❏ **DEALING WITH AN ACCIDENT**

● Use basic first aid to treat any injuries to the best of your ability.

● Try to attract the attention of anybody else who may be in the area. The **emergency signal** is six blasts on a whistle, or six flashes with a torch.

● If possible leave someone with the casualty while others go for help. If there is nobody else, you have a dilemma. If you decide to get help leave all spare clothing and food with the casualty.

● Telephone ☎ **999** and ask for the coastguard. They are responsible for dealing with any emergency that occurs on the coast or at sea. Make sure you know exactly where you are before you call.

● Report the exact position of the casualty and their condition.

Blisters can make or break a walk and the best treatment for them really is prevention. All methods of prevention work on the idea of reducing friction between the skin and the boot. You need to take action as soon as you feel a rub developing, don't make the mistake of waiting just a little longer. There are many different ideas around, but one of the most effective is to strap the affected area with tape; waterproof tape that has a smooth shiny surface works best. You may need to do this for a quite a few days until the skin toughens up.

If you've left it too late and you already have a blister one of the best ways to treat it is to cover it with Compeed or Second Skin (see p44 for first-aid kit). Another way is to build a layer of 'Moleskin' around the blister. Keep a careful eye on blisters to make sure they don't become infected.

WEATHER AND WEATHER FORECASTS

It is a good idea to listen to weather forecasts and in particular pay attention to wind and gale warnings. Winds on any coastline can get very strong and if the wind is high it is advisable not to walk. Walking in high winds is difficult particularly if you are carrying a pack which can act as a sail. If you are walking on a steep incline or above high cliffs it is dangerous. Even if the wind direction is inland it can literally blow you right over (unpleasant if there are gorse bushes around!), or if it suddenly stops or eddies (a common phenomenon when strong winds hit cliffs) it can cause you to lose your balance and stagger in the direction in which you have been leaning, ie towards the cliffs!

Another hazard on the coast is sea mist or fog which can dramatically decrease visibility. If a coastal fog blows over take extreme care where the path runs close to cliff edges.

Detailed weather forecasts for Cornwall and Devon are available through 🖥 bbc.co.uk/weather; 🖥 www.metcheck.com is also a useful source of information.

4 ROUTE GUIDE & MAPS

Using this guide

The trail guide and maps have not been divided into rigid daily stages since people walk at different speeds and have different interests. The **route summaries** below describe the trail between significant places and are written as if walking the coast path from Bude to Plymouth. To enable you to plan your own itinerary, **practical information** is presented clearly on the trail maps. This includes walking times, all places to stay, camp and eat, as well as shops where you can buy supplies. Further **service details** are given in the text under the entry for each place. For a condensed overview of this information see the **town and village facilities table** on pp32-5.

For **overview maps** and **profiles** see the colour pages at the end of the book.

TRAIL MAPS [see key map inside cover; symbols key p338]

Scale and walking times

The trail maps are to a scale of 1:20,000 (1cm = 200m; 3¹/8 inches = one mile). Walking times are given along the side of each map and the arrow shows the direction to which the time refers. Black triangles indicate the points between which the times have been taken. **See important note below on walking times**.

The time-bars are a tool and are not there to judge your walking ability. There are so many variables that affect walking speed, from the weather conditions to how many beers you drank the previous evening. After the first hour or two of walking you will be able to see how your speed relates to the timings on the maps. Note also that time spent on ferry crossings is not included on time-bars.

Up or down?

On the trail maps in this book, the walking trail is shown as a dashed red line. An arrow across the trail indicates the slope; two arrows show that it is steep. Note that the arrow points towards the higher part of the trail. If, for example, you are walking from A (at 80m) to B (at

---

❏ **IMPORTANT NOTE – WALKING TIMES**

Unless otherwise specified, **all times in this book refer only to the time spent walking**. You will need to add 20-30% to allow for rests, photography, drinking water etc. When planning the day's hike count on 5-7 hours' actual walking.

200m) and the trail between the two is short and steep it would be shown thus: A— — — >> — — – B. Reversed arrow heads indicate a downward gradient.

Other features

The numbered GPS waypoints refer to the list on pp330-5. Other features are marked on the map when pertinent to navigation. To avoid cluttering the maps and making them unusable not all features have been marked each time they occur.

ACCOMMODATION

Apart from in large towns where some selection has been necessary, the maps and text indicate almost every place to stay that is within easy reach of the trail and willing to take one-night stays. For **B&B-style accommodation** the number and type of rooms is given after each entry: **S** = **single** (one single bed), **T** = **twin** (two single beds), **D** = **double** (one double bed), **Tr** = **triple** (three single beds or one double and one single) **Qd** = **quad**. Note that many of the triple/quad rooms have a double bed and either one/two single beds, or bunk beds, thus in a group of three or four, two people would have to share the double bed, but it also means the room can be used as a double or twin. Many places describe these rooms as family rooms – **F** = **family room**.

Rates quoted are **per person** (pp) per night based on two sharing, unless indicated otherwise. The rate for single occupancy (**sgl occ**) of a double/twin is also shown where appropriate. Some B&Bs don't accept credit/debit cards but most guesthouses, hostels and hotels do, as do most of the large campsites.

The text also mentions whether the rooms are en suite, or have private or shared facilities, and if a **bath** (🛁) is available for at least one room. Also noted is whether premises offer **packed lunches** (Ⓛ) if requested in advance; and if **dogs** (🐕) are welcome. Most places will not take more than one dog in a room and also accept them only subject to prior arrangement. Some make an additional charge (usually per night but occasionally per stay) while others may require a deposit which is refundable if the dog doesn't make a mess. See also pp336-8.

It is safe to assume nowadays that if a place to stay and/or eat has a **website**, it will also have WI-FI that is free unless otherwise stated. It can be useful to check the **Facebook page** (**fb**) before arriving, especially for small or seasonal businesses, as these tend to be kept more up-to-date with changes to opening times than regular websites.

Many places do not usually accept advance **bookings** for a single-night stay at weekends or in peak holiday periods, shown in the text as (**min 2/3 nights**) but they might if someone calls near the actual date or on the day. Whether booking ahead or not, you will almost always get the best rates by booking direct with the accommodation. Booking is sometimes needed at **campsites** in school holidays but is usually not necessary at other times. Always remember to tell campsites that you are walking the coast path when you call ahead. Many campsites will find room for walkers even if they are officially full. You'll also often get a cheaper rate.

The route guide

[For the route guide from Devon along the coast path north of Bude see pp321-9]

BUDE

Bude is a small, compact seaside town with plenty of charm and character that sprawls out from its famous beach, Summerleaze.

Summer and public holidays are when this normally sleepy little town springs into life and it can become quite hectic, but arrive at any other time and you shouldn't have any trouble booking accommodation and making your way around town.

Built in 1830, the town's small **castle** (🖳 thecastlebude.org.uk; daily 10am-4/5pm winter/summer; free) is worth exploring. Its **heritage centre** contains exhibitions on shipwrecks and lifeboats as well as displays on the Bude Canal and the geology of the Cornish coast. Inside too is **Willoughby Gallery**, which holds local art exhibitions, a gift shop and the pleasant Limelight Café (see Where to eat).

Pretty **Bude Canal** (see box on p83) runs from the beach past the castle and can be followed for a mile or so along the towpath or in **boats** (£10/30 mins). Also nearby is **Bude Light**, a Millennium project built to commemorate the life of Sir Goldsworthy Gurney, a Cornish scientist and inventor for whom the castle was originally built.

The marvellous **Bude Sea Pool** (🖳 budeseapool.org; **fb**; open year-round; free) is a man-made tidal swimming pool, built in 1930 to provide a safe place for people to go sea swimming.

Bude is also known for its **Jazz Festival** (see p16).

Services

The excellent **Bude Tourist Information and Canal Centre** (☎ 01288-354240, 🖳 visitbude.info; **fb**; Easter-Oct Mon-Sat 10am-5pm, Sun 10am-4pm, Oct-Easter daily to 4pm; WI-FI free via Facebook or £1/3hrs) has a comprehensive listing of accommodation in the area (you can book accommodation in the centre and through its

website too) and the enthusiastic staff are willing to help. They are happy to store luggage for the day (£1.50). Hot drinks are available here too.

There is **internet access** (free for 30 mins) at **Bude Library** (Mon, Wed & Fri 9.30am-5pm, Sat 10am-1pm), which has a good Cornish reference section. All cafés, restaurants and pubs have free wi-fi.

Bude's main **post office** (Mon-Fri 9am-5pm, Sat 9am-12.30pm) is at the top of Belle Vue, the main shopping street. There's also a **sub-post office** which is part of a newsagent (daily 7am-5.30pm) almost directly opposite the tourist office.

For **food** shopping, head to Sainsbury's (Mon-Sat 8am-8pm, Sun 10am-4pm) or the Co-op (daily 7am-10pm). There is a Boots **pharmacy** (Mon-Sat 9am-5.30pm, Sun 10am-4pm) while, for **walking and camping gear**, there is a Mountain Warehouse (Mon-Sat 9am-5.30pm, Sun 10am-4pm).

Spencer Thorn Bookshop (☎ 01288-352518; Mon-Sat 9am-5pm, summer school hols Sun 10am-4pm) has a good selection of books on Cornwall, including Trailblazer's *Cornwall Coast Path*.

There are **banks** including a TSB and a Barclays, both of which have **ATMs**. You will also find ATMs outside the town's supermarkets.

There's a **launderette** (Mon-Thur 8.30am-5pm, Fri to 8pm, Sat 9am-5pm, Sun 10am-5pm) tucked away off Lansdown Rd.

Where to stay

Campsites The recently opened *Efford Farm Camping* (☎ 07495-915659 or ☎ 07870-472448, 🖳 effordcamping.co.uk; Easter to Sep) is now the closest campsite to the centre of the town. It's just off Vicarage Rd and charges £10 for hikers. It's no-frills camping – just an open field really – but has portacabin toilets and showers.

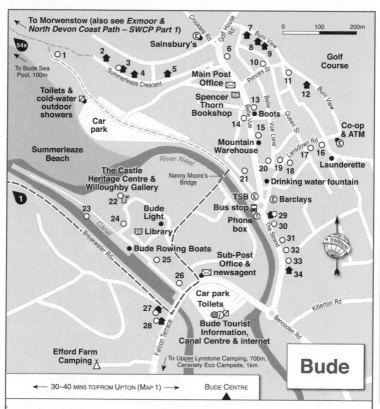

To Morwenstow (also see *Exmoor & North Devon Coast Path – SWCP Part 1*)

54x

To Bude Sea Pool, 100m

Toilets & cold-water outdoor showers

Car park

Summerleaze Beach

Crocklets Rd

Golf House Rd

Sainsbury's

Summerleaze Crescent

Main Post Office ✉

Spencer Thorn Bookshop

Mountain Warehouse

River Neet

The Castle Heritage Centre & Willoughby Gallery

Nanny Moore's Bridge

Bude Light

Library

Bude Rowing Boats

Breakwater Rd

Canal

Efford Farm Camping

Falcon Terrace

Burn View

Princes St

Belle Vue

Belle Vue Lane

Queen St

Boots

Lansdown Rd

Golf Course

Co-op & ATM

Launderette

Drinking water fountain

TSB

Barclays

Bus stop

Phone box

The Strand

Sub-Post Office & newsagent

Car park Toilets

Bude Tourist Information, Canal Centre & internet

Bencoolen Rd

Killerton Rd

To Upper Lynstone Camping, 700m, Cerenety Eco Campsite, 1km

Bude

0   100   200m

Golf Course

← 30–40 MINS TO/FROM UPTON (MAP 1) →   BUDE CENTRE

Where to stay
2 The Beach
3 The Edgcumbe
4 Atlantic House Hotel
5 The Grosvenor
7 Tee-Side Guest House
8 Sunrise
9 Links Side Guest House
12 Sea Jade Guest House
27 Falcon Hotel
28 Brendon Arms
29 The Globe Hotel
34 Premier Inn

Where to eat and drink
1 Life's a Beach
3 The Deck (at The Edgcumbe)
6 The Coffee Pot
10 The Ultimate Fish Co
11 Bude Tandoori
13 Butter Bun
14 A Taste of Cornwall
15 Costa Coffee
16 The Barrel at Bude
17 Coffee Shop
18 Lansdowne Bakery
19 Scrummies
20 Pengenna's Pasties
21 Temple

22 Limelight Café (in the Castle)
23 The Barge
24 Lock Gates Tea Rm
25 The Kitchen Front
26 Olive Tree Coffee House & Bistro
27 Falcon Hotel
28 Brendon Arms
29 The Globe Hotel
30 Tiandi
31 Silver River Chinese Takeaway
32 Carriers Inn
33 La Bocca Pizza Kitchen

For something more comfortable, continue along Vicarage Rd for around 10 minutes to reach *Upper Lynstone Caravan & Camping Park* (☎ 01288-352017, 🖳 upper lynstone.co.uk; 🐾 on lead; Apr-Sep; walker & small tent £10-13, 2 people & tent £16-23). The quiet location is perfect for those continuing on the trail as it backs on to the cliffs and the coastal path to Upton and Widemouth Bay. There is a well-stocked **shop** and **laundry** facilities; the free showers are roomy and spotlessly clean. To get here, keep walking along Falcon Terrace, which becomes Vicarage Road, and the campsite will eventually be on your right.

A third camping option is the delightful *Cerenety Eco Campsite* (Map 1; ☎ 07789-718446, 🖳 cerenetycampsite.co.uk; 🐾; £5pp). It's in Upton, just off the coast path towards Crackington Haven, so not really in Bude itself, although not much further away than Upper Lynstone. It's basic (solar-heated showers, compost toilets) but very friendly, well organised and genuinely eco-conscious. There's usually a food truck on site during peak season, for breakfasts and occasional evening meals, as well as open fires for self-caterers. Oh, and the alpacas are exceptionally cute. To get here, walk to Upper Lynstone Caravan & Camping Park, opposite which you'll see a sign for Cerenety pointing you down a road called The Grange. The campsite is about 200m down this road, on the right.

B&Bs & guesthouses B&B-style accommodation is mostly located at the northern end of town, near the golf course. On Burn View you will find: *Links Side Guest House* (☎ 01288-352410, 🖳 links sidebude.co.uk; **fb**; 2S/5D/1T, most en suite) with B&B from £32.50pp (sgl/sgl occ from £45); *Sea Jade Guest House* (☎ 01288-353404, 🖳 seajadeguesthouse.co.uk; **fb**; 3D/4Tr, most en suite) from £37.50pp (sgl occ £35-55); *Sunrise* (☎ 01288-353214, 🖳 sunrise-bude.co.uk; **fb**; 2S/1T/3D/1D or T, all en suite; 🛏; 🐾), which charges from £40pp; and *Tee-Side Guest House* (☎ 01288-352351, 🖳 tee-side.co.uk; **fb**; 1S private facilities, 4D or T, all en suite; from £40pp), overlooking the golf course.

Hotels & pubs Overlooking the beach from a great vantage point on the edge of Summerleaze Down, *The Beach* (☎ 01288-389800, 🖳 thebeachatbude.co.uk; 2T/14D, all en suite; 🛏; from £70pp winter/£100pp summer, sgl occ from £135) is Bude's most boutique hotel, with sea views from some of its very smart, modern rooms. At time of research it was also temporarily home to restaurant-café *Elements* (see p84).

On the same road, *The Edgcumbe* (☎ 01288-353846, 🖳 edgcumbe-hotel.co.uk; **fb**; 6D/5D or T/1Tr, all en suite; 🛏; Feb-Dec; from £75pp, sgl occ from £70) is friendly with a young vibe, and fresh, modern rooms. There's a small bar-restaurant with excellent meals, and a handy drying room for wet tents and soggy walking boots.

Atlantic House (☎ 01288-352451, 🖳 atlantichousehotel.com; **fb**; 1S private bathroom, 12D/3D or T, all en suite; 🛏) has some nice sea-view rooms, although some of the rear rooms are a bit poky. Rates are £45-87.50pp (sgl from £45, sgl occ £70-150). Next door is *The Grosvenor* (☎ 01288-352062, 🖳 thegrosvenorbude.co.uk; 2D/3D or T/1Qd, all en suite; Mar-Nov; min 2 nights Jul-Sep), which has two rooms with sea views. They charge £37-57pp.

On the other side of the canal, the impressive *Falcon Hotel* (☎ 01288-352005, 🖳 falconhotel.com; **fb**; 4S/7T/18D, all en suite; 🛏; from £67.50pp, sgl occ from £112.50) is a more traditional, classier alternative to its main top-end rival, The Beach.

At the lower end of the hotel scale, *The Globe Hotel* (☎ 01288 352085, 🖳 the globehotelbude.com; 2D/2Tr) is a bit run down, but has room-only rates from just £30pp (sgl/sgl occ £50); breakfast costs an extra £7.50pp.

Nearby is a *Premier Inn* (☎ 0333-2346549, 🖳 premierinn.com) where a standard double room could be as little as £16.50pp (room only; sgl occ from £33; breakfast £9.50), but expect to pay much more at peak times. There's a café-bar area, too, which also does evening meals.

Brendon Arms (☎ 01288-354542, 🖳 brendonarms.co.uk; **fb**; 1S/5D/3T, all en suite; 🛏) is a popular pub which also has rooms (from £48pp, sgl occ from £56).

❑ BUDE CANAL

Bude Canal (🖳 bude-canal.co.uk) was dug to transport mainly sand inland from the seashore so that it could be spread on the fields to improve the soil which was rather poor in parts of north Cornwall. The Canal was the brainchild of one John Endyvean, the intention being to link up with the River Tamar at Calstock, thus providing a waterway between the Bristol Channel and the English Channel, 90 miles of canal to span just 28 miles as the crow flies. The full scheme was never realised although by 1823 some 35 miles of canal were in operation. Once the railways were built the use of the canal began to decline and by World War II it became ineffective as a waterway. Today only a short stretch remains between Bude and Helebridge.

A project to restore the canal with the aid of a £45m grant from the Heritage Lottery Fund was completed in 2009. Whilst the lock-gates giving access to the open sea suffered damage in the early part of 2008 during some huge storms, the canal itself is currently in good working order. At the Helebridge end, **Weir Nature Centre** at Whalesborough Farm opened in 2011. It is a 40-minute walk by the side of the canal.

Near the castle, a small **boat-rental kiosk** (Easter-Sep 10am-5pm) has rowing boats (£15/hr), canoes and pedalos (£20/hr) for trips along the canal.

Where to eat and drink

Cafés & bakeries There are numerous options for coffee and a freshly baked snack in Bude. Inside the castle is *Limelight Café* (daily 10am-4pm). On Lansdown Rd *The Coffee Shop* (☎ 01288-355973; fb; Mar-Nov daily 10am-6.30pm, Dec-Feb 10.30am-4pm) sells freshly baked goods from *Lansdowne Bakery* (fb; daily 9am-5pm), or there's nearby *Pengenna Pasties* (daily 9am-5pm). On the outskirts of town, *The Coffee Pot* (☎ 01288-356142; fb; daily Jun-Sep 8am-6pm, winter 8.30am-3pm; 🐾) is friendly, while on Belle Vue is the pocket-sized *Butter Bun* (fb; 9.30am-4pm) and *Costa Coffee* (Mon-Sat 7am-6.30pm, Sun 9am-5pm) which opens early.

For a hot or cold lunch or cream tea by the canal try *The Barge* (☎ 01288-356786, 🖳 thebargebude.co.uk; fb; Mon-Sat 10am-5pm, Sun 10am-4pm), a café on a boat; nearby *Lock Gates Tearoom* (fb; summer Tue-Sun 10am-5pm) or *The Kitchen Front* (☎ 01288-350107, 🖳 thekitchenfront.co.uk; fb; Mon-Thur 10am-5pm, Fri & Sat to 3.30pm, closed Sun, winter hours variable) a quirky wartime-themed tearoom.

Overlooking the river, *Temple* (☎ 01288-354739, 🖳 templecornwall.com; fb; lunch Wed-Sun 11.30am-2.30pm, evening daily 5.30-8.30pm, booking essential) is the hipsters' choice of café, with old school classroom table and chairs, a health-conscious menu (lunchtime small plates £4-9, evening set menu £28) and good tunes.

Taste of Cornwall (daily 10am-6pm) has 24 different ice cream flavours on offer.

Restaurants & takeaways Café by day, bistro by night, *Olive Tree Coffee House and Bistro* (☎ 01288-359577, 🖳 olivetree bude.co.uk; fb; daily 10am-4pm, summer Mon-Sat 10am-8pm) serves a good variety of gluten-free and vegetarian dishes.

More affordable, *Scrummies* (summer Mon-Sat 8am-9pm, Sun 9am-9pm, winter opening varies) is owned by local fisherman Cliff Bowden who catches, prepares and cooks 60-70% of the fish himself and offers a gigantic cod 'n' chips.

On The Strand *La Bocca Pizza Kitchen* (☎ 01288-255855, 🖳 laboccabude .co.uk; fb; daily noon-9pm, takeaway deliveries 5-9pm) does excellent pizza to eat in or takeaway. Also on this stretch are the two Chinese restaurants, *Tiandi* (☎ 01288-359686; fb; daily 5-10pm), which also does Thai cuisine, and *Silver River Chinese Takeaway* (☎ 01288-352028; fb; mid Feb to mid Jan Tue-Sun 5-10pm).

The best Indian restaurant in town is *Bude Tandoori* (☎ 01288-359994, 🖳 bude tandoori.co.uk; daily 5-11.30pm), which, unusually, has some outdoor seating too.

For no-nonsense fish 'n' chips try *The Ultimate Fish Co* (☎ 01288-356331, **fb**; daily 1-3.30pm & 4.30-9pm), an eat-in or takeaway chippy at 9 Princes St.

In terms of location, *Life's a Beach* (☎ 01288-355222, ⌨ lifesabeach.info; **fb**; summer Sun-Tue 10am-4pm, Wed-Sat 10am-8pm, winter hours vary) is the pick of the bunch, with fabulous beach views from its terrace. Evening fine dining includes good seafood (mains £16.50-22.50, 2/3 courses £25.50/29.50), and is indoors only.

Pubs Next to the canal, the ever-popular *Brendon Arms* (see Where to stay; food daily noon-2pm & 6-9pm, summer hols noon-9pm) is a 150-year-old pub with plenty of garden seating out front. Next door, *Falcon Hotel* (see Where to stay) has a bar (food daily 10am-9pm; 🐾) and a restaurant (daily 6.30-9pm, Sun noon-2.30pm; booking preferred) with fairly standard pub grub. *The Deck* (☎ 01288-353846, ⌨ thedeckbude.co.uk; **fb**; Tue-Sat 4-8.30pm, summer daily), at The Edgcumbe (see Where to stay), can also be recommended.

At the bottom of The Strand, *Carriers Inn* (☎ 01288-352459; **fb**; food Mon-Sat noon-3pm & 6-9pm, Sun noon-5.30pm; 🐾) sometimes has live music. Just along the road *The Globe Hotel* (see Where to Stay; food noon-2.30pm & 6-9pm) has cheap pub food, real ales and friendly staff.

If you just fancy a drink, it's well worth hunting down *The Barrel at Bude* (☎ 01288-356113, ⌨ thebarrelatbude.com; **fb**; Thur-Sat 4-9pm), a pint-sized smugglers bar serving Cornish craft ales, ciders and gin.

Transport
[See pp52-5] Some Stagecoach No 85 **bus** services go from here to Barnstaple, and the nearest **railway station**. Alternatively, their No 6A runs to Exeter. The No 217 operates to Morwenstow and the 218/219 service travels to Hartland from where you can connect with the 319 to Bideford and Barnstaple. The No 12 service heads to Launceston, while the 95 runs to Truro. Buses stop on The Strand.

For a **taxi**, try Trev's Taxi (☎ 07799-663217, ⌨ trevstaxi.co.uk).

BUDE TO CRACKINGTON HAVEN   MAPS 1-5

The first **10 miles (16km, 4-5hrs)** start benignly enough following a grassy cliff-top for about a mile before unexpectedly meeting a road with a small cluster of houses, **Upton**. Next is **Widemouth Bay** (pronounced 'Widmouth'), the first of many beaches popular with surfers and sun-seekers alike and adequately supplied with cafés and places to stay. Once past these early distractions the hard work begins with a punishing ascent onto **Penhalt Cliff**, the first of several more ups and downs (Millook, Chipman Point and Castle Point) on the trek to **Crackington Haven**. Despite these testing beginnings there is still time to appreciate the beautiful green cliffs that slope down to the waves below and, once you reach Crackington, you'll be rewarded with a lovely village tucked around a sheltered cove and a sense of satisfaction at completing a strenuous first day's walk.

UPTON   [MAP 1]
Upton is a satellite village of Bude with two excellent **campsites** (see p80 and p82): *Upper Lynstone Camping* and *Cerenety Eco Campsite*. For **B&B**, advertised on a sign beside the road is lovely *Upton Cross Bed & Breakfast* (☎ 01288-355310, **fb**; 3D or T/1Tr; ➤; 🐾; from £35pp, sgl occ £60). The owner will run guests into Bude for an evening meal and is used to walkers.

Up on a hill a quarter of a mile further on but reached from the cliff path is *Elements* (☎ 01288-352386, ⌨ elements-life.co.uk). Sadly this boutique hotel was devastated by fire in August 2021 but at the time of research had temporarily relocated its excellent **restaurant-café** to *The Beach* in Bude (see p82).

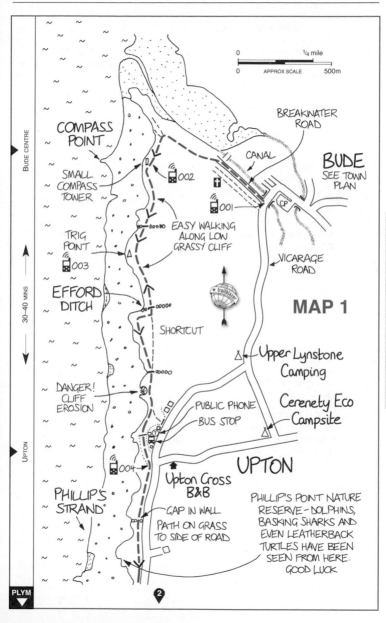

ROUTE GUIDE AND MAPS

BUDE CENTRE

30-40 MINS

UPTON

PLYM

0   ¼ mile
APPROX SCALE
0   500m

BREAKWATER
ROAD

CANAL

BUDE
SEE TOWN
PLAN

COMPASS
POINT

002

SMALL
COMPASS
TOWER

001

CP

TRIG
POINT

003

EASY WALKING
ALONG LOW
GRASSY CLIFF

VICARAGE
ROAD

EFFORD
DITCH

★ trailblazer

MAP 1

SHORTCUT

Upper Lynstone
Camping

DANGER!
CLIFF
EROSION

Cerenety Eco
Campsite

PUBLIC PHONE
BUS STOP

UPTON

004

PHILLIP'S
STRAND

Upton Cross
B&B

GAP IN WALL
PATH ON GRASS
TO SIDE OF ROAD

PHILLIP'S POINT NATURE
RESERVE – DOLPHINS,
BASKING SHARKS AND
EVEN LEATHERBACK
TURTLES HAVE BEEN
SEEN FROM HERE.
GOOD LUCK

2

WIDEMOUTH BAY
[MAP 2; MAP 3, p88]

The village, which gets very busy in the summer, is strung out rather randomly along the main road behind the long beach but it has a **general store** (Mon-Sat 8am-5pm, Sun 8am-2pm) selling all the essentials including alcohol.

Campers have two options. The first requires a steep climb from the trail to the pleasant *Penhalt Farm Holiday Park* (Map 3; ☎ 01288-361210 or 07970-521549, ⏴ penhaltfarm.co.uk; 🐾; Easter-Oct; hiker & tent £10). They have a small shop for basic provisions and accept card payments. The second option, *Widemouth Bay Caravan Park* (Map 3; ☎ 01288-361208, ⏴ john fowlerholidays.com; WI-FI; 🐾), is less of a hike from Widemouth Bay, but is a less endearing, oversized site. The facilities are excellent – they even have an indoor swimming pool – but the atmosphere is more Butlins than South West Coast Path, and in peak season costs £30 for a pitch.

For **rooms**, set back from the beach is *The Bay View Inn* (☎ 01288-361273, ⏴ bayviewinn.co.uk; 4D/2Qd for 2 adults & 2 children only; 🐶; from £52.50pp) with decent rooms. The pub is the heartbeat of the surfing community but is happy to welcome walkers. The modern bar opens to an extensive area of decking – a good place to sit out and enjoy a pint. **Food** (Mon-Fri noon-2.30pm & 5.30-9pm, Sat noon-9pm, Sun noon-8pm; book for indoor table) is served in three or four different areas.

Next to the general store is the *Beach House* (☎ 01288-361256, ⏴ beachhouse widemouth.co.uk; 6D/1T/1Tr/2Qd; from £40pp, sgl occ from £60). Rooms are small, but most come with sea views. There's a good **restaurant**, a more informal café and a bar, plus picnic tables scattered around the back garden, which leads down to the beach.

A short walk inland from the path is the pub, *Widemouth Manor* (Map 3; ☎ 01288-361207, ⏴ widemouthmanor.co.uk; 3S/5D/1Tr/1Qd), which has simple but smart en suite rooms (from £40pp, sgl/sgl occ from £50/75) and a decent **restaurant** (Mon-Sat 12.30-2.30pm & 5-8.30pm, Sun noon-5pm; book for indoor table) with a good quality menu (most mains £12.50-16) and lovely views from the back garden.

Passing walkers are more likely to grab food at one of the two very popular (seasonal) cafés. *Widemouth Bay Café* (fb; Mon-Fri 10am-5pm, Sat-Sun 9.30am-5pm) has a more extensive menu, more seating and better sea views. *Black Rock Café* (fb; 9am-5pm) is smaller, but arguably does better food, including burgers, pizzas and pasties.

The No 95 **bus** service stops here. [See pp52-5 for details].

CRACKINGTON HAVEN
[MAP 5, p91]

Crackington Haven lies at the head of the cove of the same name and can get busy in summer thanks to its atmospheric, cliff-backed beach, which is ideal for families. Overlooking the beach, the friendly pub, *Coombe Barton Inn* (☎ 01840-230345, ⏴ coombebarton.co.uk; 4D/1T/1Tr, some en suite; from £55pp, from £70 sgl occ; 🐾) is the focal point for the village. **Rooms** are nicely appointed, one with a sea-facing balcony. There also's a self-catering lodge that sleeps four (1D/1T with bunkbeds, £120) The restaurant (**food** daily noon-2.30pm & 6.30-9.30pm) has an excellent pub-grub menu, including locally caught fish and slow-cooked curries. There's no ATM in the village, but you can get cashback at the pub.

Lower Tresmorn Farm (☎ 01840-230667, ⏴ lowertresmorn.co.uk; 4D/2Tr, most en suite; 🐶; from £45pp, sgl occ £50; min 2 nights) is a lovely old building up on the cliffs before you reach the Haven, only five minutes from the coast path. One room has a four-poster bed and views to Lundy Island. Closer to the village is *Trewartha B&B* (☎ 01840-230420, ⏴ bychy.co.uk; 1D en suite; from £40pp), which has a room in the main house, plus a self-catering chalet (1D/1T with bunks) called By Chy, at the bottom of the owner's peacock-filled garden. (cont'd on p90)

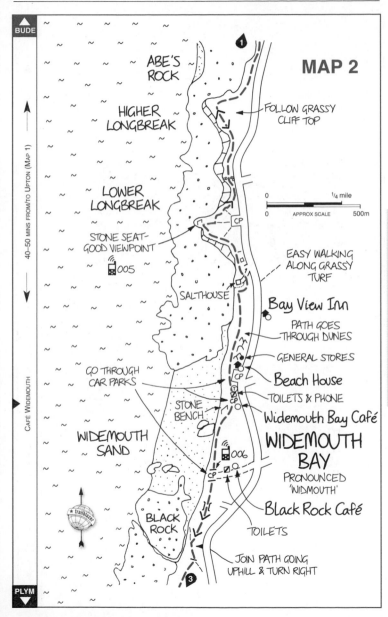

BUDE

40–50 MINS FROM/TO UPTON (MAP 1)

Café Widemouth

PLYM

ABE'S ROCK

HIGHER LONGBREAK

LOWER LONGBREAK

STONE SEAT- GOOD VIEWPOINT
005

SALTHOUSE

GO THROUGH CAR PARKS

STONE BENCH

WIDEMOUTH SAND

BLACK ROCK

MAP 2

FOLLOW GRASSY CLIFF TOP

0   1/4 mile
0   APPROX SCALE   500m

EASY WALKING ALONG GRASSY TURF

Bay View Inn
PATH GOES THROUGH DUNES
GENERAL STORES
Beach House
TOILETS & PHONE
Widemouth Bay Café

WIDEMOUTH BAY
PRONOUNCED 'WIDMOUTH'
006

Black Rock Café
TOILETS

JOIN PATH GOING UPHILL & TURN RIGHT

CP

trailblazer

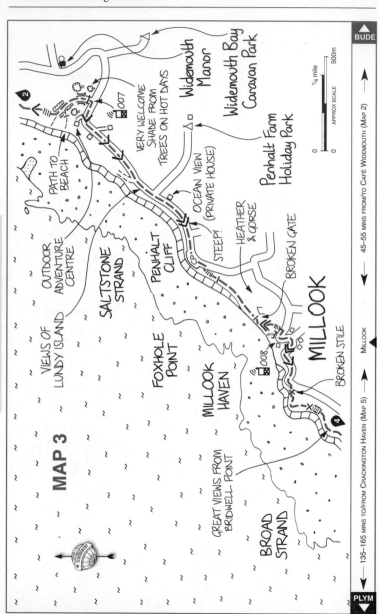

MAP 3

BUDE ▲

PLYM ▼

45–55 MINS FROM/TO CAFÉ WIDEMOUTH (MAP 2) →

← Millook ►

← 135–165 MINS TO/FROM CRACKINGTON HAVEN (MAP 5) →

Widemouth Bay Caravan Park

Widemouth Manor

Penhalt Farm Holiday Park

007

VERY WELCOME SHADE FROM TREES ON HOT DAYS

PATH TO BEACH

OCEAN VIEW (PRIVATE HOUSE)

STEEP!

HEATHER & GORSE

BROKEN GATE

OUTDOOR ADVENTURE CENTRE

VIEWS OF LUNDY ISLAND

SALTSTONE STRAND

PENHALT CLIFF

FOXHOLE POINT

MILLOOK HAVEN

008

MILLOOK

BROKEN STILE

GREAT VIEWS FROM BRIDWELL POINT

BROAD STRAND

¼ mile
500m
0
0
APPROX SCALE

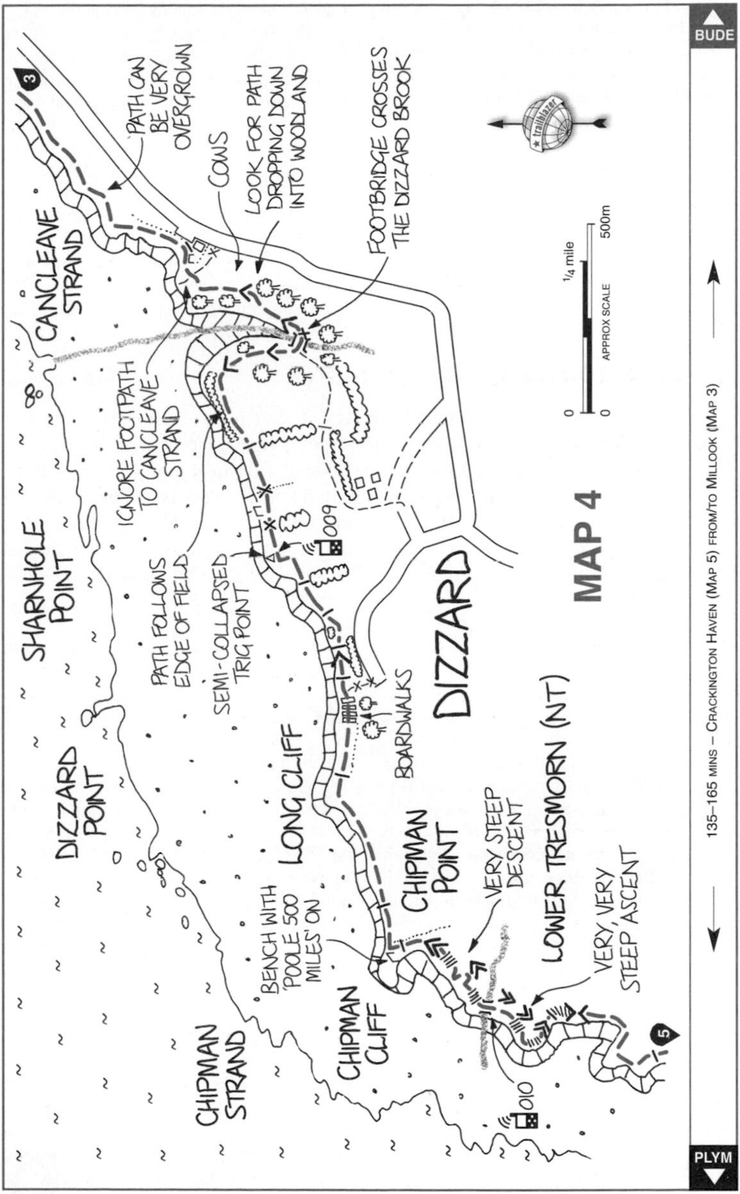
BUDE
PLYM
MAP 4
DIZZARD
CANCLEAVE STRAND
SHARNHOLE POINT
DIZZARD POINT
LONG CLIFF
CHIPMAN POINT
CHIPMAN CLIFF
CHIPMAN STRAND
LOWER TRESMORN (NT)
PATH CAN BE VERY OVERGROWN
COWS
LOOK FOR PATH DROPPING DOWN INTO WOODLAND
FOOTBRIDGE CROSSES THE DIZZARD BROOK
IGNORE FOOTPATH TO CANCLEAVE STRAND
PATH FOLLOWS EDGE OF FIELD
SEMI-COLLAPSED TRIG POINT
BOARDWALKS
BENCH WITH 'POOLE 500 MILES' ON
VERY STEEP DESCENT
VERY, VERY STEEP ASCENT
009
010
3
5
0
1/4 mile
APPROX SCALE
0
500m
135–165 MINS – CRACKINGTON HAVEN (MAP 5) FROM/TO MILLOOK (MAP 3)

It's a bit of a hike uphill from the path, but they'll pick you up if you have a booking.

Campers must walk half a mile past Trewartha B&B to the welcoming *Coxford Meadow Campsite* (☎ 01840-230707, 🖳 north-cornwall-accommodation.com, **fb**; £8pp); turn left when you get to Tremayna Methodist Church and the campsite entrance will be on your right. It's a small, family-run site with lovely countryside views. Note you could take a short cut through St Gennys to get here. The 95 bus stops outside Tremayna Methodist Church.

There are two cafés competing to supply your need for a cup of tea and a scone:

Cabin Café (🖳 cabincafecrackington.co.uk, **fb**; 🐾; 9am-5pm) is the better of the two, and also does breakfasts. It has a large terrace with views of the beach and surrounding cliffs and serves up bacon baps, baguettes and jacket potatoes plus freshly baked pasties, pastries and cakes. *Haven Café* (daily 10am-4pm), which also has terrace seating, is good for a drink and a lunchtime sandwich or pasty. Both do ice creams too.

There's a **public toilet** by the bus stop. The **bus** service is the No 95, running on the Bude/Camelford to Truro routes. [See pp52-5 for details].

CRACKINGTON HAVEN TO BOSCASTLE   [MAPS 5-8]

The cliffs on this **7-mile (11km, 2½-3½hrs)** stretch are some of the highest in Cornwall (**High Cliff**, 731ft, is the highest point on the Cornish coast path and the highest sea cliff in the county); the path is careful to keep to the top of them.

If you feel the urge to head for the beach the only access is at **The Strangles** (Map 6) which can be reached by a detour down a steep path. There are some beautiful rugged coves and clefts on the approach to Boscastle, particularly at **Pentargon** (Map 8) where a small waterfall freefalls over a lip into the sea below.

BOSCASTLE   [MAP 8, p95]

Beautiful Boscastle is tucked into a small but deep green valley that ends in a sheltered natural harbour. During the 18th and 19th centuries roads to the harbour were rough and narrow so the village relied on the sea for trade and transport. Leading away from the harbour is the medieval part of the village, based round the site of the 12th-century **Bottreaux Castle** from which the village derives its name, but of which there is little trace these days.

In 2004 the village made headline news when a devastating flash flood swept through the streets carrying away houses and cars and creating chaos, although miraculously there were no fatalities. A year later most of the buildings had been faithfully restored to their original state and today the village looks smart and spruce.

Most visitors while away the time in cafés or relaxing down by the harbour, which is also popular with swimmers, but it's also worth popping into the fascinating **Museum of Witchcraft and Magic**

(☎ 01840-250111, 🖳 museumofwitchcraft.com; May-Nov Mon-Fri 10am-5pm, also Sun in summer hols; adult/child £7/5; pre-booking essential).

Services

The village is well supplied with shops and places of refreshment all within a small area. The **post office** (daily 8am-5pm) and an **ATM** are in the well-stocked Spar **supermarket** (Mon-Sat 6am-8pm, Sun 6.30am-8pm). You can buy hiking and camping gear (but not camping-stove gas) at the **outdoor shop** Cornish Rambler (daily 10am-5pm), and there is a **public toilet** at the main car park where the buses stop.

Where to stay

For **camping**, the nearest option is *Trebyla Farm Caravan & Camping* (off Map 8; ☎ 01840-250308, 🖳 boscastlecampsite.co.uk; £6-7pp), a simple, friendly, family-run campsite, about half a mile past Boscastle Farm Shop & Café.

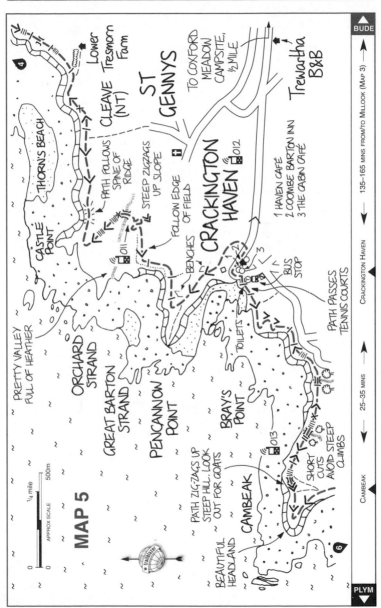

MAP 5

APPROX SCALE
¼ mile
500m

BUDE

135–165 MINS FROM/TO MILLOOK (MAP 3)

ROUTE GUIDE AND MAPS

BUDE

Trewartha B&B

TO COXFORD MEADOW CAMPSITE, ½ MILE

ST GENNYS

Lower Tresmorn Farm

CLEAVE (NT)

PATH FOLLOWS SPINE OF RIDGE

THORN'S BEACH

CASTLE POINT

STEEP ZIGZAGS UP SLOPE

FOLLOW EDGE OF FIELD

O11

O11

BENCHES

CRACKINGTON HAVEN

O12

1 HAVEN CAFE
2 COOMBE BARTON INN
3 THE CABIN CAFÉ

3

1
2

BUS STOP

PATH PASSES TENNIS COURTS

TOILETS

CRACKINGTON HAVEN

PRETTY VALLEY FULL OF HEATHER

ORCHARD STRAND

GREAT BARTON STRAND

PENCANNOW POINT

BRAY'S POINT

25–35 MINS

O13

SHORT CUTS AVOID STEEP CLIMBS

PATH ZIG-ZAGS UP STEEP HILL. LOOK OUT FOR GOATS

CAMBEAK

CAMBEAK

BEAUTIFUL HEADLAND

trailblazer

PLYM

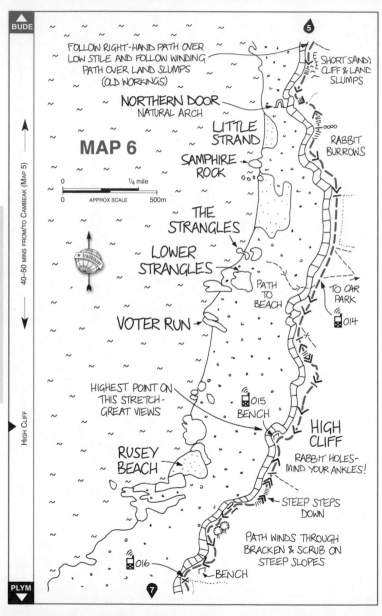

BUDE ▲

FOLLOW RIGHT-HAND PATH OVER
LOW STILE AND FOLLOW WINDING
PATH OVER LAND SLUMPS
(OLD WORKINGS)

NORTHERN DOOR
NATURAL ARCH

LITTLE
STRAND

SAMPHIRE
ROCK

MAP 6

0   ¼ mile
0   APPROX SCALE   500m

THE
STRANGLES

LOWER
STRANGLES

VOTER RUN

PATH
TO
BEACH

TO CAR
PARK
014

015
BENCH

HIGHEST POINT ON
THIS STRETCH-
GREAT VIEWS

RUSEY
BEACH

HIGH
CLIFF

RABBIT HOLES-
MIND YOUR ANKLES!

STEEP STEPS
DOWN

PATH WINDS THROUGH
BRACKEN & SCRUB ON
STEEP SLOPES

016

BENCH

PLYM ▼

5

SHORT SANDY
CLIFF & LAND
SLUMPS

RABBIT
BURROWS

7

ROUTE GUIDE AND MAPS

40–50 MINS FROM/TO CAMBEAK (MAP 5)

High Cliff

YHA Boscastle (☎ 0845-371 9006, 🖳 yha.org.uk/hostel/boscastle; 20 bunk beds & 4 double beds; from £16pp; reception open 8-10am & 5-10pm; Mar-Oct, group bookings only Nov-Feb) has very helpful staff, self-catering facilities and a lovely location beside the canal leading down to the harbour.

For **B&B**, right in the heart of the village is *Bridge House* (☎ 01840-250011, 🖳 bridgehouse-boscastle.co.uk, **fb**; 2D/2T, all en suite, from £40pp, sgl occ from £75; min 2 nights), a typically charming stone-built building with a friendly welcome and a tea room attached.

Next to the bridge, *The Riverside* (☎ 01840-250216, 🖳 riversideboscastle.co.uk, **fb**; 1S/7D/3T/2Tr; ☞; £50-60pp, sgl £54, sgl occ £77, plus £7.50 for 1-night stays) occupies a building built by Sir Richard Grenville of Revenge fame ('At Flores in the Azores Sir Richard Grenville lay...'); it's a lovely place to stay.

The premier hotel in the village is *The Wellington* (☎ 01840-250202, 🖳 wellingtonhotelboscastle.com; 3S/7D/3T/1F; ☞; 🐾; £62.50-92.50pp, sgl £60-80), with 14 en suite rooms including two spacious turret rooms with views down to the harbour.

Where to eat and drink

Right on the trail as you come into Boscastle is the award-winning *Boscastle Farm Shop & Café* (☎ 01840-250827, 🖳 boscastlefarmshop.co.uk, **fb**; café 9am-4pm, shop 9am-5pm; 🐾) with a fabulous food menu, and a well-stocked shop and deli. The emphasis is on farm-grown or locally sourced food and drinks, and there's a large back garden with wonderful sea views and a children's play area.

There is a wide choice of sustenance in the town itself, from Cornish cream teas to pasties, fish & chips, pub grub and restaurants. If you need supplies for the trail, *Boscastle Bakery* (Mon-Sat 9am-4pm, Sun 10am-4pm) does an excellent line in pasties as well as good-value rolls and sandwiches. Nearby there's also a grocery store, *Cornish Stores* (daily 9am-6pm) with fresh fruit and veg, and the decent-sized **Spar supermarket** (see Services), both of which also serve coffee.

Harbour Light Tea Garden (☎ 01840-250953; Easter-Oct Thur-Sun 9am-5pm) was originally housed in a 16th-century building – one of the many destroyed by the floods. Rebuilt beautifully in 2006, this has always been one of the most popular stops

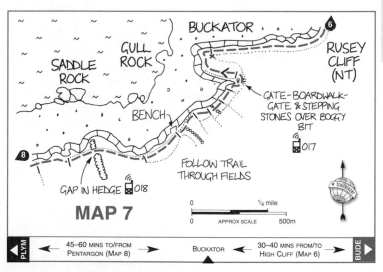

MAP 7

with walkers, with its location right on the path and lovely food, though it's now only open four days a week and surprisingly no longer serves cream teas.

Another nice café option is *Pilchard Cellar Café* (summer 10am-5pm, winter 10.30am-4pm; 🐾), which is attached to the **National Trust gift shop** (same hours). You can get a decent soup here plus good-value pasties, teacakes and scones, and they serve bottles of Tintagel Brewery Ale as well as tea and coffee.

The tea room at *Bridge House* (see Where to stay) is another lovely option for Cornish delights such as cream teas, pasties and various seafood offerings.

Toby Jug Café (daily 10am-4pm) has plenty of roadside seating and has a wide selection of gluten-free and vegan options on its menu.

For pub food, the *Cobweb Inn* (☎ 01840-250278, 🖳 cobwebinn.com, **fb**; food daily noon-3pm & 5-9pm) is popular with pub-classic mains ranging from £10 to £14. Their range of beers includes Sharp's Doom Bar and St Austell's Tribute.

Nearby former pub *Old Manor House* (☎ 01840-250251; summer daily 11am-9pm, winter hours vary) is now a licensed coffee shop being run by next door *Sharon's Plaice* (same hours) where you can take away fish & chips, pizza or pasties or eat in their lovely garden.

Riverside Restaurant (see Where to stay; Mon 6-10pm, Tue-Sun 10am-10pm, winter hours shorter) has a delightful garden by the stream which runs down to the harbour, and serves a good range of locally caught fish. Lunchtime mains cost £7-10, though the crab sandwiches are more, while most evening mains range from £12 to £20.

At the top end of the market, *The Wellington* (see Where to stay) has a swanky restaurant (daily 6.30-9pm, booking advisable), where most mains will cost £15-20, but you can also eat main meals as well as sandwiches and cream teas in the bar (food noon-8pm) with a pint of Cornish cider or ale.

Transport [See pp52-5 for details] The No 95 **bus** service between Bude and Truro stops here as well as at Crackington Haven and Tintagel.

For a **taxi**, ring BosCars (☎ 07790-983911, 🖳 boscars.uk).

BOSCASTLE TO TINTAGEL   [MAPS 8-11]

For the next **5 miles (8km, 2-2½hrs)** you leave the high cliffs behind. You start by passing the site of the **Willapark Iron Age fort**, where there now stands a **National Coastwatch tower** (and where you may stumble across some very cute ponies), before following a convoluted and rugged section of coastline, decorated with small bays, coves and headlands. The walking is not too strenuous and there are plenty of tempting places for a break, not least the dramatic rock arch known as **Lady's Window** (Map 9) and the sheltered **Rocky Valley** (Map 10), a narrow gorge just before **Bossiney** that provides welcome shade on hot summer days.

At the end of this leg are the ruins of **Tintagel Castle**, a fittingly mystical spot for a fortress that is reputed to be the birthplace of the legendary King Arthur.

❏ **IMPORTANT NOTE – WALKING TIMES**

Unless otherwise specified, **all times in this book refer only to the time spent walking**. You will need to add 20-30% to allow for rests, photography, checking the map, drinking water etc, not to mention time simply to stop and stare. When planning the day's hike count on 5-7 hours' actual walking.

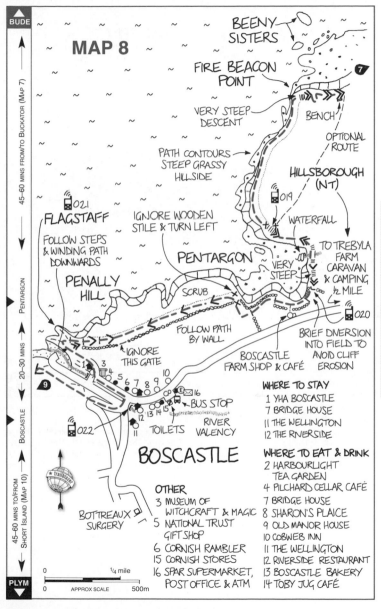

BUDE

45–60 MINS FROM/TO BUCKATOR (MAP 7)

PENTARGON

20–30 MINS

BOSCASTLE

45–60 MINS TO/FROM SHORT ISLAND (MAP 10)

PLYM

MAP 8

BEENY SISTERS

FIRE BEACON POINT

VERY STEEP DESCENT

BENCH

OPTIONAL ROUTE

HILLSBOROUGH (NT)

019

WATERFALL

PATH CONTOURS STEEP GRASSY HILLSIDE

021

FLAGSTAFF

IGNORE WOODEN STILE & TURN LEFT

FOLLOW STEPS & WINDING PATH DOWNWARDS

PENTARGON

PENALLY HILL

SCRUB

VERY STEEP

TO TREBYLA FARM CARAVAN & CAMPING ½ MILE

020

FOLLOW PATH BY WALL

IGNORE THIS GATE

BRIEF DIVERSION INTO FIELD TO AVOID CLIFF EROSION

BOSCASTLE FARM SHOP & CAFÉ

1 2 3 4

5 6 7 8 9 10

CP 16

BUS STOP

12 13 14 15

022

TOILETS

RIVER VALENCY

BOSCASTLE

BOTTREAUX SURGERY

0   ¼ mile
0   APPROX SCALE   500m

WHERE TO STAY
1 YHA BOSCASTLE
7 BRIDGE HOUSE
11 THE WELLINGTON
12 THE RIVERSIDE

WHERE TO EAT & DRINK
2 HARBOURLIGHT TEA GARDEN
4 PILCHARD CELLAR CAFÉ
7 BRIDGE HOUSE
8 SHARON'S PLAICE
9 OLD MANOR HOUSE
10 COBWEB INN
11 THE WELLINGTON
12 RIVERSIDE RESTAURANT
13 BOSCASTLE BAKERY
14 TOBY JUG CAFÉ

OTHER
3 MUSEUM OF WITCHCRAFT & MAGIC
5 NATIONAL TRUST GIFT SHOP
6 CORNISH RAMBLER
15 CORNISH STORES
16 SPAR SUPERMARKET, POST OFFICE & ATM

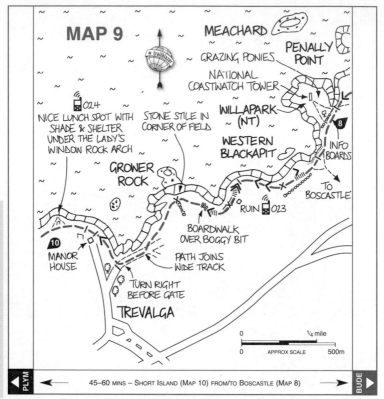

MAP 9

MEACHARD

PENALLY POINT

GRAZING PONIES

NATIONAL COASTWATCH TOWER

024
NICE LUNCH SPOT WITH SHADE & SHELTER UNDER THE LADY'S WINDOW ROCK ARCH

STONE STILE IN CORNER OF FIELD

WILLAPARK (NT)

WESTERN BLACKAPIT

INFO BOARDS

8

GROWER ROCK

RUIN 023

TO BOSCASTLE

BOARDWALK OVER BOGGY BIT

10

MANOR HOUSE

PATH JOINS WIDE TRACK

TURN RIGHT BEFORE GATE

TREVALGA

0   ¼ mile
0   APPROX SCALE   500m

45–60 MINS – SHORT ISLAND (MAP 10) FROM/TO BOSCASTLE (MAP 8)

PLYM

BUDE

ROUTE GUIDE AND MAPS

BOSSINEY [MAP 10]

The small village of Bossiney is essentially an offshoot of Tintagel and is only really worth the detour if you intend staying the night – take the path that runs off the coast path at Bossiney Haven. **Bossiney Mound**, an ancient earthen mound beside a small stone chapel, is thought to be the site of a former Norman castle. It is said to be where Arthur's Round Table lies buried.

Sir Francis Drake, who lived in nearby **Old Borough House**, was elected MP for Bossiney in 1584 after giving his election speech from Bossiney Mound.

You can't miss *Trewethett Farm Caravan and Campsite* (☎ 01840-770222, 🖥 caravanclub.co.uk; Mar-Oct; 🐾), with its glorious cliff-top location right by the path. It's a Caravan Club site with a **shop** (summer daily 9am-7pm), excellent shower facilities, and unrivalled sunset views. A walker & tent costs £14 in high season.

The No 95 **bus** service between Bude and Truro stops here. [For details see pp52-5].

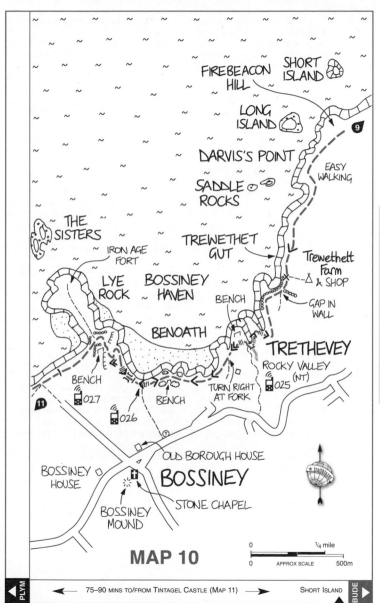

FIREBEACON HILL

SHORT ISLAND

LONG ISLAND

DARVIS'S POINT

EASY WALKING

SADDLE ROCKS

THE SISTERS

IRON AGE FORT

TREWETHET GUT

Trewethet Farm & SHOP

LYE ROCK

BOSSINEY HAVEN

BENCH

GAP IN WALL

BENOATH

TRETHEVEY

ROCKY VALLEY (NT)

025

BENCH

027

TURN RIGHT AT FORK

BENCH

026

OLD BOROUGH HOUSE

BOSSINEY HOUSE

BOSSINEY

STONE CHAPEL

BOSSINEY MOUND

MAP 10

0   ¼ mile

0   APPROX SCALE   500m

ROUTE GUIDE AND MAPS

PLYM

75–90 MINS TO/FROM TINTAGEL CASTLE (MAP 11)

SHORT ISLAND

BUDE

TINTAGEL [map p101]

There has been a settlement here since the Iron Age. However, Tintagel is associated in many minds with the legend of King Arthur who is supposed to have been born at the site of **Tintagel Castle** (Map 11; ☎ 01840-770328, 🖥 english-heritage.org.uk; Apr-Sep daily 10am-6pm, Oct to 5pm, winter check online; adult/child £17/10; online bookings only), built in AD1236 and which, even in its ruined state, dominates the narrow inlet on its rocky promontory. The castle was a stronghold of the dukes of Cornwall but whilst the position is stunning only a few walls remain. In 2019 a **suspension bridge** was installed to span the 190ft gorge, reuniting the two halves of the castle for the first time in over 500 years. The site is hugely atmospheric, especially on a cold, quiet winter's day with the sun setting as the wind whistles about the ancient ramparts. There's a *café* outside the exit and a free **exhibition gallery** opposite it. The toilets are here too.

There is more to find out about the Arthurian legend back in the town itself, at **King Arthur's Great Halls** (☎ 01840-770526; 🖥 kingarthursgreathalls.co.uk; Mar-Oct Tue-Sun 10am-5pm, last entry 4pm) where **guided tours** (adult/child £5/3) tell the story of both the halls and Arthurian legend, after which you can shop for memorabilia to your heart's content.

Now owned by the National Trust, the **Old Post Office** (☎ 01840-770024, 🖥 nationaltrust.org.uk; Mar-Oct Fri-Tue 11am-5pm; adult/child £5/2.50) is a 600-year-old medieval 'hall house' with a famously undulating slate roof. It hasn't been used as a post office since Victorian times.

Services

You'll find **Tintagel Visitor Centre** (☎ 01840-779084; Mon-Fri 10am-1pm, Sat-Sun 10am-5pm) beside the bus stop. There are **public toilets** behind it. There is no longer an actual **post office**, but there is a mobile one in the visitor centre (Tue, Wed & Fri 9-11am).

For provisions there is a Spar **supermarket** (daily 7am-9pm) and an equally well-stocked Premier supermarket (Mon-Sat 7am-9pm, Sun 8am-8pm), both of

---

❏ THE KING ARTHUR MYTH

Given the high profile accorded King Arthur in Tintagel where the name is purloined for pubs, pasties and pizzas it is worth pausing for a moment to ask exactly who he was. Disappointingly, it seems the answer is that he is a figure predominantly from the imagination. Whether the saga in Geoffrey of Monmouth's *History of the Kings of Britain* from the 12th century was drawn from legend or not, this dubious work came out hundreds of years after the events described. It was Tennyson who popularised the myth drawing on Malory's *Morte d'Arthur* and the Victorians lapped it up thanks to its dreamy, romantic imagery and nostalgia for an era when good prevailed over evil but at a terrible cost.

The 20th century re-working of the story brought us *The Sword in the Stone* and *The Once and Future King* by TH White, later translated into film versions that help to keep the myth alive. Arthur's adoption by the hippie community ensures that the torch is passed on. Don't be disappointed. Somewhere back in the 6th century a real king called Arthur did actually exist although the stuff about knights and round tables and Merlin the Wizard is fiction. It's a great story and who could fail to be stirred by Tennyson's description of the last battle:

> *So all day long the noise of battle rolled*
> *Among the mountains by the winter sea*
> *Until King Arthur's table, man by man,*
> *Had fallen in Lyonesse about their Lord.*
> **Alfred, Lord Tennyson**, *Morte d'Arthur,* 1885

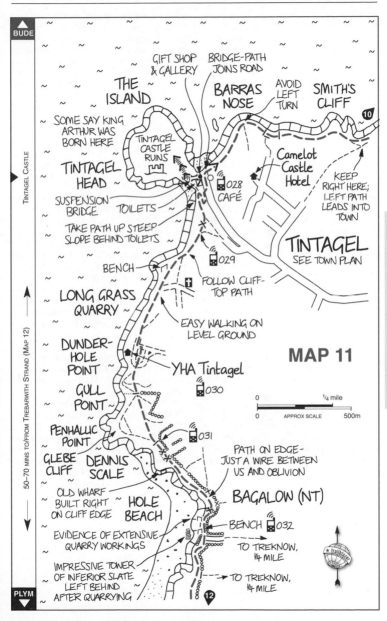

BUDE

PLYM

TINTAGEL CASTLE

50-70 MINS TO/FROM TREBARWITH STRAND (MAP 12)

THE ISLAND

GIFT SHOP & GALLERY

BRIDGE-PATH JOINS ROAD

BARRAS NOSE

AVOID LEFT TURN

SMITH'S CLIFF

10

SOME SAY KING ARTHUR WAS BORN HERE

TINTAGEL CASTLE RUINS

TINTAGEL HEAD

SUSPENSION BRIDGE

TOILETS

TAKE PATH UP STEEP SLOPE BEHIND TOILETS

028 CAFÉ

Camelot Castle Hotel

KEEP RIGHT HERE; LEFT PATH LEADS INTO TOWN

TINTAGEL SEE TOWN PLAN

BENCH

029

FOLLOW CLIFF-TOP PATH

LONG GRASS QUARRY

EASY WALKING ON LEVEL GROUND

MAP 11

DUNDER-HOLE POINT

YHA Tintagel

030

GULL POINT

0   ¼ mile

0   500m
APPROX SCALE

PENHALLIC POINT

031

GLEBE CLIFF

DENNIS SCALE

PATH ON EDGE - JUST A WIRE BETWEEN US AND OBLIVION

OLD WHARF BUILT RIGHT ON CLIFF EDGE

HOLE BEACH

BAGALOW (NT)

EVIDENCE OF EXTENSIVE QUARRY WORKINGS

BENCH 032

TO TREKNOW, ¼ MILE

IMPRESSIVE TOWER OF INFERIOR SLATE LEFT BEHIND AFTER QUARRYING

TO TREKNOW, ¼ MILE

12

trailblazer

which have free **ATMs** inside. Boots **pharmacy** (Mon-Sat 9am-5.30pm) is on Fore St.

Tintagel **launderette** (daily 8am-6pm) is opposite the visitor centre on Bossiney Rd. Next door is The Hardware Shop (Mon-Sat 9am-5pm), which stocks a small selection of **outdoor gear** and camping equipment.

Where to stay

Campers can head for *Headland Caravan and Camping Park* (☎ 01840-770239, 🖥 headlandcaravanpark.co.uk, **fb**; Easter/ Apr-Oct; WI-FI; laundry), a well-equipped, centrally located campsite, but be prepared to pay £25 if you're a solo hiker. Getting together in a group is better value; two small tents on the same pitch cost £27.50.

Those intending to stay at *YHA Tintagel* (Map 11; ☎ 01840-770334 or ☎ 0845-371 9145, 🖥 yha.org.uk/hostel/yha-tintagel; Apr-Oct; 22 beds, from £15pp; self-catering only) will need to keep going past Tintagel for 30 minutes to Dunderhole Point. In a fantastic position perched right on the cliff top, the building was once the manager's office for the quarry workings on the cliffs. There are four bunk-bed dormitories, with communal bathroom facilities, plus one twin room in an annexe with a sink but no private bathroom.

For something more central, try *Dolphins Backpackers* (☎ 07740-976326, 🖥 dolphinsbackpackers.co.uk, **fb**; 2x4-bed, 1x8-bed, 1x10-bed; 🐾; £26pp), a sociable no-frills hostel with bunk-bed dorms, a mix of shared and en suite bathrooms and a communal kitchen. The 10-bed bunkbarn has its own pool table and TV lounge. The hostel is accessed from the alleyway beside the Tintagel Arms Hotel on Fore St.

For **B&B** accommodation, if money is tight you could do far worse than stay at *Castle View* (☎ 01840-770421, 🖥 castle

viewbandb@aol.com, **fb**; 1S/1D/1T, shared bathroom; 🛁; £30pp, sgl £30; room-only rate £25pp); it may not be as chic as some of the others on offer in the village but the view is great, the service friendly and it's close to the path.

At the right-angle bend in the road, *Pendrin Guest House* (☎ 01840-770524, 🖥 pendrintintagel.co.uk, **fb**; 1S/3D/2D or T/1T, most en suite; from £45pp, sgl from £55) has homely-feeling rooms. Practically next door is the more modern *Bosayne Guest House* (☎ 01840-770514, 🖥 bosayne.co.uk, **fb**; 3S/3D/1T/1F; 🛁; from £37.50pp, sgl £45). Both welcome walkers and cyclists.

A few of the town's nice old **pubs** have rooms too. In the heart of things, *King Arthur's Arms* (☎ 01840-770628, 🖥 kingarthursarms.co.uk; 5 flexible rooms; from £49.50pp, sgl occ £88) has decent rooms but it can get a bit hectic downstairs. On Fore St, and a bit classier, *Ye Olde Malthouse* (☎ 01840-770461, 🖥 malthousetintagel.com, **fb**; 1S/4D/1T/1Tr; 🛁; 🐾; from £42.50pp, sgl from £65) boasts rooms befitting a building steeped in such character. Another pub on the same strip is *The Cornishman Inn* (☎ 01840-770238, 🖥 cornishmaninn.com, **fb**; 1S/4D/3T/3F; from £40pp, sgl from £70). Recently refurbished, B&B at *The Wootons Inn* (☎ 01840-770170, **fb**; 5D/3T/2F; 🛁; 🐾) starts at £50pp.

The *Tintagel Arms Hotel* (☎ 01840-770780, 🖥 thetintagelarmshotel.co.uk, **fb**; 5D/1T; 🛁; 🐾; from £27.50pp, sgl occ from £45), on Fore St, is more like a pub with fairly standard rooms (though some have four-poster beds). It does have a small heated outdoor swimming pool, though.

The enormous *Camelot Castle Hotel* (☎ 01840-770202, 🖥 camelotcastle.com; 50 rooms; 🛁; 🐾; from £52.50pp, sgl from

---

Symbols used in text (see also p79)
🛁 Bathtub in, or for, at least one room
Ⓛ packed lunch available if requested in advance
fb signifies places that post their current opening hours on their Facebook page
🐾 Dogs allowed; if for accommodation this is subject to prior arrangement (see p338)

£95) is impossible to miss and although it's more suitable for tour groups, the prices for the cheapest rooms aren't extortionate.

Where to eat and drink

Tintagel is full of pubs and cafés, all strung out along Fore St and its extensions.

Cafés & restaurants One of the first places you'll come to is the popular chain *The Cornish Bakery* (🖳 thecornishbakery

.com; daily 8am-6pm); bustling and busy, and serving up pasties, pastries and tea and coffee. You can eat in as well as takeaway.

Opposite is *Pengenna's Pasties* (daily 10am-5pm), another regional chain that crops up all along the coast. The speciality pasties are best bought freshly made so get here early, but beware; some cost as much as £9 each! There's plenty of space to eat in, and some outdoor seating in a back garden too. Next door is the cosier *King Arthur's*

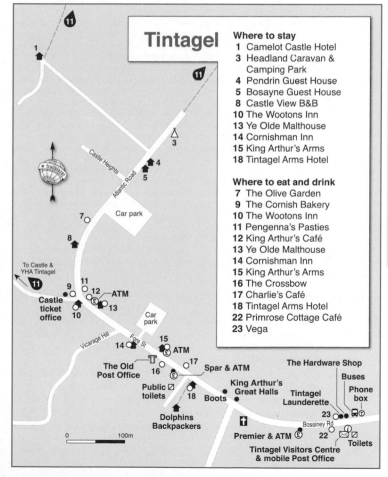

Tintagel

Where to stay
1 Camelot Castle Hotel
3 Headland Caravan & Camping Park
4 Pendrin Guest House
5 Bosayne Guest House
8 Castle View B&B
10 The Wootons Inn
13 Ye Olde Malthouse
14 Cornishman Inn
15 King Arthur's Arms
18 Tintagel Arms Hotel

Where to eat and drink
7 The Olive Garden
9 The Cornish Bakery
10 The Wootons Inn
11 Pengenna's Pasties
12 King Arthur's Café
13 Ye Olde Malthouse
14 Cornishman Inn
15 King Arthur's Arms
16 The Crossbow
17 Charlie's Café
18 Tintagel Arms Hotel
22 Primrose Cottage Café
23 Vega

ROUTE GUIDE AND MAPS

Castle Heights
Atlantic Road
Car park
Castle ticket office
To Castle & YHA Tintagel
Trailblazer
ATM
Vicarage Hill
Fore St
Car park
ATM
The Old Post Office
Spar & ATM
The Hardware Shop
Public toilets
Boots
King Arthur's Great Halls
Tintagel Launderette
Buses
Phone box
Dolphins Backpackers
Bossiney Rd
Premier & ATM
Tintagel Visitors Centre & mobile Post Office
Toilets

0   100m

Café (daily 10am-4.30pm): down-to-earth, with full-English breakfasts and the like, but also good coffee and gluten free scones.

Further up the road on Fore St, you'll find the cute *Charlie's Café* (🖳 charlies.cafe, **fb**; Mon-Sat 10am-5pm) with breakfasts, sandwiches and cream teas, plus a decent wine list. They also have a deli counter with fresh bread and cheeses. Further along still, on Bossiney Rd, is pretty *Primrose Cottage Café* (**fb**; summer Tue-Sun 10am-4pm, winter closed) serving the omnipresent cream teas, as well as breakfasts and lunches (baguettes, quiche, ploughman's).

Opposite is the wonderfully unique *Vega* (☎ 01840-770460, 🖳 vegatintagel .wordpress.com, **fb**; summer Wed-Sun noon-3pm & 6-9pm, winter hours vary; 🐾), which serves 100% vegan food and drinks and donates 50% of its profits to animal welfare charities. As well as a tapas menu (dishes £2-4) – the idea being you can try numerous vegan dishes in order to sample how tasty they are – there are vegan curries, chillis, lasagnes and pasta dishes on offer (all £8).

The Crossbow Café & Grill (☎ 01840-770330; Mon-Fri 9.30am-4pm, Sat 10am-8pm, Sun 10.30am-4pm), right on Fore St, is a busy place but a great spot to soak up Cornwall's hectic tourist vibe, with mains from £12 and their signature mixed grill (steak, pork chop, gammon, chicken fillet, sausage, fried egg & chips) for £18.95.

Slightly away from the main hub, *The Olive Garden* (☎ 01840-779270, **fb**; food daily 6-9.30pm) on Atlantic Rd is an unassuming place serving up a predominantly Italian menu (mains £10-14), including decent pizza.

Pubs [see Where to stay for all contact details] Big and brash *King Arthur's Arms* (summer daily 9am-9pm, winter 10am-3pm & 6-9pm; 🐾) does standard pub fare including their 'famous' King Arthur's mighty breakfast (£9.95) served all day from 9am onwards. Most evening mains cost £10-14, and there are real ales, three of which are brewed in Tintagel. The *Cornishman Inn* (food daily 12.30-2.30pm & 6-9pm) is cheap and cheerful, with most mains costing around £10. There's the usual pub classics plus a pizza menu. The main draught beer is Sharp's Doom Bar

Ye Olde Malthouse (Tue-Sat noon-3pm & 6-9pm) serves fabulous food, with evening mains (£15-20) including wild mushroom, fennel and asparagus risotto and pan-seared hake with chorizo and garlic mash. *The Tintagel Arms Hotel* (noon-3pm & 6.30-9pm; mains £9-10) does good-value standard pub food. *The Wootons Inn* (daily noon-2.45pm & 6.30-8.45pm) has similar fare for slightly higher prices.

Transport
[See pp52-5] The No 95 **bus** between Bude and Truro stops here on Bossiney Rd.

TINTAGEL TO PORT ISAAC   [MAPS 11-15]

This testing **9-mile (15km, 3½-4½hrs)** section begins with an easy stroll past old slate quarry workings (see box p104) and tin-mine workings (see box p180) on a level cliff-top. However, once past the attractive hamlet at **Trebarwith Strand** things get decidedly tougher.

Indeed the path between Trebarwith and Port Gaverne is one of the most challenging legs of the whole walk. The trail itself is well-trodden and easy to follow but there is a series of ascents and descents that may have the weak-willed swearing to hang up their boots. If your calf muscles are aching, take comfort in the dramatic views on this lonely coastline, kept hidden from most holidaymakers by its inaccessibility.

The hard work is over as soon as you reach the pretty twin villages of **Port Gaverne** and **Port Isaac**.

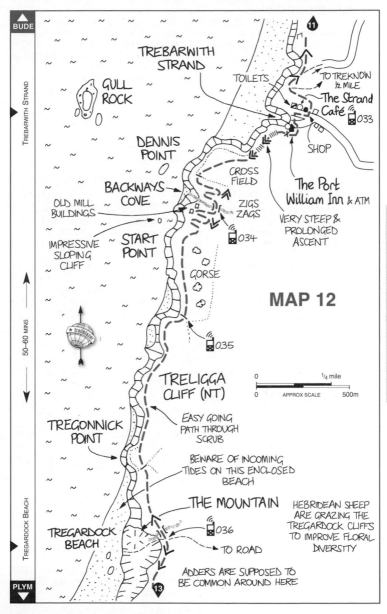

BUDE

TREBARWITH STRAND

50-60 MINS

TREGARDOCK BEACH

PLYM

GULL ROCK

TREBARWITH STRAND

TOILETS

TO TREKNOW ½ MILE

The Strand Café 🛰 033

DENNIS POINT

SHOP

CROSS FIELD

The Port William Inn & ATM

BACKWAYS COVE

ZIGS ZAGS

🛰 034

OLD MILL BUILDINGS

VERY STEEP & PROLONGED ASCENT

IMPRESSIVE SLOPING CLIFF

START POINT

GORSE

MAP 12

🛰 035

trailblazer

TRELIGGA CLIFF (NT)

0   ¼ mile

0   APPROX SCALE   500m

TREGONNICK POINT

EASY GOING PATH THROUGH SCRUB

BEWARE OF INCOMING TIDES ON THIS ENCLOSED BEACH

THE MOUNTAIN

HEBRIDEAN SHEEP ARE GRAZING THE TREGARDOCK CLIFFS TO IMPROVE FLORAL DIVERSITY

TREGARDOCK BEACH

🛰 036

TO ROAD

ADDERS ARE SUPPOSED TO BE COMMON AROUND HERE

ROUTE GUIDE AND MAPS

TREBARWITH STRAND
[MAP 12, p103]

This tiny settlement squeezed into a narrow defile overlooks a sandy beach and would be an ideal spot for lunch if it were not within an hour's walk from Tintagel, where most walkers will have stayed the night.

Those who do stop here make a bee-line for *The Strand Café* (☎ 01840-770276, fb; Easter-Sep 10am-4pm, weather dependent) right on the slipway to the beach. As well as good coffee they do excellent sandwiches, soups, fresh prawns, homemade burgers and cream teas. Next door is a small **shop** selling ice creams, snacks and drinks. Across the slipway is *The Port William Inn* (☎ 01840-770230, 🖥 theportwilliam.co.uk, fb; 7D/1T; ☞; 🐾; £55-80pp; food daily noon-3pm & 5-9pm), a decent pub sitting in an elevated position above the cove, and with a large sea-facing terrace. The bar, which has an **ATM**, has a certain nautical bias and the menu (most mains £12-16) reflects this with several seafood specials. Note, there's no phone signal here, but the pub does have two pay phones on site.

❑ SLATE QUARRIES ON THE CLIFFS

Between Tintagel and Trebarwith Strand evidence of a once-thriving slate industry can still be seen on the cliffs. There were two ways of getting the slate: the first was by digging a hole in the ground in the area of known deposits and winching it to the surface; the other was by getting at the slate that had been exposed by cliff erosion.

Lanterdan and West quarries, both passed on the coastal path, are remarkable for the volume of slate extracted during the 300 years they are known to have been worked. The isolated pinnacle of Lanterdan is thought to have been left as the fixing point for a cable necessary for winching the slate out of the cliff workings although another explanation is that it contains inferior slate and was left as not worth the effort to extract. The so-called 'wharf' at Penhallic Point was used as a loading gantry whereby cut slate could be lowered onto ships which were eased close in to the cliffs which would have been trimmed to allow the ships to approach as closely as possible.

Slate was split on the cliff tops by hand and the remains can be seen in the area around YHA Tintagel (see Map 11) on Glebe Cliff, which was formerly one of the quarry buildings.

PORT GAVERNE   [MAP 14, p106]

Port Gaverne is more peaceful than its near neighbour Port Isaac; it consists of a slipway, a café-cum-restaurant, and a hotel with a few cottages scattered nearby.

There's also a small campsite; the only one near Port Isaac: *Brooklands Farm Campsite* (☎ 01208-880259; £5pp; showers £1; Easter-Oct) is a simple, single-field set-up which has been run by the welcoming Ann Cleave and her husband Barry for years. It's only around 20 minutes' walk from the centre of Port Isaac.

If you have some cash to splash, *Port Gaverne Hotel* (☎ 01208-880244, 🖥 port gavernehotel.co.uk, fb; 10D/3T/2Tr; ☞; 🐾; £75-150pp; food daily noon-2.30pm & 6-9pm) has a lot of character. The food is excellent too, though not cheap. Lunchtime mains are £16-25, while the evening set menu costs £35/45 for two/three courses.

Facing the harbour and owned by the hotel is *Pilchards Café* (☎ 01208-880891, 🖥 portgavernehotel.co.uk/restaurant/pilchards-cafe; drinks 11am-10.30pm, food noon-9pm, winter hours vary); the food is no less mouthwatering but slightly cheaper. There's a lovely beer garden outside… and a tuk-tuk stop (!), which connects the café with Stargazy Inn, up the hill in Port Isaac (see pp108-9): don't be tempted to cheat on your coastal walk!

The adventure activities outfit Cornish Rock Tors (9am-5pm) has a **coffee** machine in its office by the slipway.

PORT ISAAC [map p108]

Over the hill from Port Gaverne is the picturesque village of Port Isaac. The steep lanes and alleyways are lined on each side by white-washed fishermen's cottages and down by the tiny cove are the still-thriving **fish cellars**.

If you are here for a night in the main season go down to The Platt and listen to either St Breward Silver Band (usually Thursdays) or Cornwall's most famous shanty singers Fisherman's Friends (🖥 the fishermansfriends.com; often Fridays).

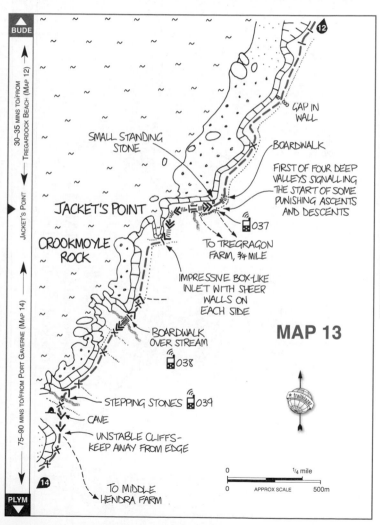

BUDE

30-35 MINS TO/FROM TREGARDOCK BEACH (MAP 12)

JACKET'S POINT

75-90 MINS TO/FROM PORT GAVERNE (MAP 14)

PLYM

GAP IN WALL

BOARDWALK

FIRST OF FOUR DEEP VALLEYS SIGNALLING THE START OF SOME PUNISHING ASCENTS AND DESCENTS

SMALL STANDING STONE

JACKET'S POINT

CROOKMOYLE ROCK

📱037

TO TREGRAGON FARM, ¾ MILE

IMPRESSIVE BOX-LIKE INLET WITH SHEER WALLS ON EACH SIDE

BOARDWALK OVER STREAM

MAP 13

📱038

STEPPING STONES 📱039

CAVE

UNSTABLE CLIFFS - KEEP AWAY FROM EDGE

14

TO MIDDLE HENDRA FARM

0   ¼ mile
0   APPROX SCALE   500m

ROUTE GUIDE AND MAPS

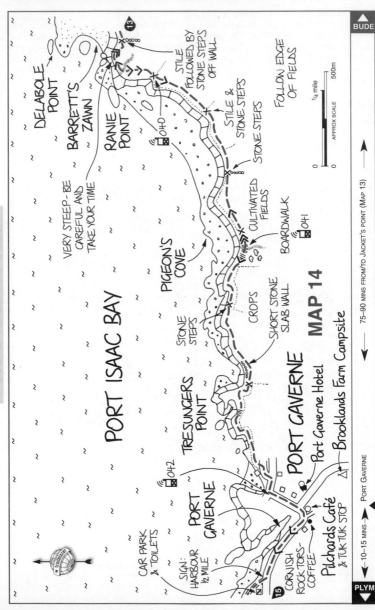

BUDE

DELABOLE POINT

BARRETT'S ZAWN

RANIE POINT

STILE FOLLOWED BY STONE STEPS OFF WALL

FOLLOW EDGE OF FIELDS

STILE & STONE STEPS

STONE STEPS

CULTIVATED FIELDS

BOARDWALK

◻41

◻40

VERY STEEP - BE CAREFUL AND TAKE YOUR TIME

PIGEON'S COVE

CROPS

SHORT STONE SLAB WALL

STONE STEPS

PORT ISAAC BAY

TRESUNGERS POINT

MAP 14

PORT GAVERNE

Port Gaverne Hotel

Brooklands Farm Campsite

◻42

CAR PARK & TOILETS

SIGN: HARBOUR ½ MILE

PORT GAVERNE

CORNISH ROCK TORS COFFEE

Pitchards Café & TUK TUK STOP

15

0   ¼ mile   500m
APPROX SCALE

◄── 75-90 MINS FROM/TO JACKET'S POINT (MAP 13)

◄── 10-15 MINS ──► PORT GAVERNE

PLYM

trailblazer

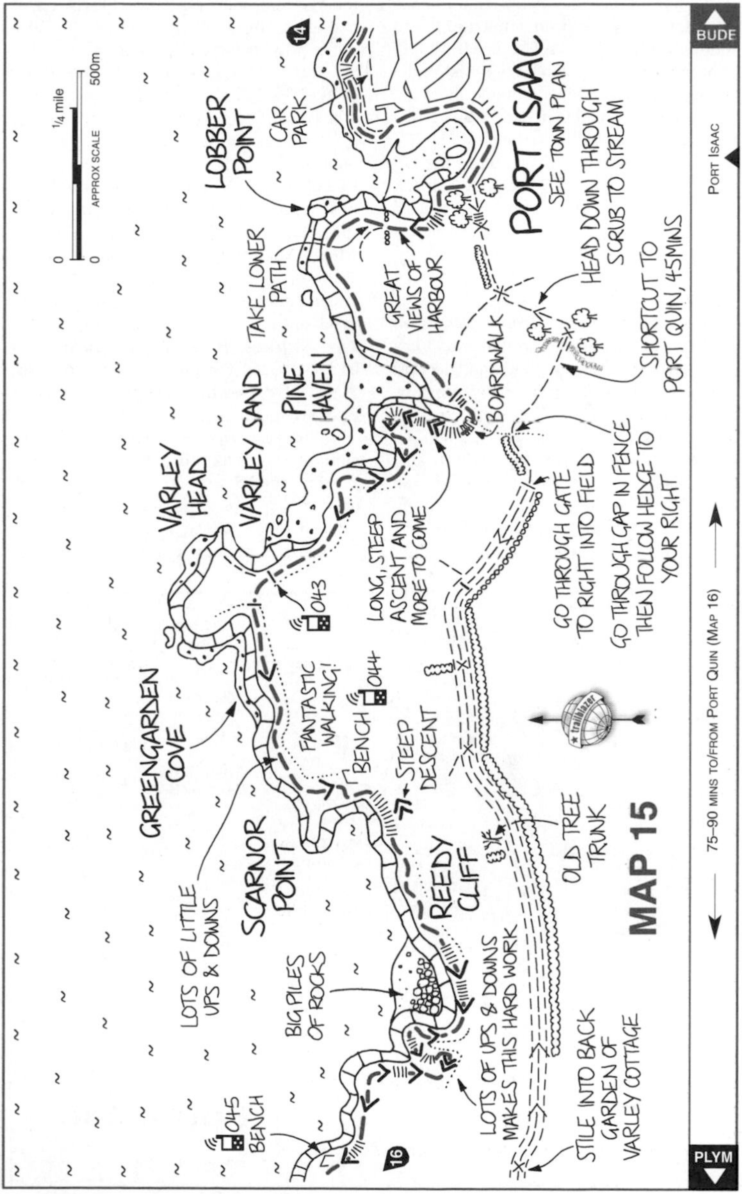

MAP 15

BUDE

PORT ISAAC

PLYM

75–90 MINS TO/FROM PORT QUIN (MAP 16)

Within the map:

PORT ISAAC
SEE TOWN PLAN

LOBBER POINT

CAR PARK

HEAD DOWN THROUGH SCRUB TO STREAM

SHORTCUT TO PORT QUIN, 45MINS

GREAT VIEWS OF HARBOUR

BOARDWALK

TAKE LOWER PATH

VARLEY SAND

PINE HAVEN

VARLEY HEAD

GO THROUGH GATE TO RIGHT INTO FIELD

GO THROUGH GAP IN FENCE THEN FOLLOW HEDGE TO YOUR RIGHT

043

LONG, STEEP ASCENT AND MORE TO COME

FANTASTIC WALKING!

BENCH 044

STEEP DESCENT

OLD TREE TRUNK

GREENGARDEN COVE

SCARNOR POINT

LOTS OF LITTLE UPS & DOWNS

BIG PILES OF ROCKS

REEDY CLIFF

LOTS OF UPS & DOWNS MAKES THIS HARD WORK

STILE INTO BACK GARDEN OF VARLEY COTTAGE

045 BENCH

¼ mile

500m

APPROX SCALE

14

16

Aside from the bucket-and-spade shops there is a Co-op **supermarket** (7am-10pm daily), with an **ATM** inside, uphill from the harbour. Like other Cornish hideaways, artists have moved in and there are some informal galleries exhibiting their work. Port Isaac is the setting for the TV drama *Doc Martin* which can make the village very busy with 'TV location tourists' in the summer and also seems to have had a significant influence on the rather overinflated room rates in the village.

Where to stay

Campers should head to *Brooklands Farm Campsite* (see p104) in Port Gaverne.

B&Bs are thin on the ground in Port Isaac these days; it seems many are now holiday homes. The sea-view rooms at *Gallery B&B* (☎ 01208-881032; 1T/2D; ✆; 🐾; from £70pp; min 2 nights), also known as Harbour View B&B, are above an artist's studio with work in progress lying about. *Three Gates Meadows B&B* (☎ 01208-880609, 🖳 cornwall-online.co.uk/

threegatesmeadow-portisaac; 1T/1D shared bathroom; from £40pp), cheaper but also more basic, is close to the Co-op.

The *Old School Hotel & Restaurant* (☎ 01208-880721, 🖳 theoldschoolhotel.co.uk, **fb**; 2S/9D/1Qd; ✆; 🐾; from £45pp, sgl £52, sgl occ from £74) is a gorgeous building (c1875), which features as the school in the TV series *Doc Martin*. It has well turned-out rooms named after school subjects. 'Latin' has the best sea views, while 'Mathematics' is the family room, sleeping up to four people. Some of the larger doubles can sleep three if requested in advance. Right in the heart of the action, *The Slipway Hotel & Restaurant* (☎ 01208-880264, 🖳 portisaachotel.com, **fb**; 5D/1T/1Qd; ✆; from £60pp; adults only) also has smart rooms.

Stargazy Inn (☎ 01208-811516, 🖳 stargazyinn.co.uk, **fb**; 9 rooms; from £120pp, sgl occ full room rate), offers luxury B&B in mostly double or twin rooms, though some can sleep three or four people. It also has a fine restaurant and featured as

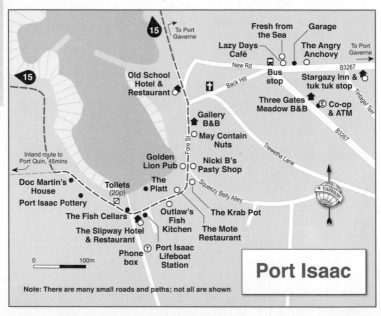

Note: There are many small roads and paths; not all are shown

Port Isaac

Wenn House in *Doc Martin*. The tuk-tuk which you may have seen on your trek up the hill to Port Isaac connects the inn with Pilchards Café in Port Gaverne.

Where to eat and drink

The first establishment you'll see (especially if you've arrived by tuk-tuk) will be the *Stargazy Inn* (see Where to stay; food Tue-Sat) which is open for light lunches (mussels, salads, cheese boards), dinner (mains £17-30) and cocktails. On the opposite side of the road there are a couple of places worth considering. The excellent *Fresh from the Sea* (☎ 01208-880849, 🖥 freshfromthesea.co.uk; Mon-Sat 10am-4pm) is unusual in that the fish is caught by the owner then cooked on site. They do sandwiches with crab, lobster or smoked salmon (£8-12), or else try the scrumptious mackerel pâté on toast (£8.50). Next door, the bright and cheery *Lazy Days Café* (☎ 01208-881113, 🖥 lazydayscafe.co.uk, **fb**; Tue-Sun 9am-4pm; 🐾) does breakfast baps, excellent pasties and freshly made sandwiches. In the evening, *The Angry Anchovy* (☎ 01208-881384, 🖥 theangryanchovy.co.uk, **fb**; Tue-Sat 7-10pm; 🐾) is Port Isaac's only dedicated pizzeria (pizza £6-13.50). They do takeaway too.

Down the hill towards the harbour, *May Contain Nuts* (**fb**; daily 9.30am-4pm) sells pasties, as does, unsurprisingly, *Nicki B's Pasty Shop* (daily 8.30am to when sold out, usually around 4.30pm), whilst *The Krab Pot* (☎ 01208-880826; 🐾; daily

10.45am-2.30pm) is a delightful seafood-based café with stand-out crab sandwiches.

For pub food, there are two fine options: choose between the 300-year-old *Golden Lion* (☎ 01208-880336, 🖥 thegoldenlionportisaac.co.uk, **fb**) serving pub classics and local seafood (Thur-Mon noon-9pm) with wonderful views across the harbour from its upstairs restaurant, or *The Mote* (☎ 01208-880226, 🖥 the-mote.co.uk, **fb**; Feb-Dec daily noon-9pm), a top culinary venue for foodies with fish dominating the menu (most mains £15-20).

Outlaw's Fish Kitchen (☎ 01208-881183, 🖥 outlaws.co.uk; Mon-Sat lunch & dinner; adults only) is Port Isaac's stand-out seafood restaurant, with a fixed-price £80pp set menu.

Nearby, *The Slipway Hotel & Restaurant* (see Where to stay; food daily noon-2.30pm & 6.30-8pm) serves locally sourced ingredients where possible and the fish (including crab, lobster and the catch of the day) comes from the fish cellar over the road. Mains cost £13-22. Equally refined, the *Old School Hotel & Restaurant* (see Where to stay; daily 9am-9.30pm), serves some fantastic food, including breakfasts and all-day cream teas. Evening mains cost £14-24, but at lunchtime you can get cheaper light bites and sandwiches.

Transport

[See pp52-5 for details] The No 10 **bus** service between Launceston and Bodmin Parkway stops here.

PORT ISAAC TO PADSTOW [MAPS 15-20]

If medals were ever to be given out for the toughest section of the SWCP then the initial three miles of this winding **12-mile (19km, 4-5hrs)** stage would certainly stand somewhere on the podium. (Note, you can actually avoid this difficult start by taking the signposted diversion off left, just past Doc Martin's house, which takes you through farmland to Port Quin in half the time; see Map 15). Indeed, you may want to prepare for it by buying a pasty before you set off, especially since the first chance of refreshment is nine miles away in Polzeath.

Taken as a whole, this stage is fairly wild and lonely, though once past Port Quin it poses few difficulties. Add to this the pretty beaches tucked between sheer cliffs and the very attractive hamlet of **Port Quin**, with its tiny cove housing a sheltered beach, and you have the ingredients for a very enjoyable day's walking. *(cont'd on p112)*

ROUTE GUIDE AND MAPS

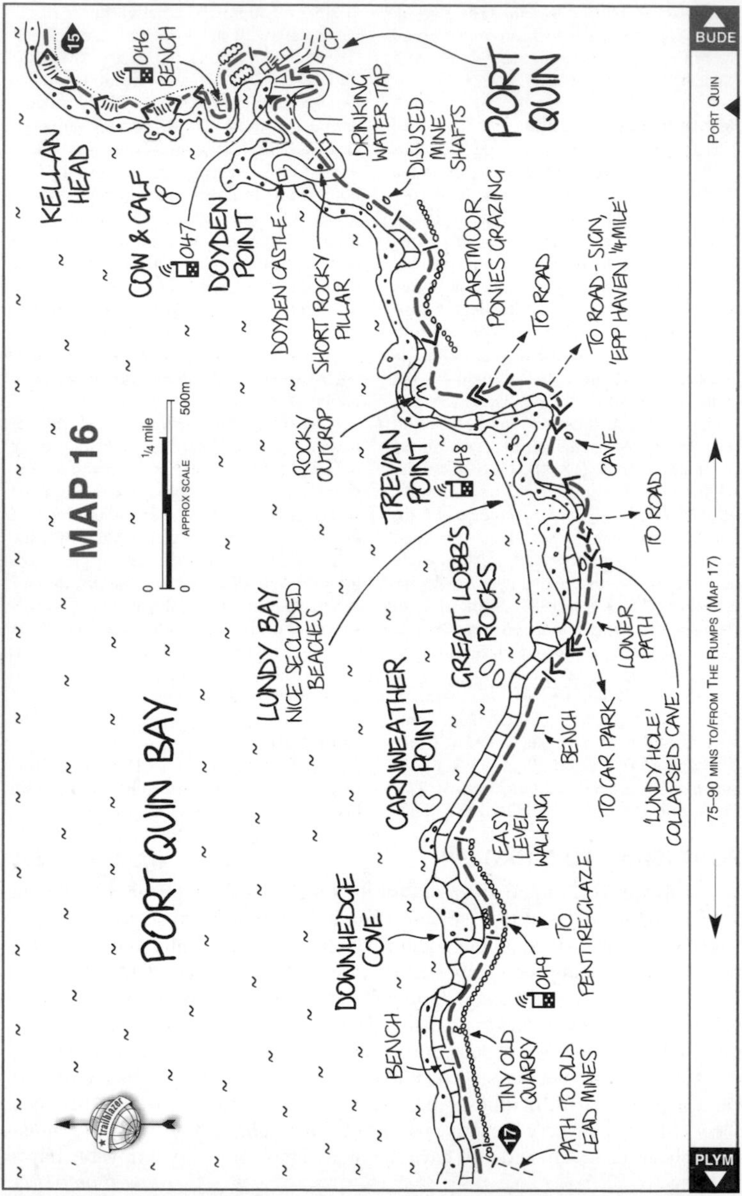

ROUTE GUIDE AND MAPS

MAP 16

¼ mile

500m

0

APPROX SCALE

PORT QUIN BAY

KELLAN HEAD

COW & CALF

DOYDEN POINT

046 BENCH

CP

DRINKING WATER TAP

DISUSED MINE SHAFTS

PORT QUIN

047

DOYDEN CASTLE

SHORT ROCKY PILLAR

DARTMOOR PONIES GRAZING

TO ROAD

TO ROAD - SIGN, 'EPP HAVEN ¼ MILE'

ROCKY OUTCROP

TREVAN POINT

048

CAVE

CAVE

TO ROAD

LUNDY BAY
NICE SECLUDED BEACHES

CARNWEATHER POINT

GREAT LOBB'S ROCKS

LOWER PATH

TO CAR PARK

BENCH

'LUNDY HOLE' COLLAPSED CAVE

DOWNHEDGE COVE

EASY LEVEL WALKING

TO PENTIREGLAZE

049

BENCH

TINY OLD QUARRY

PATH TO OLD LEAD MINES

15

17

BUDE

PORT QUIN

PLYM

75-90 MINS TO/FROM THE RUMPS (MAP 17)

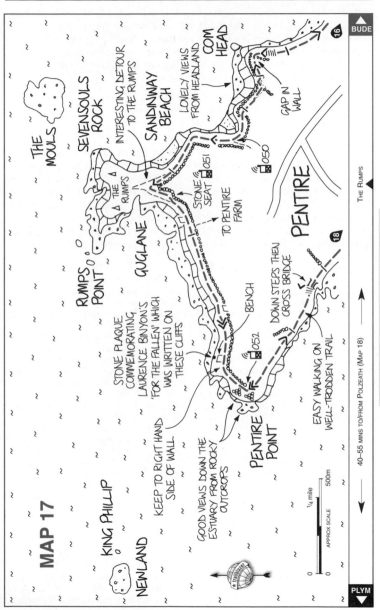

MAP 17

KING PHILLIP

NEWLAND

THE MOULS

SEVENSOULS ROCK

RUMPS POINT

THE RUMPS

GUGLANE

INTERESTING DETOUR TO THE RUMPS

SANDINWAY BEACH

LONELY VIEWS FROM HEADLAND

COM HEAD

BUDE

16

GAP IN WALL

050

STONE SEAT

051

TO PENTIRE FARM

PENTIRE

STONE PLAQUE COMMEMORATING LAURENCE BINYON'S 'FOR THE FALLEN' WHICH WAS WRITTEN ON THESE CLIFFS

KEEP TO RIGHT HAND SIDE OF WALL

GOOD VIEWS DOWN THE ESTUARY FROM ROCKY OUTCROPS

052

BENCH

DOWN STEPS THEN CROSS BRIDGE

PENTIRE POINT

EASY WALKING ON WELL-TRODDEN TRAIL

18

0   ¼ mile   500m
0
APPROX SCALE

THE RUMPS

40–55 MINS TO/FROM POLZEATH (MAP 18)

PLYM

(cont'd from p109) After the windswept and beautiful headland at **The Rumps**, the path swings by **Pentire Point** and the vast **Padstow Bay** comes into view. Along the stretch between The Rumps and Pentire Point is a small plaque commemorating the moving war poem For the Fallen, written somewhere on this point by Laurence Binyon in 1914 at the start of WWI. The plaque bears the poem's fourth (and most famous) stanza:

> *They shall grow not old, as we that are left grow old*
> *Age shall not weary them, nor the years condemn*
> *At the going down of the sun and in the morning*
> *We will remember them.*

From Pentire Point, if the tide is out you will be able to marvel at the acres and acres of sand filling the **Camel Estuary** as it sweeps back to Padstow. At the holiday town of **Polzeath** you leave the cliffs behind and follow an easy path by the beach and through the dunes to **Trebetherick** where there is a beach **shop/café** (Map 18; Easter-Oct 10.30am-5.30pm) which sells pasties, ice creams and hot and cold drinks. From here it's a short hop to **Rock**, where a passenger ferry leaves frequently for Padstow. It is worth making a detour to **St Enodoc Church** (see Map 18 and box on p114) where John Betjeman is buried.

POLZEATH [MAP 18]

Polzeath (pronounced Pol-zeth) is a seaside resort, a place for holidaymakers, for families, days on the beach and rock pools. It is also a place for surfers and during the season wetsuits and boards can be hired by the hour or day (£5/15). Nowadays your only option for a single night here is camping, but there are plenty of places to eat and drink, or to stock up on supplies, so it's a decent pitstop for walkers en route to Padstow.

All the services are concentrated along the strip facing Hayle Bay including a Spar **supermarket** (daily 7.30am-9pm). The **ATM** opposite charges £1.85; or ask for cashback in the Spar.

Frustratingly for **campers**, the two large caravan parks in the bay (Valley Caravan Park, 🖳 valleycaravanpark.co.uk; and Tristram Caravan & Camping Park, 🖳 polzeathcamping.co.uk) no longer welcome backpackers with tents (though you could ask anyway), but just over half a mile inland you'll find *Southwinds Campsite* (☎ 01208-863267, 🖳 polzeathcamping.co.uk, **fb**; Apr-Oct; hikers £15), which is walker-friendly, has hot showers, a laundry and even an on-site **café** (Sun-Wed 10am-9pm).

Food options are better. As you approach Polzeath you'll pass *Surfside*

(☎ 01208-862931, 🖳 surfsidepolzeath.com; Easter-Oct, noon-3pm & 6-9pm), a laidback beach bar specialising in oysters (£4 each) and rum cocktails, but also serving crab rolls (£16) and moules marinière (£17).

Also on the beach is *TJ's Surf Café* (🖳 tjssurfshop.co.uk/surf-cafe; daily 9.30am-8.30pm; weather dependent) which has a more typical café menu (paninis, burgers, coffees, smoothies) and a terrace overlooking the sand. Following the beach round, you'll come to *Galleon Beach Café* (**fb**; daily 10am-9pm), a seaside shack selling perky coffee, pizza and bacon baps.

Up on the road, near the Spar supermarket, is *Vanilla* (daily 10.30am-5.30pm, until 7pm on sunny evenings), a small café that does simply sumptuous ice creams.

Further along the road, *The Waterfront* (☎ 01208-869655, 🖳 waterfrontpolzeath.co .uk; daily Easter-Sep/Oct 10am-9pm, winter Thur-Sun lunch & dinner only; 🐾; mains £16-26) is a first-floor bar & grill restaurant serving pizza, burgers and the like. Up the hill a little, *The Tube Station* (☎ 01208-869200, 🖳 tubestation.org, **fb**; Tue-Sat 10am-4pm), on your left just before you leave the seafront road to rejoin the path, is a café, art gallery and community church.

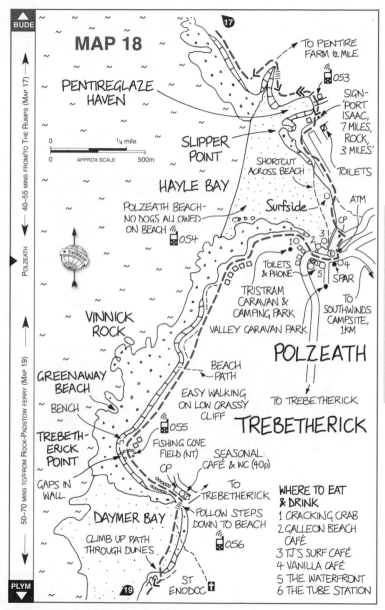

MAP 18

BUDE

40–55 MINS FROM/TO THE RUMPS (MAP 17)

POLZEATH

50–70 MINS TO/FROM ROCK-PADSTOW FERRY (MAP 19)

PLYM

ROUTE GUIDE AND MAPS

17

TO PENTIRE FARM ½ MILE

053

SIGN-
'PORT
ISAAC,
7 MILES,
ROCK,
3 MILES'

PENTIREGLAZE
HAVEN

SLIPPER
POINT

SHORTCUT
ACROSS BEACH

TOILETS

¼ mile

APPROX SCALE   500m

HAYLE BAY

Surfside

ATM

POLZEATH BEACH–
NO DOGS ALLOWED
ON BEACH
054

CP

3 1

1   2

E

5   O4

TOILETS
& PHONE

SPAR

VINNICK
ROCK

TRISTRAM
CARAVAN &
CAMPING PARK

VALLEY CARAVAN PARK

TO
SOUTHWINDS
CAMPSITE,
1KM

POLZEATH

GREENAWAY
BEACH

BEACH
PATH

TO TREBETHERICK

BENCH

EASY WALKING
ON LOW GRASSY
CLIFF

TREBETHERICK

TREBETH-
ERICK
POINT

055

FISHING COVE
FIELD (NT)

CP

SEASONAL
CAFÉ & WC (40p)

GAPS IN
WALL

TO
TREBETHERICK

WHERE TO EAT
& DRINK
1 CRACKING CRAB
2 GALLEON BEACH
  CAFÉ
3 TJ'S SURF CAFÉ
4 VANILLA CAFÉ
5 THE WATERFRONT
6 THE TUBE STATION

DAYMER BAY

FOLLOW STEPS
DOWN TO BEACH

056

CLIMB UP PATH
THROUGH DUNES

ST
ENODOC

19

❏ CHURCH OF ST ENODOC AND JOHN BETJEMAN'S GRAVE

A worthwhile and easy detour since it's only a few hundred yards off the coast path, the Church of St Enodoc is named, like most Cornish churches, after an obscure Celtic saint. The approach from the beach across the golf course brings you to the church path that crosses the fairway, a delightful walk.

© Philip Thomas

Protected now by tamarisk the church is set in a hollow, its 13th-century spire visible above the sand dunes of Daymer Bay. Battered by storms over the centuries, it slowly succumbed to the advancing sand which piled high against the walls, blocked the door and began to fill the aisles. By the early 1800s the church had been almost abandoned and the only access was through the roof. Restoration began in the mid-19th century by local craftsmen using as much of the original stone as possible so it has retained an atmosphere of earliest Christianity even in its final Victorian, basically Norman-style, restoration.

John Betjeman (Poet Laureate 1972-84) is best known for his poetry but he was also a journalist and broadcaster. There is a memorial to his father, his mother is buried here and he had his own grave so placed that the ornate headstone is set looking out to sea over the view he loved.

The Trebetherick area and Betjeman

John Betjeman's love of Cornwall and in particular North Cornwall went back to early childhood when every year his family made the day-long journey by the Great Western Railway from London's Waterloo station to Wadebridge where they'd be met by horse-drawn brake '*out of Derry's stables*'; its carriage lamps lighting their uphill way

© Philip Thomas

> '*past haunted wood and on*
> *To far Trebetherick by the sandy sea.*'
> Soon he'd '*safe in bed*' be watching the insects
> '*drawn to the candle flame*
> *While through the open window came the roar*
> *Of full Atlantic rollers on the beach.*'

> Before breakfast he'd run along '*monarch of miles of sand*
> *Its shining stretches satin-smooth and vein'd.*
> *I felt beneath bare feet the lugworm casts*
> *And walked where only gulls and oyster-catchers*
> *Had stepped before me to the water's edge.*'

He writes of '*fan-shaped scallop shells, the backs of crabs, bits of old driftwood worn to reptile shapes*' and how the sandhoppers leapt around him if he lifted up '*heaps of bladder wrack*' left by the outgoing tide. He felt they all welcomed him back and he returned almost annually throughout his life until, staying for longer than usual, he died at Trebetherick in 1984.

Patricia Major

As you leave Polzeath on the coast path, you'll pass *Cracking Crab* (☎ 01208-862333, 🖳 winkingprawngroup.co.uk/cracking-crab; summer 11.30am-3.30pm & 5-9pm; winter hours vary; evening booking essential) a seafood specialist overlooking the beach from its cliff-top perch

with spectacular sunsets. This is Polzeath's best restaurant. As well as whole cracked crab (£20.95) and crab sandwiches it has a quality evening menu (mains £17-30).

The No 10 **bus** service between Launceston and Bodmin Parkway stops here. [For details see pp52-5].

ROCK   [Map p116]

Originally a small fishing village, these days Rock has a reputation for being exclusive and pricey. It's true that second-homers have snapped up all the available property and in the summer the Porsche count is high, but for the rest of the year, it's a quiet residential neighbourhood with a wonderful waterfront.

Keen ale drinkers might like to sample a pint of Doom Bar, the UK's best-selling cask ale, on its home turf. But note, only the cask version is still brewed at the Sharp's

Brewery here in Rock. Bottled Doom Bar is now brewed in Burton upon Trent.

As with many popular Cornish villages you may find it difficult to book a room here for one night in peak season; it's far more convenient to stay in Padstow if you can.

Where to stay, eat and drink

Rock's **B&B** accommodation is limited, and a fair hike from the coast path. Just over a mile inland from the ferry jetty, the

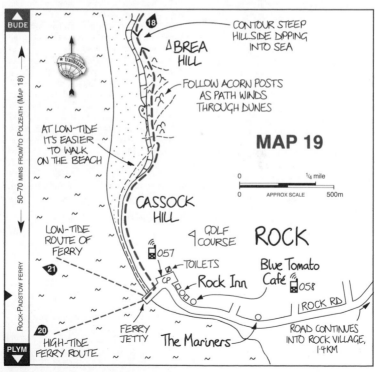

ROUTE GUIDE AND MAPS

BUDE

BREA HILL

CONTOUR STEEP HILLSIDE DIPPING INTO SEA

FOLLOW ACORN POSTS AS PATH WINDS THROUGH DUNES

AT LOW-TIDE IT'S EASIER TO WALK ON THE BEACH

MAP 19

CASSOCK HILL

0   1/4 mile
0   APPROX SCALE   500m

50-70 MINS FROM/TO POLZEATH (MAP 18)

LOW-TIDE ROUTE OF FERRY

GOLF COURSE

ROCK

057

TOILETS

Blue Tomato Café

058

CP

Rock Inn

ROCK RD

ROCK-PADSTOW FERRY

FERRY JETTY

The Mariners

ROAD CONTINUES INTO ROCK VILLAGE, 1.4KM

20

HIGH-TIDE FERRY ROUTE

PLYM

21

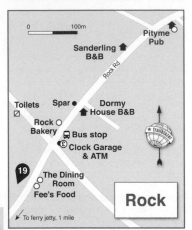

0   100m

Pityme
Pub

Sanderling
B&B

Rock Rd

Toilets   Spar●   Dormy
♿   House B&B

Rock ○
Bakery   🚏 Bus stop
          Ⓔ Clock Garage
          & ATM

★ trailblazer

19   ○ The Dining
      ○ Room
Fee's Food

Rock

↙ To ferry jetty, 1 mile

ROUTE GUIDE AND MAPS

Nearby, popular ***Blue Tomato*** (Map 19; ☎ 01208-863841, 🖥 bluetomatocafe.co .uk, **fb**; summer Mon-Wed 9am-5pm, Thur-Sun 9am-8pm, winter hours vary; 🐕) serves restaurant-quality food, including dishes such as Thai mussels, Moroccan sweet potato soup and Cornish scallops. Their breakfasts and sandwiches are delicious, and there's even a menu for dogs.

Just along Rock Rd is ***The Mariners*** (Map 19; ☎ 01841-532093, 🖥 paul-ains worth.co.uk/the-mariners, **fb**; food Mon-Sat 11.45am-9.30pm, Sun noon-5pm; 🐕), taken under the wing of celebrity chef Paul Ainsworth in 2019. The food is top quality (mains £12-22, sides £4-10), there's Doom Bar on tap and the shaded sea-view terrace is a delightful spot on which to while away a sunny summer afternoon.

In the village centre is a cluster of shops and eateries (see Rock map). The first you reach is ***Fee's Food*** (☎ 01208-869222, 🖥 feesfood.co.uk, **fb**; Mon-Sat 8am-6pm, Sun 9am-2pm) a deli/café/wine bar serving coffee, sandwiches, cheese and olives, and bottles of chilled rosé. Nearby is ***The Dining Room*** (☎ 01208-862622, 🖥 thediningroomrock.co.uk; Wed-Mon 6.30-9pm), a fine-dining restaurant with set menus costing from £47.50. Carrying on past Clock Garage, which has an **ATM** (£1.99 charge) outside it, you reach ***Rock Bakery*** (aka ***Malcolm Barnecutt***, 🖥 barne cutt.co.uk; Mon-Fri 7.30am-3pm, Sat to 2.30pm), a superb bakery and sandwich shop that also sells fruit. Further on there's the Spar **supermarket** (Mon-Sat 8am-6pm, Sun 8.30am-1pm).

Transport

[See pp52-5 for details] The No 10 **bus** service between Launceston and Bodmin Parkway stops by Clock Garage. For the ferry to Padstow, see box opposite.

relaxed ***Dormy House*** (☎ 01208-863845, 🖥 dormyhouserock.co.uk; 3D or T; £60pp, sgl occ £90) is run with Scandinavian flair and efficiency by the Anglo-Swedish owners. Slightly further still, the smaller ***Sanderling*** (☎ 01208-862420, 🖥 sander ling-rock.co.uk; 2D or T; 🐕; 🐾; room-only from £40pp) has two self-contained rooms, one in the garden with its own breakfast room, one above the garage. Both have their own fridge and kettle.

A further 400m up the road, you'll come to a pub with the curious name of ***The Pityme Inn*** (☎ 01208-862228, 🖥 pityme inn.co.uk, **fb**; 4D; food daily 9am-10pm 🐕; room-only from £70pp); breakfast here costs extra.

Just back from the ferry jetty (see Map 19), the first place you see is ***Rock Inn*** (☎ 01208-863498, 🖥 therockinnrock.co.uk, **fb**; summer daily 10am-9.30pm, winter Tue-Sat 10am-9.30pm; mains £14-19) with a gastro-pub menu (pies, curries, chilli, seafood) and sea-view terrace seating.

❑ THE DOOM BAR

The Camel Estuary forms a rare natural harbour guarded by a particularly dangerous sand bar across its entrance known as the Doom Bar, created by the Celtic Sea meeting the River Camel. Over 300 vessels have been wrecked or stranded on the bar which you can see at low tide.

❑ ROCK TO PADSTOW FERRY

Black Tor Ferry (☎ 01841-532239) operates daily between Padstow and Rock. The service starts at 8am from Padstow and runs every 20 minutes. The times for the last ferry of the day from Padstow (20 mins earlier for last ferry from Rock) are: Nov-Mar 5pm; Apr-May 6pm; June to mid July 7pm; mid July to Aug 8pm; 1st Sep to mid Sep 7pm; mid Sep to end Oct 6pm. No Sunday service early Nov to mid Feb. The fare is adult/child £3/1.50, single tickets only. In Padstow passengers embark at North Quay when the tide is in but at low tide the ferry operates from the lower beach (see Map 21), clearly signposted. Dogs can be taken on the ferry.

In addition to this, an evening service is maintained by **Rock Water Taxi** (☎ 07778-105297, 💻 wavehunters.co.uk/water-taxi; Easter-Oct 7pm-midnight weather and tide permitting, from 7.30pm mid July to end Aug; £7 single, £9 return), although in winter the service operates on Sundays only 9.30am-4.30pm.

PADSTOW   [MAP 20, p119]

Originally called Petrocstow, after St Petroc established a monastery here in the 6th century, pretty Padstow clusters around the harbour; cosy and sheltered from the prevailing wind. The parish church of **St Petroc's** was built between 1425 and 1450 but the lower part of the tower was built even earlier. The pulpit is decorated with carved scallop shells to honour pilgrims to the shrine of St James in Santiago, Spain.

Padstow is the most important and the most sheltered port on the north coast although the **Doom Bar** keeps large vessels out (see box opposite).

This is definitely a place to dawdle, eat fish & chips and watch the goings-on in the harbour. Boat trips are advertised by men calling out as you pass 'Pay when you come back. If you don't come back you don't pay!' Padstow has become synonymous with the TV chef Rick Stein who has made the place his own with numerous establishments under his name.

For a bit of history visit **Padstow Museum** (☎ 01841-532752, 💻 padstow museum.co.uk; free; Apr-Oct 10.30am-4.30pm, Nov-Mar 11am-3pm) in the town's former railway station, Old Station House, on Station Rd. Another option for a rainy day is the **National Lobster Hatchery** (☎ 01841-533877, 💻 nationallobsterhatchery .co.uk; adult/child £7.50/4; 10am-4pm); it is a conservation research centre where you can see tiny juvenile lobsters being reared, before they are released into the seas.

Padstow is the start/end-point of the very popular cycle route, the Camel Trail, which runs for 18 miles along a disused railway track between Padstow and Wenfordbridge via Wadebridge and Bodmin. It can easily be done in a day, there and back. If you want to rent bikes, **Padstow Cycle Hire** (☎ 01841 533533, 💻 padstowcyclehire.com; 9am-5pm; bike rental per day £18-20, helmets free) has everything you need, even dog trailers.

'Obby 'Oss Day (see box on p120) is held here every May, and Carnival Week is in July (see p15).

Services

The town centre is compact with everything you need within a few paces of the harbour. On South Quay, the **tourist information centre** (TIC; ☎ 01841-533449, 💻 padstow live.com; Easter-Oct Mon-Fri 9am-5.30pm, Sat & Sun 10am-4pm, winter Mon-Sat 10am-4pm, Sun closed) is very useful. They will find you a room even when the town is at bursting point.

Around Market Place is Barclays **bank**, and the **post office** (Mon-Sat 8am-6pm, Sat to noon), which is inside the small Spar **supermarket** (daily 7am-10pm).

There is a branch of Boots **pharmacy** (Mon-Fri 9am-5.30pm, Sat to 5pm, Sun 10am-4pm) centrally too.

Up the hill above the town is **Padstow Surgery** (☎ 01841-532346; daily 8.30am-6pm) on Boyd Avenue and a big Tesco

supermarket (Mon-Sat 7am-9pm, Sun 10am-4pm), which has an **ATM** outside.

For **camping necessities**, including fuel for stoves, Mountain Warehouse (9am-5.30pm), near the tourist information centre, is well stocked.

Where to stay

You can **camp** at the very welcoming *Dennis Cove Camping* (☎ 01841-532349, 🖥 denniscovecampsite.co.uk, **fb**; walkers £11.50-12.50; call ahead Jul & Aug) about 10 minutes from the harbour and close to the Camel Cycle Trail, where they will always try to accommodate walkers if they possibly can. Shower facilities are excellent here, there's a laundry room and even a small drying room for wet gear. They have three camping fields; the main one beside reception at the end of Dennis Rd and nearest to the best showers, a 'wild field' immediately above that which catches the late evening sun, and 'The Foreshore' down by the Camel Trail, overlooking the estuary.

Padstow is an exceedingly busy resort. **B&B**s frequently get booked up during the height of the season, especially at weekends, so book well ahead at these times and be prepared to stay more than one night, using buses to get to and from the coast path.

Close to the harbour is the fabulously central *South Quay B&B* (☎ 01841-532383, 🖥 southquaybedandbreakfastpadstow.co.uk; 2D; 🛏; 🐾; £42.50-47.50pp, sgl occ £70), also known as Cullinan's B&B. One of the rooms is on the top floor, with a balcony overlooking the harbour.

Up the hill leading away from South Quay is *Treverbyn House* (☎ 01841-532855 or 07534-095961, 🖥 treverbynhouse.com, Station Rd; 3D; 🛏; from £65pp, sgl occ £115; min 2 nights), a large turreted house with spacious rooms, period furniture and lovely views over the estuary.

On colourful, pastel-painted Duke St, *Cyntwell* (☎ 01841-533447, 🖥 cyntwell.co.uk; 3D/1T; 🛏; £44-49pp, sgl occ from £60; room only) has a friendly welcome. It's pronounced 'Sintwell', in case you wondered.

Plenty of Padstow's historic **pubs** have rooms too. *The Old Ship Hotel* (☎ 01841-532357, 🖥 oldshiphotel-padstow.co.uk, **fb**;

3S/9D/2Tr/1Qd; 🛏; 🐾; from £60pp, sgl £75) is central and gives discounts for stays of more than one night. At 6 Lanadwell St, the *London Inn* (☎ 01841-532554, 🖥 londoninnpadstow.co.uk, **fb**; 3D/1Qd; 🐾; from £50pp), is a proper locals' pub with good food, great ale and rooms up top.

Opposite, *The Golden Lion* (☎ 01841-532797, 🖥 goldenlionpadstow.com, **fb**; 2D/1T or D; £67.50pp) is the oldest pub in town and has been run by the same family for over 30 years. *Old Custom House* (☎ 01841-532359, 🖥 oldcustomhousepadstow.co.uk, **fb**; 23 rooms; 🛏; from £55pp) is a very slick, hotel-like operation, with smart rooms attached to the old pub, but with a separate reception area next door.

At the pricier end of the market, Rick Stein has a number of options, the most affordable being the rooms above *Rick Stein's Café* (central reservations ☎ 01841-532700, 🖥 rickstein.com; 3D; 🛏; 🐾; from £67pp). See online or phone for information about other accommodation possibilities.

The iconic Metropole Hotel has had a major refurb, and is now *Padstow Harbour Hotel* (☎ 01841-532486, 🖥 harbourhotels.co.uk; 58 rooms; 🛏; 🐾; from £70pp, sgl occ from £130; food daily to 9pm). Built in 1904, it still has a traditional feel, although the rooms themselves, all whites and pastels, now have the air of seaside cafés. Most have sea views.

Where to eat and drink

Cafés & takeaways The permanently packed *Padstow Fish and Chip Café* (☎ 01841-532915; daily summer 11.30am-9pm, winter 11.30am-4.30pm), on the harbour, and the more down-to-earth chippy, *Chip Ahoy* (☎ 01841-534753; Mon-Sat noon-2.30pm & 4.30-8/9pm, Sun noon-8pm), on Broad St, are equally good. However, fish & chip shops in Padstow must feel somewhat upstaged by the rightly lauded *Stein's Fish and Chips* (South Quay; 11.30am-3pm & 5-9pm) which is the cheapest of the many Rick Stein eateries in town (fish & chips £10.95).

For something in the rucksack, try *Chough Bakery* (3 The Strand; **fb**; daily 9am-5pm) or *Stein's Deli* (Sun-Thur

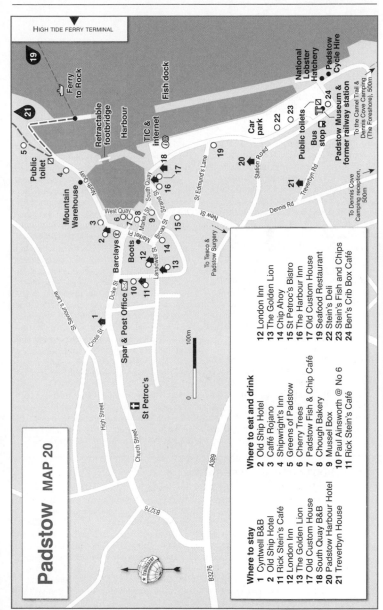

Padstow MAP 20

Where to stay
1 Cyntwell B&B
2 Old Ship Hotel
11 Rick Stein's Café
12 London Inn
13 The Golden Lion
17 Old Custom House
18 South Quay B&B
20 Padstow Harbour Hotel
21 Treverbyn House

Where to eat and drink
2 Old Ship Hotel
3 Caffè Rojano
4 Shipwright's Inn
5 Greens of Padstow
6 Cherry Trees
7 Padstow Fish & Chip Café
8 Chough Bakery
9 Mussel Box
10 Paul Ainsworth @ No 6
11 Rick Stein's Café

12 London Inn
13 The Golden Lion
14 Chip Ahoy
15 St Petroc's Bistro
16 The Harbour Inn
17 Old Custom House
19 Seafood Restaurant
22 Stein's Deli
23 Stein's Fish and Chips
24 Ben's Crib Box Café

10am-5pm, Fri-Sat 9.30am-5.30pm). Cute cafés are dotted around the harbour. *Cherry Trees* (**fb**; 8.30am-5pm daily) is particularly popular, with breakfasts and lunchtime paninis (£6-8). Look out for their end-of-day £1 pasties. *Ben's Crib Box Café* (**fb**; Mon-Sat 8am-2.30pm) is the closest thing Padstow has to a builders' café, and is the cheapest place to get a decent breakfast.

Pubs There is no shortage of lovely old pubs. The two most popular are *Old Custom House* (see Where to stay; food daily 10am-9.30pm), and the *Shipwright's Inn* (☎ 01841-532451; 🖳 shipwrightspadstow.co .uk; food daily noon-3pm & 5-9pm), largely because of their harbour-side locations.

For a more down-to-earth local, try *The Harbour Inn* (☎ 01841-533148, 🖳 harbourinnpadstow.co.uk; 🐾; food 12.30-8.30pm); *The London Inn* (see Where to stay; food noon-3pm & 6-8.30pm) with its low-beamed ceilings and fine ales; or the *Golden Lion* (see Where to stay; food Mon-Sat noon-2pm & 5-8pm, Sun noon-6pm).

The *Old Ship Hotel* (see Where to stay; daily Easter-Oct 10am-10pm, Nov-Mar noon-9pm) has fairly standard pub grub, but plenty of outdoor seating out front.

Restaurants By the harbour, on the alleyway known as The Drang, lively *Mussel Box* (☎ 01841-532846, 🖳 mussel box.co.uk, **fb**; Mon-Sat 9am-9pm, Sun 9am-5pm) serves fresh fish, shellfish and, of course, plenty of mussels (£10-16; other evening mains £15-20) plus breakfasts and takeaway boxes.

Caffé Rojano (Central reservations: ☎ 01841-532093, 🖳 paul-ainsworth.co.uk; Mar-Nov daily 8.30-10.30am & noon-10pm), at 9 Mill Square, is a pleasant and refined place with Italian tendencies (pizza £12-16, other mains £15-25). Under the same ownership, *Paul Ainsworth @ No 6* (see Central reservations above; Tue-Sat noon-2.30pm & 6-10pm; open bank holiday Mondays) is Ainsworth's flagship Michelin-star restaurant with a high-quality menu and prices to match (four courses £105).

Few people would contemplate a visit to Padstow without giving some thought to trying one of Rick Stein's restaurants, all booked via the central reservation service (see Where to stay). Reasonably priced is *Rick Stein's Café* (see Where to stay; 8am-3pm & 4-9.45pm; 🐾 in the courtyard), though in truth it's more of a restaurant than a café. Mains cost £15-23. Stein's flagship *Seafood Restaurant* (summer daily noon-2.30pm & 6.30-10pm, winter noon-2pm & 7-10pm) is a mecca for foodies. Most mains will set you back around £30. The three-course lunchtime set-menu is £39.95. At *St Petroc's Bistro* (daily 11.30am-10pm) you can eat outdoors under awnings in fine weather. The food here is also superb and slightly cheaper (mains £16-30).

As you leave Padstow on the coast path, you'll pass *Greens of Padstow* (☎ 01841-532002, 🖳 greenspadstow.co.uk, **fb**; summer daily from 10am, winter hours vary), a licensed café-restaurant (mains £14-22) overlooking the harbour with a quirky mini-golf course (adult/child £7.50/5.50) in the gardens above it.

❏ THE HOBBY HORSE CELEBRATION

On May Day bank holiday the **'Obby 'Oss,** a man wearing a head mask set on a circular wooden hoop about 6ft in diameter, dances through Padstow town. He is preceded by a Teazer who leads the dance with theatrical movements. The accompanying retinue are dressed in white with added ribbons and flowers.

This celebration has been performed for centuries and there are many theories about its origins. Some say it has pagan roots while others think it began during one of England's numerous wars with France, when the women of the town dressed up to frighten off an enemy landing while all the men were at sea. Or perhaps it is simply a welcome to the summer, a tradition that has both persisted and changed over the years.

Be aware that if you are passing through Padstow at this time of year you will have to book your accommodation well in advance.

Transport

[See pp52-5 for details] The **bus** terminus is at the bottom of Station Rd beside the former railway station, which now houses the town's museum. The No 11/11A service goes to Bodmin Parkway station and Plymouth, the No 56 goes to Newquay and in summer the Atlantic Coaster follows the coast road to St Ives.

See the box on p117 for details of the **ferry** service between Rock and Padstow.

If you need a **taxi** try Ocean Taxis (☎ 07980-001323; 🖳 oceantaxiscornwall.co .uk).

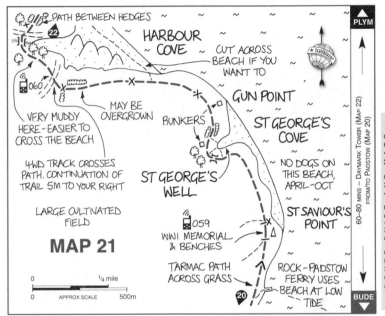

MAP 21

0 — ¼ mile
0 — APPROX SCALE — 500m

ROUTE GUIDE AND MAPS

60-80 MINS – DAYMARK TOWER (MAP 22) FROM/TO PADSTOW (MAP 20)

PADSTOW TO TREVONE   [MAPS 20-23]

It's an easy and enjoyable **5 miles (8km, 1¾-2¼hrs)** to Trevone with cliff-top scenery at its best and without the sharp ascents and descents characteristic of the path up to now. The path soon leaves Padstow behind and you begin to experience what coastal walking is all about.

Two pretty little coves (Harbour and Hawker's) lead you to *Rest A While Tea Garden* (Map 22; ☎ 01841-532919; daily 10.30am-4.30pm, weather dependent) where morning coffees, light lunches and afternoon tea are on offer, should you not have replenished calories sufficiently in Padstow.

Past **Stepper Point** you head for a 19th-century stone Daymark Tower, an early aid to navigation, and a pause here gives time to take in the Camel Estuary behind and the rugged coastline ahead. Marvellous.

The **Merope Islands** are huge chunks of rock that have split away from the mainland like fragments of broken teeth. *(cont'd on p124)*

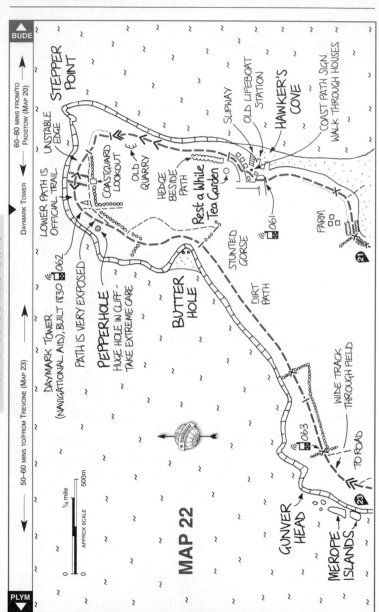

60–80 MINS FROM/TO Padstow (MAP 20)

DAYMARK TOWER

50–60 MINS TO/FROM Trevone (MAP 23)

BUDE

PLYM

STEPPER POINT

UNSTABLE EDGE

LOWER PATH IS OFFICIAL TRAIL

COASTGUARD LOOKOUT

OLD QUARRY

SLIPWAY

OLD LIFEBOAT STATION

HAWKER'S COVE

COAST PATH SIGN. WALK THROUGH HOUSES

HEDGE BESIDE PATH

Rest a While Tea Garden

1061

FARM

21

STUNTED GORSE

DAYMARK TOWER (NAVIGATIONAL AID), BUILT 1830

1062

PATH IS VERY EXPOSED

PEPPERHOLE
HUGE HOLE IN CLIFF – TAKE EXTREME CARE

BUTTER HOLE

DIRT PATH

1063

WIDE TRACK THROUGH FIELD

TO ROAD

23

GUNVER HEAD

MEROPE ISLANDS

MAP 22

¼ mile

500m

APPROX SCALE

0

0

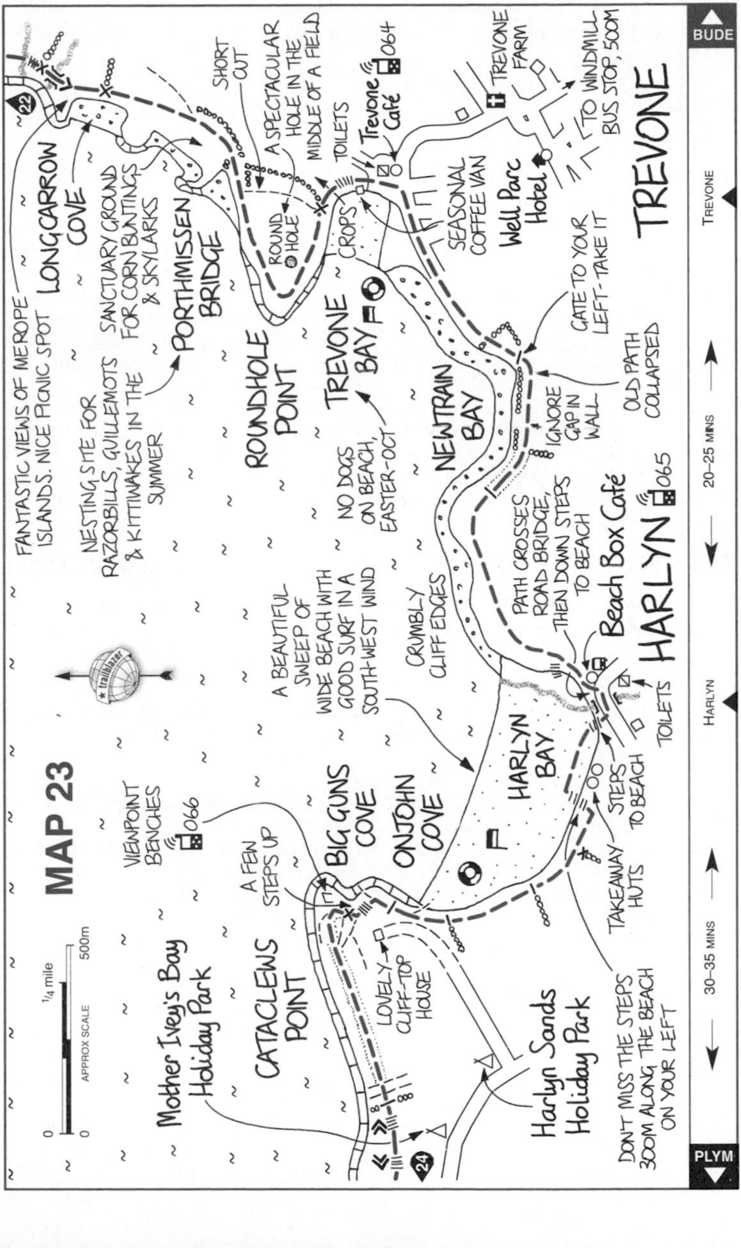

MAP 23

¼ mile
500m
APPROX SCALE
0

FANTASTIC VIEWS OF MEROPE ISLANDS. NICE PICNIC SPOT

NESTING SITE FOR RAZORBILLS, GUILLEMOTS & KITTIWAKES IN THE SUMMER

LONGCARROW COVE

SANCTUARY GROUND FOR CORN BUNTINGS & SKYLARKS

SHORT CUT

A SPECTACULAR HOLE IN THE MIDDLE OF A FIELD

PORTHMISSEN BRIDGE

ROUND HOLE

TOILETS

CROPS

Trevone Café ☐ 064

TREVONE FARM

TO WINDMILL BUS STOP, 500M

SEASONAL COFFEE VAN

Well Parc Hotel

TREVONE

ROUNDHOLE POINT

TREVONE BAY ☐

NO DOGS ON BEACH, EASTER–OCT

GATE TO YOUR LEFT—TAKE IT

NEWTRAIN BAY

IGNORE GAP IN WALL

OLD PATH COLLAPSED

A BEAUTIFUL SWEEP OF WIDE BEACH WITH GOOD SURF IN A SOUTH-WEST WIND

CRUMBLY CLIFF EDGES

PATH CROSSES ROAD BRIDGE, THEN DOWN STEPS TO BEACH

Beach Box Café

HARLYN ☐ 065

TOILETS

VIEWPOINT BENCHES ☐ 066

A FEW STEPS UP

BIG GUNS COVE

ONJOHN COVE

HARLYN BAY

STEPS TO BEACH

Mother Ivey's Bay Holiday Park

CATACLEWS POINT

A FEW STEPS UP

LOVELY CLIFF-TOP HOUSE

TAKEAWAY HUTS

Harlyn Sands Holiday Park

DON'T MISS THE STEPS 300M ALONG THE BEACH ON YOUR LEFT

BUDE
TREVONE
HARLYN
20–25 MINS
30–35 MINS
PLYM

22
24
8

(cont'd from p121) The sudden gaping holes that have opened up in the turf – terrifying to contemplate going near – are two of the strange features of the morning's walk.

Note the increase in the carpet of wild flowers – sea pinks, cornflowers, kidney vetch – particularly during May. Sometimes the flowers reach down the cliffs almost into the sea.

TREVONE   [MAP 23, p123]

This is the first bay after leaving Padstow with seasonal cafés and shops catering for the influx of holidaymakers who populate the place in the season. The **shop** (9am-9pm) attached to Trevone Café sells essentials such as milk, eggs and newspapers, as well as beachwear.

To find **accommodation**, you need to take the road away from the beach into the village where you'll find *The Well Parc* (☎ 01841-520318, 🖳 wellparc.co.uk, fb; 4D/1Tr/2Qd; ✿; £50pp). **Food** is served daily all day Easter to September, and noon-2pm & 7-9.30pm the rest of the year. More of a hub during the daytime is

Trevone Café (☎ 01841-520275, fb; 8.30am-10.30pm, last food orders 8pm; shorter hours in winter; licensed) where you can eat in, or sit out on the large terrace. They do pulled-pork burgers, have their own pizza oven and serve booze to sup while you enjoy their occasional live music nights. There's also a **seasonal coffee van** right on the path.

The No 56 bus between Padstow and Newquay and the Atlantic Coaster between Padstow and St Ives stop at Trevone but not at the beach: you have to walk just over a mile to the junction with the B3278 at Windmill. [See pp52-5 for details].

TREVONE TO TREYARNON   [MAPS 23-24]

This section of **5 miles (8km, 2-2½hrs)** is mostly fairly flat with a lovely spot of beach walking at **Harlyn Bay**, perfect for its kind, then out to Trevose Head past the lighthouse. The cliffs above **Mother Ivey's Bay** are great for a long picnic.

Booby's Bay and **Constantine Bay** are popular surf beaches with a scattering of houses along the low-lying foreshore. Constantine Bay in particular has a reputation as one of the best surf-pullers in North Cornwall.

HARLYN BAY & MOTHER IVEY'S
BAY   [MAP 23, p123]

If you need a break, you can find sustenance at the takeaway shack, *Beach Box Café* (8am-6pm) in the car park. They do toasties, wraps, coffee and ice cream and have some picnic benches to sit on.

Around 40 years ago, though just a stone's throw away, across the bridge from the café, an intact **Iron Age cemetery** was found on the site of what for a long time was a pub but is soon to be more houses; the site contained over a hundred slate coffins with human remains and bronze and iron ornaments. The finds are in Truro Museum.

The stretch above Harlyn Bay and Mother Ivey's Bay (see Map 24) is rather overwhelmed by two large caravan sites.

Harlyn Sands Holiday Park (☎ 01841-520720, 🖳 www.harlynsands.co.uk) is monstrous. Facilities include restaurants and a leisure pool, but there are no special rates for hikers or one-night stays, meaning in high season you'll pay a whopping £45 (the family rate for two nights) even if you're camping solo for just one night.

Mother Ivey's Bay Holiday Park (☎ 01841-520990, 🖳 motheriveysbay.com, fb; 2 walkers & tent £10-25; Apr-Oct) makes walkers feel more welcome, although you'll still pay £25 as a solo hiker in high season. There's a well-stocked shop here, which closes at 6pm, but no restaurant.

The No 56 **bus** stops at the bridge. [See pp52-5 for details].

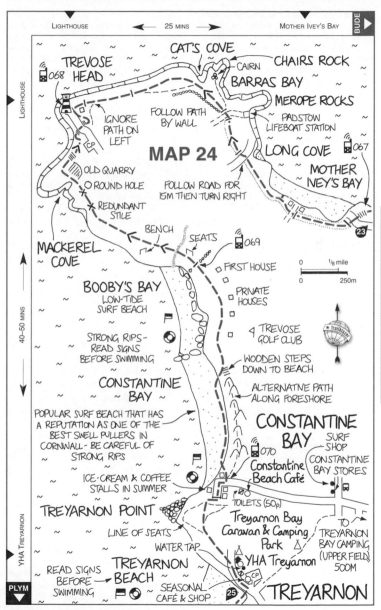

CAT'S COVE

CHAIRS ROCK

CAIRN

BARRAS BAY

TREVOSE HEAD

📶 068

MEROPE ROCKS

FOLLOW PATH BY WALL

PADSTOW LIFEBOAT STATION

IGNORE PATH ON LEFT

MAP 24

LONG COVE

📶 067

CP

MOTHER IVEY'S BAY

OLD QUARRY

ROUND HOLE

FOLLOW ROAD FOR 15M THEN TURN RIGHT

REDUNDANT STILE

BENCH

SEATS

📶 069

23

MACKEREL COVE

FIRST HOUSE

BOOBY'S BAY

LOW-TIDE SURF BEACH

PRIVATE HOUSES

0   1/8 mile
0   250m

STRONG RIPS – READ SIGNS BEFORE SWIMMING

TREVOSE GOLF CLUB

▲ trailblazer

CONSTANTINE BAY

WOODEN STEPS DOWN TO BEACH

POPULAR SURF BEACH THAT HAS A REPUTATION AS ONE OF THE BEST SWELL PULLERS IN CORNWALL – BE CAREFUL OF STRONG RIPS

ALTERNATIVE PATH ALONG FORESHORE

CONSTANTINE BAY

SURF SHOP

📶 070

CONSTANTINE BAY STORES

Constantine Beach Café

ICE-CREAM & COFFEE STALLS IN SUMMER

TOILETS (50p)

TREYARNON POINT

LINE OF SEATS

Treyarnon Bay Caravan & Camping Park

TO TREYARNON BAY CAMPING (UPPER FIELD), 500M

WATER TAP

YHA Treyarnon

READ SIGNS BEFORE SWIMMING

TREYARNON BEACH

SEASONAL CAFÉ & SHOP

25

TREYARNON

CONSTANTINE BAY & TREYARNON
[MAP 24, p125]

YHA Treyarnon (☎ 0345-3719664, 🖥 yha
.org.uk/hostel/yha-treyarnon-bay; 53 dorm
beds, £15pp; 7 private rooms sleep 3-6, from
£25pp; camping £16pp; bell tents & pods
sleep 4-5, from £90) is a gem, and the heartbeat of this area. They have space for 40 to
camp, plus bell tents (Apr-Oct) and camping
pods with beds and bedding. The **café**
(10am-9pm) is open to all, and pulls in the
crowds with live music on summer weekends. The garden terrace has fabulous sea
views with magical sunsets. They have real
ale on tap, and evening meals are available.

There are a further two camping sites at
Treyarnon Bay Caravan & Camping Park
(☎ 01841-520681, 🖥 treyarnonbayholidays
.co.uk; 🐾 in upper field; Apr-Sep). At the
main camping park it's £12-17 per two-man
tent. In their upper field (15 mins away),
it's £10 per group (no matter how many
tents). The upper field has (somewhat grot-
ty) toilets and a drinking tap, but no showers. However, you can use the showers (£1)
in the main park.

At the well-stocked **Constantine Bay
Stores** (Mon-Sat 8am-5pm, Sun 8am-4pm)
you can get picnic supplies, **cashback** and
takeaway hot drinks. Closer to the beach,
Constantine Beach Café (10am-4pm) does
pasties and paninis. There are also seasonal
coffee and burger vans in the car park by
Treyarnon Beach, and a seasonal **coffee
shack** on the other side of the beach.

The No 56 Newquay to Padstow **bus**
service stops here. [See pp52-5 for details].

TREYARNON TO MAWGAN PORTH
[MAPS 24-27]

This **7 miles (11km, 2-2¾hrs)** of cliff-top walking is relatively easy with plenty of opportunity to enjoy the impressive scenery. You first pass **Warren** and
Pepper coves where weather and the sea have effectively split an **iron-age fort**
into three. The clearly visible ditches and ramparts give you a good idea of what
to look for at the numerous other forts and castles along the Cornish coast.

At **Porthcothan** (Map 25) there is an excellent **shop**, Porthcothan Bay
Stores (daily 8.30am-5pm in summer; limited hours in the winter), which sells
coffee, pasties and cakes. There are **toilets** (in the car park), and a **bus** stop, too:
the No 56 and the Atlantic Coaster bus services stop here between Padstow and
Newquay. Then it's up to one of the most beautiful stretches of coast, **Park
Head** to **Bedruthan Steps**, which gets quite crowded in summer.

Leaving the day trippers behind, you're then bound for **Mawgan Porth**
where there are plenty of places to take a breather and refreshments.

BEDRUTHAN STEPS [MAP 26, p128]

This spectacular section of the coast was a
popular spot with the Victorians who were
much taken with the wild sea cliffs, and still
pulls in the day-trippers. Note, the
National Trust-managed **steps** down to the
wonderful beaches here were closed at the
time of research, due to a rock fall in winter 2019/20 which rendered them unsafe.

Campers can pitch at *Bedruthan Steps
Campsite* (☎ 07877-240015, 🖥 bedruth
ansteps.com; 🐾; Jul & Aug only; £10pp), a
simple cliff-top campsite with a small shower block and to-die-for sea views.

Nearby is a seasonal coffee kiosk
called *Stacks* (Tue-Sun 10am-2pm), but
most people fill up at the National Trust-run
Carnewas Tearoom (**fb**; daily 10.30am-
5pm, hot food until 3pm), just beyond
Bedruthan Steps by the viewpoint for an
iron-age fort. It's pleasant with lots of seating, and serves soups, filled baguettes,
toasties, pasties and cream teas. There's
also a National Trust **gift shop** here.

The Atlantic Coaster **bus** between
Padstow and St Ives stops at Carnewas on
the B3276. [For details see pp52-5].

MAWGAN PORTH   [MAP 27, p129]

Mawgan Porth is a cluster of old-fashioned retail shops and properties around the cove catering for visitors to its large beach. The well-stocked *Cornish Fresh Village Stores* (Mon-Sat 8am-8pm, Sun 8am-7pm) has pasties and coffee too. **Betty's News** (8am-6pm) has a **cashpoint** (£1.95 charge).

The nearest campsite is *Magic Cove Touring Park* (☎ 01637-860263, 🖳 www .magiccove.co.uk), just 300 yards from the beach. It's well-appointed with very clean

toilets and level grassy pitches but although they do have special hikers' rates (single £6-10, couples £10-14) they can be booked up months in advance in peak season.

If so, about another mile up the road (turn left off the forest-trail footpath when you reach Sun Haven Valley Country Holiday Park) is *Rettorick Mill Campsite* (☎ 01637-860460, 🖳 retorrickmill.co.uk, **fb**; camping adult/child £8/5), which is more likely to have space for hikers. Also on

(cont'd on p130)

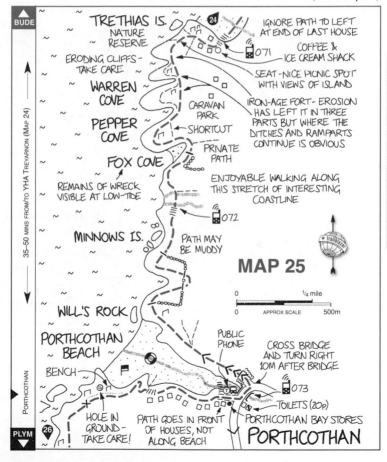

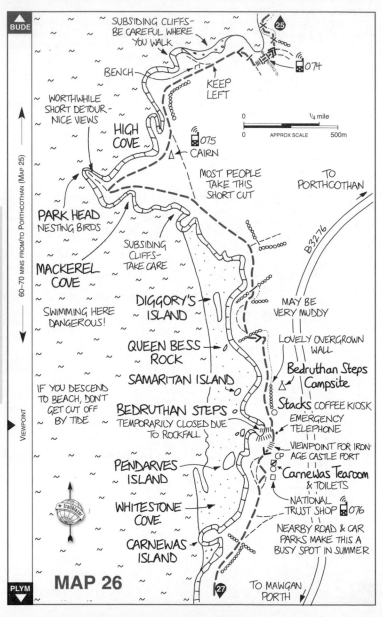

BUDE

SUBSIDING CLIFFS—
BE CAREFUL WHERE
YOU WALK

25

074

BENCH

KEEP
LEFT

WORTHWHILE
SHORT DETOUR -
NICE VIEWS

HIGH
COVE

075
CAIRN

MOST PEOPLE
TAKE THIS
SHORT CUT

TO
PORTHCOTHAN

B3276

PARK HEAD
NESTING BIRDS

SUBSIDING
CLIFFS—
TAKE CARE

MACKEREL
COVE

SWIMMING HERE
DANGEROUS!

DIGGORY'S
~ ISLAND

MAY BE
VERY MUDDY

LOVELY OVERGROWN
WALL

QUEEN BESS
~ ROCK

Bedruthan Steps
Campsite

SAMARITAN ISLAND

Stacks COFFEE KIOSK

IF YOU DESCEND
TO BEACH, DON'T
GET CUT OFF
~ BY TIDE

BEDRUTHAN STEPS
TEMPORARILY CLOSED DUE
TO ROCKFALL

EMERGENCY
TELEPHONE

VIEWPOINT FOR IRON-
AGE CASTLE FORT

CP

PENDARVES
~ ISLAND

Carnewas Tearoom
& TOILETS

NATIONAL
TRUST SHOP 076

WHITESTONE
COVE

NEARBY ROAD & CAR
PARKS MAKE THIS A
BUSY SPOT IN SUMMER

CARNEWAS ~
ISLAND

MAP 26

27

TO MAWGAN
PORTH

trailblazer

0   ¼ mile
0   500m
APPROX SCALE

PLYM

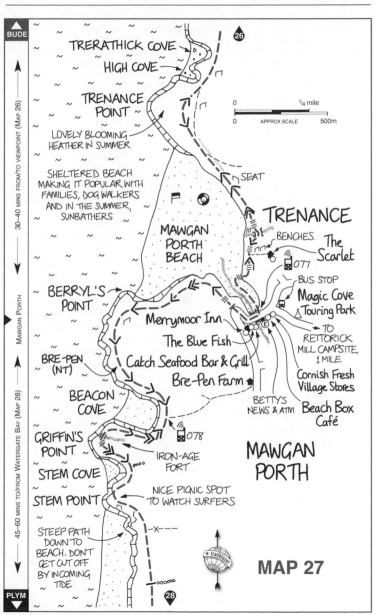

BUDE

30-40 MINS FROM/TO VIEWPOINT (MAP 26)

MAWGAN PORTH

45-60 MINS TO/FROM WATERGATE BAY (MAP 28)

PLYM

TRERATHICK COVE

HIGH COVE

TRENANCE POINT

LOVELY BLOOMING HEATHER IN SUMMER

SHELTERED BEACH MAKING IT POPULAR WITH FAMILIES, DOG WALKERS AND IN THE SUMMER, SUNBATHERS

MAWGAN PORTH BEACH

BERRYL'S POINT

BRE-PEN (NT)

BEACON COVE

GRIFFIN'S POINT

STEM COVE

STEM POINT

STEEP PATH DOWN TO BEACH. DON'T GET CUT OFF BY INCOMING TIDE

26

0   ¼ mile
0   APPROX SCALE   500m

SEAT

TRENANCE

BENCHES   The Scarlet

077

BUS STOP

Magic Cove Touring Park

Merrymoor Inn

The Blue Fish

Catch Seafood Bar & Grill

Bre-Pen Farm

BETTY'S NEWS & ATM

TO RETTORICK MILL CAMPSITE, 1 MILE

Cornish Fresh Village Stores

Beach Box Café

078

IRON-AGE FORT

NICE PICNIC SPOT TO WATCH SURFERS

MAWGAN PORTH

MAP 27

28

ROUTE GUIDE AND MAPS

site here is *Scott & Babs* (☎ 01637 861746, 🖥 woodfireatthemill.com; from 5pm; booking recommended even if camping here), a very popular barnhouse restaurant specialising in wood-fired food.

If you fancy a splurge, consider a stay (or at least a meal – muddy boots and dogs welcome) at *The Scarlet* (☎ 01637-861800, 🖥 scarlethotel.co.uk, **fb**; 🍷; 🐾; 37D; from £195pp; adults only), a sumptuous spa-hotel and restaurant nestled into the hillside just above the coast path as you approach Mawgan Porth. Rooms are bright and luxurious, while the **restaurant** (8-11am, noon-2pm & 6-9.30pm; open to all) is equally top notch. Lunchtime mains start at £14.

The beachfront is dominated by *The Merrymoor Inn* (☎ 01637-860258, 🖥 merrymoorinn.com, **fb**; 1S/1T/5D; 🐾; from £50pp, sgl occ from £80), a no-nonsense pub serving good-value food (daily summer 10am-9pm; winter noon-2.30pm & 6-9pm), and local ales.

A little way out of the village, up a steep hill, is lovely *Bre-Pen Farm* (☎ 01637-860420, 🖥 bre-penfarm.co.uk; 1T/ 3D; from £40pp, sgl occ £75), with comfortable rooms and hearty Cornish breakfasts.

Back in Mawgan Porth proper is *Beach Box Café* (🖥 beachboxcornwall.co .uk; daily 8am-6pm), while *The Blue Fish Bar* (☎ 01637-860554, 🖥 bluefishbar.co .uk; summer 12.30-2pm & 5-8pm, winter closed) is a traditional seaside chippy. Next door at the fairly upmarket *Catch Seafood Bar & Grill* (☎ 01637-860372, 🖥 catch mawganporthbeach.co.uk, **fb**; daily 9am-11pm-ish, call to check), a seafood main will cost £17-29.

The invaluable Atlantic Coaster and the No 56 **bus** services stop on Mawgan Rd. [For more details see pp52-5].

MAWGAN PORTH TO NEWQUAY   [MAPS 27-30]

The first part of this **6-mile (10km, 1½-2hrs)** stretch is perfectly easy once the initial climb out of Mawgan Porth is over with, and apart from a minor descent to **Beacon Cove**, a climb to the Iron Age fort at **Griffin's Point** and a short descent to **Stem Cove**, it's plain sailing to **Watergate Bay**. Watergate Beach looks inviting but the path follows the cliffs above it to arrive at the bay. There are fine views over the beach and, if there is a strong swell, you'll see crowds of surfers, some flying gracefully with the waves, others spectacularly wiping out.

It would be nice to walk along the beach from Watergate but the tide prevents it so the coast path remains on the cliffs until the first buildings (Sands Resort Hotel) begin to appear. You can walk on the pavement down the hill to **Porth Beach** but it's more pleasant to take the cliff path out to **Trevelgue Head** where a narrow footbridge leads across to the island on which was built one of Cornwall's largest Iron Age forts. As usual there is little of the fort remaining, though the walk to and around it is gentle, with plenty of benches for you to rest upon, nearly all dedicated to the memory of people 'who loved this spot'. It's not difficult to see why.

The route from Porth to Newquay is mostly on tarmac, though there are some things of interest to look at including the sporting activities on the cliffs above **Lusty Glaze Beach** where adrenaline seekers kitted out in safety helmets and harnesses can be seen abseiling from fixed lines on the cliffs. Once into the town you can take the old tramway route, which is now a pedestrian walkway, for about 400m (turn right after the Travelodge), before joining up again with the main shopping strip, and working your way along the town, above **Newquay's beaches** – Tolcarne, Great Western Sands and Towan Sands – to the little harbour that's still home to fishing boats.

WATERGATE BAY   [MAP 28]

Surfing hotspot Watergate Bay is another gastronomic haven with two restaurants for foodies, both owned by the classy but very expensive *Watergate Bay Hotel* (☎ 01637-860543, 🖥 watergatebay.co.uk; ☻; 🐾; 80

rooms; from £105pp) where in summer a double room often costs more than £200pp.

The more affordable of the two restaurants, *The Beach Hut* (☎ 01637-860877, 🖥 watergatebay.co.uk/eat/the-beach-hut; daily

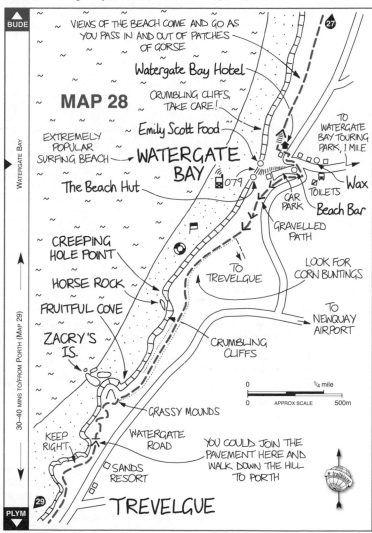

BUDE

VIEWS OF THE BEACH COME AND GO AS YOU PASS IN AND OUT OF PATCHES OF GORSE

Watergate Bay Hotel

MAP 28

CRUMBLING CLIFFS, TAKE CARE!

Emily Scott Food

EXTREMELY POPULAR SURFING BEACH

WATERGATE BAY

TO WATERGATE BAY TOURING PARK, I MILE

The Beach Hut

079

Wax

CAR PARK

TOILETS

Beach Bar

GRAVELLED PATH

CREEPING HOLE POINT

LOOK FOR CORN BUNTINGS

HORSE ROCK

TO TREVELGUE

FRUITFUL COVE

TO NEWQUAY AIRPORT

ZACRY'S IS.

CRUMBLING CLIFFS

0   ¼ mile
0   APPROX SCALE   500m

GRASSY MOUNDS

KEEP RIGHT

WATERGATE ROAD

YOU COULD JOIN THE PAVEMENT HERE AND WALK DOWN THE HILL TO PORTH

SANDS RESORT

TREVELGUE

WATERGATE BAY

30-40 MINS TO/FROM PORTH (MAP 29)

PLYM

ROUTE GUIDE AND MAPS

Easter-Sep 9am-9pm; winter Sun-Thur noon-4pm, Fri & Sat noon-9pm), is right on the beach. Mains cost £14-22 and include excellent seafood. Next door, and also overlooking the beach, *Emily Scott Food* (☎ 01637-818184, 🖳 emilyscottfood.com; Wed-Sat noon-2.30pm & 6.30-9.30pm; booking essential) has fabulous sea views and an ever-changing menu (most mains £20-40) including dishes like whole Cornish lobster with seaweed butter and burnt lime.

For those who don't fancy fine dining, there's *Wax* (☎ 01637-860353, 🖳 waxwater gate.co.uk, **fb**; daily noon-9pm), or the even

more informal *Beach Bar* (11am-8pm), both serving the likes of burgers, fish & chips, pizza (£12-14) and ice cream.

You can **camp** at *Watergate Bay Touring Park* (☎ 01637-860387, 🖳 water gatebaytouringpark.co.uk, **fb**; 🐾; camping £10-15pp) which is about a mile inland. The park has a shop, café, launderette and swimming pool. It's a steep climb to get to it, although they do usually lay on a free minibus to and from the beach in high season; alternatively, the Atlantic Coaster and the No 56 **buses** stop right outside. They also stop opposite Wax. [See pp52-5].

PORTH   [MAP 29]
Porth is an outpost of Newquay but has enough sleeping and eating options to make it a popular choice among walkers reluctant to face the overly hedonistic tendencies of many of Newquay's visitors. It is quiet and has a lovely beach; who could ask for more?

For **campers** there's the excellent, if pricey, *Porth Beach Holiday Park* (☎ 01637-876531, 🖳 porthbeach.co.uk, **fb**; from £39 per pitch; glamping pods sleep 4 £45-75; 🐾; Mar-Oct), with a stream running alongside the park.

For **B&B** try the boutique *Porth Beach Hotel* (☎ 01637-838225, 🖳 porthbeach hotel.co.uk, **fb**; 11D; 🛏; from £70pp).

Right on the beach is the colourful *Mermaid Inn* (☎ 01637-872954; 🖳 themer maidinn.co.uk, **fb**; **food** daily 11.30am-9pm). The pub isn't the prettiest, but it's friendly with a large outdoor seating area and a menu (mains £8-14) of pub classics. It also has an **ATM**. Right across the road is

the *Estrella Morada Bar de Tapas* (☎ 01637-877271, **fb**; summer daily 10.30am-3pm & 6.30-9pm; adults only), a laidback bar that also serves good tapas (£4-7).

Down at the far end of the beach towards Newquay, *Café Coast* (☎ 01637-871962; daily Apr-Sep, 10am-5pm) and nearby family-run *Gwenna Tea House* (☎ 01637-871962; 🖳 gwennateahouse.co.uk, **fb**; summer Wed-Mon 9.30am-4.30pm, winter hours variable) both offer cake, cream teas, salads and sandwiches.

For something a bit different, climb down the steep flight of 133 steps to *Lusty Glaze Restaurant* (☎ 01637-872444, 🖳 lustyglaze.co.uk, **fb**; Easter-Oct daily 10am-late, winter hours variable; evening mains £9-24), nestled in a secluded, privately-owned cove.

First Kernow's 56 and the Atlantic Coaster **bus** services call here. [See pp52-5 for details].

NEWQUAY   [MAP 30, p135]
Newquay is the surf capital of Cornwall and the major UK competitions are held on Fistral Beach (see box p136). Not surprisingly therefore, there are numerous shops selling surfing equipment and gear. The town has also become a favourite venue for stag and hen parties, to the dismay of many. If a night out on streets filled with practically paralytic 20-somethings doesn't sound like your cup of tea, then consider other options either before or after Newquay.

Services
The **tourist information centre** (☎ 01637-854020, 🖳 visitnewquay.org; Mon-Fri 9am-5pm, Sat & Sun 10am-3/4pm) is on Marcus Hill. Bank St has branches of Barclays, HSBC and NatWest **banks**, all with **ATMs**, and a Boots **pharmacy** (Mon-Sat 9am-5.30pm), a WH Smith **newsagent** (Mon-Sat 8.30am-5.30pm, Sun 10am-4pm) and a number of **bakeries** for pasties and the like.

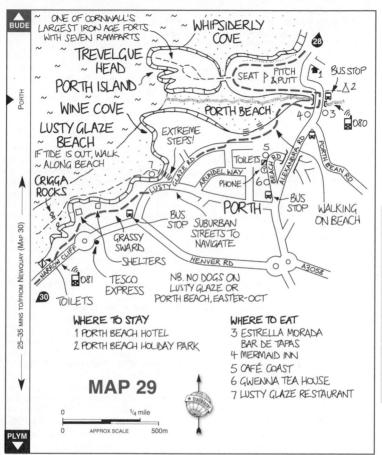

~ ONE OF CORNWALL'S ~
LARGEST IRON AGE FORTS
WITH SEVEN RAMPARTS

~ WHIPSIDERLY ~
COVE

~ TREVELGUE ~
~ HEAD ~

PORTH ISLAND

~ WINE COVE ~

LUSTY GLAZE ~
~ BEACH
IF TIDE IS OUT, WALK
~ ALONG BEACH

CRIGGA ~
ROCKS

EXTREME
STEPS!

28

SEAT PITCH
& PUTT

1 BUS STOP

2

PORTH BEACH

4 3

080

5
TOILETS

ARUNDEL WAY

PHONE

LUSTY

7

LUSTY GLAZE RD

BEACH RD

6

ALEXANDRA RD

PORTH BEAN RD

PORTH

BUS
STOP

WALKING
ON BEACH

BUS
STOP

SUBURBAN
STREETS TO
NAVIGATE

GRASSY
SWARD

SHELTERS

HENVER RD

A3058

NARROW CLIFF

081

30

TESCO
EXPRESS

TOILETS

NB. NO DOGS ON
LUSTY GLAZE OR
PORTH BEACH, EASTER-OCT

WHERE TO STAY
1 PORTH BEACH HOTEL
2 PORTH BEACH HOLIDAY PARK

WHERE TO EAT
3 ESTRELLA MORADA
BAR DE TAPAS
4 MERMAID INN
5 CAFÉ COAST
6 GWENNA TEA HOUSE
7 LUSTY GLAZE RESTAURANT

MAP 29

0 .... 1/4 mile
0 ...APPROX SCALE... 500m

★ trailblazer

On Cliff Rd, opposite the approach to the railway station, Newquay Camping (☎ 01637-877619, 🖳 newquaycampingshop .com; daily 9am-7pm) is a long-time family-run camping shop stocking **camping gear** including fuel. There's also a Mountain Warehouse (Mon-Sat 9am-5.30pm, Sun 10am-4pm) and a Millets (Mon-Sat 9am-6pm, Sun 10am-4pm) on Bank St.

There are **launderettes** on East St (Mon-Sat 9am-6pm, Sun 10am-4pm) and

Tower Rd (Mon-Sat 8am-8pm, Sun 10am-8pm). **Supermarkets** include Sainsbury's (Mon-Sat 7am-9pm, Sun 10am-4pm) on Fore St, Aldi (Mon-Sat 8am-10pm, Sun 11am-5pm) on Cliff Rd, and Asda (7am-11pm, Sun 11am-5pm), just off Cliff Rd, plus a smaller Spar supermarket on Tower Rd (Mon-Sat 7am-10pm, Sun 10am-4pm). All have **ATMs** outside.

The main **post office** (Mon-Fri 9am-5.30pm, Sat 9am-12.30pm) is on East St.

Where to stay
Camping & hostels
The nearest campsite to the town centre is *Trenance Holiday Park* (☎ 01637 873447, 🖳 trenanceholiday park.co.uk) on Edgcumbe Ave; it's popular and often full during the season, but they might squeeze in a hiker's tent (£11pp). They have a launderette and a breakfast van.

Although many so-called hostels cater primarily to the stag-/hen-do crowds these days, one old-style surfer haunt that has survived is *Newquay International Backpackers* (☎ 01637-879366, 🖳 backpackers.co.uk, **fb**, 69-73 Tower Rd; 50 beds; dorm £28-39pp, T/D £30-35pp, some en suite), which has bunk-bed dorms, single-bed dorms and private rooms, plus a self-catering kitchen, lounge and dining areas, and a large wet room with drying racks.

B&Bs
Newquay has a huge variety of accommodation but most of it is geared towards seaside holidaymakers staying for the week rather than overnighting coast-path walkers with their muddy boots, rucksacks and wet gear.

St Bernard's Guest House (☎ 01637-872932, 🖳 stbernardsguesthouse.com, **fb**; 5D/2D or T; 🐾; from £32.50pp, sgl occ from £48), at 9 Berry Rd, has a guest lounge plus a relaxation room with a sauna and a massage chair.

Almost next door is *Wenden Guest House* (☎ 01637-872604, 🖳 newquay-hol idays.co.uk; 5D; 🐾 in winter; £40-42.50pp, sgl occ room rate; couples only).

At No 6 Trenance Rd is *Alderberry Lodge* (☎ 01637-851683, 🖳 alderberry lodge.co.uk, **fb**; 3D; £25-35pp) with clean, unfussy rooms and very welcoming hosts.

Towards the Headland as you leave the town, comfortable *Treheveras* (☎ 01637-874079, 🖳 treheveras.co.uk; 3D or T; from £37.50pp), at 2a Dane Rd, is welcoming, walker friendly and right on the trail, so a great choice for an early start the next day.

If you prefer to stay in a pub, try the *Griffin Inn* (☎ 01637-874067, 🖳 griffin-inn-newquay.co.uk, **fb**; 1S/9D/4T/1Qd; from £42.50pp, sgl occ from £60) near the train station. Knock off £5pp for room-only rates. Note, it's in a noisy part of town.

Hotels
Next to Aldi, *Travelodge* (☎ 0871 9846244, 🖳 travelodge.co.uk; 72 rooms; from £35pp, breakfast £8.75) offers dependable, if bland, accommodation.

The beautifully restored *Harbour Hotel* (☎ 01637-873040, 🖳 harbourhotel.co.uk; 4D/1T; 🍽; 🐾; £55-112.50pp) on North Quay Hill has exquisitely decorated rooms with balconies overlooking the harbour. High-season prices start at £90pp.

Further round towards Beacon Cove, the large *Atlantic Hotel* (☎ 01637-872244, 🖳 atlantichotelnewquay.co.uk, **fb**; 1S/4T/52D, all with sea view; 🍽; from £50pp, sgl from £71), with its deep-pile carpets and mahogany panelling, exudes affluence and comfort from every pore. It also has a top-quality restaurant and a lovely outdoor pool.

If that's not luxurious enough for you, consider treating yourself to *The Headland* (Map 31; 01637-872211; 🖳 headland hotel.co.uk; 96 rooms; 🍽; 🐾; from £82.50pp, sgl occ from £115), Newquay's iconic, Grade II-listed, luxury hotel. You'll have to pay at least £130pp in high season.

Where to eat and drink
Approaching from the railway station, the options come thick and fast with Chinese, Indian, Italian, Mexican and fast-food restaurants following one after another. On Cliff Rd, *The Maharajah* (☎ 01637-877377, 🖳 maharajah-restaurant.co.uk; daily 5.30-10pm) is Newquay's most popular Indian restaurant, and has wonderful sea views. By the post office, *Señor Dick's* (☎ 01637-870350, 🖳 senor-dicks.co.uk, **fb**; daily 6-10pm) is a Mexican restaurant with most mains from £14 to £20.

Back on Cliff Rd, *The Cod End* (noon-8.30pm) is arguably Newquay's best fish & chip restaurant. Cod & chips cost £8.95 and can be enjoyed with fabulous sea views from its backyard terrace.

For pub grub, *Fort Inn* (☎ 01637-875700, 🖳 fortinnnewquay.co.uk, **fb**; daily noon-3pm & 5-9pm) is one of the better choices, with St Austell beers on tap, a good-value menu (most mains £10-12) and sea-view terrace seating.

Also owned by the St Austell Brewery, *The Central* (☎ 01637-873810, 🖳 thecen

ROUTE GUIDE AND MAPS

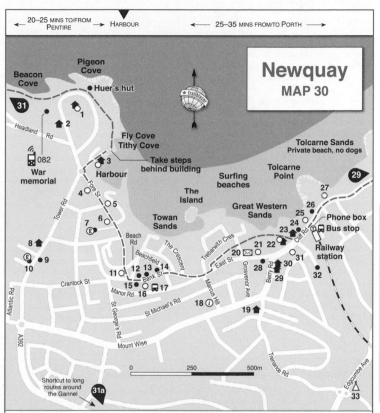

Newquay MAP 30

20–25 MINS TO/FROM PENTIRE ← → HARBOUR ← 25–35 MINS FROM/TO PORTH →

Pigeon Cove

Beacon Cove

Huer's hut

31

Headland Rd

082

War memorial

Fly Cove
Tithy Cove

Take steps behind building

Harbour

Tolcarne Sands
Private beach, no dogs

Tolcarne Point

Surfing beaches

The Island

Towan Sands

Great Western Sands

27

26

25

24

Phone box

Bus stop

Railway station

29

23

Tower Rd

Fore St

Beach Rd

Beachfield

The Crescent

Trebarwith Cres

East St

Grosvenor Ave

Cliff Rd

21 22

20

28

31

30

29

32

Atlantic Rd

Crantock St

Manor Rd

Bank St

11 12 13 14

15 16 17

St George's Rd

St Michael's Rd

Marcus Hill

18

19

Mount Wise

Trenance Rd

Edgcumbe Ave

0   250   500m

Shortcut to long routes around the Gannel

31a

33

Where to stay
1 Atlantic Hotel
2 Treheveras
3 Harbour Hotel
8 Newquay International Backpackers
19 Alderberry Lodge
22 Griffin Inn
23 Travelodge
29 Wenden Guest House
30 St Bernard's Guesthouse
33 Trenance Holiday Park

Where to eat/drink
1 Silks Bistro
3 Harbour Fish & Grill
4 Box & Barber
5 Fort Inn
6 Café Cloud
11 The Central
16 Pauline's Creamery
21 Senor Dick's
22 Griffin Inn
25 The Cod End
27 The Maharajah
31 Towan Blystra

Other
7 Sainsbury's
9 Launderette
10 Spar
12 Mountain Warehouse
13 Boots pharmacy
14 WH Smith
15 Millets
17 Bus station
18 Tourist Info
20 Post Office
24 Aldi Supermarket
26 Newquay Camping
28 Launderette
32 Asda

ROUTE GUIDE AND MAPS

tralnewquay.co.uk; daily noon-3pm & 5-9pm) is probably the main party pub in town, with crowds spilling out onto the pavement seating area. The food menu (most mains £9-13) includes burgers, grilled chicken, nachos and the like.

Up towards the station on Cliff Rd, *Griffin Inn* (see Where to stay) serves food daily from noon-2.30pm & 5-8pm (mains £9-14), while Wetherspoon's *Towan Blystra* (☎ 01637-852970, 🖳 jdwether spoon.co.uk; food daily 8am-9pm) is directly opposite, with popular roadside seating.

Cute cafés are dotted around town, particularly on Fore St. *Café Cloud* (fb; 9am-4.15pm) has a cool-blue interior and a relaxing atmosphere in which to sample cream teas, coffees, cakes and scones. Nearby, and also very popular, *Box & Barber* (fb; 7am-4pm), does fabulous coffee plus healthy breakfasts and lunches, including lots of vegan options. *Paulines Creamery* (🖳 paulinesnewquay.co.uk, fb; daily 9am-6pm) is a good-value bakery and tearoom that's been going since 1971 and serves an array of cakes, pastries, pasties, sandwiches and baguettes. They also do packed-lunch boxes and takeaway cream teas.

For fine dining, the excellent *Harbour Fish & Grill* (☎ 01637-873040, 🖳 the harbourfishandgrill.com; 10am-10pm) at Harbour Hotel (see Where to stay) has wonderful views over Newquay's harbour and beaches, especially from its terrace.

Silks Bistro and Champagne Bar at the Atlantic Hotel (see Where to stay; bar 11am-10.30pm; food served noon-3pm & 6-10.30pm), is also top class, with an ambience just on the formal side of relaxed and daily specials with a seafood bias.

Beyond the Headland, *Rick Stein Fistral* (Map 31; ☎ 01637-808437, 🖳 rick stein.com; noon-9pm) is the best of a cluster of café-restaurants overlooking Fistral Beach, and one of the few Rick Stein establishments that won't break the bank; burgers for less than a tenner, cod and chips £12.95. There's also a selection of Indian curries and Thai noodles (£9-12).

Transport

[See pp50-5 for details] A number of services operate from the **bus** station in the centre of town: the No 85 to Truro via Crantock, the Atlantic Coaster between Padstow and St Ives, the No 56 to Padstow and the U1/U1A to Falmouth via Perranporth. Newquay's **railway station**, just off Cliff Rd, has trains to Par from where you can change for Penzance and

---

❑ **SURFING, BODY BOARDING & PADDLEBOARDING**

If you fancy a day on the waves there are loads of surf shops up and down the coast offering lessons and equipment hire. If you've never surfed before the best way to begin is with a lesson. They will start you off on a long (7-8ft), soft, foam board which is more buoyant than a normal board and easier to paddle thus making it easier to take off on a wave. You'll be taught the basics like how to leap to your feet but after that it's practice, and lots of it. Most places charge £30-40 for lessons which includes all equipment and transport to the beach, if needed. However, it pays to shop around and ask lots of questions; the price may be for a one-to-one lesson or with a group of twenty people.

Alternatively, try body boarding or SUP (stand-up paddleboarding) which are both much more straightforward and with equipment that's also easy to hire (body boards around £5/10 per hr/day, SUPs £20/30 per hr/day). **Fistral Beach Surf School** (Map 31; ☎ 01637-850737, 🖳 fistralbeachsurfschool.co.uk, fb; daily 9am-5pm; 2hr group surf lessons from £40pp) is one option in Newquay.

If you prefer to keep your feet dry you may be lucky enough to catch one of the major surf competitions held in Newquay each year, such as the English National Surfing Championships which take place over the May Day public holiday and the British Cup Surfing over the last weekend in May.

Bodmin Parkway. Some London trains even stop at Par. There's no ticket office at Newquay; just buy your ticket once on the train.

There are three National Express **coach** services (see box p51) a day.

Newquay Airport (☎ 01637-860600, 🖥 newquaycornwallairport.com) has flights to a number of UK airports.

For a **taxi**, try calling A2B Taxis (☎ 01637-877777; 🖥 a2bnewquay.com).

NEWQUAY TO CRANTOCK [MAPS 30-31 & 31a]

This simple **2-mile (3km, 35-45 mins** if using ferry; longer for other options) stretch leaves Newquay by way of the headland, crosses inland of Fistral Beach through the dunes and becomes involved with suburban streets, most of them with Pentire in the name; choose your route. The only obstacle of the route is the crossing of the tidal **Gannel River** and how easy this is will depend on the state of the tide (see box on p138). You can cross by ferry at high tide, by the Penpol footbridge, or by walking the long way round by the Laurie footbridge at Trevemper (see options in detail below).

Once across the Gannel, you may decide to walk the short distance inland to the lovely old village of **Crantock** (see p138), or carry on the official route, or if it is low tide walk along the beach through the dunes.

Crossing the Gannel River [Map 31, p139; Map 31a, p140]

If you haven't already checked the tide times (see box p138), now is the time to do so. There are four ways to cross the Gannel; which one you take depends on the time of year and the state of the tide. On the **Pentire** side, at the top of the steps leading down to the river, light refreshments, including sandwiches, cakes and hot drinks, are available at *Fern Pit Café* (🖥 fernpit.co.uk, **fb**; May-Sep, daily 9.30am-6pm), along with fantastic views over the Gannel. It's open whether the ferry is running or not. On the opposite side is *Beachcomber Café* (**fb**; daily 9am-6pm) with less spectacular views but decent-value food. Note all distances are Newquay–Crantock. See Map 31 (p139) for **timings** for each route.

● The official crossing (2 miles/3km) is via the **Fern Pit Ferry (A; Map 31)** (☎ 01637-873181, 🖥 fernpit.co.uk). This is the quickest and easiest option but the ferry (adult/child £1.40/70p each way) only operates from late May to mid September, daily 9.30am-6pm. If the tide is out you can walk across their footbridge (note this is also closed during the winter) for free.

● The second option (3 miles/5km) is to cross the **Penpol Footbridge (B; Map 31)**. This footbridge is tidal but you should be able to cross two to four hours either side of low tide. If you are in any doubt whatsoever it is very easy to continue walking from here to the next bridge further up the Gannel.

● The third option (5 miles/8km) is the **Laurie Bridge (C; Map 31a)**, which is also a bridleway. The only time it's not possible to cross this bridge is one hour either side of a high spring tide.

● The final option (6 miles/9.5km) is to follow the **main road** (A392) right around the Gannel. However, this is a long and boring walk with the constant smell of exhaust fumes. You really would do much better to wait for the tides, plan ahead, or catch a bus (Go Cornwall Bus's No 85; see pp52-5).

ROUTE GUIDE AND MAPS

❑ TIDES

Tides are the regular rise and fall of the ocean caused by the gravitational pull of the moon. They are actually very long waves which follow the path of the moon across the ocean. Twice a day there is a high tide and a low tide and there are approximately 6¼ hours between high and low water.

Spring tides (derived from the German word *springan* meaning to jump) are tides with a very large range that occur just after the full- and new-moon phases when the gravitational forces of the sun and the moon line up. High tides are higher and low tides lower than normal. Spring tides occur twice every month.

Neap tides occur halfway between each spring tide and are tides with the smallest range, so you get comparatively high low tides and low high tides. They occur at the first and third quarters of the moon when the sun, moon and earth are all at right angles to each other, hence the gravitational forces of the sun and moon are weakened.

It is a good idea to carry a tide table with you; they can be purchased for about £1.50 from newsagents or TICs in coastal areas. Tide times are also available online at 🖳 tidetimes.org.uk, then select your location.

CRANTOCK & PORTH JOKE
[MAPS 31-2] Crantock is a traditional Cornish village with thatched cottages clustered round a village green, a ten-minute walk uphill from Crantock Beach.

There is a curious enclosure known as **Crantock Round Garden**. It used to be a pound (a place to keep stray cattle in until they could be claimed). You can even check out the stocks, last used in the 19th century, round the back of the church.

Londis **store** (Mon-Sat 8am-8pm, Sun 8am-7pm) and **post office** (Mon-Fri 9am-5.30pm, Sat 9am-12.30pm) has a good range of essentials including sandwiches and fruit. It also does coffee.

Although **camping** is the only option for accommodation in Crantock these days, campers are spoilt for choice. *Quarryfield Caravan and Camping Park* (☎ 01637-872792, 🖳 quarryfield.co.uk; ✖; £7-10pp; Easter-Oct), has a lovely hilltop location between Crantock Beach and Crantock Village. Alternatively there are three campsites almost side-by-side, accessible either from Crantock or from Porth Joke (Map 32).

Closest to Crantock is the excellent *Treago Farm Campsite* (☎ 01637-830277, 🖳 treagofarm.co.uk; hiker £10; ✖) which has a really well-stocked **shop** (8am-8pm) selling hot coffee and camping gas as well as groceries, plus a **café** (9am-5pm) and a games room. A little further on, *Higher*

Moor Campsite (☎ 01637-830928, 🖳 highermoor.co.uk; adults £8-10, children £4-5, peak season £30 minimum; ✖) has 22 tent pitches, each with its own picnic table. Continuing on, or take a half-mile stroll inland from Porth Joke, at *Polly Joke Campsite* (☎ 01637-830213; £10) hikers with small tents are always welcomed. The showers are a bit cramped, in individual portacabins, but are piping hot.

Two lovely old **pubs** stand opposite each other beside Crantock church. *The Old Albion* (☎ 01637-830243, 🖳 oldalbioncrantock.com; ✖; May-Sep food Wed-Sat 12.30-2.30pm & 4-9pm, Sun noon-4pm) is a 400-year-old traditional village pub with a thatched roof. Note, it's closed on Mondays and doesn't serve food on Tuesdays. *The Cornishman* (☎ 01637-520226, **fb**; ✖; food Mon-Sat 4-9pm; Sun noon-6pm) has occasional live music nights and serves food such as seafood chowder (£13) and their ever-popular pies.

Alternatively, *Jam Jar* (🖳 jamjar.cafe; daily 10am-8.30pm) is a lovely little café hidden away down an alley, en route to the pubs, and serves coffee, cake and pastries from 10am to 4pm, then wood-fired sourdough pizzas until closing. It's licensed and has a pleasant shaded garden courtyard.

Go Cornwall Bus's No 85 **bus** service stops here. [See pp52-5 for details].

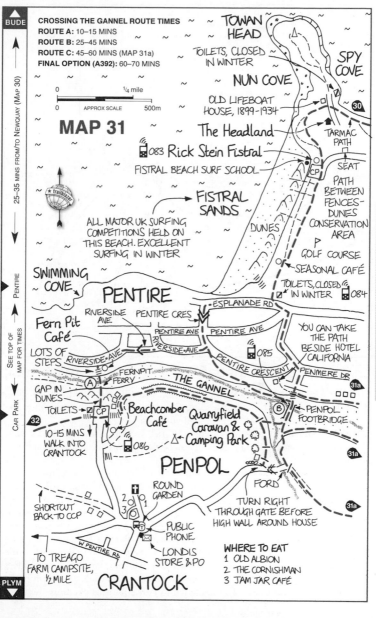

CROSSING THE GANNEL ROUTE TIMES
ROUTE A: 10–15 MINS
ROUTE B: 25–45 MINS
ROUTE C: 45–60 MINS (MAP 31a)
FINAL OPTION (A392): 60–70 MINS

TOWAN HEAD

TOILETS, CLOSED IN WINTER

SPY COVE

NUN COVE

OLD LIFEBOAT HOUSE, 1899-1934

The Headland

30

TARMAC PATH

083 Rick Stein Fistral

FISTRAL BEACH SURF SCHOOL

CP

SEAT

PATH BETWEEN FENCES- DUNES CONSERVATION AREA

FISTRAL SANDS

DUNES

GOLF COURSE

SEASONAL CAFÉ

TOILETS, CLOSED IN WINTER 084

ALL MAJOR UK SURFING COMPETITIONS HELD ON THIS BEACH. EXCELLENT SURFING IN WINTER

0   ¼ mile
0   APPROX SCALE   500m

MAP 31

SWIMMING COVE

PENTIRE

RIVERSIDE AVE   PENTIRE CRES

Fern Pit Café

ESPLANADE RD

PENTIRE AVE   PENTIRE AVE

LOTS OF STEPS   RIVERSIDE AVE

RIVERSIDE AVE

085

YOU CAN TAKE THE PATH BESIDE HOTEL CALIFORNIA

PENTIRE CRESCENT

PENMERE DR

FERNPIT FERRY

A

THE GANNEL

GAP IN DUNES

B

31a

PENPOL FOOTBRIDGE

TOILETS   CP

32

Beachcomber Café

Quarryfield Caravan & Camping Park

31a

10-15 MINS WALK INTO CRANTOCK

086

PENPOL

ROUND GARDEN

FORD

TURN RIGHT THROUGH GATE BEFORE HIGH WALL AROUND HOUSE

31a

SHORTCUT BACK TO CCP

2 1
3

PUBLIC PHONE

LONDIS STORE & PO

WHERE TO EAT
1 OLD ALBION
2 THE CORNISHMAN
3 JAM JAR CAFÉ

TO TREAGO FARM CAMPSITE, ½ MILE

W PENTIRE RD

CRANTOCK

BUDE

25–35 MINS FROM/TO NEWQUAY (MAP 30)

SEE TOP OF MAP FOR TIMES

PENTIRE

CAR PARK

PLYM

ROUTE GUIDE AND MAPS

trailblazer

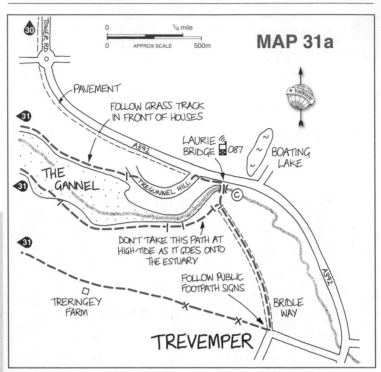

CRANTOCK TO PERRANPORTH   **[MAPS 31-34]**

The next **8 miles (13km, 2-3hrs)** provide classic cliff-top walking with some
sharp ups and downs soon after leaving Crantock, including the descent to the
secluded beach at **Porth Joke**, accessible only on foot.

Kelsey Head with its huge expanse of grass is a place to linger and savour
so don't keep charging ahead. Slow the pace down a bit and make the most of
an exquisite area.

Next comes **Holywell** with two pubs and a large holiday park after which
the coast path skirts the scattered installations of **Penhale Camp**, MoD property, which is heavily fenced. You imagine that somebody has you under observation as you pass by the concrete barracks and communications masts and hear
the noise of small-arms fire from the ranges. Once behind this, a narrow, heart-
stopping path brings you by stages to the start of **Perran Beach**, a two-mile
long stretch of golden sand bordered by dunes, the walk along the edge of the
tide making a welcome change. You'll see dog walkers, families, horse-riders
and, if the wind is up, sand yachts whistling across the beach; you'll probably
want to take your boots off. The approach to Perranporth is exciting, the town

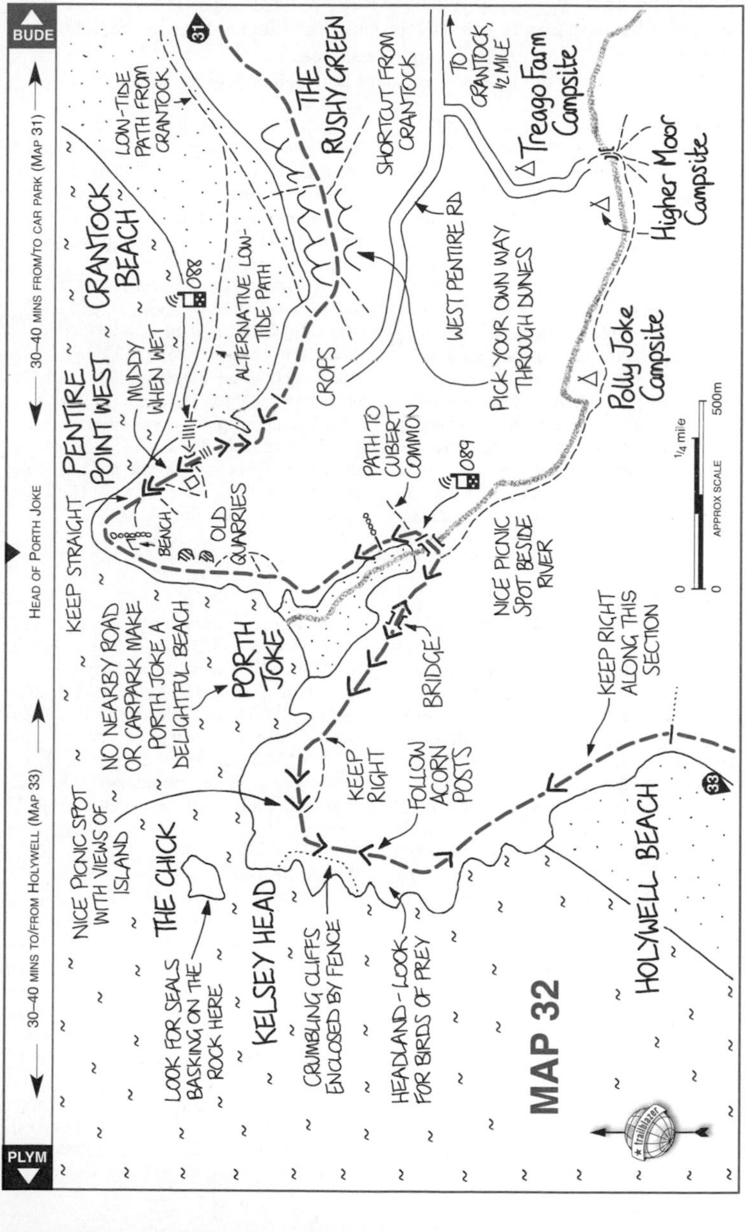

MAP 32

BUDE

PLYM

30-40 MINS FROM/TO CAR PARK (MAP 31)

Head of Porth Joke

30-40 MINS TO/FROM HOLWELL (MAP 33)

31

LOW-TIDE PATH FROM CRANTOCK

CRANTOCK BEACH

PENTIRE POINT WEST

KEEP STRAIGHT

MUDDY WHEN WET

088

BENCH

OLD QUARRIES

ALTERNATIVE LOW-TIDE PATH

THE RUSHY GREEN

SHORTCUT FROM CRANTOCK

TO CRANTOCK, ½ MILE

△ Treago Farm Campsite

△ Higher Moor Campsite

WEST PENTIRE RD

PICK YOUR OWN WAY THROUGH DUNES

△ Polly Joke Campsite

CROPS

PATH TO CUBERT COMMON

089

NICE PICNIC SPOT BESIDE RIVER

NO NEARBY ROAD OR CARPARK MAKE PORTH JOKE A DELIGHTFUL BEACH

PORTH JOKE

KEEP RIGHT

BRIDGE

KEEP RIGHT

FOLLOW ACORN POSTS

KEEP RIGHT ALONG THIS SECTION

33

NICE PICNIC SPOT WITH VIEWS OF ISLAND

THE CHICK

LOOK FOR SEALS BASKING ON THE ROCK HERE

KELSEY HEAD

CRUMBLING CLIFFS ENCLOSED BY FENCE

HEADLAND - LOOK FOR BIRDS OF PREY

HOLYWELL BEACH

MAP 32

0   ¼ mile

0   500m

APPROX SCALE

★ trailblazer

coming into sight only as you round the rocky outcrop of **Cotty's Point**. At high tide it will be necessary to leave the beach at the lifeguard station and continue on the last leg to Perranporth through the dunes.

Perranporth is the largest settlement between Newquay and St Ives.

HOLYWELL [MAP 33]

Holywell's beach is very popular with families. It has **seasonal beach shops** and two places to eat, one of which offers **B&B**. There is some dispute over the exact site of the holy well this village is named after. Some say it's in the caves on the northern end of the beach, others that it's further inland along the road.

The venerable *Treguth Inn* (☎ 01637-830248, 🖳 thetreguthinn.com; food Mon-Sat noon-2pm & 6-8pm, Sun noon-2pm) is a converted 13th-century farmhouse with a thatched roof. It's open all day May to October and serves pub classics (mains £10-14) with some veggie options.

Right on the coast path, is the revamped *Gull Rocks Bar & Coffee House* (☎ 01637-830205, 🖳 gullrocksbar.co.uk,

fb; 2D en suite, £60pp room only; summer food 10-11.45am, noon-2.30pm & 5.30-7.30pm; winter hours vary), which used to be known as St Piran's Inn. They are licensed and serve hot and cold sandwiches, pub-grub mains and pizza.

Meadow Holiday Park (☎ 01872-572752, 🖳 holywellholidaypark.co.uk; Mar-Oct; hiker & tent £13-14) is quite small so it's wise to phone ahead to reserve a tent pitch. There are other, larger holiday parks here too, but you're less likely to snag a last-minute pitch at these in high season.

Go Cornwall Bus's No 85 **bus** service stops here. [For details see pp52-5]. The bus stop is five minutes' walk from the beach near Treguth Inn.

PERRANPORTH
[MAP 34, p145 & map p146]

Named after St Piran (see box on p144), the patron saint of Cornwall, Perranporth is a small, old-fashioned seaside town that depends on the holiday trade for its existence. Perran Beach is a major drawcard and a spell of nice weather sees it crowded with sun- and fun-seekers of all ages.

Perranzabuloe Museum (☎ 01872-573321, 🖳 perranzabuloemuseum.co.uk, Ponsmere Rd; Easter-Oct Mon-Fri 10.30am-4.30pm, Sat 11am-1pm; free) provides some useful information on the area's industrial past with displays on mining, fishing and farming.

The tourist office has closed here, but you can get **tourist information** through their website (🖳 perranporthinfo.co.uk), which is kept updated.

Both Co-op **supermarkets** (daily 7am-10pm) have **ATMs**. For **groceries** there is also a Premier (daily summer 7am-10pm; ATM) on St George's Hill. The **post office** (Mon-Fri 9am-1pm & 2-5pm, Sat 9am-12.30pm) is on St Piran's Rd, and

there's **internet access** at the **library** (Tue 10am-noon & 1-4pm, Thur 1-4pm, Fri & Sat 10am-noon), attached to the museum.

There is a **launderette** (daily 8am-8pm) on The Gounce. Nearby on Beach Rd is **Perranporth Surgery** (☎ 01872-572255, Mon-Fri 8am-12.30pm & 1.30-6pm) with a Boots **pharmacy** (Mon-Fri 8.30am-6.15pm, Sat 9am-5.30pm) next door.

Where to stay

The hideously large Perran Sands Caravan & Camping Park dominates the dunes behind Perran Beach, like a small Disney-esque village, with restaurants, rides and even its own 'high street'. Luckily, hikers can skip such nonsense and continue on to the excellent, family-run *Tollgate Farm Caravan and Camping Park* (off Map 34; ☎ 01872-572130, 🖳 tollgatefarm.co.uk; Easter to end Sep; hiker & tent £14; 🐾) at the other side of the Perran Sands site. It has good shower facilities, a launderette, a farm shop selling beer and wine, and various visiting

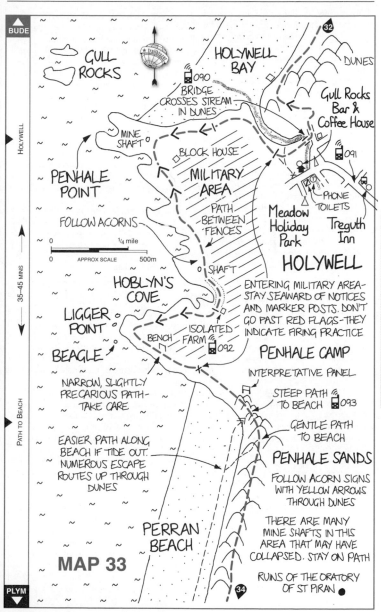

BUDE

HOLYWELL

35-45 MINS

PATH TO BEACH

PLYM

GULL ROCKS

HOLYWELL BAY

DUNES

090
BRIDGE CROSSES STREAM IN DUNES

Gull Rocks Bar & Coffee House

MINE SHAFT

BLOCK HOUSE

091

PENHALE POINT

MILITARY AREA

PHONE
TOILETS

FOLLOW ACORNS

PATH BETWEEN FENCES

Meadow Holiday Park

Treguth Inn

0   ¼ mile
0   APPROX SCALE   500m

SHAFT

HOLYWELL

HOBLYN'S COVE

ENTERING MILITARY AREA-STAY SEAWARD OF NOTICES AND MARKER POSTS. DON'T GO PAST RED FLAGS-THEY INDICATE FIRING PRACTICE

LIGGER POINT

BENCH

ISOLATED FARM
092

PENHALE CAMP

BEAGLE

INTERPRETATIVE PANEL

NARROW, SLIGHTLY PRECARIOUS PATH-TAKE CARE

STEEP PATH TO BEACH   093

GENTLE PATH TO BEACH

EASIER PATH ALONG BEACH IF TIDE OUT. NUMEROUS ESCAPE ROUTES UP THROUGH DUNES

PENHALE SANDS

FOLLOW ACORN SIGNS WITH YELLOW ARROWS THROUGH DUNES

PERRAN BEACH

THERE ARE MANY MINE SHAFTS IN THIS AREA THAT MAY HAVE COLLAPSED. STAY ON PATH

MAP 33

RUINS OF THE ORATORY OF ST PIRAN

ROUTE GUIDE AND MAPS

takeaway vans serving coffee and pastries for breakfasts, and fish & chips or pizza for dinner. It's a fair walk to town from here, but First Kernow's Atlantic Coaster and U1/U1A buses stop outside (the bus stop is called 'Perran Sands').

YHA Perranporth (Map 34; ☎ 0345-371 9755, ☐ yha.org.uk/hostel/yha-perran porth; Mar-Nov; 24 beds; from £18pp; self-catering only) is up on the hill on the cliffs at Droskyn Point; a fantastic location overlooking Perran Beach, and a prime spot for watching the sunset, brew in hand. There are two 4-bed private rooms, and two 8-bed dorms. You can also **camp** here (from £14).

B&B accommodation is thin on the ground. There's the pub *Seiners* (☎ 01872-573118, ☐ seiners.co.uk, **fb**; 2S/6T/13D/2Qd, most en suite; ▼; ✺; from 32.50pp, sgl occ from £45), right on the sea front. For a more traditional B&B, *St George's Country House Hotel* (☎ 01872-572184 or 07470-342522, ☐ stgeorges

countryhousehotel.com; 5D/1T/1F; ▼; ✺; ⓛ; £45-75pp, sgl occ from £90; min 2 nights), on the outskirts of town, is a grand, whitewashed, detached house with dormer windows and a friendly welcome. They keep their own hens, bake their own bread and have a **bistro-bar** attached.

Where to eat and drink
For Indian cuisine, try *Jaipur* (☎ 01872-573625, ☐ jaipurindiancuisine.co.uk, **fb**; daily 5pm to late). For Chinese, *Jade House* (☎ 01872-572880; Tue-Sun 5.30-10.30pm). Next to Jade House is *Brown's Fish 'n' Chips* (Mon & Wed-Sat 4.30-8pm), which has some seating as well as a takeaway.

Tywarnhayle Inn (aka the Tye; ☎ 01872-572215, ☐ tywarnhayleinn.co.uk, **fb**; summer daily 9am-9pm, Sun to 8pm, winter noon-3pm & 6-8pm) does quality pub food for decent prices (mains £10-14.50), plus breakfasts.

❏ ST PIRAN AND THE LOST ORATORY

St Piran, the patron saint of Cornwall, supposedly arrived in Perranporth in the 6th century having floated from Ireland on a millstone. In his old age he had been captured by pagan Irish and thrown over a cliff with this millstone round his neck. The stone floated and became a raft. He built a small chapel – the Oratory of St Piran – on Penhale Sands, and lived there for many years as a hermit performing miracles for the locals. When he died his relics were kept in a shrine nearby and became a major place of medieval pilgrimage.

The forgotten Oratory was lost to the sand dunes during the Middle Ages, but rediscovered in the 18th century, and in 1910 was encased in a concrete structure to help protect it. However modern conservationists grew worried that a lack of public commitment to preserve the site might lead to its eventual demise so they took the unusual step of removing its protective structure and allowing the sand dunes to once again engulf the Oratory, for its own protection. All was not lost, though. Local campaigners recently won a 14-year-long battle to re-expose the remains of what is thought to be one of the oldest Christian edifices in the British Isles. The excavation work was finally completed in November 2014.

St Piran's popularity among the Cornish lies in the tradition that it was he who first discovered tin. He was cooking on a fireplace of black rock when he saw that the intense heat made a trickle of pure white metal ooze from the stones. He shared this knowledge with the locals and it was on this that the prosperity of Cornwall was based.

St Piran is not only remembered on St Piran's Day on 5 March, but also on the Cornish flag, a white cross on a black background symbolising the white tin seeping from the black rock, the triumph of good over evil and God's light shining out of the darkness.

For further details visit the St Piran's Trust website (☐ st-piran.com).

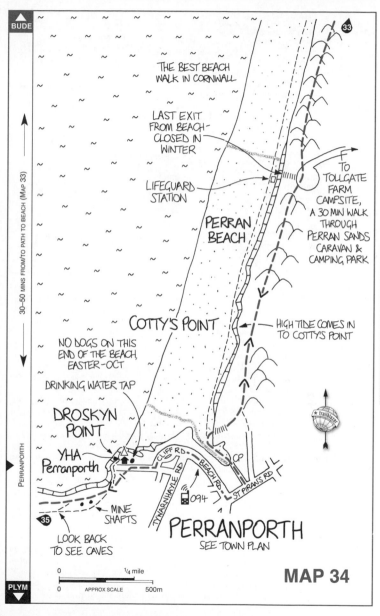

BUDE

33

THE BEST BEACH
WALK IN CORNWALL

LAST EXIT
FROM BEACH-
CLOSED IN
WINTER

TO
TOLLGATE
FARM
CAMPSITE,
A 30 MIN WALK
THROUGH
PERRAN SANDS
CARAVAN &
CAMPING PARK

LIFEGUARD
STATION

PERRAN
BEACH

30-50 MINS FROM/TO PATH TO BEACH (MAP 33)

COTTY'S POINT

HIGH TIDE COMES IN
TO COTTY'S POINT

NO DOGS ON THIS
END OF THE BEACH,
EASTER-OCT

DRINKING WATER TAP

DROSKYN
POINT

YHA
Perranporth

CLIFF RD

CP

TYNARNHAYLE RD

BEACH RD

ST PIRANS RD

094

PERRANPORTH

MINE
SHAFTS

35

LOOK BACK
TO SEE CAVES

SEE TOWN PLAN

PERRANPORTH

0   ¼ mile

0   500m
APPROX SCALE

MAP 34

ROUTE GUIDE AND MAPS

PLYM

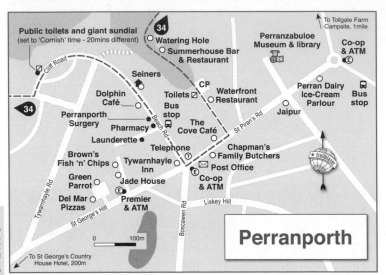

Public toilets and giant sundial
(set to 'Cornish' time - 20mins different)

To Tollgate Farm
Campsite, 1mile

Watering Hole

Summerhouse Bar
& Restaurant

Perranzabuloe
Museum & library

Co-op
& ATM

Cliff Road

Seiners

CP

Perran Dairy
Ice-Cream
Parlour

Bus
stop

Dolphin
Café

Toilets

Waterfront
Restaurant

Bus
stop

Perranporth
Surgery

Beach Rd

The
Cove Café

Jaipur

St Piran's Rd

Pharmacy

Launderette

Telephone

Chapman's
Family Butchers

Trailblazer

Brown's
Fish 'n' Chips

Tywarnhayle
Inn

Post Office

Green
Parrot

Jade House

Co-op
& ATM

Tywarnhayle Rd

Del Mar
Pizzas

Premier
& ATM

Liskey Hill

Boscawen Rd

St George's Hill

0   100m

Perranporth

To St George's Country
House Hotel, 200m

Seiners (see Where to stay; food daily noon-2.30pm & 6-8.30pm; mains £10-15) is like the lower deck of a sailing ship inside, with a range of piratical beers from Truro Brewery. Try the large bowl of mussels with chips or one of their fish specials.

Close to the beach, the *Waterfront Restaurant* (☎ 01872-573167, **fb**; Easter-Oct daily 6.30pm-late, from 5pm in July & Aug) is pub-like, with a garden cabin serving booze. The menu includes chicken wings (£10 for 10), loaded fries (£8-9) and a host of burger options (£11-12).

Right on the beach, *Summerhouse Bar & Restaurant* (☎ 01872-228222, 🖥 thesummerhouse.co.uk, **fb**; food noon-3pm & 6-8pm) is probably the classiest place to eat and drink. It's open from 11am till late for drinks, serves lunches (mains £10-13) and evening meals (mains £13-20), and has outdoor decking as well as a bright interior restaurant. Dishes include butter-roasted lamb loin and moules marinière.

Also on the beach – in fact, literally on the sand – is the more laidback *Watering Hole* (☎ 01872-572888, 🖥 thewateringhole .co.uk, **fb**; 🐾; Sun-Thur 9am-11pm, Fri-Sat 9am-1am; food 9am-9pm), a beach bar

with long opening hours, magical sunsets and a menu (mains £10-19) including burgers, fajitas, and fish and chips as well as breakfast baps (£5-7) and wraps (£10).

Green Parrot (☎ 01872-574990, 🖥 jdwetherspoon.com; St George's Hill; food daily 8am-11pm) is a Wetherspoon's serving inexpensive pub fare (mains from £6). Sharing the pub's car park is *Del Mar Italian Restaurant and Pizzeria* (☎ 01872-572878, 🖥 delmarrestaurant.co.uk, **fb**; summer daily noon-2pm & 5-11pm, winter Mon-Fri 5-11pm, Sat & Sun noon-2pm & 5-11pm), specialising in pizzas (£11-14), but also offering pasta, risotto, seafood, grilled meats and plenty of vegetarian options (most mains £12-18).

Popular *Cove Café* (☎ 01872-571487, **fb**; daily summer 8.30am-4pm, winter hours vary), on St Piran's Rd, does a decent breakfast, paninis and cream teas, plus a range of sandwiches.

All your Cornish ice cream cravings can be met at *Perran Dairy Ice-Cream Parlour* (**fb**; 10am-9pm, winter to 5pm), which also does coffee and paninis.

Dolphin Café (8am-4.30pm, later in summer) is more of a no-frills place, serving good value fry-up breakfasts as well as fish and chips. There's some outdoor seating with beach views.

For the best pasty in town, locals swear by *Chapman's Family Butcher's* (Mon-Sat 8am-5pm).

Transport

[See pp52-5 for details] First Kernow's U1/U1A and the Atlantic Coaster **bus** services stop on Beach Rd.

For a **taxi** try Atlantic Taxis (☎ 01872-571111; ✉ atlantic-taxis.business.site).

PERRANPORTH TO PORTHTOWAN [MAPS 34-38]

This **8-mile (13km, 2½-3hrs)** section passes through terrain that is mostly heathland which at one time covered the whole of the west of Cornwall. The walking is relatively easy and you should be able to crack on and make light of the few ups and downs, the most severe of which is down to **Chapel Porth**, where there is a seasonal **beach café** (Map 37; Apr-Oct daily 10am-5pm, winter Fri-Sun only). It is here that you first begin to encounter the remains of Cornwall's mining industry at **Wheal Coates** and **Towan Roath** mines, the abandoned engine houses lonely relics of a once-thriving period. You'll also notice the heads of many shafts close to the path, most of them fenced and in some cases topped with a steel-wire pyramid-shaped cage for safety. They have become colonised by the greater horseshoe bat, an endangered species you are unlikely to see unless you are passing at dusk.

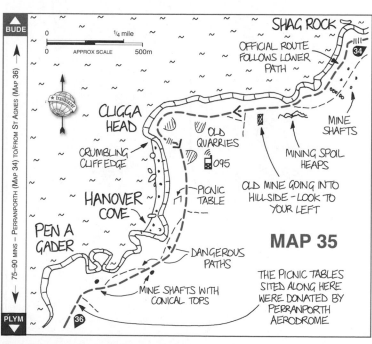

ROUTE GUIDE AND MAPS

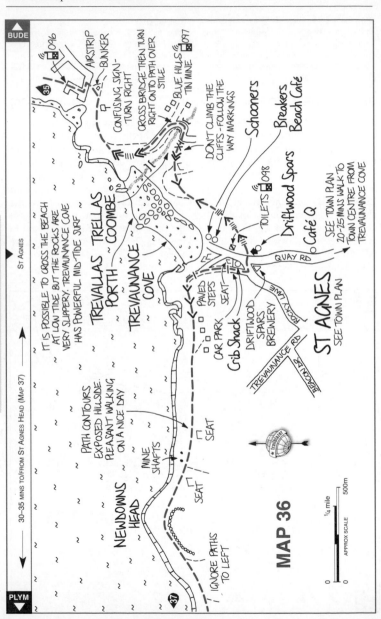

ROUTE GUIDE AND MAPS

BUDE

PLYM

St Agnes

30-35 MINS TO/FROM St Agnes Head (MAP 37)

AIRSTRIP
BUNKER
096
CONFUSING SIGN-
TURN RIGHT
CROSS BRIDGE THEN TURN
RIGHT ONTO PATH OVER
STILE
BLUE HILLS 097
TIN MINE
35
DON'T CLIMB THE
CLIFFS - FOLLOW THE
WAY MARKINGS
Schooners
Breakers
Beach Café
IT IS POSSIBLE TO CROSS THE BEACH
AT LOW TIDE BUT THE ROCKS ARE
VERY SLIPPERY. TREVAUNANCE COVE
HAS POWERFUL MID-TIDE SURF
TREVALLAS TRELLAS
PORTH ~ COOMBE
TREVAUNANCE
COVE
TOILETS 098
Driftwood Spars
Café Q
SEE TOWN PLAN
20-25 MINS WALK TO
TOWN CENTRE FROM
TREVAUNANCE COVE
QUAY RD
PAVED
STEPS
SEAT
CAR PARK
Crib Shack
Driftwood
Spars
Brewery
ST AGNES
SEE TOWN PLAN
ROCKY LANE
TREVAUNANCE RD
BEACON DR
PATH CONTOURS
EXPOSED HILLSIDE.
PLEASANT WALKING
ON A NICE DAY
MINE
SHAFTS
SEAT
SEAT
NEWDOWNS
HEAD
IGNORE PATHS
TO LEFT
37
MAP 36
¼ mile
500m
0
0
APPROX SCALE
trailblazer

TREVAUNANCE COVE MAP 36

Trevaunance Cove is small and rocky with a sandy beach at low tide. At mid tide the surf can be powerful. There is a pub with rooms and a couple of cafés here, or head inland to St Agnes for more options.

B&B is available at popular *Driftwood Spars* (☎ 01872-552428, 🖳 driftwoodspars .co.uk, **fb**; Quay Rd; 1S/9D/1T & 4Qd for families only; ☛; 🐾; from £41pp, sgl £52-61, sgl occ from £63), a tastefully decorated and enthusiastically run pub and restaurant, housed in a whitewashed 17th-century building. They serve decent pub food (Mon-

Sat noon-2.30pm & 6-9pm, Sun noon-8pm), and have extra outdoor seating in the *Crib Shack*, opposite the pub. They also own the small **Driftwood Spars Brewery** (☎ 01872-552591, 🖳 driftwoodsparsbrewery.co.uk; Tue-Sat noon-5pm) opposite, which brews half a dozen beers on site, including the award-winning Alfie's Revenge.

Nearby, *Schooners* (☎ 01872-553149, 🖳 schoonerscornwall.com, **fb**; summer daily noon-8pm; winter hours vary) peers over the beach with some choice tables outside on a narrow terrace. There's an extensive, if not cheap, menu to choose from as well as daily specials.

Next door, *Breakers Beach Café* (**fb**; daily 10am-4pm) has pasties and sandwiches. Following Quay Rd towards St Agnes you'll pass dog-friendly *Café Q* (☎ 01872-857045, **fb**; 🐾; daily 9am-4pm), with good coffee, pancakes and paninis.

ST AGNES

The 20- to 25-minute walk inland to the village of St Agnes is dotted with houses and cottages along the way.

A well-known local landmark not to be missed is the **Stippy Stappy**, a row of mine workers' cottages that climb the hill like steps. Also worth visiting is the small **St Agnes Museum** (☎ 01872-553228, 🖳 st agnesmuseum.org.uk; Penwinnick Rd; Easter-Oct daily 10.30am-5pm, free), housed inside the 19th-century Chapel of Rest. It has exhibits on the area's rich mining and maritime history.

For **groceries** there's Select Convenience (Mon-Sat 7.30am-10pm, Sun 8.30am-10pm), which also houses the local **post office** and an **ATM**, and Spar (daily 8am-10pm). There's also a Barclays ATM outside Fission Chip Shop. Boots **pharmacy** (Mon-Fri 9am-6pm, Sat 9am-5.30pm) is further up Vicarage Rd.

See p15 for details of the **Giant Bolster Festival** held here in May.

Where to stay

Campers need to go a little way out of the village to find *Presingoll Farm Caravan and Camping Park* (☎ 01872-552333, 🖳

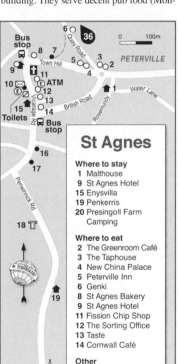

St Agnes

Where to stay
1 Malthouse
9 St Agnes Hotel
15 Enysvilla
19 Penkerris
20 Presingoll Farm Camping

Where to eat
2 The Greenroom Café
3 The Taphouse
4 New China Palace
5 Peterville Inn
6 Genki
8 St Agnes Bakery
9 St Agnes Hotel
11 Fission Chip Shop
12 The Sorting Office
13 Taste
14 Cornwall Café

Other
7 Stippy Stappy
10 Select Convenience ATM & PO
16 Boots Pharmacy
17 Spar
18 St Agnes Museum

ROUTE GUIDE AND MAPS

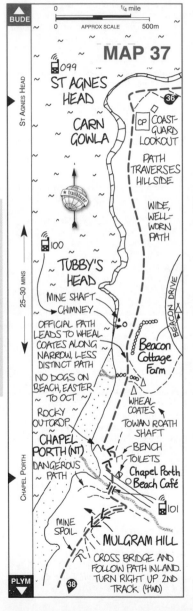

presingolfarm.co.uk, Penwinnick Rd; 🐾; adult/child £10/1.50), a working farm with a well-run campsite. There's a small **shop** and a laundry. Alternatively, further along the coast path towards Porthtowan is *Beacon Cottage Farm* (Map 37; ☎ 01872-552347, 🖳 beaconcottagefarmholidays .co.uk; 🐾; £12 for walkers; Easter-Oct), another nicely run site with a lovely sea-view location and a small **shop** selling essentials.

In the village proper, *Enysvilla* (☎ 01872-552137, 🖳 enysvilla.co.uk; 1D/2D, T or Tr; 🐾; £40-55, sgl occ £50-65) welcomes walkers.

In nearby Peterville, the ever-popular *Malthouse* (☎ 01872-553318, 07808-030034, 🖳 themalthousestagnes.co.uk; 2D en suite/2D shared facilities; 🐾; ⓛ £40pp, sgl occ £55) is the kind of B&B you seldom find now; a home from home, with a wonderfully welcoming host.

On Penwinnick Rd, just out of the village is *Penkerris* (☎ 01872-552262 or 07504-496037; 4D/1T/2D or Tr, most en suite; 🍷; 🐾; £25-42.50pp), a lovely detached Edwardian house with Virginia creeper climbing over it and a slightly fading ambience that only adds to the experience of staying here. It has been run by the same redoubtable lady for the past 20 years; she welcomes walkers and has written a book on local walks.

For pub accommodation, try *St Agnes Hotel* (☎ 01872-552307, 🖳 stagneshotel.co .uk; 1T/4D/1Qd; 🍷; 🐾; £50-80pp, sgl occ £80-140), opposite the church. They are refreshingly dog-friendly.

Where to eat and drink
Beach hut café *Genki* (☎ 01872-555858, 🖳 genkicornwall.co.uk, **fb**; Tue-Sun 9.30am-2pm) may be small in size but it's full of big flavours and fantastic food.

In Peterville, *The Taphouse* (☎ 01872-553095, 🖳 the-taphouse.com, **fb**; daily noon-3pm & 5-9pm) is a lively, unconventional, brightly coloured pub with decent food, more than 80 types of gin and live music some evenings.

Nearby, *The Peterville Inn* (☎ 01872-552406; 🖳 thepetervilleinn.co.uk, **fb**; food

Mon-Sat noon-2.30pm & 6-9pm) has some quality seafood on its menu (£14-22).

Beside The Taphouse, *The Greenroom Café* (**fb**; daily 9am-3.30pm) serves good coffee and breakfasts, plus cream teas.

Beside The Peterville Inn, *New China Palace* (☎ 01872-552688, **fb**; daily noon-2pm & 5-11pm) does Chinese food to take-away and eat-in.

Up in St Agnes itself, *St Agnes Bakery* (**fb**; 7.30am-3pm) is a hugely popular café with standout pastries, cakes and pasties, plus filled sandwiches and excellent coffee.

Over the road, the pub restaurant at *St Agnes Hotel* (see Where to stay; food daily 8am-9pm; open to all) also has a garden pizza shack (Mon-Fri 3-10pm, Sat-Sun noon-10pm).

Continuing along Vicarage Rd you'll pass the local chippy, *Fission Chip Shop*

(**fb**; Tue-Sat 5-8.30pm), before reaching *The Sorting Office* (**fb**; Mon-Fri 9am-3.30pm, Sat 9am-3pm, Sun 10am-3pm), a tiny coffee shop serving great coffee, filled baguettes and warm pastries. Then follows *Taste* (☎ 01872-552194, **fb**; Tue-Sat noon-2pm & 7-9pm, Sun noon-2pm), a good option for seafood as well as other locally sourced dishes (lunch mains £7-17, evening mains £15-25), but could be friendlier.

The quirky *Cornwall Café* (9.30am-4.30pm) is a crockery-filled Aladdin's cave of tea cups and china plates; and the perfect spot for a Cornish cream tea.

Transport

[See pp52-5 for details] Hopley's No 315 and the U1/U1A and Atlantic Coaster **bus** services all call here.

For a **taxi** call St Agnes Taxis (☎ 07778-436753, 🖳 stagnestaxis.com).

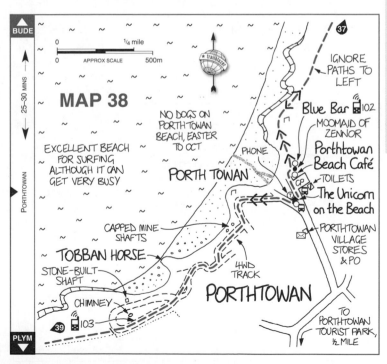

PORTHTOWAN   [MAP 38, p151]

Tiny Porthtowan is hardly even a village, but it has a fine beach. **Porthtowan Village Stores & Post Office** (☎ 01209-891210; daily 8am-7pm) stocks basic supplies, including bread and pasties.

The nearest **campsite** is *Porthtowan Tourist Park* (☎ 01209-890256, 🖳 porthtowantouristpark.co.uk; hiker & tent £14.95-19.95; Apr-Oct) about a mile away. It has a laundry room and a **shop** (daily 8.30-10.30am & 4.30-7.30pm) selling a few essentials like bread, milk, eggs and bacon.

The Unicorn on the Beach (☎ 01209-890381, 🖳 theunicornonthebeach.com), has had quite a revival since being taken over by new owners but, currently, if you wish to stay here the only accommodation is in a 12-bed surf house that has a 7-night minimum stay (4-night Oct-Mar). See their website for details. If it's just food and drink you're after, it's a great place for a pint and

some good quality pub grub (mains £14-18), either inside by the fire in winter, or out on the large decked terrace in summer.

Another fine place for food is the long-standing, hugely popular *Blue Bar* (☎ 01209-890329, 🖳 blue-bar.co.uk, **fb**; 🐾; food summer daily 10am-3pm & 6-9pm) which entices many walkers off the path with its unpretentious atmosphere, fine ales and no-nonsense menu (try the spice-tinged 'Dirty Chips' – chips with pulled pork, cheese and jalapeño peppers). Next door, *Porthtowan Beach Café* (🖳 porthtowanbeachcafe.com, **fb**; daily 10am-4pm plus summer evenings) does breakfasts, toasties, paninis and other light lunches.

For superior, locally made ice cream, pop next door to *Moomaid of Zennor* (🖳 moomaidofzennor.com; daily 9.30am-5pm).

Bus services include Hopley's No 315 to St Agnes and 304 to Truro, and the Atlantic Coaster. [See pp52-5 for details].

PORTHTOWAN TO PORTREATH   [MAPS 38-40]

For most of these **3 miles (5km, 1-1¼hrs)** the walking is alongside heavily fenced **MoD land** with frequent signs warning of dire penalties for straying from the path. It keeps to the cliff tops with spectacular views on the sea side but it is hard to ignore the concrete buildings and chain link fencing of Penhale Camp.

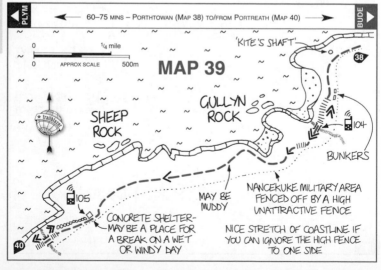

60–75 MINS – PORTHTOWAN (MAP 38) TO/FROM PORTREATH (MAP 40)

MAP 39

KITE'S SHAFT

GULLYN ROCK

SHEEP ROCK

BUNKERS

NANCEKUKE MILITARY AREA FENCED OFF BY A HIGH UNATTRACTIVE FENCE

MAY BE MUDDY

CONCRETE SHELTER- MAY BE A PLACE FOR A BREAK ON A WET OR WINDY DAY

NICE STRETCH OF COASTLINE IF YOU CAN IGNORE THE HIGH FENCE TO ONE SIDE

PEPPERPOT; WIND VANE AND SEAT. GOOD PLACE FOR A BREAK OR PICNIC WITH VIEWS OVER BEACH

PORTREATH BEACH CAN GET HEAVY SURF AND STRONG RIPS

NO ACCESS TO PIER AS TOO MANY PEOPLE HAVE BEEN WASHED OFF

GULL ROCK

MAY-SEPT

TURN LEFT IN FRONT OF HOUSES

GOODEN HEANE POINT

HORSE ROCK

PATH CLOSED DUE TO EROSION

MoD LAND

BLOCKHOUSE

PORTREATH BEACH

PORTREATH

SIGN SAYS GWITHIAN 6½ MILES

TURN RIGHT UP BATTERY HILL

TOILETS

CAR PARK

PO & ATM COSTCUTTER

TO YHA PORTREATH & NANCE FARM, 2 MILES

NO DOGS ON PORTREATH BEACH, EASTER-OCT

MAP 40

0 ¼ mile
0 APPROX SCALE 500m

WHERE TO STAY & EAT
1 CLIFF HOUSE
2 PORTREATH ARMS
3 PORTREATH BAKERY
4 TUNGSING CANTONESE
5 THE BASSET ARMS
6 THE HUB
7 THE WATERFRONT INN
8 THE ATLANTIC
9 BEACH CAFÉ

PORTREATH [MAP 40]

Portreath is a small community with options for refreshment or an overnight stop on the way to St Ives.

The row of shops opposite the Portreath Arms consists of a Costcutter **store** (daily 8am-9pm), which houses the **post office** (Mon-Wed & Fri 9am-1pm, 2-5pm, Sat 10am-12.30pm) and an **ATM** (£1.95 charge), and *Portreath Bakery* (☎ 01209-842612, ☐ portreathbakery.com; Mon-Sat 8am-4pm, Sun 9am-4pm) for

fresh coffee, filled rolls, pasties and marvellous pastry goods.

Where to stay

YHA Portreath (off Map 40; ☎ 01209-842244, ☐ yha.org.uk/hostel/yha-portreath, or ☐ mary.alway@btinternet.com; open all year; 21 beds; from £18pp) is at Nance Farm, in **Illogan**, a village 1½ miles from Portreath. It's a converted barn on a working farm, with a self-catering kitchen and drying room, but is a bit tricky to find; you'll probably need to call for directions. The No 47 **bus** (see pp52-5) goes to Illogan, but it is a half-mile walk to the hostel from Paynters Lane End bus stop.

B&B is available at the attractive *Cliff House* (☎ 01209-843847, 🖳 cliffhouseport reath.co.uk; 1D/1T/1Tr en suite, 2S shared facilities; 🐾; from £42.50pp, sgl £55, sgl occ £75), an ideal stopover and a great favourite with coast-path walkers. In the conservatory at the front of the house there are some fascinating old photos of Portreath when it was a thriving port for sailing ships.

Alternatively there are smart rooms at *Portreath Arms* (☎ 01209-842259, 🖳 the portreatharms.co.uk; 3D/2T/1Tr, most en suite; 🐾; from £37.50pp, sgl occ £55).

Where to eat

The windswept *Beach Café* (9.30am-3pm) is the only place that's genuinely by the beach. It does bacon baps (£3), burgers (£4-5) plus tea, coffee and snacks.

The Atlantic (☎ 01209-843490, **fb**; café 10am-5.30pm, takeaway to 6.30pm) is a good-looking modern place serving café food, booze and fish and chips; there's a takeaway window to one side.

Nearby, *The Hub* (**fb**; daily 9am-5pm) is also a licensed café, with seating in sun-warmed conservatories as well as outside beside a small stream. They do pizza (£7-11) and jacket potatoes (£5-6) plus cream teas (£6), paninis (£5.50) and the like.

As well as the *Portreath Arms* (see Where to Stay; food Mon-Sat noon-2pm & 6-9pm), which has a bar menu (mains £10-12) and a restaurant menu (most mains £12-15), there are two other pubs here: *The Waterfront Inn* (☎ 01209-842777, 🖳 the waterfrontinn.webs.com, **fb**; food Mon-Sat noon-3pm & 6-9pm, Sun noon-3pm) sits oddly alone in the middle of a car park, but does standard pub food at reasonable prices. The *Basset Arms* (☎ 01209-842077; 🖳 the bassetarms-portreath.foodanddrinksites.co .uk, **fb**; food daily noon-2pm & 5-8pm), set back from the road as you leave Portreath, is a better bet. The food is decent pub grub and the atmosphere more pleasant. They often have live music on Sunday afternoons.

Further down the same road is a Chinese restaurant, *Tungsing Cantonese* (☎ 01209-844672; Wed-Mon 4.45-8.45pm), which is closed on Tuesdays.

The No 47 and the Atlantic Coaster **bus** services call here. [See pp52-5].

PORTREATH TO GWITHIAN [MAPS 40-44]

This **8-mile (13km, 2-2¾hrs)** leg is nearly all on the cliff top through gorse and shrub with only a narrow path to walk on. Once you reach Hudder Cove and the spectacularly named **Hell's Mouth** you are well rewarded as the cliffs are filled with nesting birds while grey seals breed in the caves below Navax Point. The path here has been surfaced to suit the heavy use that it now gets from dog walkers and joggers who are able to park in the car parks close to the cliff edge.

Hell's Mouth Coffee House (**fb**; Map 43; summer Mon-Fri 10am-4.30pm, Sat-Sun 9.30am-5pm), just across the road from the coast path, makes for a

---

❏ **BEWARE, THESE CLIFFS ARE UNSTABLE...**

You are likely to see black and yellow triangular warning signs bearing these or similar words at several points along the South-West Coast Path, but they have particular significance at North Cliff, near Deadman's Cove (Map 42). On 23rd September 2011, geologist Richard Hocking captured video footage here of an estimated 200,000 tonnes of rock face collapsing into the sea, just days after the coastal path was diverted inland. So don't ignore those warning signs!

pleasant pitstop. They do bottled beers as well as coffees, breakfast baps (£3.50), ciabattas (£5.50-7) and ice creams.

Godrevy Point is in the care of the National Trust and is a popular place for picnics and recreation. The offshore lighthouse was the inspiration for Virginia Woolf's classic novel, *To the Lighthouse*. Written in 1927, it drew on her memories of holidays with her parents in St Ives; the lighthouse in the book is merely a device for the development of the plot. Plans to switch off the light permanently were shelved after vocal protests by fishermen and Virginia Woolf fans. From the NT car park at Godrevy the path follows a long stretch of dunes into **Gwithian** so you may want a break at Godrevy Beach Café (p157), which is in the car park, right by the coast path.

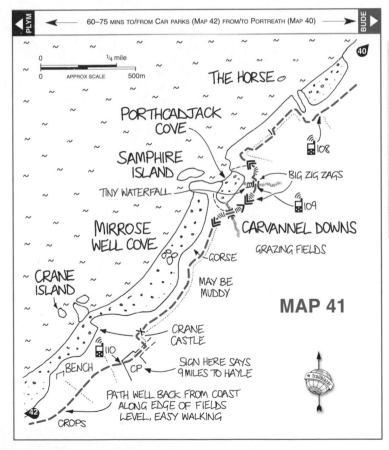

GWITHIAN [MAP 44, p158]

Gwithian is a sandy sort of place just inland from the dunes with the main road running through it bordered by a few houses. It offers several refreshment choices, but accommodation is rather limited.

In fact the only option for a single night here now is for **campers**, on the family-run *Gwithian Farm Campsite* (☎ 01736-753127, 🖳 gwithianfarm.co.uk; 🐾; hiker and tent £8-10), a welcoming, well-run site

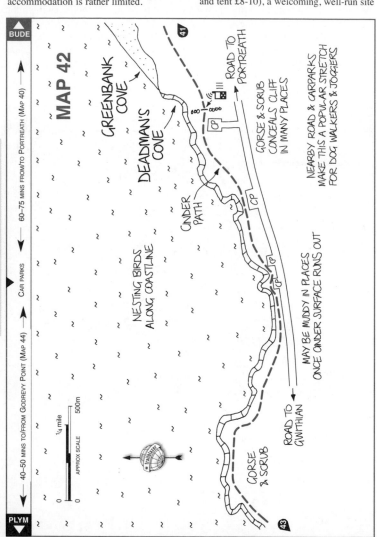

MAP 42

BUDE

PLYM

60-75 MINS FROM/TO PORTREATH (MAP 40)

CAR PARKS

40-50 MINS TO/FROM GODREVY POINT (MAP 44)

GREENBANK COVE

DEADMAN'S COVE

CINDER PATH

NESTING BIRDS ALONG COASTLINE

ROAD TO PORTREATH

GORSE & SCRUB CONCEALS CLIFF IN MANY PLACES

NEARBY ROAD & CARPARKS MAKE THIS A POPULAR STRETCH FOR DOG WALKERS & JOGGERS

CP

CP

CP

MAY BE MUDDY IN PLACES ONCE CINDER SURFACE RUNS OUT

ROAD TO GWITHIAN

GORSE & SCRUB

¼ mile

500m

APPROX SCALE

0

0

41

43

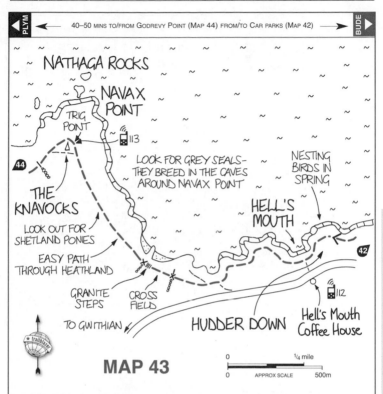

NATHAGA ROCKS

NAVAX POINT

TRIG POINT

113

LOOK FOR GREY SEALS– THEY BREED IN THE CAVES AROUND NAVAX POINT

NESTING BIRDS IN SPRING

THE KNAVOCKS

LOOK OUT FOR SHETLAND PONIES

EASY PATH THROUGH HEATHLAND

HELL'S MOUTH

42

GRANITE STEPS

CROSS FIELD

TO GWITHIAN

HUDDER DOWN

Hell's Mouth Coffee House

112

MAP 43

0   ¼ mile
0   APPROX SCALE   500m

ROUTE GUIDE AND MAPS

with a **shop** (8.30am-6.30pm), a coffee van (8am-noon), laundry and a clean, spacious shower block. They are happy to charge phones, and never turn walkers away.

For **food**, *Godrevy Beach Café* (☎ 01736-757999, **fb**; 10am-4/5pm) is handy, doing coffee, light bites and ice cream right beside the coast path. From here a pathway leads to the back of *The Rockpool* (☎ 01736-449990, 🖳 therockpoolbeachcafe .co.uk, **fb**; daily 10am-8pm), a more upmarket café, bar and grill serving burgers, pizza and seafood (mains from £13).

Further along the beach, though back slightly, through the dunes, is *The Jampot* (**fb**; summer daily 10am-5pm, winter Wed-Sun 10am-4pm), a laidback café serving

home-made cakes, toasties, hot rolls and cream teas. The food is cheap and there's local art on the walls.

Nearby, *Sunset Surf* (**fb**; 10am-4pm, plus Aug evenings) is very popular. This family-friendly café-bar serves breakfasts, cream teas, burgers and pasta and has plenty of garden seating.

The local pub, *The Red River Inn* (☎ 01736-753223, 🖳 red-river-inn.co.uk, **fb**; food noon-3pm & 4-9pm) does good food (mains £10-13, tapas £17 for four dishes), real ale and has a beer garden over the road.

The Atlantic Coaster **bus** stops here. [For details see pp52-5].

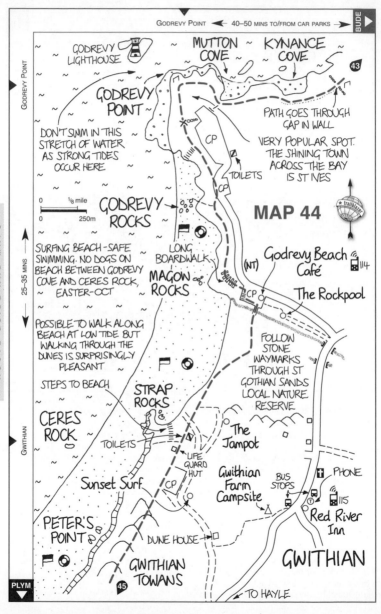

GODREVY POINT ◀— 40–50 MINS TO/FROM CAR PARKS —▶ BUDE ▶

GODREVY
LIGHTHOUSE

MUTTON ~ KYNANCE
COVE ~ COVE

43

GODREVY
POINT

Godrevy Point

PATH GOES THROUGH
GAP IN WALL

CP

DON'T SWIM IN THIS
STRETCH OF WATER
AS STRONG TIDES
OCCUR HERE

TOILETS

VERY POPULAR SPOT.
THE SHINING TOWN
ACROSS THE BAY
IS ST IVES

CP

★ trailblazer

0   ⅛ mile
0   250m

GODREVY
ROCKS

MAP 44

LONG
BOARDWALK

SURFING BEACH – SAFE
SWIMMING. NO DOGS ON
BEACH BETWEEN GODREVY
COVE AND CERES ROCK,
EASTER–OCT

MAGOW
ROCKS

(NT)

CP

Godrevy Beach
Café 114

The Rockpool

POSSIBLE TO WALK ALONG
BEACH AT LOW TIDE BUT
WALKING THROUGH THE
DUNES IS SURPRISINGLY
PLEASANT

FOLLOW
STONE
WAYMARKS
THROUGH ST
GOTHIAN SANDS
LOCAL NATURE
RESERVE

STEPS TO BEACH

STRAP
ROCKS

The Jampot

CERES
ROCK

TOILETS

LIFE
GUARD
HUT

Gwithian
Farm
Campsite

BUS
STOPS

PHONE

115

Sunset Surf

CP

Red River
Inn

PETER'S
POINT

DUNE HOUSE

GWITHIAN

45

GWITHIAN
TOWANS

TO HAYLE

ROUTE GUIDE AND MAPS

Godrevy Point

25–35 MINS

Gwithian

GWITHIAN TO HAYLE [MAPS 44-46]

For these **4 miles (6km, 1-1¼hrs)** you have the choice of either walking along the beach (very easy, with firm sand all the way), or taking the official coast path through the dunes.

Although it is continually up and down, the walk through the dunes is actually quite pleasant. It's a game of connect the dots as you follow the acorn posts with their yellow arrows from dune to dune and the sleepy undemanding scenery allows your mind to wander. Be aware, however, that if the sun is out, the dunes trap the heat and shelter you from the breeze; it can get very hot so take plenty of water.

The last part of this section, from **Hayle Towans** to **Hayle**, is through a small industrial area.

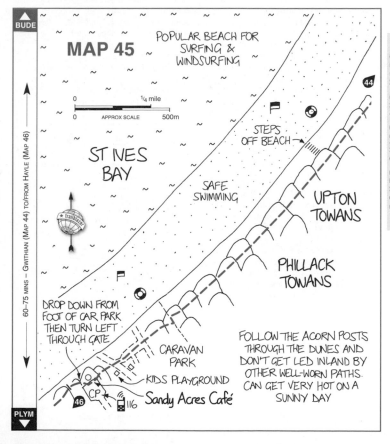

MAP 45

ST IVES BAY

POPULAR BEACH FOR SURFING & WINDSURFING

0   ¼ mile
0   APPROX SCALE   500m

STEPS OFF BEACH →

SAFE SWIMMING

UPTON TOWANS

PHILLACK TOWANS

DROP DOWN FROM FOOT OF CAR PARK THEN TURN LEFT THROUGH GATE

CARAVAN PARK

KIDS PLAYGROUND

CP

116

Sandy Acres Café

FOLLOW THE ACORN POSTS THROUGH THE DUNES AND DON'T GET LED INLAND BY OTHER WELL-WORN PATHS. CAN GET VERY HOT ON A SUNNY DAY

BUDE ▲

PLYM ▼

60–75 MINS – GWITHIAN (MAP 44) TO/FROM HAYLE (MAP 46)

ROUTE GUIDE AND MAPS

44

46

HAYLE TOWANS & HAYLE [MAP 46]

Hayle (*heyl* meaning estuary in Cornish) is recorded as having supplied tin as early as 1500BC and the Romans sailed their ships up as far as St Erth. Today the estuary is home to lobster boats, their catch going mostly to the continent.

For keen birdwatchers the muddy flats are good twitching territory and the RSPB owns a **nature reserve** on the estuary. Autumn and winter are particularly good for migrating and wintering wild fowl such as widgeon, teal, shelduck and waders, including dunlin, curlew and grey plover.

There are a few amenities in **Hayle Towans** (*towan* is Cornish for sand dune), before you reach **Hayle** proper, which has two centres: Copperhouse, around Fore Street, and Foundry Square, south of the railway station. It is a fair-sized town with services including a **post office** (Mon-Fri 9am-5.30pm) at 13 Penpol Terrace inside McColl's **newsagent** (Mon-Sat 6am-8pm, Sun 7am-8pm; with ATM). The **tourist information centre** (☎ 01736-754399; Mon, Wed & Fri 9.30am-1pm & 2-5pm, Sat 9.30am-12.30pm) is in the **library** (same hours) with **internet access** and wi-fi.

Also on Penpol Terrace is a small Spar **supermarket** (7am-10pm), or head to the huge Asda (Mon-Sat 7am-11pm, Sun 10am-4pm; with ATM) by South Quay.

There's a Boots **pharmacy** (Mon-Fri 8.30am-6pm, Sat 9am-1pm) at 44 Fore St and a **launderette** (Mon-Sat 9am-5pm) on Foundry Square.

One surprise for walkers coming out of the dunes may be the open-air **swimming pool** (**fb**; ☎ 01736-755005; May-Sep daily 11am-6pm; £3/2hrs), on East Quay, with the cute **Café Riviere** (11am-4pm) beside it.

The **Heritage Festival** (see p16) is held here every summer.

Hayle Towans

Campers can head to *Beachside Holiday Park* (☎ 01736-753080, 🖳 beachside.co .uk; tent pitch £12-38), one of a cluster of large holiday parks along the coast here. It's more set up for caravans, but walkers can pitch tents here too, albeit at a very high price in summer. Facilities include a shop, a

bar and even an outdoor pool. At the spacious *Penellen B&B* (☎ 01736-753777, 🖳 bedandbreakfasthotelcornwall.co.uk; 3D/ 2Tr, all en suite; £47.50-72.50pp) each room has a wonderful sea view, some from private balconies.

Approaching Hayle along the beach you pass a few cafés and bars, including tiny *Sandy Acres Café* (Map 45; daily 10am-5pm) which is on the dunes and has some outside seating, *The Bluff Inn* (**fb**; 9am-10pm), a café, bar and grill with a huge sea-facing terrace, then once past Hayle Towans, you'll see *Lula Shack* (☎ 01736-653653, 🖳 lulashack.co.uk, **fb**; 9am-9.30pm) which serves lots of seafood and BBQ offerings as well as more typical café fare.

Hayle

For **B&B** there's the modest but friendly *Mad Hatter* (☎ 01736-754241, 🖳 www. madhatterbandb-hayle.co.uk; 1D or T en suite, 1D/1T/1S/1Tr share facilities; ▼;

HAYLE – MAP KEY

Where to stay, eat and drink
1 The Cornubian Inn
2 Balti King
3 Mad Hatter
6 The Terrace
7 Eastern Empire
8 Café Riviere
9 Philp's Bakery
10 Lewy's Fish & Chips
11 Mr B's ice creams
14 Warrens Bakery
16 Salt
18 White Hart Hotel

Other
4 Boots Pharmacy
5 Tourist Information, library & internet access
12 McColl's newsagent, Post Office & ATM
13 SPAR supermarket
15 Asda supermarket
17 Launderette

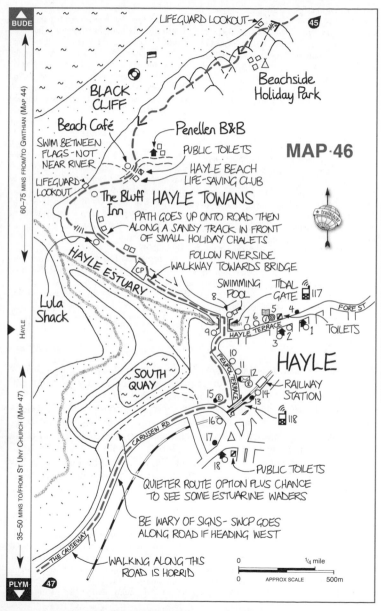

🐾; from £40pp, sgl occ £65, sgl £45) at 73 Fore St. Alternatively, there are rooms at **The Cornubia Inn** (☎ 01736-753351, 🖥 thecornubiainn.co.uk, **fb**; 3D/1T en suite; £45-60pp), a pub on Fore St, and at **White Hart Hotel** (☎ 01736-752322, 🖥 white harthotel-hayle.co.uk; 2S/15D/5'1'/2F; 🛏; from £50pp, sgl £90, sgl occ £100), an old coaching inn, housed in an elegant Regency building dating from 1838.

If everywhere in Hayle is full, you could also try *The Old Quay House* (see below) on the way to Lelant.

There are plenty of **food** options here. Grab Mediterranean dishes and pizza at **The Terrace** (☎ 01736-753745, 🖥 theter racehayle.com; daily 5.30-9.30pm; pizza £11-15), Indian at **Balti King** (☎ 01736-752001, 🖥 baltikingrestaurant.co.uk; daily 5.30-11.30pm), fish & chips at **Lewy's Fish and Chips** (**fb**; daily noon-2pm & 5-9pm) or Chinese at **Eastern Empire** (☎ 01736-753272, **fb**; daily 5.30-10pm).

For ice cream, look no further than **Mr B's** (☎ 01736-755808, 🖥 mrbsicecream.co .uk, **fb**; daily 11am-5pm).

One place that is very popular is **Philp's Bakery** (☎ 01736-755661, 🖥 philps bakery.co.uk; Mon-Sat 8.30am-6pm, Sun 10.30am-4.30pm), on East Quay, reckoned by some to bake the best pasties in Cornwall. It's hard to disagree. The more central **Warrens Bakery** (Mon-Sat 8.30am-5pm, Sun 10am-4pm) is good for pastries and a coffee.

Food is also served in **White Hart Hotel** (see Where to stay; daily noon-2pm & 6-8.30pm) and at the little **tearoom** attached to **Mad Hatter B&B** (**fb**; see Where to stay; Easter-Oct 10am-5pm); Cornish cream teas (£6) are, of course, available.

For a gastro pub experience, try **Salt** (☎ 01736-755862, 🖥 salt-hayle.co.uk; 🐾; 10am-late), with steaks (£14-16) and gourmet burgers (£11-13) on an otherwise fairly standard pub-grub menu. They have cocktails and live music on Friday evenings.

The Cornubia Inn (see Where to Stay) also does pub food.

Transport

[See pp50-5] The Atlantic Coaster **bus** service calls here as does the National Express 104 **coach** service.

Hayle is also a stop on the **railway** line (operated by GWR) to Penzance.

For a **taxi** ring Hayle Town Cars (☎ 07902-192090, 🖥 hayletowncars.co.uk.

HAYLE TO ST IVES   [MAPS 46-49]

This **6-mile (9.5km, 1¾-2½hrs)** stretch leaves Hayle along the busy Carnsew Rd and The Causeway crossing to the other side of the estuary. It's a delightful – if noisy to begin with – excursion in a stunning seascape.

Thankfully, the path soon leaves the busy roads behind and briefly follows the B3301 beneath the branch line between St Erth and St Ives. From here the route follows The Saltings; a quiet suburban walk through the outskirts of **Lelant**.

From **St Uny Church** the coast path follows the railway line into St Ives, firstly through more dunes then past **Carbis Bay**. The path beyond Carbis Bay winds its way through wooded cliffs to arrive at the broad sands of **Porthminster Beach** where there is an upmarket beach café (see p169) complete with decking.

LELANT & CARBIS BAY
                [MAP 47; MAP 48, p164]

Just before you reach **Lelant** (Map 47) you'll pass **The Old Quay House** (☎ 01736-753445, 🖥 quayhousehayle.co.uk, **fb**; 2D/2T/2Tr; from £75pp) which does pub **food** (noon-2.15pm & 5.30-8.15pm) and has six en suite **B&B** lodges set around a water-side garden; and **Birdies Bistro** (☎ 01736-759307, 🖥 birdiesbistro.co.uk, **fb**; Sun-Wed 9am-5pm, Thur-Sat 9am-10pm) with unusual offerings such as kedgeree (£14) and vegan dhal (£13) on the menu

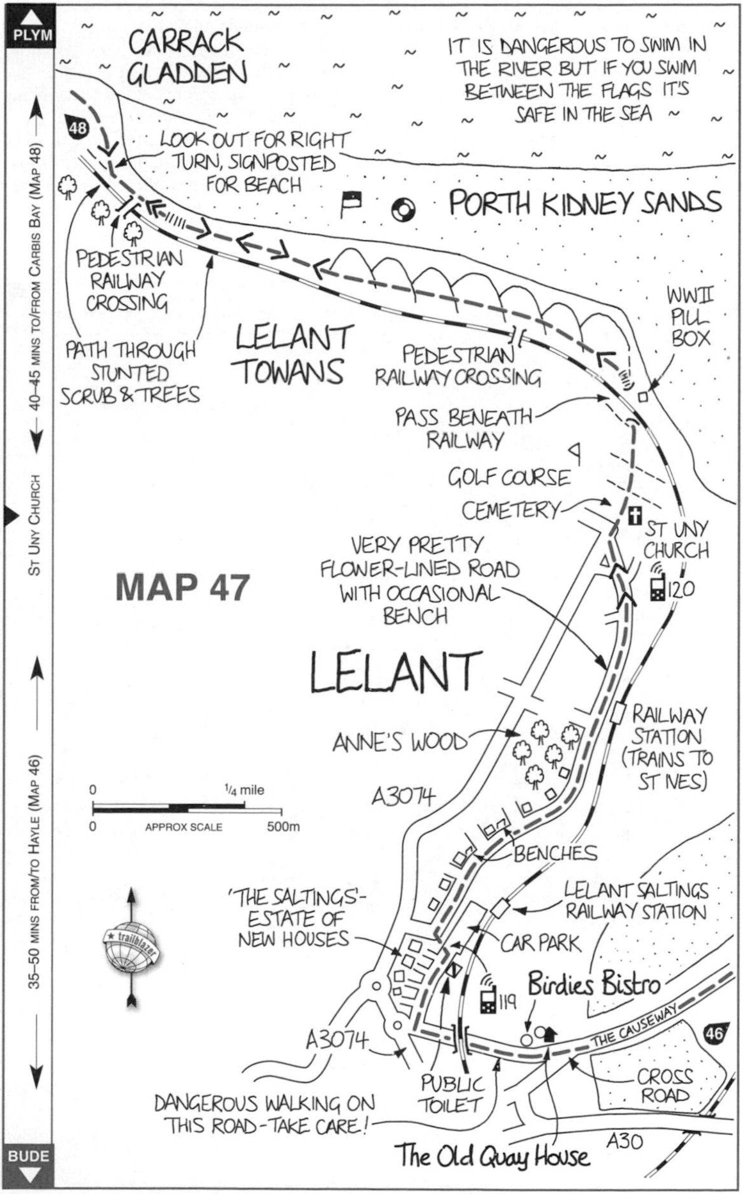

CARRACK GLADDEN

IT IS DANGEROUS TO SWIM IN THE RIVER BUT IF YOU SWIM BETWEEN THE FLAGS IT'S SAFE IN THE SEA

LOOK OUT FOR RIGHT TURN, SIGNPOSTED FOR BEACH

PORTH KIDNEY SANDS

PEDESTRIAN RAILWAY CROSSING

PATH THROUGH STUNTED SCRUB & TREES

LELANT TOWANS

PEDESTRIAN RAILWAY CROSSING

WWII PILL BOX

PASS BENEATH RAILWAY

GOLF COURSE

CEMETERY

VERY PRETTY FLOWER-LINED ROAD WITH OCCASIONAL BENCH

ST UNY CHURCH

MAP 47

120

LELANT

ANNE'S WOOD

A3074

RAILWAY STATION (TRAINS TO ST IVES)

0   ¼ mile
0   APPROX SCALE   500m

BENCHES

'THE SALTINGS' ESTATE OF NEW HOUSES

LELANT SALTINGS RAILWAY STATION

CAR PARK

Birdies Bistro

119

A3074

THE CAUSEWAY

46

CROSS ROAD

PUBLIC TOILET

A30

DANGEROUS WALKING ON THIS ROAD-TAKE CARE!

The Old Quay House

PLYM

48

40-45 MINS TO/FROM CARBIS BAY (MAP 48)

St UNY CHURCH

35-50 MINS FROM/TO HAYLE (MAP 46)

BUDE

ROUTE GUIDE AND MAPS

alongside burgers and salads. They also have prime views over the estuary from their garden.

In **Carbis Bay** (Map 48) there's a Tesco **supermarket** (Mon-Sat 8am-8pm, Sun 10am-4pm) and a number of B&Bs along the A3074, including the very smart *Chy-an-Gwedhen* (☎ 01736-798684, 🖥 chyangwedhen.com; 1S/3D/1T, all en suite; from £40pp, sgl £60-80; min 2 nights), with fabulous views over St Ives bay and local

oak-smoked haddock on offer for breakfast. As you continue on towards St Ives, you'll pass right by the multi-award-winning *Porthminster Beach Café* (see p169) with its gorgeous setting overlooking Porthminster beach and St Ives bay.

The Land's End Coaster, T2 and No 17 **bus** services stop at both places and St Ives Bus Co's No 1 stops at Tesco Carbis Bay. [See pp52-5 for details.]

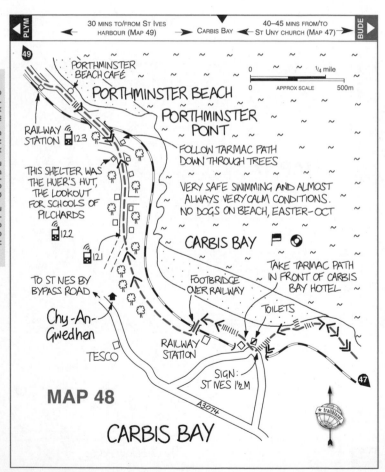

MAP 48

CARBIS BAY

ST IVES [MAP 49, p167]

Pretty St Ives has attracted artists for years and is certainly a place worth spending some time in, even if it's just to chill out, and soak up the charms of its harbour and tightly packed fishermen's cottages. It is a very popular destination, though, so can get incredibly overcrowded with tourists in the height of summer. If you are coming in the main season (particularly July and August) it is advisable to book accommodation well in advance.

The flagship gallery is **Tate St Ives** (see box p168), Porthmeor Beach. It's well worth a visit and has a fine top-floor *café* (Mar-Oct daily 10am-4.50pm, Nov-Feb Tue-Sun 10am-4.50pm). If you're interested in art you should put an hour aside to visit the **Barbara Hepworth Museum** (also see box p168).

There are numerous small **galleries** in St Ives with art on display but also usually for sale with prices ranging from moderately expensive to ludicrous. Your wanders round the town might also bring you to the doors of the **St Ives Museum** (☎ 01736-796005; Easter-Oct Mon-Fri 10.30am-4.30pm, Sat 10.30am-3.30pm, last admission 30 mins before closing; £3), at Wheal Dream, by the harbour front. The exhibits include memorabilia of local significance such as the fishing industry, shipwrecks, lighthouses and lifeboats.

In addition to all this several **festivals** (see pp15-16) are held here every year.

Services

The **tourist information centre** (☎ 01736-796297, 🖳 visitstives.org.uk; daily Mon-Sat 9.30am-5pm, Sun 10am-3pm, winter closed Sun) is in the **library** (☎ 01736-795377 or ☎ 0300-1234111, 🖳 cornwall.gov.uk/library; Mon-Sat 9.30am-4pm), on Gabriel St, which offers **internet access** for one hour at a time.

Various **banks,** including Barclays and HSBC, have branches with ATMs on High St. The main **post office** (Mon-Fri 9am-5.30pm, Sat 9am-12.30pm) is at the end of Fore St on the harbour front and has an **ATM** outside it. On The Stennack is a **launderette** (daily 8.30am-8.30pm) with

an enormous mural on its outside wall. Further up the same road is a **medical centre** (Stennack Surgery; ☎ 01736-793333, 🖳 thestennacksurgery.co.uk) which has a minor injuries unit (Mon-Fri 8am-8pm). There are several **pharmacies** including Leddra Chemist (Mon-Fri 9am-12.30pm & 1.30-5.30pm, Sat 1.30-5.30pm) at 7 Fore St. There are also several **convenience stores** dotted around town, including two branches of the Co-op (7am-11pm), one on The Stennack and the other on Tregenna Hill.

For **camping gear**, there's a Mountain Warehouse (Mon-Fri 9am-7pm, Sat 9am-5.30pm, Sun 11am-5pm) on Fore St.

St Ives Bookseller (🖳 stives-bookseller.co.uk; Mon-Fri 9am-9pm, Sat 9am-8pm, Sun 10am-4pm) has lots of local-interest books, including some St Ives-themed children's books.

The **cinema** is opposite **St Ives Theatre** (🖳 www.stives-cornwall.co.uk/st-ives-theatre), the venue used by an enterprising local drama company, Kidz-R-Us (🖳 kidzrus.net).

Where to stay

Campsites and hostels For **campers,** *Ayr Holiday Park* (off Map 49; ☎ 01736-795855, 🖳 ayrholidaypark.co.uk; tent & two adults £18-31) is about 10 to 15 minutes' walk from the harbour. Solo hikers are charged £16 in high season. Alternatively, consider Trevalgan Touring Park, see p172.

Hostel accommodation is available at *Cohort Hostel* (☎ 01736-791664, 🖳 stayatcohort.co.uk; 2T/1Tr/40 dorm beds; from £20pp), a modern hostel that is clean, colourful and well-run. Common areas are large, comfortable and well-equipped (sofas, TVs, kitchen, outdoor courtyard), and the bunks are solidly made and of good quality, but some of the dorms, and the showers, are extremely cramped. There's no café, but they do sell coffee and booze in the common room.

B&Bs, pubs and guesthouses There are some B&Bs up by the bus terminus, overlooking the harbour.

The Rookery (☎ 01736-799401, 🖥 therookerystives.com; 1S/4D/1Tr/1Qd all en suite; ➤; from £42.50pp, sgl £55-65), at 8 The Terrace, welcomes walkers. Most rooms have a sea view. A couple of doors up, at No 10, is *Golden Hind B&B* (☎ 01736-796632, 🖥 goldenhindstives.com; 3D, all en suite; from £67.50pp; min 2/3 nights), with beautful rooms, each with sea views.

Just round the corner, at 7 Porthminster Terrace, is *Rivendell* (☎ 01736-794923, 🖥 rivendell-stives.co.uk; 4D/1T, all en suite; from £50pp; min 2 nights), a smart Edwardian former Sea Captain's house. Next door, at No 9, is *Carlill* (☎ 01736-796738, 🖥 carlillguesthouse.co.uk; 1S/2D/1T/1Tr; Ⓛ; £40-50pp), which also offers luggage transfer.

In the old part of town, down by the harbour, there are some lovely, intimate, fisherman's cottages, some of which offer B&B. On Bunker's Hill, a cobbled lane just off Fore St, *Grey Mullet* (☎ 01736-796635, greymulletguesthouse@gmail.com, **fb**; 1S/5D/1T; ➤; from £35pp), with hanging baskets festooning the front, and low wood-beamed ceilings inside, is housed in an old stone building that dates from 1776, and is an absolute pleasure to stay in.

Also characterful, *Downlong Cottage* (☎ 01736-798107, 🖥 downlongcottage.co

.uk; 3D/1T/1Tr, all en suite; £40-50pp) is at 95 Back Rd East and welcomes one-night stays.

There are also B&B rooms at nearby *Sloop Inn* (☎ 01736-796584, 🖥 sloop-inn .co.uk, **fb**; 12D/3T/4Qd, most en suite; ➤; 🐾; £65-85pp, sgl occ 25% off room rate; min 3 nights). Believed to date from around 1312, it's one of Cornwall's oldest pubs.

Overlooking Harbour Beach, *Lifeboat Inn* (☎ 01736-794123; 🖥 lifeboatinnst ives.co.uk, **fb**; 3D or T/2Qd all en suite; 🐾; from 75pp, sgl occ from £150; min 2 nights) has smart sea-facing rooms, plus two apartments that can sleep four people.

At 2 High St, *The Queens Hotel* (☎ 01736-796468, 🖥 queenshotelstives.com; 8D/2F; from £80pp; min 2 nights) is a smart, central gastropub with bright, modern rooms.

Hotels At *The Western Hotel* (☎ 01736-795277, 🖥 hotelstives.com; 2S/7D/2T/3Tr; ➤; from £60pp, sgl from £90), on Gabriel St, rooms are simple but smart enough, and breakfast costs an extra £5. The bar here is the lively Kettle 'n' Wink, known as the 'Kidleywink'; good for live music. The name comes from a time when ale houses kept smuggled brandy in a kettle; to order a glass, you needed to wink surreptitiously in the direction of the kettle.

ST IVES – MAP KEY

Where to stay
1 Downlong Cottage
4 Sloop Inn
6 Grey Mullet
15 Lifeboat Inn
18 Queens Hotel
21 Cohort Hostel
22 The Western Hotel
26 Pedn-Olva Hotel
27 The Rookery
28 Golden Hind B&B
29 Carlill
30 Rivendell

Where to eat and drink
2 Mermaid Seafood Restaurant
3 Beachcomber Café
4 Sloop Inn
5 Balancing Eel
7 Porthmeor Café & Bar
8 The Beach Restaurant
9 St Ives Bakery
10 Myrings Fudge & Rock Shop
11 Peppers Pasta & Pizzeria

12 The Union Inn
13 The Castle Inn
14 Talat Thai Tapas
15 Lifeboat Inn
16 Harbour Fish & Chips
17 Scoff Troff Café
18 Queens Hotel
19 The Golden Lion
20 Coasters
23 Rajpoot
24 The Mex
25 Blas Burger Works

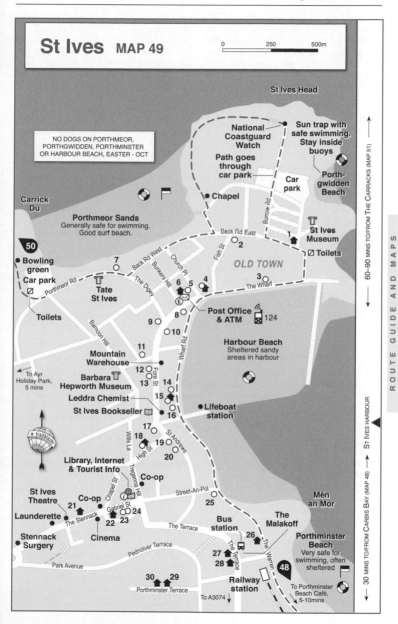

St Ives MAP 49

0   250   500m

St Ives Head

National Coastguard Watch

Sun trap with safe swimming. Stay inside buoys

Path goes through car park

Porthgwidden Beach

Car park

Chapel

NO DOGS ON PORTHMEOR, PORTHGWIDDEN, PORTHMINSTER OR HARBOUR BEACH, EASTER - OCT

Carrick Du

Porthmeor Sands
Generally safe for swimming. Good surf beach.

St Ives Museum

Toilets

Back Rd East

50

Bowling green
Car park

7

Back Rd West

Church Pl

Burkers Hill

The Digey

Porthmeor Rd

Fish St

OLD TOWN

2

5   4

6

3

The Wharf

1

Tate St Ives

Post Office & ATM

124

8

9

10

Harbour Beach
Sheltered sandy areas in harbour

Barmoon Hill

11

Mountain Warehouse

To Ayr Holiday Park, 5 mins

12

Fore St

13

14

Barbara Hepworth Museum

15

Leddra Chemist

16

St Ives Bookseller

Lifeboat station

17

Wills La

18

19

St Andrews

20

High St

Library, Internet & Tourist Info

Tregenna Hill

Co-op

Chapel St

St Ives Theatre

Co-op

21

Gabriel St

Street-An-Pol

25

Mén an Mor

Launderette

The Stennack

22

23

24

Cinema

The Terrace

Bus station

26

The Malakoff

Porthminster Beach
Very safe for swimming, often sheltered

Stennack Surgery

Pednolver Terrace

Park Avenue

27

28

The Warren

The Terrace

30   29

Porthminster Terrace

Railway station

To A3074

To Porthminster Beach Café, 5-10mins

48

60–90 MINS TO/FROM THE CARRACKS (MAP 51)

ST IVES HARBOUR

30 MINS TO/FROM CARBIS BAY (MAP 48)

ROUTE GUIDE AND MAPS

Close to the bus station, down the steps to The Warren, is a lovely hotel, **Pedn-Olva** (☎ 01736-796222, 🖳 pednolva .co.uk, **fb**; 2S/19D/4T/2Tr/3Qd; 🍴; from £62.50pp, sgl from £120), albeit with very high room rates in peak season. It is owned by St Austell Brewery and has a bar/restaurant looking out over the bay.

Where to eat and drink

St Ives has a seemingly endless number of eateries, suiting all tastes and budgets. Of course, fresh fish is often the order of the day, with langoustine, crab, line-caught bass, bream, monkfish and scallops all featuring prominently on menus around the harbour.

Fast food For a gourmet take on traditional fish & chips, try **Harbour Fish & Chips** (☎ 01736-799295, 🖳 harbourfish andchips.co.uk; noon-10pm), which has restaurant seating and sells beer and wine too. **The Beach Restaurant** (☎ 01736-798798, 🖳 beachrestaurant.co.uk, **fb**; 9.30am-10pm) is similar, with eat-in or takeaway options. For a traditional fish 'n'

chip takeaway head to **Balancing Eel** (**fb**; noon-2pm & 5-7.30pm). **Rajpoot** (☎ 01736-795307, 🖳 rajpootstives.co.uk, **fb**; 5-6 Gabriel St; daily 5.30-10.30pm) is a good bet for Indian food, but bring your own booze as it's unlicensed. Practically next door is **The Mex** (☎ 01736-797658, 🖳 themex-stives.co.uk, **fb**; Mon-Sat 5-8pm) where Mexican mains cost £10-13.

Those with a sweet tooth shouldn't miss a visit to **Myrings Fudge & Rock Shop** (10am-5pm), a family-run Cornish fudge business that's been going for more than 30 years. If you want to thank the neighbour for feeding the cat while you're away, they also do mail order so you can send a box home rather than lugging it round with you.

There are nearly as many bakeries in St Ives as there are seagulls. Our favourite is **St Ives Bakery** (☎ 01736-79888, 🖳 stivesbakery.co.uk; Mon-Fri 9am-5pm, Sat-Sun 9am-4pm) on the corner of Fore St and The Digey.

Pubs There are numerous old pubs in the town. Most people gravitate to the harbour

---

❏ ART IN ST IVES

It was the quality of light and the landscape which first attracted artists to St Ives and is still inspiring them today. Most modern art histories of Cornwall start with Turner's visit in 1811; however, 1928 is when the development of St Ives as an artists' colony really began with a meeting of Alfred Wallis, Ben Nicholson and Christopher Wood.

Tate St Ives (☎ 01736-796226, 🖳 tate.org.uk/visit/tate-st-ives; Mar-Oct daily 10am-5.20pm, last admission 5pm, Nov-Feb Tue-Sun 10am-4.20pm, last admission 4pm; £10.50) was built on the site of the town's old gas works. The gallery has no static collection and instead displays exhibitions of selected works from the national Tate collection. Even if you are not a supporter of modern art you are bound to find something of interest.

Barbara Hepworth Museum and Sculpture Garden (☎ 01736-796226, 🖳 tate.org.uk/visit/tate-st-ives/barbara-hepworth-museum; same opening hours as the Tate; £7) is on the site of the former studio of Barbara Hepworth, a well-known sculptor who worked mainly with stone and bronze. Some of her sculptures are big enough to walk inside and around so that you can study every angle. Her studio has been preserved exactly as it was when she died in 1975 and there is a collection of her sculptures in the garden; a very peaceful place to spend a morning or afternoon watching each work change with the movement of the sun.

You can buy a joint ticket to both the Tate and Barbara Hepworth Museum for £14.50. At the time of research, tickets had to be purchased online in advance.

for an evening stroll, and the *Lifeboat Inn* (see Where to stay; food daily noon-3pm & 5-9pm) is right at the heart of things; there's a decent range of seafood here, as well as pub classics (most mains £12-14). Has Sky TV too. The *Sloop Inn* (see Where to stay; food served 9-11am, noon-3pm & 5-10pm) has plenty of character with low beams, slate floors and wooden benches. You can eat in the main pub (if you can find a table), on the Upper Deck terrace (adults only), or upstairs at **The Captain's Table** (☎ 01736-796584; daily 6-10pm), where booking is advisable. Most mains are £11-15.

The Castle Inn (☎ 01736-796833; 🖳 the-castle-cornwall.co.uk, **fb**; 🐾 ; food Mon-Sat noon-2.30pm & 6-8.30pm, Sun noon-5pm), 16 Fore St, lies back from the seafront and feels a little off the tourist trail, though there is plenty to attract you here, including the building's old granite walls, stained-glass windows, fine real ales and reasonably priced food. Next door is *The Union Inn* (☎ 01736-796486, **fb**; food daily noon-3pm & 5.30-9pm), where most mains cost £10-14.

The Golden Lion (☎ 01736-797935, **fb**; food noon-9.30pm; 🐾) is central and is good value too, with a number of mains costing less than a tenner. It's also the place to come in the town if you're after local cider. Up the road, *The Queens Hotel* (see Where to stay; food Mon-Sat noon-2.30pm & 5.30-9pm, Sun noon-3.30pm & 5-9pm) serves burgers and good-quality pub classics (mains £11.50-13.50).

Cafés The friendliest café in town, and certainly the most family-focused, is *Scoff Troff Café* (☎ 01736-797341; 🖳 scofftroff .co.uk, **fb**; Mon & Tue 8am-5pm, Wed-Sat 8am-9pm, Sun 9am-5pm), where you'll be greeted with a warm welcome, good strong coffee and all-day breakfasts that include veggie and vegan options. There's pizza, pasta dishes and other delights some evenings.

Another friendly café, and off the main strip in a side street so usually a bit quieter than other places, is *Coasters* (10am-6pm) where you can get toasties (£6.50), coffee and cakes, and cream teas (£6.95).

Further along The Wharf, so with great views over the harbour, *Beachcomber Café* (**fb**; daily 10am-5pm) does standout cakes and scones, plus light lunches such as crab sandwiches. It's only small, but has seating inside and out.

For proper beach-side cafés, you need to walk away from the harbour a short distance. With its greenhouse-like all-glass walls, *Porthmeor Café & Bar* (☎ 01736-793366, 🖳 porthmeor-beach.co.uk; summer 9am-10.30pm, winter 9am-5pm, Fri & Sat 6-9pm) offers unrivalled sea views from its perch overlooking Porthmeor beach. They do lunchtime tapas (£2.75-9.95) and evening meals (£12.95-18.50) as well as coffee, cream teas and breakfasts.

Even better, though you may need to book a table, is the multi-award-winning *Porthminster Beach Café* (Map 48; ☎ 01736-795352, 🖳 porthminstercafe.co.uk; summer daily 9am-10pm, winter Tue-Sun noon-3pm & 6-9pm), 15 minutes' walk south of the harbour. You can have coffee on the decked area right on the beach or dine inside on something more substantial, looking out over St Ives Bay. Expect to pay restaurant prices for lunchtime and evening meals (seafood mains £16-32).

Restaurants An absolute gem is *Blas Burgerworks* (☎ 01736-797272, 🖳 blas burgerworks.co.uk, **fb**; The Warren; Feb-Nov Tue-Sat 5-10pm; peak season daily noon-9.30pm) an intimate restaurant with only a small number of tables. Local organic produce is their focus, and their burgers (£14-15) are stupendously tasty.

For Italian, head to *Peppers Pasta & Pizzeria* (☎ 01736-794014, 🖳 peppers-st ives.co.uk, 22 Fore St; daily 5.30-9.30pm).

A seafood restaurant quietly operating away from the mayhem surrounding the harbour is *Mermaid Seafood Restaurant* (☎ 01736-796816, 🖳 mermaidstives.co.uk, **fb**; Mon-Sat 6-9pm, most mains £16-23), aptly located at 21 Fish St.

There's Thai tapas (£5-9) amongst other spicy dishes back on the harbour at *Talay Thai* (☎ 01736-795157, 🖳 talaythai .kitchen; daily Mon-Thur 4-10pm, Fri-Sun noon-10pm; eat in or takeaway).

Transport

[See pp50-5] Services from the **bus station** at The Malakoff include the Atlantic Coaster, the Land's End Coaster, No 17 to Penzance and 16A to Zennor, plus St Ives Bus Co's No 1.

The **railway station** is at Porthminster Beach. Trains (operated by GWR) run to St Erth where you must change for mainline services but the ride to Lelant Saltings is a delightful short journey. Many folk do the trip both ways for the sheer fun of it but you could walk to Lelant and get the train back in an afternoon; a great little excursion.

For a **taxi**, try ACE Cars (☎ 01736-797799, 🖥 acecarstives.co.uk).

ST IVES TO ZENNOR HEAD [MAPS 49-52]

Although the next **6 miles (10km, 1¾-2½hrs)** are pretty hard going, they are also amongst the most stunning. Often cited as the toughest section of the whole path, this is mostly due to what is underfoot rather than any particularly nasty ascent. The path hugs the contours of the coastline, sending you on an endless series of ups and downs as it travels through boggy fields and across rough and rocky terrain. The gradients aren't as severe as the sections around Port Isaac or Crackington Haven. The problem is you need to keep your eyes on the ground, particularly in wet weather, which prolongs the section.

While the weathered and windblown landscape is reward enough, there's also much evidence of its ancient occupation, if you care to venture a little inland, in the form of ancient stone circles and quoits (see box on p174). It is little wonder that many artists found inspiration here.

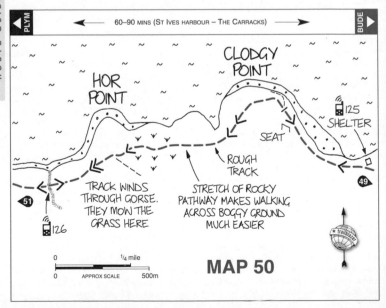

MAP 50

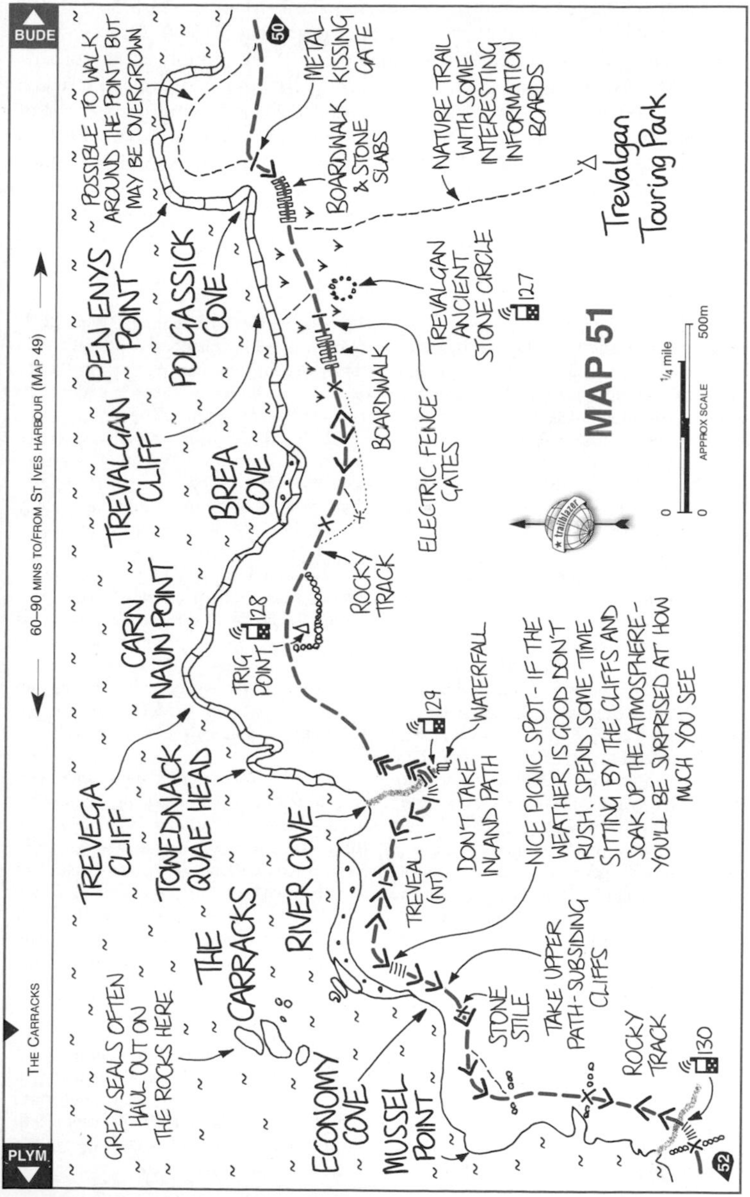

BUDE

← 60–90 MINS TO/FROM ST IVES HARBOUR (MAP 49) →

THE CARRACKS

PLYM

50

POSSIBLE TO WALK AROUND THE POINT BUT MAY BE OVERGROWN

METAL KISSING GATE

BOARDWALK & STONE SLABS

NATURE TRAIL WITH SOME INTERESTING INFORMATION BOARDS

Trevalgan Touring Park

PEN ENYS ~ POINT

TREVALGAN CLIFF

POLGASSICK COVE

BREA COVE

TREVALGAN ANCIENT STONE CIRCLE

127

BOARDWALK

ELECTRIC FENCE GATES

MAP 51

¼ mile

0   500m

0   APPROX SCALE

CARN NAUN POINT

ROCKY TRACK

TRIG POINT 128

TREVEGA CLIFF

TOWEDNACK QUAE HEAD

RIVER COVE

129

WATERFALL

DON'T TAKE INLAND PATH

TREVEAL (NT)

NICE PICNIC SPOT – IF THE WEATHER IS GOOD DON'T RUSH, SPEND SOME TIME SITTING BY THE CLIFFS AND SOAK UP THE ATMOSPHERE – YOU'LL BE SURPRISED AT HOW MUCH YOU SEE

THE ~ CARRACKS

GREY SEALS OFTEN HAUL OUT ON THE ROCKS HERE

ECONOMY COVE

MUSSEL POINT

STONE STILE

TAKE UPPER PATH-SUBSIDING CLIFFS

ROCKY TRACK

130

52

ROUTE GUIDE AND MAPS

Campers can stay at *Trevalgan Touring Park* (Map 51; ☎ 01736-791892, 🖳 trevalgantouringpark.co.uk, **fb**; non-electric pitches £13.50-39; May-Sep), halfway along this stage, but it is hideously expensive in high season for solo hikers who have to pay the full rate for a pitch (£39), and at the time of research you had to book pitches in advance. It's reached from the path by a series of signposts describing the flora and fauna of the area. You can also get here on Royal Buses No 44 service (🖳 royalbuses.co.uk; July-end Sep daily 1-2/hr) from Stennack Surgery in St Ives.

Although the tiny village of **Zennor** is a 10- to 15-minute walk inland, walkers who don't visit are missing a treat.

ZENNOR   [MAP 52]

Zennor seems to emerge from the rocky landscape itself, surrounded as it is by granite tors and outcrops, boulder-strewn fields with their high stone walls and the slate and granite cliffs of the coastline. The village has attracted its share of outsiders for centuries, not least the author DH Lawrence and his wife Frieda who lived at Higher Tregerthen Farm, near Zennor, for a period during World War I.

Zennor is a tiny place with the few houses clustered together round the *Tinners Arms* pub (see Where to stay, eat and drink) and the 12th-century granite **church of St Senara** (🖳 zennorchurch .com), neither of which should be missed.

Take a moment to look inside the church at the **Mermaid's Chair**, with its carving of a mermaid on a medieval bench end. The date of the carving is unknown but is thought to be from the 15th century. At that time the symbol of a mermaid was used to teach Cornish church-goers about the two natures of Christ – human and divine. Mermaids and mermen were often portrayed in carvings and paintings in Cornish churches, but this is one of the very few which has survived.

Where to stay, eat and drink

The famous *Tinners Arms* (☎ 01736-796927, 🖳 tinnersarms.com; 2S share facilities/2D en suite; 🐾; £60-75pp, sgl £70-80) has accommodation in an adjoining building called the **White House** (🖳 whitehousezennor.com). The lovely, simple bedrooms are a pleasure with crisp white linen and plain white walls. The pub also

serves great **food** (daily noon-3.30pm & 5-7pm); the menu changes frequently with choices such as moules marinière (£12.50) or salmon and cod fishcakes in sweet chilli sauce (£14). The stone-flagged floors, oak benches and Cornish beer all add to the charm. On Thursday nights musicians gather in the pub (outside in summer) and sessions begin with fiddles, guitar and penny whistle until closing time; all in all, a fantastic Cornish experience.

About half a mile along the road, in the direction of Gurnard's Head (Treen), is a lovely **B&B** called *Tregeraint House* (☎ 01736-797061, 🖳 www.cornwall-online.co .uk/tregeraint-house; 2D/1T, shared facilities; from £45pp, sgl occ £50), artistically decorated and in a secluded setting. Walkers are made to feel very welcome here.

A short walk from the pub is the lovely cafe-tearoom *Moomaid of Zennor* (☎ 01736-793591, 🖳 moomaidofzennor.com, **fb**; daily 9.30am-5.30pm) which serves teas, coffees, sandwiches, cakes, cream teas and its own speciality ice cream, which you'll find at other places along the coast path. The location is charming, too: beside a small stream within the grounds of the former Old Wayside Museum.

Transport

[See pp52-5] The **bus** stop is on the main road, a sharp sprint from the pub if you have lingered too long over your pint. Zennor is on the Land's End Coaster route; the 16A also stops here, as does the No 7.

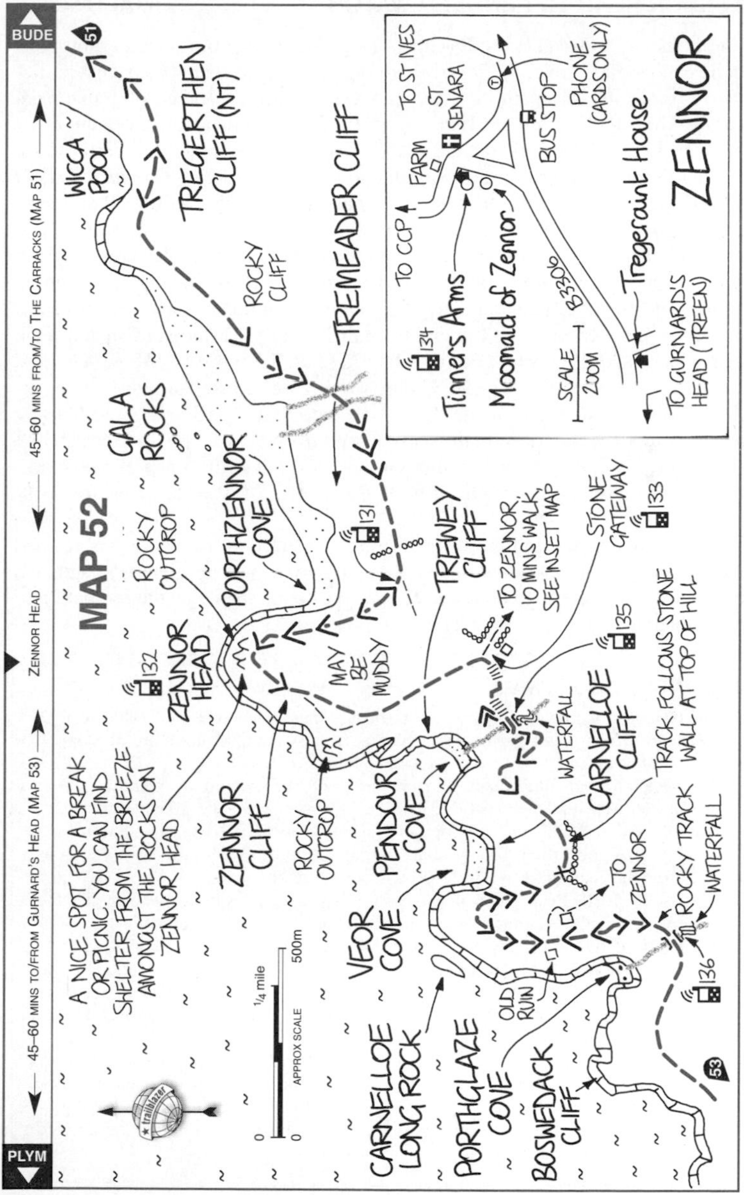

BUDE
51

TREGERTHEN CLIFF (NT)

WICCA POOL

45–60 MINS FROM/to The Carracks (MAP 51)

TREMEADER CLIFF

ROCKY CLIFF

GALA ROCKS

ROCKY OUTCROP

PORTHZENNOR COVE

MAP 52

ZENNOR HEAD

ZENNOR HEAD

ZENNOR CLIFF

131

MAY BE MUDDY

TRENEY CLIFF

132

A NICE SPOT FOR A BREAK OR PICNIC. YOU CAN FIND SHELTER FROM THE BREEZE AMONGST THE ROCKS ON ZENNOR HEAD

45–60 MINS TO/FROM GURNARD'S HEAD (MAP 53)

ZENNOR HEAD

ROCKY OUTCROP

VEOR COVE

PENDOUR COVE

TO ZENNOR, 10 MINS WALK, SEE INSET MAP

STONE GATEWAY

133

135

WATERFALL

CARNELLOE CLIFF

TRACK FOLLOWS STONE WALL AT TOP OF HILL

CARNELLOE LONG ROCK

PORTHGLAZE COVE

BOSWEDACK CLIFF

OLD RUIN

TO ZENNOR

ROCKY TRACK

WATERFALL

136

53

N

APPROX SCALE

0   ¼ mile

0   500m

PLYM

INSET:

TO ST IVES
ST SENARA

PHONE (CARDS ONLY)

FARM

TO CCP

BUS STOP

Tinners Arms

134

Moomaid of Zennor

Tregeraint House

ZENNOR

SCALE
200m

TO GURNARD'S HEAD (TREEN)

B3306

ZENNOR HEAD TO PENDEEN WATCH   [MAPS 52-56]

For the next **7 miles (11km, 2¼-3hrs)** the going is sometimes rocky along this quite challenging stretch with some damp places unless there has been a particularly dry spell. The path cuts across the long, graceful neck of **Gurnard's Head**. The small settlement here, lying 10 minutes inland (turn off the coast path at **Lean Point**), is technically Treen but is generally referred to as Gurnard's Head. Here, by the road junction, you'll find *The Gurnard's Head Hotel* (Map 53; ☎ 01736-796928, 🖳 gurnardshead.co.uk, **fb**; 4D/3D or T; ☛; 🐾; £70-102.50pp, sgl occ from £90), a fine pub with very comfortable **B&B** rooms. This place has won awards for its **food** (daily 5-9pm, plus noon-3pm on Mon, Thur & Sun), and booking ahead is certainly recommended for evening meals. The menu changes regularly but is always sumptuous and features local produce wherever possible. Lunchtime mains cost £8-12 (though fish and steak dishes are £20-25). Sunday lunch is £22.50/27.50 for two/three courses. Evening set menus cost £29.50/35 for two/three courses. The wine list is fittingly sophisticated; one of the best along the coast. The Land's End Coaster and 16A **bus** services stop by the pub, as does the No 7 (see pp52-5 for details).

The route finding is easier after Gurnard's Head with improved waymarking across the boulder-strewn cliffs of **Bosigran**, a favourite haunt for rock-climbers.

Approaching the lighthouse of **Pendeen Watch** you meet a tarmac road which leads to the facilities at Pendeen village, a half-mile walk inland. It's more pleasant, though, to continue on the coast path, then take the footpath into the village just before Geevor Tin Mine museum.

❏ ANCIENT CORNWALL

The history of Cornwall goes back a lot further than its churches and the arrival of the saints. There is another history which is far less tangible and more mysterious with most of its secrets yet to be unlocked by modern man.

Mesolithic nomadic hunters and gatherers were the first settlers after the Ice Age but they left few remains. Neolithic man arrived from across the Atlantic in 3500BC, bringing both the skills to rear crops and raise flocks *and* the art of building *quoits*, the stone chambers used for communal burials. **Zennor Quoit** is relatively easy to visit from the coast path and is signposted from Zennor church (see Map 52).

In 2000BC the Beaker Folk arrived and many believe it was they who erected the stone circles and standing stones, enigmas to modern science and thinking. The **Merry Maidens** and the **Pipers** (see box p194 and Map 65) are worth visiting.

It was Bronze-Age man, 1500-700BC, who made the discovery of adding tin to copper. **Ballowal Barrow** (see Map 58), right on the coast path, is thought to be late Bronze Age or early Iron Age. Its purpose is unknown, but one speculation is that the *barrows* were used for religious ceremonies.

The Iron Age Celts, 700BC, introduced the iron-making process from north-west Europe. They organised themselves into clans and formed alliances under kings. As you walk the coast path you pass many signs of Celtic occupation in the form of hillforts and cliff castles. It has even been suggested that the name Cornwall was derived from the Cornish word *cornovii*, meaning cliff castles.

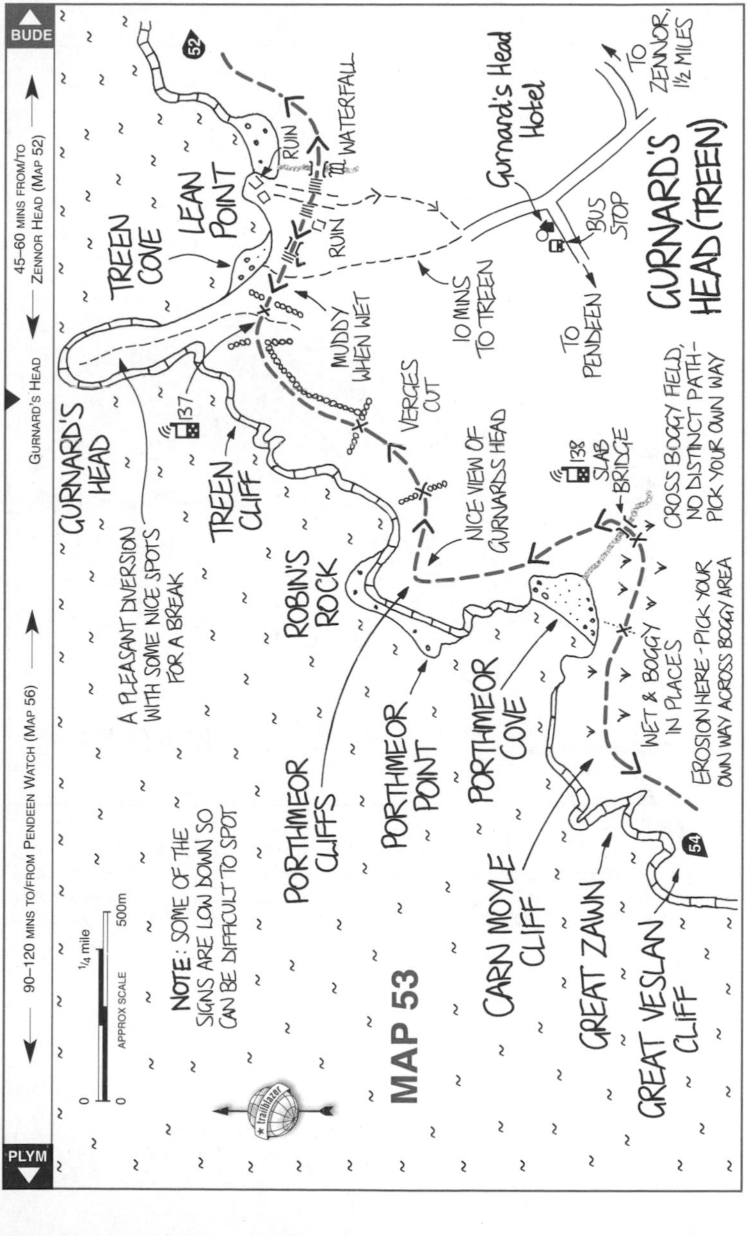

90–120 MINS TO/FROM PENDEEN WATCH (MAP 56)

GURNARD'S HEAD

45–60 MINS FROM/to ZENNOR HEAD (MAP 52)

0 1/4 mile
0 500m
APPROX SCALE

NOTE: SOME OF THE SIGNS ARE LOW DOWN SO CAN BE DIFFICULT TO SPOT

MAP 53

TREEN COVE

LEAN POINT

52

RUIN

WATERFALL

RUIN

RUIN

MUDDY WHEN WET

GURNARD'S HEAD

137

TREEN CLIFF

A PLEASANT DIVERSION WITH SOME NICE SPOTS FOR A BREAK

ROBIN'S ROCK

PORTHMEOR CLIFFS

PORTHMEOR POINT

CARN MOYLE CLIFF

GREAT ZAWN

GREAT VESLAN CLIFF

54

VERGES CUT

NICE VIEW OF GURNARDS HEAD

SLAB BRIDGE

138

CROSS BOGGY FIELD, NO DISTINCT PATH– PICK YOUR OWN WAY

WET & BOGGY IN PLACES

EROSION HERE – PICK YOUR OWN WAY ACROSS BOGGY AREA

PORTHMEOR COVE

Gurnard's Head Hotel

TO ZENNOR, 1½ MILES

BUS STOP

TO PENDEEN

10 MINS TO TREEN

GURNARD'S HEAD (TREEN)

53

DON'T GET LED TO THE CLIFF TOP BY CLIMBERS' PATHS

HALLDRINE COVE

BOSIGRAN CASTLE

BOSIGRAN CLIFF
LOOK FOR ROCK CLIMBERS

PORTHMOINA COVE

📱139

PICK YOUR WAY ACROSS ROCKY FIELD. PATH INDISTINCT AND NOT MARKED

NESTING BIRDS INCLUDING KITTIWAKES

BRANDY'S ROCKS

RUIN

FOLLOW PATH ACROSS BRIDGE, **NOT** INLAND!

📱140

OLD MINES

TREVOWHAN CLIFF

WHIRL POOL

📱141

TO TREEN

OLD MINE

STEPPING STONES

REMEMBER TO LATCH GATE

55

B3306

TREVEAN CLIFF

PATH MEANDERS UP & DOWN, WELL ABOVE CLIFF

NARROW & BOGGY

↓ TO PENDEEN

0 ___ ¼ mile
0 ___ APPROX SCALE ___ 500m

★ trailblazer

MAP 54

ROUTE GUIDE AND MAPS

MORVAH [MAP 55]

This is one of the smallest parishes in Cornwall with about 70 residents but is a community bursting with energy. At its heart is **The Schoolhouse**; originally a chapel, dating from 1744, but now a gallery, craft centre and great-value *café* (☎ 01736-787808, 🖥 morvah.com, **fb**; café daily 10am-4pm, gallery to 5pm) serving home-made soup, pies and Ploughman's plus cakes, scones and cream teas. Have a look at the community created stained-glass door depicting scenes from daily life in the area.

Close by is *Morvah Wild Camping* (☎ 01736-788309 or ☎ 07733-486347, adult/child £5/2), a simple camping field with toilets but no shower.

The Land's End Coaster **bus** service stops here. [For details see pp52-5.]

❑ **IMPORTANT NOTE – WALKING TIMES**

Unless otherwise specified, **all times in this book refer only to the time spent walking**. Add 20-30% to allow for rests, photography, checking the map, drinking water etc.

PENDEEN   [MAP 56, p178]

Pendeen has a **post office** (Mon-Wed & Fri 9am-5pm, Thur 9am-1pm, Sat 9am-noon) and a Spar **convenience store** (Boscaswell Stores; daily 6.30am-9pm) which sells hot pasties and sausage rolls.

Next door is the friendly fish and chip shop *Lil's Chippy* (Tue, Fri & Sat 11.45am-1.15pm & 5-7pm, Wed & Thur 5-7pm), which serves fish and chips during the above opening hours, but confusingly also opens for hot drinks, breakfast baps and sandwiches at the following times: Mon, Wed & Thur 8am-11pm, Tue, Fri & Sat 8am-1.15pm.

Near the church is the cute little tapas-café *Maria Chica* (☎ 01736-787596, 🖳 mariachica.co.uk; Tue, Wed & Sun 10am-3pm, Thur-Sat 10am-3pm & 6-10pm) which has a typical café breakfast menu but also a great selection of tapas (£4-6) for lunch or dinner.

Campers can stay in the back field belonging to *The North Inn* (☎ 01736-788417, 🖳 thenorthinnpendeen.co.uk, **fb**; 3Tr/1D; 🛏; 🐾; campers £7pp, B&B from £45pp; food daily noon-2.30pm & 6.30-8.30pm), a traditional local with St Austell real ale and good-value pub grub, including curry specials. Campers get use of the showers attached to the pub. The four **B&B** rooms are in an annexe behind the main building.

Radjel Inn (☎ 01736-788446, 🖳 the radjelinn@aol.com) weren't serving food or B&B at the time of research; it is likely they will serve food in the main season but they were unsure if or when they would offer B&B so contact them for an update.

A number of **buses** stop here: the Land's End Coaster, the No 7 and No 18 to Penzance via St Just. [See pp52-5 for details.]

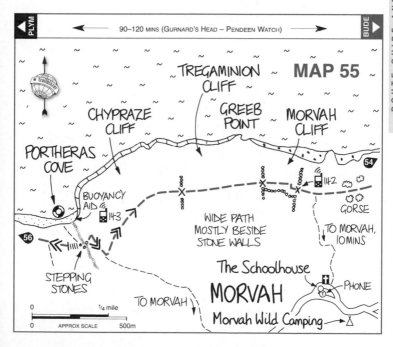

ROUTE GUIDE AND MAPS

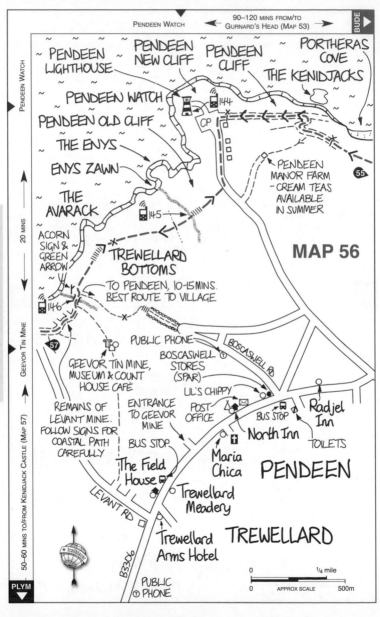

ROUTE GUIDE AND MAPS

PENDEEN WATCH

20 MINS

GEEVOR TIN MINE

50–60 MINS TO/FROM KENIDJACK CASTLE (Map 57)

PLYM

PENDEEN WATCH ← 90–120 MINS FROM/TO → BUDE
GURNARD'S HEAD (Map 53)

~ PENDEEN ~ PENDEEN PENDEEN ~ PORTHERAS ~
LIGHTHOUSE ~ NEW CLIFF CLIFF ~ ~ COVE ~
~ THE KENIDJACKS

~ PENDEEN WATCH ~ 📱144

PENDEEN OLD CLIFF CP

~ THE ENYS ~

ENYS ZAWN ~

~ THE
AVARACK

📱145 → PENDEEN
MANOR FARM
– CREAM TEAS
AVAILABLE
IN SUMMER

ACORN
SIGN &
GREEN
ARROW ✕ TREWELLARD
BOTTOMS

📱146

MAP 56

TO PENDEEN, 10-15 MINS.
BEST ROUTE TO VILLAGE

57

PUBLIC PHONE BOSCASWELL RD

GEEVOR TIN MINE,
MUSEUM & COUNT
HOUSE CAFÉ

BOSCASWELL
STORES
(SPAR)

LIL'S CHIPPY

ENTRANCE
TO GEEVOR
MINE

POST
OFFICE

BUS STOP Radjel
Inn

North Inn TOILETS

REMAINS OF
LEVANT MINE.
FOLLOW SIGNS FOR
COASTAL PATH
CAREFULLY

BUS STOP

The Field
House

Maria
Chica PENDEEN

LEVANT RD Trewellard
Meadery

TREWELLARD

Trewellard
Arms Hotel

B3306

PUBLIC
PHONE

trailblazer

0 ¼ mile

0 500m
APPROX SCALE

TREWELLARD [MAP 56]

Trewellard, right next to Pendeen, has a few more options for food and accommodation, including *The Field House* (☎ 01736-788097, ☐ www.cornwall-online.co.uk/field-house; 2D; £35-40pp), a lovely place boasting a sea view and a rooftop terrace with a private sitting room. Equally lovely here is the **food** (served April-Sep on Thur & Fri, from 7pm; take your own wine), which is available to non-residents too. The set menu (from £18.50) includes delights such as Aga-baked Newlyn hake fillet with mango, chilli and tomato salsa.

You can also get a decent meal at *Trewellard Arms Hotel* (☎ 01736-788634, **fb**; Mon-Sat noon-3pm & 5.30-8.30pm, Sun noon-3pm, booking essential; 🐾), which

serves some great fresh fish dishes as well as standard pub fare, plus half a dozen real ales, including the ever-popular Doom Bar.

Another, more unusual option for dinner is the atmospheric, gothic-themed *Trewellard Meadery* (☎ 01736-788345, **fb**; summer daily 6.30-8.30pm, winter Thur-Sun only, booking essential). The menu includes mead (honey wine) and their speciality quarter or half a chicken and chips which, like the rest of the food, is served 'in the rough' – that is, on wooden platters and eaten with fingers (although cutlery is available on request!). They also do takeaways.

For a **bus** there's the Land's End Coaster to Penzance via St Just. [See pp52-5 for details.]

PENDEEN WATCH TO CAPE CORNWALL [MAPS 56-58]

There is a lot to see on this **4-mile (6km, 1½-1¾hrs)** section, scattered with tin-mining ruins, and with views from the cliff tops all the way. Just off the path and signposted from it are the remains of **Geevor Tin Mine** (see box 'Mining in Cornwall' on p180), closed in 1990 but now a museum where you can get a coffee or cream tea (entry to the *café* is free) and a tour underground.

The surroundings here are post-industrial and offer a fascinating insight into what it must have been like when the mine was in full operation. The path then passes right by the remains of **Levant Mine** and on to the eyrie cliff-top location of **Crown Mine**, both of which had starring roles in the 2015-19 TV adaptation of Winston Graham's *Poldark*. The old engine houses appear dotted along the coast as if guarding it like sentinels.

The backdrop changes again by the time you reach the site of the Iron Age fort known as **Kenidjack Castle**, a nice place to take a break and admire the views towards Cape Cornwall.

Once thought to be the most westerly point in the British Isles, **Cape Cornwall** (see box p182) is often referred to as 'the connoisseur's Land's End'. It is certainly everything that Land's End could have been in different hands. A cape is defined as a headland where two oceans or channels meet; in this case the English Channel and St George's Channel. There's a **snack caravan** in the car park during the season, open all day depending on the weather. The coast path doesn't actually go out to the very point of the Cape but there's nothing to stop you from making the short diversion just to say you've done it, and perhaps to get a photo of the remains of the tiny **St Helen's chapel**.

The thriving community of **St Just** is another town popular with artists and is well worth the detour for lunch or a coffee, even if you're not scheduled to stay there. Take the road out of the car park – it should take you 15-20 minutes on foot. You can then rejoin the path near YHA Land's End.

BOTALLACK   [MAP 57]

There's a good **campsite** here: *Trevaylor Caravan and Camping Park* (☎ 01736-787016, 🖳 cornishcamping.co.uk, **fb**; 🐾; WI-FI; pitch for two people £16.50), with an on-site bar and restaurant and a shop selling most essentials including camping gas.

At the lively *Queen's Arms* (☎ 01736-788318, 🖳 queensarmscornwall.co.uk; daily noon-2.30pm & 6-8pm; most mains £11-13) the food is great, and they have Press Gang cider on tap, as well as real ales. Note the ornate ceiling above the stairs, which is thought to be around 150 years old and is one reason why this lovely 17th-century building is Grade II listed.

The Land's End Coaster, the No 7 and No 18 **bus** services stop right outside the pub. [For details see pp52-5.]

☐ MINING IN CORNWALL

For at least two thousand years tin, copper and lead have been extracted from the Cornish peninsula. Tin found in streams was first utilised by Bronze-Age people. As these sources became exhausted, miners began to dig out veins of ore from solid rock. It wasn't until the early 19th century that the technology of steam-driven pumps allowed mines to be worked below the water table. With the invention of dynamite, mining literally exploded. Shafts could be constructed to depths of over 300m (1000ft) and could even be extended below the seabed. At Levant Mine it is said that miners could hear the rumble of boulders being rolled across the seabed during bad storms.

Life in the mines was tough. Poor pay and extreme conditions such as constant dampness and the intense heat given off by the rock itself led to an average life expectancy of less than forty years. When the market collapsed due to cheaper sources being discovered in South America and Australia many Cornishmen emigrated, taking their knowledge to these countries.

Today all that can be seen of this once huge industry are the engine houses left on the surface. The hundreds of miles of underground galleries and shafts lie forgotten, destined to become yet another secret clutched to the bosom of the earth.

Between Pendeen Watch and Cape Cornwall are two popular mining attractions. The first is **Geevor Tin Mine** (Map 56; ☎ 01736-788662, 🖳 geevor.com; Apr-Oct Sun-Thur 9am-5pm, Nov-Mar to 4pm; admission £16.10) which closed as a mine in 1990 and is now a museum where you can don a helmet to be guided on a half-hour underground tour. There's also the excellent *Count House Café* (☎ 01736-788864, 🖳 counthousecafe.com, **fb**; Sun-Thur 9am-5pm, Sat 9am-1pm; no mine ticket needed) with hearty Cornish food and lovely sea views; the pasties and home-made soup are recommended.

The second place, well worth a visit, is the National Trust's **Levant Engine House** (Map 57; ☎ 01736-786156, 🖳 nationaltrust.org.uk/levant-mine; Mar 15-Nov 1 10.30am-5pm Sun-Thur; admission £10) where the cliff-top engine house and steam-powered beam engine have been restored to their former glory. The engine, which from 1840 to 1930 lifted copper and tin ore to the surface, is now steamed up for the public in the main season; phone beforehand to check opening. The Levant Mine was the site of a tragic disaster in 1919 when the lift collapsed killing 31 miners. For a mind-boggling insight into the harsh realities of life in the mines join one of the free tours here which really help to make sense of all the mines you see on your walk.

Cornwall and West Devon's industrial heritage is of international importance. For several centuries the region was the world's largest producer of tin and copper providing some of the main raw materials for the industrialisation of the world. In recognition of the importance of this, the mining sites of the region were granted World Heritage site status.

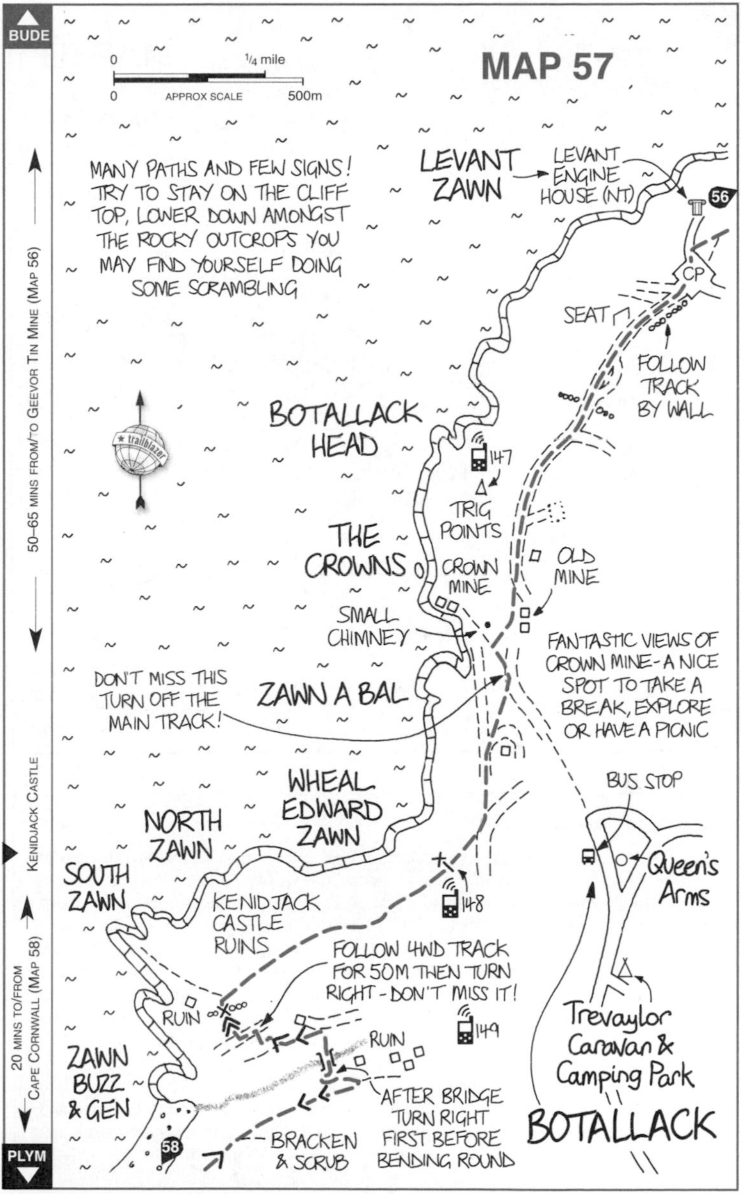

MAP 57

BUDE ▲

0 ____ ¼ mile
0 ____ APPROX SCALE ____ 500m

50–65 MINS FROM/'O GEEVOR TIN MINE (MAP 56)

MANY PATHS AND FEW SIGNS! TRY TO STAY ON THE CLIFF TOP, LOWER DOWN AMONGST THE ROCKY OUTCROPS YOU MAY FIND YOURSELF DOING SOME SCRAMBLING

trailblazer

LEVANT ZAWN

LEVANT ENGINE HOUSE (NT)

56

CP

SEAT

FOLLOW TRACK BY WALL

BOTALLACK HEAD

📱147

△ TRIG POINTS

THE CROWNS

CROWN MINE

OLD MINE

SMALL CHIMNEY

FANTASTIC VIEWS OF CROWN MINE - A NICE SPOT TO TAKE A BREAK, EXPLORE OR HAVE A PICNIC

DON'T MISS THIS TURN OFF THE MAIN TRACK!

ZAWN A BAL

WHEAL EDWARD ZAWN

BUS STOP

NORTH ZAWN

SOUTH ZAWN

KENIDJACK CASTLE RUINS

📱148

Queen's Arms

KENIDJACK CASTLE

ZAWN BUZZ & GEN

RUIN

FOLLOW 4WD TRACK FOR 50M THEN TURN RIGHT - DON'T MISS IT!

📱149

RUIN

AFTER BRIDGE TURN RIGHT FIRST BEFORE BENDING ROUND

BRACKEN & SCRUB

58

Trevaylor Caravan & Camping Park

BOTALLACK

20 MINS TO/FROM CAPE CORNWALL (MAP 58)

PLYM ▼

ROUTE GUIDE AND MAPS

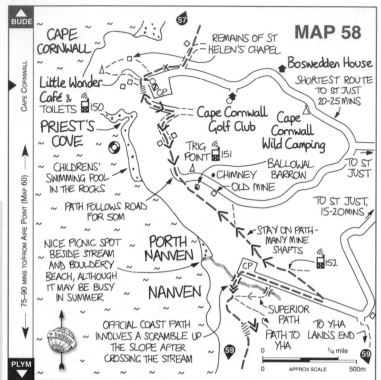

BUDE

CAPE CORNWALL

75-90 MINS TO/FROM AIRE POINT (MAP 60)

ROUTE GUIDE AND MAPS

PLYM

CAPE CORNWALL

57

REMAINS OF ST HELEN'S CHAPEL

MAP 58

Boswedden House

SHORTEST ROUTE TO ST JUST 20-25 MINS

Little Wonder Café & TOILETS 150

Cape Cornwall Golf Club

Cape Cornwall Wild Camping

PRIEST'S COVE

CHILDRENS' SWIMMING POOL IN THE ROCKS

TRIG POINT 151

CHIMNEY OLD MINE

BALLOWAL BARROW

TO ST JUST

PATH FOLLOWS ROAD FOR 50M

PORTH NANVEN

TO ST JUST, 15-20 MINS

STAY ON PATH - MANY MINE SHAFTS

152

NICE PICNIC SPOT BESIDE STREAM AND BOULDERY BEACH, ALTHOUGH IT MAY BE BUSY IN SUMMER

NANVEN

CP

SUPERIOR PATH

TO YHA

OFFICIAL COAST PATH INVOLVES A SCRAMBLE UP THE SLOPE AFTER CROSSING THE STREAM

59

PATH TO YHA

PATH TO LANDS END

trailblazer

0   ¼ mile

0   APPROX SCALE   500m

59

❏ CAPE CORNWALL

Cape Cornwall is a headland four miles north of Land's End which was thought at one time to be the most westerly point in mainland Britain. It turned out later not to be so after calculations proved Land's End to have that distinction. It is a place of stunning beauty once the crowds have left. The cape is the point at which the current divides, going south into the English Channel and north into St George's Channel. There is an old chimney at the highest point left over from the days when tin mining dominated the area and shafts extended right out under the sea. The chimney dates from 1850 and served the Cape Cornwall Mine extracting tin and copper from beneath the sea bed between 1836 and 1879 when the mine merged with the St Just United Mine further south.

In the early 20th century the Cape was owned by Captain Francis Oates: he had started work at 12 years old and worked his way up to become owner of the Cape and managing director of de Beers in South Africa. On retirement, in 1909, he returned to Cornwall and built Porthledden House near St Just as his family home.

CAPE CORNWALL [MAP 58]

If you're just passing through, ***Little Wonder Café*** (**fb**; Feb-Oct daily 10.30am-4.30pm), a small coffee shack in the Cape car park, sells hot drinks, cakes, ice creams and pasties.

In summer, **campers** can find a pitch at ***Cape Cornwall Wild Camping*** (☎ 07533-002762, **fb**; £10), a simple camping field with two toilets and a water tap.

Cape Cornwall Club (☎ 01736-788611, 🖳 capecornwallclub.com, **fb**; 15 en suite rooms, £40-90pp, sgl occ from £60; ▼; food daily 8am-9pm) has some lovely **B&B accommodation**, a good restaurant and a bar. The bright, modern and characterful rooms are in converted barn buildings, and rates include access to the pool, sauna and Jacuzzi. In the **restaurant**, mains cost £11-19 and include gourmet burgers, ribeye steak and wild mushroom risotto.

The other accommodation option here is ***Boswedden House*** (☎ 01736-788733, 🖳 boswedden.org.uk, **fb**; 1S/5D or T/1T/1Qd, all en suite; ▼; £35-50pp), a retreat and healing centre with B&B. Rooms are immaculate. There's also a heated indoor **pool** (open to the public 9am-6pm; £6; booking essential) and sauna to ease aching muscles.

ST JUST

Dear Lord, we hope that there be no shipwrecks, but if there be, let them be in St Just for the benefit of the inhabitants. Spoken in St Just Church by **Parson Amos Mason**, 1650

St Just is the most westerly town in England and, as if in deference to the Atlantic weather, built from granite arranged in a charmingly rugged way. Despite its isolated location St Just is a surprisingly cosmopolitan place with art shops and an active social life throughout the year. Whereas most of the villages round here have only a weekend of events for their annual carnivals, St Just's Lafrowda Festival (see p16) lasts a whole week. More than 50 artists have made St Just their home and their work can be seen at the many **galleries** around the town. The **church** is worth a visit for its two splendid medieval frescoes, *St George* and *Christ of all Trades*. Also note the wooden plaque near the door listing all the vicars and rectors since 1297.

Tourist information (☎ 01736-788165, 🖳 stjusttourist@cornwall.gov.uk) is based at the **library** (☎ 01736-788669; Tue & Thur 9.30am-5pm, Wed 9.30am-1.30pm, Sat 10am-1pm) where **internet access** is available. There are public **toilets** opposite. Cape Cornwall **doctors' surgery** (☎ 01736-788306, 🖳 atlanticmedicalgroup.co.uk; Mon-Fri 8am-1pm & 2-6pm) is behind the library. The town also has a **pharmacy** (Mon-Fri 9am-1pm & 2-6pm, Sat 9am-12.30pm). For supplies, the Co-op

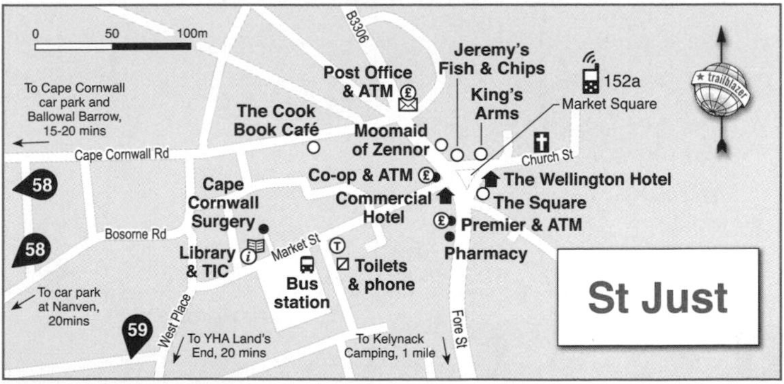

supermarket (daily 7am-10pm), and Premier (7am-10pm), both with **ATMs** outside, are by Market Square.

The **post office** (Mon-Sat 7am-6pm, Sun 7am-1.30pm) also has an ATM outside.

As well as the **campsites** at Botallack (p180), Kelynack (p185) and Cape Cornwall (p184), there's also budget accommodation at YHA Land's End (see p185), a 20-minute walk from St Just.

In the village itself you can **stay** and **eat** at two of the pubs: ***Commercial Hotel*** (☎ 01736-788455, 🖳 commercial-hotel.co.uk; 1S/4D/6T; 🐕; from £32.50pp, sgl from £69) has nice airy rooms and a lovely conservatory dining area (food noon-2pm & 6-9pm; mains £11-15). ***Wellington Hotel*** (☎ 01736-787319, 🖳 wellingtonhotelcornwall.co.uk; 2T/5D/4Qd; ☕; from £37.50pp, sgl occ from £60; food daily noon-2pm & 6-9pm, winter to 8.30pm) is your other option.

St Just has a cluster of pleasant **cafés**. Amongst the more unusual is ***The Cook Book*** (☎ 01736-787266, 🖳 thecookbookcafe.co.uk, **fb**; Tue-Sat 9am-4pm, Sun 9am-noon; 🐕) which as well as serving excellent coffee and delicious cakes, sandwiches, soups and breakfasts, has more than 5000 rare and second-hand books on display for customers to browse and buy. Also serving excellent coffee, as well as pastries and their house-speciality ice creams, is ***Moomaid of Zennor*** (🖳 moomaidofzennor.com; daily 9am-6pm), on Market Square. Across the way is ***The Square*** (**fb**; Wed-Sat 9am-8pm), a café serving breakfasts, light lunches and then, from 4pm, pizza (£9-14).

For a **pub** oozing character look no further than ***The King's Arms*** (☎ 01736-

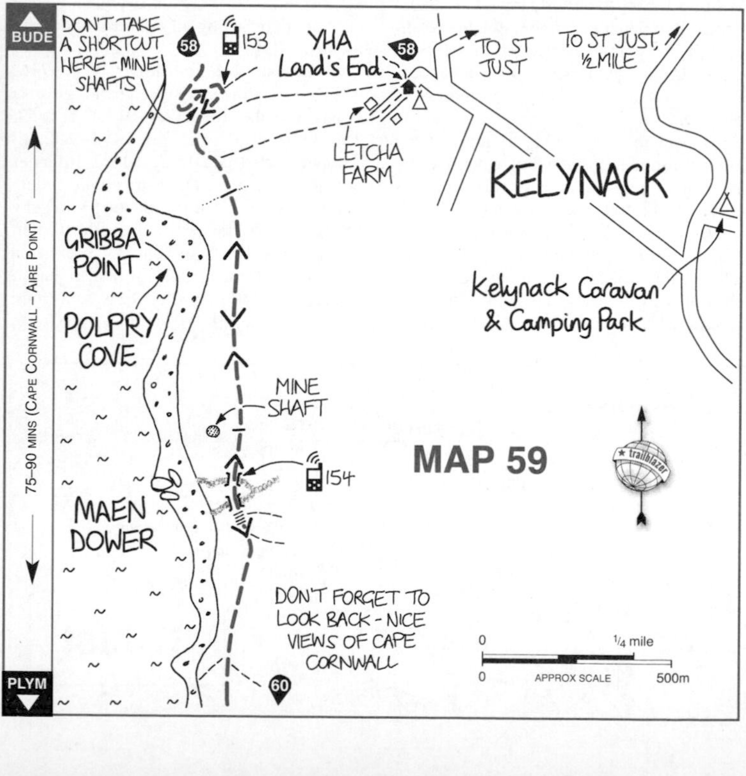

788545; food Mon-Sat noon-2pm & 5-9pm, Sun noon-3pm; 🐾), on Market Square, which was constructed in the 14th century to house the builders of the church next door. The menu is classic pub grub, plus a range of burgers. Next door to The King's Arms is *Jeremy's Fish and Chips*

(**fb**; Tue-Sat noon-2pm & 4.30-8pm), a takeaway which has some seating upstairs.

St Just **bus** services include the Land's End Coaster, the No 7, No 8 and the No 18. Buses stop at the large car park opposite the library. [See pp52-5 for details].

CAPE CORNWALL TO SENNEN COVE [MAPS 58-61]

This is a fine walk of **5 miles (8km, 1¾-2hrs)** along the cliffs, gradually flattening out to provide a gentle approach through the dunes to **Whitesand Bay**. Practically everyone will find this walk a real pleasure and as a day walk it is very popular. The cliffs are honeycombed with old mine workings so it is best to keep to the path. Leaving Cape Cornwall the path climbs to the trig point on **Ballowal Barrow** then it wanders through fields to descend into the **Cot Valley** where a tarmac road leads to a car park for people going to the tiny, geologically significant beach of **Porth Nanven** with its curious round boulders.

The views back to Cape Cornwall are great and you may see seals popping their heads up for a look around. Dolphins are not an unusual sighting either, and basking sharks are occasionally seen. Look up and you may even catch a glimpse of that most iconic of Cornish birds, the red-legged Cornish chough (see box p63).

Zig-zag paths take you round **Gribba Point** from where the path is quite easy and level, with one down and up at **Maen Dower**. **Sennen Cove** comes into sight and you may like to take to the beach as an alternative to the official route through the dunes.

KELYNACK [MAP 59]

Lovely *YHA Land's End* (☎ 01736-788437, 🖳 yha.org.uk/hostel/yha-lands-end; 28 dorm beds/1T/2D or F; from £21pp), at Letcha Vean, is secreted away amongst the trees in the Cot Valley. **Camping** (Apr to mid Oct; £10-14pp) is available in the garden where there are also two **camping pods** (£59-79; 🐾) that sleep four people on one double and two single beds (bedding included). There are self-catering kitchen facilities, and breakfast and evening meals are available too – and there's a licensed bar.

An alternative is *Kelynack Caravan and Camping Park* (☎ 01736-787633, 🖳 kelynackholidays.co.uk; 🐾) where **camping** costs £8-9pp and there's a small **shop** (open daily in season 8.30-10am & 5.30-7pm) selling groceries including fresh milk and fruit. There's a sheltered dining area for campers, a laundry and a sparkling clean toilet block.

Bus services here are the hourly Land's End Coaster and the No 7. [See pp52-5 for details.]

SENNEN & MAYON [MAP 60, p186]

Most people will want to stay as close to Land's End as possible, but this small settlement, on top of the hill above Sennen Cove, gives you another couple of options. It actually comprises Mayon and Sennen but tends to be known collectively as Sennen. It takes around half an hour to

climb up to here from places on the coast path such as Sennen Cove, Gwnver Beach or Land's End.

You can buy food for the day at the Costcutter **convenience store** (daily 8am-8pm), which also houses the **post office** (same hours) and has an **ATM**. There's also

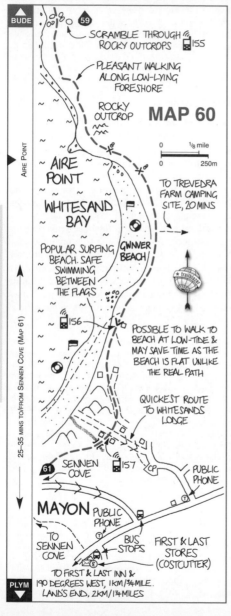

SCRAMBLE THROUGH ROCKY OUTCROPS

PLEASANT WALKING ALONG LOW-LYING FORESHORE

ROCKY OUTCROP

MAP 60

0   1/8 mile
0   250m

AIRE POINT

WHITESAND BAY

POPULAR SURFING BEACH. SAFE SWIMMING BETWEEN THE FLAGS

GWNVER BEACH

TO TREVEDRA FARM CAMPING SITE, 20 MINS

POSSIBLE TO WALK TO BEACH AT LOW-TIDE & MAY SAVE TIME AS THE BEACH IS FLAT UNLIKE THE REAL PATH

QUICKEST ROUTE TO WHITESANDS LODGE

SENNEN COVE

MAYON PUBLIC PHONE

PUBLIC PHONE

TO SENNEN COVE

BUS STOPS

FIRST & LAST STORES (COSTCUTTER)

TO FIRST & LAST INN & 190 DEGREES WEST, 1KM/¾ MILE. LAND'S END, 2KM/1¼ MILES

BUDE

PLYM

a good **fish & chip shop** here, called *190 Degrees West* (☎ 01736-872723; Tue & Wed 5-7.30pm, Thur & Sat 5-8pm, Fri noon-2pm & 5-8pm).

Campers should head to *Trevedra Farm* (off Map 60; ☎ 01736-871818, 🖥 trevedrafarm .co.uk, **fb**; hiker & tent £11-14; 🐾 ; Apr-Oct), a working farm with a campsite and **shop** (daily all day in peak season; limited hours at other times) selling fresh bread, milk and pasties. The campsite is about a mile inland: take the steps off Gwnver Beach, climb up, cross a lane, a stile and two fields. To camp closer to Land's End, try Land's End Camping (p188).

Alongside **St Sennen Church** (founded in AD520, although the oldest part of the current structure is 13th century), *The First and Last Inn* (off Map 60; ☎ 01736-871680, 🖥 firstandlastinn.co.uk, **fb**; food daily May-Sep noon-9pm; Oct-Apr noon-2pm & 6-9pm; mains £10-12.50) dates from at least 1620 and is a famous old smugglers' haunt with a fascinating history. Beside the bar, a deep well (now glass-topped) is said to have once been the start of a smuggling tunnel that led all the way to cliffs. Former landlady Ann Treeve was reportedly sentenced to death by drowning for her part in the illicit operation. The pub's very spacious **rooms** (☎ 01736-871844, 🖥 saddleandstable rooms.co.uk; 3D or T; 🛏; from £55pp, room only) are in beautifully converted stables by the pub, and have well-equipped kitchenettes. There's also an **apartment** that sleeps four (min 2 nights).

As well as the steep road, there's a footpath that leads down to Sennen Cove from opposite Costcutter.

The Land's End Coaster **bus** stops at the First and Last Inn, as does the No 7. [See pp52-5].

❏ NATIONAL COASTWATCH

Modern technology, such as accurate positioning systems, has made coastal waters much safer, but it can still fail in distress situations close to shore. The **National Coastwatch Institution** (🖥 nci.org.uk) was reformed in 1994 to re-instate a visual lookout along the British coastline and is manned by volunteers. If they see anyone in distress including yachtsmen, divers, walkers, climbers or people in difficulty the watchkeeper immediately informs the nearest HM Coastguard Rescue Centre to alert the rescue services. There are now 46 stations operating around the coast. The NCI is funded entirely by public donations and company sponsorships.

SENNEN COVE   [MAP 61, p189]

Sennen Cove is a small beach-side community where fishing and the tourist trade are the only source of employment. The winter weather is too wild for the boats to go out so from November onwards the quay is piled high with lobster pots and the fishermen spend their time maintaining their boats and nets.

There is a **shop**, The Old Boathouse (**fb**; Mar-Nov daily 8.30am-6pm), which sells groceries and good-value pasties (£2.60), above the southern end of the beach.

The *Old Success Inn* (🕿 01736-871232, 🖥 oldsuccess.co.uk, **fb**; 24 rooms; ➤; 🐾; from £42.50pp, sgl occ from £85) is under St Austell Brewery, so the beers are Tribute, HSD and Proper Job. **Food** (noon-3pm & 5-8.30pm; most mains £12-16) is served daily in summer. Some of their

B&B rooms are above the pub with more in other nearby buildings.

Back along the coast path, as you enter Sennen Cove, *Surf Beach Bar* (🕿 01736-871191, 🖥 surfbeachbar.co.uk, **fb**; noon-8pm) is your first chance to get refreshments. There's pizza, nachos, drinks and snacks, and seating inside and out. Further along the coast path, cute *Sennen Cove Café* (daily 9am-3.30pm) does hearty breakfasts, decent coffee and lunchtime sandwiches. They also have beer on tap. Close by, *Blue Lagoon* (daily noon-8pm) a no-frills café and fish-and-chip shop where you can eat in or takeaway.

The Land's End Coaster and No 7 **buses** stop here. [See pp52-5].

If you want a **taxi** ring Logan Rock Cars (🕿 01736-871786, 🖥 loganrockcars .co.uk).

SENNEN COVE TO PORTHCURNO   [MAPS 61-63]

This **6-mile (9.5km, 1¾-2½hrs)** section contains some spectacular cliff-top walking including the rounding of Land's End, a big milestone on the coast path. The mile from Sennen Cove to Land's End is an easy walk on a wide, hard-packed path, virtually a stroll in the park. However, in bad weather it can be very exposed, particularly across Land's End and **Gwennap Head**, as there is barely a rock or bush to shelter behind. **Dr Syntax's Head** is the true most westerly point of mainland England; a Cornwall flagpole marks the spot.

A few hundred metres south of this is the **Land's End** complex, home of the much-photographed Land's End signpost, with distance markers for New York and John O'Groats; though these days in high season you'll have to pay £10.95 for the privilege of having your photo taken next it! This is also where you'll find (perhaps to your horror), a theme park to rival any seaside town in England. Thankfully, there's also a bar and restaurant in the hotel here, so you can grab a beer to celebrate reaching this far.

As you leave the Land's End complex, you'll pass Greeb Animal Farm (adult/child £4/3), an 18th-century farm with pigs, goats, chickens and the like.

From here, the cliff architecture is full of arches and holes, such as the natural land-bridge of **Tol-Pedn-Penwith**, or holed headland, created by the ceaseless battering of the sea, and which you can walk across. If you keep on the alert, your chances of seeing grey seals are high, although your pace slows as you watch for them to pop up then disappear again. The path passes through **Porthgwarra** where there is a **seasonal café** (Map 62; daily 9am-4pm) and toilets.

LAND'S END   [MAP 61]

Land's End stirs all sorts of emotions in coast-path walkers. No one who comes here can be unaffected by the beauty of the rugged coastline and the windswept heath; nor the sense of accomplishment at having come this far. However, the development of the West Country Shopping Village, and the abundance of children's theme-park rides, does tend to dispel one's sense of wonder. The **Visitor Centre** (☎ 0871-7200044, 🖳 landsend-landmark.co.uk; daily 10am-5pm, Tue & Thur to 9pm, winter hours vary) is more of a ticket office for the attractions, some of which are quite interesting (the RSPB has a Wildlife Discovery Centre here), than a place for tourist information. There's an **ATM** in the shopping village, but it charges for withdrawals.

Campers should head to nearby *Land's End Camping* (☎ 07376-535822, 🖳 landsendcamp.co.uk, **fb**; £11.50pp; Apr-Oct) which has good showers, a drying room and a coffee kiosk on site. There are also seven camping pods (£85; open all year; min 3 nights) that can sleep two adults and two children, and have their own mini bathrooms, kitchenettes and roof terrace. There's also camping at *Seaview Holiday Park* (☎ 01736-871266, 🖳 seaview.org.uk; hiker & tent £18; Apr-Oct; booking recommended), but they are less hiker-friendly and prefer week-long stays in peak season.

Close by, but not related to its namesake campsite, there are **rooms** at the friendly *Seaview House B&B* (☎ 01736-871984 or 07581-417595, 🖳 seaviewhousebandb sennencornwall.com, **fb**; 1D/1D or T; from £45pp). And, just back off the main road, is *Treeve Moor House* (☎ 01736-871284, 🖳 treevemoorhouse.co.uk; 1D en suite, 1T private facilities; 🛏; from £45pp, sgl occ £60)

with two sea-view rooms that are often in demand from cyclists about to start the End-to-End cycle ride to John O'Groats.

The rather grand *Land's End Hotel* (☎ 01736-871844, 🖳 landsendhotel.co.uk, **fb**; 30 flexible rooms; 🛏; 🐾; from £60pp, sgl from £70) has a range of room styles. The **restaurant-bar** (noon-8.45pm) serves lunches, cream teas and evening meals with an uninspiring menu but a fabulous view. There are several places for light refreshments, including *The Bakehouse* (11am-4pm; takeaway kiosk open until 5.30pm) which also does pasties and jacket potatoes. *The Cornish Pantry* (9.30am-4pm) is your best bet for a cheap sit-down meal, with buffet-style cafeteria food, including unlimited coffee refills and indoor seating with some sea-view tables.

Hikers, backpackers and cyclists looking for a place to stay tend to prefer *Land's End Hostel* (☎ 07585-625774, 🖳 landsend holidays.co.uk; 14 beds/2D or T; from £30pp), a family-run hostel in a converted barnhouse and about as close as you can be to Land's End other than the Land's End Hotel. The rate for a private room (£44pp) includes breakfast. For those in dorms, a continental 'breakfast in a basket' is available for £6. For *YHA Land's End* see p185.

Close to Land's End Hostel is the lovely *Apple Tree Café* (☎ 01736-872753, 🖳 appletreecafe.co.uk, **fb**; Wed-Sun 10am-4pm, closed Jan), a charming tearoom in an old stone cottage with garden seating. The menu includes healthy breakfasts and lunches as well as less healthy (but delicious) homemade cakes. They do cream teas (naturally) and are licensed.

The Land's End Coaster and No 7 **buses** stop here. [See pp52-5].

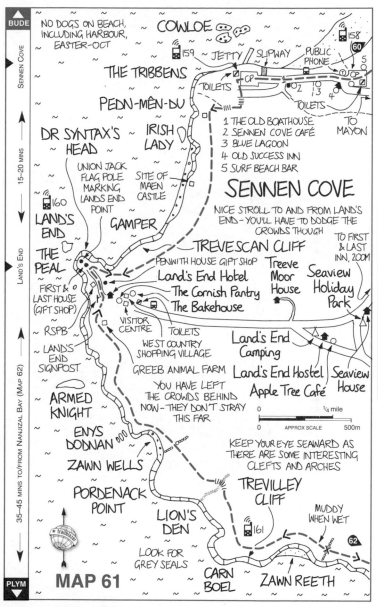

SENNEN COVE

15-20 MINS

LAND'S END

35-45 MINS TO/FROM NANJIZAL BAY (MAP 62)

PLYM

NO DOGS ON BEACH, INCLUDING HARBOUR, EASTER-OCT

COWLOE

159

JETTY SLIPWAY

158
60
5

PUBLIC PHONE

THE TRIBBENS

TOILETS CP

CP

2 1
3

4

PEDN-MÊN-DU

TOILETS

TO MAYON

DR SYNTAX'S HEAD

IRISH LADY

1 THE OLD BOATHOUSE
2 SENNEN COVE CAFÉ
3 BLUE LAGOON
4 OLD SUCCESS INN
5 SURF BEACH BAR

UNION JACK FLAG POLE MARKING LANDS END POINT

SITE OF MAEN CASTLE

SENNEN COVE

160

LAND'S END

GAMPER

NICE STROLL TO AND FROM LAND'S END - YOU'LL HAVE TO DODGE THE CROWDS THOUGH

TO FIRST & LAST INN, 200M

THE PEAL

TREVESCAN CLIFF

PENWITH HOUSE GIFT SHOP

Land's End Hotel

The Cornish Pantry

The Bakehouse

Treeve Moor House

Seaview Holiday Park

FIRST & LAST HOUSE (GIFT SHOP)

RSPB

LAND'S END SIGNPOST

VISITOR CENTRE

TOILETS

WEST COUNTRY SHOPPING VILLAGE

GREEB ANIMAL FARM

Land's End Camping

Land's End Hostel

Seaview House

ARMED KNIGHT

YOU HAVE LEFT THE CROWDS BEHIND NOW - THEY DON'T STRAY THIS FAR

Apple Tree Café

0   ¼ mile

0   APPROX SCALE   500m

ENYS DODNAN

ZAWN WELLS

KEEP YOUR EYE SEAWARD AS THERE ARE SOME INTERESTING CLEFTS AND ARCHES

PORDENACK POINT

trailblazer

LION'S DEN

TREVILLEY CLIFF

MUDDY WHEN WET

161

62

LOOK FOR GREY SEALS

MAP 61

CARN BOEL

ZAWN REETH

ROUTE GUIDE AND MAPS

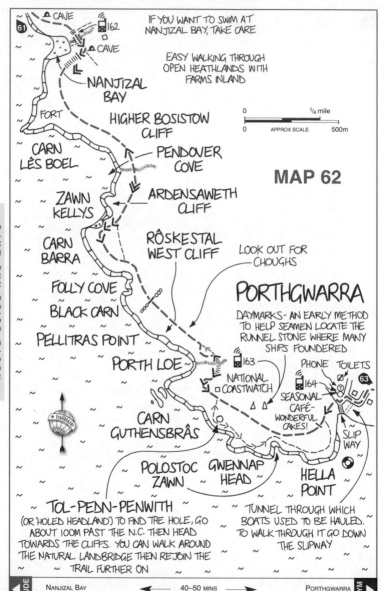

CAVE

61

162

CAVE

NANJIZAL
BAY

IF YOU WANT TO SWIM AT
NANJIZAL BAY, TAKE CARE

EASY WALKING THROUGH
OPEN HEATHLANDS WITH
FARMS INLAND

FORT

HIGHER BOSISTOW
CLIFF

0   ¼ mile

0   APPROX SCALE   500m

CARN
LÊS BOEL

PENDOVER
COVE

MAP 62

ZAWN
KELLYS

ARDENSAWETH
CLIFF

CARN
BARRA

RÔSKESTAL
WEST CLIFF

LOOK OUT FOR
CHOUGHS

FOLLY COVE

BLACK CARN

PORTHGWARRA

PELLITRAS POINT

DAYMARKS - AN EARLY METHOD
TO HELP SEAMEN LOCATE THE
RUNNEL STONE WHERE MANY
SHIPS FOUNDERED

PORTH LOE

163

NATIONAL
COASTWATCH

PHONE TOILETS

164

63

SEASONAL
CAFÉ -
WONDERFUL
CAKES!

SLIP
WAY

CARN
GUTHENSBRÂS

POLOSTOC
ZAWN

GWENNAP
HEAD

HELLA
POINT

TOL-PEDN-PENWITH
(OR 'HOLED HEADLAND') TO FIND THE HOLE, GO
ABOUT 100M PAST THE N.C. THEN HEAD
TOWARDS THE CLIFFS. YOU CAN WALK AROUND
THE NATURAL LANDBRIDGE THEN REJOIN THE
TRAIL FURTHER ON

TUNNEL THROUGH WHICH
BOATS USED TO BE HAULED.
TO WALK THROUGH IT GO DOWN
THE SLIPWAY

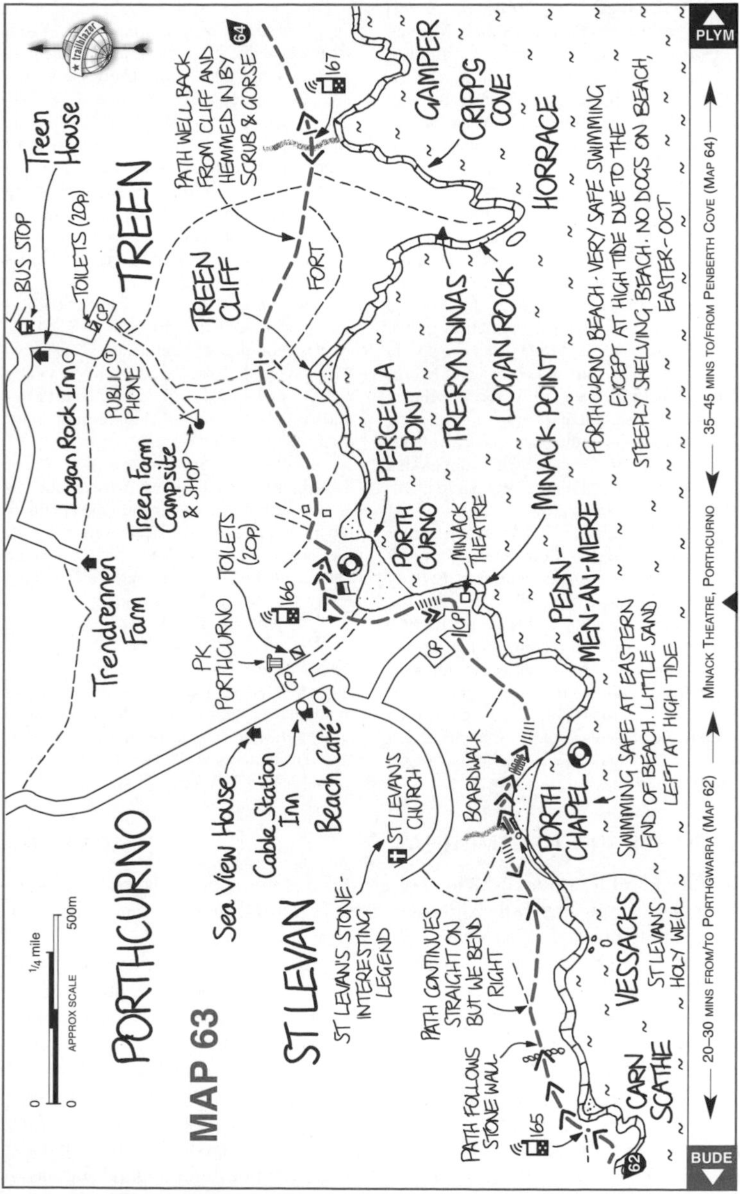

MAP 63

PORTHCURNO

ST LEVAN

0

APPROX SCALE

1/4 mile

500m

Trendrennen Farm

Treen House

Treen Farm Campsite & Shop

BUS STOP

TOILETS (20p)

Logan Rock Inn

PUBLIC PHONE

TREEN

PATH WELL BACK FROM CLIFF AND HEMMED IN BY SCRUB & GORSE

64

167

GAMPER

CRIPPS COVE

FORT

TREEN CLIFF

HORRACE

PERCELLA POINT

PORTH CURNO

TRERYN DINAS

LOGAN ROCK

MINACK POINT

MINACK THEATRE

166

TOILETS (20p)

PK PORTHCURNO

CP

PORTHCURNO BEACH: VERY SAFE SWIMMING EXCEPT AT HIGH TIDE DUE TO THE STEEPLY SHELVING BEACH. NO DOGS ON BEACH, EASTER-OCT

PENN-MÊN-AN-MERE

Sea View House

Cable Station Inn

Beach Café

ST LEVAN'S CHURCH

ST LEVAN'S STONE - INTERESTING LEGEND

BOARDWALK

SWIMMING SAFE AT EASTERN END OF BEACH. LITTLE SAND LEFT AT HIGH TIDE

PORTH CHAPEL

VESSACKS

ST LEVAN'S HOLY WELL

PATH CONTINUES STRAIGHT ON BUT WE BEND RIGHT

PATH FOLLOWS STONE WALL

165

62

CARN SCATHE

20-30 MINS FROM/TO PORTHGWARRA (MAP 62) MINACK THEATRE, PORTHCURNO 35-45 MINS TO/FROM PENBERTH COVE (MAP 64)

PLYM

BUDE

PORTHCURNO [MAP 63, p191]

A visit to the spectacular open-air **Minack Theatre** (☎ 01736-810181, ☐ minack .com, **fb**; Apr-Sep daily 9.30am-5pm, Oct-Mar 10am-4.30pm; £7.50; must be pre-booked) is essential even if you are unable to see a performance. The theatre and fabulous sub-tropical gardens are open for visits throughout the year but the hours can vary so check in advance. The theatre programme (May-Sep, usually daily 2pm & 7.30pm; £10-30) may include anything from musicals to Shakespeare.

This remarkable place, perched on the top of the cliff, was the brainchild of the late Rowena Cade (1893-1983) who, in 1930, with the help of a couple of workman, transformed the gully above Minack Rock into a rudimentary stage and seating area, so that she could stage a performance of *The Tempest*. Over time, she developed the site into the stunning, Greek-style open-air theatre you see today.

Also interesting is **PK Porthcurno: Museum of Global Communications** (☎ 01736-810966, ☐ pkporthcurno.com; daily Apr-Oct 10am-5pm, Nov-Mar Sat-Mon 10.30am-4pm; adult/child £9/5.50; 🐾). Porthcurno was the landing point for the first international telegraph cable connecting Britain and India in 1870, and the museum tells the remarkable story of the men who overcame the obstacles to lay undersea telegraph cables. There's a **café** and **gift shop** inside.

It's also worth visiting **St Levan's Church** with its 12th-century font and medieval carvings in the Celtic style. On the pew ends are figures such as eagles, fish, a bishop and a shepherd, and in the churchyard is a large stone said to have been split in half by St Levan himself so that people would have something by which to remember him. Opinions vary as to its true origin but its supposed pagan significance was neutralised by the stone cross standing close by.

Sea View House (☎ 01736-810638, ☐ seaviewhouseporthcurno.com; 1S/2D/2T, en suite or private facilities; Ⓛ; £42.50-45pp, sgl £60-65, sgl occ £70) has washing and drying facilities, offers luggage transfer and accepts credit cards. Single-night stays aren't usually available in August.

The *Cable Station Inn* (☎ 01736-810479, **fb**) is the only pub in town and was closed pending a change of ownership at the time of research. It previously served food and had two rooms in a beautiful stone cottage next door so it's worth calling them for an update on reopening plans.

Porthcurno Beach Café (☎ 01736-811108; ☐ porthcurnobeachcafe.co.uk; Apr-Sep daily 10am-5.30pm; 🐾) is a great spot for lunch; there's booze and tapas available as well as your normal paninis and sandwiches and jacket potatoes.

The Land's End Coaster **bus** calls here. [See pp52-5 for details].

PORTHCURNO TO LAMORNA [MAPS 63-66]

The next **5 miles (8km, 2-2½hrs)** of coastline are sometimes described as subtropical. The undergrowth is denser than previously, in some places growing overhead to provide a shady tunnel through which to walk.

After passing the turn-off to **Treen** you may like to make the short detour to the **Logan Rock** (see box opposite). From here you can make quick progress, one moment walking up high amongst the scrub and gorse, the next dipping down for a taste of the sea at numerous exquisite little coves, all tempting you to stop and explore. The cove at **Penberth** is usually entirely free of tourists, and to pass through it seems almost an intrusion on the people who make their living here from the sea. Look out for the now disused 19th-century capstan winch, which used to haul boats up onto the beach. Dogs are discouraged here, and dog owners are asked to take a diversion inland to keep them from fouling the slipway.

Beyond **Trevedran Cliff** the path crosses an area of heathland with rough, dry-stone walls before turning down to the verdant valley of **St Loy**.

The path crosses the beach on boulders before regaining the cliffs and passing the lighthouse of **Tater-Du** (not open to the public) down to the right. Built in 1965, it was fully automated from the start. The name is Cornish for 'black loaf', after the rocks hereabouts.

Between the lighthouse and Lamorna is the unobtrusive entrance to the **Minack Chronicles Nature Reserve** (⌨ minack.info), set up by the late authors Derek and Jeannie Tangye, who lived here in a cliff-top daffodil farm called Dorminack. Derek was the author of *The Minack Chronicles* (p48), and they set up this small reserve, only accessible from the coast path, as a place for local wildlife to thrive. It wasn't intended for visitors, but those who wish to 'seek solitude, enjoy peace, and contemplate nature and the elements' are welcome to walk around it.

TREEN   [MAP 63, p191]

A short jaunt up a dirt track, the tiny hamlet of Treen feels like a well-kept secret. Not to be confused with Treen near Gurnard's Head (Map 53) on the north coast, this Treen has a few farmhouses and the warm and homely *Logan Rock Inn* (☎ 01736-810495, ⌨ theloganrockinn.co.uk, **fb**). **Food** is served daily (noon-8pm); the menu has typical pub classics (mains £12-15), but also includes steamed mussels (£18) and Logan Rock fish pie (£15).

The very friendly folks at *Treen Farm Campsite* (☎ 01736-810273 or ☎ 07598-469322, ⌨ treenfarmcampsite.com, hiker and tent £12-14; 🐾; Easter-Oct) don't take bookings, but never turn walkers away. They have laundry facilities, the camping fields are dotted with handy picnic tables, and their **shop** (daily 8am-7pm in season) does coffee and sells homemade pasties, bread, milk and booze.

Just past the pub, *Treen House* (☎ 01736-810379, ⌨ treenhousebedandbreakfast.co.uk; ➽; 2D/1T or Tr; £45-50pp) is a

B&B with lovely en suite rooms and a very friendly welcome.

Further from the village, there's also a nice B&B at *Trendrennen Farm* (☎ 01736-810585, ⌨ trendrennen.com; 1D en suite/1D private bathroom/1Qd; ➽; from £45pp). Sit out in the huge garden and admire the view. The quad is an adjacent self-catering cottage.

About two miles (3km) further on, just past Porthguarnon, is another welcoming **campsite**, at *Treverven Farm* (off Map 64; ☎ 01736-810200, ⌨ treverventouringpark .co.uk; hiker & tent £8; Easter-Oct), which is signposted from the coast path. It's a well-run, well-appointed site on a working dairy farm, with a **shop** (8.30-10am & 5.30-7pm) selling basics for self-caterers, and a pop-up café in high season.

The Land's End Coaster **bus** service stops in Treen. [See pp52-5].

For a **taxi** try Logan Rock Cars (☎ 01736-871786, ⌨ loganrockcars.co.uk).

❑ **THE LOGAN ROCK**   [MAP 63, p191]

Right out on the headland of **Treryn Dinas** sits a massive 70-tonne boulder that could once be rocked by pushing it gently. That is until Lieutenant Goldsmith succeeded in pushing it right off its perch in 1824. Villagers were incensed as two local people had been employed as guides to the stone. The lieutenant promised to restore it to its original position, but despite help from Admiralty lifting equipment, was unable to restore its fine balance, although it can still be rocked with some difficulty.

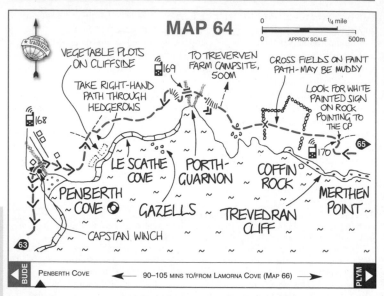

MAP 64

0 — ¼ mile
0 — APPROX SCALE — 500m

VEGETABLE PLOTS ON CLIFFSIDE

📱169

TO TREVERVEN FARM CAMPSITE, 500M

CROSS FIELDS ON FAINT PATH - MAY BE MUDDY

TAKE RIGHT-HAND PATH THROUGH HEDGEROWS

LOOK FOR WHITE PAINTED SIGN ON ROCK POINTING TO THE CP

📱168

📱170

65

LE SCATHE COVE

PORTH-GUARNON

COFFIN ROCK

MERTHEN POINT

PENBERTH COVE

GAZELLS

TREVEDRAN CLIFF

CAPSTAN WINCH

63

BUDE — PENBERTH COVE ◄— 90–105 MINS TO/FROM LAMORNA COVE (MAP 66) —► PLYM

LAMORNA [MAP 66, p196]

Lamorna is one of the few wooded coves along the coast path. Note that it is privately owned so you must keep your dog on a lead here or risk a fine. There isn't much in the way of services but walkers will be glad to discover *Lamorna Cove Café* (daily 10am-4pm, later in peak season), with ice cream, teas, pasties, and lunches served on the decking opposite. If your water bottle needs filling there's a tap outside the café.

You may prefer to head further up the cove road to the local pub, the *Lamorna Wink* (☎ 01736-731566; food Tue-Sun 11.30am-2pm & 6-9pm, closed Mon), which has a nautical theme with charts and maps on the walls and a ship's wheel above the fireplace. The name harks back to when spirits were banned but smuggled brandy could be had with a wink to the publican. Martha Grimes' murder mystery *The Lamorna Wink* is set in the area and is a good read.

The closest **B&B** is 1½ miles up the road: *Lamorna Pottery* (off Map 66; ☎ 01736-810330, 🖥 lamornapottery.co.uk; 1D/1T, both en suite; £52.50-57.50pp, sgl occ £95-105) has two lovely rooms, one

---

❑ MERRY MAIDENS AND PIPERS

Inland from the coast are two ancient sites, the **Merry Maidens** stone circle and the **Pipers**, two large standing stones nearby. According to legend the Merry Maidens were nineteen young girls dancing in the fields to the tunes of the two nearby Pipers when they should have been attending vespers on the Sabbath. For their sins they were all turned to stone.

You could visit these sites by walking inland (see Map 65) and then staying on the road and walking to Lamorna (see Map 66) but this involves walking along narrow roads which get busy in the summer. The alternative is to return on the same path.

with its own garden, and a *café* (**fb**; Wed-Sun 11am-5pm) with a tasty lunchtime menu including salads, quiches, soups and homemade curries. Evening meals are available by arrangement. It first opened as a **pottery** in 1948, and you can still buy locally crafted ceramics here.

First's Land's End Coaster **bus** service stops at what they call Lamorna Turn, a junction about a one-mile walk uphill from the cove. Apparently, if buses drove all the way down to the cove they'd struggle to get back up to the main road. [See pp52-5 for details].

LAMORNA TO MOUSEHOLE [MAPS 66-68]

In truth, this straightforward **2-mile (3km, 40-50 mins)** section isn't the most pleasant stretch you'll walk on this trip as much of it is very overgrown; at times the path can feel claustrophobic, your arms and legs will get scratched and stung, and if it's wet your clothes will get soaked.

The route begins comfortably enough, passing through the pine forest of the **Kemyel Crease Nature Reserve**, but then heads inland through the overgrown scrub before finally popping you out at the top of the hill above Mousehole. On reaching the road you turn right and walk down into the tiny village acclaimed by Dylan Thomas as 'the loveliest village in England'.

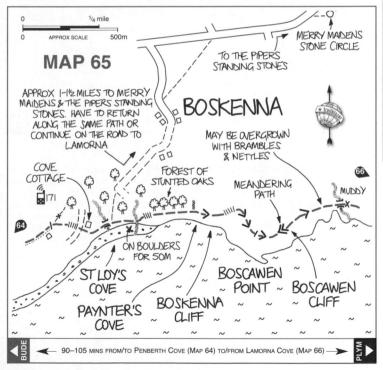

TO LAMORNA POTTERY B&B, 2¼ MILES
& LAMORNA TURN, ½ MILE

PUBLIC PHONE

Lamorna Wink

MAP 66   LAMORNA

BOULDERS & ROCKS

0   ¼ mile

174 Lamorna Cove Café

0   APPROX SCALE   500m

67

ROCKY PATH, PLEASANT WALKING

LAMORNA COVE

TREGURNOW CLIFF

CARN MELLYN

CELTIC CROSS

ENTRANCE TO MINACK CHRONICLES NATURE RESERVE

173

LAMORNA POINT

SAFE SWIMMING WITHIN THE HARBOUR

METAL GATES

172

65

CARN BARGES

GAZELL

TATER-DU LIGHTHOUSE

TATER-DU

BUDE

← 90–105 MINS FROM/TO PENBERTH COVE (MAP 64) →   LAMORNA COVE

ROUTE GUIDE AND MAPS

PLYM

MOUSEHOLE
[map p198 & MAP 68, p199]

Pronounced 'mowzell', possibly from the Cornish *mouz hel* or 'maiden's brook' or alternatively because the entrance to the harbour was so tight that getting through it was like trying to sail through a mouse hole, Mousehole is a former pilchard fishing village. The old stone quay and cottages are hardly equal to the volume of visitors that crowd in during the season, and traffic can be an issue at times on the narrow streets, but the village is like a film-set; a romantic notion of what a Cornish village should look like and one of the most appealing on the coast path.

There are plenty of services available to the walker although with Penzance only five miles away, a couple of hours on foot or 15 minutes on the bus, many will push on to the much bigger destination. Anyone walking the coast path in December may like to be here for **Mousehole Lights**, when the village is illuminated by a display of Christmas lights, and **Tom Bawcock's Eve** (see p16) on the 23rd.

Coming down the hill into the village you pass the **Wild Bird Hospital** (Map 68; ☎ 01736-731386, **fb**; daily 10am-4.30pm; free) for injured, orphaned or oiled birds, which you might decide to visit.

In the centre of the village is a **newsagent/post office** (Mon-Sat 8am-5.30pm, Sun 8am-noon) with some limited groceries. *Hole Foods Deli* (**fb**; 8am-5pm,

Sun 9am-noon) is a **café** and **deli** rolled into one, selling various goodies and groceries, and serving healthy breakfasts (poached eggs with avocado and chilli) and exotic lunches (sweet potato and harissa tagine) alongside fine wines and ciders.

There's an **ATM** (£1.50 charge) in the Ship Inn (see Where to Stay).

Where to stay
Campers should head to Mousehole Camping (see p198), a mile uphill in the village of Paul.

There are some very smart **B&B** rooms, some with sea views, at *The Ship Inn* (☎ 01736-731234, 🖳 shipinnmouse hole.co.uk, **fb**; 1S/6D/1Qd, 🍽; 🐾; from £50pp, sgl occ full room rate, sgl £95), an old pub which celebrates the local festival, Tom Bawcock's Eve (see p16) on 23rd December. For something much more upmarket, *The Old Coastguard Hotel* (☎ 01736-731222, 🖳 oldcoastguardhotel.co

.uk, **fb**; 14D; 🍽; 🐾; £79-132.50pp, sgl occ from £110) has regal rooms and fabulous sea views across Mount's Bay.

Where to eat and drink
As you come down into the village, you'll pass *Old Pilchard Press Café* (☎ 01736-731154, **fb**; 8 Old Quay St; summer Sun-Thur 11am-3pm, winter hours vary) which does breakfasts, cream teas (with scones freshly baked every day), ploughman's, paninis and salads.

For a traditional tearoom, the best in the village is *Four Teas Café* (☎ 01736-731532; summer daily 9am-5pm, winter hours vary) – inspired by the 1940s, hence the name. The welcome is warm and friendly and the Cornish cream teas are unrivalled; the sandwiches aren't half bad either.

Tiny *Jessie's Dairy* (**fb**; daily 10.30am-4.30pm) is difficult to pass by on a hot day. They have all sorts of ice cream including gooseberry and wild cherry. They

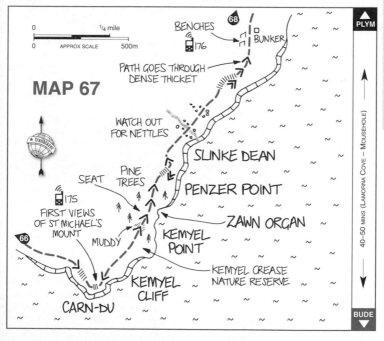

MAP 67

ROUTE GUIDE AND MAPS

40-50 MINS (LAMORNA COVE – MOUSEHOLE)

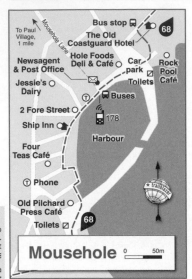

Bus stop
To Paul Village, 1 mile
Mousehole Lane
68
The Old Coastguard Hotel
Hole Foods Deli & Café
Newsagent & Post Office
Car park
Rock Pool Café
Jessie's Dairy
Toilets
Buses
2 Fore Street
178
Ship Inn
Harbour
Four Teas Café
Phone
trailblazer
Old Pilchard Press Café
68
Toilets

Mousehole 0 ____ 50m

the usual pub classics (£12-14) plus the local 'catch of the day' fish dish (£16).

For more refined dining, seek out the well-regarded licensed bistro *2 Fore Street* (☎ 01736-731164, 🖳 2forestreet.co.uk, **fb**; Feb-Dec 9am-10.30am, noon-3.30pm & 5-9.30pm). Choose whether to eat inside or in the garden if the weather is good. Evening mains (£10-20) feature lamb cutlets, portobello mushroom burgers and Newlyn crab.

Even classier is the restaurant at *The Old Coastguard Hotel* (see Where to stay; food served noon-2.30pm & 5.30-9pm; booking recommended). The food is fantastic, as are the sea views, and there are some fine real ales on tap too.

As you leave Mousehole, you'll see a sign pointing you down towards the rocky seafront where *Rock Pool Café* (☎ 01736-732645, 🖳 rockpoolmousehole.co.uk, **fb**; summer daily 10am-6pm, winter hours vary; ✖), with its weathered wooden tables perched above Mousehole's small sea pool, awaits to ply you with cakes, coffee and smoked salmon bagels, before sending you on your way towards Penzance.

also serve Cornish pasties and takeaway sandwiches.

For a good-value evening meal, try the pub-grub menu at *The Ship Inn* (see Where to stay; Mon noon-8.30pm, Thur-Sun 1.30-8.30pm, closed Tue & Wed), which includes

Transport
[See pp52-5 for details]   First Kernow's MOUS **bus** to Penzance runs throughout the day.

PAUL   [MAP 68]
A mile to the north of Mousehole, this tiny village is where you'll find *Mousehole Camping* (☎ 07470-920006, 🖳 mouseholecamping.co.uk, **fb**; £10) based at the local football club, Mousehole AFC. From Mousehole, walk north up Mousehole Lane and take the second left after Paul Parish Church. Opposite the church is a good pub with rooms, *The King's Arms* (01736-

731224, 🖳 thekings armspaul.com; 2D/1D, T or Tr/1Qd, en suite; from £45pp, sgl occ from £60). The family room has a double bed and bunks. They also do **food** (Mon-Fri 5.30-9pm, Sat-Sun noon-2pm & 5.30-8pm; most mains £12-15) and have St Austell brewery ales.

The No 5 **bus** service calls in Paul. [For details see pp52-5.]

MOUSEHOLE TO PENZANCE   [MAPS 68-70]

The **4-mile (6km, 1-1¼hrs) section** between Mousehole and Penzance is all on tarmac. From the harbour car park the path stays close to the shore on the concrete sea wall but soon leaves it to join a cycle path all the way through **Newlyn** to **Penzance**. On the way you'll pass the memorial to the Penlee lifeboat, the *Solomon Browne*, lost with all hands in 1981 whilst trying to rescue the crew of the *Union Star*, an event of national importance at the time.

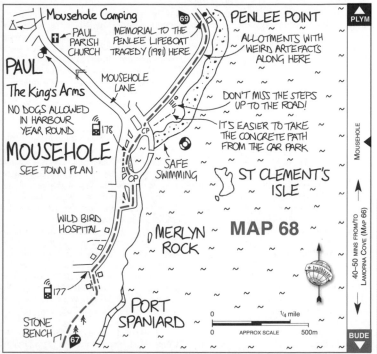

❑ CORNWALL'S FISHING INDUSTRY

One of Cornwall's oldest fishing industries is that of fishing for pilchard. Shoals containing millions of fish would appear seasonally off the Cornish coast and a lookout man, called a *huer*, would be stationed on top of the cliffs to alert the community of a sighting. When the pilchards were spotted he would cry 'hevva' (shoal) and then use semaphore to direct the waiting fishermen to surround the fish with their nets.

Over-fishing brought the industry to an end by the 1920s, although recently pilchards have once again been caught off Cornwall. Pressing and salting of pilchards is still carried out by traditional methods in Newlyn with the end product being exported to Italy as was traditionally done.

The number of fishing boats in Cornwall continues to decrease. According to the news website Cornwall Live, in 2019 there were just 543 boats and 917 fishermen working along the Cornwall coast (down from 724 and 1141 in 2000), although interestingly the value of the fish they landed increased significantly during the same period, from £26 million in 2000 to £43 million in 2019.

In the smaller harbours most of the fishing boats you see are landing crabs and lobsters using various types of crab pot, although they may also use nets to fish for spider crabs, ray and anglerfish depending on the season. These vessels tend not to work more than five to ten miles away from their respective ports.

NEWLYN [MAP 69]

Newlyn is a working fishing port that stead-fastly refuses to be turned into a nostalgia trip for the benefit of the tourists. The Fish Festival (see p16) is held here in August.

Newlyn also is famous for a colony of artists who arrived in the 19th century, drawn by the seascapes and its similarity to Brittany, in France. Although their names may be unfamiliar to many of us, in their day the work of Stanhope Forbes, Walter Langley and Edwin Harris was widely applauded and can be seen at Penlee House Gallery (see p202) in Penzance. **Newlyn Art Gallery** (☎ 01736-363715, 💻 newlynartgall ery.co.uk; Tue-Sat 10am-5pm; **café** same hours; £4.50) beautifully showcases work by contemporary artists of local provenance.

For **food** supplies, there's a **Co-op** (daily 7am-11pm; **ATM** inside), while **The Little Greengrocer** (Tue-Sat 10am-noon) does wonderfully fresh fruit and veg. **Newlyn Pharmacy** (Mon-Fri 8.45am-5.30pm, Sat 8.45am-noon) is on The Strand.

Where to stay

There's a lovely **B&B** as you walk in to Newlyn from Mousehole: *The Smugglers* (☎ 01736-331501, 💻 smugglersnewlyn.co .uk; 4D; from £55pp; usually min 2 nights) overlooks the dock and beyond, across the curve of Mount's Bay to Penzance, and is arguably one of the best B&Bs along the coast path. Named after different Newlyn artists, the rooms are large and comfortable with king-sized beds and sea views.

You could also try the *Swordfish Inn* (☎ 01736-362830, 💻 swordfishinn.co.uk, **fb**; 4D; from £45pp, sgl occ from £80) for en suite accommodation. Rooms are bright and spacious, and the showers are decent.

Where to eat and drink

If you're self catering, Newlyn is *the* place to purchase fresh fish; there are several places selling the day's catch along the harbour front.

For breakfast, lunch or just a caffeine fix, there are several options. *Aunty May's* (**fb**; Mon-Sat 9am-3pm), which has been going since 1996, is just the place for freshly baked pasties. Across the road *Lovetts*

(💻 lovetts-newlyn.co.uk; 9am-2pm & 5-10pm) is a tiny barista coffee shop that transforms into a small wine bar come evening. Larger, and set back slightly from the main road, *Duke St Café* (☎ 01736-368000, **fb**; Mon-Sat 9am-4pm, Sun 9am-1pm) is a popular, flower-filled tearoom.

Pub-wise, the *Red Lion Inn* (☎ 01736-362012, **fb**; food summer daily noon-2.30pm & 5-8pm, winter noon-2pm only) is renowned for its crab soup.

The Smugglers Restaurant (see Where to stay; summer Wed-Sat 6.30-9.30pm, winter hours may vary) has a wonderful view of the harbour; the very boats you are watching have probably brought in the fish you are eating. Most mains cost from £12 to £16, and they have Camel Valley wines available too.

On the bridge, *Mackerel Sky Seafood Bar* (☎ 01736-367199, 💻 mackerelsky cafe.co.uk, **fb**; summer daily noon-9pm, winter hours vary) is a charming riverside seafood restaurant, which doesn't take bookings. They serve tapas-style tasting plates (around £7-10) to share, such as mussels, crab claws, scallops and smoked mackerel pâté.

For fast food, try *Lewis's Fish 'n' Chips* (Mon, Tue, Thur & Fri 11am-2pm & 4.45-9pm, Wed & Sat 4.45-9pm) or *China Garden* (☎ 01736-367483; Tue-Sun 5.10-11pm), a Chinese takeaway. There's also a decent Italian, *The Bridge* (☎ 01736-363446, 💻 thebridgenewlyn.com, **fb**; Mon-Sat 11am-2.30pm & 6-9pm, Sun 6-9pm), which does pizza, pasta and various seafood specials. Takeaway is available too.

A mention must also go to *Jelbert's* (daily from 11am), an ice cream shop selling one flavour only (vanilla), but which has built up an international reputation over the years. Single-scoop cones cost £2.

Transport

[See pp52-5 for details] First Kernow's Land's End Coaster and MOUS **bus** services pass through Newlyn, as does the No 5.

For a **taxi** there's Stone's Taxis (☎ 01736-363400, 💻 stones.taxi).

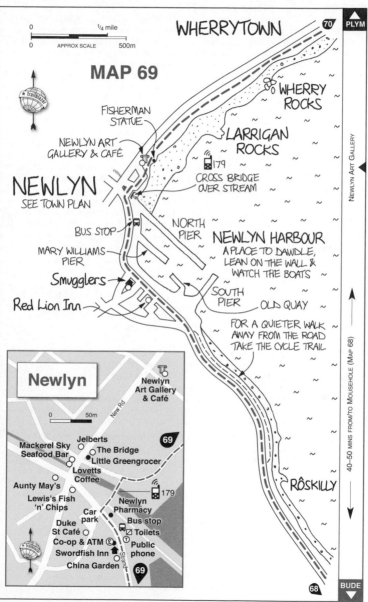

WHERRYTOWN

0   ¼ mile
0   APPROX SCALE   500m

MAP 69

PLYM

70

★ trailblazer

FISHERMAN STATUE

NEWLYN ART GALLERY & CAFÉ

WHERRY ROCKS

LARRIGAN ROCKS

179

CROSS BRIDGE OVER STREAM

NEWLYN
SEE TOWN PLAN

BUS STOP

MARY WILLIAMS PIER

NORTH PIER

NEWLYN HARBOUR
A PLACE TO DAWDLE, LEAN ON THE WALL & WATCH THE BOATS

Smugglers

Red Lion Inn

SOUTH PIER

OLD QUAY

FOR A QUIETER WALK AWAY FROM THE ROAD TAKE THE CYCLE TRAIL

RÔSKILLY

NEWLYN ART GALLERY

40–50 MINS FROM/TO MOUSEHOLE (MAP 68)

BUDE

68

Newlyn

0   50m

New Rd

Newlyn Art Gallery & Café

69

Jelberts
Mackerel Sky Seafood Bar
The Bridge
Little Greengrocer
Lovetts Coffee
Aunty May's
Lewis's Fish 'n' Chips
Duke St Café
Co-op & ATM
Swordfish Inn
China Garden

Newlyn Pharmacy
Bus stop
Toilets
Public phone

Car park

179

Strand

★ trailblazer

69

ROUTE GUIDE AND MAPS

PENZANCE [MAP 70, p204]

The heyday of busy, bustling Penzance was in the 19th century when it was the commercial centre of the tin-mining industry. A statue of **Sir Humphry Davy**, born in the town and inventor of the miners' safety lamp, stands outside the Market House.

The town is a happy hunting ground for those who love galleries, rivalling St Ives in its artistic prominence. The flagship is **Penlee House Gallery** (☎ 01736-363625, 🖳 penleehouse.org.uk, Morrab Rd; Apr-Oct Mon-Sat 10am-5pm, Nov-Mar to 4.30pm, £6), inside a grand Victorian house in the leafy grounds of **Penlee Park**. The gallery has a wide-ranging collection from archaeology to photography documenting the life and history of west Cornwall, as well as an art collection from the late 19th century painted by well-known Newlyn artists. A close second, under the same umbrella as the Newlyn Gallery, is **The Exchange** (☎ 01736-363715, 🖳 newlynartgallery.co.uk, Princes St; Jul-mid Sep daily 10am-5pm, mid Sep-Jun Tue-Sat only; £4.50; café same hours) in the town's former telephone exchange, showcasing the best of contemporary art.

Also in Penlee Park is a small **outdoor theatre** (☎ 01726-285367, 🖳 penleeparktheatre.com; tickets £10-16, child £5-10) which puts on performances in July and August. Shows range from Shakespeare plays to Cornish sea shanty concerts, and tend to start at 7.30pm, with occasional matinées. There's a licensed bar and you can even order a pre-show veggie curry (£6.50) through the website when you book tickets.

Don't miss a walk along historic **Chapel Street**, in some ways charmingly unchanged since the 19th century. The Grade 1 listed **Egyptian House**, with its extraordinary facade, dates back to 1835.

❏ VISITING THE ISLES OF SCILLY

Penzance is one of the gateways to the Isles of Scilly, an archipelago of five inhabited islands and numerous small rocky islets, 28 miles off Cornwall, with a population of around 2300. They are promoted for their peace and tranquillity, and can make a fantastic short break from the rigours of coast-path walking.

You have three options for travelling to the Isles of Scilly:

● **Ferry** With **Isles of Scilly Travel** (☎ 01736-334220, 🖳 islesofscilly-travel.co.uk). *Scillonian III* (Mar-Nov; adult/child sgl from £61.95/34.25, day rtn enquire for rates) sails from Penzance once a day to the main island of St Mary's. Services operate daily in season except during the World Pilot Gig Championships (early May), although can be cancelled due to weather conditions. Departure times vary depending on the tides, but the boat leaves Penzance in the morning (between 8.30am and 10.30am) and returns in the afternoon (between 3pm and 4.30pm). The journey takes 2hrs 45mins.

● **Plane** Also with Isles of Scilly Travel. The Skybus service from Land's End to St Mary's (all year, adult/child sgl from £97.95/76.25, day return Mon-Fri only, enquire for rates) takes 20 minutes with at least half a dozen flights each day. Single flights are also available from Newquay (30 mins, all year) and Exeter (60 mins, Mar-Nov).

You can buy a fly-sail combo day-return ticket from £84 (child £64.50).

In Penzance, the Isles of Scilly Travel's **ticket office** (Mon-Fri 8am-4pm) is on Quay St, just up from the dock.

● **Helicopter** After the closure of the old Penzance heliport in 2012, there was no helicopter service for several years until, with huge local support, a new heliport was built at Eastern Green and services recommenced in 2020. **Penzance Helicopters** (☎ 01736-780828, 🖳 penzancehelicopters.co.uk; sgl adult/child £129.50/108.50; day return £185) fly to both St Mary's and Tresco, running up to 17 flights a day, six days a week, taking just 15 minutes. They also offer a last-minute day return for 'spontaneous sorts or weather watchers' of £129, bookable within 24 hours of departure.

Built in 1935, the wonderful art-deco outdoor swimming pool, the **Jubilee Pool** (☎ 01736-369224, 🖳 jubileepool.co.uk; daily 9.30am-1pm & 1.30-5pm; £6) is also worth a visit. The main pool is open from May to September, but there's also a heated geo-thermal pool (£11.75) that's open year round. There's a *café* here too.

Golowan Festival (see p15) in June, is a celebration of the arts that includes theatre, music, carnival and fireworks.

Services

The **tourist information centre** (☎ 01736-335530; Mon-Fri 10am-4pm) is right outside the railway station.

The main shopping street is Market Jew St, with a couple of **supermarkets** including Co-op (Mon-Sat 7am-10pm, Sun 10.30am-4.30pm), Tesco Express (daily 7am-10pm), and the **newsagent** WH Smith (Mon-Sat 8.30am-5.30pm, Sun 10am-4pm), which houses the **post office** (Mon-Fri 9am-5.30pm, Sat 9am-2pm).

Millets Outdoor Shop (Mon-Fri 9am-5.30pm, Sat to 6pm, Sun 10am-4pm) and Mountain Warehouse (Mon-Fri 9am-5pm, Sat to 5.30pm, Sun 10am-4pm) both have plenty of **camping supplies** including camping-stove gas.

Also on Market Jew St are several **banks**, including HSBC, Barclays and NatWest, all with **ATMs**.

For free **internet access** try Penzance Library (☎ 01736-363954, Alverton Rd; Mon-Fri 9am-5pm, Sat 10am-1pm; WI-FI), on Alverton St. England and Wales library members get one hour's free use; non members 30 minutes.

There are some good **bookshops** including The Edge of the World Bookshop (Mon-Sat 9am-5.30pm, Sun 10am-4pm) at 23 Market Jew St.

Suds & Surf **launderette** (☎ 01736-364815; daily 9am-8pm) is near the railway station.

Causeway Head often has **fruit and vegetable stalls** on its pedestrianised strip; there's also a small **cinema** on this street. This way also leads to **West Cornwall Hospital** (☎ 01736-874000), which has a 24hr Urgent Care Centre, while down Morrab Rd there's a **medical surgery** (☎

01736-363866, 🖳 morrabsurgery.co.uk; Mon-Fri 8.30am-5.30pm) with a **dental surgery** next door.

Back on Market Jew St there are a couple of **pharmacies** including branches of Boots (Mon-Sat 9am-5.30pm; second branch on Morrab Rd, Mon-Fri 8.30am-6pm, Sat 9am-1pm), and Superdrug (Mon-Sat 9am-5.30pm, Sun 10am-4pm).

Where to stay

There's a wide choice of accommodation in Penzance, particularly B&Bs, but be aware that very few places accept advance bookings for one-night stays in the main season.

Hostels & camping *YHA Penzance* (☎ 0345-371 9653, 🖳 yha.org.uk/hostel/yha-penzance; 100 beds; £17-25pp) is housed inside a lovely Georgian Mansion, but is a bit out of the way, over the A30 at Castle Horneck. There are dorm beds, private doubles and twins, and even some family rooms. You can **camp** (£8-14pp) in the grounds; campers have their own shower block but can use the other facilities in the hostel. They also have accommodation in bell tents (sleep 5, from £99, inc bedding). There's a games room, a barbecue area and a **bar-café** with real ales on tap, and food available three times a day. It's about a 15-minute walk from the coast path: to get here walk up Alexandra Rd, left onto Alverton Rd, then right on Castle Horneck Rd and across the A30.

Much closer to the path is *Ponsandane Campsite* (Map 71; ☎ 01736-351777, 🖳 ponsandane.co.uk; Jul-Sep; 🐾; hiker & tent £10), beside the Tesco superstore as you leave Penzance. It has clean showers and toilets, and a small breakfast café.

B&Bs At 29 Lannoweth Rd, the owners of *easyPZ Stay* (☎ 01736-368136, 🖳 easypz .info; 2D en suite, 1D private facilities; £40-45pp), have turned their small backpackers hostel into a B&B with a difference. Breakfast is self-serve, set up in the shared kitchen, which guests can also use to make other meals. There's free tea and coffee throughout the day, and a communal lounge (with DVDs to watch, and a computer that guests can use) and garden to hang out in. The rooms are spotless, decorated artistically and generally un-hostel like, though the atmosphere is still relaxed.

Alexandra Rd is lined with more traditional B&Bs. Built in the 19th century following the arrival of the trains, many of these buildings are known as 'gentlemen's residences' as they were built for the local professionals. The following are all of a reasonable standard: *Torwood House* (☎ 01736-360063, 🖳 torwoodhousehotel.co .uk; 1S/1T/3D/2Tr; ☕; 🐾; £35-37.50pp;

sgl occ £45-55) is a nice cheerful place and has been welcoming guests for more than 30 years; *Tremont House* (☎ 01736-362614, 🖳 tremonthotel.co.uk; 2S/6D/2T; from £40pp, sgl from £45, sgl occ from £70; min 3 nights) is a lovely friendly place with breakfasts so good they've won awards. They've also received a green tourism award for their eco-friendly approach to running their B&B. On this same strip is *The Dunedin* (☎ 01736-362652, 🖳 dunedinhotel.co.uk; 1S/4D/

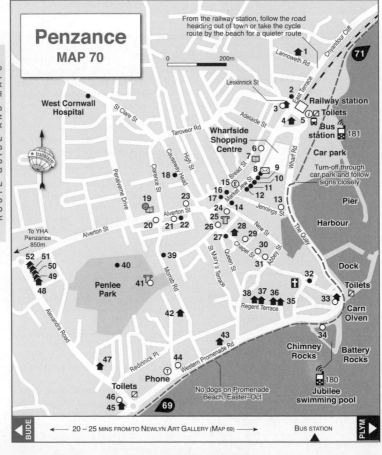

Penzance
MAP 70

ROUTE GUIDE AND MAPS

From the railway station, follow the road heading out of town or take the cycle route by the beach for a quieter route

Chyandour Cliff

71

0   200m

Lannoweth Rd   1

West Cornwall Hospital

St Clare St

Leskinnick St

East Terrace

2

Railway station

3   i **Toilets**

Adelaide St

4   5   **Bus station**   181

Taroveor Rd

Wharfside Shopping Centre

Wharf Rd

Car park

Turn-off through car park and follow signs closely

High St

Clarence St

Causewayhead

Bread St

6

7

8   9

10

Pier

18

15

16

17

11

12

13

Market Jew St

Jennings St

Harbour

19

23

24

14

Alverton St

25

26

28

29

New St

To YHA Penzance 850m

20   21   22

27

30

Chapel St

31

Dock

52 51

50

49

48

39

40

41

Morrab Rd

St Mary's Terrace

Queen St

Abbey St

32

Toilets

33

Carn Olven

Penlee Park

38 37 36

35

Regent Terrace

Alexandra Road

42

43

34

Chimney Rocks

Battery Rocks

47

44

Redinnick Pl

Western Promenade Rd

Phone

180

46

45

69

Toilets

No dogs on Promenade Beach, Easter–Oct

Jubilee swimming pool

2Tr; from £40pp, sgl occ from £60; min 2/3 nights); and *The Pendennis* (☎ 01736-691301, 🖳 thependennis.co.uk; 2S/5D/1T; ➥; from £37.50pp, sgl/sgl occ from £70).

At *Keigwin House* (☎ 01736-363930, 🖳 keigwinhouse.co.uk; 2S/1T/2T or D/3D/1Tr, most en suite; ➥; from £38, sgl occ from £60pp) there is a warm welcome for hikers as the owners are also keen walkers.

Back down the hill near the front, walkers are also very welcome at *Treventon Guest House* (☎ 01736-332730, 🖳 treventon.co.uk; 4D/1T/1Tr; ➥; from £35pp).

Nearby Morrab Rd also has some accommodation, including *The Lynwood* (☎ 01736-365871, 🖳 lynwood-guesthouse .co.uk; 2S/2T/2D, some en suite; £35-50pp, sgl £45 55; adults only) at No 41, which provides dressing gowns for some rooms and has drying facilities.

Continuing along Western Promenade you reach Regent Terrace with several guest houses to choose from, including: *Warwick House* (☎ 01736-363881, 🖳 war wickhousepenzance.co.uk; 2S/3D/2T; ➥; from £34pp, sgl from £67; min 3 nights) at No 17; *Lombard House* (☎ 01736-364897, 🖳 lombardhousehotel.com; 6 flexible rooms, ➥; from £50pp, sgl occ from £75, sgl from £53.50) at No 16; *Blue Seas Hotel* (☎ 01736-364744, 🖳 blueseashotel-pen zance.co.uk; Mar-Dec; 4D/1D orT/2Tr; ➥; from £50pp, sgl occ from £73) at No 13; and *Camilla House Hotel* (☎ 01736-363771, 🖳 camillahouse.co.uk; 2S/6D or T; £60-70pp, sgl from £70) at No 12.

Hotels & pubs On the Promenade is the smart, recently refurbished *Beachfield Hotel* (☎ 01736-331100, 🖳 beachfield .co.uk; 6S/4T/4D/4F; ➥; 🐾; from £90pp,

---

PENZANCE – MAP KEY

Where to stay
1 EasyPZ Stay
3 The Longboat Inn
4 Premier Inn
28 Union Hotel
33 Dolphin Tavern
35 Warwick House
36 Lombard House
37 Blue Seas
38 Camilla House Hotel
42 Lynwood
43 Lugger Inn
45 Beachfield Hotel
47 Treventon Guest House
48 Torwood House
49 Pendennis
50 Keigwin House
51 Tremont House
52 The Dunedin

Where to eat and drink
3 The Longboat Inn
6 Quirky Bird Café
13 Old Lifeboat House Bistro
20 The Shore
21 Lavenders Café
23 New Hong Kong
24 Harris's Restaurant
26 Curry Corner
29 The Bakehouse
30 Turks Head
31 Admiral Benbow
33 Dolphin Tavern
34 Jubilee Pool Café
41 Orangery Café
44 Fraser's
46 Thai Moon

Other
2 Suds & Surf Launderette
5 Tourist Information
7 Edge of the World Books

Other (*cont'd*)
8 WH Smith & Post Office
9 Superdrug
10 Mountain Warehouse
11 Boots
12 Tesco Express
14 Co-op
15 Barclays Bank & ATM
16 Millets
17 Sir Humphrey Davy statue
18 Cinema
19 Library & internet access
22 Boots Pharmacy
25 The Exchange
27 The Egyptian House
32 Isles of Scilly Travel Ticket Office
39 Surgery
40 Open-air theatre
41 Penlee House Gallery

ROUTE GUIDE AND MAPS

sgl from £170; room only; breakfast £9.95) with sea views and a restaurant. Further along the Promenade is the less refined, but arguably more welcoming *Lugger Inn* (☎ 01736-363236, 🖳 thelugger.co.uk; Ⓛ; 20 rooms; from £32.50pp, sgl occ from £60) which also has a restaurant and bar with very popular road-side terrace seating.

Dating back to the 17th century, *The Union Hotel* (☎ 01736-362319, 🖳 union hotel.co.uk; 28 rooms; 🖤; from £46pp, sgl/ sgl occ from £75/82), on Chapel St, offers old-fashioned rooms but bags of history. Charles Dickens once stayed, and from here the victory at the Battle of Trafalgar was first announced to the public in 1805.

For something more modern, there's a *Premier Inn* (☎ 0330-1281340 or ☎ 01736 805950, 🖳 premierinn.com; 61 rooms; 🖤; from £20pp room only) beside the railway station. Breakfast costs £9.50.

For a pub with rooms, there's *The Longboat Inn* (☎ 01736-364137, 🖳 long boatinn.co.uk; 1S/2T/3D/1F; from £54pp, sgl from £65), close to the railway station; or *The Dolphin Tavern* (☎ 01736-364106, 🖳 dolphintavern.co.uk; 3D; from £55pp) down by the docks. Both get good reviews.

Where to eat and drink

Cafés There are plenty of tearooms and coffee houses in town including the stylish licensed café *Orangery* (☎ 01736-361325, 🖳 penleehouse.org.uk/cafe; Apr-Oct Mon-Sat 10am-5pm, winter to 4.30pm), overlooking the gardens at Penlee House Gallery. Nearby, the excellent *Lavenders Café* (🖳 lavendersdelibakery.co.uk, **fb**; Mon-Sat 9am-6pm) is attached to a deli and bakery, while on Market Jew St is the friendly and down-to-earth *Quirky Bird Café* (☎ 01736-448340, **fb**; Mon-Sat 8am-4.30pm, Sun 10am-4pm) with good-value food and art on the walls you can purchase.

Pubs & restaurants There are two wonderful old pubs on historic Chapel St: the swashbuckling *Admiral Benbow* (☎ 01736-363448, 🖳 thebenbow.com, **fb**; food Tue-Fri 6-9.15pm, Sat & Sun noon-9.15pm) is named after a 17th-century seafarer whose story is told in the menu notes (mains £10-12). No less nautical in theme,

though with a more extensive menu, is the nearby *Turks Head* (☎ 01736-363093, 🖳 turksheadpenzance.co.uk, **fb**; daily noon-9.30pm; most mains £12-15). You could also try *The Longboat Inn* (see Where to stay; **fb**; food daily 7am-9pm; 🐾; evening mains £12-14), which does food all day and popular Sunday roasts, or *The Dolphin Tavern* (see Where to stay; food daily 11am-10pm; 🐾) offering burgers, curries, veggie options and plenty of seafood (mains £12-18).

The charming *Old Lifeboat House Bistro* (☎ 01736-369409, 🖳 oldlifeboat housebistro.com, **fb**; 🐾; daily 5.30-9pm, Sat & Sun also 3-5pm) is a great place to come for some seafood. Mains (£14-21) include their speciality fish pie as well as dishes such as pan-roasted duck breast.

For something even more chic, the intimate little *Bakehouse* (☎ 01736-331331, 🖳 bakehouserestaurant.co.uk, **fb**; Tue 6-8.30pm, Wed-Sat noon-2pm & 6-8.30pm), found through an archway off Chapel St, has a well-devised menu (evening mains £16-28), including a range of steaks.

Held by some to be the best restaurant in Penzance, *Harris's Restaurant* (☎ 01736-364408, 🖳 harrissrestaurant.co.uk; Tue-Sat 6.30-9.30pm) is at 46 New St. The menu (mains £22-42) includes such culinary delights as roasted monkfish, Newlyn crab and grilled goats' cheese with walnuts. The whole lobster (£42.50) is pretty special too.

Receiving rave reviews, another fine-dining option for seafood is *The Shore* (☎ 01736-362444, 🖳 theshorerestaurant.uk; Tue-Sat 7-9pm; set menu £69pp; booking essential), at 13/14 Alverton St. It's intimate (only 14 seats), but the food is outstanding; Chef Bruce Rennie goes to Newlyn market every morning to source fresh fish and bakes all his own bread.

On the corner of Alexandra Rd and the Promenade, *Thai Moon* (☎ 01736-369699, 🖳 thaimoon.co.uk; Mon-Sat 5-10pm) is a friendly and popular Thai restaurant which also does takeaway.

Takeaways There are lots of **fish & chip shops** in Penzance, but a good choice is *Fraser's* (🖳 frasersfishandchips.co.uk; Mon-Tue 4-8.30pm, Wed-Sun noon-

8.30/9pm) on the Promenade. Next door to a small **Chinese supermarket** on Alverton St, you can get Chinese food at *New Hong Kong* (☎ 01736-362707; daily 5.30-11pm). For Indian food, *Curry Corner* (☎ 01736-331558; Mon-Sat noon-2pm, Sun-Thur 5pm-midnight, Fri & Sat to 1am) is a sound choice.

Transport
[See pp50-5 for details] **Train** services, operated by GWR, run hourly to St Erth (change for St Ives), Par (for Newquay) and Plymouth. There are many direct trains daily to London Paddington (about 5hrs), mostly in the morning. There's also the 'Night Riviera' sleeper train (9.45pm; 7hrs).

Bus services include the Land's End Coaster and Falmouth Coaster, and the Nos 2, 5, 7, 8, 16/16A, 17 and 18. Penzance is also served by National Express **coach** services (Nos 104, 406 & 504).

For a **taxi**, try Penzance Taxis (☎ 01736-366366, 🖳 penzancetaxis.co.uk).

PENZANCE TO MARAZION
[MAPS 70-73]

The walk to Marazion (**3 miles/ 5km, 45-50 mins**) is on a cycle path between the railway line and the beach and makes for quite a pleasant stroll with the whole prospect of Mount's Bay to add to the enjoyment.

On the way to Marazion, at **Long Rock**, you pass *The Station House* (☎ 01736-350459, 🖳 thesta tionhouse.webs.com; food 12.30-2.30pm & 5.30-9.30pm), a friendly **pub** with views of St Michael's Mount, and *Jordan's Café* (Map 71; ☎ 01736-360502, **fb**; Tue-Sun 10am-4.30pm), with freshly baked pizza and hot and cold baguettes, to eat in or take away. But most walkers push on to Marazion.

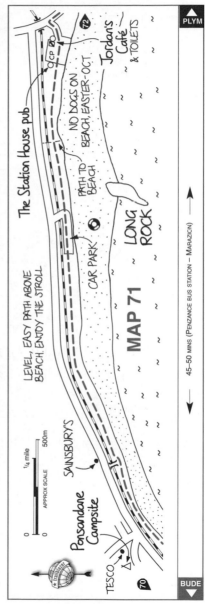

ROUTE GUIDE AND MAPS

MARAZION [MAPS 72 & 73]

The name derives from the Cornish *marghas byghan* or 'small market' from the days when the village held two markets, the marghas byghan and the *marghas yow* or 'Thursday market'. Over time these have become Marazion and Market Jew, the latter now the name of the main street in Penzance.

The iconic island of **St Michael's Mount** (see box p210) attracts huge numbers of visitors every year. The village itself is quaint and has much to satisfy the curious wanderer. The little **Marazion**

Museum (Easter-Oct 10am-4pm; £1), inside the Town Hall building, was once the jail and a typical cell has been reconstructed. Of interest to nature lovers is the **RSPB Nature Reserve** (☎ 01736-711682; open 24hrs; free) on Marazion Marsh, which has Cornwall's largest reed bed.

Cobble Corner Newsagents and **shop** (Mon-Sat 7am-6.30pm, Sun 7am-2pm) houses the **post office** (same hours) and has a free **ATM** inside. Nearby, there's a **pharmacy** (Mon-Fri 9am-1pm & 2-5.30pm, Sat 9am-noon).

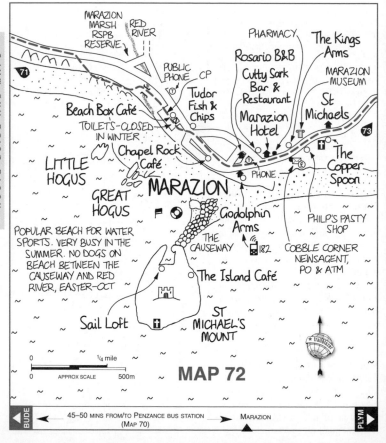

MARAZION MARSH RSPB RESERVE

RED RIVER

PHARMACY

The Kings Arms

71

PUBLIC PHONE   CP

Rosario B&B

Cutty Sark Bar & Restaurant

MARAZION MUSEUM

Beach Box Café

Tudor Fish & Chips

Marazion Hotel

St Michaels

73

TOILETS-CLOSED IN WINTER

Chapel Rock Café

PHONE

The Copper Spoon

LITTLE HOGUS

MARAZION

GREAT HOGUS

Godolphin Arms

PHILP'S PASTY SHOP

POPULAR BEACH FOR WATER SPORTS. VERY BUSY IN THE SUMMER. NO DOGS ON BEACH BETWEEN THE CAUSEWAY AND RED RIVER, EASTER-OCT

THE CAUSEWAY

182

COBBLE CORNER NEWSAGENT, PO & ATM

The Island Café

Sail Loft

ST MICHAEL'S MOUNT

0   ¼ mile

0   500m
APPROX SCALE

MAP 72

Where to stay

The nearest place to **camp** is *Wheal Rodney Holiday Park* (off Map 73; ☎ 01736-710605, 🖳 whealrodney.co.uk, **fb**; tent & 2 people £15-23; Easter-Oct), a 10-minute walk inland from the path. They have a **shop** (daily 8.30am-7.30pm) and an indoor pool on what is a nicely appointed site.

There are several options if you want to stay in Marazion. *Rosario B&B* (☎ 01736-711998, 🖳 rosario-marazion.co.uk; 1S/2D/1T; 🐾; £45-50pp, sgl from £45), on The Square, is a charming establishment with a **tea garden** serving crab sandwiches, cream teas and coffee. *St Michaels* (☎ 01736-711348, 🖳 stmichaels-bedandbreak fast.co.uk; 4D/2D or T; £50-60pp, sgl occ

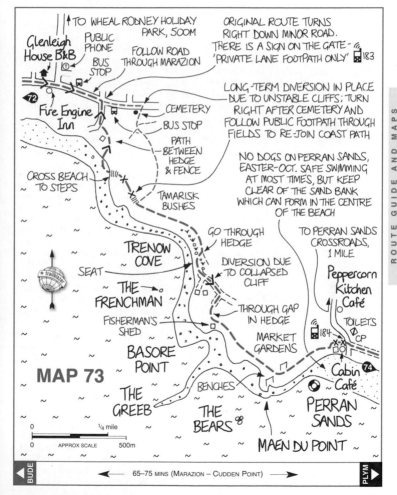

TO WHEAL RODNEY HOLIDAY PARK, 500M

Glenleigh House B&B

PUBLIC PHONE

FOLLOW ROAD THROUGH MARAZION

BUS STOP

72

Fire Engine Inn

ORIGINAL ROUTE TURNS RIGHT DOWN MINOR ROAD. THERE IS A SIGN ON THE GATE - 'PRIVATE LANE FOOTPATH ONLY' 📱183

LONG-TERM DIVERSION IN PLACE DUE TO UNSTABLE CLIFFS; TURN RIGHT AFTER CEMETERY AND FOLLOW PUBLIC FOOTPATH THROUGH FIELDS TO RE-JOIN COAST PATH

CEMETERY

BUS STOP

PATH BETWEEN HEDGE & FENCE

CROSS BEACH TO STEPS

TAMARISK BUSHES

NO DOGS ON PERRAN SANDS, EASTER-OCT. SAFE SWIMMING AT MOST TIMES, BUT KEEP CLEAR OF THE SAND BANK WHICH CAN FORM IN THE CENTRE OF THE BEACH

GO THROUGH HEDGE

TO PERRAN SANDS CROSSROADS, 1 MILE

TRENOW COVE

SEAT

THE FRENCHMAN

DIVERSION DUE TO COLLAPSED CLIFF

Peppercorn Kitchen Café

FISHERMAN'S SHED

THROUGH GAP IN HEDGE

📱184

TOILETS CP

MARKET GARDENS

BASORE POINT

MAP 73

THE GREEB

BENCHES

THE BEARS

Cabin Café

74

PERRAN SANDS

MAEN DU POINT

0 — 1/4 mile
0 — APPROX SCALE — 500m

ROUTE GUIDE AND MAPS

☐ **ST MICHAEL'S MOUNT** [MAP 72, p208]

St Michael's Mount (☎ 01736-710265, 🖥 stmichaelsmount.co.uk) is steeped in history. In one of the earliest written records of Cornwall, Greek historian Diodorus Siculus wrote that in the 1st century BC tin was taken on wagons to Ictis (St Michael's Mount) at low tide, thence by sea to Brittany, France, and from there overland to the Mediterranean. Much later, in 1645 during the Civil War, it was one of the last Royalist strongholds and was only eventually taken after a long siege. The spectacular 14th-century castle on the Mount was originally a 12th century Benedictine Priory, the daughter-house of the famous Mont St Michel in Normandy, France. It is now the home of the St Aubyn family.

You can climb the steep cobbled hill to the **castle** (Mar-Nov, Sun-Fri, 9.30am-5pm; Jul & Aug to 5.30pm, closed Sat; £14, National Trust members free) and the **gardens** (Apr-Jun, Mon-Fri, 10.30am-5pm; Jul & Aug Thur & Fri only, 10.30am-5.30pm; Sep to 5pm; £10). The island has a **shop** and two eateries: *The Island Café*, which was once the castle laundry, has plenty of picnic tables outside; and *Sail Loft*, a coffee house with cakes, pastries and cream teas. All are open the same hours as the castle. Dogs are not allowed in the castle or gardens.

To get to the island you can walk across the causeway from Marazion at low tide all year round, or catch one of the regular ferry boats which ply back and forth during the summer months. They charge £2.50 each way and leave from one of three slipways depending on the state of the tide. All visits are also subject to the weather.

£90-110; min 2 nights), on Fore St, is a little pricier. Also on Fore St *Glenleigh House B&B* (Map 73; ☎ 01736-710308, 🖥 glenleigh-marazion.co.uk; 1S/5D/2T; 🐾; £50-65pp, sgl £75) is full of Victorian-era charm.

Rather more up-market is *Marazion Hotel* (☎ 01736-710334, 🖥 marazionhotel.co.uk; fb; 11D or T, all en suite; 👜; winter/summer from £65/90pp; min 2 nights).

Equally salubrious, but with the choice location overlooking St Michael's Mount, is *The Godolphin Arms* (☎ 01736-888510, 🖥 godolphinarms.co.uk; 7D/2D or T/1Qd; 🐾; winter/summer from £65/85pp; sgl occ from £130), with modern rooms in immaculate condition.

Where to eat and drink

You'll pass *Beach Box Café* (9am-6pm) on the walk into the village. It does breakfast naans (!) and lunchtime burgers.

In the village itself, the slimline *Chapel Rock Café* (☎ 01736-719468; fb; Apr-Oct Mon-Fri 9am-6pm, Sat-Sun 10am-6pm) serves soups, crab sandwiches, pizza and coffee, plus a range of breakfasts, while *The Copper Spoon* (☎ 01736-711607; fb; 🐾; Tue, Wed, Sat & Sun 10am-4pm) does

stone-baked pizza as well as café treats. The back terrace of *The Godolphin Arms* (see Where to stay; food 8-11am & noon-9pm) looks out over the causeway to St Michael's Mount, a fabulous vista in the setting sun, and a very popular spot with holidaymakers as well as thirsty walkers. Locally caught fish are well-represented on the menu.

The King's Arms (☎ 01736-710291, 🖥 kingsarmsmarazion.co.uk; food daily noon-8.30pm) does good-value pub grub, cask ales and has some road-side seating.

With an emphasis on local produce, *Cutty Sark Bar & Restaurant* (food daily noon-2pm & 6-8pm; most mains £13-17) belongs to next door Marazion Hotel (see Where to stay), and has a beer garden as well as an indoor restaurant.

For **takeaway**, there's *Tudor Fish & Chips* (☎ 01736-711889, fb; Apr-Sep Mon-Fri noon-3pm & 4-8pm, Sat 5-8pm, Sun noon-3pm & 4-7pm) as well as *Philp's Pasty Shop* (fb; Mon-Sat 9am-4pm, Sun 10am-4pm). Pasty fans will remember Philp's from Hayle; they're one of the best.

Up the hill as you leave the village is the ever-so-friendly *Fire Engine Inn* (Map 73; ☎ 01736-710771, 🖥 thefireenginemara zion.pub, **fb**; food Wed 6-8.30pm, Thur-Sat noon-2pm & 6-8.30pm, Sun noon-2.30pm & 6-8pm; Mon closed). They serve top-notch pub grub (mains £12-17), the location overlooking St Michael's Mount, is impressive, and so too is the sign by the door: 'Walking boots welcome!'

Transport

[See pp52-5 for details] First Kernow's U4 **bus** service calls here en route between Penryn and Penzance, as do the Land's End and Falmouth Coasters, and Transport for Cornwall's No 2.

MARAZION TO PRAA SANDS [MAPS 73-76]

The first half of these **6¼ miles (10km, 1¾-2hrs)** provides fairly uninteresting walking on low-lying cliffs devoted to market gardening, and requires close attention in following the waymarker posts. There's a long-term diversion to the

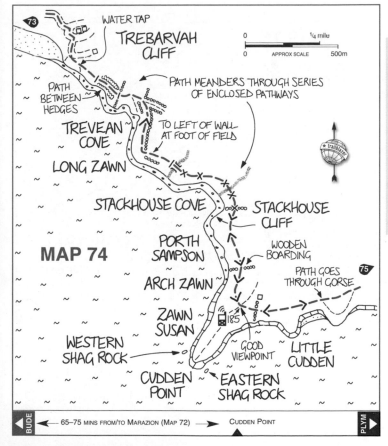

old route out of Marazion, due to unstable cliffs; you now need to turn right off the main road just after the cemetery (Map 73), then follow the public footpath through fields down to the coast path.

Things liven up at **Perran Sands** (Map 73) where there are two great cafés. *The Cabin Café* (**fb**; summer daily 9.30am-5pm; winter 10am-4pm) is down on the seafront with inside and outside seating, plus great coffee. Well worth the short walk up the hill, at *Peppercorn Kitchen Café* (**fb**; Wed-Sun 9.30am-5pm; 🐕) all the food is freshly made and they serve Origin coffee locally roasted in Porthleven. First Kernow's U4 **bus** (see pp52-5) calls at Perran (Crossroads).

From Perran Sands the walking gets a little more interesting. **Prussia Cove** (see box below), however, makes the effort worthwhile with Bessy's Cove below a real smugglers' landing place. From here good cliff-top walking takes you to the impressive beach at Praa Sands.

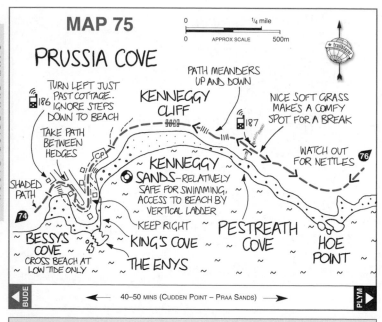

MAP 75

0   ¼ mile

0   APPROX SCALE   500m

PRUSSIA COVE

TURN LEFT JUST PAST COTTAGE. IGNORE STEPS DOWN TO BEACH 📱186

TAKE PATH BETWEEN HEDGES

PATH MEANDERS UP AND DOWN

KENNEGGY CLIFF

NICE SOFT GRASS MAKES A COMFY SPOT FOR A BREAK

📱187

WATCH OUT FOR NETTLES 76

SHADED PATH

CP

74

KENNEGGY SANDS – RELATIVELY SAFE FOR SWIMMING, ACCESS TO BEACH BY VERTICAL LADDER

KEEP RIGHT

PESTREATH COVE

HOE POINT

BESSY'S COVE

CROSS BEACH AT LOW TIDE ONLY

KING'S COVE

THE ENYS

BUDE   ← 40–50 MINS (CUDDEN POINT – PRAA SANDS) →   PLYM

❏ **PRUSSIA COVE**   **[MAP 75]**

Prussia Cove derives its name from the former King of Prussia Inn which stood on the cliff. It was run by the notorious Carter family whose smuggling exploits have guaranteed them a place in local folklore. The size of their operation was of such a scale that they needed to mount a small battery of guns to ward off the customs men. More recently, in 1979, a smuggling racket was busted by Customs and Excise who confiscated £3 million worth of marijuana.

PRAA SANDS [MAP 76]

Praa (pronounced 'pray' locally) Sands is a mini holiday resort that gets very busy in the summer and is stone dead in winter.

A short walk from the beach is **Pengersick Castle** (☎ 01736-763973; 💻 pengersickcastle.com; castle & gardens £7.50, guided tour £15; pre-booking is essential for both) is a Grade II-listed fortified manor house, dating from the late Middle Ages (14th century). It features one of the few towers of its type preserved in Britain.

On Pengersick Lane there's a pop-up **post office** (Mon noon-12.45pm & Fri

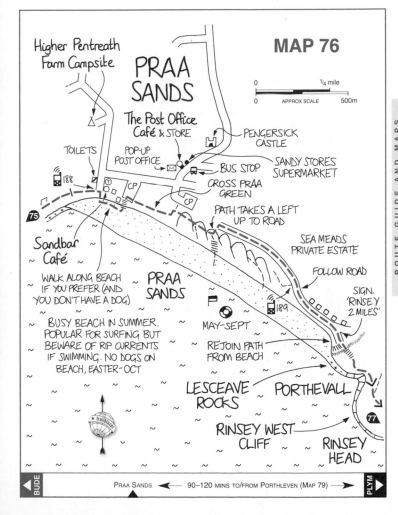

11.30am-12.30pm) behind *The Post Office Café and Store* (☎ 01736-780893, 🖳 post officecafe.co.uk, **fb**; Thur & Sun 10am-6pm, Fri & Sat 10am-8pm), which sells an eclectic mix of provisions and serves pizzas, toasties, cakes and coffee. Next door is a much better stocked **mini-supermarket**, Sandy Stores (☎ 01736-762197, 🖳 sandystores.co.uk; daily 8am-8pm).

There are no longer any B&Bs here, but if you want to camp, *Higher Pentreath Farm Campsite* (☎ 01736-763240, 🖳 higherpentreathcampsite.co.uk; 🐾; 2 hikers & tent £13.50; May-Sep)

is a small, welcoming, family-run place with lovely sea views. It's a five-minute walk uphill from the beach.

Back down by the beach, most people gravitate towards *Sandbar* (☎ 01736-763516, 🖳 sandbarpraasands.co.uk; **fb**; 10am-11pm, food to 9pm), a large beach café that's the focal point of Praa Sands with occasional live music on summer evenings, when it becomes more of a bar-restaurant with real ales and decent pub grub.

The U4 **bus** stops outside the post office, as does the No 2 to Penzance. [For details see pp52-5].

PRAA SANDS TO PORTHLEVEN [MAPS 76-79]

This **4½-mile (7km, 1½-2hrs)** stretch of harder walking returns you to the clifftops again after the lower-level terrain between Marazion and Praa Sands. This is another area of old copper workings and you pass some weathered spoil tips that have begun to blend with their surroundings.

As you get nearer to **Porthleven** you'll find some of the cliffs are subsiding and the path has been fenced off to keep it well back from what is at present the edge. On the last headland there is a **memorial** (see Map 79, p216) to the many mariners drowned off these coasts.

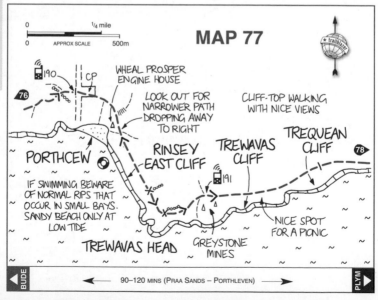

MAP 77

0 — ¼ mile
0 — APPROX SCALE — 500m

★ trailblazer

190 CP WHEAL PROSPER ENGINE HOUSE

76

LOOK OUT FOR NARROWER PATH DROPPING AWAY TO RIGHT

CLIFF-TOP WALKING WITH NICE VIEWS

PORTHCEW

RINSEY EAST CLIFF

TREWAVAS CLIFF

TREQUEAN CLIFF

78

191

IF SWIMMING BEWARE OF NORMAL RIPS THAT OCCUR IN SMALL BAYS. SANDY BEACH ONLY AT LOW TIDE

NICE SPOT FOR A PICNIC

TREWAVAS HEAD

GREYSTONE MINES

BUDE ◄   ◄ 90–120 MINS (PRAA SANDS – PORTHLEVEN) ►   PLYM ►

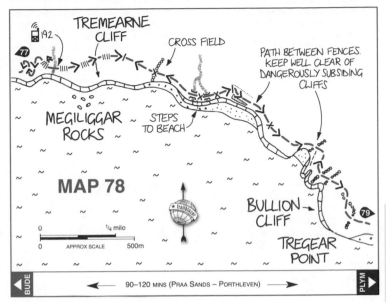

TREMEARNE CLIFF

192

77

CROSS FIELD

PATH BETWEEN FENCES.
KEEP WELL CLEAR OF
DANGEROUSLY SUBSIDING
CLIFFS

MEGILIGGAR ROCKS

STEPS TO BEACH

MAP 78

0   ¼ milo
0   APPROX SCALE   500m

BULLION CLIFF

79

TREGEAR POINT

BUDE ◄   ◄── 90–120 MINS (PRAA SANDS – PORTHLEVEN) ──►   PLYM

ROUTE GUIDE AND MAPS

PORTHLEVEN   [map p217]

Porthleven Harbour was built using prisoners from the Napoleonic wars for manpower, and once housed a fishing fleet which harvested the huge shoals of pilchards and mackerel in the bay. Today it depends on tourism and winters must be endured. The coast is subject to ferocious storms and waves sometimes crash right over the harbour wall to wreck the boats sheltering within. The few fishing boats left work the local reefs for crab and lobster during the summer, some of the catch going to local restaurants and the rest to Newlyn for export abroad.

There's a large, very well-stocked local **supermarket**, Pengelly's (Mon-Fri 7.15am-9pm, Sat-Sun 8am-9pm; **ATM** inside) with groceries and even camping-stove gas.

Boots **pharmacy** (Mon-Sat 9am-5.30pm) is on Fore St, while the **post office** (Mon, Wed & Fri 1.30-4.30pm) is a mobile service in the car park by the supermarket.

Where to stay

Mill Lane Campsite (☎ 01326-573881, **fb**; £20 per tent) is a small campsite run by a local pub called Out of the Blue, beside Porthleven AFC's football ground. The toilets and showers are in the pub building, but can be used round the clock.

Also on Mill Lane, but back towards the harbour, is *Wellmore End Cottage B&B* (☎ 01326-569310, 🖳 wellmoreend .co.uk; 1D/1Qd; from £45pp, sgl occ £70), with cosy rooms and a cracking fruit-filled breakfast. On the corner of Well Lane and Harbour View, at No 1 Harbour View, is *Fisherman's Cottage B&B* (☎ 01326-573713; 1D or Tr; from £45pp), with one en suite room and a friendly welcome.

You can also find good-quality B&B accommodation at the St Austell Brewery owned *Harbour Inn* (☎ 01326-573876, 🖳 harbourinnporthleven.co.uk; **fb**; 1S/1T/10D/3Qd; ♥; winter from £40pp, summer from £59pp, sgl occ room rate).

Also on the harbour is *Kota* (☎ 01326-562407, 🖳 kotarestaurant.co.uk, **fb**; 2D/1Tr, all en suite; from £50pp, sgl occ from £85; min 2 nights), a fine-dining restaurant with three lovely, spacious rooms. The harbour views are a treat, as is the home-smoked salmon for breakfast.

Where to eat and drink

It would be hard to go hungry in Porthleven. From chippies to bakeries, and pub grub to fine dining, it has most bases covered.

There's a proliferation of **cafés** here. Popular *Harbour View Café* (☎ 07498-61380, **fb**; Tue-Sun 10am-4pm) has a great location. The service could be more cheery,

but the food (all-day breakfasts, sandwiches, soups) is excellent.

Friendlier, but with no sea views, *Twisted Currant* (☎ 01326-565999, 🖥 twistedcurrant.co.uk, **fb**; Mon-Sat 9am-5pm, Sun 10am-4pm; 🐾) is a very pleasant tearoom with a small garden. They do lovely breakfasts, cakes, toasties and salads, and are happy to refill water bottles. They also do takeaway picnic boxes. Next door, *The Corner Deli* (☎ 01326-565554, 🖥

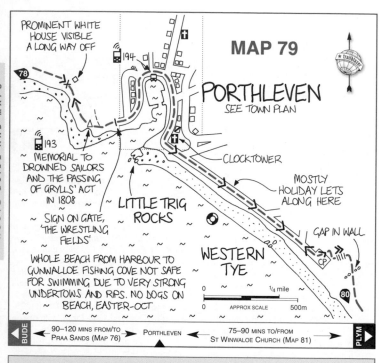

ROUTE GUIDE AND MAPS

PROMINENT WHITE HOUSE VISIBLE A LONG WAY OFF

194

MAP 79

PORTHLEVEN
SEE TOWN PLAN

trailhero

193

~ MEMORIAL TO DROWNED SAILORS AND THE PASSING OF GRYLLS' ACT IN 1808

CLOCKTOWER

MOSTLY HOLIDAY LETS ALONG HERE

~ SIGN ON GATE, 'THE WRESTLING FIELDS'

LITTLE TRIG ROCKS

WHOLE BEACH FROM HARBOUR TO GUNWALLOE FISHING COVE NOT SAFE FOR SWIMMING DUE TO VERY STRONG UNDERTOWS AND RIPS. NO DOGS ON BEACH, EASTER-OCT

WESTERN TYE

GAP IN WALL

CP

0   ¼ mile
0   APPROX SCALE   500m

BUDE ◀ | 90-120 MINS FROM/TO PRAA SANDS (MAP 76) ◀ PORTHLEVEN ◀ 75-90 MINS TO/FROM ST WINWALOE CHURCH (MAP 81) ▶ | PLYM ▶

☐ **GRYLLS' ACT**

Passed in 1808, Grylls' Act, drafted by local solicitor Thomas Grylls, allowed bodies washed up by the sea to be buried in the nearest consecrated ground. Before this all bodies were buried on the cliff tops as it was not possible to distinguish between Christians and non-Christians. The memorial (see Map 79) marks the passing of this Act, which was prompted by the wrecking of the 44-gun frigate *HMS Anson* the previous year, in which 130 people drowned.

thecornerdeliporthleven.co.uk, **fb**; Mon-Sat 9am-9pm) does outstanding wood-fired pizza, as well as paninis, bagels and homemade quiche and soups.

On your way out of town, *Nauti but Ice* (☎ 01326-573747, 🖳 www.nautibutice.co.uk, **fb**; daily 9am-5pm, food to 3pm) is a cross between a café, a sandwich shop

and an ice cream parlour, and has some terrace seating. Next door is their pizzeria *Go Nauti Pizza* (summer Wed-Sat 5-10pm).

As nice as all these cafés are, though, the best coffee in town is at *Origin Coffee* (☎ 01326-574337, 🖳 origincoffee.co.uk, **fb**; daily 9am-4pm), a multi-award-winning, ethically minded local roastery which will

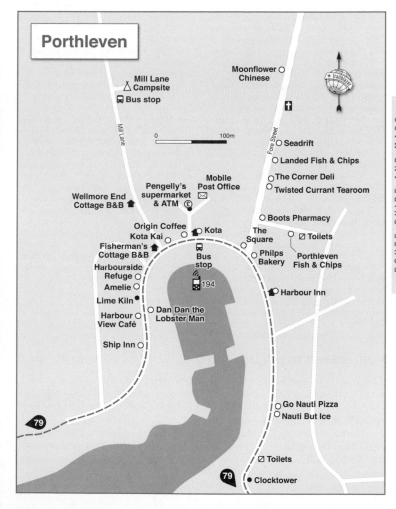

tempt you inside with the rich scent of freshly roasted beans wafting across the pavement.

Of the two or three **pubs** near the harbour, the 17th-century *Ship Inn* (☎ 01326-564204, 🖳 theshipinnporthleven.co.uk, **fb**; daily noon-2.30pm & 5.30-8.30pm, winter no food Sun evenings) has the most atmosphere. If it's available don't pass up the Porthleven crab. The Cornish fish pie is also very good. Around the other side of the harbour, the menu at *Harbour Inn* (see Where to stay; daily noon-9pm; mains £12-16), includes steamed mussels, fish & chips and Thai vegetable curry. The great food at *The Square* (☎ 01326-573911, 🖳 the squareatporthleven.co.uk, **fb**; summer daily noon-2pm & 6-9pm, winter closed Sun) has been awarded Michelin Bib Gourmand status for 'standout food at a good value'. Evening mains (£15-20) include roasted skate wing (£20) and pork belly with celeriac & apple (£18.50). Their exquisite ice creams are made on the premises, too.

Restaurants include *Seadrift* (☎ 01326-558783, 🖳 seadriftporthleven.co .uk, **fb**; Tue & Sat 6-9pm, Wed-Fri noon-2.30pm & 6-9pm; 🐾) a small, welcoming place with mains (£15-23) including wild mushroom risotto and chargrilled monk fish.

More established is the multi-award-winning *Kota* (see Where to stay; Tue-Sat 5.30-9pm) where two/three-course set menus cost £24/28 and include the likes of peppered venison steak, hake lentil dahl and pan-fried mackerel. A few doors down, their more affordable restaurant-café, *Kota Kai* (☎ 01326 727707, 🖳 kotakai.co.uk, **fb**; Mon-Tue & Thur-Sat noon-2.30pm & 5.30-

9pm) is open for lunch too. The Asian-influenced menu (most mains £12-15) also includes plenty of Cornish seafood.

There's more fine dining at *Amelie* (☎ 01326-653653, 🖳 ameliesporthleven.co .uk, **fb**; daily noon-3pm & 5-9.30pm; mains £13-21), with harbour views too. The menu is dominated by seafood and shellfish, but includes gourmet burgers and wood-fired oven pizzas too. Next door, *Harbourside Refuge* (☎ 01326-331758, 🖳 theharbour siderefuge.co.uk; Wed-Sun noon-9pm; mains £14-25) is owned by Michelin-star chef Michael Caines MBE, and serves shellfish linguini, chargrilled curried monkfish and sumptuous burgers.

For **takeaway**, *Philps Bakery* (Mon-Sat 9am-4pm, Sun 10am-4pm) – yes, it's them again – is an excellent source of rucksack fillers, with outstanding pasties. For fish and chips there's *Porthleven Fish & Chips* (☎ 01326-554257, **fb**; daily 11.45am-3pm & 4.30-8/9pm) or *Landed* (☎ 01326-531507, **fb**; 🖳 landedporthleven.co .uk; Mon & Wed 4-8.30pm, Thur-Sat noon-3pm & 5-8.30pm, Sun noon-8pm). For **Chinese** cuisine, there's *Moonflower* (☎ 01326-562973, **fb**; daily 5-11pm; eat-in or takeaway), but for a takeaway with a difference, try *Dan Dan the Lobster Man* (**fb**; daily 10am-6.30pm) who serves fabulously fresh lobster rolls (£16.50) and crab sandwiches (£13.50) from a shipping container perched on the harbour wall.

Transport
[See pp52-5] First Kernow's U4 **bus** service operates to Penzance and Helston. The Falmouth Coaster also stops here.

PORTHLEVEN TO MULLION COVE [MAPS 79-82]

This is an enjoyable **6-mile (10km, 2-2½hrs)** walk with lots of diversity. You leave Porthleven past the iconic clock tower, over which heavy seas sometimes crash in winter storms, and climb the hill past all the holiday cottages to the open spaces high above Western Tye beach.

Next you come to **Loe Bar**, a shingle bank that cuts off the sea from the fresh water lagoon known as The Loe (see box p220). Keen birdwatchers passing in winter will want to spend some time here; it is possible to walk around the lagoon. It was on Loe Bar that *HMS Anson* (see box p216) was wrecked in 1807; this is commemorated by a bright, white-painted cross which you pass as you

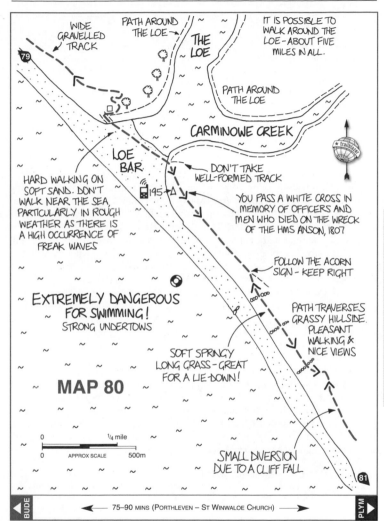

ROUTE GUIDE AND MAPS

❑ **WARNING [MAP 80]**

Although the sea may look innocuous on a calm day there are powerful undertows here and the geology of the sea floor on Mount's Bay causes unusually high numbers of freak waves to occur; please **don't consider swimming**. In rough weather it is not advisable to even walk near the sea.

□ **THE LOE** [MAP 80, p219]

The Loe is Cornwall's largest natural freshwater lake. Originally the Loe was the estuary of the river Cober but it was dammed by the shingle bar around 800 years ago. The National Trust owns all the land surrounding the Loe and it has been designated a Site of Special Scientific Interest (see box p66).

It is mostly known for its bird population and over-wintering wildfowl but such a place inevitably attracts legends of its own, one of which is that Sir Bedivere cast Excalibur, the sword of the dying King Arthur, into this lake.

The walk around the Loe is about five miles (8km), mostly along the water's edge. The path is easy to follow but it can get muddy on the eastern side.

---

climb up onto the cliffs again. The coastal path then meanders along to the beach at **Gunwalloe**, where you can take a short detour inland to the charming 15th-century pub, *Halzephron Inn* (Map 81; ☎ 01326-240406, 🖥 halzephron-inn.co.uk, **fb**; 2D; from £50pp, sgl occ £65; food daily noon-2.30pm & 6-8.30pm; 🐾), with good food, real ale and two **B&B** rooms.

You'll soon reach **Halzephron Cove**, then **Dollar Cove**, where the church of St Winwaloe (see box opposite) huddles in the dunes, and where you'll also find a small, seasonal, National Trust-run **coffee kiosk** (Map 81; summer daily 10am-4pm, winter weekends only) serving hot drinks and snacks.

After **Dollar Cove** you come to **Poldhu Cove** which has historic significance in the development of radio signals (see box p224). There's also a good café here, *Poldhu Beach Café* (☎ 01326-240530, 🖥 poldhu.com, **fb**; daily 9.30am-5.30pm, winter hours vary); their bacon sandwiches are good, and on Fridays they serve stonebaked pizzas to 7pm. The No 34 and L1 **bus** services (see pp52-5 for details) call at the cove.

After Poldhu Cove, it's **Polurrian Cove** which boasts the fine hotel, *Polurrian on the Lizard* (Map 82; ☎ 01326-240421, 🖥 polurrianhotel.com, **fb**; 41 rooms; 🐾; winter from £65pp, summer from £85pp) before the huge edifice of Mullion Cove Hotel announces your arrival at perhaps the quintessential Cornish harbour, **Mullion Cove**. The coast path doesn't go into **Mullion village**, which is about a mile inland, but it's worth the diversion if you need food, accommodation or general supplies.

MULLION COVE [MAP 82, p223]

One of the more unusual attractions round here is *The Chocolate Factory* (☎ 01326 241311, 🖥 the-chocolatefactory.co.uk; daily 10am-5pm), between Mullion Cove and Mullion Village. Cornish chocolate is hand-made here, and there's a **shop** and an excellent **café**, too.

Campers should head for the National Trust-managed *Teneriffe Farm Caravan and Camping Park* (Map 83; ☎ 01326-240293; 🖥 nationaltrust.org.uk/holidays/

teneriffe-farm-campsite; hiker & tent £6-10; Mar-Oct) about a mile south of Mullion Cove. Walker-friendly, they also have four unfurnished camping pods for up to three adults (£25-45).

The plushest place to stay in the area is *Mullion Cove Hotel* (☎ 01326-240328, 🖥 mullion-cove.co.uk; 12T/15D/3F; ▼; 🐾; winter from £57.50pp, summer from £87.50) with an unsurpassable location and a reputation for hospitality and two

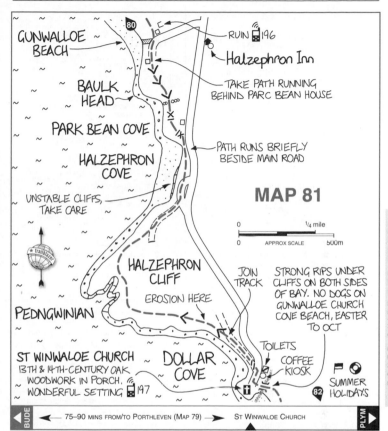

GUNWALLOE ~ BEACH

80

RUIN 📱196

Halzephron Inn

TAKE PATH RUNNING BEHIND PARC BEAN HOUSE

BAULK HEAD

PARK BEAN COVE

HALZEPHRON COVE

PATH RUNS BRIEFLY BESIDE MAIN ROAD

MAP 81

UNSTABLE CLIFFS, TAKE CARE

0 ————— 1/4 mile
0 ————— 500m
APPROX SCALE

trailblazer

HALZEPHRON CLIFF

EROSION HERE

JOIN TRACK

STRONG RIPS UNDER CLIFFS ON BOTH SIDES OF BAY. NO DOGS ON GUNWALLOE CHURCH COVE BEACH, EASTER TO OCT

PEDNGWINIAN

ST WINWALOE CHURCH
13TH & 14TH-CENTURY OAK WOODWORK IN PORCH, WONDERFUL SETTING 📱197

DOLLAR COVE

TOILETS

COFFEE KIOSK

SUMMER HOLIDAYS

82

◄ BUDE   ◄— 75–90 MINS FROM/TO PORTHLEVEN (MAP 79) —►   ST WINWALOE CHURCH   PLYM ►

ROUTE GUIDE AND MAPS

❑ ST WINWALOE CHURCH, GUNWALLOE   [MAP 81]

The present church has been restored over the generations but there has been a church here since the 14th century or even earlier. Some of the carved woodwork in the porch has been dated to the 13th century although storms have caused havoc periodically resulting in restoration work by the community determined to keep the faith alive in this inhospitable spot. The burial registers dating from 1716 record shipwrecks and drownings along the coast – a Spanish ship with a cargo of silver dollars was wrecked just to the north in the 1780s – and these have been the object of many searches ever since, so far without success. Dollar Cove (also known as Jangye Ryn) preserves the legend, or truth, of the incident.

St Winwaloe, whose statue greets the visitor to the church, was an abbot who came from Brittany, France, in the 6th century and founded the first sacred place on this site which has come to be known as the Church of the Storms.

restaurants; it would be a great place for a special break.

There is also a seasonal café: *Porthmellin Café* (☎ 01326-240941; 10.30am-4.30pm) that has cream teas, pasties and all-day breakfasts amongst many tempting offerings. A **kiosk** next door has the same opening hours and sells ice creams and cold drinks.

MULLION

The **post office** is in the Co-op **supermarket** (daily 7am-11pm), with an **ATM** outside.

Nearer to the centre of the village is a Spar **shop** (daily 6am-9pm) which also has an **ATM** and a **bakery** with a lovely selection of warm pasties, fresh bread and coffee. There's also a **pharmacy** (Mon-Fri 9am-6pm, Sat 9am-5.30pm).

Where to stay

There's **B&B** at the spacious *Old Vicarage* (☎ 01326-240898, ☐ bandbmullion@hotmail.com; 2D/1Tr/1Qd; £47-50pp, sgl occ £50-60), a lovely old house in the heart of the village, which welcomes walkers and accepts single-night bookings. It is said that Sir Arthur Conan Doyle stayed here and the house is mentioned in the Sherlock Holmes story *The Devil's Foot*.

The two pubs here also do B&B; rooms at *Old Inn* (☎ 01326-240240, ☐ oldinnmullion.co.uk, **fb**; 2T/3D or Tr; ✖; from £36pp, sgl occ from £65) are light and airy; while *Mounts Bay Inn* (☎ 01326-240221, ☐ mountsbaymullion.co.uk, **fb**; 1T/3D/2Tr; from £48.50pp, sgl occ from £80; min 2 nights) has distant sea views.

Where to eat and drink

Both pubs also do food. *Mounts Bay Inn* (see above; food Mon-Sat noon-5pm & 6-9pm, Sun noon-3pm & 6-8pm) is a lively place with a beer garden, and is popular with both locals and holidaymakers. Mains (£10-20) include steaks, burgers and seafood, but there are also vegetarian options and specials.

Old Inn (see above; Sat-Mon noon-9pm, Tue-Fri noon-2.30pm & 6-9pm) is equally busy and has a menu (most mains £11-14) of burgers, curries and speciality

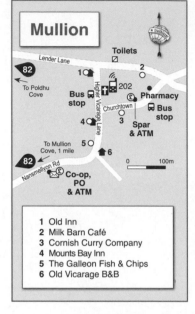

1 Old Inn
2 Milk Barn Café
3 Cornish Curry Company
4 Mounts Bay Inn
5 The Galleon Fish & Chips
6 Old Vicarage B&B

homemade pies. Beers on tap include St Austell's Tribute, HSD, Proper Job and IPA.

The friendly *Milk Barn Café* (☎ 01326-241007, **fb**; daily 10am-4pm) has a good-value menu including breakfast baps, sandwiches and baguettes, jacket potatoes, and plenty of cakes, plus Sunday roast lunch (booking recommended). As well as hot drinks, they do excellent milk shakes.

The village also boasts a great fish & chip restaurant: *The Galleon* (Tue-Fri 11am-2pm & 4.30-8.30pm, Sat 11am-8.30pm) does all-day breakfasts and proper coffee as well as chip-shop fare.

For homemade takeaway curries, *Cornish Curry Company* (☎ 01326-240016; Easter-Oct Tue & Thur 5.30-8pm) offers five types of veg, chicken or prawn curry (£6.20-6.80).

Transport

[See pp52-5 for details] The No 34 **bus** stops here.

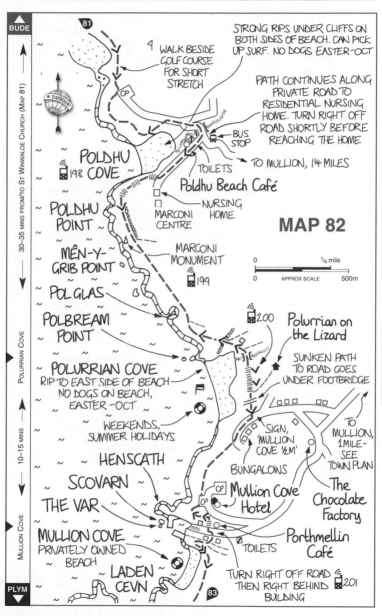

BUDE

30-35 MINS FROM/TO ST WINWALOE CHURCH (MAP 81)

POLURRIAN COVE

10-15 MINS

MULLION COVE

PLYM

81

WALK BESIDE GOLF COURSE FOR SHORT STRETCH

STRONG RIPS UNDER CLIFFS ON BOTH SIDES OF BEACH. CAN PICK UP SURF. NO DOGS EASTER-OCT

PATH CONTINUES ALONG PRIVATE ROAD TO RESIDENTIAL NURSING HOME. TURN RIGHT OFF ROAD SHORTLY BEFORE REACHING THE HOME

BUS STOP

POLDHU COVE 198

TOILETS

Poldhu Beach Café

TO MULLION, 1¼ MILES

POLDHU POINT

NURSING HOME

MARCONI CENTRE

MÊN-Y-GRIB POINT

MARCONI MONUMENT 199

MAP 82

0   ¼ mile
0   APPROX SCALE   500m

POL GLAS

POLBREAM POINT

200

Polurrian on the Lizard

SUNKEN PATH TO ROAD GOES UNDER FOOTBRIDGE

POLURRIAN COVE
RIP TO EAST SIDE OF BEACH NO DOGS ON BEACH, EASTER-OCT

WEEKENDS, SUMMER HOLIDAYS

SIGN, 'MULLION COVE ½M'

TO MULLION, 1 MILE – SEE TOWN PLAN

HENSCATH

BUNGALOWS

SCOVARN

CP Mullion Cove Hotel

CP

The Chocolate Factory

THE VAR

MULLION COVE
PRIVATELY OWNED BEACH

TOILETS

Porthmellin Café

LADEN CEVN

TURN RIGHT OFF ROAD THEN RIGHT BEHIND BUILDING 201

83

ROUTE GUIDE AND MAPS

❏ THE MARCONI MONUMENT   [MAP 82, p223]

❏ THE MARCONI MONUMENT   [MAP 82, p223]
Walkers passing the stone obelisk on the cliffs near Poldhu might do well to pause
and consider what it commemorates. Guglielmo Marconi chose this spot from which
to transmit the very first message ever to cross the Atlantic by wireless. On December
12th 1901, a morse signal sent from a station on Angrouse Cliff was received by
Marconi in Newfoundland. Twenty years later the world's first short-wave beam signals were transmitted from the same spot and history was made. Poldhu became a
research centre and when it closed in 1934 Marconi gave the site to the National Trust
(NT) and erected the memorial.
    The other significant radio station, Marconi's Lizard Wireless Station (see Map
86, p229) was also bought by the NT and can be seen along the coast path just north
of the Lizard lighthouse.

MULLION COVE TO LIZARD POINT   [MAPS 82-86]

The next **6 miles** (**10km, 2½-3¼hrs**) are along exposed cliff tops giving some of
the best coastal walking in South Cornwall with superb views of the treacherous
rocks on which so many ships have been wrecked. The terrain underfoot can get
boggy at times due to poor drainage.

    You might spot the New Forest ponies brought in by the National Trust to
crop the gorse, clearing the ground to allow unique and fragile plant species to
come through.

    Kynance Cove is a delightful spot where the intrusion of summer visitors
has not spoiled a unique cove that deserves a longer stay than most walkers allow
it. *Kynance Café* (see Map 85, p227; 🖥 kynancecovecafe.co.uk) is open daily
from 9am to 4.30pm in the main season.

    As you get nearer to Lizard Point the coastline becomes increasingly spec-
tacular and if this is your first visit it's hard not to be impressed by its wildness
and beauty. The Lizard has been called Cornwall's big toe dipped into the ocean.
Rare clovers and heathers grow here and nowhere else, and some exotics such as
gunneras and tree ferns flourish in the sub-tropical conditions.

    After **Pentreath Beach** several paths lead away from the coast to Lizard
Village (see below) where you may have decided to spend the night or get a pasty.
The temptation is to take the first path in and the last path out but this would mean
missing **Lizard Point.** The shortest route into **Lizard Village** is from Housel Cove
but it's only about 15 minutes along the path from near Shag Rock. Alternatively,
there's a pretty walk from Church Cove past thatched-roofed houses.

LIZARD VILLAGE
                    [map p228 & MAP 86, p229]
Lizard Village has a somewhat Bohemian
feel to it, making the passing traveller feel
very much at home. You'll see brightly
painted buildings dotted around the place,
home-made sculptures on front lawns and,
if you stay at Henry's Campsite (see p226),

broods of chickens running about the place.
The distinctive, 260-year-old twin towers
of **Lizard Lighthouse** (☎ 01326-290222,
🖥 trinityhouse.co.uk; Apr-Oct Sun-Thur
11am-5pm; Heritage Centre £4.50, inc
Lighthouse Tour £8.50) mark the most
southerly point of mainland Britain, where

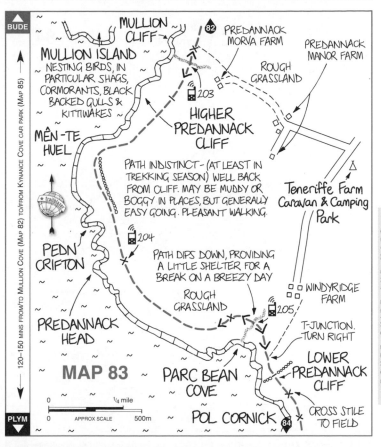

MULLION CLIFF

82

PREDANNACK MORVA FARM

PREDANNACK MANOR FARM

MULLION ISLAND
~ NESTING BIRDS, IN PARTICULAR SHAGS, CORMORANTS, BLACK BACKED GULLS & KITTIWAKES ~

ROUGH GRASSLAND

📱 203

MÊN-TE HUEL

HIGHER PREDANNACK CLIFF

PATH INDISTINCT - (AT LEAST IN TREKKING SEASON) WELL BACK FROM CLIFF. MAY BE MUDDY OR BOGGY IN PLACES, BUT GENERALLY EASY GOING. PLEASANT WALKING.

Teneriffe Farm Caravan & Camping Park

★ trailblazer

📱 204

PEDN CRIFTON

PATH DIPS DOWN, PROVIDING A LITTLE SHELTER FOR A BREAK ON A BREEZY DAY

ROUGH GRASSLAND

📱 205

WINDYRIDGE FARM

PREDANNACK HEAD

T-JUNCTION. TURN RIGHT

MAP 83

PARC BEAN COVE

LOWER PREDANNACK CLIFF

0   ¼ mile

0   APPROX SCALE   500m

POL CORNICK

84

CROSS STILE TO FIELD

❑ GEOLOGY OF THE LIZARD

Even the most ungeologically minded can't miss the colourful serpentine rock around the Lizard; great streaks of green cliffs reminiscent of a snake's skin giving the stone its name. Spanning 20 square miles, this is the largest outcrop of serpentine in mainland Britain. It is actually part of the Earth's mantle, which would normally be about 20km, on average, below the surface. Local sculptors still carve ornaments from the serpentine rock which reached their height of popularity during the Victorian era, although they're probably a little too heavy to carry away in your pack.

Lizard Point isn't just famed as the most southerly point of mainland Britain. The offshore islets from Lizard Point are 500 million years old, a leftover crumb of the collision between the super-continents of Gondwanaland and Euramerica.

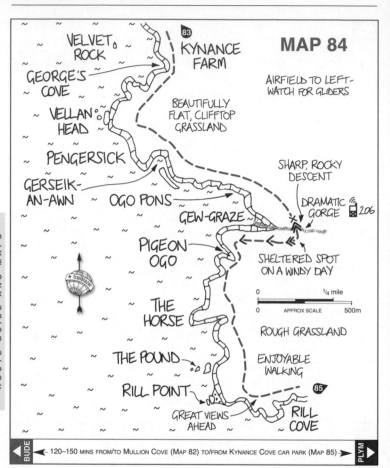

MAP 84

KYNANCE FARM

83

VELVET ROCK

GEORGE'S COVE

VELLAN HEAD

PENGERSICK

GERSEIK-AN-AWN ~ OGO PONS

GEW-GRAZE

PIGEON OGO

THE HORSE

THE POUND

RILL POINT

GREAT VIEWS AHEAD

AIRFIELD TO LEFT-WATCH FOR GLIDERS

BEAUTIFULLY FLAT, CLIFFTOP GRASSLAND

SHARP, ROCKY DESCENT

DRAMATIC GORGE 206

SHELTERED SPOT ON A WINDY DAY

ROUGH GRASSLAND

ENJOYABLE WALKING

RILL COVE

85

0   1/4 mile
0   APPROX SCALE   500m

120–150 MINS FROM/TO MULLION COVE (MAP 82) TO/FROM KYNANCE COVE CAR PARK (MAP 85)

BUDE

PLYM

there is a heritage centre for visitors, who can take a guided tour of the complex.

Lizard Village has some basic services. There is a **post office** (Mon-Thur 9am-noon & 1-5pm, Fri 9am-noon), and you can get fresh provisions in the **butcher & greengrocer**, C&E Retallack (Mon-Fri 9am-3pm, Sat 9am-1pm).

Where to stay

Campers need look no further than *Henry's Campsite* (☎ 01326-290596, 🖳 henryscamp

site.co.uk; 🐾; hiker & tent £12), still our favourite campsite on the whole of the Cornwall Coast Path. Like staying in a small farmyard commune, there's a wonderful atmosphere: pigs, chickens, goats and alpacas keep the kids amused, while parents home in on the fresh coffee and croissants served for breakfast, or the bottles of real ale and Cornish cider sold in the well-stocked shop. You can buy firewood and rent fire braziers, and there's a communal fire pit for everyone to share. Oh, and the sea-view sunsets are stunning. Don't forget to say you're a walker when you call ahead; they almost always find room for walkers even if the campsite is otherwise full.

If Henry's really is chock-a-block, there's *Kynance Camping* (off Map 85 & 86; ☎ 07534-616006, **fb**; Apr-Sep 🐾; £20 per tent), a spacious site with clean showers, a few hundred metres north of the village.

Occupying the buildings of a former Victorian hotel, at *YHA Lizard Point* (see Map 86; ☎ 01326-291145, 🖥 www.yha.org .uk/hostel/yha-lizard-point; 28 beds, from £25pp; Mar-Dec only; booking recommended) there is a huge self-catering kitchen and oodles of space throughout.

For B&B, *The Caerthillian* (☎ 01326-290019; 1S/1T/3D; 🛁; 🐾; from £40pp, sgl occ £40) is a lovely blue and white painted house in the heart of the village with very welcoming owners. Alternatively, enjoy panoramic sea views, and freshly baked bread for breakfast, at *Haelarcher Farm* (☎ 01326-291188, 🖥 haelarcher.co.uk; 1S/2D; from £45pp, sgl occ from £60). Both welcome one-night-stay walkers.

The Top House Inn (☎ 01326-450098, 🖥 thetophouseinn.co.uk, **fb**; 5D/2T/1Qd; from £45pp) is a friendly pub with very comfortable B&B rooms.

Where to eat and drink
In the village centre is the famed *Ann's Pasties* (☎ 01326-572282, 🖥 annspasties.co .uk, **fb**; Mon-Sat 3-9pm), which also does cakes, flapjacks, ice creams, and even beer!

MAP 85

0 — ¼ mile
0 — APPROX SCALE — 500m

GREAT VIEWS OF THE ISLAND

AT HIGH TIDE WHEN YOU CAN'T CROSS THE BEACH, TAKE THE ROAD - IT'S ONLY A SHORT DIVERSION

KYNANCE CLIFF

Kynance Café (SEASONAL)

TOILETS

GRAVELLED PATH

84

trailblazer

THE BELLOWS

ASPARAGUS ISLAND

NANTIVET ROCK
LOOK FOR GREEN SERPENTINE ROCK

GULL ROCK

THE BISHOP

KYNANCE COVE

207

CP — TOILETS

TO KYNANCE CAMPING, 1KM

GREAT VIEWS

86

ENYS YEAN

LION ROCK

AT LOW TIDE IT'S POSSIBLE TO EXPLORE THE ISLANDS AND CAVES. ALWAYS BE AWARE OF THE INCOMING TIDE, PARTICULARLY IF ON THIS SIDE - CAN HAVE VERY DANGEROUS SURF & RIPS

NO DOGS ON BEACH EASTER-OCT

BUDE ◄ ← 120-150 MINS FROM/TO MULLION COVE (MAP 82) → KYNANCE COVE CAR PARK ← 35-45 MINS TO/FROM LIZARD POINT (MAP 86) → PLYM ▶

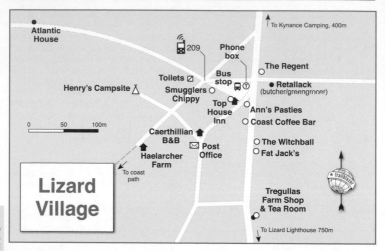

To Kynance Camping, 400m

Atlantic House

209

Phone box

The Regent

Toilets

Bus stop

Retallack (butcher/greengrocer)

Henry's Campsite

Smugglers Chippy

Top House Inn

Ann's Pasties

Coast Coffee Bar

Caerthillian B&B

Post Office

The Witchball

Fat Jack's

Haelarcher Farm

To coast path

0   50   100m

Lizard Village

Tregullas Farm Shop & Tea Room

To Lizard Lighthouse 750m

ROUTE GUIDE AND MAPS

For pub food, head to *The Top House Inn* (see Where to stay; food daily noon-8pm, Fri & Sat to 8.30pm) which does pub classics, fresh seafood and a separate pizza menu (£10-13). Nearby, *Smugglers* (☎ 01326-290763, **fb**; daily 4.30-8pm) is the place to go for fish & chips (£7.50).

Also close by, you'll find plenty of outdoor seating at *Coast Coffee Bar* (**fb**; Wed-Sat 9.30am-8pm, Sun-Tue 9.30am-5pm); good for breakfasts, cream teas and sandwiches, but with a decent evening menu too.

The Regent (☎ 01326-761049; 🖥 the regentcafe.co.uk; Sun-Thur 9am-7.30pm, Fri & Sat to 8pm) is a no-frills café and grill serving an extensive, reasonably priced menu (mains £7-12) including crab mac and cheese, giant hot dogs and scampi and chips. Between village and coast *Tregullas Farm Shop and Tea Rooms* (☎ 01326-290122; 🖥 tregullasfarm.co.uk, **fb**; daily 9am-5pm; 🐾) dishes up some fabulous Cornish breakfasts plus tarts, pies, sundaes, scones, ice cream, cakes... you get the idea. Delicious.

The Witchball (☎ 01326-290662, 🖥 witchball.co.uk; food daily noon-3pm & 5-9pm, booking advised) is a popular bar and restaurant serving pizza, burgers and some excellent seafood (most mains £9-11). They also serve Cadgwith Crabber Ale, brewed

by Cornish Chough Brewery right here in the village, and their front terrace is lively on summer evenings. In case you were wondering, a 'witch ball' is a hollow sphere of glass hung in a cottage window to ward off evil spirits.

Next door, café *Fat Jack's* (**fb**; Sun-Mon & Wed-Thur 9.30am-6pm, Tue & Sat 9am-5pm) serves sandwiches, pasties, ice cream and coffee.

The most southerly café on mainland Britain, *Polpeor Café* (see Map 86; ☎ 01326-290939, **fb**; summer daily 9am-5/6pm, winter 11am-3pm; bring your own wine) at Lizard Point has one of the best terraces anywhere, with a view over the rocks and sea that is second to none; you'd be hard-pressed to imagine anywhere more evocative. Nearby, though not quite as far south, the licensed *Wavecrest Café* (Map 86; ☎ 01326-290898; 🖥 wavecrestcornwall .co.uk, **fb**; daily 10am-4pm) has been serving holidaymakers since the 1930s, and also has fabulous sea views from its terrace.

Transport

[For details see pp52-5] The No 34 **bus** service calls here, as does the open-topped L1 tourist bus.

For a **taxi**, ring Meneage Taxis (☎ 07773-817156).

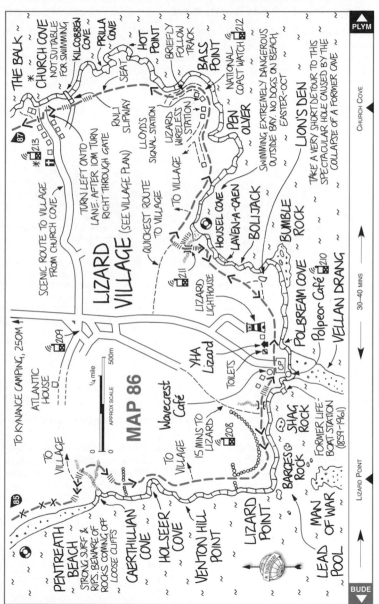

PLYM

TO KYNANCE CAMPING, 250M

ATLANTIC HOUSE

🔌 209

MAP 86

APPROX SCALE

0   ¼ mile
0   500m

TO VILLAGE

TO VILLAGE

Wavecrest Café

15 MINS TO LIZARD

🔌 208

PENTREATH BEACH

STRONG SURF & RIPS. BEWARE OF ROCKS COMING OFF LOOSE CLIFFS

85

CAERTHILLIAN COVE

HOLSEER COVE

VENTON HILL POINT

LIZARD POINT

MAN OF WAR

BARGES & ROCK

SHAG ROCK

FORMER LIFE-BOAT STATION (1859–1961)

LEAD POOL

Trailblazer

THE BALK

CHURCH COVE
NOT SUITABLE FOR SWIMMING

KILCOBBEN COVE

PRILLA COVE

HOT POINT

BRIEFLY FOLLOW TRACK

BASS POINT

NATIONAL COAST WATCH 🔌 212

PEN OLVER

LION'S DEN

TAKE A VERY SHORT DETOUR TO THIS SPECTACULAR HOLE CAUSED BY THE COLLAPSE OF A FORMER CAVE

87 213

SCENIC ROUTE TO VILLAGE FROM CHURCH COVE

TURN LEFT ONTO LANE: AFTER 10M TURN RIGHT THROUGH GATE

LIZARD VILLAGE (SEE VILLAGE PLAN)

QUICKEST ROUTE TO VILLAGE

TO VILLAGE

SEAT

RNLI SLIPWAY

LLOYDS SIGNAL STATION

LIZARD WIRELESS STATION

HOUSEL COVE

LAVEN-A-CAEN

BOLJACK

BUMBLE ROCK

SWIMMING EXTREMELY DANGEROUS OUTSIDE BAY. NO DOGS ON BEACH EASTER–OCT

🔌 211

LIZARD LIGHTHOUSE

YHA Lizard

TOILETS

CP

POLBREAM COVE ROCK

Polpeor Café 🔌 210

VELLAN DRANG

CHURCH COVE

30–40 MINS

LIZARD POINT

BUDE

LIZARD POINT TO CADGWITH COVE [MAPS 86-87]

This **4-mile (6km, 1½-1¾hrs)** stretch is quite popular and no wonder, given the superb views back to the lighthouse. The blue-ish serpentine rock can be seen on the path and on the slabs used for the stiles. It becomes quite slippery when wet, and even on dry days it is easy to slip where there has been constant polishing by boots. Serpentine provides the craftsmen with the raw material for the pendants and lighthouse ornaments that you can buy in the gift shops in the area, and in Lizard Village you can watch them at work.

CADGWITH [MAP 87]

This tiny village is a collection of lobster pots, fishing floats and boats clustered around the one pub, *Cadgwith Cove Inn* (☎ 01326-290513, ☐ cadgwithcoveinn.com, **fb**; 3D/2D or T/1Tr, some en suite; ✻; from £30pp, sgl occ from £54) an intriguing survivor from a simpler age, with newly refurbished **B&B** rooms. On a Friday you could be in for a sing-song since the Cadgwith Singers meet to work on their sea shanties. The **food** (summer daily noon-8.30pm, winter daily noon-3pm & 6-8.30pm) includes standard pub fare, plus dishes such as moules marinière and seafood chowder. The beers are Betty Stoggs, Doom Bar and Otter.

Next door, down the hill, seafood is also the speciality at *The Old Cellars* (☎ 01326-290727, **fb**; Easter-Oct Mon-Sat 11.30am-3pm & 6-8.30pm, Sun 11am-4pm), perhaps unsurprisingly given its proximity to the harbour. They do an array of sandwiches and baguettes, too, and a cracking Ploughman's (£8.95). You can also enjoy cakes, cream teas and coffee outside the usual food-serving hours, as you sit amongst the hanging baskets and nesting swallows of the courtyard.

If you just fancy grabbing a **snack** on the go, you can buy takeaway pasties, croissants, cake and ice cream at *The Watch House* (☐ thewatchhouse.co.uk), which also serves tea and coffee as well as souvenirs, from what is the village's 200-year-old former customs and excise house.

The nearest campsite is two miles further on at Kennack Sands (see p232).

The **bus** doesn't visit Cadgwith; instead, walk half a mile inland to **Ruan Minor** and get the No 34 (The Lizard to Helston) bus. [See pp52-5 for details].

CADGWITH COVE TO COVERACK [MAPS 87-91]

The next **7 miles (11km, 2½-3hrs)** are over a mixed terrain that makes for varied walking from quite dull to exhilarating.

After you leave Cadgwith the cliffs are relatively low-lying and the path traverses country thick with blackthorn, gorse and bracken. You'll soon pass the ruins of the **Serpentine works**, a once-thriving Victorian serpentine rock factory. Later you cross the beach at **Kennack Sands** (see p232), which has two beach cafés, before continuing with a sharp descent at **Downas Cove** followed by the inevitable climb up out of it.

A further descent has to be tackled at **Beagles Hole**, soon after which you'll reach Black Head, where you'll find **Black Head Lookout**, a National Trust hut with information boards inside, detailing facts about this part of the coastline, and with a sea-facing bench outside it that's perfect for a pitstop.

From here it's a skip around **Chynhalls Point** followed by an easy amble into the secretive little harbour village of Coverack.

ROUTE GUIDE AND MAPS

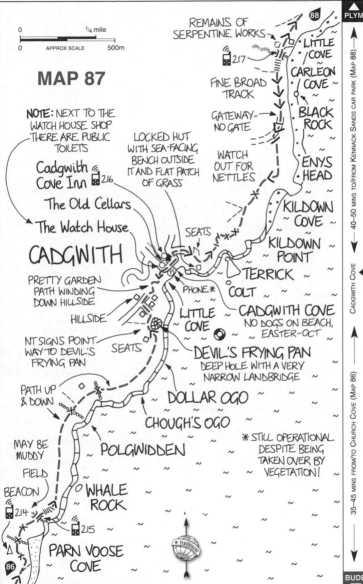

MAP 87

REMAINS OF SERPENTINE WORKS

📱217

FINE BROAD TRACK

GATEWAY – NO GATE

WATCH OUT FOR NETTLES

LITTLE COVE

CARLEON COVE

BLACK ROCK

ENYS HEAD

NOTE: NEXT TO THE WATCH HOUSE SHOP THERE ARE PUBLIC TOILETS

LOCKED HUT WITH SEA-FACING BENCH OUTSIDE IT AND FLAT PATCH OF GRASS

Cadgwith Cove Inn 📱216

The Old Cellars

The Watch House

CADGWITH

SEATS

KILDOWN COVE

KILDOWN POINT

TERRICK

COLT

PRETTY GARDEN PATH WINDING DOWN HILLSIDE

HILLSIDE

PHONE *

CADGWITH COVE
NO DOGS ON BEACH, EASTER–OCT

NT SIGNS POINT WAY TO DEVIL'S FRYING PAN

SEATS

LITTLE COVE

DEVIL'S FRYING PAN
DEEP HOLE WITH A VERY NARROW LANDBRIDGE

PATH UP & DOWN

DOLLAR OGO

CHOUGH'S OGO

* STILL OPERATIONAL DESPITE BEING TAKEN OVER BY VEGETATION!

MAY BE MUDDY

POLGWIDDEN

FIELD

BEACON
📱214

WHALE ROCK

📱215

PARN VOOSE COVE

86

0 ¼ mile
0 APPROX SCALE 500m

trailblazer

PLYM

ROUTE GUIDE AND MAPS ← 35–45 MINS FROM/TO CHURCH COVE (MAP 86) — CADGWITH COVE — 40–50 MINS TO/FROM KENNACK SANDS CAR PARK (MAP 88)

88

BUDE

KENNACK SANDS [MAP 88]

The beach here is popular with surfers.

At *Silver Sands Camp Site* (☎ 01326-290631, 🖥 silversandsholidaypark.co.uk; two adults & tent £14-22; Apr-Sep; 🐾) coastal walkers are always welcome and

you can exercise dogs in the campsite's one-acre field.

There's also *The Beach Hut* (Easter-Oct; daily 9.30am-7pm) and *Kennack Sands Beach Café* (daily 9am-6pm) with teacakes, scones and other Cornish delights.

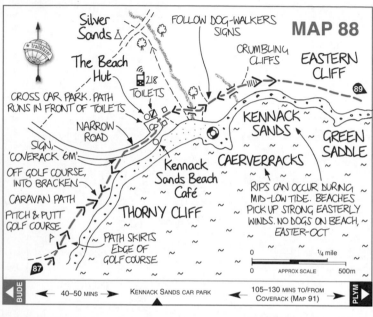

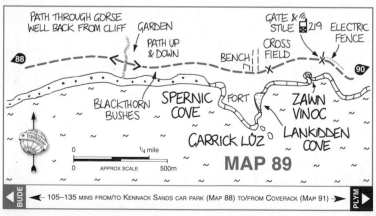

ROUTE GUIDE AND MAPS

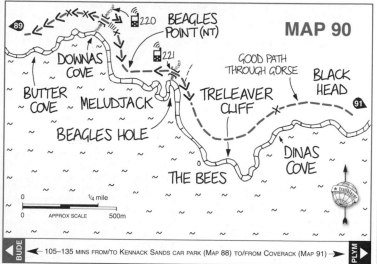

← 105–135 MINS FROM/TO KENNACK SANDS CAR PARK (MAP 88) TO/FROM COVERACK (MAP 91) →

COVERACK   [MAP 91, p234]

The foreshore at Coverack has an unusual claim to fame as one of only three places in Britain where you can see exposed *Moho*, the geological boundary between the Earth's crust and the Earth's mantle. The rocks you see at the surface here would have been 5km underground 380 million years ago. The Serpentine rocks to the south of the beach were the deepest, and once formed part of the Earth's mantle. The Gabbro rocks to the north of the beach once formed part of the Earth's crust, above the mantle. The beach is effectively the transition zone between the two – the *Moho* – and contains a jumble of intermingling rocks from both the mantle and the crust. Unsurprisingly perhaps, Coverack goes about its business in blissful ignorance of such matters, concerning itself more with coping with the huge influx of holidaymakers in the summer. It is one of the nicest little villages in the whole of this part of the coast – one with a great community spirit – and has avoided the seaside commercialisation of many other places.

Coverack Village Stores (**fb**; Mon-Sat 8.30am-5pm, Sun 9am-4pm) is good for takeaway hot drinks, sandwiches, fruit and veg, snacks and general supplies. **The Old Mill Shop** has a great range of second-hand **books**. There's a pop-up **post office** (Mon & Thur 1.30-4.30pm) in St Peter's Hall.

Where to stay

For accommodation listings, and other village information see 🖳 coverack.org.uk.

YHA Coverack (☎ 01326-280687, 🖳 yha.org.uk/hostel/yha-coverack; 33 beds, in dorms & private rooms; from £25pp; Apr-Oct) is a splendid Victorian country house, high up on School Hill; it's well-run and welcoming with a bar, self-catering kitchen and laundry. There is **camping** (£14-15) in the orchard behind. Campers have separate shower and kitchen facilities, but can use the main house too. They also have two popular bell tents (£99-149; sleep 5; booking essential). If the YHA campsite is full, the nearest **campsite** is about a mile further up the road at *Little Trevothan* (off Map 91; ☎ 01326-280260, 🖳 littletrevothan.co.uk, **fb**; tent & one/two people £10/15; Easter-Oct), which has a small **shop** and a games room.

For **B&B**, consider swish *Boak House* (☎ 01326-280329, 🖳 bridgetyoung@hot

BUDE

PLYM

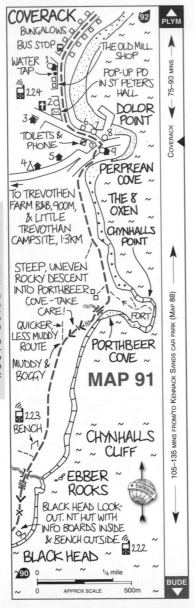

mail.co.uk; 3D/1T; ☞; ⚐; from £50pp, sgl occ £60), with light, bright rooms and fantastic sea views from the front of the house.

About another half a mile up School Hill is *Trevothen Farm B&B* (off Map 91; ☎ 01326-360647, ⌨ trevothen-farm.business.site; 1D en suite; from £40pp), which has a lovely room with its own entrance.

On Chymbloth Way, *Fernleigh* (☎ 01326-280626, ⌨ fernleighcoverack.co.uk; 1D/1D or T/1Qd; ☞; ⚐; from £40pp, sgl occ from £50) is nicely appointed with very welcoming owners.

You can also stay in bright, modern rooms at the only pub in the village, *Paris Hotel* (☎ 01326-280258, ⌨ pariscoverack.com; 2T/4D; ⚐; from £45pp, sgl occ £60), named after the ocean liner *SS Paris*, which was wrecked on the headland in 1899.

At the top end of the scale, overlooking the beach, is the charming *Bay Hotel* (☎ 01326-280464, ⌨ thebayhotel.co.uk; 12D, 2 suites; Mar-Nov; ☞; ⚐; from £60, sgl occ from £96) where comfort and a good welcome are assured, and where all rooms have sea views.

Where to eat and drink

Food-wise, there are several places in town but Coverack's humble chippy is the best known: the award-winning *Lifeboat House* (☎ 01326-281400, ⌨ thelifeboathouse.co.uk, **fb**; restaurant Wed-Sun 10am-8pm,

---

COVERACK – MAP KEY

Where to stay
1 The Bay Hotel
3 Fernleigh
4 YHA Coverack
5 Boak House
9 Paris Hotel

Where to eat and drink
1 The Bay Hotel
2 Harbour Lights Café
7 Archie's Loft
8 The Lifeboat House
9 Paris Hotel

Other
6 Coverack Village Stores

takeaway Wed-Fri 4-8pm, Sat noon-8pm, Sun noon-7pm) is as good as ever; the haddock & chips are fantastic, and the sea views are sublime. The restaurant has its own bar with Cornish ales on tap.

Paris Hotel (see Where to stay; daily noon-2.30pm & 6-9pm) has lovely sea views from its restaurant extension. The menu (most mains £11-13) changes regularly but seafood is pre-eminent.

Archie's Loft (daily 10am-5.30pm, winter hours vary) is a tiny tea room serving Origin coffee, Roskilly's ice cream, toasted sandwiches, baguettes (£4.95), pizzas and cream teas (£4.50); ideal for a quick snack before hitting the trail.

Further along is a pleasant café, *Harbour Lights* (☎ 01326-280612; fb; Tue-Sun 9.30am-4pm, winter hours vary).

The owner and head chef is a Coverack local who tries to source as much produce as possible from the immediate area.

Posh hotels sometimes turn their noses up at hikers and their muddy boots. Not *Bay Hotel* (see Where to Stay; lunch noon-2pm, afternoon tea 2-4pm, dinner 6.15-8.30pm; 🐾; booking recommended), which welcomes walkers in their bar, lounge or garden restaurant. Lunches include crab sandwiches (£12.50), their cream teas cost £10, and evening mains (£17-28) include roast lamb, pan-fried salted cod and Coverack lobster.

Transport

[See pp52-5] The No 36 **bus** service calls at Coverack. The bus turns at the bend north of the village, right on the coast path.

COVERACK TO PORTHALLOW   [MAPS 91-94]

This **5-mile (8km, 1¾-2¼hrs)** section leaves Coverack along a lane lined with bungalows with gardens full of sub-tropical plants that you won't see at home. You then follow the shore through fields to the monstrous obstacle that is **Dean Quarry**. The way through the quarry is well signposted; be sure to follow the signs carefully. Once past the quarry the path is taken inland; the former official route was abandoned to avoid more of the quarry's workings as well as some extensive flood damage, though there is talk of opening it up again between Porthoustock and Porthallow, so look out for coastpath signs round here.

Porthoustock (Map 93) has no services other than toilets and a public phone box, but there's an excellent café and a pleasant pub at **Porthallow**.

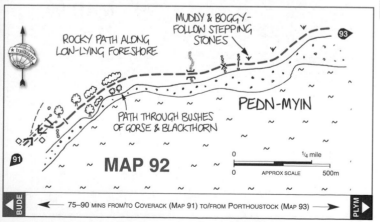

MUDDY & BOGGY - FOLLOW STEPPING STONES

ROCKY PATH ALONG LON-LYING FORESHORE

★ trailblazer

PEDN-MYIN

PATH THROUGH BUSHES OF GORSE & BLACKTHORN

MAP 92

0   ¼ mile

0   APPROX SCALE   500m

91   93

BUDE ◀ ──── 75–90 MINS FROM/TO COVERACK (MAP 91) TO/FROM PORTHOUSTOCK (MAP 93) ───▶ PLYM ▶

ROUTE GUIDE AND MAPS

ROUTE GUIDE AND MAPS

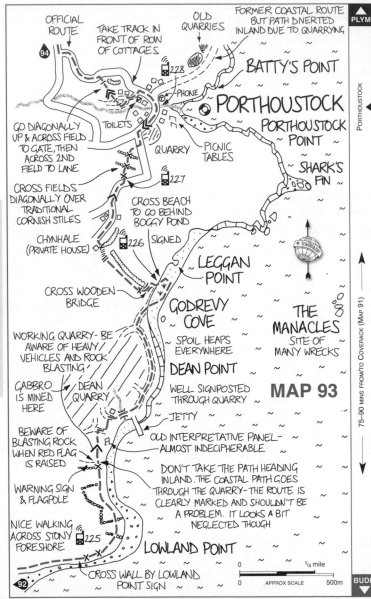

OFFICIAL ROUTE

TAKE TRACK IN FRONT OF ROW OF COTTAGES

OLD QUARRIES

FORMER COASTAL ROUTE BUT PATH DIVERTED INLAND DUE TO QUARRYING

94

228

BATTY'S POINT

PHONE

PORTHOUSTOCK

PORTHOUSTOCK POINT

GO DIAGONALLY UP & ACROSS FIELD TO GATE, THEN ACROSS 2ND FIELD TO LANE

TOILETS

QUARRY

PICNIC TABLES

SHARK'S FIN

CROSS FIELDS DIAGONALLY OVER TRADITIONAL CORNISH STILES

227

CHYNHALE (PRIVATE HOUSE)

CROSS BEACH TO GO BEHIND BOGGY POND

226 SIGNED

LEGGAN POINT

CROSS WOODEN BRIDGE

GODREVY COVE

THE MANACLES SITE OF MANY WRECKS

WORKING QUARRY - BE AWARE OF HEAVY VEHICLES AND ROCK BLASTING

SPOIL HEAPS EVERYWHERE

DEAN POINT

GABBRO IS MINED HERE

DEAN QUARRY

WELL SIGNPOSTED THROUGH QUARRY

MAP 93

JETTY

BEWARE OF BLASTING ROCK WHEN RED FLAG IS RAISED

OLD INTERPRETATIVE PANEL - ALMOST INDECIPHERABLE

WARNING SIGN & FLAGPOLE

DON'T TAKE THE PATH HEADING INLAND. THE COASTAL PATH GOES THROUGH THE QUARRY - THE ROUTE IS CLEARLY MARKED AND SHOULDN'T BE A PROBLEM. IT LOOKS A BIT NEGLECTED THOUGH

NICE WALKING ACROSS STONY FORESHORE

225

LOWLAND POINT

92

CROSS WALL BY LOWLAND POINT SIGN

PLYM

PORTHOUSTOCK

75-90 MINS FROM/TO COVERACK (MAP 91)

BUDE

0   1/4 mile
0   APPROX SCALE   500m

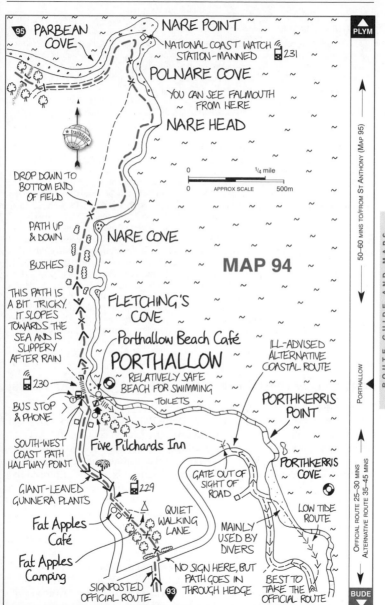

❏ **THE MANACLES**   **[MAP 93, p236]**

This treacherous reef lies a mile out to sea from Dean Quarry, dangerously close to the shipping lanes in and out of Falmouth. Hundreds of people have lost their lives here. In 1809 two ships were wrecked on the same night: *HMS Dispatch*, which was carrying troops, and *HMS Primrose*; only eight survived the tragedy. Many shipwreck victims are buried in the churchyard at St Keverne.

More positively, The Manacles provide good fishing grounds for boats from Porthallow and Porthoustock who mainly use handlines to catch bass here.

PORTHALLOW   [MAP 94, p237]

For coastal walkers Porthallow holds a very special significance, for here is a sculpture, unveiled in 2009, to celebrate the halfway point on the South-West Coast Path – it's 315 miles (517km) from here to Minehead in Somerset, and 315 miles to South Haven Point near Poole in Dorset. On one side of the sculpture is a list of flora and fauna that may be seen on the path, from orchids to oystercatchers, while on the other is a poem, *Fading Voices*, by writer Stephen Hall, which commemorates the life of Pralla (aka Porthallow) and coastal Cornwall in general.

On the approach into the village, you'll pass the wonderful *Fat Apples Café* (☎ 01326-281559, ▫ fatapplescafe.uk; **fb**; Apr-Sep Tue/Wed-Sun 9.30am-4pm, winter hours vary), which does breakfasts, fresh coffee, sandwiches and homemade cakes.

They also offer **camping** (£8 per tent) in a forested area behind the café, with showers and toilets available round the clock.

In the village itself, the pint-sized *Porthallow Beach Café* (**fb**; summer daily 10.30am-5.30pm; winter hours vary) is just a stone's throw from the shingle beach, and is good for drinks, ice creams, bacon rolls and pasties. Also here is *The Five Pilchards Inn* (☎ 01326-280256, or ☎ 01326-280751, ▫ thefivepilchards.co.uk; 2D/2D or T/1Tr; from £50pp, sgl occ £100), which serves good pub **food** (noon-3pm & 5.30-8.30pm) and has very smart rooms for **B&B**.

OTS Falmouth's No 33 **bus** from St Keverne to Helston, via Helford and Mawgan, stops here twice a day on weekdays (once a day in winter). [For details see p52-5].

PORTHALLOW TO HELFORD   **[MAPS 94-96]**

The next **7¼ miles (11.75km, 1¾-2¼hrs)** are fairly straightforward, though the path can be slippery after rain. Once past **Nare Point**, where there is a National Coastwatch Station manned by volunteers, the path encounters the inlet of **Gillan Creek**, which can only be forded one hour either side of low tide (stepping stones magically appear). So you must either wait for the tide to go out or take the 45-minute walk round the estuary. There may be one other possibility: an enterprising boatman in **St Anthony-in-Meneage** will sometimes ferry people across for £3 per person (minimum £5 per trip) between 9am and 6pm.

Across the creek, St Anthony is simply some cottages, mostly holiday lets, grouped round the church but it gives you something to aim for when wading across. A small gift shop opposite the church sells coffee, ice creams and snacks.

Beyond **Dennis Head** the sweep of the Helford River offers great views across to Falmouth. Large ships can be seen standing off until a berth becomes available in the docks. The path meanders through some lovely little wooded stretches, passes **Ponsence Cove** and **Bosahan Cove** and enters the riverside village of Helford by the back door, through a car park.

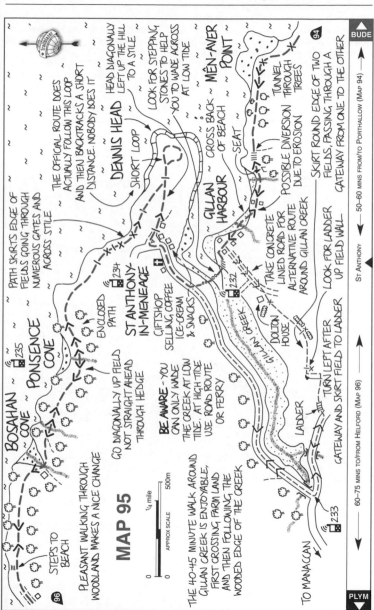

MAP 95

¼ mile

0   500m

0

APPROX SCALE

STEPS TO BEACH

PLEASANT WALKING THROUGH WOODLAND MAKES A NICE CHANGE

BOSAHAN COVE

PONSENCE COVE

🏕 235

GO DIAGONALLY UP FIELD NOT STRAIGHT AHEAD THROUGH HEDGE

PATH SKIRTS EDGE OF FIELDS GOING THROUGH NUMEROUS GATES AND ACROSS STILE

THE OFFICIAL ROUTE DOES ACTUALLY FOLLOW THIS LOOP AND THEN BACKTRACKS A SHORT DISTANCE. NOBODY DOES IT

DENNIS HEAD

HEADS DIAGONALLY LEFT UP THE HILL TO A STILE

SHORT LOOP

LOOK FOR STEPPING STONES TO HELP YOU TO WADE ACROSS AT LOW TIDE

MÊN-AVER POINT

94
BUDE ▲

TUNNEL THROUGH TREES

CROSS BACK ~ SEAT

GILLAN HARBOUR

ENCLOSED PATH

ST ANTHONY-IN-MENEAGE

🏕 234

✝

GIFTSHOP SELLING COFFEE, ICE-CREAM & SNACKS

BE AWARE - YOU CAN ONLY WADE THE CREEK AT LOW TIDE. AT HIGH TIDE USE ROAD ROUTE OR FERRY

THE 40-45 MINUTE WALK AROUND GILLAN CREEK IS ENJOYABLE, FIRST CROSSING FARM LAND AND THEN FOLLOWING THE WOODED EDGE OF THE CREEK

TO MANACCAN

🏕 233

LADDER

GATEWAY AND SKIRT FIELD TO LADDER

TURN LEFT AFTER

DOLON HOUSE

132

TAKE CONCRETE LINED ROAD FOR ALTERNATIVE ROUTE AROUND GILLAN CREEK

GILLAN CREEK

LOOK FOR LADDER UP FIELD WALL

POSSIBLE DIVERSION DUE TO EROSION

SKIRT ROUND EDGE OF TWO FIELDS, PASSING THROUGH A GATEWAY FROM ONE TO THE OTHER

─── 60-75 MINS TO/FROM HELFORD (MAP 96) ─── St ANTHONY ─── 50-60 MINS FROM/TO PORTHALLOW (MAP 94) ───

96

HELFORD [MAP 96]

Helford is a picture-postcard village beside an inlet of the Helford River, which drains completely at low tide. **Helford Village Stores** (daily 9am-3pm) sells pasties, a few baked goods and other groceries. They'll also fill water bottles for walkers.

Just before the footbridge, *Holy Mackerel Café* (☎01326-231008; Sat-Wed 11am-4pm, winter closed; **fb**; 🐾) serves light lunches, cream teas, Ploughman's and crab sandwiches and also has Cornish craft ales, cider and lager. The pub, *Shipwright's Arms* (☎ 01326-231235, 🖥 shipwrights helford.co.uk; summer daily noon-3pm & 6-8.30pm, winter hours vary; 🐾) is a lovely old inn with a thatched roof and a garden right beside the creek. The food is good-quality pub grub, plus pasties.

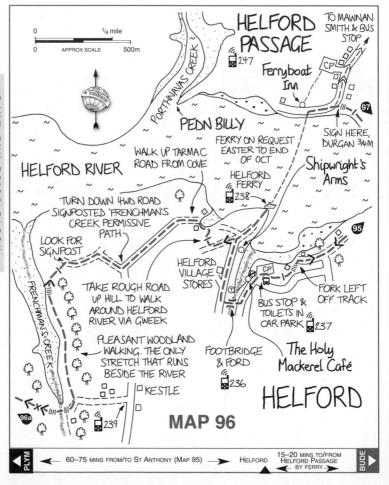

HELFORD TO HELFORD PASSAGE [MAPS 96 & 96a-d]

The most convenient crossing of the Helford River is by **Helford Ferry** (☎ 01326-250770, 🖳 helford-river-boats.co.uk; Apr-Jun & Sep-Oct daily 9.30am-5pm, Jul & Aug daily 9.30am-9.30pm; adults/under-12s £5/3) which runs all day, apart from an hour either side of low tide (check online at 🖳 tidetimes.org.uk/helford-river-entrance-tide-times) when all you can do is wait. The ferry operates on request – if it's not at the slipway when you arrive, you must display a yellow disc erected on the jetty for the purpose of alerting the ferryman. See below for how to get around Helford River if walking the coast path out of season.

GETTING AROUND THE HELFORD RIVER IN WINTER (ON FOOT)

On foot (Map 96 and 96a-96d, pp242-5) It is a **10-mile (16km, 3-4hrs)** walk around Helford River. The walk starts off promisingly along the wooded Frenchman's Creek but from Mudgeon Farm to Gweek it's all on tarmac with only tantalising glimpses of the river. However, in winter there won't be many cars and the pretty country lanes can provide some enjoyable walking away from the sea. *Gear Farm* (Map 96a, p242; ☎ 07968-778631, 🖳 campinghelfordriver.co.uk), owned by a welcoming couple, offers **camping** (£9pp; June-Sep). Also small and friendly, *Helford River Camping* (☎ 07971-540644, 🖳 helfordrivercamping.co.uk; Easter-Sep; tents £13-16) is right across the road. The next village, **Mawgan**, has a pub, *The Ship Inn* (Map 96b; ☎ 01326-221240, 🖳 shipinnmawgan.co.uk), that does really good food (Tue-Sat 6-9pm, closed Mon & Tue) in the evening, and **Mawgan Stores** (Mon-Sat 8am-7pm, Sun 9am-6pm), which is well stocked with groceries.

Gweek (see below) is a pleasant halfway point. If you are tired of walking it is possible to go by **bus** (the No 35; see p55) to Helford Passage (p246).

Between Gweek and Helford Passage there are a few shortcuts across fields taking you briefly off the roads. You pass through **Nancenoy** (see p244; Map 96c) with a popular pub (Trengilly Wartha Inn) right on the route.

You rarely see the river but instead are teased every now and again by a steep descent down to a connecting creek and an equally steep climb away from it; the two creeks are Polwheveral and Porth Navas before you reach **Helford Passage**.

Or by taxi If you decide this option, try Autocabs (☎ 01326-333337, 🖳 autocabshelston.co.uk) or Telstar (☎ 01326-221007, 🖳 telstartravel.co.uk).

GWEEK [MAP 96b, p243]

Gweek can provide some rest and relaxation although the services are limited. Those who failed to spot a single seal on their coastal wanderings may like to visit the **Cornish Seal Sanctuary** (☎ 01326-221361, 🖳 sealsanctuary.sealifetrust.org; daily summer 10am-6pm, winter 10am-4pm; adult/child £15.50/12.50). Nearby is a Premier **shop** (Mon-Sat 8am-8pm, Sun 9am-6pm) which also houses the local **post office** (Mon-Fri 9am-5.30pm, Sat 9am-12.30pm). Across the road, *The Black Swan* (☎ 01326-221502, 🖳 theblackswangweek.co.uk; **fb**; 4D en suite; from £42.50pp, sgl occ £70) has a wide selection of real ales, some decent pub **food** (Tue 5-9pm, Wed-Sat noon-2.30pm & 5-9pm, Sun noon-4pm), and **B&B** rooms.

OTS Falmouth's No 35A **bus** service between Falmouth and Helston stops here. [See pp52-5 for details.]

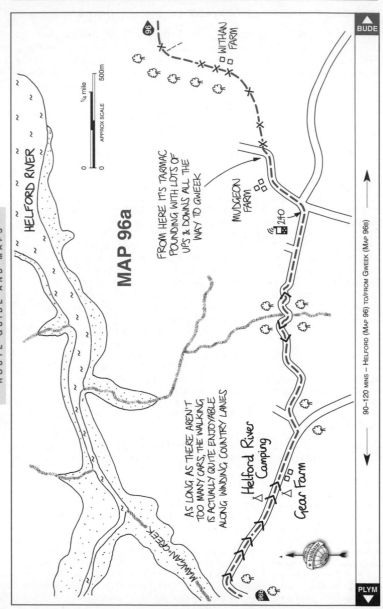

MAP 96a

HELFORD RIVER

WITHAN FARM

96

FROM HERE IT'S TARMAC POUNDING WITH LOTS OF UPS & DOWNS ALL THE WAY TO GWEEK

MUDGEON FARM

240

AS LONG AS THERE AREN'T TOO MANY CARS, THE WALKING IS ACTUALLY QUITE ENJOYABLE ALONG WINDING COUNTRY LANES

Helford River Camping

Gear Farm

MAWGAN CREEK

96b

¼ mile
APPROX SCALE
0   500m

90–120 MINS – HELFORD (MAP 96) TO/FROM GWEEK (MAP 96B)

BUDE

PLYM

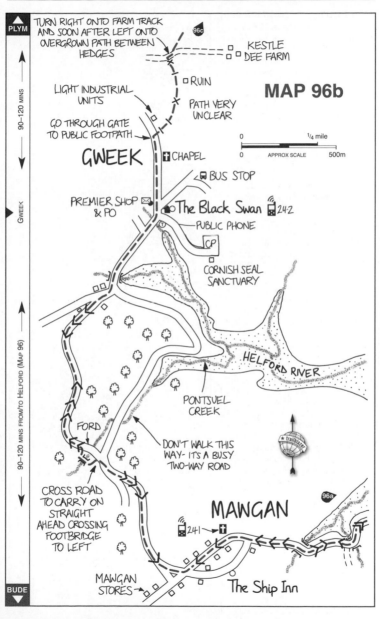

PLYM

90–120 MINS

GWEEK

90–120 MINS FROM/TO HELFORD (Map 96)

BUDE

TURN RIGHT ONTO FARM TRACK AND SOON AFTER LEFT ONTO OVERGROWN PATH BETWEEN HEDGES

96c

KESTLE DEE FARM

RUIN

LIGHT INDUSTRIAL UNITS

MAP 96b

PATH VERY UNCLEAR

GO THROUGH GATE TO PUBLIC FOOTPATH

GWEEK

0 ¼ mile
0 500m
APPROX SCALE

✝ CHAPEL

🚌 BUS STOP

PREMIER SHOP ✉ & PO

The Black Swan 📱242

PUBLIC PHONE

CP

CORNISH SEAL SANCTUARY

HELFORD RIVER

PONTJUEL CREEK

FORD

DON'T WALK THIS WAY- ITS A BUSY TWO-WAY ROAD

CROSS ROAD TO CARRY ON STRAIGHT AHEAD CROSSING FOOTBRIDGE TO LEFT

MAWGAN

📱241 ➔ ✝

MAWGAN STORES ➔

The Ship Inn

96a

ROUTE GUIDE AND MAPS

NANCENOY   **[MAP 96c]**

You might like to drop in at ***Trengilly Wartha Inn*** (☎ 01326-340332, 💻 trengilly.co.uk; **fb**; food Mon-Sat 3-9pm, Sun noon-6pm), well-known and a favourite locally. Their food has won many awards; the two-/three-course set menu changes frequently and costs £22/27. They also offer **B&B** (5D/1T/1Qd, all en suite; 🛏; 🐕; £42-54.50pp, sgl occ from £77).

❑ TREBAH & GLENDURGAN GARDENS (MAP 97, p247)

For garden and plant lovers there are two beautiful gardens slightly inland between Helford Passage and Mawnan Smith which would make an exceptionally pleasant and relaxing day of gentle wandering. Both can be reached by walking up the lane from Helford Passage. OTS Falmouth's No 35 (see p55) **bus** stops here.

● **Trebah Gardens** (☎ 01326-252200, 💻 trebahgarden.co.uk; daily 10am-5pm; adult/child £12/6; pre-book online) descends 200ft down a steeply wooded ravine to a private beach. The stream meanders through ponds containing giant Koi (carp) and through two acres of blue and white hydrangeas before spilling onto the beach. There's also a licensed **restaurant** that sells lunches and cream teas.

● **Glendurgan Gardens** (☎ 01326-252020, 💻 nationaltrust .org.uk; Feb-Oct Tue-Sun 10.30am-5pm, last entry 4pm; adult/child £10/5, NT members free) is owned by the National Trust. The valley garden was created in the 1820s and is rich in fine trees and rare and exotic plants and also features a maze. Spring time brings outstanding displays of magnolias and camellias. There's also a **tearoom** serving light refreshments.

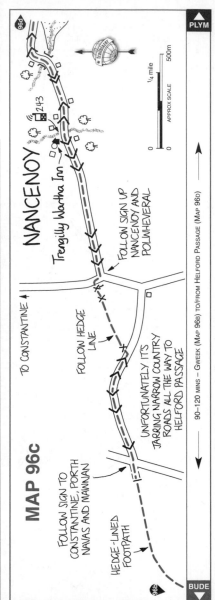

MAP 96c

NANCENOY

Trengilly Wartha Inn

TO CONSTANTINE

FOLLOW SIGN UP NANCENOY AND POLWHEVERAL

FOLLOW HEDGE LINE

UNFORTUNATELY IT'S JARRING NARROW COUNTRY ROADS ALL THE WAY TO HELFORD PASSAGE

FOLLOW SIGN TO CONSTANTINE, PORTH NAVAS AND MAWNAN

HEDGE-LINED FOOTPATH

90–120 MINS – GWEEK (MAP 96b) TO/FROM HELFORD PASSAGE (MAP 96d)

¼ mile   500m

APPROX SCALE

PLYM

BUDE

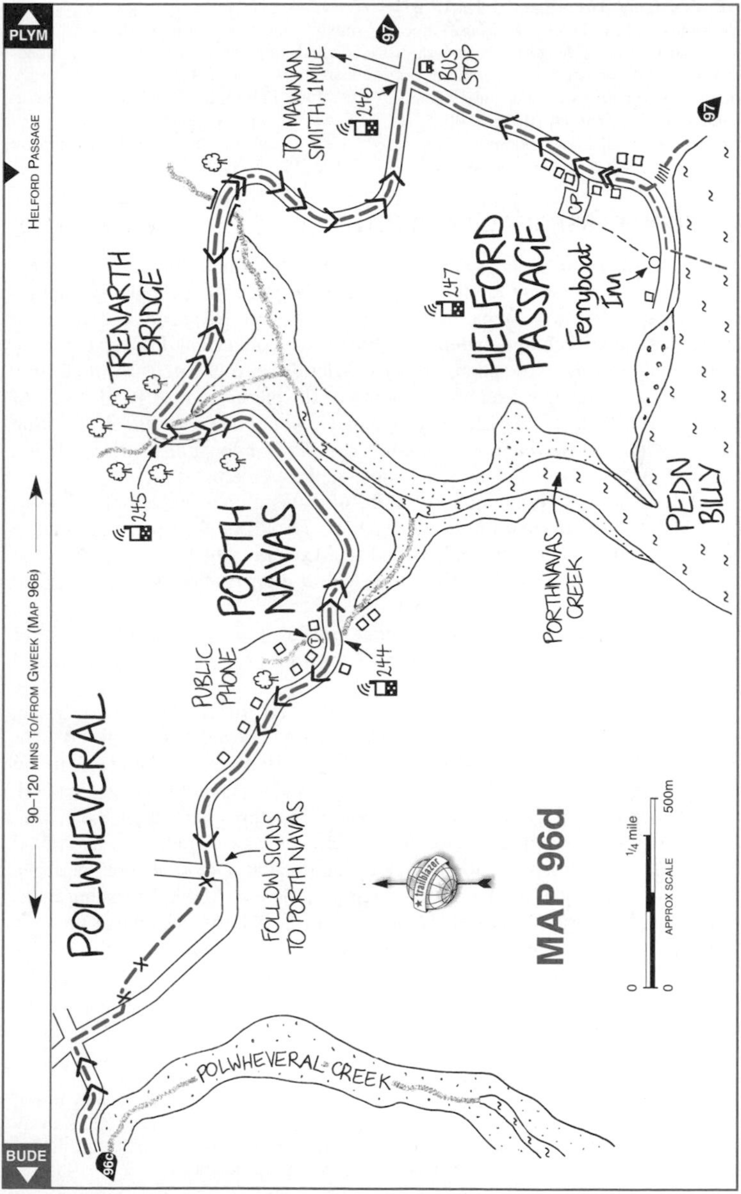

PLYM

HELFORD PASSAGE

← 90–120 MINS TO/FROM GWEEK (MAP 96B) →

PLYM

HELFORD PASSAGE

TO MAWNAN SMITH, 1 MILE

97

BUS STOP

📱 246

97

TRENARTH BRIDGE

HELFORD PASSAGE

📱 247

CP

Ferryboat Inn

PEDN BILLY

📱 245

PORTH NAVAS

PORTHNAVAS CREEK

PUBLIC PHONE

📱 244

POLWHEVERAL

FOLLOW SIGNS TO PORTH NAVAS

MAP 96d

¼ mile

500m

APPROX SCALE

0

0

trailblazer

POLWHEVERAL CREEK

96c

BUDE

ROUTE GUIDE AND MAPS

HELFORD PASSAGE   [MAP 97]

Helford Passage is directly opposite Helford on the north bank of the wide rivermouth. It is alive with the boating set in summer but rather quiet out of season. The only amenity is the *Ferryboat Inn* (☎ 01326-250625, 🖳 ferryboatcornwall.co.uk; food noon-3pm & 5-8pm), which has seating both inside and outside, and a decent pub menu (mains £9-14) that includes crab toast, smokey three-bean chilli and stonebaked sourdough pizza.

OTS Falmouth's No 35 **bus** calls here. [See pp52-5 for details].

You can also try local **taxi** company Telstar (☎ 07889-535009).

HELFORD PASSAGE TO FALMOUTH   [MAPS 97-100]

The **10 miles (16km, 2-2¾hrs)** to Falmouth provide wonderful gentle walking. On leaving the foreshore at Helford Passage the path climbs a grassy bank to lead by narrow ways to Trebah Beach where American troops embarked for the D-Day landings. **Trebah Gardens** (see box p244) come right down to the shore and the path passes below them, as it does **Glendurgan Gardens** a little further on. There are wide views across the mouth of the picturesque Helford River. At **Durgan**, you'll pass **The Fish Cellar** (Map 97; 🖳 nationaltrust.org.uk; Tue-Sun 11am-4.30pm, but volunteer-run so hours can vary), a local history information centre, which also sells second-hand books and ice creams.

Before the rocky promontory of **Toll Point** there are a couple of paths leading inland to **Mawnan Smith** (see below): after Toll Point the path enters steep woodland and another path leads inland to **Mawnan** which has an interesting church dedicated to St Maunanus, a Celtic saint. Then it loops out to **Rosemullion Head**, a superb viewpoint.

A series of little beaches follows, including Gatamala Cove and Bream Cove before the lovely expanse of **Maenporth Beach** (see p248) where there's a café and a smarter restaurant.

From Maenporth the path is well travelled. At the family-friendly beach, **Swanpool**, there's a popular restaurant, *Hooked on the Rocks* (Map 99; ☎ 01326-311866, 🖳 hookedontherocksfalmouth.com, **fb**; daily noon-2pm & 5-10pm; booking recommended), with a sea-view terrace and a menu of tapas and seafood, plus a **beach café** (daily 9am-5pm) with outdoor seating overlooking the beach.

After Gyllyngvase Beach suburban pavements take you all the way around **Pendennis Point** and past Falmouth Docks, a popular spot to lean on the fence for a while and watch the boats being repaired below. About 20 fishing boats work from this port of which half either trawl for whitefish or dredge for scallops. There is a native oyster fishery situated in the River Fal.

Then on through the streets of **Falmouth** (p248) jostling for space with the shoppers. There are plenty of pubs and restaurants here where you can celebrate your achievement so far.

MAWNAN SMITH   [map p248]

This village used to have four blacksmiths so acquired the name to distinguish it from nearby Mawnan. The 200-year-old **Old Smithy Workshops** (Mon-Fri 10.30am-5.30pm, Sat 11am-4pm) is the only one of the four still in operation, and offers a very rare opportunity to see a fully functioning traditional blacksmith's.

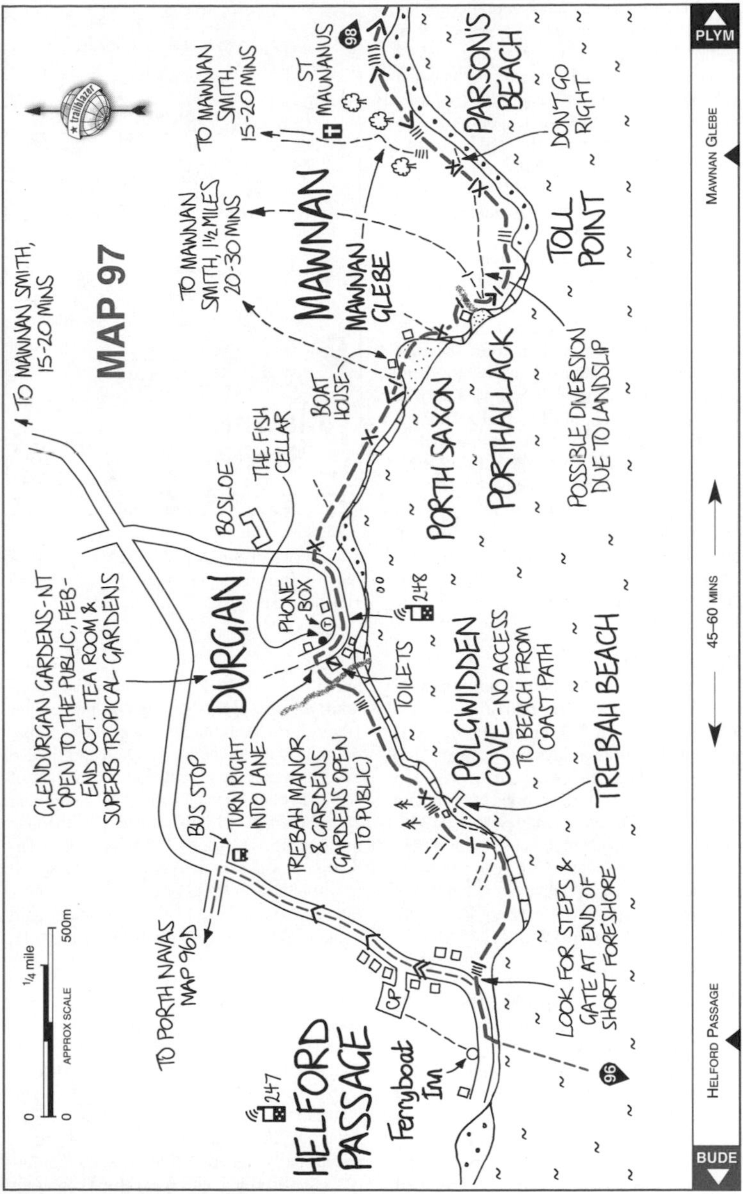

MAP 97

TO MAWNAN SMITH, 15-20 MINS

GLENDURGAN GARDENS - NT OPEN TO THE PUBLIC, FEB-ENDS OCT. TEA ROOM & SUPERB TROPICAL GARDENS

TO PORTH NAVAS MAP 96D

¼ mile
500m
APPROX SCALE

HELFORD PASSAGE

Ferryboat Inn

🏠 247

BUS STOP

TURN RIGHT INTO LANE

Trebah Manor & Gardens (Gardens Open to Public)

CP

Look for steps & gate at end of short foreshore

96

DURGAN

BOSLOE

THE FISH CELLAR

PHONE BOX

TOILETS

🏠 248

POLGWIDDEN COVE - NO ACCESS TO BEACH FROM COAST PATH

TREBAH BEACH

BOAT HOUSE

PORTH SAXON

PORTHALLACK

POSSIBLE DIVERSION DUE TO LANDSLIP

TO MAWNAN SMITH, 1½ MILES 20-30 MINS

TO MAWNAN SMITH, 15-20 MINS

ST MAWNANUS

MAWNAN

MAWNAN GLEBE

DON'T GO RIGHT

TOLL POINT

PARSON'S BEACH

98

PLYM

MAWNAN GLEBE

45-60 MINS

HELFORD PASSAGE

BUDE

ROUTE GUIDE AND MAPS

Mawnan Smith isn't actually on the coast path but it can easily be reached by walking from Helford Passage (25-30 mins), Durgan (15-20 mins), or Mawnan (15-20 mins). The **Village Shop** (Mon-Fri 9.30am-4pm, Sat 9.30am-12.30pm) is very well stocked with fresh fruit and other groceries including sandwiches.

Trevarn B&B (☎ 01326-251245, 💻 trevarn.co.uk; 2D/1T one en suite, two private facilities; from £50pp, sgl occ £100) is the only B&B left in the village. It's small but bright and comfortable, and the owners are friendly and helpful.

The thatched **Red Lion** (☎ 01326-250026, 💻 redlioncornwall.com, fb; food noon-3pm & 5-8.30pm) is a pub to spend time in; a true beauty with real ales such as Old Speckled Hen and Doom Bar on tap. The food is excellent, with a menu including Ploughman's (£10) and ciabattas (£8.25) as well as pub-classic mains (£11-14).

Just across the road, *AWNA Coffeehouse* (fb; Tue-Sat 9.30am-4pm, Sun 10am-3pm) is a modern, minimalist barista café serving top-notch coffee and delicious pastries and cakes.

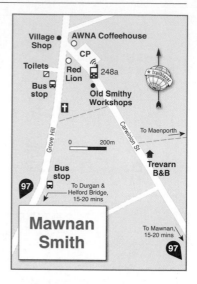

Mawnan Smith is on OTS Falmouth's No 35 **bus** route between Falmouth and Helston. [See pp52-5 for details].

MAENPORTH　　　　　　[MAP 98]

The beach here is a real gem. **Campers** have two choices nearby. *Tregedna Farm* (Map 99; ☎ 01326-250529 or 07798-622351, 💻 tregednafarmholidays.co.uk; Apr-Oct; £10pp) has bags of space and good clean showers. Slightly further on is family-run *Pennance Mill Farm* (Map 99; ☎ 01326-317431, 💻 pennancemill.co.uk; hiker & tent £13-15; Easter-Oct). Both can also be accessed from Swanpool beach (Map 99).

There are also two **food** choices. Café *Life's a Beach* (☎ 01326-251176, 💻 lifes

abeachcafe.co.uk, fb; daily summer 9am-5pm, plus Fri pizza evenings 6-9pm, winter 10am-3pm), does burgers, baguettes, ciabattas and excellent ice cream. Maenporth also has an upmarket beach restaurant. Part of celebrity chef Michael Caines' collection, at *The Cove* (☎ 01326-251136, 💻 thecove maenporth.co.uk; daily 8.30-10am & noon-8.30pm) you can sit out on the deck and have breakfast (£6-12) or a coffee, or tuck into a main menu (£15-35) adorned with quality seafood, grilled meats and fine wine.

FALMOUTH　　　　[MAP 100, p253]

Falmouth is a working port and holiday resort rolled into one. Just a small fishing village in the 17th century, it was developed by the Killigrew family who made their money from privateering and piracy, a lucrative trade in those days. Falmouth is still defined by the sea and the ships that sail in thanks to its large expanse of sheltered

water. It is said that an entire navy can anchor safely in Carrick Roads, the body of water between Falmouth and St Mawes. One of Britain's major yachting centres, it is often the first port of call for trans-Atlantic sailors, and the Tall Ships (large, traditionally rigged sailing vessels) regularly visit, bringing out the crowds in their

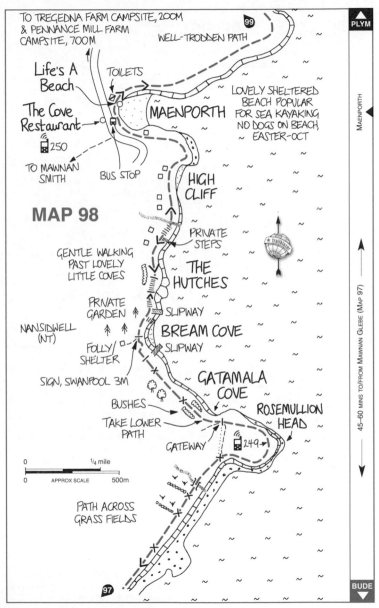

TO TREGEDNA FARM CAMPSITE, 200M
& PENNANCE MILL FARM
CAMPSITE, 700M

99

WELL-TRODDEN PATH

PLYM

Life's A
Beach

TOILETS

The Cove
Restaurant

250

MAENPORTH

LOVELY SHELTERED
BEACH POPULAR
FOR SEA KAYAKING
NO DOGS ON BEACH,
~ EASTER-OCT

MAENPORTH

TO MAWNAN
SMITH

BUS STOP

HIGH
CLIFF

MAP 98

PRIVATE
STEPS

GENTLE WALKING
PAST LOVELY
LITTLE COVES

THE
HUTCHES

PRIVATE
GARDEN

SLIPWAY

NANSIDWELL
(NT)

BREAM COVE

FOLLY/
SHELTER

SLIPWAY

45-60 MINS TO/FROM MAWNAN GLEBE (MAP 97)

ROUTE GUIDE AND MAPS

SIGN, SWANPOOL 3M

GATAMALA
COVE

BUSHES

ROSEMULLION
HEAD

TAKE LOWER
PATH

GATEWAY

249

0   ¼ mile

0   APPROX SCALE   500m

PATH ACROSS
GRASS FIELDS

97

BUDE

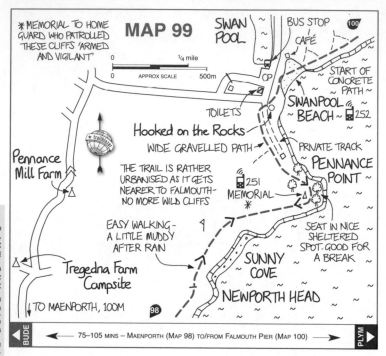

* MEMORIAL TO HOME GUARD WHO PATROLLED THESE CLIFFS 'ARMED AND VIGILANT'

MAP 99

0 — ¼ mile

0 — APPROX SCALE — 500m

SWAN POOL

BUS STOP 100

CAFÉ

CP

START OF CONCRETE PATH

TOILETS

SWANPOOL BEACH 252

Hooked on the Rocks

WIDE GRAVELLED PATH

PRIVATE TRACK

Pennance Mill Farm

THE TRAIL IS RATHER URBANISED AS IT GETS NEARER TO FALMOUTH – NO MORE WILD CLIFFS

251

MEMORIAL *

PENNANCE POINT

EASY WALKING – A LITTLE MUDDY AFTER RAIN

SEAT IN NICE SHELTERED SPOT. GOOD FOR A BREAK

Tregedna Farm Campsite

SUNNY COVE

NEWPORTH HEAD

↓ TO MAENPORTH, 100M

98

◄ BUDE   ← 75–105 MINS – MAENPORTH (MAP 98) TO/FROM FALMOUTH PIER (MAP 100) →   PLYM ►

tens of thousands. Two festivals worth attending are **Falmouth Regatta Week** and the **Oyster Festival** (see p16). The entrance to Carrick Roads is guarded by two castles built by Henry VIII, Pendennis Castle on the western promontory and the other across the water at St Mawes (see p255). **Pendennis Castle** (☎ 01326-316594, 🖳 english-heritage.org.uk; Mar-Oct daily 10am-5/6pm; winter weekends only; adult/child £13.10/7.90) is well worth a visit.

On Discovery Quay, the **National Maritime Museum** (☎ 01326-313388, 🖳 nmmc.co.uk; daily 10am-5pm; adult/child £14.95/7.50) tells the stories of Cornwall's nautical past. Don't miss The Lookout Tower, with panoramic views across the harbour, and The Tidal Zone, where you can see the underwater world changing with the tides from below the water line through two (immensely thick) windows.

Falmouth Art Gallery (☎ 01326-313863, 🖳 www.falmouthartgallery.com; Mon-Fri 10am-4pm, Sat 10am-1pm; free), on The Moor above the library, has a permanent collection of work by mainly Cornish artists with occasional visiting exhibitions. The independent **Poly Cinema** (☎ 01326-319461, 🖳 thepoly.org; box office Mon-Sat 10am-5pm), on Church St, shows art-house films.

Services
The staff at the **visitor centre** (☎ 01326-741194, 🖳 falmouth.co.uk or 🖳 falriver.co.uk; Mon-Sat 10am-3pm), on Prince of Wales Pier, are volunteers and very helpful. The **post office** (daily 8am-8pm) is in a branch of Spar supermarket (8am to midnight). The **library** (Mon, Tue, Thur & Fri 9.30am-4pm, Wed & Sat 9.30am-1pm) provides free **internet access**.

There are **banks** with **ATMs** along Market St and a Tesco Express **supermarket** (6am-midnight) at Discovery Quay which has an ATM outside it. There's also an ATM outside most other supermarkets in town. The most central **launderette** is Bubbles (Mon-Sat 9am-4pm, Sun 10am-2pm), on Killigrew St. The **medical centre** Westover Surgery (☎ 01326-212120, ☐ westoversurgery.co.uk; Mon-Fri 8am-6.30pm) is on Western Terrace. There is a Boots **pharmacy** (Mon-Sat 9am-5.30pm, Sun 10.30am-4.30pm) on Market St. You can find **camping equipment** at Mountain Warehouse (Mon-Sat 9am-5.30pm, Sun 10am-4pm). Nearby, there's a branch of the **newsagent** WH Smith (Mon-Sat 8.30am-5.30pm, Sun 10am-4pm).

Where to stay

Campsites and hostels The nearest places for **camping** are at Maenporth (see p248), a couple of miles from the centre. The only **hostel** in town is the very welcoming *Falmouth Backpackers* (☎ 01326-319996, ☐ falmouthbackpackers.co.uk; 18 dorm beds, 1D/1F; dorms from £19pp, private rooms £27pp, sgl occ £39), at 9 Gyllyngvase Terrace, with clean, decent-sized rooms, friendly staff and a simple toast-and-coffee breakfast.

B&Bs and guesthouses The following is just a selection from Falmouth's huge choice of B&B accommodation, all of similar quality. In summer, and for events such as the Tall Ships' gathering (see p16), the town can get booked up so keep this in mind when planning your trip.

B&Bs are plentiful in the Melvill Rd/ Avenue Rd area. On Melvill Rd are two guesthouses side by side: *Melvill House* (☎ 01326-316645, ☐ melvill-house-falmouth .co.uk; 2T/3D/2F; ☞; £35-45pp), at 52 Melvill Rd; and the very welcoming *Dolvean House* (☎ 01326-313658, ☐ dolvean.co.uk; 2S/2T/6D; ☞; 🐾; £50-62.50pp, sgl from £65), at No 50, which has a licensed bar.

On the corner of Gyllyngvase Rd and Melville Rd, the attractive *Gyllyngvase House* (☎ 01326-312956, ☐ gyllyngvase .co.uk; 3S/2T/7D, most en suite; ☞; from £70pp, sgl £80) has a restaurant and bar. *Camelot* (☎ 01326-312480, ☐ camelotfal mouth.com; 2S/1T/5D, all en suite; from £37.50pp, sgl occ from £60, sgl from £45) is at No 5 Avenue Rd. *Braemar* (☎ 01326-311285; 4D/1T; ☞; 🐾; from £75pp, sgl occ £100) is at No 9, and has rooms with their own kitchen facilities, though does still provide a continental breakfast.

At 17 Western Terrace is the family-run and highly recommended *Lyonesse Guest-house* (☎ 01326-313017, ☐ lyon essefalmouth.co.uk; 1D/2D or T; ☞; from £40pp, sgl occ from £60) with lovely en suite rooms and a very warm welcome.

Hotels Opposite Discovery Quay, is the modest 10-room hotel *Cutty Sark Inn* (☎ 01326-210861, ☐ cuttysarkfalmouth.co.uk; 7D/1T/2D or T, some en suite; from £45pp; min 2 nights) with some reasonable rooms (though the twin has metal-framed bunk beds rather than two single beds).

If you're in need of pampering, *St Michael's Hotel & Spa* (☎ 01326-312707, ☐ stmichaelshotel.co.uk; 61 rooms; ☞; from £65pp, sgl occ from £90, sgl from £65), near Gyllyngvase Beach, is a smart, 4-star hotel in leafy grounds. Non-residents can use the **pool** and **spa** too. Check online for special offers.

Less plush, but with plenty of character, *Merchant's Manor* (☎ 01326-312734, ☐ merchantsmanor.com; 39 rooms; ☞; 🐾; in summer from £100pp, in winter from £45pp) is a 1913 manor house with small but stylish rooms, plus a pool and gym.

Where to eat and drink

Falmouth is packed with places to eat, ranging from fish & chip joints and low-key cafés through to intimate bistros and fine-dining restaurants. Naturally enough seafood predominates.

Discovery Quay is the most buzzing part of town on a summer's evening, and events are often held on the square, which is surrounded by restaurants, cafés and bars. During the day, the numerous cafés, pubs and small restaurants on and around Market St and Church St are your best bet.

Cafés *De Wynns* (☎ 01326-319259, **fb**; Apr-Oct Mon-Sat 10am-5pm, Sun 11am-4pm; Nov-Mar Mon-Fri 10am-4pm, Sat 10am-5pm), at 55 Church St, is a lovely 30-year-old coffee house and tearoom that does pleasant lunches and breakfasts. Dishes include a fine Cornish rarebit and a decent selection of teas and coffees.

It's tough to resist the smell of roasted coffee beans that wafts across the pavement as you approach *Espressini* (**fb**; Tue-Sat 8am-4pm), a modern Italian-style café with fabulous coffee, plus healthier-than-usual breakfasts (eggs Benedict, avocado on toast, smoked haddock potato cakes). Nearby *Good Vibes Café* (☎ 01326-211870, **fb**; Mon-Sat 8am-3pm, Sun 9am-2pm) is rightly popular, with excellent vegetarian and vegan options and outstanding coffee.

Back on Church St, *Picnic* (**fb**; daily 9am-5pm), with tables spilling out onto the pavement, and *Ragamuffins* (Mon-Sat 9am-4pm), with harbour views at the back, are both cute little cafés.

Gylly Beach Café (☎ 01326-312884; 🖥 gyllybeach.com, **fb**; Wed-Sun 9am-8pm; takeaway daily 9am-6pm) has a nice perch above the ever-popular Gyllyngvase Beach, and does excellent food for a beach café, occasionally accompanied by live music on Sunday evenings.

Pasty fans should look no further than the much-loved *Oggies Cornish Kitchen* (**fb**; Mon-Sat 8am-5.30pm, Sun 9am-5.30pm). They have more than a dozen different types, ranging from the unusual (Keralan cauliflower, spinach and ricotta) to the classics, and you can eat in or take away.

Pubs Traditional pubs that serve food include the 17th-century *Chain Locker* (☎ 01326-311085, 🖥 chainlockerfalmouth.co.uk, **fb**; food daily noon-3pm & 5-9pm; 🐾), on Quay Hill, which has quayside seating.

FALMOUTH – MAP KEY

Where to stay
9 Lyonesse Guesthouse
11 Merchant's Manor
36 Cutty Sark Inn
37 Melvill House
38 Dolvean House
39 Braemar
40 Camelot
41 Falmouth Backpackers
42 Gyllyngvase House
43 St Michael's Hotel & Spa

Where to eat and drink
7 Nepalese Gurkha
12 Espressini
13 Pennycomequick
14 Good Vibes
16 Beerwolf Books
18 Picnic
20 Oggies
21 The Grapes
22 Ragamuffins
23 De Wynns
24 Ming's Garden
25 The Seafood Bar
26 Ploi Thai
27 The Chain Locker
28 The Stable
29 The Front

Where to eat and drink *(cont'd)*
30 Harbour Lights
33 The Shed
34 The Ranch
35 5 Degrees West
44 Gylly Beach Café

Other
1 SPAR, Post Office & ATM
2 Visitor Centre
3 Mountain Warehouse
4 Boots Pharmacy
5 Tesco Metro & ATM
6 Art Gallery & Library
8 Launderette
10 Medical Centre
15 Lloyds Bank
16 Beerwolf Books
17 WH Smith
19 Poly Cinema
31 Tesco Express & ATM
32 National Maritime Museum

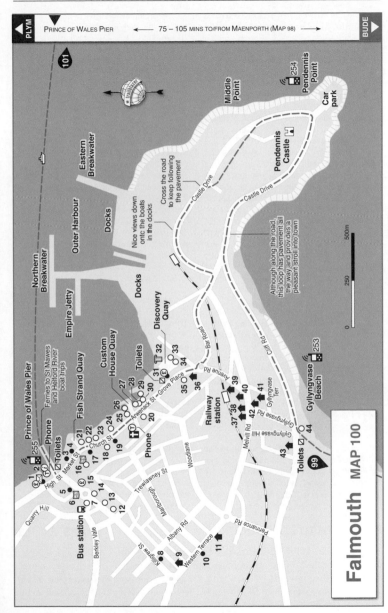

101

Middle Point

254
Pendennis Point

Car park

Eastern Breakwater

Pendennis Castle

Cross the road to keep following the pavement

Castle Drive

Castle Drive

Nice views down onto the boats in the docks

Northern Breakwater

Outer Harbour

Docks

Docks

Although along the road, this loop has pavement all the way and provides a pleasant stroll into town

Empire Jetty

Discovery Quay

Bar Road

500m

0   250

Prince of Wales Pier

Ferries to St Mawes and Helford River boat trips

Fish Strand Quay

Custom House Quay

Toilets

32

33

34

Phone

Toilets

High St Market St

21
22
23
24

Church St

17
18
19

16
15
14
13
12

Arwenack St — Grove Place

25
26
27
28
29
30
31

20

35

36

Avenue Rd

Railway station

Cliff Rd

37·38
42
40
41
39

Gyllyngvase Terr

Gyllyngvase Rd

Gyllyngvase Hill

253
Gyllyngvase Beach

44

43

Toilets

99

255

Phone

5
1 2
3 4

Bus station

6

7

8

9

10

11

Quarry Hill

Berkley Vale

Killigrew St

Western Terrace

Albany Rd

Marlborough

Trelawney St

Woodlane

Melvill Rd

Penwerris Rd

Penwerris Rd

Falmouth   MAP 100

Nearby at 64 Church St, *The Grapes* (☎ 01326-314704, 🖥 grapesalehouse.co.uk, **fb**; food daily noon-3pm & 6-9pm, winter hours vary) is an old alehouse with fine pub food, including plenty of seafood specials.

Closer to the railway station, *5 Degrees West* (☎ 01326-311288, 🖥 fivewest.co, **fb**; daily noon-10pm; 🐾) is great for a pint and a pizza (£9-14) and serves food later than most places. Near the bus station is cosy 18th-century *Pennycomequick* (☎ 01326-311912, 🖥 pennycomequick.co.uk, **fb**; food Mon-Sat 5-10pm, Sun noon-3pm & 6-9pm), serving excellent food. There are a couple of places that don't do food but let you bring your own to have with your pint. Literary real ale enthusiasts will love *Beerwolf Books* (☎ 01326-618474, 🖥 beerwolfbooks.com, **fb**; Mon-Sat 10am-midnight, Sun noon-11pm; 🐾) where you can indulge in numerous ales and lagers and peruse their bookshop. It's tucked away in Bells Court just off Market St. *The Front* (**fb**; 11am-11pm) is a real-ale pub on the quay, with outside seating.

Asian cuisine Housed inside the splendid 18th-century Grade II-listed building known as Bank House, *Ming's Garden Restaurant* (☎ 01326-314413; Tue-Sun 4.30-9.30pm) is a decent place to come for Chinese food. For Thai cuisine, try *Ploi Thai* (☎ 01326-210333; Wed-Mon 5-9.30pm) on Quay St. More unusual is *Nepalese Gurkha* (☎ 01326-311483, 🖥 gurkhafalmouth.co.uk; Wed-Mon 5.30-10.30pm), at 2a The Moor, for high-quality Nepalese curries.

Seafood For great value, you can't beat *Harbour Lights* (☎ 01326-316934, 🖥 harbourlights.co.uk, **fb**; daily noon-3pm & 5-8.30pm, takeaway noon-9.30pm, winter hours vary), serving quality fish & chips with a view of the harbour for £6-10.

Secreted away down a small lane leading to the harbour, *The Seafood Bar* (☎ 01326-315129; 🖥 verdantbrewing.co/pages/seafoodbar, **fb**; food Tue-Sat noon-3pm & 5-10pm, drinks noon-midnight) is an intimate independent restaurant specialising in locally caught fish and shellfish, as well as homemade desserts. Great beer, too, courtesy of local brewmasters, Verdant Brewing.

Restaurants Two restaurants that spill out onto Discovery Quay are standout steakhouse *The Ranch* (☎ 01326-210989, 🖥 the ranchfalmouth.co.uk, **fb**; noon-3pm & 6-9.30pm), and *The Shed* (☎ 01326-318502, 🖥 theshedfalmouth.co.uk, **fb**; daily 9.30am-10pm), with burgers, thin tortilla-crust pizzas and nachos (from £9.50).

Up towards Church St, family-friendly *The Stable* (☎ 01326-211199, 🖥 stable pizza.com/falmouth, **fb**; 11.30am-10pm, kitchen closed 3.30-4.30pm) offers pizza, pies and cider and has a large harbourside terrace out back.

Transport
[See pp50-5] There are **bus** services to Truro (U1) and to Mawnan Smith, Gweek, Helford Passage & Helston (35/35A) and the Falmouth Coaster to Penzance. **Trains**, operated by GWR, go to Truro hourly.

The 406 and 504 National Express **coach** services also operate here.

Ferry from Falmouth to St Mawes
The 20-minute ferry ride (☎ 01326-741194, 🖥 falriver.co.uk; 1-2/hr, approx 8am-5pm; £7.50) between bustling Falmouth and sleepy St Mawes runs year-round. It departs from the Prince of Wales dock in the heart of Falmouth, with a second ferry (1/hr) in summer from Custom House Quay in Falmouth. A combination ticket including the St Mawes to Place ferry costs £12.50.

FALMOUTH TO PORTSCATHO [MAPS 100-103]

This **6¼-mile (10km; 2-2½hrs not including ferry time)** jaunt begins with a couple of **ferries**: the one from Falmouth to St Mawes runs all year (see above), while the other links St Mawes with the tiny settlement of Place (see p255). There's an easy walk from St Mawes to Place round Trethem Creek if the ferries aren't operating; see p256.

ST MAWES

St Mawes, named after the 5th-century Celtic saint Maudez, is the gateway to, and largest town on, the Roseland Peninsula and was once a busy fishing port but now relies on tourism. Though less than a mile separates it from Falmouth, it's a shame that most coast path walkers don't experience more of this town than the harbour, where the ferry to Falmouth docks and from where a second ferry, to Place, sets sail.

Facilities in town include **Roseland Visitor Centre** (☎ 01326-270440, 💻 st mawesandtheroseland.co.uk; Mon-Sat 10am-4pm), with public toilets and an **ATM** beside it, a Co-op **supermarket** (daily 7am-10pm), a **post office** (Mon-Sat 7.30am-5.30pm, Sun to 5pm) and **St Mawes Pharmacy** (Mon-Tue 9am-6pm, Wed 9am-1pm, Thur-Fri 9am-5pm, Sat 10am-3pm).

Where to stay and eat

For a fabulous **B&B**, walk up the lane beside The Watchhouse restaurant, then turn right up the very steep Grove Hill and you'll soon see, on your right, the entrance to the exquisite *Braganza* (☎ 01326-270281, 💻 braganza-stmawes.co.uk; 1S/4D or T; 🐾; £62.50-70pp, sgl £65-70; min 2 nights peak season), a beautifully decorated period building with stunning harbour views. They are very accommodating to passing walkers.

Back down at the harbour, *The Rising Sun* (☎ 01326-270233, 💻 risingsunstmaw es.co.uk, **fb**; 1S/3D/2T/2F; 🍺; 🐾; from £60pp, sgl from £70) is a pub with rooms, some with panoramic sea views. They also do **food** (daily 8.30-10am, noon-2.30pm & 5.30-8.30pm; mains from £12).

Nearby *Idle Rocks Hotel* (☎ 01326-270270, 💻 idlerocks.co.uk; 19 rooms; 🍺; 🐾; from £155pp; min 2 nights; food noon-2pm & 6.30-9pm) is proper gorgeous, but proper expensive. Its sister property, *St Mawes Hotel* (☎ 01326-270270, 💻 stma weshotel.com; 5D/2D or T; from £110pp; food daily noon-3pm & 6-9pm) is slightly cheaper. Passing walkers will be tempted by its 'coffee and a treat' deal (£5) but it also has decent pub food (mains £12-18).

For outstanding pasties head to *St Mawes Bakery* (☎ 01326-270292, 💻

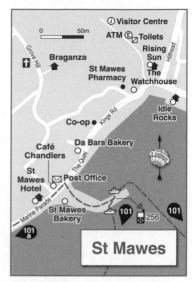

stmawespasty.co.uk; daily 8am-3pm) on the quay. The wooden tables outside it are for *Café Chandlers* (daily 8.30am-5pm), a friendly place across the road that does good coffee, cakes and flapjacks. Smarter and more spacious is *Da Bara Bakery* (💻 dabara.co.uk; daily 8am-5pm), with excellent breads and pastries, plus artisan ice creams.

For more formal dining there's *The Watchhouse* (☎ 01326-270038, 💻 watch housestmawes.co.uk; daily noon-3pm & 6-9pm; evening mains £14-24.50), where you can get a splendid lunch for £10-15.

Transport

The No 50 **bus** runs to Portscatho & Truro. [See pp52-5 for details.]

Ferry from St Mawes to Place

The ferry (☎ 01326-741194; 9am-5.30pm every 30 mins; journey time 10 mins; £6.50, or £12.50 for combination ticket with Falmouth ferry) between St Mawes and Place runs in summer only. So from November to Easter you'll need to either rely on the local bus services or take the walk described overleaf.

ROUTE GUIDE AND MAPS

ST MAWES TO PLACE VIA THE INLAND ROUTE

This route is a lovely, flat stroll and full of interest. Highlights include a Henry VIII castle, a gorgeous 13th-century church and some delightful ambling through woods lining the creek. The only part that is in any way 'difficult' is the central section as you cross from the banks of the Carrick Roads (separating Falmouth from St Mawes) to Gerrans, because you're not on the national trail now, so the clearly marked path with all its waymarks and signposts is conspicuous in its absence. As a result, it *can* be slightly tricky finding your way. But follow the directions in this guide closely and it shouldn't be too demanding.

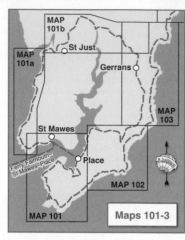

Maps 101-3

St Mawes Castle (Map 101a; ☎ 01326-270526, 🖳 english-heritage .org.uk; Apr-Oct daily 10am-5pm, Jul & Aug to 6pm, Nov-Feb Sat & Sun only 10am-4pm, Mar Wed-Sun 10am-4pm; adult/child £6.90/4.10) lies just to the west of St Mawes looking towards Falmouth. A superior example of Henry VIII's artillery castles, the fortifications are built in a clover-leaf shape. Despite its utilitarian purpose, the castle is not without decoration including inscriptions in Latin praising the king and his son Edward VI.

A succession of sometimes-muddy cattle fields and a somnolent harbour leads from the castle to the next attraction, the beautiful 13th-century **Church of St Just** (Map 101b), surrounded by palm trees and set in some of the prettiest semi-tropical gardens of any church. The path passes through the gardens, and rounds the church, where you'll see *Miss V's Cornish Cream Tea* (🖳 missvs.co.uk; May-Oct 10am-5pm), a delightful café with seating indoors and out. Continuing to skirt the edge of the church grounds opposite the café, you then drop down to the small natural spring or fountain where, just beyond, the path takes a sharp right up the hill through the trees to the road.

More fields are crossed before another road is reached, which you follow down past *Trethem Mill Touring Park* (☎ 01872-580504, 🖳 trethem.com; Easter-Oct; tent & two people £26-29; adults only), an award-winning campsite with a lovely rural setting. At the end of this stretch of road, turn left across the bridge, then immediately right, up a path off the road, before crossing more fields until another road is joined. Turn right here, then follow the road to Polhendra Cottage, where you turn left through the second gate and drop down towards a stream. There's no discernible path through this field, but try aiming for the line of trees on the slopes opposite. Follow that line of trees, keeping them on your left as you climb up to a track that crosses two fields before emerging on a lane leading to **Gerrans Church** (Map 103). Those who have taken the bus (the No 50; see p55) will be dropped off here. There's another excellent campsite here and a village pub – see p260.

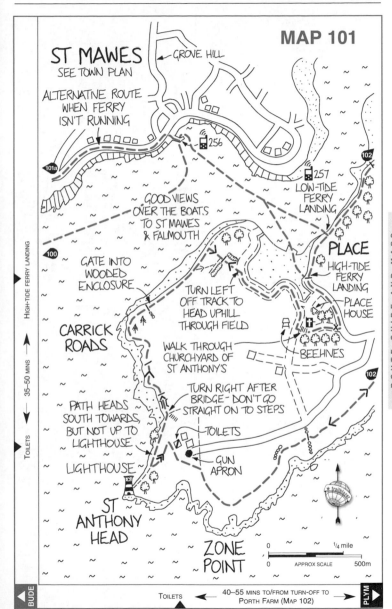

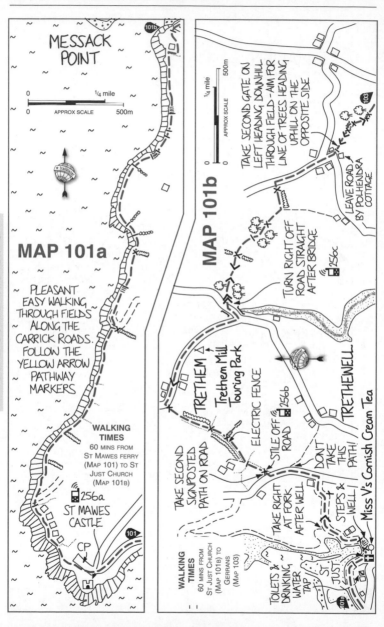

MESSACK POINT

0 — 1/4 mile
APPROX SCALE
0 — 500m

MAP 101a

~ PLEASANT
EASY WALKING
THROUGH FIELDS
~ ALONG THE
CARRICK ROADS.
FOLLOW THE
YELLOW ARROW
PATHWAY
MARKERS

**WALKING
TIMES**
60 MINS FROM
ST MAWES ferry
(MAP 101) TO ST
JUST CHURCH
(MAP 101B)

256a
ST MAWES
CASTLE

CP

101

MAP 101b

TAKE SECOND GATE ON
LEFT HEADING DOWNHILL
THROUGH FIELD - AIM FOR
LINE OF TREES HEADING
UPHILL ON THE
OPPOSITE SIDE

0 — 1/4 mile
APPROX SCALE
0 — 500m

103

LEAVE ROAD
BY POLHENDRA
COTTAGE

256c

TURN RIGHT OFF
ROAD STRAIGHT
AFTER BRIDGE

TRETHEM
Trethem Mill
Touring Park

ELECTRIC FENCE

256b

STILE OFF
ROAD

TRETHEWELL

Miss V's Cornish Cream Tea

TAKE SECOND
SIGNPOSTED
PATH ON ROAD

DON'T
TAKE
THIS
PATH!

TAKE RIGHT
AT FORK
AFTER WELL

STEPS &
WELL

ST
JUST

**WALKING
TIMES**
60 MINS FROM
ST JUST CHURCH
(MAP 101B) TO
GERRANS (MAP 103)

TOILETS &
DRINKING
WATER
TAP

101b

At this point a choice is available: take the road left after the church and a five-minute descent will bring you to Portscatho. Alternatively, to follow the coast path religiously continue by taking the track (Treloan Lane) by the Royal Standard pub and follow this all the way down to a road, where you should turn right. Leave the road on the left by the bridge to follow Porth Creek and the Percuil River that will eventually lead you to the ferry launch at Place.

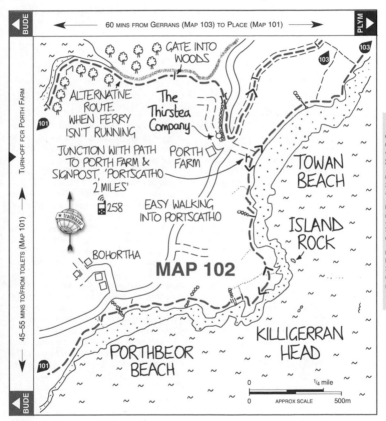

Assuming you're starting at **Place**, where the ferry docks, the path begins with a saunter around picturesque **Place House** to the neighbouring church and from there up to the top of the ridge with lovely views of St Mawes Harbour and, in the distance, Falmouth itself. **St Anthony Head**, the southernmost tip of the **Roseland Peninsula**, with its historic lighthouse, is the next destination (though the path actually turns off east before reaching the lighthouse). All around the point are the silent remnants of defensive fortifications such as a WWII gun battery as well as earlier, 19th-century relics. The whole Head is owned by the National Trust and there are toilets here.

From here the path squeezes between the old military road and the sea, high above the sailors and surfers. The landmarks of **Killigerran Head** and **Greeb Point** are ticked off without too much difficulty. Between the two, you can get **refreshments** at *The Thirstea Company* (Map 102; ☎ 01872-580773, 🖳 the thirsteacompany.co.uk, **fb**; Apr-Oct, daily 10am-5pm, winter hours vary) above Towan Beach.

After Greeb Point, the path passes a memorial to those who fell in Burma during WWII, then rounds the small geographical pimple of **Pencabe** that shelters the former pilchard-fishing harbour of **Portscatho**.

PORTSCATHO & GERRANS
[MAP 103]

Portscatho's history is typical of this part of Cornwall. A former fishing village that once survived on the seemingly endless supplies of pilchards that flourished in the balmy waters here, it now relies on tourism, with a bare remnant of the fishing industry still clinging on gamely.

The centre of Portscatho is a square where you'll find a decent restaurant, a very well-stocked store and a busy pub. The **store** is Ralph's (☎ 01872-580702; daily 7am-7pm), a mini supermarket really, with baked goods and fresh fruit and veg, plus the village's **post office** (same hours) inside it.

Nearby, *The Boathouse* (☎ 01872-580326, 🖳 theboathouseportscatho.com, **fb**; Mon-Sat 10am-9pm, Sun till 5pm) is a licensed café with a quality menu that includes plenty of freshly caught fish. The pub menu at *Plume of Feathers* (☎ 01872-580321, 🖳 plumeoffeathers-roseland.com; daily 9am-9pm) includes Cornish mussels and pan-roasted hake as well as pub classics (from £15). They also have **rooms** (3D/2D or T, all en suite; 🐾; from £47.50pp; weekends min 2 nights).

Down by the slipway is *Tatams* (🖳 tatams.co, **fb**; summer daily 9am-4pm, plus 5-9pm Fri & Sat), a seasonal coffee hut that does great coffee, pastry and cakes and is lovely spot for a rest.

Around 5-10 minutes up the hill is the neighbouring village of **Gerrans**, home to a lovely old 13th-century church dedicated to the obscure St Gerendus.

Here you'll find the lovely 18th-century *Royal Standard* (☎ 01872-580271, 🖳 royalstandard-gerrans.co.uk; food summer daily noon-2pm & 6-9pm; winter hours vary; 🐾).

There is an excellent **campsite** here called *Treloan* (☎ 01872-580989, 🖳 treloancoastalholidays.co.uk; 🐾), which is often busy, but always makes room for coast-path walkers (£10); expect flat, grassy pitches, sea views and a very warm welcome. They also have a wooden 'Snug' (sleeps 2, £43) and a yurt (sleeps 3, £60) which can be rented by the night outside the school summer holidays.

The nearest B&B, about a mile north of Portscatho, is *Trewithian Farm* (Map 104; ☎ 01872-580293, 🖳 trewithianfarm.co.uk; 2D/2T/1Tr/1Qd; 🐾; from £37.50pp, sgl occ from £55), a 400-year-old stone farmhouse with spacious rooms. To get here, take the lane running north from Porthcurnick Beach (see Map 103), past Rosevine, then turn left at the sign for St Mawes and Truro, and walk to the end of the lane.

The No 50 **bus** passes through Gerrans and Portscatho en route between St Mawes and Truro. [For details see pp52-5.]

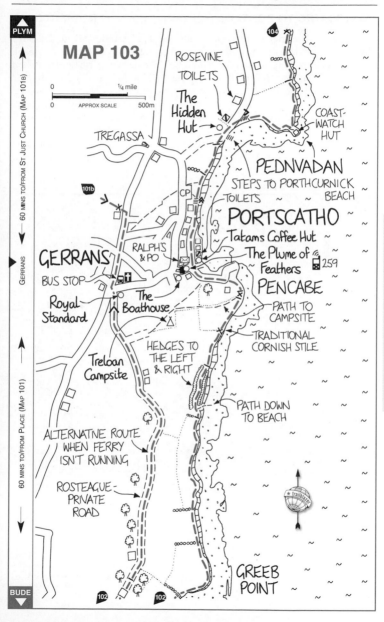

MAP 103

PLYM

0   1/4 mile
0   500m
APPROX SCALE

60 MINS TO/FROM ST JUST CHURCH (MAP 101B)

GERRANS

60 MINS TO/FROM PLACE (MAP 101)

BUDE

104

ROSEVINE

TOILETS

The Hidden Hut

TREGASSA

101b

CP

COAST-WATCH HUT

PEDNVADAN

STEPS TO PORTHCURNICK BEACH

TOILETS

PORTSCATHO

Tatams Coffee Hut

GERRANS

RALPH'S & PO

The Plume of Feathers   259

BUS STOP

PENCABE

Royal Standard

The Boathouse

PATH TO CAMPSITE

TRADITIONAL CORNISH STILE

Treloan Campsite

HEDGES TO THE LEFT & RIGHT

PATH DOWN TO BEACH

ALTERNATIVE ROUTE WHEN FERRY ISN'T RUNNING

ROSTEAGUE PRIVATE ROAD

GREEB POINT

102   102

trailblazer

PORTSCATHO TO PORTLOE   [MAPS 103-106]

Things get a little trickier after Portscatho on this **7½-mile** (**12km; 2½-3hrs**) stage. The path initially describes an arc bending eastwards around sizeable **Gerrans Bay**, passing some lovely little beaches such as Porthcurnick (where you can seek out *The Hidden Hut* café; Map 103; 🖳 hiddenhut.co.uk, **fb**; Mar-Oct daily 11am-5pm, lunch served noon-3pm), Pendower (where you can grab refreshments at the wonderfully named and good value *Shallikabooky Beach Hut*; Map 105; **fb**; daily 10am-5pm), and neighbouring Carne (just before which you'll find the luxury *Nare Hotel* (Map 105; ☎ 01872-501111, 🖳 narehotel.co .uk; 36 rooms; low season from £160pp, sgl from £174, high season from £210pp, sgl from £242). At low tide these beaches unite to form one huge, very inviting expanse of sand.

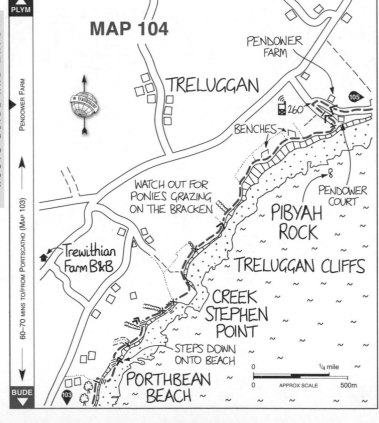

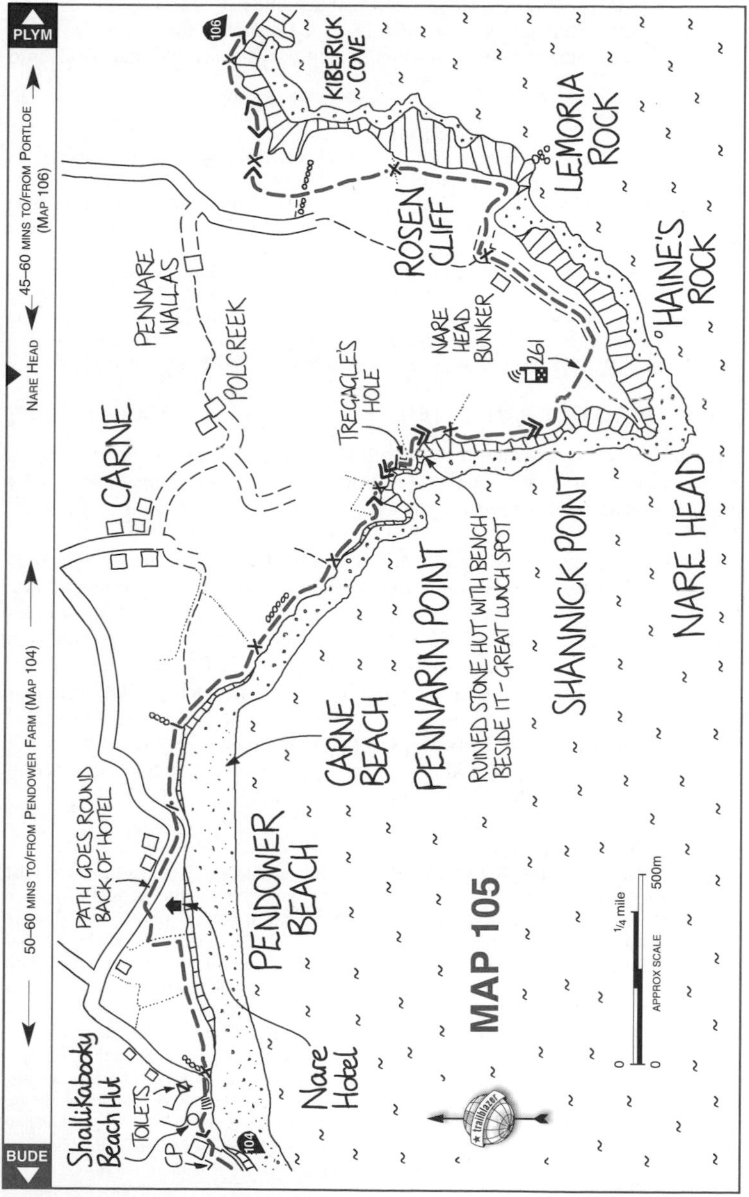

ROUTE GUIDE AND MAPS

PLYM

BUDE

NARE HEAD ← 45–60 MINS TO/FROM PORTLOE (MAP 106)

50–60 MINS TO/FROM PENDOWER FARM (MAP 104)

106

KIBERICK ~ COVE

LEMORIA ROCK

ROSEN CLIFF

HAINE'S ROCK

PENNARE WALLAS

POLCREEK

NARE HEAD BUNKER

261

TREGGLE'S HOLE

CARNE

NARE HEAD

PENNARIN POINT

SHANNICK POINT

RUINED STONE HUT WITH BENCH
BESIDE IT – GREAT LUNCH SPOT

CARNE BEACH

PENDOWER BEACH

MAP 105

PATH GOES ROUND
BACK OF HOTEL

Nare Hotel

Shallikabooky Beach Hut

TOILETS

CP

104

¼ mile

500m

APPROX SCALE

0

0

Nare Head provides the stage's first real test, the path undulating ever more severely before culminating in a steep al-fresco staircase that soars up to the Head. From here, the path becomes kinder as it drops gently through fields into the slumbering fishing village of Portloe.

PORTLOE   [MAP 106]

Yet another pretty little fishing harbour, this one is tinier and even more tranquil than most. The centre of life in the village lies a short jaunt up the road from the harbour at *The Ship Inn* (☎ 01872-228393, **fb**; 2D/1T; from £40pp, sgl occ £60), with cosy rooms, St Austell ales on tap, and fabulous pub **food** (daily noon-4pm & 5-9pm).

Back down on the path, the upmarket *Lugger Hotel* (☎ 01872-501322, 🖳 lugger hotel.com; 24D; ➡; 🐾; from £80pp, sgl occ from £110; min 2 nights at weekends; food daily 12.30-2pm & 7-9pm) has a lovely location on the water's edge and is open for morning coffee. Every room is en suite with a deep bath and a deluge shower.

The No 51 **bus** is Portloe's link to the outside world. To get to Portscatho you would need to transfer onto the No 50 at Tregony. [See pp52-5 for details.]

PORTLOE TO GORRAN HAVEN   [MAPS 106-110]

This relatively easy **9-mile** (**14.5km; 2-3hrs**) stage is one of the prettiest in southern Cornwall. A fairly uneventful stretch of clifftop marching, broken up by a couple of stiff gradients, brings you eventually to the twin hamlets of **West** and **East Portholland**.

You may need some sustenance at **Porthluney Cove's** fine *beach café* (Map 108; *YHA Boswinger* is also on Map 108 with details on p269) in preparation for the hike up to Dodman Point, which is embellished with a large stone cross that was erected at the end of the 19th century as a navigational aid. **Dodman Point** was actually once the location of a huge Iron Age fort, the biggest in the South-West. Reasons as to why early Britons should have chosen to build their fortifications here quickly become obvious on a clear day, with views to Lizard Point in one direction and Berry Head in the other. It's a lovely spot for a rest.

After Dodman, the path follows a fairly gentle course down to the peaceful village of **Gorran Haven**.

WEST & EAST PORTHOLLAND
[MAP 107, p266]

Both Porthollands combined only have around 40 residents and form part of the gorgeous estate of **Caerhays Castle** (☎ 01872-501310, 🖳 visit.caerhays.co.uk; gardens mid Feb to mid June daily 10am-4pm; castle open only for guided tours, mid Mar to mid June Mon-Fri at noon, 1.30pm & 3pm; gardens/castle/both £10/13/20), which peers above the trees to your left on reaching **Porthluney Cove** (Map 108). The castle itself was designed by Georgian architect John Nash, most famous as the man behind Buckingham Palace, Marble Arch and much of Regency London. East Portholland boasts the delightfully cute *Pebbles Café and Crafts* (☎ 01872-501036, **fb**; Easter-Sep Mon-Thur & Sat 9am-5pm, Sun 10.30am-5pm), where you can recharge with a hot drink, a pasty or a light lunch. Their rock cakes are delicious.

At Porthluney Cove the seasonal *beach café* (Map 108; **fb**; 11am-5pm) is excellent. It's set back from the beach without sea views but there are views of the castle, and the food is very good. They open later than usual on some summer evenings with occasional live music.

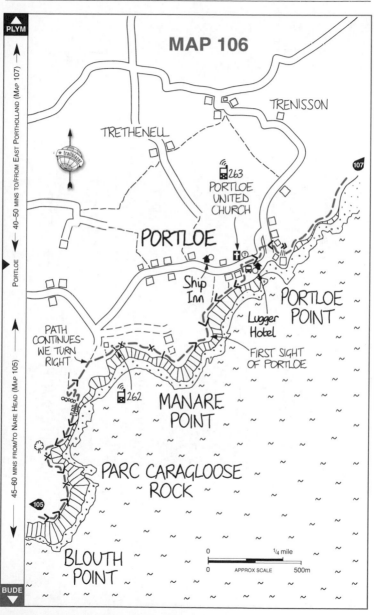

MAP 106

PLYM

← 40-50 MINS TO/FROM EAST PORTHOLLAND (MAP 107) →

← PORTLOE →

← 45-60 MINS FROM/TO NARE HEAD (MAP 105) →

BUDE

TRENISSON

TRETHENELL

📱263
PORTLOE
UNITED
CHURCH

107

PORTLOE

Ship
Inn

PORTLOE
POINT

Lugger
Hotel

FIRST SIGHT
OF PORTLOE

PATH
CONTINUES-
WE TURN
RIGHT

📱262

MANARE
POINT

PARC CARAGLOOSE
ROCK

105

BLOUTH
POINT

0   ¼ mile
0   500m
APPROX SCALE

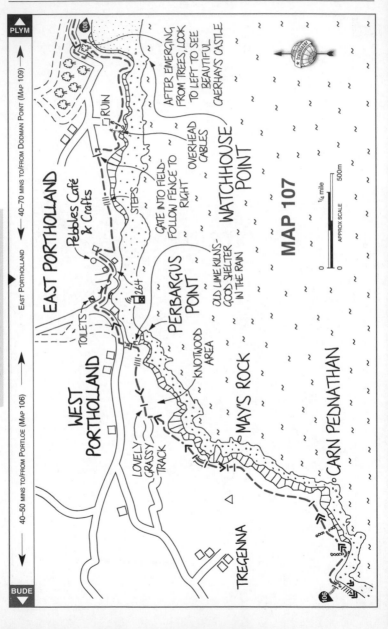

PLYM ▲

◀— 40–70 MINS TO/FROM DODMAN POINT (MAP 109) —▶

East Portholland

▲— 40–50 MINS TO/FROM PORTLOE (MAP 106) —▶

BUDE ▼

108

AFTER EMERGING FROM TREES, LOOK TO LEFT TO SEE BEAUTIFUL CAERHAYS CASTLE

RUIN

WATCHHOUSE POINT

Pebbles Café & Crafts

EAST PORTHOLLAND

STEPS

GATE INTO FIELD - FOLLOW FENCE TO RIGHT

OVERHEAD CABLES

MAP 107

TOILETS

264

PERBARGUS POINT

OLD LIME KILNS - GOOD SHELTER IN THE RAIN

¼ mile

500m

0   APPROX SCALE   0

WEST PORTHOLLAND

KNOTWOOD AREA

MAY'S ROCK

CARN PEDNATHAN

LONELY GRASSY TRACK

½

TREGENNA

106

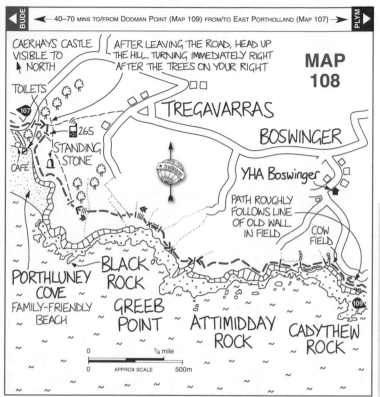

CAERHAYS CASTLE
VISIBLE TO
↑ NORTH

AFTER LEAVING THE ROAD, HEAD UP
THE HILL, TURNING IMMEDIATELY RIGHT
AFTER THE TREES ON YOUR RIGHT

MAP 108

TOILETS

107

TREGAVARRAS

265

BOSWINGER

STANDING
STONE

CAFE

YHA Boswinger

PATH ROUGHLY
FOLLOWS LINE
OF OLD WALL
IN FIELD

COW
FIELD

PORTHLUNEY
~ COVE ~
FAMILY-FRIENDLY
BEACH

BLACK
ROCK

GREEB
POINT

~ ATTIMIDDAY
ROCK ~

109

CADYTHEW
~ ROCK ~

0 ____ 1/4 mile
0 ____ APPROX SCALE ____ 500m

traiblazer

ROUTE GUIDE AND MAPS

GORRAN HAVEN [MAP 110, p269]

Sheltered from the wind by Dodman Point, Gorran Haven is popular with families, with sandy beaches that are amongst the safest in the county. See ⌨ gorranhaven.org.uk for tourist information. Perhaps uniquely for Cornwall, there is no pub here. Other facilities are thin on the ground too, though the very friendly folks at **Cakebreads shop** (fb; Mon-Sat 8am-5.30pm, Sun 8.45am-3pm) have a bakery and the village **post office** (Mon-Fri 9am-5.30pm, Sat 9am-5pm). Alongside it is *Cakebreads Café* (summer Mon-Sat 8am-4pm, Sun 8.45am-3pm, winter hours vary), a licensed café in a marquee, which does a hearty Cornish breakfast (£7.95) plus baps, paninis and the like.

There are two **campsites** nearby. About three-quarters of a mile from the path is *Trelispen* (off Map 110; ☎ 01726-843501, ⌨ trelispen.co.uk; Apr-Oct; 🐾; 2 people & tent £13-18), a family-run site that gives walkers a warm welcome. To get here, walk along Chute Lane, past the Llawnroc Hotel, then take the second right (Trewollock Lane) and continue to a T-junction; turn left here and the campsite will soon be on your right. A similar distance away to the south is the larger *Treveague Campsite* (Map 109; ☎ 01726-844027, ⌨ treveaguecampsite.co.uk; hiker & tent £10), with its own restaurant, café and bar, plus a shop selling basics including camping gas.

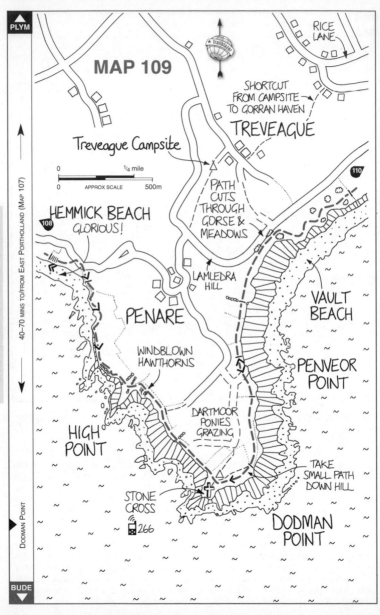

PLYM

MAP 109

RICE LANE

trailblazer

SHORTCUT FROM CAMPSITE TO GORRAN HAVEN

TREVEAGUE

Treveague Campsite

0   1/4 mile
0   APPROX SCALE   500m

PATH CUTS THROUGH GORSE & MEADOWS

HEMMICK BEACH
GLORIOUS!

108

LAMLEDRA HILL

VAULT BEACH

PENARE

PENVEOR POINT

WINDBLOWN HAWTHORNS

DARTMOOR PONIES GRAZING

HIGH POINT

STONE CROSS

📱266

TAKE SMALL PATH DOWN HILL

DODMAN POINT

110

ROUTE GUIDE AND MAPS

40–70 MINS TO/FROM EAST PORTHOLLAND (MAP 107)

DODMAN POINT

BUDE

Back beyond Dodman Point is *YHA Boswinger* (Map 108; ☎ 0345-371 9107, 🖳 yha.org.uk/hostel/yha-boswinger; 38 beds, private rooms available; £16-25pp; Mar-Oct). Walking via Penare (Map 109) is quickest, if you're going west.

The only **B&B** option nowadays is the modern but pricey *Llawnroc Hotel* (☎ 01726-843461, 🖳 thellawnrochotel.co.uk; 18 rooms; 🐾; winter from £62.50pp, summer from £87.50pp). The hotel's *Gwineas Bar & Bistro* (food daily noon-9.30pm, bar Mon-Sat 11am-11pm, Sun noon-10.30pm;

mains £13-17) is the closest thing Gorran Haven has to a pub, and you can just pop in for a pint. In case you haven't spotted it, 'Llawnroc' is 'Cornwall' backwards!

The Haven Fish & Chips (**fb**; summer Tue-Sun 11.30am-9pm, winter hours vary) is a popular chippy, but the standout place for some light food is lovely community-run *Coast Path Café* (**fb**; Thur-Sat 10.30am-4.30pm, Sun 2-4.30pm), staffed entirely by volunteers who serve home-made cakes, sandwiches, tea and coffee from their perch right on the coast path. At

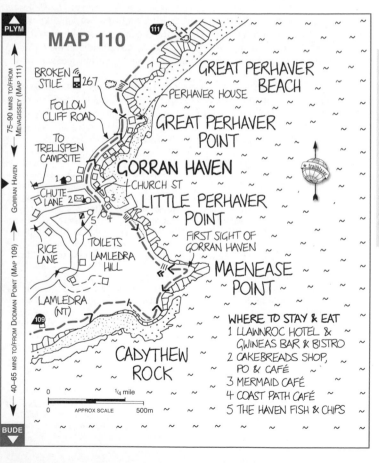

MAP 110

PLYM

← 75-90 MINS TO/FROM MEVAGISSEY (MAP 111) →

← GORRAN HAVEN →

← 40-65 MINS TO/FROM DODMAN POINT (MAP 109) →

BUDE

BROKEN STILE 🚌 267
FOLLOW CLIFF ROAD
TO TRELISPEN CAMPSITE
GORRAN HAVEN
CHUTE LANE 2
RICE LANE
TOILETS
LAMLEDRA HILL
LAMLEDRA (NT)
109

GREAT PERHAVER BEACH
PERHAVER HOUSE
GREAT PERHAVER POINT
CHURCH ST
LITTLE PERHAVER POINT
FIRST SIGHT OF GORRAN HAVEN
MAENEASE POINT

trailblazer

CADYTHEW ROCK

WHERE TO STAY & EAT
1 LLAWNROC HOTEL & GWINEAS BAR & BISTRO
2 CAKEBREADS SHOP, PO & CAFÉ
3 MERMAID CAFÉ
4 COAST PATH CAFÉ
5 THE HAVEN FISH & CHIPS

0   ¼ mile
0   APPROX SCALE   500m

ROUTE GUIDE AND MAPS

the time of research it was temporarily closed because of fire damage, but should reopen soon. Another gem is *The Mermaid Café* (☎ 01726-843654, 🖳 themermaid cafe.co.uk, **fb**; Easter-Oct daily 10am-5pm) where, as the sign says, you can get 'breakfast, lunch and tea, right beside the sea'.

The limited community-run Gorran Bus (☎ 01726-844933, 🖳 gorranbus.org; reservations recommended) G1, G3 & G4 **bus** services go to St Austell, Truro and Plymouth. The No 23 goes to St Austell via Mevagissey. [See pp52-5 for details.]

GORRAN HAVEN TO MEVAGISSEY [MAPS 110-111]

A relatively easy **3½-mile (5.5km; 1¼-1½hrs)** amble across a small headland separates Gorran Haven from Mevagissey, a picturesque stroll that takes in the lovely cottages at **Chapel Point**, built in the 1930s (using stone quarried from the point itself) and which featured in Daphne du Maurier's novel *The House on the Strand*. The point is preceded on the trail by a clifftop meadow known as **Bodrugan's Leap**, named after Sir Henry Bodrugan who is said to have successfully leapt off the cliffs to a waiting boat in the cove below in his efforts to evade his pursuer, Sir Richard Edgcumbe of Cothele, during the War of the Roses in the 15th century.

Soon afterwards you reach the Mevagissey suburb of **Portmellon**, where the 17th-century pub, *The Rising Sun Inn* (Map 111; ☎ 01726-843235, 🖳 therising suninn.com; 1S/1T/2D/1Tr; from £40pp; food 12.30-2.30pm & 6-8pm) serves good-value **food** (most mains around £10), fine Cornish ales, and has rooms available for **B&B**. The path then follows the road into Mevagissey itself.

MEVAGISSEY [map p272]

Named after two saints, Meva and Issey, Mevagissey's busy, bustling working harbour is one of the highlights of the south Cornish coast. There is believed to have been a settlement on this site as early as the Bronze Age and it was mentioned in records from the early 14th century (then called Porthhilly). However, the town only truly thrived with the rise of the pilchard industry. The fish provided both a source of nutrition *and* a source of power, a power station having been built in the village in 1895 that ran on pilchard oil! As a result, Mevagissey claims to be the first village in England to have had electric street lighting.

Today at least a morning or even a day of gentle meandering and munching can be enjoyably passed here. Set between harbour and sea, the **Mevagissey Museum** (☎ 01726-843568, 🖳 mevagisseymuseum .com; Easter-Oct 11am-4pm, July & Aug 10am-5pm; free) is interesting. Housed in a building that dates back to the 1740s, it has some diverting curios including a £1 note

from the Bank of Mevagissey, and photos of the village from the 19th and 20th centuries.

Also worth a quick look is the **Mevagissey Aquarium** (🖳 mevagisseyhar bour.co.uk/aquarium; Easter-Oct Mon-Sat 10am-6pm; free), in the former lifeboat house at the mouth of the harbour, with nine small tanks displaying local marine life.

Services
Visitor Information can be found in the marvellous **bookshop** Hurley Books (☎ 01726-842200, 🖳 hurleybooks.co.uk; daily 10am-4/5pm) on Jetty St. The **post office** is in the Premier **shop** (Mon-Sat 7am-8pm, Sun to 7pm) just off Market Sq on River St. Boots **pharmacy** (Mon-Fri 9am-6pm, Sat 9am-5pm) is on Fore St.

Where to stay
Right in the centre, *The Ship Inn* (☎ 01726-843324, 🖳 theshipinnmeva.co.uk; 3D/1Tr/1Qd; ●; 🐾; from £45pp, sgl occ £60-75), on Fore St, is an old-fashioned

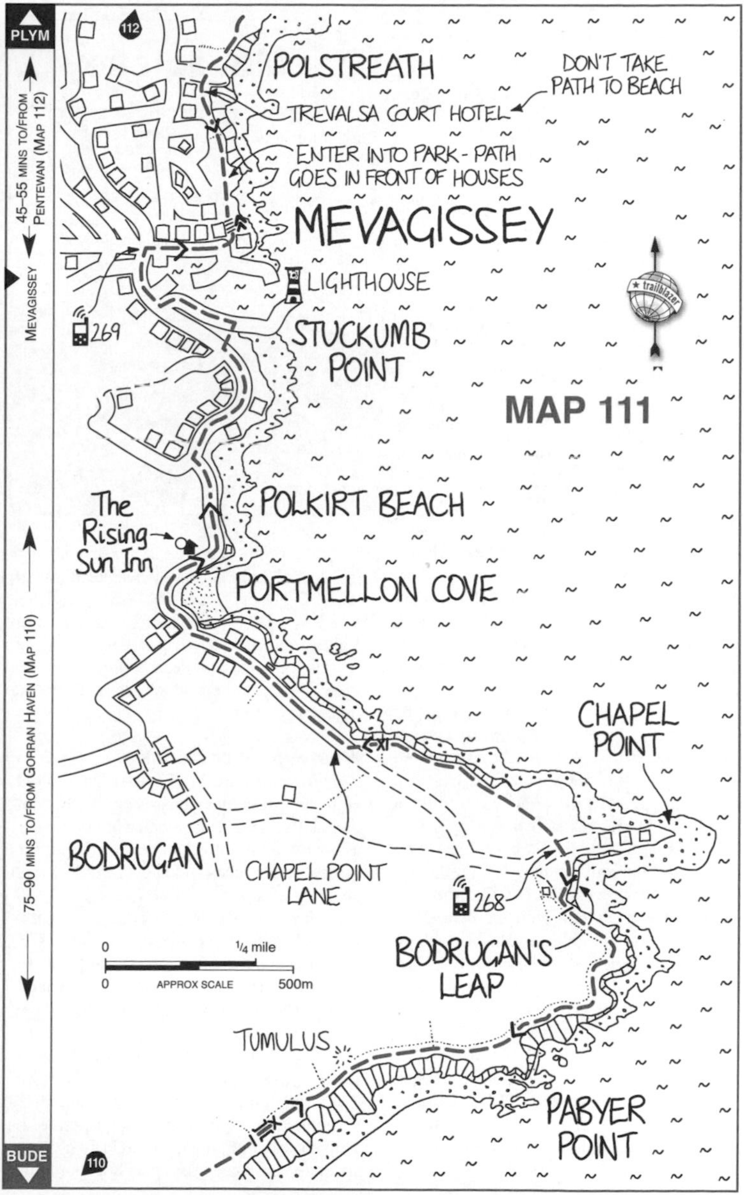

PLYM

112

POLSTREATH

DON'T TAKE
PATH TO BEACH

TREVALSA COURT HOTEL

ENTER INTO PARK - PATH
GOES IN FRONT OF HOUSES

45–55 MINS TO/FROM Pentewan (Map 112)

MEVAGISSEY

MEVAGISSEY

LIGHTHOUSE

269

STUCKUMB
POINT

MAP 111

POLKIRT BEACH

The
Rising
Sun Inn

PORTMELLON COVE

75–90 MINS TO/FROM GORRAN HAVEN (MAP 110)

CHAPEL
POINT

BODRUGAN

CHAPEL POINT
LANE

268

BODRUGAN'S
LEAP

0   ¼ mile

0   APPROX SCALE   500m

TUMULUS

PABYER
POINT

BUDE

110

ROUTE GUIDE AND MAPS

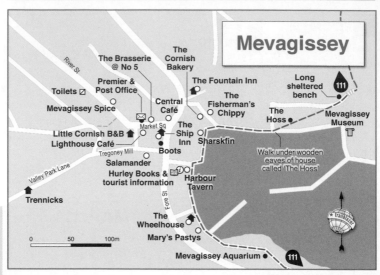

Mevagissey

The Brasserie @ No 5

The Cornish Bakery

River St

Premier & Post Office

Toilets ☑

Mevagissey Spice

The Fountain Inn

Long sheltered bench 111

The Fisherman's Chippy

Central Café

The Hoss ●

Mevagissey Museum

Little Cornish B&B 🏠

Lighthouse Café

Market Sq

Tregoney Mill

The Ship Inn

Boots

Sharskfin

Walk under wooden eaves of house called 'The Hoss'

Salamander

Valley Park Lane

Hurley Books & tourist information

Harbour Tavern

Fore St

Trennicks

The Wheelhouse

Mary's Pastys

Mevagissey Aquarium ● 111

0   50   100m

★ trailblazer

Cornish fisherman's pub with low ceilings and decent rooms. Sitting right on the harbourfront, *The Wheelhouse Restaurant and Guest-house* (☎ 01726-339029, 🖥 wheelhouserestaurant.co.uk; 3D; from £45pp, sgl occ from £85) has rooms with great harbour views.

The best pub in town, though, is the oldest: the 15th-century *Fountain Inn* (☎ 01726-842320, 🖥 mevagissey.net/fountain .htm; 2D en suite, 1D private facilities; 🐾; £37.50-50pp, sgl occ £65-90), a hidden gem of a place, secreted away in a side alley just back from the harbour. It has two bars; Front Bar and Smugglers Bar, the latter still displaying evidence (a floor pit, and holes in the walls that held the beams for the presses) of its time used as a pilchard press in the 18th and 19th centuries. They serve Cornish ales, great pub grub and host sea-shanty singers some evenings.

One of the cutest **B&Bs** is *The Little Cornish B&B* (☎ 01726-842563, 🖥 little cornishbandb.co.uk, **fb**; 3D; from £48pp, sgl occ £65), a traditional 1752 Cornish cottage, at 1-2 River Terrace. It's a quirky, friendly place with helpful hosts and a memorable candlelit breakfast.

Near the centre is *Trennicks* (☎ 01726-842235, 🖥 trennicksguesthouse.co .uk; 2D/1D or T; £42.50-47.50pp, sgl occ £70-85; adults only; min 2/3 nights), on Valley Park Lane. Its elevated position makes for some wonderful harbour and sea views – enjoy them after a lazy dip in the outdoor pool.

Where to eat and drink
The Brasserie at No 5 (☎ 01726-844422, 🖥 numberfiveinmevagissey.co.uk, **fb**; summer daily 9am-11pm, winter hours vary) is a lovely place offering healthy breakfasts (£5-8), sandwiches and baguettes (£6-7) and an array of tapas (£4.50-7).

For no-frills café food, try nearby *Central Café* (Mon-Sat 9.30am-3pm & 5-7.30pm, winter hours vary; 🐾), or for more vegetarian and vegan options, friendly *Lighthouse Café* (Mon-Fri 9.30am-5pm, Sun 10am-4pm).

You'll find the usual collection of lovely **pubs** with good menus in the town. *The Ship Inn* (see Where to stay; daily summer noon-9pm; winter noon-3pm & 6-9pm) has varied, locally-caught fish on the specials board each day, plus hot sourdough rolls and pub-grub classics (most mains £12-15). The intriguing old *Fountain Inn* (See opposite; food noon-2pm & 6-9pm) serves great pub grub (rump steak, home-made fish pie; £12-14), and has St Austell ales on tap in its two, history-laden bars. Children, dogs and walkers all welcome.

Now pirate-themed, *The Wheelhouse* (see Where to stay; food daily Mar-Oct 9am-9pm, Nov-Feb to 4pm) is thought to date back to the early 19th century, and was a net loft in a previous incarnation, where it is said the Methodist John Wesley preached his first sermon. Food consists of break-fasts, paninis, stonebaked pizzas, and pub-type evening meals (6-9pm; £12-14).

The large, open-plan **restaurant** and bar, *Harbour Tavern* (☎ 01726-842220, ☐ harbourtavern.com; food 11am-11pm), serves local seafood, Cornish-inspired tapas and stonebaked pizza (mains £14-16, pizza £9-12). Further along the harbour front, *The Sharksfin* (☎ 01726-842969; ☐ thesharksfin.co.uk, **fb**; food noon-9pm) is a similar bar-restaurant, offering burgers and seafood (mains £14-18).

Arguably the best restaurant in Mevagissey, however, is *Salamander* (☎ 01726-842254, ☐ salamander-restaurant .co.uk; Tue-Sat 5.30-9.30pm, daily in summer), a lovely little place with a tastebud-tantalising menu featuring choices such as fried Cornish Camembert, St Austell Bay scallops, or pumpkin and apple falafel. A 2/3-course set meal is £25/30.

For something a little hotter, *Mevagissey Spice* (☎ 01726-844701; daily 5.30-11pm, Sun noon-10pm), at 3-4 River St, is the town's local Indian restaurant.

For **takeaway** treats, options include *Fishermen's Chippy* (☐ thefishermens chippy.co.uk; daily noon-3pm & 4-8pm); and for a pasty head to *The Cornish Bakery* (daily 8.30am-6.30pm) or harbourfront *Mary's Pastys* (**fb**; daily 9am-5pm).

Transport

[For details see pp52-5] For **buses**, the No 24 will transport you to Fowey via Pentewan, St Austell, Charleston and Par. For Gorran Haven there's the GorranBus (see p276), and the No 23 from St Austell.

MEVAGISSEY TO CHARLESTOWN [MAPS 111-114]

This 7¼-mile (**11.75km; 2¾-3¾hrs**) stage is one of the toughest on the Cornish south coast, superseded perhaps only by the later stretch between Polruan and Polperro.

It starts gently enough, with a straightforward stroll to **Pentewan** (see p274), a small and unassuming village squashed hard by coast and caravan park. However, things get decidedly more dramatic as the path tackles the often sharp ascents leading to Black Head, the route seeming to take an almost perverse pleasure in finding gradients to climb. A secluded woodland valley decorated here and there with wooden statues provides some distraction from the sweat-inducing slopes as you approach **Black Head**, which was yet another location for an Iron Age fort. The path doesn't visit the head itself, preferring instead to take a sharp left by a large stone memorial to the Cornish poet and historian AL Rowse – the stone at least providing you with an excuse to tarry awhile before tackling more of the path.

A couple of climbs later and you find yourself entering into the Cornish nature reserve of **Ropehaven** – famed for its fulmars which nest on ledges in the cliff-face – alas, not visible from the trail itself.

A few more steep gradients separate you from the beach at **Porthpean**. Note, periodic cliff erosion in recent years means that the coastal path on the final stretch into **Charlestown** (see p276), is sometimes diverted inland along Porthpean Beach Rd (Map 114). Follow the signpost instructions.

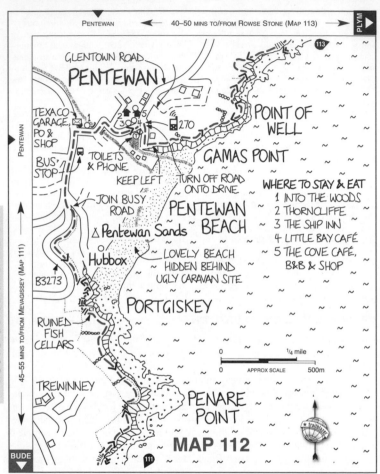

GLENTOWN ROAD
PENTEWAN

TEXACO GARAGE, PO & SHOP

BUS STOP

TOILETS & PHONE

KEEP LEFT

JOIN BUSY ROAD

△ Pentewan Sands

Hubbox

B3273

RUINED FISH CELLARS

TREWINNEY

270

POINT OF WELL

GAMAS POINT

TURN OFF ROAD ONTO DRIVE

PENTEWAN BEACH

LOVELY BEACH HIDDEN BEHIND UGLY CARAVAN SITE

PORTGISKEY

PENARE POINT

MAP 112

WHERE TO STAY & EAT
1 INTO THE WOODS
2 THORNCLIFFE
3 THE SHIP INN
4 LITTLE BAY CAFÉ
5 THE COVE CAFÉ, B&B & SHOP

0   1/4 mile
0   APPROX SCALE   500m

ROUTE GUIDE AND MAPS

PENTEWAN [MAP 112]

45-55 MINS TO/FROM MEVAGISSEY (MAP 111)

BUDE ▼

PENTEWAN   [MAP 112]

The name Pentewan comes from the Cornish 'Pen', meaning headland, and 'Towan', which means sand dunes. As with most headlands on this stretch there was once an Iron Age fort here, and in the 19th century the town was a major port for the china clay industry, big enough to rival nearby Charlestown and to handle about a third of all the china clay produced in the country. Since the 1950s, however, the village has been better known for – and dwarfed by – the huge caravan site that you probably just walked past.

Services are limited, though the village website (🖳 pentewanvillage.co.uk) is surprisingly informative given the size of the place. On the village outskirts is a Texaco garage which has a **shop** (Mon-Sat

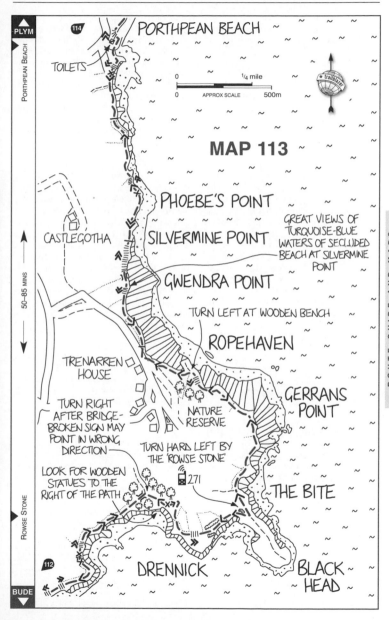

PLYM

PORTHPEAN BEACH

50-85 MINS

ROWSE STONE

BUDE

114

PORTHPEAN BEACH

TOILETS

0   ¼ mile
0   APPROX SCALE   500m

MAP 113

PHOEBE'S POINT

CASTLEGOTHA

SILVERMINE POINT

GREAT VIEWS OF
TURQUOISE-BLUE
WATERS OF SECLUDED
BEACH AT SILVERMINE
POINT

GWENDRA POINT

TURN LEFT AT WOODEN BENCH

ROPEHAVEN

TRENARREN
HOUSE

GERRANS
POINT

TURN RIGHT
AFTER BRIDGE -
BROKEN SIGN MAY
POINT IN WRONG
DIRECTION

NATURE
RESERVE

TURN HARD LEFT BY
THE 'ROWSE STONE'

LOOK FOR WOODEN
STATUES TO THE
RIGHT OF THE PATH

271

THE BITE

112

DRENNICK

BLACK
HEAD

7am-7pm, to 6pm in winter, Sun 9am-6pm, to 2pm in winter) and also houses the **post office** (Mon-Fri 9am-5.30pm, Sat to 12.30pm).

Where to stay

It's not everyone's cup of tea, and it's hideously expensive in July and August, but you can **camp** at the large beachside holiday park, *Pentewan Sands* (☎ 01726-843485, 🖳 pentewan.co.uk; Mar-Oct; tent & two people £16.50-40.80).

Otherwise, accommodation is limited to the two B&Bs in the village, both of which lie within a stone's throw of the path. The short row of traditional Cornish granite terraces leads on to Higher West End where you'll find *Thorncliffe* (☎ 01726-843583, 🖳 pentewanbedandbreakfast.co.uk; Mar-Sep; 1D/1T shared facilities; from £33.50pp), with a warm welcome and sea views. The second, *The Cove B&B* (☎ 01726-843781, 🖳 pentewanbandb.co.uk; 1T/1D/1Tr, all en suite; 🐾; from £47.50pp, sgl occ from £50), is above its namesake café and offers breakfast either indoors or outside on their sun terrace.

Where to eat and drink

Hubbox (☎ 01726-844189, 🖳 hubbox.co .uk, fb; daily 9.30am-10pm) is a popular beach shack with indoor and outdoor seating, serving gourmet burgers (£7-12) and hotdogs as well as beer on tap. The family-run *Cove Café* (🖳 creamteastaustell pentewan.co.uk; Easter-Oct Mon-Fri 10am-5pm, Sun 10am-4pm) does tea, coffee, sandwiches and light lunches, plus cracking Cornish cream teas, while the adjoining *Cove Shop* (Apr-Sep daily 10am-5pm) sells cold drinks and ice creams.

Nearby, the *Little Bay Café* (☎ 01726-844667, fb; summer daily 10am-3pm, winter weekends only) is certainly little, with just a couple of tables and a small wooden-decked terrace outside, but it packs a punch with its delicious cream teas (the scones here are amazing), and does sandwiches, pastries and jacket potatoes to boot.

The Ship Inn (☎ 01726-842855, 🖳 theshipinnpentewan.co.uk; food Tue-Sun noon-4pm & 5-8pm, winter hours vary; 🐾) is lovely, serving Cornish ales and ciders, decent pub grub (steak and ale pie, cod and chips; mains £10-13) and with a pleasant waterside beer garden across the road.

On your way into the village, *Into the Woods* (☎ 01726-844639; 🖳 into-the-woods-bar-restaurant.business.site, fb; bar noon-11.45pm; food daily noon-9pm, winter hours vary) is a family-run bar and restaurant serving Cornish ales and lagers and decent food.

Transport

[See pp52-5] The No 23 and No 24 **bus** services connect the village with the surrounding area. GorranBus's G1, G3 & G4 also pass through (☎ 01726-844933; seat reservation recommended).

CHARLESTOWN [MAP 114]

One of the lovelier spots on the whole path, the unspoilt harbour village of Charlestown was partly developed by – and named after – local landowner Charles Rashleigh in the late 18th century as a port for the booming china clay industry. Once a thriving dock, its history is charted at the **Shipwreck and Heritage Centre** (☎ 01726-69897, 🖳 wreckcharlestown.com; Mar-Oct 10am-5pm; 🐾; adult/child £6.50/4.50) which has 8000 finds from over 100 wrecks.

There are no small grocery stores in the village. The nearest **supermarket** is Tesco (Mon 8am-6pm, Tue-Sat 6am-midnight, Sun 10am-4pm; free **ATM**), half a mile out of town; turn right along Church Rd, then left at the small roundabout. In the village itself, there's an ATM (£1.50 charge) in The Rashleigh Arms.

Where to stay

There is a small **campsite** (12 pitches) on the eastern edge of the village at *Broadmeadow House* (☎ 01726-76636, 🖳 broadmeadowhouse.com; 🐾; hiker & tent £10; booking recommended). It's one of the best little campsites on the path, run by a knowledgeable local lady with lots of useful tips on the surrounding area. There is a 'Camp and Breakfast' deal where, after a

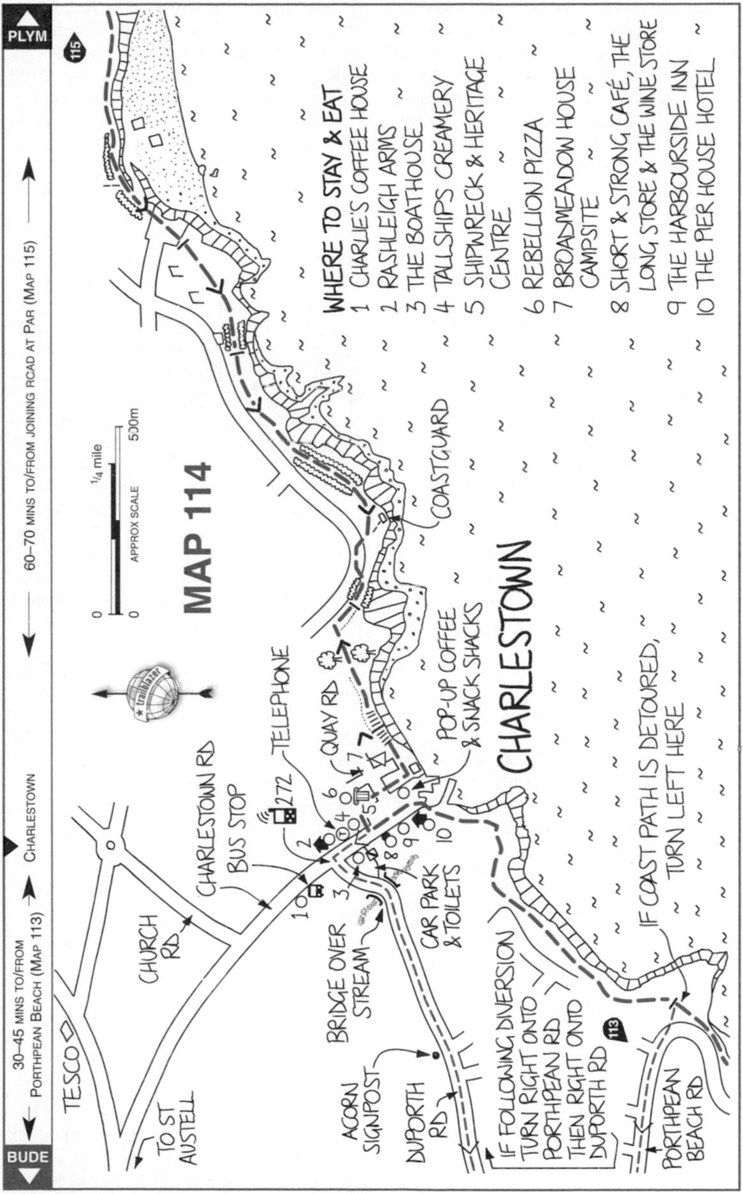

MAP 114

APPROX SCALE

0 ¼ mile
0 500m

WHERE TO STAY & EAT

1 CHARLIE'S COFFEE HOUSE
2 RASHLEIGH ARMS
3 THE BOATHOUSE
4 TALLSHIPS CREAMERY
5 SHIPWRECK & HERITAGE CENTRE
6 REBELLION PIZZA
7 BROADMEADOW HOUSE CAMPSITE
8 SHORT & STRONG CAFÉ, THE LONG STORE & THE WINE STORE
9 THE HARBOURSIDE INN
10 THE PIER HOUSE HOTEL

TESCO

CHURCH RD

TO ST AUSTELL

CHARLESTOWN RD

BUS STOP

TELEPHONE

QUAY RD

POP-UP COFFEE & SNACK SHACKS

COASTGUARD

CHARLESTOWN

BRIDGE OVER STREAM

CAR PARK & TOILETS

ACORN SIGNPOST

DUPORTH RD

IF FOLLOWING DIVERSION TURN RIGHT ONTO PORTHPEAN RD THEN RIGHT ONTO DUPORTH RD

IF COAST PATH IS DETOURED, TURN LEFT HERE

PORTHPEAN BEACH RD

113

night under canvas, you can look forward to your pre-ordered breakfast basket (£7). If that site is full, head to the also excellent *Carlyon Bay Camping Park* (Map 115; ☎ 01726-812735, 💻 carlyonbay.net; 🐾; hiker & tent £8-10), a large but friendly holiday park run by the same family for three generations, which never turns away walkers. They have a well-stocked **shop**, a large sheltered eating area, and even a heated outdoor pool! Walk across the golf course between here and Par, and under the railway bridge.

The Rashleigh Arms (☎ 01726-73635, 💻 rashleigharms.co.uk; 18 rooms; ☞; 🐾; winter/summer from £47.50/67.50pp), on Charlestown Rd, is a 150-year-old pub with eight of its rooms in an attached annexe. There are glimpses of the harbour, and the tall ships which sometimes frequent it, from some of the upper rooms.

Built in 1794, *The Pier House Hotel* (☎ 01726-67955, 💻 pierhousehotel.com; 27 rooms; ☞; winter/summer from £55/70pp, sgl from £99/125) on the harbour-front represents Charlestown's most expensive and luxurious accommodation. Note that none of the single rooms has a sea view.

Where to eat and drink

Pop-up coffee and snack shacks line the harbourside in summer.

If simply passing through, *Tallships Creamery* (fb; summer 9am-6pm, winter 11am-5pm) is right by the trail and can supply you with a drink, a pasty, a cake, or one of its award-winning ice creams.

Congenial *Charlie's Coffee House* (☎ 01726-67421; May-Sep Mon-Fri 9am-4pm, Sat 10am-4pm, Oct-Apr closed Mon), at 79 Charlestown Rd, has an emphasis on local produce such as their smoked salmon breakfast, paninis and homemade cakes. Also does great bagels and pancakes.

Down the hill a bit is *The Boathouse* (☎ 01726-63322; 💻 theboathousecharles town.co.uk, fb; Wed-Sun 10am-9pm), a light and airy café-bistro (mains £13-16) with wooden beams and a beer garden.

Further down still, is the popular *Short & Strong Café* (☎ 01726-68598; 💻 short andstrong.co.uk, fb; daily 9am-5pm) serving artisan coffee, cakes and sandwiches from its often busy roadside patio and newly restored stone building, which also houses its sister steakhouse (*The Long Store*; ☎ 01726-68598, 💻 thelongstore.co .uk, fb; Mon-Fri 4.30pm-late, Sat & Sun noon-2.30pm & 4.30pm-late; mains £14-30) and tapas and wine bar (*The Wine Store*; fb; Mon-Thur 4-10pm, Fri & Sat noon-11pm, Sun noon-5.30pm).

The Rashleigh Arms (see Where to stay; food daily noon-9pm; mains £12-16) does standard pub fare with the occasional surprise, such as Cornish whiting goujons.

Sister-inn to The Pier House Hotel, *The Harbourside Inn* (☎ 01726-839888, 💻 harboursideinncharlestown.co.uk; food 4-9pm) is a St Austell Brewery pub with restaurant-quality food (duck ragu, steamed mussels, Thai spring curry; mains £14-20) and a good selection of real ales. The **restaurant** adjoining *The Pier House Hotel* (see Where to stay) shares the same menu.

Another option is *Rebellion* (☎ 01726-839888, 💻 rebellionroasthouse.co.uk, fb; Mar-Oct Mon-Wed 9.30am-9pm, Thur-Sat to 11pm, Sun to 5pm) a roasthouse and pizzeria situated beside and above the Shipwreck and Heritage Centre. The mussels here are good, and there's a huge beer-and-cocktails terrace out front.

Transport

[See pp52-5] The No 24 and 25 **bus** services stop here.

CHARLESTOWN TO FOWEY   [MAPS 114-117]

After the exertions of the previous stage these **11½ miles** (**18.5km; 3-4hrs**) are positively gentle. Unfortunately, there is a price to pay for this leniency, the path taking you firstly beside a golf course and then around the back of **Par Docks**. True, the docks and the china-clay plant that they serve do have some history, having been established back in the 19th century; but that does little to make them, or the section of road walking you have to undertake to circumvent them,

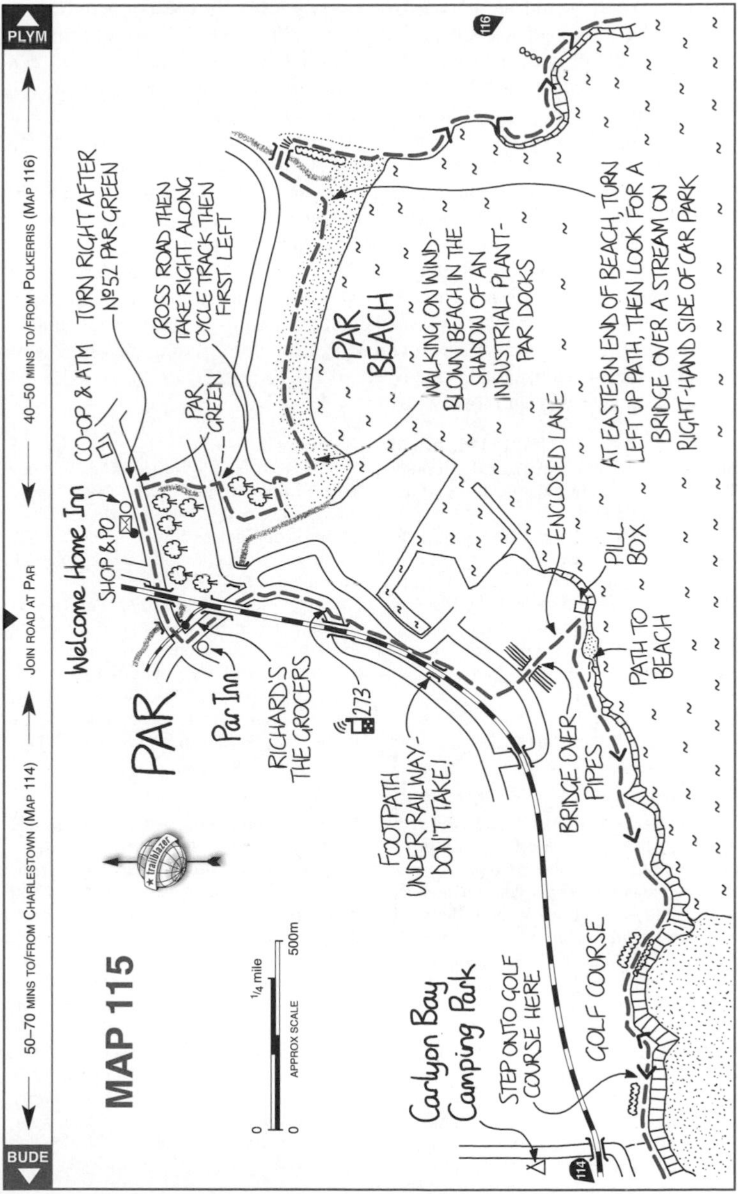
PLYM
BUDE
50–70 MINS TO/FROM CHARLESTOWN (MAP 114)
JOIN ROAD AT PAR
40–50 MINS TO/FROM POLKERRIS (MAP 116)
MAP 115
0
¼ mile
0
500m
APPROX SCALE
trailblazer
PAR
Welcome Home Inn
SHOP & PO
CO-OP & ATM
TURN RIGHT AFTER
Nº52 PAR GREEN
PAR
GREEN
CROSS ROAD THEN
TAKE RIGHT ALONG
CYCLE TRACK THEN
FIRST LEFT
Par Inn
RICHARD'S
THE GROCERS
273
PAR
BEACH
WALKING ON WIND-
BLOWN BEACH IN THE
SHADOW OF AN
INDUSTRIAL PLANT-
PAR DOCKS
ENCLOSED LANE
AT EASTERN END OF BEACH, TURN
LEFT UP PATH, THEN LOOK FOR A
BRIDGE OVER A STREAM ON
RIGHT-HAND SIDE OF CAR PARK
PILL
BOX
PATH TO
BEACH
FOOTPATH
UNDER RAILWAY-
DON'T TAKE!
BRIDGE OVER
PIPES
Carlyon Bay
Camping Park
STEP ONTO GOLF
COURSE HERE
GOLF COURSE
114
116

ROUTE GUIDE AND MAPS

any more attractive. Indeed, it's one of those stages that the coast path throws up occasionally to remind walkers that they are still in the real world. Still, the beach at the end of **Par** is nice enough and backed by some interesting dunes that actually form a nature reserve – though with the industrial plant so close, you may want to save your swimming for later.

Climbing away from the sands, the path is fairly straightforward to **Polkerris** and its lovely little enclosed beach. From Polkerris the path continues its relatively gentle way to the red and white tower, or **daymark**, at **Gribbin Head**, built in 1832 as a navigational aid to help sailors distinguish this promontory from neighbouring Dodman Point and St Anthony Head.

From here the gradients get a little more severe as you descend to **Polridmouth** – the house here providing the inspiration for the beach house in Daphne du Maurier's novel *Rebecca* (the author used to live just up the valley; see box p286) – then round **Southground Point** before passing the remains of **St Catherine's Castle**, another one of Henry VIII's many Cornish coastal fortifications, on your way into lovely Fowey.

PAR [MAP 115, p279]

Most walkers scuttle fairly quickly through Par, though there are some facilities which you may find useful.

Richard's (Mon-Fri 6am-5.30pm, Sat to 5pm) is a long-standing family **grocer**, and a great place to pick up fresh fruit. Over the other side of the railway line is a **shop** (Mon-Sat 6.30am-5.30pm, Sun to 1pm) which contains a small **bakery** and the **post office** (Mon 8am-2pm, Tue-Sat 8am-1pm).

Further along there's an **ATM** inside the Co-op (daily 7am-10pm).

Next to the post office, *The Welcome Home Inn* (☎ 01726-816894; 🐾) is indeed welcoming, and serves great-value **food** (daily noon-2pm & 5-8pm; mains £8-10). They have a large beer garden out the back and an open fire inside in winter.

Opposite Richard's, *The Par Inn* (☎ 01726-815695; **fb**; 🐾) is good for a pint (St Austell's beers), but doesn't do food.

The Nos 24 & 25 **bus** services stop in Par en route between St Austell and Fowey. Par is also a stop on several of GWR's **train** services. [See pp50-5 for details.]

POLKERRIS [MAP 116]

Watersports are the focus for many who visit this sandy little beach. Most walkers, however, will be far more interested in the calories and liquids they can consume whilst watching those windsurfing and sailing.

The Rashleigh Inn (☎ 01726-814685, 🖳 therashleighinn.co.uk, **fb**; food daily summer noon-8pm, winter noon-3pm & 6-8pm; 🐾) serves up some great **food** including moules marinière (£9/16.50), buttermilk fried chicken burger (£12.50) and Newlyn crab sandwich (£14.50). To wash it down there are half a dozen real ales on tap, including those from Skinners, St Austell brewery and Timothy Taylor. There are also ciders by both Stowford

Press and Addlestones, and a wood-decked terrace overlooking the beach.

Sam's on the Beach (☎ 01726-812255, 🖳 samscornwall.co.uk, **fb**; food noon-9pm; 🐾 on terrace) is next door to the pub and also has a terrace overlooking the beach. Their menu includes stone-baked pizza (£13-17) and slow roasted pork belly (£18.95) plus an extensive wine list. You may need to reserve a table for an evening meal on summer weekends.

For something more affordable, or if you're just passing through, *The Hungry Sailor Café* (Easter-Oct daily 9am-5pm, hot food to 3pm) does takeaway coffee, ice cream, pasties and bacon baps.

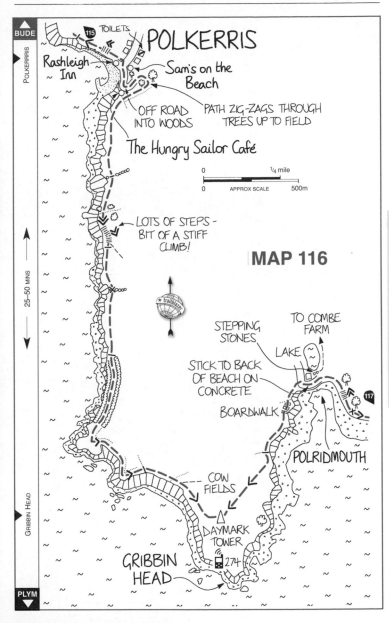

POLKERRIS

TOILETS

Rashleigh Inn

Sam's on the Beach

OFF ROAD INTO WOODS

PATH ZIG-ZAGS THROUGH TREES UP TO FIELD

The Hungry Sailor Café

0 — 1/4 mile
0 — 500m — APPROX SCALE

LOTS OF STEPS - BIT OF A STIFF CLIMB!

MAP 116

STEPPING STONES

TO COMBE FARM

LAKE

STICK TO BACK OF BEACH ON CONCRETE

BOARDWALK

POLRIDMOUTH

COW FIELDS

DAYMARK TOWER

274

GRIBBIN HEAD

BUDE
POLKERRIS
25–50 MINS
GRIBBIN HEAD
PLYM

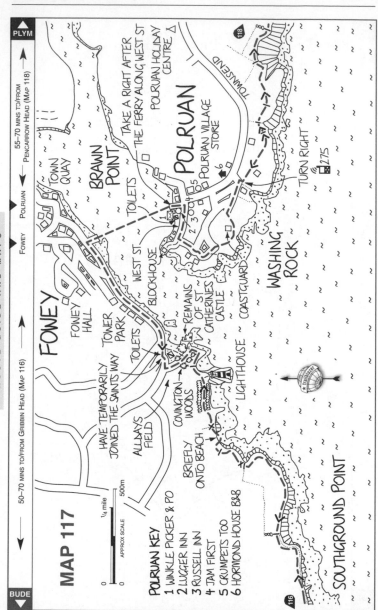

PLYM ▲

55–70 MINS TO/FROM PENCARROW HEAD (MAP 118) ↑

▲ POLRUAN

▲ FOWEY

50–70 MINS TO/FROM GRIBBIN HEAD (MAP 116) →

BUDE ▼

MAP 117

APPROX SCALE

0 .... 500m
0 .... ¼ mile

POLRUAN KEY
1 WINKLE PICKER & PO
2 LUGGER INN
3 RUSSELL INN
4 JAM FIRST
5 CRUMPETS TOO
6 HORMOND HOUSE B&B

FOWEY

FOWEY HALL

TOWER PARK

HAVE TEMPORARILY JOINED THE SAINTS WAY

ALLDAYS FIELD

COVINGTON WOODS

BRIEFLY ONTO BEACH

TOILETS

WEST ST

BLOCKHOUSE

REMAINS OF ST CATHERINES CASTLE

LIGHTHOUSE

COASTGUARD

SOUTHGROUND POINT

116

TOWN QUAY

BRAZEN POINT

TOILETS

TAKE A RIGHT AFTER THE FERRY ALONG WEST ST

POLRUAN HOLIDAY CENTRE △

POLRUAN

POLRUAN VILLAGE STORE

6

2 3 4 5
1

TOWNSEND

118

TURN RIGHT

275

WASHING ROCK

FOWEY [map p284]

It seems strange to think that what now seems an incredibly quaint, laid back and serene little Cornish town – one of the most attractive on the whole coast path – was once a major trading and industrial port. The medieval defences that you walk past on your way into the town, however, such as **St Catherine's Castle** and the two **blockhouses** that stand on either side of the river at the harbour entrance, provide an indication of just how commercially important this town was in the 15th and 16th centuries. Unfortunately for Fowey (pronounced 'Foy'), Plymouth's fortune was to be largely at Fowey's expense and the locals returned to fishing and smuggling to make a living.

The town enjoyed a renaissance in the 19th century owing to the rise of the china clay industry. Initially, as other harbours at Charlestown, Par and Pentewan were established they took most of the trade. However, once Fowey harbour was developed in 1869, its natural deep-water anchorage offered a considerable advantage over the shallower artificial harbours of neighbours, despite being further from the tin mines and clay works that produced the cargo to be shipped. The beacon tower at Gribben Head also helped to improve navigation into Fowey which further increased its popularity. While some china clay is still exported from the harbour, the mines have all now shut and the old cargo boats and steamers have largely been replaced by the yachts and pleasure craft of the amateur sailor. Indeed, it is estimated that around 7000 yachts visit in any one season, swelling the large numbers of visiting tourists that throng the main street in summer.

Services

There's no longer a tourist information office here, but the website (🖳 fowey.co .uk) is useful. For **supplies**, Fowey Minimarket (Mon-Sat 7am-8pm, Sun 7.30am-6pm), which also houses the **post office** (Mon-Fri 8am-5.30pm, Sat & Sun 8am-noon) is on the main drag, Fore St. So too is a branch of Boots **pharmacy** (Mon-Sat 9am-5.30pm) and a wonderful independent **bookshop**, Shrew Books (☎ 01726-833361, 🖳 shrewbooks.co.uk; Mon-Sat 10am-5pm), which stocks a huge collection of books on Cornwall, including plenty of Daphne du Maurier. You'll pass an off-licence and **newsagent**, Shipmates of Fowey (daily 9am-7pm) along the Esplanade. For **camping supplies** there's a Mountain Warehouse (Mon-Sat 9am-

---

❑ ST CATHERINE'S CASTLE AND FORTIFICATIONS AROUND FOWEY

When walking east from Polkerris, it is quite striking to note just how many fortifications have been built to defend Fowey down the centuries. The town was once a fairly major port and following Henry VIII's perceived attack on the Catholic Church after the Reformation and dissolution of the monasteries, it was decided that the fortifications around Britain's southern coastline needed boosting, with (largely Catholic) France and Spain threatening. The D-shaped St Catherine's Castle was built on the highest available point, with good views that encompassed the estuary as well as out to sea. Indeed, such were the strategic advantages of the site that it was utilised for defensive purposes up until the end of WWII, when it was used as a gun battery and observation point.

St Catherine's Castle, however, was not the earliest fortification protecting Fowey and its river. Prior to the castle, two **blockhouses** stood on either side of the river – medieval fortifications between which, at one time, a chain would have stretched across the river to prevent access to the harbour by invading French warships and, on occasion, rapacious pirates. The blockhouse on the Fowey side is now, alas, in a parlous state but that on the Polruan side is in reasonable condition and can be visited by taking a small detour off the coast path as you walk out of the village.

5.30pm, Sun 10am-4.30pm) on Fore St. There's an **ATM** near the museum.

The sweet little **Fowey Aquarium** (☎ 07815-840467, 💻 foweyaquarium.co.uk; Feb-Oct daily 10.30am-4pm; adult/child £5/3.50) is located on land that was previously part of the covered market. **Fowey Museum** (Easter-Sep Mon-Fri 10.30am-4.30pm; £1) celebrates the history of Fowey and has some unusual exhibits including, oddly, a cloak that once belonged to Italian hero General Garibaldi.

Where to stay

The nearest **campsite** is across the Fowey River, above Polruan (see p287).

For **B&B**, you could do far worse than *The Well House* (☎ 01726-435346, 💻 wellhousefowey.co.uk, **fb**; 3D; 🛏; 🐾;

£50-60pp, sgl occ from £60), at 31-35 Fore St, housed in a gorgeous old building with low ceilings and period décor.

Several **pubs** offer accommodation, including *The Ship Inn* (☎ 01726-832230, 💻 shipfowey.co.uk, **fb**; 3D/1T; 🛏; from £50pp, sgl occ from £45), which dates from 1570; and the 17th-century *King of Prussia* (☎ 01726-833694, 💻 kingofprussiafowey .co.uk, **fb**; 4D or T/2D; 🛏; £70-90pp, sgl occ full room rate, with all its rooms overlooking the harbour. The name is believed to have come from the smuggler John Carter, who resided at the inn in the 1780s and was nicknamed the 'King of Prussia' (see box p212). Another riverside pub-with-rooms option is *The Galleon Inn* (☎ 01726-833014, 💻 galleon-inn.co.uk, **fb**; 3D/3D or T/2Tr/1Qd; 🛏; from £60pp, sgl

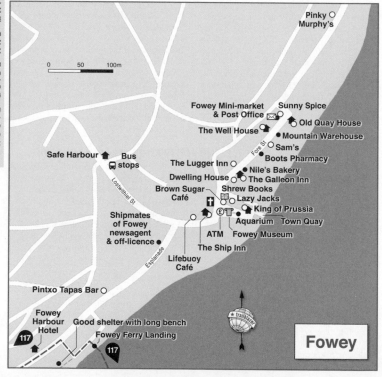

Fowey

occ from £100), with some rooms overlooking the river. Away from the water, *The Safe Harbour Inn* (☎ 01726-833379, 🖳 safeharbourinn.com, **fb**; 3S/3D/1Tr/1Qd; 🛏, 🐾; £40-70pp) is a fourth pub option. It's a short climb up Lostwithiel St, at No 58, with views over the town.

For **hotel** accommodation, *Old Quay House* (☎ 01726-833302, 🖳 theoldquay house.com; 13D; 🛏; £77-137pp; min 2 nights) is ultra-modern and super-swish, with prices to match its swankiness. For something more traditional, *Fowey Harbour Hotel* (☎ 01726 832551, 🖳 harbourhotels.co.uk/fowey; 37 rooms; 🛏; 🐾; from £56/110pp, sgl occ £104/196) is now part of the Harbour Hotels group, but dates from 1882 and is still all class.

Where to eat and drink

For simple food on the go, *Nile's Bakery* (**fb**; daily 9am-5pm) won't let you down. Alternatively, there's sandwich shop *Lazy Jack's* (**fb**; daily 9.30am-4.30pm). In the heart of the action, *Brown Sugar Café* (🖳 brownsugarfowey.com; daily 8.30am-5pm) is very popular and has roadside seating. Less busy, though not quiet by any means, on Lostwithiel St is *Lifebuoy Café* (☎ 07825-835863; Tue-Sat 9am-3.30pm); or for a café away from the crowds, head to colourful *Pinky Murphy's* (☎ 01726-832512, 🖳 pinkymurphys.co.uk; 9.30am-4.30pm; 🐾), a quirky, yet very relaxed and friendly place, on a quiet lane north of the centre, with river views from the tables on the small front terrace.

If you're looking for a more traditional tearoom for a spot of cream tea head to the delightful *Well House* (see Where to stay; 10am-5pm).

If you prefer a pub, *The Lugger Inn* (☎ 01726-833435, **fb**; food daily noon-2.30pm & 6-9pm) is one of several old taverns on Fore St; the food is traditional pub fare. Right on the front, *King of Prussia* (see Where to stay; food daily noon-9.30pm) serves hearty and tasty meals, including a slow-cooked pork belly. *The Ship Inn* (see Where to stay; food 9am-9.30pm; most mains around £14) is unpretentious and friendly, and opens for breakfast. *The Galleon Inn* (See Where to Stay;

food Mon-Sat noon-2.30pm & 5-9pm, Sun till. 8.30pm) does burgers, fish and chips, pizza and the like (mains £10-14).

You might remember *Sam's* (☎ 01726-832273, 🖳 samscornwall.co.uk/fowey, **fb**; food daily noon-9.30pm) from Polkerris Beach. This Fowey branch is equally lively and includes a menu that lists almost a dozen different types of burgers (£12-18) as well as plenty of fresh fish dishes.

The former tearoom, *The Dwelling House* (☎ 01726-833662; Thur-Mon 1-10pm), has restyled itself as a bistro-restaurant, and now offers light lunches, tapas and fine wines. And its small garden courtyard is a delightful escape from the tourist crowds.

For something approaching fine dining, *Old Quay House* (see Where to stay; food Easter-Sep noon-2.30pm & 6-9pm) has a lovely al-fresco area overlooking the water. The menu changes frequently but you can expect to pay £16-22 for lunchtime mains, or a set £37.50/45 for two/three courses in the evening. Cream teas (noon-3pm) are an easier-to-swallow £6.50 per person.

Indian to eat in or takeaway can be found at *Sunny Spice* (☎ 01726-833594, **fb**; daily 5-10pm), 39A Fore St, while *Pintxo* (☎ 01726-337450, 🖳 pintxo.co.uk, **fb**; Mar-Oct Mon-Sat noon-9pm, Sun noon-4pm), 38 Esplanade, dishes up some tremendous tapas (£3-10) – which may be a very welcome sight if you're entering town hungry from the south.

Transport

[See pp52-5] The No 24 (to Mevagissey) and No 25 (to St Austell) **bus** services also call at Par and Charlestown.

The official South-West Coast Path takes the **ferry** (every 15 mins; 9.45am-11.30pm; adult/child £2.50/1.10) across the Fowey River to Polruan. Make sure you have your camera ready when you board – it's a lovely crossing when the sun's shining. Daytime ferries (9.45am-5.15pm) leave from **Fowey Ferry Landing**, on Esplanade. Evening ferries (5.30-11.30pm) leave from **Town Quay**, near King of Prussia pub.

FOWEY TO POLPERRO   [MAPS 117-120]

From the Fowey ferry landing-point, this strenuous **7¼-mile (11.75km; 2½-3½hrs)** stage begins with a meander through pretty **Polruan**. Emerging by the Coastguard lookout at the top of the village, the path then leads you on a jaunt eastwards around **Lantic Bay** and its popular beach. At the end, a stiff climb brings you out above **Pencarrow Head**, with its lovely clear-day views all the way back to the Lizard. Prepare yourself: this is just the first of several steep ascents, the path unrelenting as it struggles up and down along the cliff edge at the eastern end of **Lantivet Bay**. Campers can rest up halfway at the pleasant, National Trust-run *Highertown Farm Campsite* (Map 119; ☎ 01208-265211, 🖳 nationaltrust.org.uk; May-Oct; 🐾; hiker & tent £7-9), three-quarters of a mile from the coast path in the tiny village of **Lansallos** – there's a sign to it on a gate by the path.

Back on the path, an unusual white stone cone – yet another navigational aid for seafarers – and the natural rock arch at **Blackybale Point** provide distractions from your aching legs: this is a pretty tough section. The reward for your exertions, however, is the lovely **Polperro**; more than worth the effort.

Be sure to stock up on drinks and snacks for this stretch as there's nowhere to buy anything between Polruan and Polperro.

❏ CORNWALL'S LITERARY GIANTS

Maybe it's the gorgeous scenery, the wild coastline, the spectacular weather – or simply something in the water. For whatever reason, this stretch of the southern Cornish shoreline has produced its fair share of literary talents.

Perhaps the author most identified with this corner of the UK is **Daphne du Maurier**, which is curious as she only moved here in 1943, long after she had already achieved a level of fame and renown for her works. However, the claim that Du Maurier is a Cornish author is not a fatuous one: she had actually been visiting Cornwall since her parents bought a holiday home, Ferryside, just north of Fowey, and both wrote and set many of her best-known works in the county. The first of these, *The Loving Spirit*, concerning the lives of Cornish boat builders, moved a Major Tommy Browning so much that he set sail for Cornwall with the specific intention of meeting her. They were married the next year at Llanteglos Church. *Jamaica Inn* (a real inn, situated on Bodmin Moor) and *Rebecca*, perhaps her two most famous novels, were both set at least partly in Cornwall. Indeed, the famous opening lines of *Rebecca* ('Last night I dreamt I went to Manderley again') were inspired by a 17th-century mansion, Menabilly, overlooking the sea and owned by the Rashleigh family (after which several pubs in the area, such as those at Charlestown and Polkerris, are named). She managed to secure a 25-year lease on the property in 1943 and stayed there until 1965 and the death of Major Browning, when she moved to another Rashleigh property, Kilmarth, which was immortalised in another novel, *The House on the Strand*. She died in 1989, having been made a dame 20 years earlier; her ashes were scattered on the cliffs near her home.

Another distinctive Cornish voice – indeed, he is celebrated on his memorial as the Voice of Cornwall – is **AL Rowse**. Though not as famous as Du Maurier, during his lifetime Rowse (1903-1997) published more than 100 books, his best-known works being histories of Elizabethan England and a book of poetry about Cornwall.

POLRUAN [MAP 117, p282]

Polruan is for those who like their experience of the Fowey River to be quieter and more serene. Indeed, surrounded on three sides by water, and hidden from the fourth by the steep hill, it feels like one of the more isolated settlements on the path, though Fowey is only 10 minutes away by ferry. The main sight in the village is the **blockhouse**, far more complete than its twin across the water. The town's few facilities lie at the bottom end of the main street close to the ferry point. The **post office** (Mon-Fri 9am-4.30pm, Sat 9am-1pm) is in a shop called **The Winkle Picker** (daily 7.30am-5.30pm, or after the last daytime ferry). There's also Polruan Village **Store** (Mon-Sat 9am-noon & 2-5pm, Sun 8am-11.30pm) with an **ATM** (£1.95).

For **camping**, head to pretty *Polruan Holiday Centre* (☎ 01726-870263, 🖳 polruanholidays.co.uk; one adult & tent £8-12;

🐾; summer booking recommended). It's peaceful, welcoming and well-run with sea views, good shower and laundry facilities and a **shop** selling basics, including camping gas; to find it, follow Fore St (which becomes Townsend) for half a mile up a very steep hill out of town and it's on your left shortly after Ocean View.

For **B&B**, there is *Hormond House* (☎ 07703-170969, 🖳 hormondhouse.com; 1S/1D or T/1Qd; ➖; 🐾; £42.50-47.50pp, sgl occ £60-80, sgl from £50), a pleasant family-run place on the main Fore St (No 55) with cracking views over the harbour, and a cosy fireplace in the largest of the rooms.

There are several **food** options here too. For pub grub, the friendly, family-run *Lugger Inn* (☎ 01726-870567, 🖳 lugger polruan.co.uk, **fb**; food 9am-3pm & 5-8pm; mains £11-14) has a great location overlooking the harbour. Behind it sits *The*

(cont'd on p290)

If he is known at all today, however – other than for his rather lovely memorial on Black Head, right by the coast path – it is for his rather acerbic criticism of the works of others. One who clearly enjoyed his reputation as an intellectual heavyweight (he was a graduate from Oxford and enjoyed renown as one of the foremost English scholars of his generation), he was quick to dismiss the efforts of others, memorably describing (admittedly, merely in pencil in his own copy of a magazine) John Middleton Murry's poem *In Memory of Katherine Mansfield* as 'Sentimental gush on the part of JMM. And a bad poem. A.L.R'. Though his relationship with the county wasn't as straightforward as his reputation would suggest, he did return to live out his remaining days here following his retirement in 1973, living at Trenarren House near Black Head. His bestseller, *A Cornish Childhood*, the first part of his autobiography and published in 1942, served to cement his reputation as 'The Voice of Cornwall', a title that he officially took in 1968 when made a Bard of Gorseth Kernow. His ashes are buried in the Charlestown cemetery.

One of Rowse's main influences was **Arthur Quiller-Couch**, who was born in Bodmin of two very ancient Cornish families, and returned after university to settle in Fowey in 1891. Like Rowse, he was also honoured with the title Bard of Gorseth Kernow and, also like Rowse, is perhaps best known for his critiques, reviews and anthologies of the literary efforts of others, including *Studies in Literature* (1918), *On the Art of Reading* (1920) and the impressively comprehensive *Oxford Book Of English Verse 1250-1900* (1900). All of these were published under the sobriquet, 'Q'.

Curiously, Quiller-Couch was cited by **Kenneth Grahame** as the inspiration for the character Ratty in his best-known work, *Wind in the Willows*. Though he was born in Scotland (in 1859) and spent most of his life in Cookham in Berkshire, Grahame was married in Fowey, spent his honeymoon in St Ives, and it is widely claimed that the inspiration for the first chapter of *Wind in the Willows*, in which Ratty and Mole enjoy a boat trip, came after a similar trip taken by Grahame along the Fowey River.

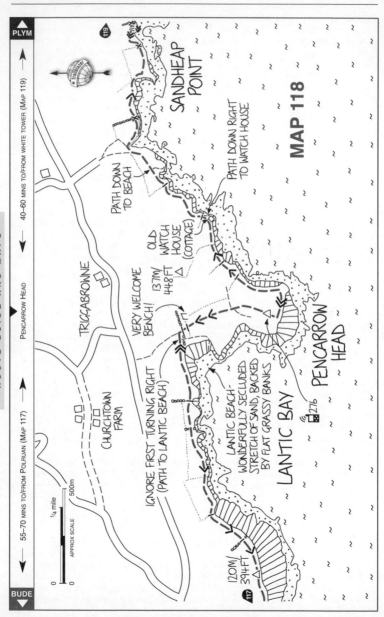

PLYM

119

SANDHEAP POINT

MAP 118

PATH DOWN RIGHT TO WATCH HOUSE

PATH DOWN TO BEACH

TRIGGABROWNE

OLD WATCH HOUSE (COTTAGE)

137M/448FT △

VERY WELCOME BENCH!

PENCARROW HEAD

CHURCHTOWN FARM

IGNORE FIRST TURNING RIGHT (PATH TO LANTIC BEACH)

LANTIC BEACH – WONDERFULLY SECLUDED STRETCH OF SAND, BACKED BY FLAT GRASSY BANKS

LANTIC BAY

276

120M/394FT

117

¼ mile

500m

APPROX SCALE

0

0

BUDE

40–60 MINS TO/FROM WHITE TOWER (MAP 119)

PENCARROW HEAD

55–70 MINS TO/FROM POLRUAN (MAP 117)

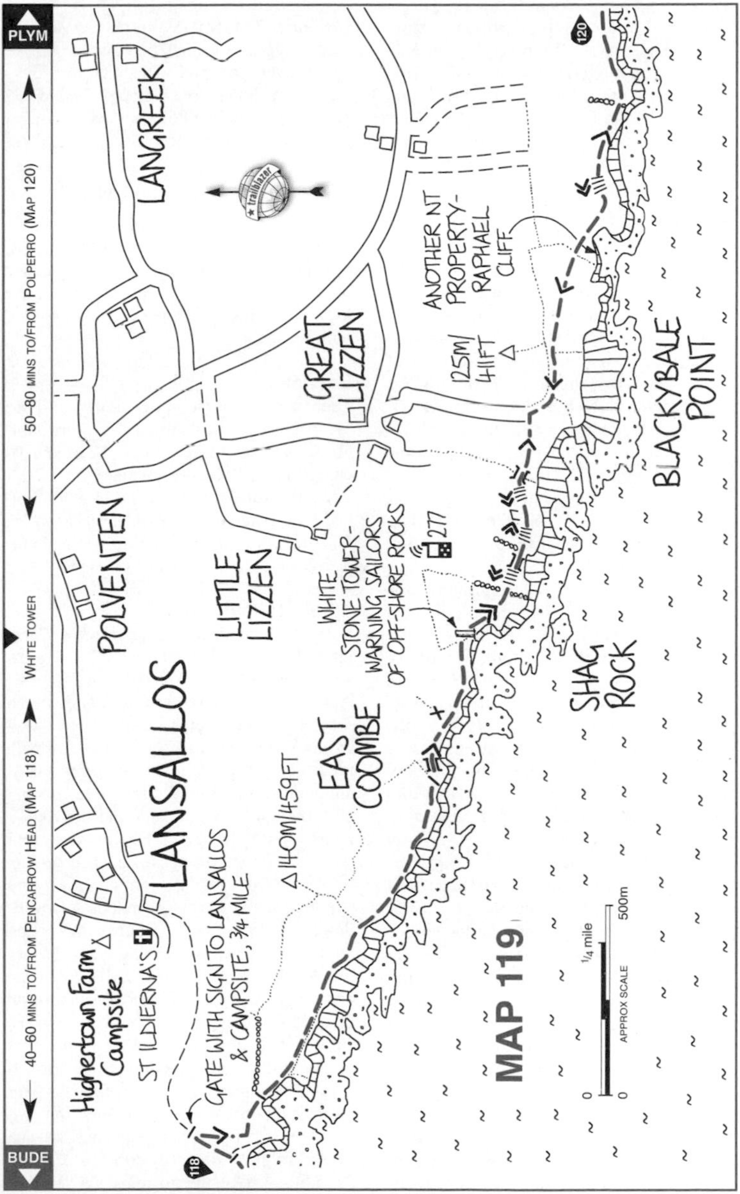

MAP 119

PLYM

BUDE

◄ 40–60 MINS TO/FROM PENCARROW HEAD (MAP 118) ▲ WHITE TOWER ▲ 50–80 MINS TO/FROM POLPERRO (MAP 120) ►

Higertown Farm Campsite

ST ILDIERNA'S

LANSALLOS

POLVENTEN

LANGREEK

GREAT LIZZEN

LITTLE LIZZEN

WHITE STONE TOWER – WARNING SAILORS OF OFF-SHORE ROCKS

EAST COOMBE

△140M/459FT

ANOTHER NT PROPERTY – RAPHAEL CLIFF

125M/411FT △

GATE WITH SIGN TO LANSALLOS & CAMPSITE, ¾ MILE

SHAG ROCK

BLACKYBALE POINT

277

118

120

¼ mile

0   500m
0
APPROX SCALE

(cont'd from p287) **Russell Inn** (☎ 01726-870707, 🖥 russellinn.co.uk, **fb**; food Mon-Sat 6-8.30pm; 🐾), a lovely old boozer with good-value pub grub in the evenings (from £10). During the day you can eat your take-away food from next door café *Jam First* (☎ 07875-293364, **fb**; summer daily 8.30am-4pm, winter hours vary) in the pub.

A short way up the hill, at 10 Fore St, *Crumpets Too* (☎ 07890-602813, Mon-Sat 8am-1.30pm) is a small bakery/tearoom.

Travel Cornwall's No 481 **bus** links Polruan with Polperro & Looe. The No 482 goes to Bodmin via Polperro. Note, neither runs at the weekend. [See pp52-5 for details.]

POLPERRO   [map p292]

Polperro is one of the more idiosyncratic towns on the entire coast path. Maybe it's the location, squeezed between high hills that, bearded with pine forests, give it a vaguely alpine feel. Maybe it's the unusual layout, the town strung along a couple of parallel roads that stretch back for almost a mile from the harbour to **Crumplehorn**. Or maybe it's the presence of a '**tram**' – actually an electric cart – which ferries people to and from the town centre and Crumplehorn. Whatever it is, in high season you will have to share it with large crowds of tourists, and may struggle to find a room for the night.

The town has an interesting history. Originally a fishing village, its isolated location gave it a significant advantage as a centre for various illegal activities, particularly smuggling and privateering. Tea, gin, brandy and tobacco were the mainstays of the smuggling industry, mostly shipped over from Guernsey. Indeed, so all-pervasive was the trade that John Wesley remarked when visiting: *'An accursed thing among them: well nigh one and all bought or sold uncustomed goods.'*

Polperro's heyday coincided with the arrival of Zephaniah Job (1749-1822). Job probably did more than anyone to ensure the town's prosperity, organising the smuggling trade, acting as accountant to the inhabitants and establishing a bank in the town. He also rebuilt the harbour following a terrible storm in 1817. Privateering brought further wealth, the Admiralty giving licence to the boats of Polperro to attack French craft and keep the cargo. Thereafter, the coastguard slowly became more organised and smuggling declined in the town, to be replaced in the 19th century by tourism. That history is recounted in the local

museum (Easter-Oct 10am-4.30pm; £2) down by the harbour, just past an eccentric private home, dubbed 'Shell House', the façade of which is almost entirely covered with seashells.

Services

There are a few facilities, mostly on Fore St, including a **post office** (Mon-Fri 9am-5pm, Sat 9am-1pm) with an **ATM** (£1.90 charge), plus Roberts **pharmacy** (☎ 01503-272250; Mon-Fri 9am-1pm & 2-5.30/6pm) and a **newsagent**, Polperro News (Mon-Fri 7.30am-5pm, Sat 8am-5pm, Sun 8am-noon) with a good stock of **groceries**.

Where to stay

For **camping**, there's *Great Kellow Farm* (off Map 120; ☎ 01503-272387, 🖥 kellowfarm.co.uk; hiker & tent £10; 🐾; Apr-Oct) which never turns walkers away. It is basic but very friendly, with a small shower block, on a working beef cattle farm with great views back over Polperro Bay, although the half-mile climb uphill to get here is quite a slog; turn left at the round-about after Milly's, then take the first right (signposted to the campsite) and keep going.

Fore St and its continuation, The Coombe, is the main place to look for **B&B**. Several are right in the heart of the action including the friendly 16th-century *House on the Props* (☎ 01503-272310, 🖥 house ontheprops.co.uk; 2D/1T; 🐾; £40-45pp, sgl occ £55-65; min 3 nights) built on props or stilts taken from a ship, *Maverine*, that foundered in the harbour back in around 1700. The rooms have views of the harbour through the lovely old leaded windows.

One of Polperro's pubs has rooms: *The Noughts and Crosses* (☎ 01503-273344, 🖥 oxopolperro.co.uk; 2S/2D; 🐾;

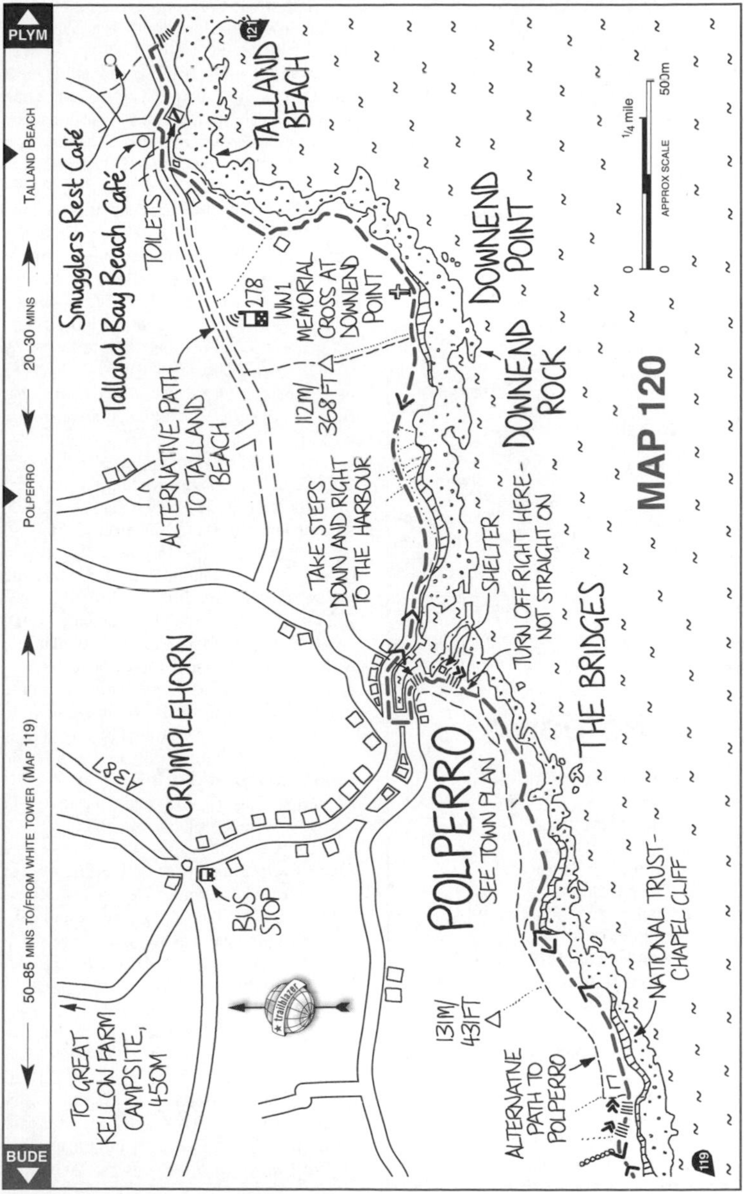

MAP 120

from £40pp, sgl from £55) was originally a 16th-century bakery named after the old custom of allowing fishermen bread on credit if poor weather scuppered their catch. Loaves marked 'X' were yet to be paid for, while 'O' showed the debt had been settled.

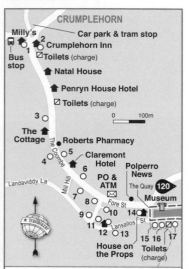

CRUMPLEHORN

Milly's
Car park & tram stop
2 Crumplehorn Inn
1
Bus stop
Toilets (charge)

Natal House

Penryn House Hotel

Toilets (charge)

0   100m

3
The Cottage
Roberts Pharmacy
5
4 6 Claremont Hotel
Polperro News
PO & ATM
The Quay 120
Landaviddy La
7
Museum
8 Fore St
9 10 14
11 Lansallos St
12 13
15 16 17
House on the Props
Toilets (charge)

Polperro

Where to eat and drink
1 Milly's
2 Crumplehorn Inn
3 The Kitchen
4 Plantation Tearooms
5 Bean & Scone
6 Harbour Greenhouse
7 Ship Inn
8 South Coast Bakery
9 Couch's Great House
10 Michelle's
11 Nelson's Restaurant
12 Noughts & Crosses
13 The Chip Ahoy
14 House on the Props
15 Wheelhouse Restaurant
16 The Three Pilchards
17 The Blue Peter Inn

The smart *Claremont Hotel* (☎ 01503-272241, 🖳 theclaremonthotel.co.uk; 1S/9D/1T/1F; ✿; 🐾; from £47.50pp, sgl from £120; adults only; min 2 nights) is near where Fore St turns into The Coombes and has come a long way since its origins as a fisherman's cottage in the 17th century.

Just up the road but still very much in the middle of it all, *The Cottage* (☎ 01503-272217, 🖳 polperrobedandbreakfast.co.uk; 6D; from £52.50pp) is a 400-year-old building with timber-beamed ceilings. Further along is large country-house style *Penryn House Hotel* (☎ 01503-272157, 🖳 penryn house.co.uk; 1S/2T/9D; ✿; 🐾; £45-55pp, sgl from £55, sgl occ £60-70), followed by friendly *Natal House* (☎ 01503-273011, 🖳 natalhouse.co.uk; 2D/1Tr/1Qd; ✿; 🐾; from £47.50pp, sgl occ £65; summer min 2 nights).

There are two more options at the top of The Coombe, a short walk (or tram ride) from the centre. *Milly's* (☎ 01503-272492, 🖳 millysbandb.co.uk; 3D; from £45pp, sgl occ £90; min 2 nights) has perfectly pleasant rooms and a restaurant attached. Opposite that, *Crumplehorn Inn & Mill* (☎ 01503-272348, 🖳 thecrumplehorninn.co.uk; 4D/3Tr/1Qd; from £50pp) is a very popular pub with eight B&B rooms, three above the pub, and five in an adjacent building. Some rooms have attached lounge areas, making this a good choice for groups of walkers.

Where to eat and drink
Eating is one of the main pastimes in Polperro – there's plenty of choice.

For Cornish pasties and the like, try *South Coast Bakery* (☎ 01503-262066; 🖳 southcoastbakery.com; Mon-Sat 8.30am-4.30pm, Sun 9.30am-4pm), a café and bakery with a nice patio at the rear. There's also a fish & chip shop, *Chip Ahoy* (fb; Mar-Oct Mon-Sat noon-8pm, Sun noon-6pm; eat in or takeaway), near the harbour.

There are several **café** options. On The Coombe, there's popular *Plantation Tea Rooms* (☎ 01503-272223; daily 11am-5pm). Nearby, *Bean and Scone* (daily 10am-5pm) is a friendly choice for cream teas, while right on the path and the harbour is *The House on the Props* (see Where to stay; food daily 9.30am-4pm), which has played a central role in the town's story of smuggling (it even once had secret stairs leading from the river) but is now more renowned for its cakes and cream teas. Unsurprisingly for an old smuggling village, **pubs** are not in short supply. The first one you reach is *The Blue Peter Inn* (☎ 01503-272743, ☐ thebluepeterinn.com, **fb**; food daily noon-2.45pm & 5-8pm) at the end of Quay Rd. It is known for its fresh seafood as well as hosting regular live entertainment. A few doors down at *The Three Pilchards* (☎ 01503-272233, ☐ threepilchardspolperro.co.uk, **fb**; food daily 11am-9pm), their pies are much lauded: try the 'famous' fish one (£16.95). Nearby, *The Noughts and Crosses* (see Where to Stay) is another option for a pint and some pub grub.

On Fore St, *Ship Inn* (☎ 01503-273424, ☐ shipinnpolperro.com, **fb**; food Mon-Sat noon-8.30pm, Sun noon-4pm) offers a fairly classic pub menu with sport on their TV. *Crumplehorn Inn & Mill* (see opposite; food daily 8.30-9.30am & noon-9pm) serves very good food, from breakfasts then light lunches through to an excellent evening menu (mains £11-13) of homemade delights such as Crumplehorn Curry, pork and chorizo pie, and falafel fritters.

In the **restaurant** line, across the road from Crumplehorn, *Milly's* (see Where to stay; Mon-Sat 9.30am-3pm & 6-9pm) specialises in tapas and fine wines, but is also open for breakfast. On the Quay in a former stable is the more formal *Wheelhouse*

Restaurant (☎ 07702-115992, **fb**; food summer daily 9am-9pm, winter hours vary), which dishes up home-cooked food including the ubiquitous Cornish crab sandwich. For fine dining there's *Couch's Great House* (☎ 01503-272554, ☐ couchspolperro.com; Mon-Sat 6.30-10pm); the executive chef honed his skills alongside Gordon Ramsay! They offer a £55 set menu which includes dishes such as beetroot tatin, rump of lamb and roasted hake.

Opposite, *Nelson's Restaurant* (☎ 01503-272366, ☐ polperro.co.uk/nelsons-restaurant, **fb**; Tue-Sun 6.30-9pm; mains from £18) specialises in seafood (with particularly good lobster) and has an old-worlde atmosphere. Nearby, *Michelle's* (☎ 01503-272459, Wed-Sat 6pm to late, Sun 12.30-3.30pm) is another great choice for seafood (most mains £15-25).

Further up the hill, *Harbour Green House* (☎ 01503-272261, **fb**, Mon-Sat 10am-8.30pm, Sun 10am-6pm) is a licensed café-restaurant with a lovely tiered front terrace, then continuing on, *The Kitchen* (☎ 01503-272812, ☐ thekitchenpolperro.com, **fb**; Mar-Oct Thur-Mon 6.30-9pm) is now a multi-award-winning licensed restaurant (mains £15-19).

Transport

To get a **bus** it's best to walk (or get the 'tram', see p290) to Crumplehorn, though a few services go to the village centre.

Bus services include the No 72 to Plymouth and Travel Cornwall's Nos 481 and 482. [See pp52-5 for details.]

POLPERRO TO LOOE   [MAPS 120-122]

These **5 miles (8km; 1¼hr-2hrs)** provide a gratifyingly gentle contrast to the severity of the previous stage. From Polperro the path climbs out of the village towards the war memorial at **Downend Point**, then takes a more northerly direction for the descent to **Talland Beach** (Map 120), home to a car park and two lovely cafés; the stylish *Talland Bay Beach Café* (☎ 01503-272088, ☐ tallandbaybeachcafe.co.uk, **fb**; Mar-Oct daily 9am-5.30pm) and *The Smuggler's Rest* (☎ 01503-272259; Easter-Nov 10.30am-5pm), with pleasant patio seating and great sea views. Curiously, Talland Bay was dubbed the Playground of Plymouth in the 19th century owing to its popularity with daytripping Victorian city-dwellers.

A further jaunt out to the point brings you the first glimpses of **St George's Island** (aka **Looe Island**) which you can actually walk to a couple of times a

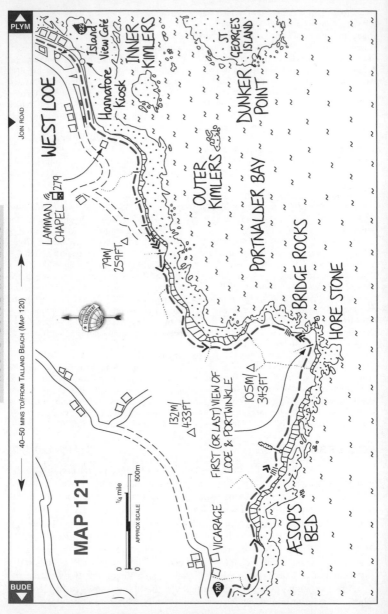

MAP 121

APPROX SCALE

1/4 mile

500m

40–50 MINS TO/FROM TALLAND BEACH (MAP 120)

JOIN ROAD

PLYM

BUDE

WEST LOOE

Island View Café

Hannafore Kiosk

INNER KIMLERS

ST GEORGE'S ISLAND

DUNKER POINT

LAMMAN CHAPEL 279

79M/259FT

OUTER KIMLERS

PORTNADLER BAY

BRIDGE ROCKS

HORE STONE

132M/433FT

FIRST (OR LAST) VIEW OF LOOE & PORTWINKLE

105M/343FT

VICARAGE

120

AESOP'S BED

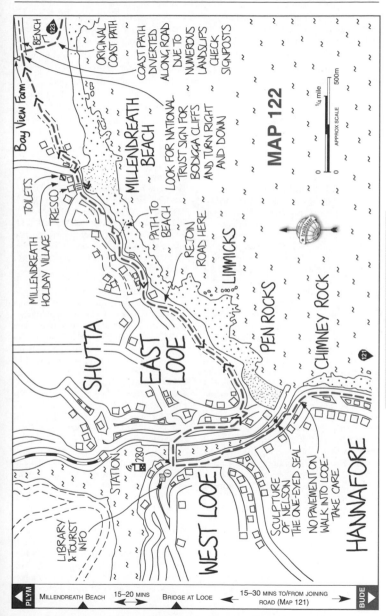

MAP 122

BENCH 123

Bay View Farm

ORIGINAL COAST PATH

COAST PATH DIVERTED ALONG ROAD DUE TO NUMEROUS LANDSLIPS CHECK SIGNPOSTS

MILLENDREATH BEACH

LOOK FOR NATIONAL TRUST SIGN FOR BODIGGA CLIFFS AND TURN RIGHT AND DOWN

TOILETS

TRESCO

MILLENDREATH HOLIDAY VILLAGE

PATH TO BEACH

REJOIN ROAD HERE

¼ mile

0   500m

APPROX SCALE

LIMMICKS

SHUTTA

EAST LOOE

PEN ROCKS

CHIMNEY ROCK

121

STATION

280

WEST LOOE

LIBRARY & TOURIST INFO

SCULPTURE OF NELSON THE ONE-EYED SEAL

NO PAVEMENT ON WALK INTO LOOE- TAKE CARE

HANNAFORE

PLYM

MILLENDREATH BEACH 15–20 MINS BRIDGE AT LOOE 15–30 MINS TO/FROM JOINING ROAD (MAP 121)

BUDE

year when the tide is particularly low. According to local legend, Jesus of Nazareth visited Looe Island with Joseph of Arimathea in order to buy tin – though presumably he didn't need to wait for the tide in order to walk out.

Soon after you spy the island the town itself comes into view, and is eventually reached after a steady but long-winded stroll through fields and the suburb of **Hannafore** (Map 121). If you need a pick-me-up before you reach Looe, you can stop for refreshments of the coffee, cake and light lunch variety here, either from picnic tables overlooking the sea at *Hannafore Kiosk* (☎ 01503-264929, 🖥 han naforekiosk.co.uk, **fb**; daily May-Sep 10am-6pm, winter hours vary), or at *Island View Café* (☎ 07443-460874, **fb**; Mar-Oct Wed-Sun 10am-5pm), where you can eat inside or out on its sea-facing front lawn.

LOOE

Looe is a medium-sized Cornish coastal town divided – East Looe and West Looe – by the river of the same name and united by an old stone Victorian bridge. It was mentioned in the *Domesday Book* and enjoyed brief prosperity in the 14th century as a boatbuilding town and commercial port, but only really grew in the 19th century with the Victorians' insatiable appetite for seaside holidays. Nevertheless, Looe still has a fishing industry and is known as a national centre for shark angling.

Although the town is sleepy in winter, it's renowned for its New Year celebrations when many local residents don fancy dress to party in the streets.

There are a couple of attractions to help pass the time on a rainy day. As you come into West Looe you'll pass the recently restored Grade-II listed **Old Sardine Factory**, which now houses the **Looe Harbour Heritage Centre** (☎ 01503-264223, 🖥 looeharbourheritagecentre.uk; Mar-Oct daily 9.30am-4pm; £3 for two) where you can learn about the history of the harbour, the river, its bridges, and all about sardines! There's a **café** here, as well as the excellent **Sardine Factory Restaurant** (see Where to Eat).

Across the river, the **Old Guildhall**, right in the heart of East Looe, is one of the oldest buildings here (it was constructed around 1450) and houses **Looe Museum** (☎ 01503-263709, 🖥 looemuseum.co.uk; Mon & Thur 11am-4pm, Tue-Wed & Fri-Sun 11am-1.30pm; £2), providing an absorbing run-through of this historic port's lengthy past.

Services

The **visitor information centre** (☎ 01503-262255, 🖥 visitlooe.co.uk; Mon & Fri 9.30am-1pm, Tue & Thur 9.30am-5pm) is at the **library** (Map 122; ☎ 0300-123 4111, 🖥 www.cornwall.gov.uk/libraries; same opening hours), at Millpool in West Looe, where you can use the library computers to get online free.

Services on East Looe's Fore St include Boots **pharmacy** (Mon 10am-4pm, Tue-Fri 9am-6pm, Sat 9am-5.30pm, Sun 10.30am-4.30pm), a Co-op **supermarket** (daily 7am-10pm), and more than one **ATM**. For **camping gear**, there's a Mountain Warehouse (Mon-Sat 9am-5.30pm, Sun 10am-5pm) on Fore St.

Where to stay

The nearest **campsite** to Looe is *Bay View Farm* (Map 122; ☎ 01503-265922, 🖥 www.looebaycaravans.co.uk; hiker & tent £10; 🐕; Feb-Dec) which overlooks Looe Bay and St George's Island from a peaceful perch right by the coast path. The owners are very welcoming. As well as normal tent pitches they also rent out wooden 'camping snugs' (sleep 2-4) for £40-50.

In central Looe, there's accommodation on both sides of the river.

West Looe One nice **B&B** option near the bus station is *Tidal Court* (☎ 01503-263695, 🖥 tidalcourt.co.uk; 2S/1T/3D/4Tr; 🚐; £25-30pp, sgl £35-45pp), at 3 Church St, which is family-run and very affordable.

Nearby, and one of several places that claim to be the oldest pub in Looe, *Ye Olde*

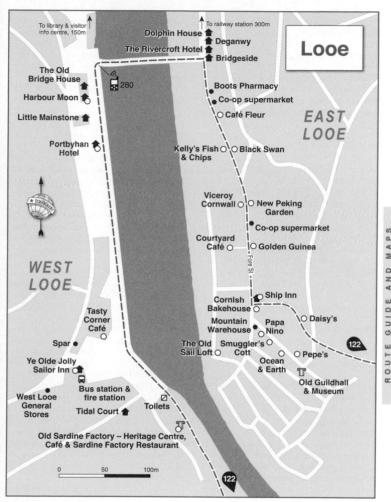

Looe

To library & visitor info centre, 150m

To railway station 300m

Dolphin House
Deganwy
The Rivercroft Hotel
Bridgeside

The Old Bridge House
Harbour Moon
Little Mainstone

Boots Pharmacy
Co-op supermarket
Café Fleur

EAST LOOE

Portbyhan Hotel

Kelly's Fish & Chips
Black Swan

Viceroy Cornwall
New Peking Garden
Co-op supermarket

Courtyard Café
Golden Guinea

Fore St.

WEST LOOE

Cornish Bakehouse
Ship Inn
Mountain Warehouse
Papa Nino
Daisy's

Tasty Corner Café

Spar

Ye Olde Jolly Sailor Inn

The Old Sail Loft
Smuggler's Cott
Ocean & Earth
Pepe's

West Looe General Stores
Tidal Court
Bus station & fire station
Toilets
Old Guildhall & Museum

Old Sardine Factory – Heritage Centre, Café & Sardine Factory Restaurant

0   50   100m

122

122

280

Jolly Sailor Inn (☎ 01503-263387, 🖥 jolly sailorlooe.co.uk, **fb**; 3D/2T; ☛; from 45pp), built in 1516, has low-beamed ceilings and bags of character.

Nearer to the bridge – and thus with great river views – are *Little Mainstone Guest House* (☎ 01503-262983, 🖥 little mainstone-looe.com; 3D/1Tr/1Qd; from £29pp; Jan-Nov) and *The Old Bridge*

House Hotel (☎ 01503-263159, 🖥 theold bridgehousehotel.co.uk; 2S/5D/2T; £46-80pp, sgl occ 10% off full room rate, sgl £57-75; min 2 nights).

Next to those two is *Harbour Moon Inn* (☎ 01503-265600, 🖥 www.theharbour moonlooe.co.uk, **fb**; 1S/2D/1T/1Tr, some en suite; ☛; from £60pp, sgl from £100), a bar and bistro with five rooms.

ROUTE GUIDE AND MAPS

A **hotel** worth considering is the modern *Portbyhan Hotel* (☎ 01503-262071, 🖳 portbyhan.com, **fb**; 4S/18D/12T/10F; 🐾; from £52.50pp, sgl from £65) which charges more for rooms with a riverside view.

East Looe By the bridge on this side of the river is the appropriately named *Bridgeside* (☎ 01503-263113, 🖳 bridge side-guesthouse-looe.co.uk; 1S/1T/1D/2D or T/2Tr/1Qd; 🐾; from £37.50pp, sgl occ from £60), Fore St. Friendly, neighbouring *Deganwy* (☎ 01503-262984, 🖳 deganwy hotel.co.uk; 6D/1D or T/1Tr; from £50pp, sgl occ from £80) and *Dolphin House* (☎ 01503-262578; 6D/1T; 🖢; 🐾; from £50pp, sgl occ from £70) both have high-spec rooms. Next door to them is *The Rivercroft Hotel* (☎ 01503-262251, 🖳 rivercrofthotel.co.uk, **fb**; 1S/11D; 🖢; £40-57.50pp, sgl occ £45-80), which has a restaurant and bar. Further down on Fore St, *Ship Inn* (☎ 01503-263124, **fb**; 🖢; 1S/1D/6T; from £60pp or £52.50pp room only) is a rival to Ye Olde Jolly Sailor (see pp296-7), if not in age then certainly in character and atmosphere.

Where to eat and drink
Most of the action, in terms of shopping, dining and drinking, happens in East Looe although there are options in West Looe.

West Looe The first place you pass on your way into Looe is the riverside *Sardine Factory Restaurant* (☎ 01503-770262, 🖳 thesardinefactorylooe.com, **fb**; Wed-Sun noon-2pm & 6-9pm), a bright, modern café-like restaurant that forms part of the recent £1.7 million restoration of Looe's Grade-II listed former sardine factory building. There are tapas dishes (£5-8) as well as mains (£15-20), and unsurprisingly seafood features prominently, including, of course, Cornish sardines on toast (£8). The attached **heritage centre** (p296) has a **café** (daily 9.30am-4pm) serving coffees, cakes and cream teas.

You can get pasties and other picnic supplies at *West Looe General Stores* (Mon-Sat 8am-6pm, Sun 10am-4pm), which has a delicatessen. There's also a

small Spar **supermarket** (Mon-Sat 7.30am-10pm, Sun 8am-10pm) on this side.

Nearby, *Tasty Corner Café* (☎ 07973-660995; Tue-Sun 8.30am-4pm) is a friendly no-frills café with plenty of breakfast and lunch options (mains £8-10).

Across the road, characterful *Ye Olde Jolly Sailor Inn* (see Where to stay; food noon-2.30pm & 5-8pm) does pasties, sandwiches and burgers for lunch (£6-12), then pub-grub classics (sausage & mash, steak & ale pie £10-13) come evening.

For a sit-down evening meal, you could try snagging one of the seats on the terrace overlooking the river at *Harbour Moon* (see Where to stay; food daily noon-8pm), though it's fairly standard pub-grub fare. Far nicer, *Portbyhan Hotel* (see Where to stay) also has a riverside restaurant (Mon-Sat noon-9pm, Sun to 8pm; most mains £15-18) with terrace seating.

East Looe Half the buildings on this side of the river seem to be eateries of one sort or another. For **pasties** to go, there's *Cornish Bakehouse* (☎ 01503-265524; daily 8am-6pm) which also does coffee and sandwiches and has some seating indoors.

Amongst the **takeaway** options are the hugely popular *Kelly's Fish & Chips* (**fb**; daily 8.30am-9pm; eat in or takeaway); and *New Peking Garden* (☎ 01503-264500. **fb**; daily 5-11pm), a classic Chinese restaurant and takeaway with an extensive menu. Spicy subcontinental suppers are on offer at *Viceroy Cornwall* (☎ 01503-265372; 🖳 viceroyofcornwall.co.uk; daily 5-11pm), while tantalising Thai tucker (curries from £6.50) is available at *Ocean and Earth* (☎ 01503-263080, daily 5.30-11pm) on Higher Market St.

Cafés of all shapes, sizes and characters are particularly prevalent. Popular *Café Fleur* (**fb**; ☎ 01503-265734; Mon-Sat 10am-3pm) does cheap breakfast baps, as well as light lunches, while further down towards the sea, *Courtyard Café* (☎ 01503-264494, **fb**; 11.30am-4pm) provides a lovely little sanctuary away from the hubbub on Fore St. It serves some great food too including Fowey River Mussels and Looe

Crab, and has an impressive wine list. However, the undisputed king of cafés in Looe is *Daisy's* (☎ 07988-803315, 🖳 daisyscafelooe.com, **fb**; Mon-Sat 9am-4pm; 🐾), up the hill a few metres on Castle St but right on the path. It's a treat for walkers – they even advertise that both dogs and muddy boots are welcome – and they do some sizeable food too, including pasties, doorstep toasties and fabulous breakfasts.

There's a cluster of lovely old **pubs** on this side of the river, most of which do food. The oldest of the lot is *Smuggler's Cott* (☎ 01503-262397, 🖳 looerestaurants .co.uk, **fb**; food daily 5.30-8.30pm, Sun carvery noon-2pm), built in 1430 and restored in 1595 with timbers said to be salvaged from the Spanish Armada! The bar is still styled on a nautical theme, and in the cellar is the entrance to a genuine smugglers' tunnel that led down to the quayside. Food-wise, aside from their renowned rib roast Sunday carvery, their regular menu is great, too, particularly their fresh lemon sole (£18.50).

Nearby on Fore St there's *Ship Inn* (see Where to stay; 🐾; food daily noon-3pm & 6-9pm), with good baguettes and some generous pub-grub mains; and the handsome *Golden Guinea* (☎ 01503-262780; noon-9pm), with its extensive pub-grub menu including griddled tuna. You can also eat out in the back garden, though with a more limited menu. *Black Swan* (☎ 01503-263002, 🖳 blackswanlooe.com; noon-9pm; **fb**) has an American diner feel to it with its booth-seating set-up.

In terms of **restaurants**, *Papa Nino* (☎ 01503-264231, 🖳 papanino.uk; Mon-Sat 4.30-10.30pm) is a great little Italian with a wide breadth of dishes (most mains £10-15), while *Pepe's Tex-Mex Kitchen* (☎ 01503-265832; summer daily 5.30-9.30pm, winter hours vary) is where to go for fajitas and burritos. For something more refined, *The Old Sail Loft* (☎ 01503-262131, 🖳 old sailloftlooe.co, **fb**; Mon 5-11pm, Tue-Sat noon-2pm & 5-11pm; most mains £11-18) serves some mouthwatering fish and steak dishes from its 16th-century premises on Quay St, alongside tapas and cocktails.

Transport

[See pp50-5] Looe railway station is on the East Looe side (see Map 122). **Trains** on Looe Valley Line (GWR 37 service) run to Liskeard where you can connect to services for Truro & Plymouth.

The No 72 **bus** calls at West & East Looe and will get you to Plymouth; while the No 73 service visits East Looe en route between Polperro & Liskeard. The No 481 links both West & East Looe with Polperro & Polruan. **Taxi** firms include Looe Taxis (☎ 01503-262405, 🖳 looetaxis.com).

LOOE TO PORTWRINKLE [MAPS 122-125]

The 7¾ **miles** (**12.5km; 2¼-3hrs**) separating the two harbours of Looe and Portwrinkle are dotted with little settlements that break up the sometimes monotonous walking, much of which is done on roads without pavements (though there is the option of taking to the sands between Seaton and Downderry).

On the other side of the bay, the original coast path goes back towards the sea and **Bodigga Cliffs**, which along with the woods above it are in the care of the National Trust. Passing a small **labyrinth** (🖳 windsworth.org.uk) cut into the grass, it enters into the woods above **Keveral Beach** before descending along the steps to more National Trust property at **Struddicks**, where the path undulates until descending on steps through a pine plantation to the road at **Seaton** (see p300). However, owing to a number of landslips in this area, you may be diverted along a road for part or all of the route into Seaton. Be sure to pay attention to the signposts by Bay View Farm (Map 122).

After Seaton, a not-entirely-safe stretch of road walking (no pavement) takes you to the village of **Downderry**. The **beach alternative route** at low tide –

which rejoins the main path just after The Inn on the Shore – is attractive. The path then continues along the road to a hairpin bend, where it finally leaves the tarmac for a climb up to and alongside farmland, negotiating a couple of sharp gradients, and a small diversion due to cliff fall, as it leads into **Portwrinkle**, which plays host to a pub, golf course, a café... and a famous ghost (see box below).

SEATON   [MAP 123]

There are a couple of places to stop for a bite here. Right on the sand *Seaton Beach Café* (☎ 01503-250621, 💻 seatonbeach cafe.com, **fb**; 🐾; summer daily 9am-4pm, winter hours vary; bring your own alcohol), has plenty of outdoor seating and an impressive menu. On the opposite side of the bay, *The Smugglers Inn* (☎ 01503-250923, 💻 thesmugglersinnseaton.co.uk, **fb**; 🐾; food Mon-Sat noon-4pm & 5.30-8.30pm, Sun

carvery noon-4pm; winter hours vary; mains £10-15) is a traditional, family-friendly pub that does light lunches as well as pub-classic mains. They also run *The Shack* (daily 10am-5pm), a takeaway coffee kiosk selling ice creams and hot pasties which has picnic benches beside it.

The No 72 bus from Plymouth to Polperro calls in Seaton, as does the No 75. [See pp52-5 for details.]

DOWNDERRY   [MAP 124, p302]

There are a couple of good choices for food here, and even some rooms. Downderry **stores** (Mon-Sat 8am-6pm, Sun 9am-5pm) is very well stocked although the **post office** hours are now very limited (Tue & Fri 1-3pm).

Down by the beach, the friendly *Inn on the Shore* (☎ 01503-250027, 💻 innon theshore.co.uk; 8D; 🐾) has smart, brightly decorated **B&B** rooms (from £50pp) and good-quality pub **food** (noon-3pm & 6-

9pm). It also has a little **coffee kiosk** (10am-4pm) on its large sea-facing terrace.

The tiny café *Summink Different* (☎ 01503-250311, **fb**; daily 9.30am-4pm) on Broads Yard Rd, does great coffee, tea and cake and has vegan options including highly recommended vegan Cornish pasties.

The No 72 bus from Plymouth to Polperro calls in Downderry, as does the No 75. [See pp52-5 for details.]

ROUTE GUIDE AND MAPS

❏ THE LEGEND OF FINNYGOOK

Notorious smuggler **Silas Finny** lived in and around **Portwrinkle** in the 18th century. He was part of a gang of successful lawbreakers who exploited the rather threadbare state of the Coastguard and law enforcement in the region to import alcohol, tobacco and lace into England. A very lucrative little operation it turned out to be, too, until one day Silas disagreed with his fellow smugglers over where to land a particular consignment. In a fit of anger, Silas revealed the landing location to the Excise men, and as a result of the information provided, several of the gang members were arrested, sentenced and deported to Australia. Of course, Silas Finny was a marked man after this and it wasn't long before he was bludgeoned to death by persons unknown – presumably friends and relatives of the exiled men, and other smugglers who wanted to make an example of Silas to show what happens if you betray them.

The story, however, doesn't end there, for since then Silas's ghost, or 'gook', has been making a nuisance of itself – to the extent that there are some local families who keep away from the hill between Portwrinkle and Crafthole after dark.

Whether his spirit actually lives on in the village is, of course, a moot point. His fame and legend, however, certainly do, with the lovely nearby pub named after him.

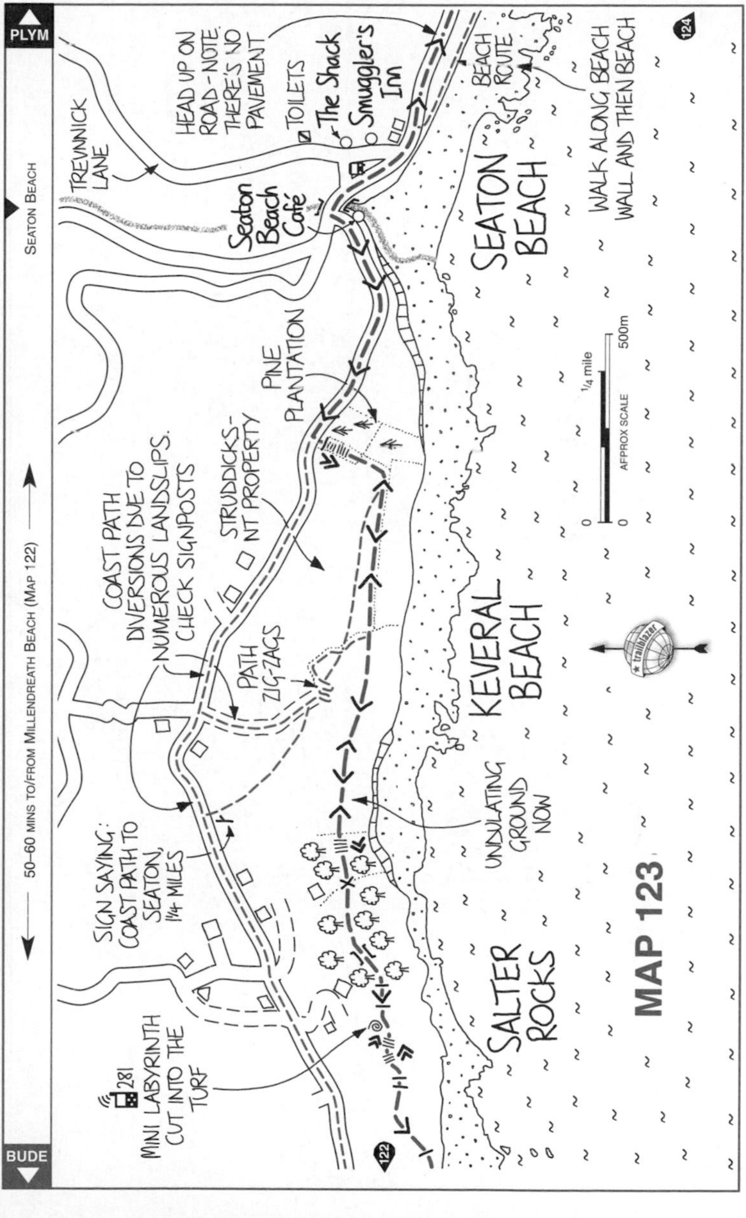

MAP 123

SEATON BEACH

PLYM ▲

SEATON BEACH ▶

HEAD UP ON ROAD – NOTE THERE'S NO PAVEMENT

TREVNNICK LANE

The Shack

Smuggler's Inn

TOILETS

Seaton Beach Café

BEACH ROUTE

WALK ALONG BEACH WALL AND THEN BEACH

SEATON BEACH

124

PINE PLANTATION

COAST PATH DIVERSIONS DUE TO NUMEROUS LANDSLIPS. CHECK SIGNPOSTS

STRUDDICKS – NT PROPERTY

PATH ZIG-ZAGS

50–60 MINS TO/FROM MILLENDREATH BEACH (MAP 122)

KEVERAL BEACH

¼ mile

500m

APPROX SCALE

0

0

Trailblazer

ROUTE GUIDE AND MAPS

SIGN SAYING: COAST PATH TO SEATON, 1¼+ MILES

MINI LABYRINTH CUT INTO THE TURF

281

UNDULATING GROUND NOW

SALTER ROCKS

MAP 123

122

BUDE ▼

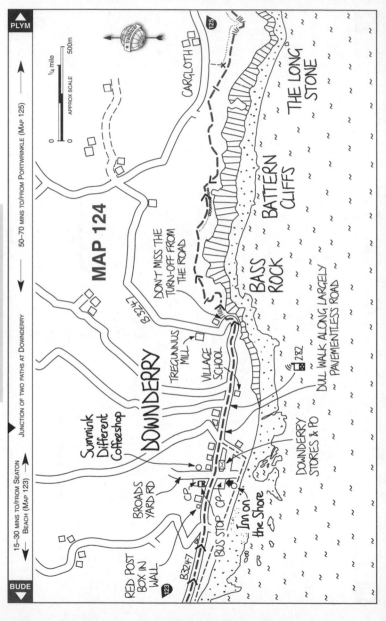

ROUTE GUIDE AND MAPS

PLYM ▲

50–70 MINS TO/FROM PORTWRINKLE (MAP 125) →

← JUNCTION OF TWO PATHS AT DOWNDERRY →

← 15–30 MINS TO/FROM SEATON BEACH (MAP 123) →

BUDE ▼

MAP 124

¼ mile
APPROX SCALE
0   500m

125

CARGLOTH

THE LONG STONE

BATTERN CLIFFS

BASS ROCK

DON'T MISS THE TURN-OFF FROM THE ROAD

DOWNDERRY

B3247

Tregunnus Mill

Village School

282

DULL WALK ALONG LARGELY PAVEMENTLESS ROAD

DOWNDERRY STORES & PO

Summink Different Coffeeshop

BROADS YARD RD

CP

BUS STOP CP

Inn on the Shore

RED POST BOX IN WALL

B3247

123

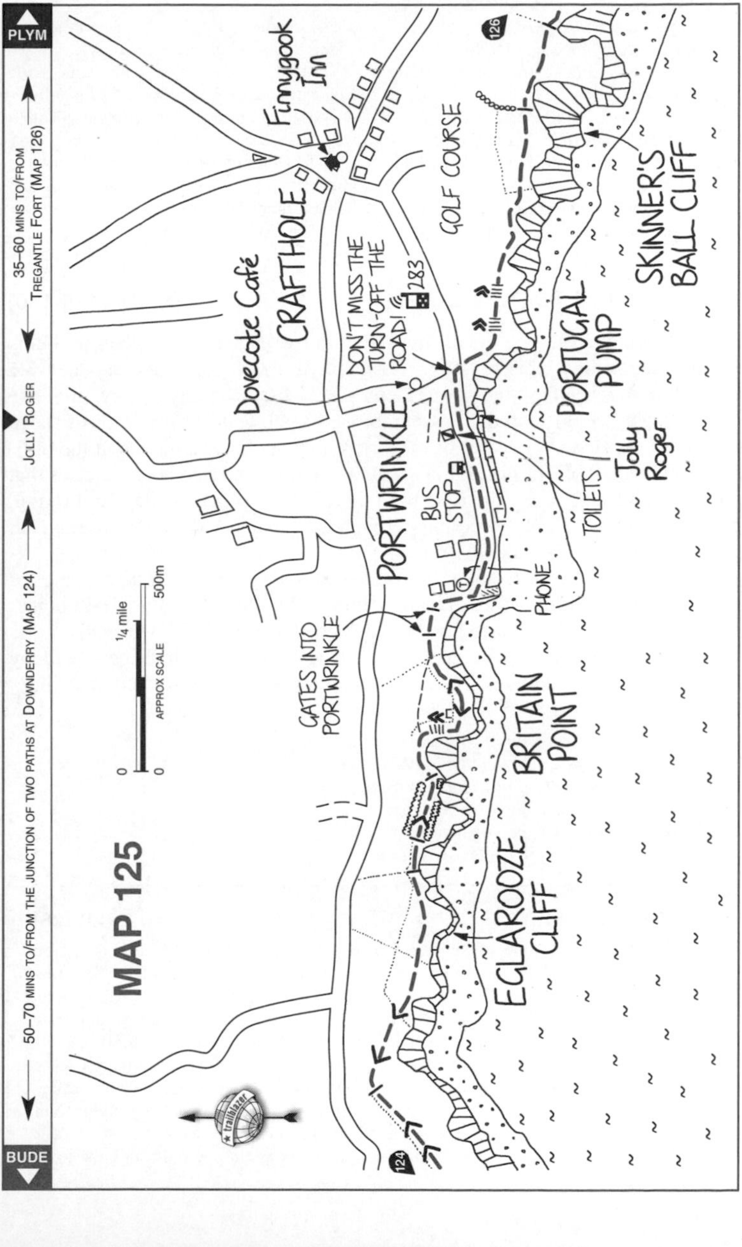
MAP 125
50–70 MINS TO/FROM THE JUNCTION OF TWO PATHS AT DOWNDERRY (MAP 124)
JOLLY ROGER
35–60 MINS TO/FROM TREGANTLE FORT (MAP 126)
PLYM
BUDE
0
0
1/4 mile
500m
APPROX SCALE
trailblazer
Finnygook Inn
CRAFTHOLE
Dovecote Café
DON'T MISS THE TURN-OFF THE ROAD!
283
GOLF COURSE
126
PORTWRINKLE
BUS STOP
TOILETS
Jolly Roger
PHONE
PORTUGAL PUMP
SKINNER'S BALL CLIFF
GATES INTO PORTWRINKLE
BRITAIN POINT
EGLAROOZE CLIFF
124

PORTWRINKLE   [MAP 125, p303]
The long-missed *Finnygook Inn* (☎ 01503-230338, 🖳 finnygook.co.uk, **fb**; 6D en suite; 🍷; 🐾; from £50pp) has finally reopened after being devastated by fire in 2017. They now have **B&B** rooms, and serve excellent pub **food** (most mains £12-16), locally sourced with fresh-off-the-boat seafood specials. They stock plenty of real ales and ciders, including 'Silas', their house-special cider, named after Portwrinkle's infamous ghost (see box p300), produced by local brewers Polbathic Cider Circle (🖳 cidercircle.co.uk).

Right on the coast path, café *Jolly Roger* (**fb**; daily 10am-5pm; 🐾) is a lovely spot for a break. Nearby, and also with a sea-view terrace, is Whitsand Bay Golf Club's *Dovecote Café* (🖳 whitsandbaygolf.com; Mon 8.30am-4.30pm, Tue-Sun 8.30am-6pm; 🐾), open to all.

The No 70B **bus** service stops here, as does the No 75. [For details see pp52-5.]

PORTWRINKLE TO PLYMOUTH   [MAPS 125-130]

The path continues to hug the clifftops after Portwrinkle at the beginning of this lengthy **13¼-mile/21.25km stage** (to Cremyll Ferry only; add another **2½ miles/4km** to reach the Mayflower Steps; **4¼-5¾hrs** to Cremyll Ferry, **plus 1hr** to Mayflower Steps). Initially passing through a golf course then fields of sheep and cattle, the first excitement of the day is only really encountered at the military firing ranges of **Tregantle Fort** (military area). A red flag here indicates that the alternative path along the road must be followed. If the red flag isn't flying, however, a superior cliffside tramp through the grounds can be enjoyed, a path that leads up to the Napoleonic fort.

Reuniting with the roadside route, the path then flirts with the tarmac for much of the next mile before actually joining it by Sharrow Point. The Point is home to **Sharrow Grotto** (Map 126), which is the work of one man, James Lugger, a Naval purser, who completed his task in 1784. Mr Lugger actually began the work in an attempt to cure his gout; as the poem inscribed on an interior wall makes clear:

But, as thou walk'st should sudden storms arise,
Red lightnings flash, or thunder shake the skies,
To Sharrows friendly grot in haste retreat,
And find safe shelter and a rocky seat.
By this, and exercise, here oft endured
The gout itself for many years was cured.

❏ **TREGANTLE FORT**   [MAP 126]

Tregantle Fort is just one of several fortifications built in the 1860s to deter the French from attacking Plymouth's naval base. The fort at Cawsand, and the batteries at Mt Edgcumbe Park and Penlee Point are further examples of these fortifications built on the orders of the then prime minister, Lord Palmerston, following a review by the Royal Commission on the Defence of the United Kingdom in 1859 that highlighted some of the weaknesses in the UK's defences. Tregantle was actually one of the larger constructions, with a capacity of one thousand personnel and over thirty large guns. However, by the early 20th century it was being used more for training than defensive purposes, and since WWII has largely been renowned for and utilised for its rifle ranges, a couple of which you walk past if taking the route through the fort.

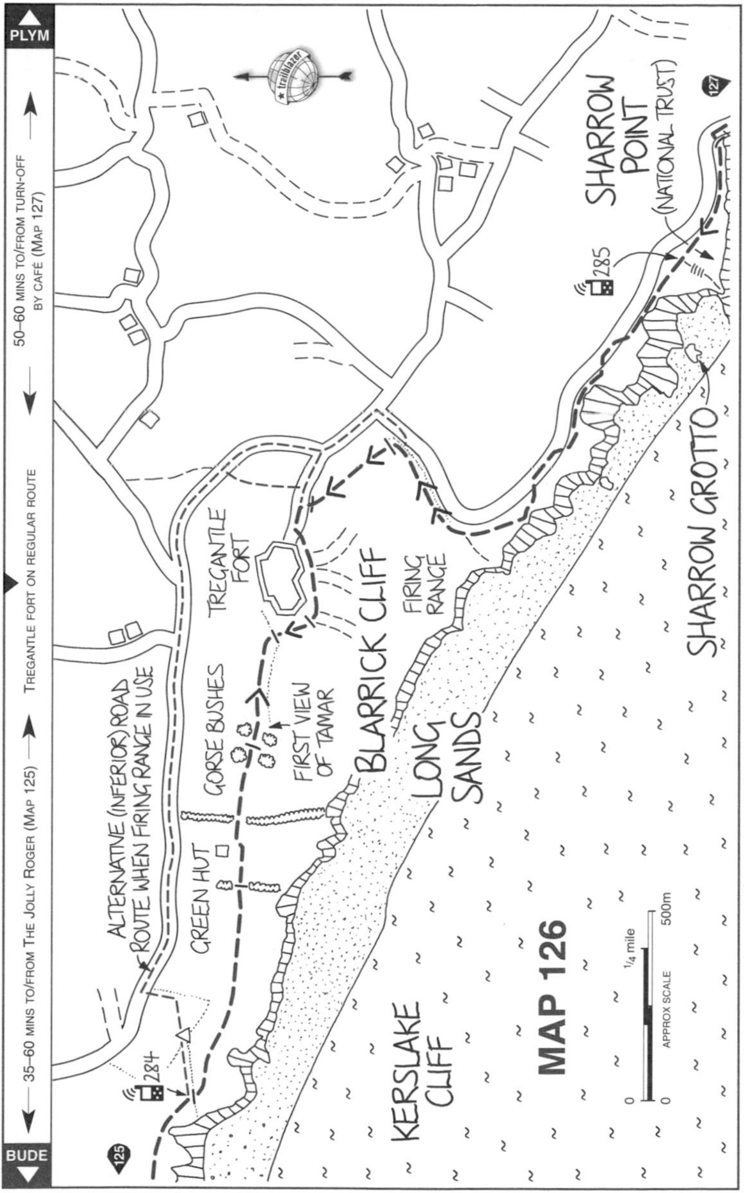

PLYM

50–60 MINS TO/FROM TURN-OFF BY CAFÉ (MAP 127)

TREGANTLE FORT ON REGULAR ROUTE

35–60 MINS TO/FROM THE JOLLY ROGER (MAP 125)

BUDE

127

SHARROW POINT (NATIONAL TRUST)

285

SHARROW GROTTO

TREGANTLE FORT

BLARRICK CLIFF

FIRING RANGE

ALTERNATIVE (INFERIOR) ROAD ROUTE WHEN FIRING RANGE IN USE

GORSE BUSHES

FIRST VIEW OF TAMAR

GREEN HUT

LONG SANDS

KERSLAKE CLIFF

MAP 126

284

125

¼ mile   500m

APPROX SCALE

0   0

ROUTE GUIDE AND MAPS

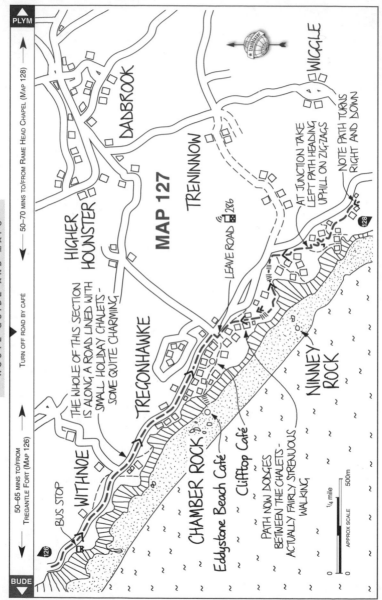

PLYM ▲

50–70 MINS TO/FROM RAME HEAD CHAPEL (MAP 128) →

← TURN OFF ROAD BY CAFÉ

50–65 MINS TO/FROM
TREGANTLE FORT (MAP 126)

DADBROOK

WICCLE

AT JUNCTION TAKE
LEFT PATH HEADING
UPHILL ON ZIGZAGS

NOTE PATH TURNS
RIGHT AND DOWN

HIGHER
HOUNSTER

TRENINNOW

MAP 127

LEAVE ROAD 🕮 286

128

THE WHOLE OF THIS SECTION
IS ALONG A ROAD LINED WITH
SMALL HOLIDAY CHALETS –
SOME QUITE CHARMING

TRECONHAWKE

NINNEY
ROCK

WITHNOE

BUS STOP

126

CHAMBER ROCK

Eddystone Beach Café

Clifftop Café

PATH NOW DODGES
BETWEEN THE CHALETS –
ACTUALLY FAIRLY STRENUOUS
WALKING

¼ mile

500m

0

0

APPROX SCALE

BUDE ▼

Back on the tarmac, the path now brings you to the conjoined villages of **Freathy** and **Tregonhawke**, an uninspiring elongated expanse of small holiday bungalows, but where you'll also find two nice little cafés (see Map 127): friendly *Clifftop Café* (**fb**; daily 10am-4pm) and beachside *Eddystone Beach Café* (**fb**; daily 10am-6pm), both offering coffee, cake and light lunches.

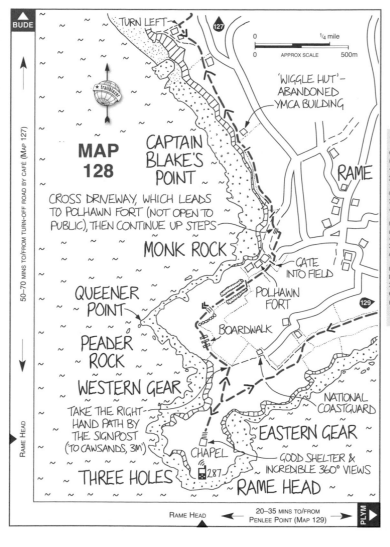

BUDE

0   ¼ mile
0   APPROX SCALE   500m

TURN LEFT

127

'WIGGLE HUT' – ABANDONED YMCA BUILDING

★ trailblazer

MAP 128

CAPTAIN BLAKE'S POINT

RAME

CROSS DRIVEWAY, WHICH LEADS TO POLHAWN FORT (NOT OPEN TO PUBLIC), THEN CONTINUE UP STEPS

MONK ROCK

GATE INTO FIELD

50–70 MINS TO/FROM TURN-OFF ROAD BY CAFÉ (MAP 127)

QUEENER POINT

POLHAWN FORT

129

PEADER ROCK

BOARDWALK

WESTERN GEAR

TAKE THE RIGHT-HAND PATH BY THE SIGNPOST (TO CAWSANDS, 3M')

NATIONAL COASTGUARD

EASTERN GEAR

CHAPEL

287

GOOD SHELTER & INCREDIBLE 360° VIEWS

THREE HOLES

RAME HEAD

RAME HEAD

ROUTE GUIDE AND MAPS

RAME HEAD   ←   20–35 MINS TO/FROM PENLEE POINT (MAP 129)   →   PLYM

Back up on the path, your uninteresting schlep along the road continues, and when the path does finally leave the road (just after a sign for one of the cafés) to dodge between the chalets on the cliffside, the numerous rises and falls do little to lighten the mood. Finally, however, the path relents and begins the gentle march to the lovely old **chapel** at **Rame Head** (Map 128). The building, dedicated to St Michael, actually dates back to the end of the 14th century and was built on the site of an even earlier Celtic hermitage. A priest would stay here and keep a beacon burning for passing ships. As with other promontories on this coastline, the headland was once the location of an Iron Age fort.

The gradients become more gentle now as you wend your way via farmland and forest, round **Penlee Battery Nature Reserve**, past the ruined **Folly Tower** – built in the 19th century for Princess Adelaide (wife of William IV, and the woman after whom Adelaide in South Australia is named) – and on to the twin villages of Cawsand and Kingsand.

CAWSAND & KINGSAND [MAP 129]

The twin villages of Cawsand and Kingsand offer a peaceful alternative to a night staying in Plymouth, and are linked to the city via a 30-minute ride on **Cawsand ferry** (see p310). The villages' narrow streets and alleyways have plenty of character and a surprisingly good choice of pubs and accommodation.

Curiously, despite their proximity, before 1844 the two villages were in different counties; a house on Garrett St bears the name Devon-Corn and stands on the old boundary between Devon (to which Kingsand belonged) and Cawsand (which has always been in Cornwall). Today the twins provide a quaint and friendly resort with a few amenities, including **The Shop in the Square** (☎ 01752-822505; daily 10am-7pm, winter hours vary) in Cawsand, which sells some takeaway food as well as general supplies, and a well-stocked Spar **convenience store** (daily 8am-9pm) at 55 Fore St, in Kingsand.

Where to stay

If you want to **camp**, *Maker Heights* (☎ 01752-822618, 🖳 makercamp.org.uk; Mar-Oct £12pp; 🐾), run by Rame Conservation Trust (🖳 rameconservationtrust.org.uk) is your nearest option. It's a site full of character and also has a small **restaurant/café** and a **shop**. To get to the site follow Jackman's Meadow Rd out of Kingsand as far as a T-junction where you turn right on

the B3247. Follow this up the hill until the campsite is signed off to the right. Alternatively follow the network of paths that begins at the top of Devonport Hill.

For **accommodation** in Cawsand, the blue-painted *Old Admiralty Boathouse B&B* (☎ 01752-822229, 🖳 cawsandbedandbreakfast.co.uk; 2D/1T or Qd, all en suite; 🐾; from £45pp) is a sunny house with great views out over the bay; it's also the closest place to the ferry slipway.

In Kingsand on the corner of Fore St, *Halfway House Inn* (☎ 01752-822279, 🖳 halfwayinnkingsand.co.uk, **fb**; 1S/4D/1T; 🛥; 🐾; from £45pp, sgl occ £80, sgl £60) is a comfortable pub with rooms.

Where to eat and drink

The Old Bakery (☎ 01752-656215, 🖳 the oldbakery-cawsand.co.uk; Apr-Oct Fri-Sun 9am-noon; takeaway pizza Mon 5.30-8pm if preordered) is a standout café and bakery that sadly isn't open every day but if your timing is right then it's the most pleasant place to eat in town. Their sourdough bread is outstanding, they do fabulous breakfasts, and great pastries and coffee.

Overlooking the ferry slipway in Cawsand, *The Bay* (☎ 01752-822706, 🖳 thebaycawsand.co.uk, **fb**; food noon-3pm & 5.30-8.30pm; summer from 10am; most mains £13-16) is a modern bar and restaurant with terrace seating beside the sea. For pub food, *The Cross Keys Inn* (☎ 01752-

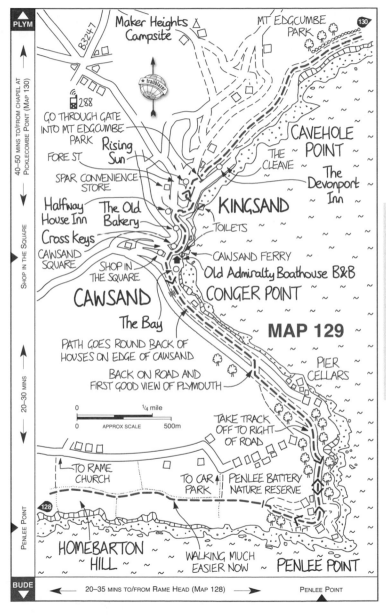

PLYM

40–50 MINS TO/FROM CHAPEL AT PICKLECOMBE POINT (MAP 130)

SHOP IN THE SQUARE

20–30 MINS

PENLEE POINT

BUDE

Maker Heights Campsite

B3247

MT EDGCUMBE PARK

130

trailblazer

288

GO THROUGH GATE INTO MT EDGCUMBE PARK

FORE ST

Rising Sun

SPAR CONVENIENCE STORE

Halfway House Inn

The Old Bakery

Cross keys

CAWSAND SQUARE

SHOP IN THE SQUARE

CAWSAND

The Bay

PATH GOES ROUND BACK OF HOUSES ON EDGE OF CAWSAND

BACK ON ROAD AND FIRST GOOD VIEW OF PLYMOUTH

0   1/4 mile
0   APPROX SCALE   500m

THE CLEAVE

CAVEHOLE POINT

The Devonport Inn

KINGSAND

TOILETS

CAWSAND FERRY

Old Admiralty Boathouse B&B

CONGER POINT

MAP 129

PIER CELLARS

TAKE TRACK OFF TO RIGHT OF ROAD

TO RAME CHURCH

TO CAR PARK

PENLEE BATTERY NATURE RESERVE

128

HOMEBARTON HILL

WALKING MUCH EASIER NOW

PENLEE POINT

ROUTE GUIDE AND MAPS

20–35 MINS TO/FROM RAME HEAD (MAP 128)

PENLEE POINT

822706, 💻 crosskeysinncawsand.com, **fb**; summer food daily noon-7pm, winter closed Mon), in Cawsand, does pretty standard pub-grub, but you can't beat the prices (most mains £8.50-10).

In Kingsand, *Halfway House Inn* (see Where to stay; food daily noon-2pm & 6-9pm; mains £10-12) serves reasonable food in modern surroundings. On The Cleave, and with drinkers spilling out onto the street in summer to soak up the sea views, *The Devonport Inn* (☎ 01752-822869, 💻 devonportinn.com, **fb**; food Mon-Sat noon-2.30pm & 6-9.30pm, Sun noon-3pm; mains from £13; 🐾) does homebaked pasties, toasted sourdoughs and some wonderful seafood including *moules frites* (mussels and chips). The smallest pub in the village,

The Rising Sun (☎ 01752-822840; food daily noon-2.30pm & 6.30-9pm, winter closed Mon) does baps and burgers as well as pub meals (mains £11-14), and has some roadside seating.

Transport

[See pp52-5 for details] The No 70/70A **bus** services call here.

The **Cawsand Ferry** (💻 plymouth boattrips.co.uk; single £5) makes the 30-minute crossing to The Barbican in Plymouth six times a day (9.30am, 11am, 12.30pm, 2pm, 3.30pm & 5pm). Return trips from Plymouth back to Cawsand are made at 9am, 10.30am, noon, 1.30pm, 3pm and 4.30pm, with an extra 6.30pm service in the school summer holidays.

A final, glorious stretch is all that separates you now from the end of the walk. Leaving Kingsand opposite The Rising Sun pub, you enter the grounds of lovely **Mount Edgcumbe Park**, dotted here and there with lakes and follies, grottoes and chapels, before passing into the Formal Gardens and on, via the 18th-century *Orangery* (☎ 01752-822586, 💻 theorangerymountedgcumbe.co.uk; summer daily 10.30am-4pm, winter weekends only) – a charming spot for one final Cornish cream tea – to the monumental gates leading to the Cremyll Ferry.

The waterside *Edgcumbe Arms* (☎ 01752-822330, 💻 edgcumbearms.co.uk; 5D/1T, en suite; from £60pp; food Sun-Thur 10am-8pm, Fri-Sat 10am-9pm; mains £13-15; 🐾) is conveniently located for a pitstop before catching the ferry.

Once across **Plymouth Sound**, the city itself is reached. For most, a B&B in the city or a train back home is the next and final destination. For those who seek a more monumental end to their monumental journey, however, we have chosen as our final stop on the path the **Mayflower Steps** by the old part of Plymouth, an area known as the Barbican. Not only does this take you along Plymouth's attractive and historic waterfront, but it also seems an appropriate place to end your journey in lands of the far west – given that the Pilgrim Fathers (see box p316) were looking to start a new chapter with their own occidental odyssey when they set sail from here in 1620.

🚢 CREMYLL FERRY

The ferry (☎ 01752-253153, 💻 plymouthboattrips.co.uk; adult/child £2/1) crosses the Tamar every 30 minutes – on the hour and half-hour – from Cremyll on Rame Head to Admiral's Hard, Stonehouse, in Plymouth. The journey takes just five minutes. In summer, the last boat leaves Cremyll at 9pm Mon-Thur, at 9.30pm Sun and at 10pm Fri-Sat. In winter it's 6.30pm Mon-Fri, 7pm Sat, and 6pm Sun.

Plymouth Citybus's Nos 70/70A/70B (see pp52-5) connect with the ferry and also travel to Plymouth by land, but take much, much longer (1hr 40 mins).

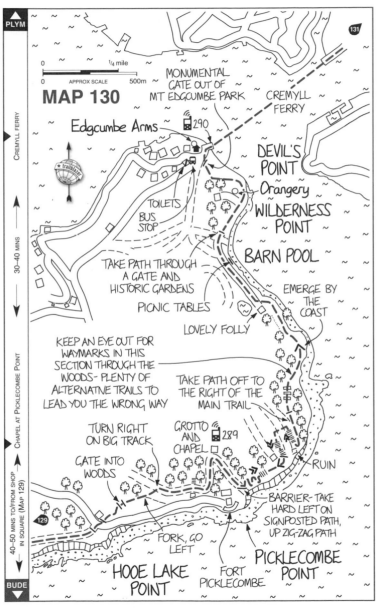

PLYMOUTH [MAP 131, p319]

'Plymouth is indeed a town of considera-tion, and of great importance to the public. The situation of it between two very large inlets of the sea, and in the bottom of a large bay [...] is very remarkable for the advantage of navigation.'

Daniel Defoe, *A Tour through the Whole Island of Great Britain*

Lying between the mouths of the rivers Plym and Tamar, Plymouth is a modern city with a rich and eventful past. The city's growth and prosperity are forever indebted to her proximity to – and relationship with – the sea. Not just as the famous departure point of the Pilgrim Fathers but also as a hub for trade (the commercial dockyards are amongst the largest in Europe) and, foremost, as a vital naval base; with a tradition that dates back to the very inception of the Royal Navy, there is much to see and do in this historic and thriving metropolis.

The first record of habitation in the area, Sudtone (Saxon for 'South Farm'), situated on the site of the present-day Barbican, can be found in the Domesday Book (1086). Initially just a small fishing village, its strategically important location soon brought prosperity and despite bouts of plague, cholera and smallpox trimming the ever-burgeoning population – as well as a concerted attempt at destruction by the Luftwaffe during the Plymouth Blitz – the city has continued to swell in size.

Much of this success is down to its sit-uation at the mouths of two rivers, a crucial location that the nascent Royal Navy in the 17th century was quick to recognise. Her Majesty's Naval Base (HMNB) Devonport opened in 1690, with further docks being built in 1727, 1762 and 1795. Isambard Kingdom Brunel then designed the Great Western Docks (1844-1850) and in 1854 the Keynham Steam Yard, built for the con-struction of steam ships, was also complet-ed. Hardly surprising, then, that most of the city's defining moments are sea based, from the defeat of the Spanish Armada (1588) to the sailing of the *Mayflower* (1620) as well as the heroic resistance the city showed in WWII when, despite enduring 59 German bombing sorties, it still played a full part in the Battle of the Atlantic and was a major embarkation point on D-Day.

ROUTE GUIDE AND MAPS

❏ THE COAST PATH THROUGH PLYMOUTH

Initially this **2¾-mile** (4.5km) trail from the Cremyll Ferry through Plymouth is a lit-tle confusing, the lack of coast path signs not helping. If you fancy some refreshment, the much-loved *Elvira's Café* (**fb**; Mon-Thur & Sat 8am-2.30pm, Fri 7.30am-2.30pm, Sun 8.30am-2.30pm; cash only) is right in front of you as you disembark from the ferry. Their breakfasts are particularly good.

Take the road opposite Elvira's (Strand St), then turn left and right onto Cremyll St. This leads you past **Ede Vinegar Works** (owned by the same family for six gen-erations) to **Royal William Yard**. Named after King William IV (who stands over-looking the entrance), the yard was built, mostly on reclaimed land, to supply the navy with beef, biscuits and beer – with a brewery, bakery and slaughterhouse on site. The yard has undergone recent restoration and is now dotted with **cafés, restaurants and bars**, making for a very pleasant stroll; and the official coast path has been re-directed through the yard, so you can explore its historic buildings without having to make any detours. You exit the yard at its far end, via a **staircase** dedicated to the late Eric Wallis MBE, who was the secretary of the South West Coast Path Association for 24 years. This brings you out over the defensive wall and into **Devil's Point Park**, with its wonderful sea views, before leading you back round the peninsula to the **Artillery Tower**, built to protect the harbour and yard but now a restaurant.

From here, make your way past the smart Georgian terraces of Durnford St, where Sir Arthur Conan Doyle worked as a doctor – which explains the **Sherlock Holmes quotes** in the pavement.

Unfortunately, where the Luftwaffe flattened Plymouth numerous ugly, concrete buildings have sprouted, making some areas rather devoid of charm. Thankfully, the seafront route to the Mayflower Steps is one of the more interesting and attractive corners of the city; the area around the steps, known as the Barbican, is one of oldest, prettiest and most vibrant, with plenty of bars and restaurants in which to toast your achievements. For this reason, after crossing the Cremyll, if you have the time – not to mention the stamina – we suggest finishing up at the Mayflower Steps (see box p316 for route), a suitably impressive finale to your Cornwall Coast Path odyssey – and the place where many before you, centuries ago, began their own incredible journeys.

What to see and do
The Hoe The green expanse that separates the modern-day city centre from the sea, The Hoe is most famous for playing host to Francis Drake's game of bowls in 1588, when, with the Spanish Armada fast approaching, he resolved to finish his game and wait for the tide to change before exchanging pleasantries with the enemy. Then during the Plymouth Blitz of WWII, Nancy Astor, Plymouth MP and great friend of TE Lawrence (of Arabia) danced with servicemen here, defiantly proclaiming that the city would go on despite the bombing.

Lighthouse lovers will be impressed by **Smeaton's Tower** (see box p315).

Other notable sites on The Hoe include a three-tier **belvedere** (a structure that has been deliberately designed to command a view) built in 1891, and the **Drake Statue** (1884), sculpted by one of the Victorian era's most pre-eminent producers of commemorative statues, Joseph Boehm. Many **war memorials** also adorn the area, fittingly so when one considers the number of servicemen and women to have departed from (and hopefully returned to) the city on various campaigns and missions over the years.

Finally, overlooked by the Smeaton Tower is **Tinside Lido** (☎ 01752-261915, 🖥 everyoneactive.com/centre/Tinside-Lido; May-Sep Mon, Wed & Fri 10am-7.30pm, Tue, Thur, Sat & Sun 10am-5pm; adult/child £5/4), an Art Deco outdoor saltwater swimming pool that first opened in 1935. After years of neglect, the pool was

---

A hard right after Stonehouse Barracks leads you onto Barrack Place, which becomes Millbay Rd, with Millbay Docks on the right.

At the next roundabout, by Duke of Cornwall Hotel, you need to turn right onto West Hoe Rd to return to the waterfront. This road leads you past the **Wall of Industrial Memories**, with its smattering of old metal signboards celebrating the heritage of the Millbay area.

You now join Hoe Road, which you follow all the way to the Barbican, passing the lovely **Tinside Lido**, on your right, and The Hoe (see above) and The Citadel (see p314) on your left.

There are still some quirky little sights on the way, including a cross in the pavement to celebrate the total eclipse of the sun that occurred in 1999, and a **marble scallop shell** in the wall near the start of The Barbican, celebrating the fact that Plymouth was one of only two ports licensed by the king from which pilgrims were allowed to embark when heading to Santiago de Compostella on the Way of St James. The shell is the symbol of St James, the patron saint of pilgrims. Another patron saint is celebrated in the same wall a little further down: **Stella Maris, the Virgin, Star of the Sea**, patron saint of seafarers, was rescued from a lost cargo of marble and now sits illuminated by the pole star shining above. Pilgrims would pray to these saints for protection during their journeys. For you, however, the journey is over; a few metres on, you'll reach the **Mayflower Steps**, marking the end of your almighty trek along Cornwall's magnificent coast path.

Grade II-listed before renovation and reopening in 2005.

The Citadel At The Hoe's eastern end is the **Royal Citadel** (☎ 07876-402728, 🖳 www.english-heritage.org.uk). A large and impressive limestone fort, it was built in the late 1660s on the orders of Charles II in response to the second Dutch War (1664-67). Encompassing a previous fort that Drake had requested to be built in the 16th century, its guns bear down on the town as well as out to sea, most likely as a reaction to Plymouth's Parliamentarian leanings during the English Civil War.

Still militarily operational today, the fort can only be visited as part of a **guided tour** (May-Oct), and strict security procedures must be followed (see the website for full details, and to book your tour).

The Barbican The Barbican is the old harbour area of the city and the heart of the old town. Fortuitously escaping much of the bombing inflicted on Plymouth during the war, the mazes of narrow **cobbled streets** (reputed to be the most extensive collection of cobbled thoroughfares in the UK) still exist in the originally medieval layout of what was then the town of Sutton.

ROUTE GUIDE AND MAPS

❏ **SIR FRANCIS DRAKE AND THE SPANISH ARMADA**

The Elizabethan era was a time of turmoil. The major European powers were often at war, with religion frequently the cause. The two main protagonists at this time were Protestant England and Catholic Spain. The latter controlled the Netherlands where Protestant ideals were popular. England, as was their wont, aided the Dutch Protestants who were being hunted by the Spanish Inquisition, and it was this decision – as well as the beheading of the Catholic Mary Queen of Scots, ordered by the Protestant Queen Elizabeth I in 1587 – that led to King Philip II of Spain's decision to defend Catholicism by invading England.

One of Queen Elizabeth I's most feared seamen was Sir Francis Drake. A buccaneering adventurer and hero to the English, the Spanish considered him a menace and he was a constant thorn in their side. Conducting his own personal Protestant crusade, by 1588 he had already harassed and harried many Spanish boats in the West Indies, occupied the ports of Cadiz and Corunna, destroying 37 Spanish ships as he did so, and plundered the treasures of Spain wherever he found them, describing his wish to 'singe the king of Spain's beard.'

King Philip II's Spanish Armada set sail from Lisbon in May 1588. Their ships were harassed by English and Dutch boats throughout their journey. The huge flotilla struggling through, the Spanish were eventually spotted off the Lizard and the news of their arrival swiftly reached Plymouth, where the English navy was waiting. Famously, Drake purportedly scoffed on being told of the arrival of the Armada, and chose to finish his game of bowls, claiming he could do so *and* defeat the Spanish. A much debated incident, if it did actually happen it is possible that Drake would have known that the tide of the Tamar was against him, preventing his boats from accessing the Channel until it turned – and thus recognised that he had ample time to complete his game.

History doesn't record whether Drake won his game of bowls. The outcome of the battle, however, is well known. Fighting between the Spanish and English navies went on for eight days before the Spaniards finally had to admit defeat, their navy beaten, burnt and scattered. Rubbing sea salt into the wounds, owing to westerly winds many of the defeated boats couldn't return straight home, but instead had to sail around the tip of Scotland and down the coast of Ireland where they were further battered by storms – as well as being executed by the English in Ireland. Drake meanwhile sailed home a hero, his legend forever cemented in English naval history for establishing England's dominance of the Atlantic – and refusing to end a game of bowls.

❏ PLYMOUTH'S HISTORY IN AND OUT OF THE BOX

Recently revamped at a cost of £46 million, and now known as **The Box** (☎ 01752-304774, 🖥 theboxplymouth.com; Tue-Sun 10am-5pm; free; no pre-booking required), Plymouth's premier **museum and art gallery** is entered through an eye-catching cuboid facade. The complex now houses a **café**, shop and bar as well as a series of new galleries and exhibition spaces, including its elevated 'archive in the sky'. Highlights include some of the earliest depictions of Plymouth (sketches and watercolours dating from the 1600s) plus, in the '100 Journeys' exhibition, effects belonging to two of the city's heroes: a side drum (the oldest in the UK) that was once Francis Drake's; and a pair of skis owned and used by Robert Falcon Scott in his 1902 Antarctic expedition.

The Box also manages two key historic sights in Plymouth. On The Hoe, **Smeaton's Tower** (Tue-Sun 10am-5pm; £5; no pre-booking required) was originally the third lighthouse to be put on Eddystone Rocks 14km south-west of Rame Head. Built in 1759, it was dismantled in 1882 and the upper portions reconstructed on The Hoe. Named after its builder John Smeaton, at 72ft high it offers striking views of Plymouth Sound and the city from its lantern room.

Close to the Barbican on New St is **Elizabethan House** (Tue-Sun 10am-5pm; guided tour £10, pre-booking essential). Built in the late 1500s, it retains much of its original structure, and has undergone major restoration as part of Plymouth's Mayflower 400 commemorations. It's been home to merchants, businessmen, fishermen, washerwomen and dressmakers, survived the Blitz and slum clearances in the early 1900s and presents a fascinating journey through the history of Plymouth.

To book tickets for Elizabethan House or for more information on winter opening hours at all venues, see 🖥 theboxplymouth.com; select 'Visit' then 'Outside the Box'.

The former location of Plymouth's fish market, the area is now more of a draw to those seeking art, antiques and alcohol.

Speaking of the latter, if you feel that a celebratory tipple is in order, on Southside St the venerable **Plymouth Gin Distillery** (☎ 01752-665292, 🖥 plymouthgin.com; Tue-Sat 11am-5.30pm, Sun noon-5pm) has been knocking out grade-A booze to discerning punters since 1793 and runs **distillery tours** (£11; 40 mins; pre-booking essential) round its building, which originally dates back to the mid 15th century. Tours include three gin tastings, plus a gin and tonic in the Refectory Bar. The building, incidentally, and more than a little ironically, was also where the Puritan Pilgrim Fathers supposedly spent their last night before embarking for America. If you're not taking a tour, you could just go for an evening pink gin in the salubrious *Refectory Bar* (Wed-Thur 6-9.30pm, Fri-Sat 6-10pm).

Only a couple of minutes away is **Elizabethan House** (see box above).

Next to the pedestrian walkway which crosses Sutton Harbour, **The Mayflower Steps** commemorate the Pilgrim Fathers' departure for the New World in 1620. The steps consist of a portico that was built in 1934 and a platform hanging out over the water's edge. Nearby, the **Mayflower Museum** (☎ 01752-306330; Apr-Oct Mon-Sat 9am-5pm, Sun 10am-4pm, Nov-Mar Mon-Fri 9am-5pm, Sat 10am-4pm; £3.50), is above the tourist information centre and tells the story of the Pilgrim Fathers.

Not technically part of the Barbican but just across the walkway from the Mayflower Steps is the **National Marine Aquarium** (☎ 0844-893 7938, 🖥 national-aquarium.co.uk; daily 10am-5pm, Aug to 6pm; £19.50-23; pre-booking essential). The UK's largest, it houses a tank that contains 2.5 million litres of water! Truly unmissable, the Atlantic Ocean display, as it is known, is home not only to ragged tooth sharks, stingrays and barracuda but also a full-sized replica of a WWII plane.

Plymouth's premier **museum and art gallery**, **The Box** (see box p315) is on Drake Circus, just north of the Barbican.

Services

As you'd expect, Plymouth has just about every amenity you need. The **tourist information centre** (☎ 01752-306330, 💻 visit plymouth.co.uk; same opening hours as Mayflower Museum) is handily placed right by the Mayflower Steps on the Barbican and is one of the friendliest and most helpful on the entire walk. There's a McColl's **supermarket** (7am-10pm), which also contains an **ATM** and a **post office** (same hours), nearby at 49-50 Southside St, plus another **post office** (Mon-Fri 9am-5.30pm, Sat 9am-2pm) inside WH Smith's (Mon-Sat 8am-6pm, Sun 10am-4pm) on New George St. There are two more handy **supermarkets** on Notte St: Tesco Express (6am-11pm; ATM outside), and Co-op (Mon-Sat 6am-11pm, Sun 7am-11pm; ATM inside).

At 167-171 Armada Way, the Central **library** (☎ 01752-305901, 💻 plymouth .gov.uk/libraries; Mon-Fri 9am-6pm, Sat 10am-4pm) has **computers** for internet access (£1.75 for 30 mins).

For **camping/trekking** supplies head to nearby New George St, north-west of the Saint Andrew's Cross Roundabout, where you'll find Millets (No 40; Mon-Sat 9am-6pm, Sun 10.30am-4.30pm) and Trespass (No 34; Mon-Sat 9am-5.30pm, Sun 10.30am-4.30pm). There are plenty of **ATMs** near here too, in what is largely a pedestrianised shopping zone. The most

---

ROUTE GUIDE AND MAPS

❑ THE MAYFLOWER AND THE PILGRIM FATHERS

Most visitors to Plymouth – and probably just about all American tourists in the city – are aware that amongst the first, and certainly the most famous, Europeans to settle in America (a group now celebrated as the Pilgrim Fathers) set sail from Plymouth in 1620. What is less well known, perhaps, is the background to their emigration and why they felt compelled to head for the New World in the first place.

The pilgrimage had its roots in Henry VIII's rejection of the Catholic Church back in 1534, an act that led to England becoming a Protestant country for the first time. Puritanism, the ideology followed by the Pilgrim fathers, emerged soon afterwards during the reign of Henry VIII's daughter, Elizabeth I. As the name suggests, the Puritans felt that Henry VIII's Church of England was neither strict nor pious enough for their rather fanatical tastes. This stance angered both Elizabeth and her successor, James I, and before long the Puritans were being persecuted for their beliefs.

In 1609 some Puritans headed for Leiden in the Netherlands to seek a land where they could practise their faith in peace. However, whilst there was less persecution, they were still unhappy with the tolerance and levity of their Dutch hosts; more worrying still for the Puritans was the way their offspring were being assimilated into Dutch culture. There seemed to be only one solution: to build their own community, away from the persecution and profanity (as they saw it) of Europe, in the New World.

Plymouth's role in their story is actually both fortuitous and fairly minor. Setting sail from Southampton in *The Mayflower* and *The Speedwell* in August 1620, they only docked in Plymouth due to a storm that damaged the already old and leaking boats as they navigated The Channel. Fully stocked and with the decision made to leave *The Speedwell* behind, a total of 102 passengers and crew (not all of whom were Puritans) finally left the city on 6 September 1620, reaching Cape Cod 66 days later to found the community they had dreamed of in Massachusetts.

The Pilgrim Fathers' travails didn't end there, though. Weakened by their journey and unprepared for winter, half of them died within the first four months of landing. However, those who did live owed their survival to the natives, a relationship cemented in the Pilgrims' first harvest of 1621 – a ceremony which would go on to become the basis for the American festival of Thanksgiving.

convenient **launderette** is Hoegate Laundromat (☎ 01752-223031; Mon-Fri 8.30am-5pm, Sat 9am-1pm) at 55 Notte St.

Where to stay
Hostels and budget accommodation
Long-standing *Plymouth Backpackers Hotel* (☎ 01752-213033, ☎ 01752-269333, 🖳 plymouthbackpackershotel.co.uk; dorm from £16pp, private twin rooms from £19.50pp; 🐾), at 102 Union St, has both dorm beds and private rooms, some en suite. They have a self-catering kitchen and can offer packed lunches and evening meals.

The most central of Plymouth's several *Premier Inns* (🖳 premierinn.com; City Centre, Derry's Cross ☎ 0871-527 8880) is at one end of Royal Parade. Close by, is a branch of *Travelodge* (☎ 0871-984 6251, 🖳 travelodge.co.uk; Derry's Cross); both chains offer advance-booking bargains.

B&Bs Plymouth has plenty of B&Bs; a useful resource is 🖳 visitplymouth.co.uk/ accommodation. Many are well situated for both the path and the city sights. Two of the most convenient for the Cremyll ferry are *The Firs* (☎ 01752-300010, 🖳 thefirsinply mouth.co.uk; 2S/1D/1T/1D or T/2Tr, some en suite; 🐾; from £36pp, sgl/sgl occ from £60), at 13 Pier St; and *The Caraneal* (☎ 01752-663589, 🖳 caranealplymouth.co.uk; 8D/2T; 🐾; from £30pp, sgl occ from £40), at 12-14 Pier St.

More central, Citadel Rd has numerous B&B options all the way along its length. At the road's eastern end, close to the Barbican, is the aptly named *Barbican Reach Guest House* (☎ 01752-220021, 🖳 barbicanreach .co.uk; 1S/2T/4D/2Qd; 🐾; from £35pp, sgl occ from £60), at No 225, with super clean rooms and a friendly welcome.

Further along, facing Hoe Park, is *The George Guesthouse* (☎ 01752-661517, 🖳 georgeguesthouse.com; 1S/5T/3Tr/1F, some en suite; 🐾; £20-27.50pp, sgl from £30; room only), at No 161, which offers very competitive rates. Next door, at No 159, the friendly *Pub on the Hoe* (☎ 01752-219183, 🖳 pubonthehoe.co.uk; 2D/1Tr; 🐾; from £32.50pp) was completely refurbished following a fire in 2020. It has reasonable rooms, good food and plenty of real ales.

Towards the western end of Citadel Rd, there are more options such as *The Kynance* (☎ 01752-266821, 🖳 kynance house.co.uk; 2S/1D/2T/2Tr/1Qd; ●; 🐾; from £37.50pp, sgl from £45), at 107-11; *Caledonia Guesthouse* (☎ 01752-229052; 1S/5D/3T/1Tr; from £40pp), at No 27 Athenaeum St; and *Tudor Guest House* (☎ 01752-661557, 🖳 tudorhouseplymouth.co .uk; 2S/1T/4D/1Tr, some en suite; from £35pp, sgl occ from £55, sgl £40-45) at No 105 Citadel Rd.

Hotels The closest hotel to the Cremyll Ferry is the grand, 150-year-old *Duke of Cornwall Hotel* (☎ 01752-275850, 🖳 the dukeofcornwall.co.uk; 72 rooms; ●; from £40pp) on Millbay Rd. You can get double rooms for as little as £80 in winter, but expect to pay at least double that in season. Nearer to The Hoe is *Invicta Hotel* (☎ 01752-664997, 🖳 invictahotel.co.uk; 4S/ 8D/6D or T/4Qd; ●; 🐾; from £40pp, sgl from £65), 11/12 Osborne Place.

Where to eat and drink
The Barbican is the place to go for food, though there are also some nice waterside spots right on the coast path along Hoe Rd.

Snacks & takeaways For **pasties**, head to *Barbican Pasty Co* (10.30am-4pm), on Southside St, or get your **fish & chips** fix at *Harbourside* (daily 11am-10.30/11pm), at 35 Southside St. *B-Bar* (🖳 b-bar.co.uk; food noon-9/10pm; eat in or takeaway) is a **Thai** noodle bar inside Barbican Theatre on Castle St, or get **kebabs** from *Favourite Food* (daily 4.30pm-1.30am) at 53 Notte St.

Cafés There's a great choice of places for coffee, cake, breakfast or light lunch, from cute and friendly to whimsical and eccentric including; *Jacka Bakery* (38 Southside St; **fb**; Wed-Mon 9am-2.30pm) with the best bread in the city; *Monty's Café* (13 The Barbican, **fb**; 8am-4pm) with standout all-day breakfasts; and *The Flower Café* (46 Southside St; **fb**; 10am-4/5pm), perfect for tea and cake in their small back garden.

Hidden away in the cobbled back streets is the quirky *Mad Merchant Coffee House* (37 New St, 🖳 themadmerchants coffeehouse.com, **fb**; Tue-Sun 10am-3.30pm), with a gorgeous flower-filled back garden and arguably the best cream teas in the city.

If you're following the coast path from the Cremyll Ferry round to the Barbican, just a short diversion off it, at 26 Pier St, is the small deli-café *By The Park* (**fb**; Tue-Sun 9.30am-4.30pm). Close by, right on the path, is *The Waterfront* (💻 waterfront-plymouth .co.uk; food 9am-9pm, drinks to 11pm), with an art deco frontage and outstanding views from a large waterside terrace. The food (seafood and pub grub) is excellent.

Pubs & bars On Southside St, *The Navy Inn* (☎ 01752-301812; food noon-9pm) has won awards for its food. It's a traditional pub with a seemingly ordinary pub-grub menu, but the results are excellent, and the

atmosphere always lively. An added bonus is the upstairs terrace with waterfront views.

Opening out onto the waterfront, *The Ship* (☎ 01752-667604, 💻 theshipply mouth.co.uk; food Mon-Fri noon-3pm & 5.30-9pm, Sat noon-9pm, Sun noon-8pm) does very good food (mains £10-15) – the fish and chips are superb.

Practically next door, *Rakuda Bar & Pizzeria* (☎ 01752-221155, 💻 rakudabar .com; food noon-9pm, drinks till 2am) has the same great outdoor seating spot as The Ship for your pasta, pizza and cocktails.

Away from the tourists, the *Pub on the Hoe* (see Where to stay; food served Mon-Sat noon-10pm, Sun noon-8pm) has a regularly changing selection of real ales, and good honest pub grub (bangers & mash, steak & ale pie), plus a selection of vegan and gluten-free dishes.

PLYMOUTH – MAP KEY

Where to stay
3 Plymouth Backpackers Hotel
4 Duke of Cornwall Hotel
5 Travelodge
6 Premier Inn
9 The Firs
10 The Caraneal
15 Caledonia Guesthouse
16 Tudor Guest House
17 The Kynance
18 Invicta Hotel
19 Pub On The Hoe
20 George Guest House
32 Barbican Reach Guest House

Where to eat & drink
1 Elvira's Café
2 Artillery Tower
11 By the Park Deli-Café
12 The Waterfront

Where to eat & drink *(cont'd)*
13 The Wet Wok
14 Maritimo
19 Pub On The Hoe
23 Yukisan
24 Favourite Food
26 Eastern Eye
27 Arribas
28 Barbican Steakhouse
29 The Thai House
30 The Bottling Plant
31 Plymouth Gin Distillery, Barbican Kitchen
34 Barbican Pasty Co
35 The Ship
36 Rakuda Bar & Pizzeria
37 The Village Restaurant
38 The Navy Inn
39 The Flower Café
41 Jacka Bakery
42 Mad Merchant Coffee House
43 Harbourside

Where to eat & drink *(cont'd)*
44 Himalayan Spice
45 Monty's Café
47 B-Bar
48 Pier Master's House

Other
7 Millets
8 Trespass
21 Tesco Express & ATM
22 Co-op
25 Hoegate Laundromat
31 Plymouth Gin Distillery
33 McColl's supermarket, Post Office & ATM
40 Elizabethan House & Gardens
46 Tourist Office & Mayflower Museum
47 Barbican Theatre

Plymouth MAP 131

To The Box (museum and art gallery), 100m

Charles Cross roundabout

Drake Circus Shopping Centre

£ ATMs

To railway station, 550m

Cornwall St

Armada Way

Mayflower St

Plymouth Coach Station

Library & Internet

Bus stops

WH Smith & Post Office

New George St

Royal Parade

A374

King St

King St

Neswick St

Octagon St

Manor St

Clarence Pl

Union St

Union St

Edgecumbe St

High St

Martin St

Bath St

Millbay Rd

Barrack Pl

Stonehouse Barracks

The Vine (pub)

Durnford St

Cremyll St

Cremyll Ferry

Ede Vinegar Works

Royal William Yard

Toilets (20p)
Water tap
Tidal pool

Wall of Industrial Memories

West Hoe Rd

Millbay Docks

Prospect Pl

Pier St

West Hoe Park

Leigham St

Toilets (20p)

Elliot St

Athenaeum St

Citadel Rd

Alfred St

Lockyer St

Holyrood Pl

Notte St

Sussex St

Zion St

Hoe St

Hoe Approach

Hoegate St

Vauxhall St

Citadel Rd E

Landpay Hill

Madeira Rd

THE BARBICAN

National Marine Aquarium 75m

Dorset & South Devon Coast Path - SWCP continues

Mayflower Steps

Stella Maris

St James Scallop Shell

The Royal Citadel

Ferries to Mountbatten Point & Cawsand

The Belvedere

Smeaton's Tower

Drake Statue

THE HOE

Hoe Promenade

Hoe Rd

Hoe Rd

Tinside Lido

trilobite

0   250   500m

ROUTE GUIDE AND MAPS

50 – 70 MINS TO/FROM CREMYLL FERRY DISEMBARKATION POINT (MAP 130)

MAYFLOWER STEPS

Restaurants Next door to The Navy Inn, *The Village Restaurant* (☎ 01752-667688, ☐ thevillagerestaurantplymouth.co.uk, **fb**; daily 11.30am-10.15pm; mains £14-19), at No 32 Southside St, is an excellent seafood restaurant which also does a terrific roast beef on Sundays. Also on Southside St, *Barbican Kitchen* (☎ 01752-604448, ☐ barbicankitchen.com, **fb**; Tue-Fri noon-2.30pm & 6-9.30pm, Sat noon-2.30pm & 5-10pm; mains £15-25) is in Plymouth Gin Distillery (see p315) and serves delights such as slow-cooked Devon lamb shoulder, and roasted sea bream. Opposite, inside the distillery's former bottling house is *The Bottling Plant* (☎ 01752-511511, ☐ the bottlingplant.co.uk, **fb**; Mon-Sat 9am-11pm, Sun 10am-9pm). With period furniture and portraits of the past, the atmosphere certainly demands an afternoon cream tea, if not a gin or two. They also do a good range of breakfasts, lunchtime and evening mains (£12-15).

With a fabulous harbourside location, *Pier Masters House* (☎ 01752-651410, ☐ piermastershouse.com, **fb**; daily 7am-11pm) is a fine choice for a meal. Its huge wood-decked terrace jutting out over the water is a very popular spot on summer evenings, and its menu (mains £12-16) of seafood, burgers and steaks doesn't disappoint. It's also open nice and early for breakfasts (£6-9). A short walk away, on Notte St, *Barbican Steakhouse* (☎ 01752-222214, ☐ barbicansteakhouse.com, **fb**; Mon-Thur 5-10.30pm, Fri-Sat 5-11pm, Sun 5-9.30pm) does a mouthwatering smothered fillet steak for £19.95.

For **Indian** cuisine, eat in or takeaway, there's *The Eastern Eye* (☎ 01752-262948, ☐ easterneyeplymouth.com; daily 4.30-10pm), at 57 Notte St, or the excellent *Himalayan Spice* (☎ 01752-252211, ☐ himalayanspice.net; daily 6-11pm), housed in a 16th-century building at 31 New St.

For **Thai** food, head to *Thai House* (☎ 01752-661600, ☐ thethaihouseplymouth .co.uk, **fb**; Mon-Thur 6-10pm, Fri-Sat 5-10.30pm) at 63 Notte St. Eat **Mexican** at *Arribas* (☎ 01752-603303, ☐ arribasmexi can.co.uk, **fb**; daily 5-10pm) at No 58. At No 51 is long-standing **Japanese** restaurant *Yukisan* (☎ 01752-250240, ☐ yukisan.co .uk; Mon-Fri noon-2.30pm & 5-10pm, Sat noon-10.30pm, Sun noon-9.30pm).

There are plenty of **Chinese** options in town, though perhaps the most unusual is *The Wet Wok* (☎ 01752-664456, ☐ wet wok.com; daily noon-2pm & 6-10pm) hidden away down a flight of steps leading to a secret perch overlooking Plymouth Sound. Service is quick (ideal for passing walkers), and the food is tasty.

Also on Hoe Rd, and also overlooking the Sound, is the cute wine and **tapas** bar *Maritimo* (☎ 01752-222938, ☐ maritimo plymouth.co.uk, **fb**; Sun-Thur 10am-9pm, Fri-Sat 10am-10pm), with a relaxed atmosphere and more great views.

Further afield, but worth the walk, *Artillery Tower* (☎ 01752-257610, ☐ art illerytower.co.uk; Wed-Sat 7-11pm, last arrivals 8pm; booking essential), is one of the more discreet places in the city; indeed, you may well have walked right past it without knowing on the way into the centre from the Cremyll ferry. Evening meals are set at £54/60 for two/three courses, and include mains such as peppered haunch of venison with red cabbage and pineapple pickle. The restaurant is located in a 15th-century defensive tower on the sea wall and overlooks Plymouth Sound.

Transport

[See pp50-5] The most convenient places to board buses for local services are the bus stops along Royal Parade. Numerous services leave from here, including: 70/70A/70B **buses** to Torpoint Ferry; the 12/12B to Bude via Launceston; the 72 operates to Looe. GorranBus's G4 runs to St Austell, Mevagissey & Gorran Haven.

National Express coaches leave from **Plymouth Coach Station** (☎ 0871-781 8181), Armada Way, with direct or connecting services to pretty much every city in mainland Britain.

Plymouth is a stop on GWR's regular **train** services between London (Paddington) and Penzance. The railway station is an easy 10-minute walk north of Royal Parade.

For a **taxi**, try Need-a-Cab (☎ 01752-666222, ☐ needacab247.com) or Tower Cabs (☎ 01752-252525, ☐ towercabs.co.uk).

APPENDIX A: HARTLAND QUAY TO BUDE

HARTLAND QUAY TO BUDE [MAPS 48x-54x]

The following section, the route from Hartland Quay in Devon over the border into Cornwall and on to Bude, is from *Exmoor & North Devon Coast Path*, the first book in this series. It's included for completeness, so that every inch of the path within Cornwall is covered in this book.

This **15½-mile (24.9km; 9hrs)** stretch is often cited as the hardest section on the entire South-West Coast Path! It's across soaring summit and plunging combe that includes, by our reckoning, ten *major* ascents and descents as you scramble across valley after valley, with no refreshments along the way (unless you divert off the path to Morwenstow, Map 51x) until right near the end.

Thankfully, the rewards are manifold: the views along the way, especially the panorama at Higher Sharpnose Point, the vista south from Steeple Point and the aspect from Yeolmouth Cliff back to Devil's Hole, are little short of magnificent. If surveying the scenery is difficult due to inclement conditions you can find shelter in the huts of writers Rev Stephen Hawker, near Morwenstow, and Ronald Duncan, above the border with Cornwall. While if the weather is good, it seems churlish not to pay a visit to the endless stretch of sand before Bude. All this, and we haven't even mentioned the waterfalls (with a particularly fine example at Speke's Mill Mouth), Iron Age forts, Roman sites, and the sheer joy of being on one of the most remote and beautiful stretches of coastline this country can offer.

HARTLAND QUAY [MAP 48x, p322]

In Tudor times this was a major port but a storm in 1887 destroyed the quay, and now there's only a small modern slipway and *Hartland Quay Hotel* (☎ 01237-441218, 🖳 hartlandquayhotel.co.uk, **fb**; 13 rooms, 12 en suite; ☛; from £55pp, sgl/sgl occ £70/80). It has its own **museum** (Easter-Oct 11am-4pm), with photos and mementoes of various local shipwrecks. (They've plenty of raw material: it's said that this coastline has about ten shipwrecks per

mile!). The hotel's bar, the *Wreckers Retreat*, serves **food** (daily noon-2.30pm & 6-8.30pm, summer also 3-5pm; mains from £10).

Campers can pitch tents at the welcoming and well-facilitated *Stoke Barton Farm* (☎ 01237-441238 or 07766-766176, 🖳 westcountry-camping.co.uk; adult/child £9/3.50; WI-FI shop only; ☛; Mar-Oct), half a mile inland in the village of Stoke.

The route

Despite the fearsome reputation of this stage, the beginning of the walk is rather gentle as you leave Hartland Quay to head towards the triangular promontory of **St Catherine's Tor**. The path ignores the scramble up the Tor (which is believed to have had a Roman villa on its summit), preferring instead to follow **Wargery Water** upstream, a waterway that ends its journey in impressive fashion by plummeting over the cliffs to the north of the Tor. Those who miss this waterfall (which, after all, is not actually on the path) needn't be too concerned, for the next valley, **Speke's Mill Mouth**, has, if anything, an even more spectacular version, and one that is easily visible just a few metres from the path.

Climbing out of the combe – the first of many calf-popping ascents – takes you up **Swansford Hill** and past the turn-off to **Elmscott**.

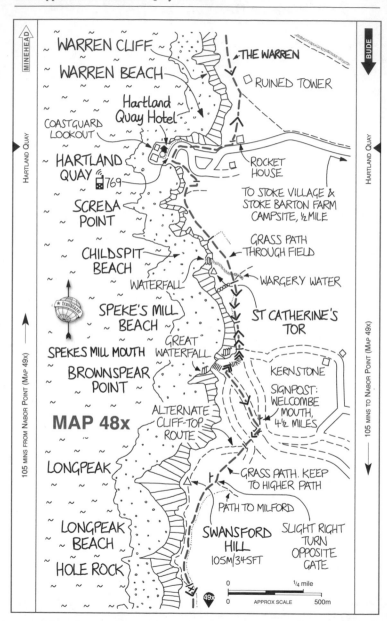

MINEHEAD

BUDE

HARTLAND QUAY

HARTLAND QUAY

105 MINS FROM NABOR POINT (MAP 49x)

105 MINS TO NABOR POINT (MAP 49x)

~ WARREN CLIFF ~

~ WARREN BEACH ~

THE WARREN

RUINED TOWER

Hartland ~ Quay Hotel

COASTGUARD LOOKOUT

~ HARTLAND QUAY

769

ROCKET HOUSE

TO STOKE VILLAGE & STOKE BARTON FARM CAMPSITE, ½ MILE

~ SCREDA POINT

~ CHILDSPIT BEACH

GRASS PATH THROUGH FIELD

WATERFALL

WARGERY WATER

~ SPEKE'S MILL BEACH ~

ST CATHERINE'S TOR

SPEKES MILL MOUTH

GREAT WATERFALL

KERNSTONE

~ BROWNSPEAR POINT

SIGNPOST: WELCOMBE MOUTH, 4½ MILES

MAP 48x

ALTERNATE CLIFF-TOP ROUTE

~ LONGPEAK

GRASS PATH. KEEP TO HIGHER PATH

PATH TO MILFORD

~ LONGPEAK BEACH ~

SWANSFORD HILL 105M/345FT

SLIGHT RIGHT TURN OPPOSITE GATE

~ HOLE ROCK

49x

0   ¼ mile

0   APPROX SCALE   500m

★ trailblazer

ELMSCOTT   [off MAP 49x, p324]

Elmscott is a 10- to 15-minute walk from the path and the accommodation is rather pleasant. Privately-owned, but YHA-affiliated, *YHA Elmscott* (☎ 01237-441367 or 01237-441276, 🖳 elmscott.org.uk, or 🖳 yha.org.uk/hostel/elmscott-bunkhouse; 32 beds, shared facilities; Mar-Oct; from £22pp) was originally a Victorian school. Now a cosy hostel, it has a small **shop** (8-10am & 5-10pm), good kitchen facilities (which is just as well as meals aren't provided) and a drying room. You can also **camp** (£10pp; booking recommended), although they only have room for four tents.

Elmscott Farm, on which it is set, is also a **B&B** (☎ 01237-441276, 🖳 elmscott.org.uk; 2D en suite/1T private bathroom; 🛒; (£); from £40pp) under the same ownership as the hostel. They don't do evening meals but will direct you to the local pub.

The path is rather uneventful to **Nabor Point**, even joining a road at one stage, and only gets exciting again at **Embury Beacon**, where the path runs alongside the defensive earthwork of an Iron Age fort. Yet another vertiginous descent follows, this time at **Welcombe Mouth**, where the path crosses the stream on stepping stones. It's a beautiful spot – and popular with wild campers – but it's surpassed in its noteworthiness for walkers only, perhaps, by the next laceration in the surface of the land: **Marsland Valley** where you'll find **Ronald Duncan's hut**. Author, poet, playwright and pacifist, Duncan is perhaps best known for writing the libretto of Benjamin's Britten's opera *The Rape of Lucretia*, but also for this lovely hut, constructed for views over the sea while writing, and restored by members of his family in recent years.

Struggle down the steps to the floor of the valley and you cross the **border into Cornwall**, the exact boundary marked by a bridge and a signpost welcoming you to 'Kernow' (as they call it round here). But while the county might have changed, the path remains as challenging as ever as you traverse yet more stamina-sapping undulations at **Litter Mouth** and **Yeol Mouth** and around **St Morwenna's Well** – so easy to write, so exhausting to hike.

Thankfully, soon after the latter, it's possible to get off the rollercoaster for a while by taking the short diversion to the hamlet of **Morwenstow**.

MORWENSTOW   [MAP 51x, p326]

There's little more to this ancient settlement than a church, a tearoom and a pub. All three, however, are full of character. The church is dedicated to St Morwenna and St John the Baptist, and while the earliest part of the current church is Norman, there is believed to have been a church on this site since Anglo-Saxon times. The Rev Hawker, of Hawker's Hut fame (see p329), was one of the vicars here.

Opposite sits the award-winning *Rectory Farm Tearoom* (☎ 01288-331251, 🖳 rectory-tearooms.co.uk, **fb**; Easter-Oct daily 11am-5pm, winter hours vary; 🐾), part of a charming 13th-century farm that's been serving cream-topped scones to hungry walkers for 60 years. Gluten- and dairy-free options are available and they also do sandwiches, pasties, cakes and tarts, as well as beer, cider, and clotted-cream ice cream.

To the south, the 13th-century *Bush Inn* (☎ 01288-331242, 🖳 thebushinnmorwenstow.com, **fb**; 2D/2T; 🛒; 🐾; from £47.50pp, sgl occ £80; summer min 2 nights) provides **B&B** and serves pub **food** (daily noon-2.30pm & 5.30-8.45pm). Ask the owners to point out some of the ancient features of the inn, including the lepers' squint, through which the diseased of the parish were fed scraps, and a monastic cross carved into a flagstone in the floor.

(cont'd on p329)

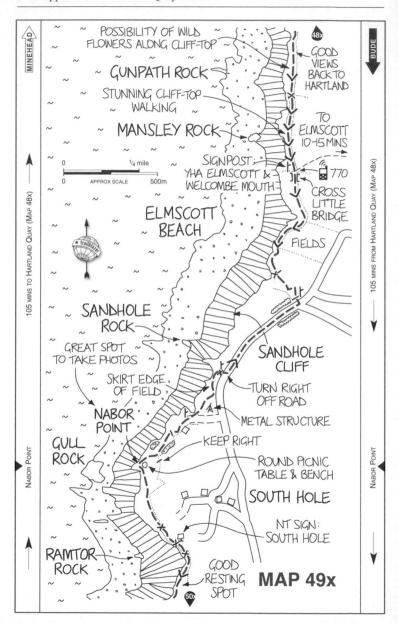

MINEHEAD

BUDE

POSSIBILITY OF WILD FLOWERS ALONG CLIFF-TOP

48x

GOOD VIEWS BACK TO HARTLAND

GUNPATH ROCK

STUNNING CLIFF-TOP WALKING

TO ELMSCOTT 10-15 MINS

MANSLEY ROCK

SIGNPOST: YHA ELMSCOTT & WELCOMBE MOUTH

770

CROSS LITTLE BRIDGE

0   ¼ mile
0   APPROX SCALE   500m

ELMSCOTT BEACH

FIELDS

trailblazer

SANDHOLE ROCK

GREAT SPOT TO TAKE PHOTOS

SANDHOLE CLIFF

SKIRT EDGE OF FIELD

TURN RIGHT OFF ROAD

METAL STRUCTURE

NABOR POINT

KEEP RIGHT

GULL ROCK

ROUND PICNIC TABLE & BENCH

SOUTH HOLE

NT SIGN: SOUTH HOLE

RAMTOR ROCK

GOOD RESTING SPOT

MAP 49x

50x

105 MINS TO HARTLAND QUAY (MAP 48x)

105 MINS FROM HARTLAND QUAY (MAP 48x)

NABOR POINT

NABOR POINT

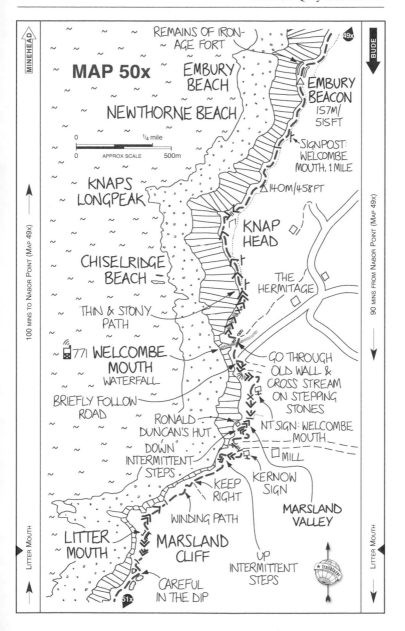

MINEHEAD

BUDE

REMAINS OF IRON-
AGE FORT

MAP 50x

EMBURY
BEACH

NEWTHORNE BEACH

EMBURY
BEACON
157M/
515FT

SIGNPOST:
WELCOMBE
MOUTH, 1 MILE

△140M/458FT

0   ¼ mile

0   APPROX SCALE   500m

KNAPS
LONGPEAK

KNAP
HEAD

CHISELRIDGE
BEACH

THE
HERMITAGE

THIN & STONY
PATH

📱771 WELCOMBE
MOUTH
WATERFALL

GO THROUGH
OLD WALL &
CROSS STREAM
ON STEPPING
STONES

BRIEFLY FOLLOW
ROAD

NT SIGN: WELCOMBE
MOUTH

RONALD
DUNCAN'S HUT

☐ MILL

DOWN
INTERMITTENT
STEPS

KERNOW
SIGN

KEEP
RIGHT

MARSLAND
VALLEY

WINDING PATH

LITTER
MOUTH

MARSLAND
CLIFF

UP
INTERMITTENT
STEPS

★ trailblazer

CAREFUL
IN THE DIP

100 MINS TO NABOR POINT (MAP 49x)

90 MINS FROM NABOR POINT (MAP 49x)

LITTER MOUTH

LITTER MOUTH

49x

51x

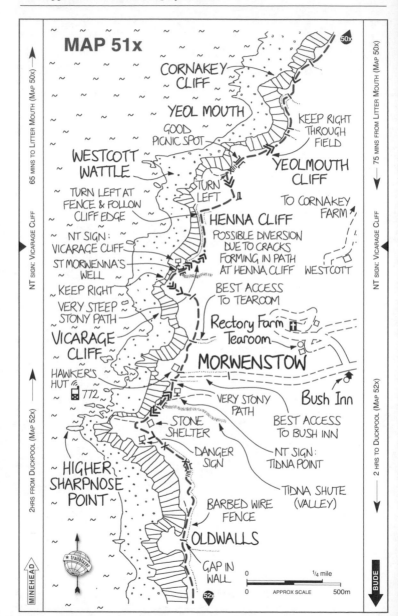

MAP 51x

65 MINS TO LITTER MOUTH (MAP 50x)

NT SIGN: VICARAGE CLIFF

2HRS FROM DUCKPOOL (MAP 52x)

MINEHEAD

50x

CORNAKEY CLIFF

YEOL MOUTH

KEEP RIGHT THROUGH FIELD

GOOD PICNIC SPOT

WESTCOTT WATTLE

YEOLMOUTH CLIFF

TURN LEFT AT FENCE & FOLLOW CLIFF EDGE

TURN LEFT

TO CORNAKEY FARM

HENNA CLIFF

NT SIGN: VICARAGE CLIFF

POSSIBLE DIVERSION DUE TO CRACKS FORMING IN PATH AT HENNA CLIFF

ST MORWENNA'S WELL

WESTCOTT

KEEP RIGHT

BEST ACCESS TO TEAROOM

VERY STEEP STONY PATH

Rectory Farm Tearoom

VICARAGE CLIFF

MORWENSTOW

HAWKER'S HUT

772

Bush Inn

VERY STONY PATH

BEST ACCESS TO BUSH INN

STONE SHELTER

DANGER SIGN

NT SIGN: TIDNA POINT

HIGHER SHARPNOSE POINT

TIDNA SHUTE (VALLEY)

BARBED WIRE FENCE

OLDWALLS

GAP IN WALL

52x

0   ¼ mile

0   APPROX SCALE   500m

trailblazer

75 MINS FROM LITTER MOUTH (MAP 50x)

NT SIGN: VICARAGE CLIFF

2 HRS TO DUCKPOOL (MAP 52x)

BUDE

MINEHEAD

BUDE

2HRS TO NT SIGN: VICARAGE CLIFF (MAP 51x)

2 HRS FROM NT SIGN: VICARAGE CLIFF (MAP 51x)

ACORN SYMBOL:
STANBURY MOUTH

KEEP RIGHT AT
INLAND FOOTPATH
SIGN

~ HIPPA
~ ROCK ~

~ STANBURY
~ MOUTH ~

INTERMITTENT STEPS-
CAN BE MUDDY!

ACORN SYMBOL-
KEEP STRAIGHT

~ LOWER
SHARPNOSE
~ POINT ~

TURN
RIGHT 773

HARSCOTT
HIGH CLIFF

GCHQ
BUDE

FIRST VIEWS OF
CORNISH SAND

FOLLOW CLIFF EDGE

~ SQUENCH ~
~ ROCK ~

NT SIGN:
STEEPLE
POINT

WALKING OVER
ROLLING CLIFFS

~ PIGSBACK ROCK

PATH GOES
THROUGH CAR
PARK &
CROSSES ROAD

~ ROCKY PATH ~

~ STEEPLE POINT ~

DUCKPOOL
COTTAGE

~ NT SIGN:
DUCKPOOL

~ DUCKPOOL ~

WARREN
POINT

~ MUSSEL ROCK ~

MAP 52x

0   ¼ mile

0   APPROX SCALE   500m

DUCKPOOL

DUCKPOOL

MINEHEAD

MINEHEAD

BUDE

53x

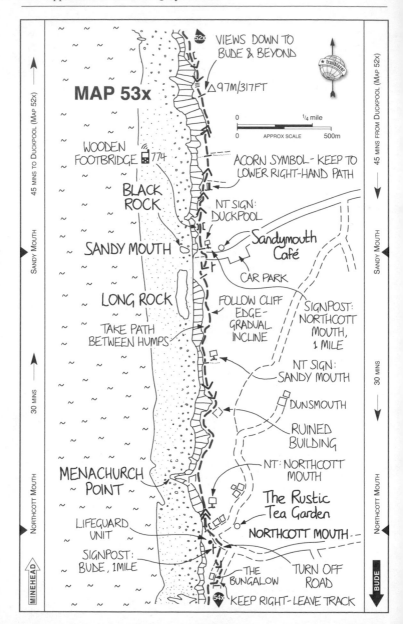

MAP 53x

VIEWS DOWN TO BUDE & BEYOND

△97M/317FT

0   ¼ mile
0   500m
APPROX SCALE

WOODEN FOOTBRIDGE ◻774

ACORN SYMBOL – KEEP TO LOWER RIGHT-HAND PATH

BLACK ROCK

NT SIGN: DUCKPOOL

SANDY MOUTH

Sandymouth Café

CAR PARK

LONG ROCK

FOLLOW CLIFF EDGE – GRADUAL INCLINE

SIGNPOST: NORTHCOTT MOUTH, 1 MILE

TAKE PATH BETWEEN HUMPS

NT SIGN: SANDY MOUTH

DUNSMOUTH

RUINED BUILDING

MENACHURCH ~ POINT ~

NT: NORTHCOTT MOUTH

The Rustic Tea Garden

NORTHCOTT MOUTH

LIFEGUARD UNIT

SIGNPOST: BUDE, 1MILE

THE BUNGALOW

TURN OFF ROAD

KEEP RIGHT – LEAVE TRACK

45 MINS TO DUCKPOOL (MAP 52x)

SANDY MOUTH

30 MINS

NORTHCOTT MOUTH

MINEHEAD

45 MINS FROM DUCKPOOL (MAP 52x)

SANDY MOUTH

30 MINS

NORTHCOTT MOUTH

BUDE

(*cont'd from p323*) Those who forego the delights of Morwenstow will instead continue along **Vicarage Cliff**, in time coming to the cliff-face path to **Hawker's Hut** (easy to miss but if you're following the path right by the cliff you'll see the sign near it), built from the timbers of shipwrecked craft by the eccentric vicar of Morwenstow, the Reverend Stephen Hawker.

Still the relentless gradients of the path continue as you clamber in and out of the valleys of **Tidna Shute** and **Stanbury Mouth**, the latter seemingly the steepest of all today's climbs. Your reward at the top is **GCHQ (Bude)** and its enormous satellite dishes from where, at its southern end, there are views of Bude.

Another steep valley, **Duckpool**, follows, where in July at dusk you can see the rare spectacle of glow worms. Duckpool is also the last serious challenge on this stage. The gradients finally relent now and the path, though still long and undulating, is more merciful than it has been previously on this stage. Cafés (see Map 53x) start to appear on the route too, including *Sandymouth Café* (☎ 01288-354286, 🖳 sandymouth.com; daily 10am-4pm, later in summer) and the lovely eatery, *The Rustic Tea Garden* (☎ 07789-283681; Easter-Oct daily 11am-4pm), by the stream at **Northcott Mouth.** Run by the redoubtable Margaret Frost for 54 years until her death in 2020, it has since been taken on by a local family who serve 'a cracking cream tea'. But by now even this idyllic place may not be enough to halt your determined march to Bude, which you should reach, weary, exhausted and happy, about 2-2½ hours after leaving Duckpool.

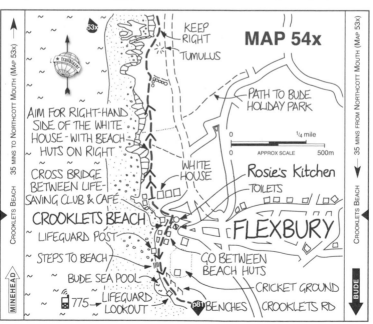

APPENDIX B: GPS WAYPOINTS

MAP	REF	GPS WAYPOINTS		DESCRIPTION
Map 1	001	50 49 601	04 32 803	Falcon Hotel, Bude
Map 1	002	50 49 685	04 33 330	Compass tower
Map 1	003	50 49 427	04 33 380	trig point
Map 1	004	50 48 861	04 33 242	Upton
Map 2	005	50 48 006	04 33 514	stone seat
Map 2	006	50 47 224	04 33 342	Black Rock Café
Map 3	007	50 46 769	04 33 519	junction with road
Map 3	008	50 46 257	04 34 494	Millook
Map 4	009	50 45 632	04 35 924	semi-collapsed trig point
Map 4	010	50 45 425	04 36 795	footbridge, Lower Tresmorn
Map 5	011	50 44 809	04 37 815	footbridge
Map 5	012	50 44 446	04 37 911	Crackington Haven
Map 5	013	50 44 287	04 38 742	boardwalk, Cambeak
Map 6	014	50 43 562	04 38 723	turning to car park
Map 6	015	50 43 039	04 38 957	bench at highest point
Map 6	016	50 42 661	04 39 303	stile
Map 7	017	50 42 458	04 39 721	boardwalk
Map 7	018	50 42 215	04 40 615	gap in hedge
Map 8	019	50 41 826	04 40 942	boardwalk
Map 8	020	50 41 717	04 40 688	gate
Map 8	021	50 41 530	04 41 669	Flagstaff, Penally
Map 8	022	50 41 403	04 41 645	Boscastle Bridge
Map 9	023	50 41 030	04 42 489	steps by ruin
Map 9	024	50 41 000	04 43 286	Lady's Window rock arch
Map 10	025	50 40 372	04 43 693	Rocky Valley
Map 10	026	50 40 201	04 44 213	path to beach
Map 10	027	50 40 315	04 44 440	bench
Map 11	028	50 40 058	04 45 399	café at castle
Map 11	029	50 39 854	04 45 277	path junction
Map 11	030	50 39 553	04 45 777	YHA Tintagel
Map 11	031	50 39 280	04 45 707	gate
Map 11	032	50 39 038	04 45 396	bench
Map 12	033	50 38 651	04 45 574	Trebarwith Strand
Map 12	034	50 38 365	04 45 818	stream crossing
Map 12	035	50 38 053	04 45 987	gate
Map 12	036	50 37 450	04 45 974	path to Tregardock Beach
Map 13	037	50 37 794	04 46 517	path to Tregragon Farm
Map 13	038	50 36 430	04 46 939	stream crossing
Map 13	039	50 36 209	04 47 190	stepping stones
Map 14	040	50 35 974	04 47 456	stile
Map 14	041	50 35 736	04 48 404	boardwalk
Map 14	042	50 35 609	04 49 200	Port Gaverne
Map 15	043	50 35 778	04 50 880	gate at Varley Sand
Map 15	044	50 35 617	04 51 254	bench at Scarnor Point
Map 15	045	50 35 655	04 52 062	bench, Kellan Head
Map 16	046	50 35 437	04 52 187	bench in memory of Sgt Roberts
Map 16	047	50 35 308	04 51 998	stile, Doyden Point
Map 16	048	50 35 097	04 52 795	Trevan Point
Map 16	049	50 34 996	04 53 930	path to Pentireglaze
Map 17	050	50 35 249	04 55 011	path to Pentire Farm

MAP	REF	GPS WAYPOINTS		DESCRIPTION
Map 17	051	50 35 477	04 55 477	stone seat, The Rumps
Map 17	052	50 35 188	04 55 988	Pentire Point
Map 18	053	50 34 770	04 54 940	Pentireglaze Haven
Map 18	054	50 34 414	04 54 989	junction with road, Polzeath
Map 18	055	50 33 838	04 55 769	Trebetherick Point
Map 18	056	50 33 679	04 55 491	steps to Daymer Bay
Map 19	057	50 32 722	04 55 496	Rock car park
Map 19	058	50 32 646	04 55 384	Blue Tomato Café, Rock
Map 21	059	50 32 808	04 56 040	War Memorial, Padstow
Map 21	060	50 33 204	04 56 957	junction with track
Map 22	061	50 33 570	04 56 892	Hawker's Cove
Map 22	062	50 34 052	04 57 090	daymark tower
Map 22	063	50 33 415	04 57 988	path to road
Map 23	064	50 32 681	04 58 601	Trevone Beach steps
Map 23	065	50 32 344	04 59 632	Harlyn Bridge
Map 23	066	50 32 728	05 00 213	bench at viewpoint
Map 24	067	50 32 581	05 00 889	junction with path
Map 24	068	50 32 892	05 02 018	Trevose Head
Map 24	069	50 32 422	05 01 489	gate near first house in Booby's Bay
Map 24	070	50 31 851	05 01 318	beach exit south
Map 25	071	50 31 491	05 01 307	steps up from beach, Constantine Bay
Map 25	072	50 31 015	05 01 571	steps
Map 25	073	50 30 521	05 01 208	bridge at Porthcothan
Map 26	074	50 30 168	05 01 998	footbridge
Map 26	075	50 29 870	05 02 409	cairn
Map 26	076	50 28 830	05 01 861	National Trust shop, Carnewas
Map 27	077	50 27 866	05 01 834	Mawgan Porth
Map 27	078	50 27 586	05 02 163	path to Bre-Pen Farm
Map 28	079	50 26 622	05 02 472	Watergate Bay
Map 29	080	50 25 522	05 03 134	bridge at Porth Beach
Map 29	081	50 25 033	05 04 236	path junction with road
Map 30	082	50 25 141	05 05 408	war memorial, Headland
Map 31	083	50 25 104	05 05 779	Rick Stein Fistral
Map 31	084	50 24 720	05 06 060	Esplanade toilets, Fistral Beach
Map 31	085	50 24 420	05 05 883	Penpol footbridge
Map 31	086	50 24 341	05 06 699	car park
Map 31a	087	50 24 319	05 04 641	Laurie Bridge
Map 32	088	50 24 253	05 07 616	Crantock Beach Steps
Map 32	089	50 24 041	05 08 972	footbridge, Porth Joke
Map 33	090	50 23 333	05 08 560	bridge crosses stream in dunes
Map 33	091	50 23 172	05 08 358	bus stop by Treguth Inn
Map 33	092	50 22 788	05 08 979	gate by isolated farm
Map 33	093	50 22 459	05 08 653	top of path to beach
Map 34	094	50 20 694	05 09 209	Beach Rd, Perranporth
Map 35	095	50 20 336	05 10 704	quarry, Cligga Head
Map 36	096	50 19 577	05 11 383	airstrip
Map 36	097	50 19 253	05 11 505	Blue Hills Tin Mine
Map 36	098	50 19 108	05 12 062	toilets, Trevaunance Cove
Map 37	099	50 19 057	05 13 888	St Agnes Head
Map 37	100	50 18 027	05 13 926	chimney, Wheal Coates
Map 37	101	50 17 976	05 14 011	Chapel Porth
Map 38	102	50 17 231	05 14 417	Porthtowan Beach

MAP	REF	GPS WAYPOINTS		DESCRIPTION
Map 38	103	50 16 755	05 15 319	chimney
Map 39	104	50 16 578	05 15 513	stream crossing, Nancekuke
Map 39	105	50 16 353	05 16 526	concrete shelter
Map 40	106	50 15 821	05 17 019	car park, Portreath
Map 40	107	50 15 645	05 17 517	Portreath beach
Map 41	108	50 15 528	05 18 117	path opposite The Horse
Map 41	109	50 15 312	05 18 466	bridge, Porthcadjack Cove
Map 41	110	50 14 915	05 18 765	car park exit
Map 42	111	50 14 408	05 19 807	car park, Deadman's Cove
Map 43	112	50 14 196	05 21 639	Hell's Mouth
Map 43	113	50 14 471	05 22 687	trig point, The Knavocks
Map 44	114	50 13 803	05 23 226	Godrevy Beach Café
Map 44	115	50 13 233	05 23 084	Gwithian
Map 45	116	50 12 287	05 24 715	Phillack Towans car park
Map 46	117	50 11 278	05 25 276	Hayle tidal gate
Map 46	118	50 11 033	05 25 211	Hayle Viaduct
Map 47	119	50 10 651	05 26 484	path leaves car park at Lelant Saltings
Map 47	120	50 11 271	05 26 129	St Uny Church
Map 48	121	50 11 804	05 27 714	road at Carbis Bay
Map 48	122	50 12 312	05 28 239	shelter, Porthminster Point
Map 48	123	50 12 538	05 28 612	Porthminster Station
Map 49	124	50 12 856	05 28 707	St Ives post office
Map 50	125	50 12 949	05 29 300	shelter
Map 50	126	50 12 862	05 30 674	stream crossing
Map 51	127	50 12 775	05 31 345	Trevalgan ancient stone circle
Map 51	128	50 12 779	05 32 168	trig point, Carn Naun Point
Map 51	129	50 12 613	05 32 534	stream, River Cove
Map 51	130	50 12 143	05 33 246	stream crossing
Map 52	131	50 11 742	05 34 421	turn for Zennor
Map 52	132	50 11 839	05 34 553	Zennor Head
Map 52	133	50 11 697	05 34 375	gap in hedge
Map 52	134	50 11 473	05 34 002	Tinner's Arms, Zennor
Map 52	135	50 11 669	05 34 485	stream, Pendour Cove
Map 52	136	50 11 385	05 35 028	stream, Porthglaze Cove
Map 53	137	50 11 300	05 35 864	path junction to Gurnard's Head
Map 53	138	50 10 817	05 36 269	stream, Porthmeor Cove
Map 54	139	50 10 503	05 37 096	Bosigran Castle
Map 54	140	50 10 397	05 37 009	stone bridge, Porthmoina Cove
Map 54	141	50 09 924	05 37 839	stream crossing, Trevowhan Cliff
Map 55	142	50 09 935	05 38 345	stile, Morvah Cliff
Map 55	143	50 09 799	05 39 328	buoyancy aid, Portheras Cove
Map 56	144	50 09 823	05 40 178	car park, Pendeen Watch
Map 56	145	50 09 567	05 40 280	stream, Enys Zawn
Map 56	146	50 09 304	05 40 699	footbridge, Geevor
Map 57	147	50 08 654	05 41 465	trig point, Botallack Head
Map 57	148	50 08 071	05 41 667	gate and stone stile
Map 57	149	50 07 926	05 41 953	change of direction to right
Map 58	150	50 07 591	05 42 224	Cape Cornwall car park
Map 58	151	50 07 325	05 42 106	trig point Ballowal Barrow
Map 58	152	50 07 049	05 41 590	junction in path
Map p183	152a	50 07 431	05 40 721	St Just Square
Map 59	153	50 06 892	05 41 843	turn in path

MAP	REF	GPS WAYPOINTS		DESCRIPTION
Map 59	154	50 06 289	05 41 742	stream crossing, Maen Dower
Map 60	155	50 05 874	05 41 699	rocky outcrop
Map 60	156	50 05 273	05 41 237	lifeguard station
Map 60	157	50 04 796	05 41 401	junction with path inland
Map 61	158	50 04 635	05 42 091	car park, Sennen Cove
Map 61	159	50 04 634	05 42 263	toilets, Sennen Cove
Map 61	160	50 04 059	05 42 859	Land's End
Map 61	161	50 03 320	05 42 207	Trevilley Cliff
Map 62	162	50 03 197	05 41 470	Nanjizal
Map 62	163	50 02 211	05 40 545	black and white daymark tower
Map 62	164	50 02 235	05 40 283	Porthgwarra
Map 63	165	50 02 333	05 39 575	Carn Scathe
Map 63	166	50 02 599	05 39 059	Porthcurno
Map 63	167	50 02 654	05 38 011	stream crossing, Gamper
Map 64	168	50 02 831	05 37 704	Penberth Cove
Map 64	169	50 03 048	05 37 107	stream, Porth Guarnon
Map 64	170	50 03 024	05 36 363	sign on rock
Map 65	171	50 03 118	05 36 066	Cove Cottage, St Loy
Map 66	172	50 03 201	05 34 887	metal gate
Map 66	173	50 03 319	05 34 096	path junction, Carn Barges
Map 66	174	50 03 657	05 33 788	Lamorna Cove
Map 67	175	50 03 639	05 33 216	steps, Carn-Du
Map 67	176	50 04 207	05 32 616	bench
Map 68	177	50 04 596	05 32 453	road junction
Map 68	178	50 04 977	05 32 283	war memorial, Mousehole
Map 69	179	50 06 366	05 32 907	Newlyn Bridge
Map 70	180	50 06 881	05 31 901	Jubilee Pool, Penzance
Map 70	181	50 07 266	05 31 888	bus station, Penzance
Map 72	182	50 07 388	05 28 424	Godolphin Arms, Marazion
Map 73	183	50 07 398	05 27 485	path leaves road, Marazion
Map 73	184	50 06 756	05 26 496	Perran Sands
Map 74	185	50 05 950	05 25 525	Cudden Point
Map 75	186	50 06 050	05 25 063	steps to beach, Bessy's Cove
Map 75	187	50 06 194	05 24 179	stream crossing, Pestreath Cove
Map 76	188	50 06 217	05 23 484	road by Sandbar Café, Praa Sands
Map 76	189	50 06 053	05 22 860	beach exit, Praa Sands
Map 77	190	50 05 703	05 22 061	car park, Porthcew
Map 77	191	50 05 428	05 21 269	Grey Stone Mine
Map 78	192	50 05 477	05 20 209	stream crossing, Tremearne Cliff
Map 79	193	50 05 053	05 19 370	Grylls' Act Memorial
Map 79	194	50 05 085	05 18 911	Porthleven Harbour
Map 80	195	50 04 034	05 17 433	HMS Anson Memorial
Map 81	196	50 03 270	05 16 601	ruin by Gunwalloe beach
Map 81	197	50 02 402	05 16 130	St Winwaloe Church
Map 82	198	50 02 005	05 15 507	Poldhu Cove
Map 82	199	50 01 704	05 15 707	Marconi Monument
Map 82	200	50 01 418	05 15 279	steps, Polurrian Cove
Map 82	201	50 00 893	05 15 385	Mullion Cove
Map 82a	202	50 01 613	05 14 488	Mullion Church
Map 83	203	50 00 515	05 15 594	stream, Mullion Cliff
Map 83	204	50 00 045	05 15 816	stile, Predannack Head
Map 83	205	49 59 860	05 15 273	stream, Parc Bean Cove

MAP	REF	GPS WAYPOINTS		DESCRIPTION
Map 84	206	49 59 008	05 14 471	gorge, Gew-Graze
Map 85	207	49 58 487	05 13 818	Kynance Cove
Map 86	208	49 57 583	05 12 541	footpath to Lizard Village
Map 86	209	49 58 092	05 12 165	Lizard Green
Map 86	210	49 57 506	05 12 308	most southerly point
Map 86	211	49 57 803	05 11 800	Housel Cove
Map 86	212	49 57 769	05 11 139	National Coast Watch, Bass Point
Map 86	213	49 58 227	05 11 267	Church Cove
Map 87	214	49 58 372	05 11 332	beacon
Map 87	215	49 58 476	05 11 209	stream crossing, Parn Voose Cove
Map 87	216	49 59 218	05 10 714	Cadgwith Cove
Map 87	217	49 59 832	05 10 337	bridge, Little Cove
Map 88	218	50 00 300	05 09 750	Kennack Sands West
Map 89	219	50 00 535	05 07 610	gate and stile, Zawn Vinoc
Map 90	220	50 00 530	05 07 306	stream, Downas Cove
Map 90	221	50 00 405	05 06 872	stream, Meludjack
Map 91	222	50 00 285	05 06 088	Black Head National Trust lookout
Map 91	223	50 00 751	05 05 906	bench, Chynhall's Cliff
Map 91	224	50 01 436	05 05 791	Coverack Harbour
Map 93	225	50 02 094	05 04 073	Lowland Point
Map 93	226	50 02 849	05 04 018	wooden bridge
Map 93	227	50 03 100	05 04 092	path leaves lane
Map 93	228	50 03 333	05 03 926	Porthoustock
Map 94	229	50 03 766	05 04 609	junction with road
Map 94	230	50 04 023	05 04 703	Porthallow
Map 94	231	50 05 087	05 04 551	Nare Point
Map 95	232	50 05 188	05 06 020	steps, Gillan Creek
Map 95	233	50 04 771	05 07 509	path to Manaccan
Map 95	234	50 05 335	05 06 018	St Anthony-in-Meneage
Map 95	235	50 05 558	05 06 496	Ponsence Cove
Map 96	236	50 05 454	05 08 083	ford, Helford
Map 96	237	50 05 512	05 08 000	bus stop, car park, Helford
Map 96	238	50 05 701	05 07 978	ferry landing, Helford
Map 96	239	50 05 184	05 08 475	Kestle
Map 96a	240	50 04 755	05 09 806	crossroads, Mudgeon Farm
Map 96b	241	50 04 851	05 12 114	Mawgan Church
Map 96b	242	50 05 791	05 12 422	The Black Swan, Gweek
Map 96c	243	50 06 634	05 10 356	Trengilly Wartha pub
Map 96d	244	50 06 405	05 08 645	Porth Navas
Map 96d	245	50 06 671	05 08 196	Trenarth Bridge
Map 96d	246	50 06 331	05 07 421	crossroads
Map 96d	247	50 05 986	05 07 660	Helford Passage
Map 97	248	50 06 202	05 06 884	Durgan
Map p248	248a	50 06 966	05 06 497	Red Lion, Mawnan Smith
Map 98	249	50 06 587	05 04 958	Rosemullion Head
Map 99	250	50 07 477	05 05 615	Maenporth Beach
Map 99	251	50 08 039	05 04 417	Home Guard Memorial
Map 99	252	50 08 423	05 04 512	beach exit, Swanpool Beach
Map 100	253	50 08 646	05 04 035	Gyllyngvase Beach
Map 100	254	50 08 780	05 02 862	Pendennis Point
Map 100	255	50 09 351	05 04 180	Visitor Centre, Prince of Wales pier
Map 101	256	50 09 464	05 00 834	ferry point St Mawes

MAP	REF	GPS WAYPOINTS		DESCRIPTION
Map 101	257	50 09 152	05 00 257	low-tide ferry landing
Map 101a	256a	50 09 354	05 01 375	St Mawes Castle
Map 101b	256b	50 11 197	05 00 579	stile off road
Map 101b	256c	50 11 331	04 59 853	turn off road
Map 102	258	50 09 432	04 59 012	junction with path to Porth Farm
Map 103	259	50 10 739	04 58 457	Plume of Feathers, Portscatho
Map 104	260	50 12 309	04 57 173	top of alleyway by Pendower Farm
Map 105	261	50 11 840	04 55 122	junction with path from Nare Head
Map 106	262	50 12 832	04 54 057	gate beside house
Map 106	263	50 13 090	04 53 495	Portloe United church
Map 107	264	50 14 118	04 51 632	East Portholland
Map 108	265	50 14 219	04 50 342	gate behind trees
Map 109	266	50 13 169	04 48 122	stone cross at Dodman Point
Map 110	267	50 14 632	04 47 128	broken stile
Map 111	268	50 15 351	04 46 197	track to Chapel Point
Map 111	269	50 16 185	04 47 137	road junction by Mevagissey Harbour
Map 112	270	50 17 537	04 46 785	turn-off road out of Pentewan
Map 113	271	50 18 011	04 45 309	Rowse Stone
Map 114	272	50 19 964	04 45 463	junction of Charlestown Rd & Duporth Rd
Map 115	273	50 20 607	04 42 442	join road leading into Par
Map 116	274	50 19 020	04 40 391	Daymark Tower
Map 117	275	50 19 582	04 37 978	right turn outside Polruan
Map 118	276	50 19 512	04 35 992	Pencarrow Head
Map 119	277	50 19 677	04 33 501	white stone tower
Map 120	278	50 19 873	04 30 151	Cross at Downend Point
Map 121	279	50 20 652	04 27 478	Lamman Chapel
Map 122	280	50 21 362	04 27 395	bridge at Looe
Map 123	281	50 21 850	04 25 054	Labyrinth
Map 124	282	50 21 689	04 21 908	main road past village school
Map 125	283	50 21 741	04 18 417	turn off from road
Map 126	284	50 21 559	04 17 369	junction of two paths
Map 126	285	50 20 899	04 15 463	path above Sharrow Point
Map 127	286	50 20 397	04 14 168	path leaves road
Map 128	287	50 18 820	04 13 389	Chapel at Rame Head
Map 129	288	50 20 075	04 12 045	gate into Edgcumbe Park
Map 130	289	50 20 749	04 10 397	grotto and chapel
Map 130	290	50 21 627	04 10 492	Cremyll Ferry

Hartland Quay to Bude

Map 48x	769	N50 59.631 W4 31.968	Hartland Quay
Map 49x	770	N50 58.069 W4 31.795	turn-off to YHA Elmscott
Map 50x	771	N50 55.988 W4 32.624	Welcombe Mouth
Map 51x	772	N50 54.389 W4 33.720	Hawker's Hut
Map 52x	773	N50 53.129 W4 33.531	right turn by radio station
Map 53x	774	N50 51.659 W4 33.224	wooden footbridge at Sandy Mouth
Map 54x	775	N50 50.121 W4 33.129	lifeguard lookout

APPENDIX C: TAKING A DOG ALONG THE PATH

The South-West Coast Path is a dog-friendly path and many are the rewards that await those prepared to make the extra effort required to bring their best friend along the trail. However, you shouldn't underestimate the amount of work involved in bringing your pooch to the path. Indeed, just about every decision you make will be influenced by the fact that you've got a dog: how you plan to travel to the start of the trail, where you're going to stay, how far you're going to walk each day, where you're going to rest and where you're going to eat in the evening etc etc.

The decision-making begins well before you've set foot on the trail. For starters, you have to ask – and be honest with – yourself: can your dog really cope with walking 10+ miles (16+km) a day, day after day, week after week? And just as importantly, will he or she actually enjoy it?

If you think the answer is yes to both, you need to start preparing accordingly. For one thing, extra thought also needs to go into your itinerary. The best starting point is to study the Village & Town Facilities table on pp32-5 (and the advice below), and plan where to stop, where to eat, where to buy food for your mutt.

Looking after your dog

To begin with, you need to make sure that your own dog is fully **inoculated** against the usual doggy illnesses, and also up to date with regard to **worm pills** (eg Drontal) and **flea preventatives** such as Frontline – they are, after all, following in the pawprints of many a dog before them, some of whom may well have left fleas or other parasites on the trail that now lie in wait for their next meal to arrive. **Pet insurance** is also a very good idea; if you've already got insurance, do check that it will cover a trip such as this.

On the subject of looking after your dog's health, perhaps the most important implement you can take with you is the **plastic tick remover**, available from vets for a couple of quid. Ticks are a real problem on the SWCP, as they hide in the long grass waiting for unsuspecting victims to trot past. These removers, while fiddly, help you to remove the tick safely (ie without leaving its head behind buried under the dog's skin).

Being in unfamiliar territory also makes it more likely that you and your dog could become separated. All dogs now have to be **microchipped**, but make sure your dog also has a **tag with your contact details on it** (a mobile phone number would be best if you are carrying one with you).

Dogs on beaches

There is no general rule regarding whether dogs are allowed on beaches or not. Some of the beaches on the SWCP are open to dogs all year; some allow them on the beach only outside the summer season (Easter or 1 May to 30 September); while a few beaches don't allow dogs at all. (Guide dogs, by the way, are usually excluded from any bans.) If in doubt, look for the noticeboards that tell you the exact rules. A useful website for further details is 🖥 cornwall-beaches.co.uk/dog-friendly. Where dogs are banned from a beach there will usually be an alternative path that you can take that avoids the sands. If there isn't an alternative, and you have no choice but to cross the beach even though dogs are officially banned, you are permitted to do so as long as you cross the beach as speedily as possible, follow the line of the path (which is usually well above the high-water mark) and keep your dog tightly under control.

Whatever the rules of access are for the beach, remember that your dog shouldn't disturb other beach-users – and you must always **clean up after your dog**.

Finally, remember that you need to bring drinking water with you on the beach as dogs can over-heat with the lack of shade.

When to keep your dog on a lead
● **On cliff tops** It's a sad fact that, every year, a few dogs lose their lives falling over the edge of the cliffs. It usually occurs when they are chasing rabbits (which know where the cliff-edge is and are able, unlike your poor pooch, to stop in time).

● **When crossing farmland**, particularly in the lambing season (around May) when your dog can scare the sheep, causing them to lose their young. Farmers are allowed by law to shoot at and kill any dogs that they consider are worrying their sheep. During lambing, most farmers would prefer it if you didn't bring your dog at all. The exception to the keep-your-dog-on-a-lead-advice is if your dog is being attacked by cows (see box p74); almost every year in the UK at least one or two walkers are trampled to death by cows, usually as they try to rescue their dogs from the attentions of cattle. The advice in this instance is to let go of the lead, head speedily to a position of safety (usually the other side of the field gate or stile) and call your dog to you.

● **On National Trust land**, where it is compulsory to keep your dog on a lead.

● **Around ground-nesting birds** It's important to keep your dog under control when crossing an area where certain species of birds nest on the ground. Most dogs love foraging around in the woods but make sure you have permission to do so; some woods are used as 'nurseries' for game birds and dogs are only allowed through them if they are on a lead.

What to pack
You've probably already got a good idea of what to bring to keep your dog alive and happy, but the following is a checklist:

● **Food/water bowl** Foldable cloth bowls are popular with walkers, being light and take up little room in the rucksack. You can also get a water-bottle-and-bowl combination, where the bottle folds into a 'trough' from which the dog can drink.

● **Lead and collar** An extendable one is probably preferable for this sort of trip. Make sure both lead and collar are in good condition – you don't want either to snap on the trail, or you may end up carrying your dog through sheep fields until a replacement can be found.

● **Medication** You'll know if you need to bring any lotions or potions.

● **Tick remover** See opposite

● **Bedding** A simple blanket may suffice, or you can opt for something more elaborate if you aren't carrying your own luggage.

● **Poo bags** Essential.

● **Hygiene wipes** For cleaning your dog after it's rolled in stuff.

● **A favourite toy** Helps prevent your dog from pining for the entire walk.

● **Food/water** Remember to bring treats as well as regular food to keep up the mutt's morale. That said, if your dog is anything like mine the chances are they'll spend most of the walk dining on rabbit droppings and sheep poo anyway.

● **Corkscrew stake** Available from camping or pet shops, this will help you to keep your dog secure in one place while you set up camp/doze.

● **Raingear** It can rain a lot!

● **Old towels** For drying your dog after the deluge.

How to pack
When it comes to packing, I always leave an exterior pocket of my rucksack empty so I can put used poo bags in there (for deposit at the first bin I come to). I always like to keep all the dog's kit together and separate from the other luggage (usually inside a plastic bag inside my rucksack). I have also seen several dogs sporting their own 'doggy rucksack', so they can carry their own food, water, poo etc – which certainly reduces the burden on their owner!

Cleaning up after your dog
It is extremely important that dog owners behave in a responsible way when walking the path. Dog excrement should be cleaned up. In towns, villages and fields where animals graze

or which will be cut for silage, hay etc, you need to pick up and bag the excrement. In other places you can possibly get away with merely flicking it with a nearby stick into the undergrowth, thus ensuring there is none left on the path to decorate the boots of others.

Staying with your dog

In this guide we have used the symbol 🐕 to denote where a hotel, pub or B&B welcomes dogs. However, this always needs to be arranged in advance and some places may charge extra. Hostels (both YHA and independent) do not permit them unless they are an assistance (guide) dog; smaller campsites tend to accept them, but some of the larger holiday parks do not. Before you turn up always double check whether the place you would like to stay accepts dogs and whether there is space for them; many places have only one or two rooms suitable for people with dogs.

When it comes to eating, most landlords allow dogs in at least a section of their pubs, though few restaurants do. Make sure you always ask first and ensure your dog doesn't run around the pub but is secured to your table or a radiator.

Henry Stedman

Map key

🔷 Where to stay	📖 Library/bookstore	● Other
○ Where to eat and drink	@ Internet	CP Car park
Λ Campsite	🎭 Museum/gallery	🚌 Bus station/stop
⊠ Post Office	✝ Church/cathedral	Rail line & station
£ Bank/ATM	☏ Telephone	▢ Park
ⓘ Tourist Information	☑ Public toilet	GPS waypoint 082
	☐ Building	

South West Coast Path	Sand dunes	Trees/woodland
Other path	Cliffs	Bog or marsh
4 x 4 track	Cornish hedge	Sand
Tarmac road	Bridge	Stones
Steps	Fence	Lighthouse
Slope	Wall	Lifeguard cover
Steep slope	Hedge	Rescue equipment
Stile	Water	Golf course
Gate	Stream/river	Map continuation

INDEX

Page references in red refer to maps

0 | 2 miles
0 | 3km

★ trailblazer

Poughill
Flexbury
Grimscott
A39
MAP 1
Bude
Stratton
Compass Point
Red Post
A3072
Lynstone
Upton
A3072
B3254
Higher Longbreak
Marhamchurch
Lower Longbreak
Bridgerule
Widemouth Sand
Widemouth Bay
MAP 2
MAP 3
A39
Millook
Poundstock
Dizzard Point
Chipman Point
Treskinnick Cross
Whitstone
MAP 5
Dizzard
MAP 4
St Gennys
Week St Mary
Crackington Haven
Middle Crackington
Jacobstow
A39

Elevation profile:
200m
150
100
Chipman Point
Widemouth Bay
Upton
50
Bude
Millook
Crackington Haven
0 miles 2 3 4 5 6 7 8 9 10

Crackington Haven — Bude

Plymouth

Maps 1–5, Bude to Crackington Haven
10 miles/16km – 4-5hrs

NOTE: Add 20-30% to these times to allow for stops

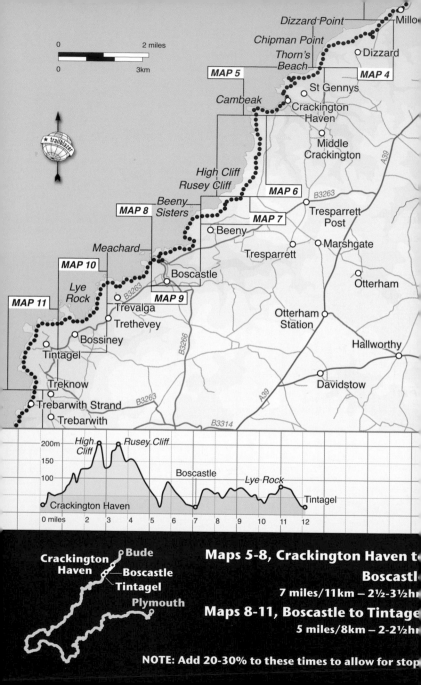

MAP 5

MAP 4

Dizzard Point

Chipman Point

Thorn's Beach

Millo

Dizzard

St Gennys

Cambeak

Crackington Haven

Middle Crackington

High Cliff

Rusey Cliff

MAP 6

B3263

MAP 8

Beeny Sisters

MAP 7

Tresparrett Post

Beeny

Meachard

Tresparrett

Marshgate

MAP 10

Boscastle

Otterham

Lye Rock

MAP 9

MAP 11

Trevalga

Trethevey

Otterham Station

B3266

Bossiney

Hallworthy

Tintagel

Treknow

A39

Trebarwith Strand

B3263

Davidstow

Trebarwith

B3314

0   2 miles

0   3km

★ trailblazer

Elevation profile:

200m
150
100

High Cliff

Rusey Cliff

Boscastle

Lye Rock

Tintagel

Crackington Haven

0 miles   2   3   4   5   6   7   8   9   10   11   12

Bude

Crackington Haven

Boscastle

Tintagel

Plymouth

Maps 5-8, Crackington Haven t

Boscastl

7 miles/11km – 2½-3½hr

Maps 8-11, Boscastle to Tintage

5 miles/8km – 2-2½hr

NOTE: Add 20-30% to these times to allow for stop

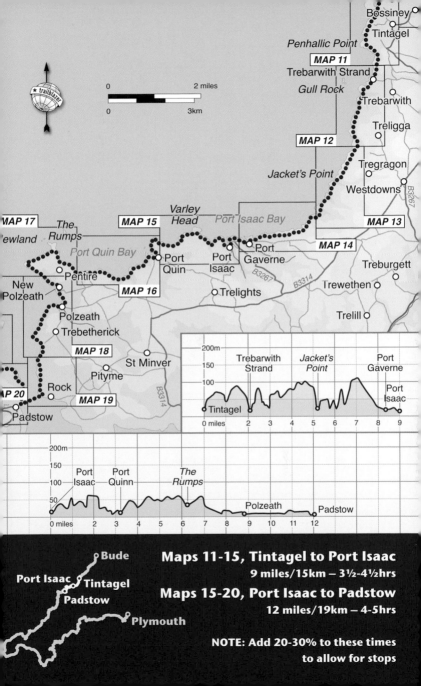

Bossiney

Tintagel

Penhallic Point

MAP 11

Trebarwith Strand

Gull Rock

Trebarwith

Treligga

MAP 12

Tregragon

Westdowns

B3267

Jacket's Point

MAP 13

Varley Head

MAP 15

Port Isaac Bay

MAP 14

The Rumps

MAP 17

Port Quin Bay

Port Quin

Port Isaac

Port Gaverne

Treburgett

ewland

New Polzeath

Pentire

MAP 16

Trelights

B3267

B3314

Trewethen

Polzeath

Trebetherick

MAP 18

St Minver

Pityme

Trelill

Trewethen

B3314

Rock

MAP 19

MAP 20

Padstow

Elevation profile (Map 11–15):

200m
150
100

Trebarwith Strand

Jacket's Point

Port Gaverne

Port Isaac

Tintagel

0 miles 1 2 3 4 5 6 7 8 9

Elevation profile (Map 15–20):

200m
150
100
50

Port Isaac

Port Quinn

The Rumps

Polzeath

Padstow

0 miles 1 2 3 4 5 6 7 8 9 10 11 12

Bude

Port Isaac   Tintagel

Padstow

Plymouth

Maps 11-15, Tintagel to Port Isaac
9 miles/15km – 3½-4½hrs

Maps 15-20, Port Isaac to Padstow
12 miles/19km – 4-5hrs

NOTE: Add 20-30% to these times
to allow for stops

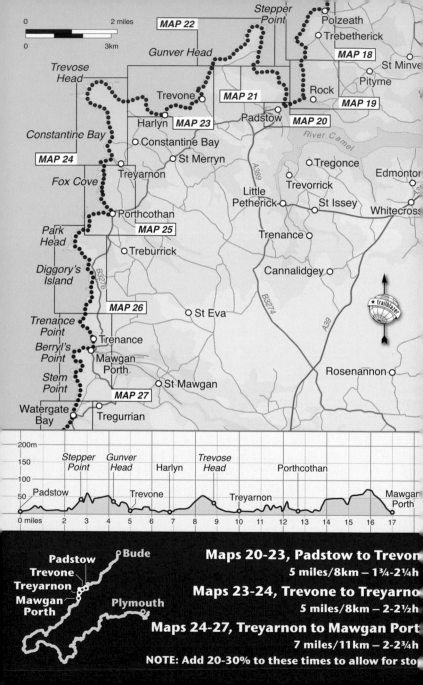

Maps 20-23, Padstow to Trevon
5 miles/8km – 1¾-2¼h

Maps 23-24, Trevone to Treyarno
5 miles/8km – 2-2½h

Maps 24-27, Treyarnon to Mawgan Port
7 miles/11km – 2-2¾h

NOTE: Add 20-30% to these times to allow for stop

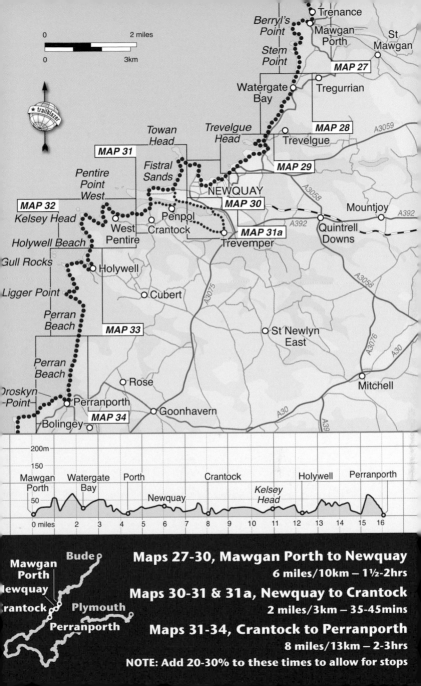

Maps 27-30, Mawgan Porth to Newquay
6 miles/10km – 1½-2hrs

Maps 30-31 & 31a, Newquay to Crantock
2 miles/3km – 35-45mins

Maps 31-34, Crantock to Perranporth
8 miles/13km – 2-3hrs

NOTE: Add 20-30% to these times to allow for stops

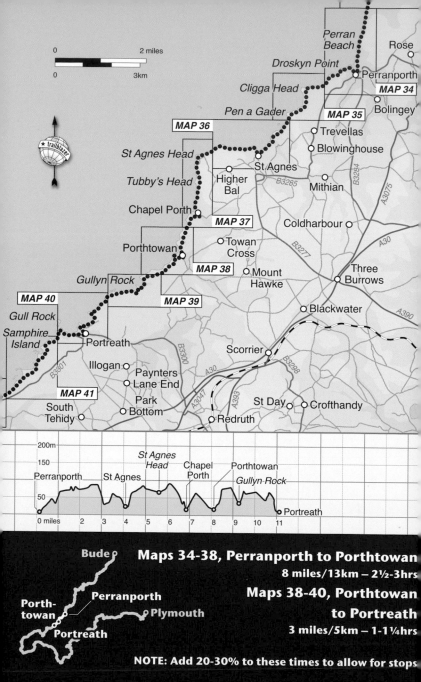

Maps 34-38, Perranporth to Porthtowan
8 miles/13km – 2½-3hrs

Maps 38-40, Porthtowan to Portreath
3 miles/5km – 1-1¼hrs

NOTE: Add 20-30% to these times to allow for stops

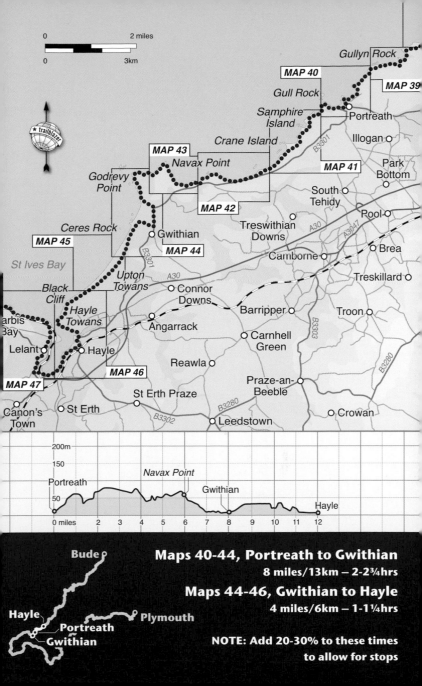

0 .... 2 miles

0 .... 3km

Gullyn Rock

MAP 40

MAP 39

Gull Rock

Samphire
Island

Portreath

Illogan

Crane Island

MAP 43

Navax Point

B3301

Park
Bottom

Godrevy
Point

MAP 41

South
Tehidy

Rool

Ceres Rock

MAP 42

Treswithian
Downs

Brea

MAP 45

Gwithian

MAP 44

A30

A3047

Camborne

Treskillard

St Ives Bay

B3301

Upton
Towans

A30

Connor
Downs

Barripper

B3303

Troon

Black
Cliff

Hayle
Towans

Angarrack

Carnhell
Green

arbis
Bay

Lelant

Hayle

Reawla

Praze-an-
Beeble

B3280

MAP 46

MAP 47

St Erth Praze

Canon's
Town

St Erth

B3302

Leedstown

Crowan

200m

150

Navax Point

Portreath

Gwithian

50

Hayle

0 miles   1   2   3   4   5   6   7   8   9   10   11   12

Bude

Maps 40-44, Portreath to Gwithian
8 miles/13km – 2-2¾hrs

Hayle

Plymouth

Maps 44-46, Gwithian to Hayle
4 miles/6km – 1-1¼hrs

Portreath

Gwithian

**NOTE: Add 20-30% to these times
to allow for stops**

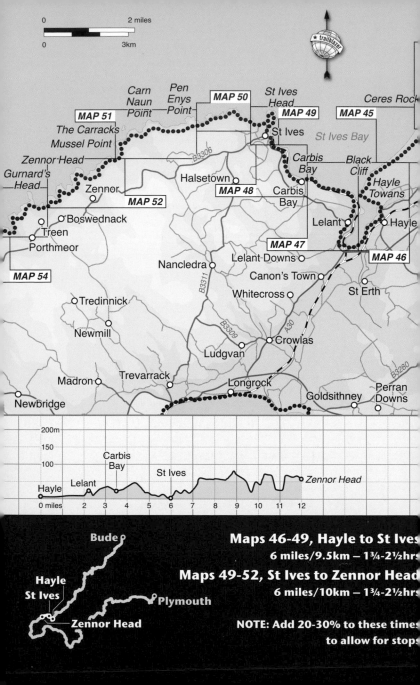

0 | 2 miles
0 | 3km

Carn Naun Point
Pen Enys Point
MAP 50
St Ives Head
Ceres Rock
MAP 51
MAP 49
MAP 45
The Carracks
Mussel Point
St Ives
St Ives Bay
Zennor Head
Carbis Bay
Black Cliff
Gurnard's Head
Halsetown
MAP 48
Carbis Bay
Hayle Towans
Zennor
MAP 52
Carbis Bay
Boswednack
Lelant
Hayle
Treen
Porthmeor
MAP 47
MAP 54
Lelant Downs
MAP 46
Nancledra
Canon's Town
Tredinnick
Whitecross
St Erth
Newmill
Crowlas
Madron
Trevarrack
Ludgvan
Perran Downs
Newbridge
Longrock
Goldsithney

200m
150
100
Carbis Bay
St Ives
Zennor Head
Hayle
Lelant
0
0 miles | 2 | 3 | 4 | 5 | 6 | 7 | 8 | 9 | 10 | 11 | 12

Bude
Hayle
St Ives
Plymouth
Zennor Head

Maps 46-49, Hayle to St Ives
6 miles/9.5km – 1¾-2½hrs

Maps 49-52, St Ives to Zennor Head
6 miles/10km – 1¾-2½hrs

NOTE: Add 20-30% to these times to allow for stops

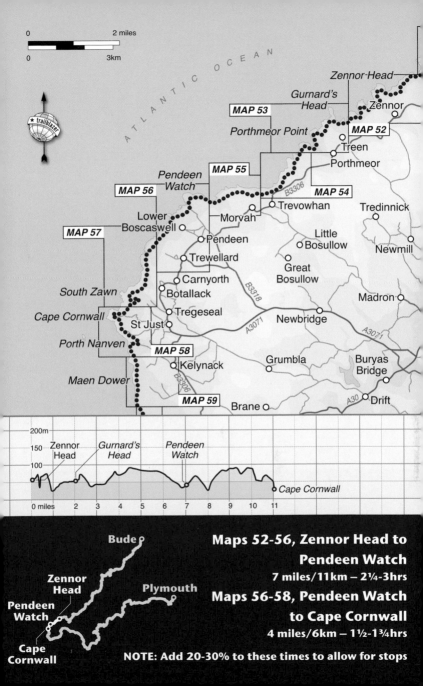

Map features

0 ___ 2 miles
0 ___ 3km

ATLANTIC OCEAN

Zennor-Head

Gurnard's Head

MAP 53

Porthmeor Point

MAP 52

Zennor

Treen

Porthmeor

Pendeen Watch

MAP 55

MAP 54

Trevowhan

Tredinnick

Morvah

MAP 56

B3306

Newmill

Lower Boscaswell

Pendeen

Little Bosullow

MAP 57

Trewellard

Great Bosullow

Carnyorth

Madron

South Zawn

B3318

Botallack

Cape Cornwall

Tregeseal

Newbridge

A3071

A3071

Porth Nanven

St Just

MAP 58

Kelynack

Grumbla

Buryas Bridge

Maen Dower

B3306

MAP 59

Brane

A30

Drift

Elevation profile

200m
150
100

Zennor Head

Gurnard's Head

Pendeen Watch

Cape Cornwall

0 miles   1   2   3   4   5   6   7   8   9   10   11

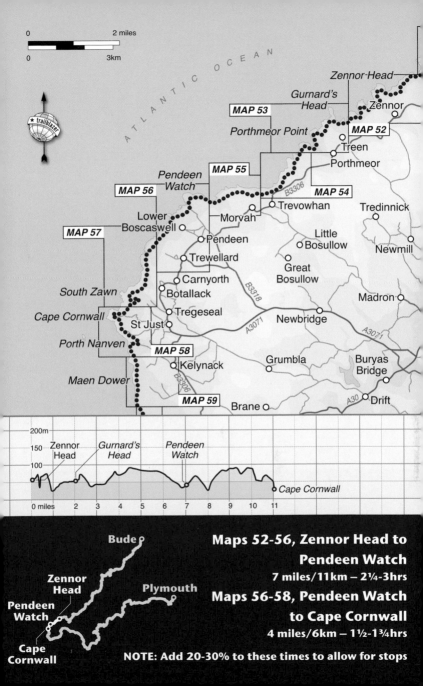

Bude

Zennor Head

Plymouth

Pendeen Watch

Cape Cornwall

Maps 52-56, Zennor Head to Pendeen Watch
7 miles/11km – 2¼-3hrs

Maps 56-58, Pendeen Watch to Cape Cornwall
4 miles/6km – 1½-1¾hrs

NOTE: Add 20-30% to these times to allow for stops

South Zawn
Carnyorth
Botallack
Tregeseal
Cape Cornwall
St Just
Porth Nanven
MAP 58
Madron
B3318
Newbridge
A3071
A3071
Kelynack
Grumbla
Buryas Bridge
Newlyn
MAP 59
B3306
Brane
Drift
Catchall
A30
Kerris
Maen Dower

Aire Point
Whitesand Bay
Sennen
Cove
Carn Towan
The Tribbens
Mayon
MAP 60
Sennen
Dr Syntax's Head
Trevescan
Armed Knight
MAP 61
Trethewey
MAP 63
Treen
MAP 64
Horrace
Carn Lês Boel
Porthcurno
St Levan
Black Carn
Gwennap Head
Porthgwarra
MAP 62
B3315
B3283
Tregadgwith
St Buryan
B3315
MAP 65
MAP 66
Lamorna
Boskenna
Tater-du
Boscawen Point

Tregadgwith

0   2 miles
0   3km

200m
150
100
Cape Cornwall
Dr Syntax's Head
Porthgwarra
Penberth Cove
Sennen Cove
Aire Point
Carn Lês Boel
Porthcurno
Boscawen Point
Lamorna

0 miles   2   3   4   5   6   7   8   9   10   11   12   13   14   15   16

Bude
Plymouth
Cape
Cornwall
Sennen
Cove
Lamorna
Porthcurno

Maps 58-61, Cape Cornwall t
Sennen Cov
5 miles/8km – 1¾-2hr

Maps 61-63, Sennen Cove t
Porthcurn
6 miles/9.5km – 1¾-2½hr

Maps 63-66, Porthcurno t
Lamorn
5 miles/8km – 2-2½hr

NOTE: Add 20-30% to these times to allow for stop

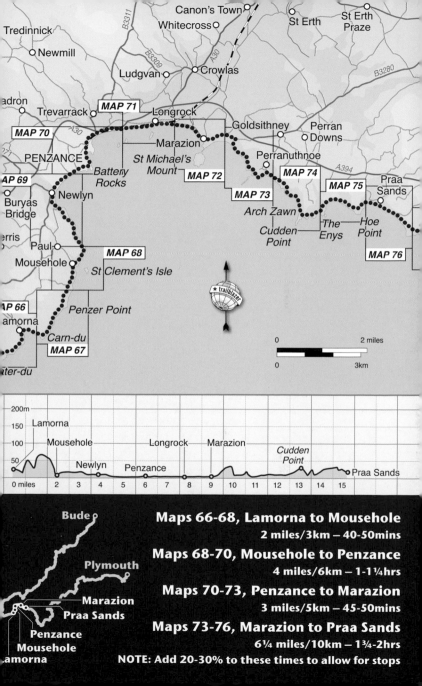

Map labels

Tredinnick
Newmill
Canon's Town
Whitecross
St Erth
St Erth Praze
Ludgvan
Crowlas
adron
Trevarrack
Longrock
MAP 71
Goldsithney
Perran Downs
MAP 70
PENZANCE
Marazion
Perranuthnoe
St Michael's Mount
MAP 72
MAP 74
Praa Sands
AP 69
Battery Rocks
MAP 73
MAP 75
Buryas Bridge
Newlyn
Arch Zawn
The Enys
Hoe Point
erris
Paul
Cudden Point
Mousehole
MAP 68
MAP 76
St Clement's Isle
AP 66
Penzer Point
amorna
Carn-du
MAP 67
ater-du

★ trailblazer

0   2 miles
0   3km

Elevation profile

200m
150
100
50

Lamorna
Mousehole
Longrock
Marazion
Cudden Point
Newlyn
Penzance
Praa Sands

0 miles   2   3   4   5   6   7   8   9   10   11   12   13   14   15

Route summary

Bude
Plymouth
Marazion
Praa Sands
Penzance
Mousehole
amorna

Maps 66-68, Lamorna to Mousehole
2 miles/3km – 40-50mins

Maps 68-70, Mousehole to Penzance
4 miles/6km – 1-1¼hrs

Maps 70-73, Penzance to Marazion
3 miles/5km – 45-50mins

Maps 73-76, Marazion to Praa Sands
6¼ miles/10km – 1¾-2hrs
NOTE: Add 20-30% to these times to allow for stops

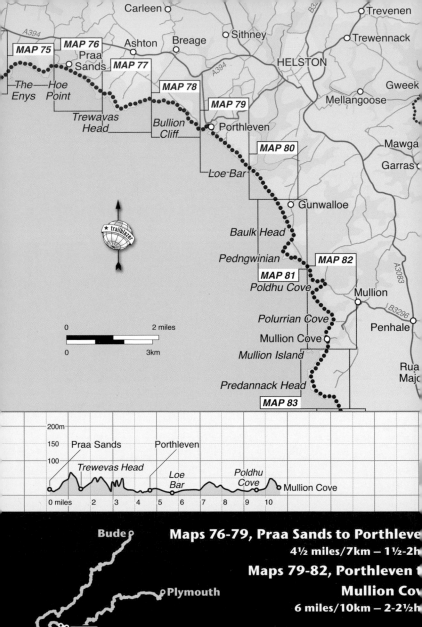

Carleen · Trevenen

MAP 75 · MAP 76 · Praa · Sands · Ashton · Breage · Sithney · Trewennack

The Enys · Hoe Point · MAP 77 · MAP 78 · HELSTON · Gweek

Trewavas Head · Bullion Cliff · MAP 79 · Porthleven · Mellangoose

MAP 80 · Mawga · Garras

Loe Bar · Gunwalloe

Baulk Head · MAP 82 · Mullion

Pedngwinian · MAP 81 · Poldhu Cove · A3083 · Penhale

Polurrian Cove · Mullion Cove · Rua Majo

Mullion Island · Predannack Head · MAP 83

A394 · B32

0 ——— 2 miles
0 ——— 3km

Elevation profile:

200m
150 — Praa Sands · Porthleven
100 — Trewavas Head · Loe Bar · Poldhu Cove · Mullion Cove

0 miles · 2 · 3 · 4 · 5 · 6 · 7 · 8 · 9 · 10

Location map:

Bude
Plymouth
Porthleven
Praa Sands · Mullion Cove

Maps 76-79, Praa Sands to Porthleve

4½ miles/7km – 1½-2h

Maps 79-82, Porthleven t
Mullion Cov

6 miles/10km – 2-2½h

NOTE: Add 20-30% to these tim
to allow for sto

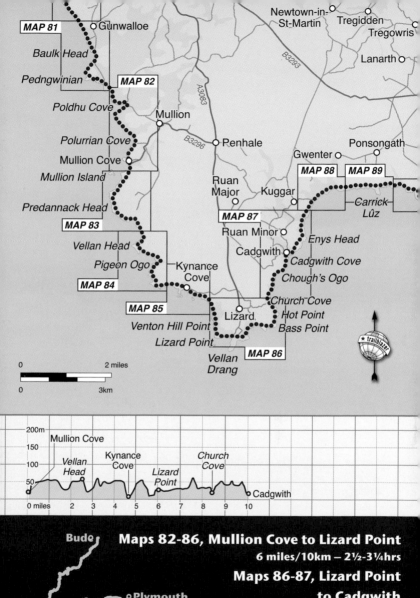

MAP 81
Gunwalloe
Baulk Head
Pedngwinian
MAP 82
Poldhu Cove
Mullion
Polurrian Cove
Mullion Cove
Mullion Island
Predannack Head
MAP 83
Vellan Head
Pigeon Ogo
MAP 84
Kynance Cove
MAP 85
Venton Hill Point
Lizard Point
Vellan Drang
MAP 86
Lizard
Newtown-in-St-Martin
Tregidden
Tregowris
Lanarth
B3293
A3083
Penhale
B3296
Gwenter
Ponsongath
MAP 88
MAP 89
Carrick Lûz
Ruan Major
Kuggar
MAP 87
Ruan Minor
Cadgwith
Enys Head
Cadgwith Cove
Chough's Ogo
Church Cove
Hot Point
Bass Point

trailblazer

0   2 miles
0   3km

200m
150
100
50

Mullion Cove
Vellan Head
Kynance Cove
Lizard Point
Church Cove
Cadgwith

0 miles   2   3   4   5   6   7   8   9   10

Bude

Maps 82-86, Mullion Cove to Lizard Point
6 miles/10km – 2½-3¼hrs

Maps 86-87, Lizard Point to Cadgwith
4 miles/6km – 1½-1¾hrs

Plymouth

Cadgwith
Lizard Point
Mullion Cove

NOTE: Add 20-30% to these times to allow for stops

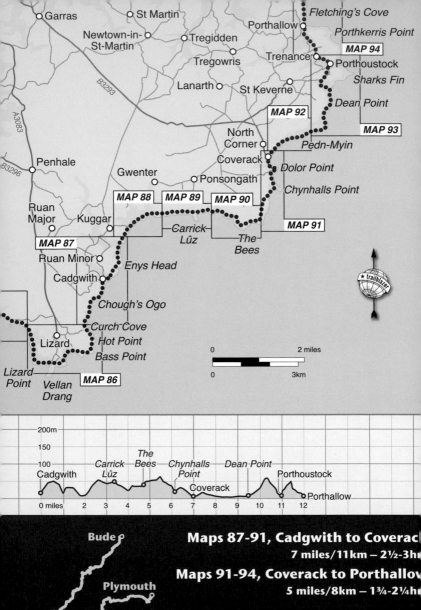

Garras
St Martin
Newtown-in-
St-Martin
Tregidden
Porthallow
Fletching's Cove
Porthkerris Point
Trenance
Tregowris
MAP 94
Tregowris
Porthoustock
Sharks Fin
B3293
Lanarth
St Keverne
St Keverne
MAP 92
Dean Point
MAP 93
A3083
North
Corner
Pedn-Myin
B3296
Penhale
Coverack
Dolor Point
Gwenter
Ponsongath
Chynhalls Point
Ruan
Major
Kuggar
MAP 88
MAP 89
MAP 90
MAP 91
MAP 87
*Carrick
Lûz*
*The
Bees*
Ruan Minor
Cadgwith
Enys Head
Chough's Ogo
Curch Cove
Lizard
Hot Point
Bass Point
*Lizard
Point*
*Vellan
Drang*
MAP 86

0		2 miles
0		3km

200m
150
100
*The
Bees*
Cadgwith
*Carrick
Lûz*
*Chynhalls
Point*
Dean Point
Porthoustock
Coverack
Porthallow
0 miles 2 3 4 5 6 7 8 9 10 11 12

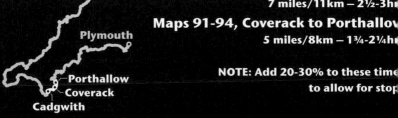

Bude

Plymouth

Porthallow
Coverack
Cadgwith

Maps 87-91, Cadgwith to Coverack
7 miles/11km – 2½-3hr

Maps 91-94, Coverack to Porthallow
5 miles/8km – 1¾-2¼hr

NOTE: Add 20-30% to these time
to allow for stop

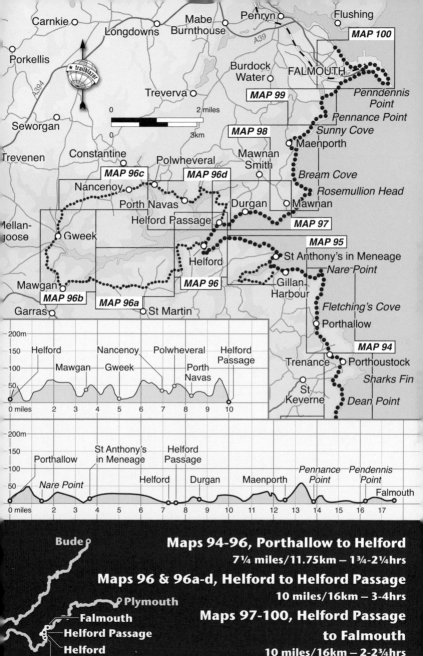

Maps 94-96, Porthallow to Helford
7¼ miles/11.75km – 1¾-2¼hrs

Maps 96 & 96a-d, Helford to Helford Passage
10 miles/16km – 3-4hrs

Maps 97-100, Helford Passage to Falmouth
10 miles/16km – 2-2¾hrs

NOTE: Add 20-30% to these times to allow for stops

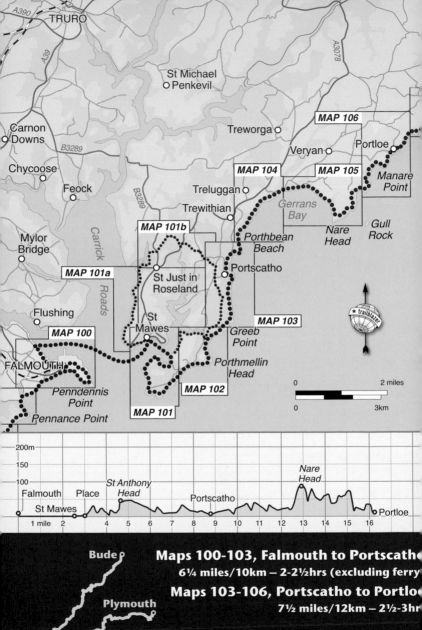

A390
TRURO
A39

St Michael
○ Penkevil

Carnon
○ Downs
B3289

Chycoose

Feock

Treworga ○

Veryan ○

MAP 106

Portloe ○

MAP 104

MAP 105

Treluggan ○

Trewithian ○

*Gerrans
Bay*

*Manare
Point*

*Gull
Rock*

*Nare
Head*

Mylor
Bridge

Carrick

Roads

MAP 101b

St Just in
Roseland

*Porthbean
Beach*

Portscatho

MAP 101a

Flushing

MAP 100

St
Mawes

MAP 103

FALMOUTH

*Penndennis
Point*

MAP 102

*Greeb
Point*

*Porthmellin
Head*

MAP 101

Pennance Point

★ trailblazer

0   2 miles

0   3km

200m
150
100

*St Anthony
Head*

*Nare
Head*

Falmouth

Place

Portscatho

St Mawes

Portloe

1 mile 2   3   4   5   6   7   8   9   10   11   12   13   14   15   16

Bude ○

**Maps 100-103, Falmouth to Portscatho
6¼ miles/10km – 2-2½hrs (excluding ferry**

Plymouth ○

**Maps 103-106, Portscatho to Portloe
7½ miles/12km – 2½-3hr**

○ Portloe
Portscatho
Falmouth

**NOTE: Add 20-30% to these time
to allow for stop**

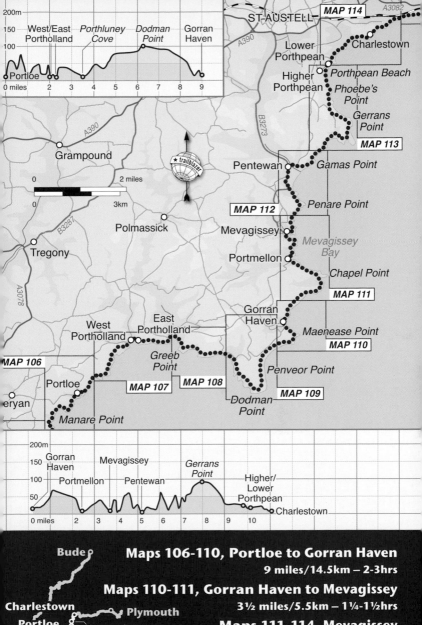

Maps 106-110, Portloe to Gorran Haven

9 miles/14.5km – 2-3hrs

Maps 110-111, Gorran Haven to Mevagissey

3½ miles/5.5km – 1¼-1½hrs

Maps 111-114, Mevagissey

to Charlestown

7¼ miles/11.75km – 2¾-3¾hrs

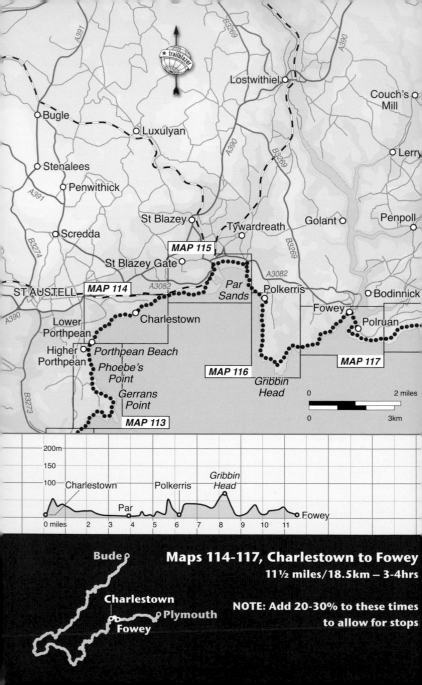

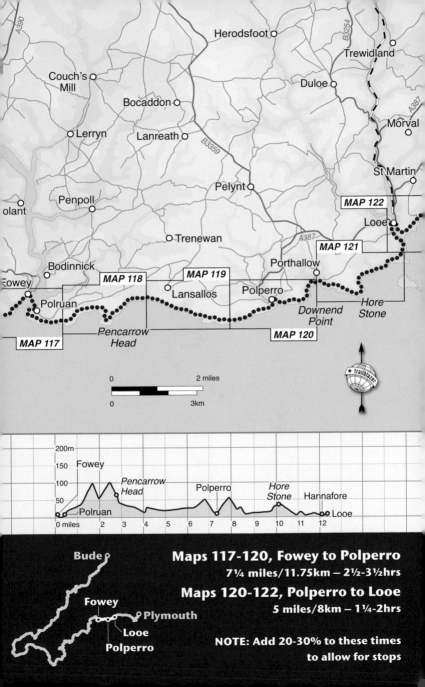

Herodsfoot

Trewidland

Couch's
Mill

Duloe

Bocaddon

Morval

Lerryn

Lanreath

St Martin

Penpoll

Pelynt

MAP 122

Looe

Trenewan

MAP 121

Bodinnick

Porthallow

MAP 118

MAP 119

Fowey

Lansallos

Polperro

Polruan

Downend
Point

Hore
Stone

MAP 117

*Pencarrow
Head*

MAP 120

0   2 miles

0   3km

★ trailblazer

200m

150   Fowey

100   *Pencarrow
Head*   Polperro   *Hore
Stone*   Hannafore

50   Polruan   Looe

0 miles   1   2   3   4   5   6   7   8   9   10   11   12

Bude

Fowey

Plymouth

Looe

Polperro

Maps 117-120, Fowey to Polperro
7¼ miles/11.75km – 2½-3½hrs

Maps 120-122, Polperro to Looe
5 miles/8km – 1¼-2hrs

**NOTE: Add 20-30% to these times
to allow for stops**

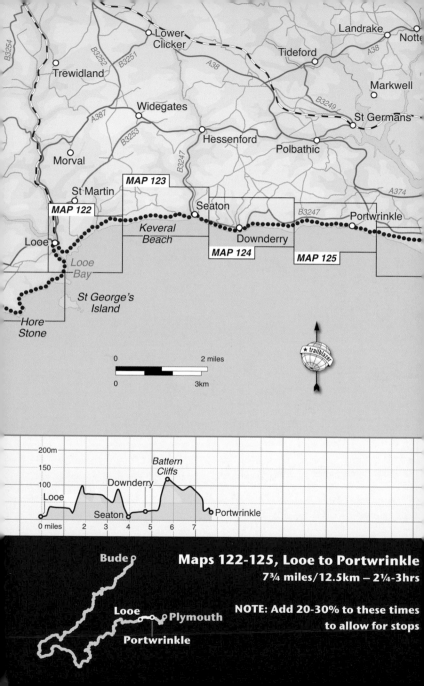

Lower Clicker

Landrake

Notte

Tideford

B3254

Trewidland

B3252

B3251

A38

Markwell

A387

Widegates

B3249

St Germans

B3253

Hessenford

Polbathic

Morval

B3247

A374

MAP 123

St Martin

Seaton

B3247

Portwrinkle

MAP 122

Keveral Beach

Downderry

Looe

MAP 124

MAP 125

Looe Bay

St George's Island

Hore Stone

0   2 miles

0   3km

★ trailblazer

200m

150

Battern Cliffs

100

Downderry

Looe

Seaton

Portwrinkle

0 miles   2   3   4   5   6   7

Bude

Maps 122-125, Looe to Portwrinkle

7¾ miles/12.5km – 2¼-3hrs

Looe   Plymouth

NOTE: Add 20-30% to these times to allow for stops

Portwrinkle

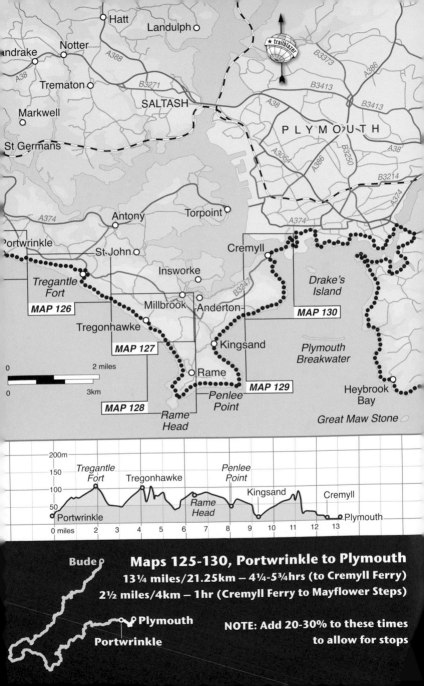

Hatt Landulph

★ trailblazer

ndrake Notter

A388

B3373 B3386

A38

Trematon

B3271

SALTASH

B3413

PLYMOUTH

B3413

Markwell

A38

St Germans

A3064 A386 B3250 A38

B3214

A374

Antony Torpoint

A374

B3374

Portwrinkle

Cremyll

St-John

Insworke

MAP 126

Drake's Island

Tregantle Fort

B3247

MAP 130

Millbrook

Anderton

Tregonhawke

MAP 127

Kingsand

Plymouth Breakwater

0   2 miles

0   3km

Rame

MAP 129

MAP 128

Penlee Point

Heybrook Bay

Rame Head

Great Maw Stone

Maps 125-130, Portwrinkle to Plymouth

13¼ miles/21.25km – 4¼-5¾hrs (to Cremyll Ferry)

2½ miles/4km – 1hr (Cremyll Ferry to Mayflower Steps)

Bude

Plymouth

Portwrinkle

NOTE: Add 20-30% to these times to allow for stops

TRAILBLAZER'S BRITISH WALKING GUIDES

We've applied to destinations which are closer to home Trailblazer's proven formula for publishing definitive practical route guides for adventurous travellers. Britain's network of long-distance trails enables the walker to explore some of the finest landscapes in the country's best walking areas. These are guides that are user-friendly, practical, informative and environmentally sensitive.

'The same attention to detail that distinguishes its other guides has been brought to bear here'.
THE SUNDAY TIMES

● **Unique mapping features** In many walking guidebooks the reader has to read a route description then try to relate it to the map. Our guides are much easier to use because walking directions, tricky junctions, places to stay and eat, points of interest and walking times are all written onto the maps themselves in the places to which they apply. With their uncluttered clarity, these are not general-purpose maps but fully edited maps drawn by walkers for walkers.

● **Largest-scale walking maps** At a scale of just under 1:20,000 (8cm or 3¹/₈ inches to one mile) the maps in these guides are bigger than even the most detailed British walking maps currently available in the shops.

● **Not just a trail guide – includes where to stay, where to eat and public transport** Our guidebooks cover the complete walking experience, not just the route. Accommodation options for all budgets are provided (pubs, hotels, B&Bs, campsites, bunkhouses, hostels) as well as places to eat. Detailed public transport information for all access points to each trail means that there are itineraries for all walkers, for hiking the entire route as well as for day or weekend walks.

Cleveland Way *Henry Stedman,* 1st edn, ISBN 978-1-905864-91-1, 240pp, 98 maps

Coast to Coast *Henry Stedman,* 9th edn, ISBN 978-1-912716-11-1, 268pp, 109 maps

Cornwall Coast Path (SW Coast Path Pt 2) *Stedman & Newton,* 7th edn, ISBN 978-1-912716-26-5, 352pp, 142 maps

Cotswold Way *Tricia & Bob Hayne,* 4th edn, ISBN 978-1-912716-04-3, 204pp, 53 maps

Dales Way *Henry Stedman,* 1st edn, ISBN 978-1-905864-78-2, 192pp, 50 maps

Dorset & South Devon (SW Coast Path Pt 3) *Stedman & Newton,* 2nd edn, ISBN 978-1-905864-94-2, 340pp, 97 maps

Exmoor & North Devon (SW Coast Path Pt I) *Stedman & Newton,* 3rd edn, ISBN 978-1-9912716-24-1, 224pp, 68 maps

Glyndŵr's Way *Chris Scott,* 1st edn, ISBN 978-1-912716-32-6, 220pp, 70 maps

Great Glen Way *Jim Manthorpe,* 2nd edn, ISBN 978-1-912716-10-4, 184pp, 50 maps

Hadrian's Wall Path *Henry Stedman,* 6th edn, ISBN 978-1-912716-12-8, 250pp, 60 maps

London LOOP *Henry Stedman,* 1st edn, ISBN 978-1-912716-21-0, 236pp, 60 maps

Norfolk Coast Path & Peddars Way *Alexander Stewart,* 1st edn, ISBN 978-1-905864-98-0, 224pp, 75 maps

North Downs Way *Henry Stedman,* 2nd edn, ISBN 978-1-905864-90-4, 240pp, 98 maps

Offa's Dyke Path *Keith Carter,* 5th edn, ISBN 978-1-912716-03-6, 268pp, 98 maps

Pembrokeshire Coast Path *Jim Manthorpe,* 6th edn, 978-1-912716-13-5, 236pp, 96 maps

Pennine Way *Stuart Greig,* 5th edn, ISBN 978-1-912716-02-9, 272pp, 138 maps

The Ridgeway *Nick Hill,* 5th edn, ISBN 978-1-912716-20-3, 208pp, 53 maps

South Downs Way *Jim Manthorpe,* 7th edn, ISBN 978-1-912716-23-4, 204pp, 60 maps

Thames Path *Joel Newton,* 3rd edn, ISBN 978-1-912716-27-2, 256pp, 99 maps

West Highland Way *Charlie Loram,* 7th edn, ISBN 978-1-912716-01-2, 218pp, 60 maps

'The Trailblazer series stands head, shoulders, waist and ankles above the rest. They are particularly strong on mapping ...'
THE SUNDAY TIMES

TRAILBLAZER TITLE LIST

For more information about Trailblazer and our
expanding range of guides, for guidebook updates or
for credit card mail order sales visit our website:

www.trailblazer-guides.com

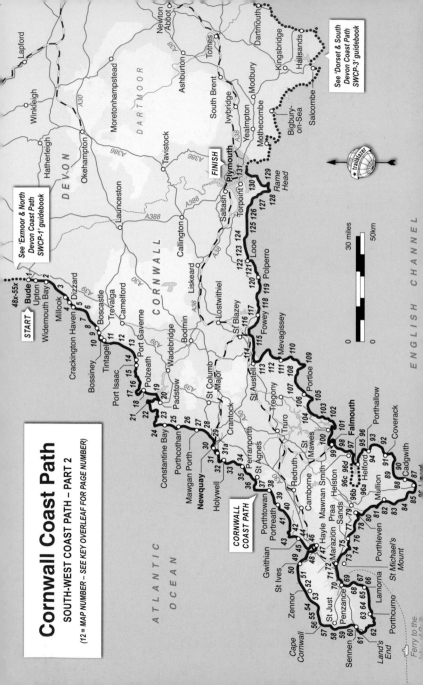

Cornwall Coast Path

SOUTH-WEST COAST PATH – PART 2

(12 = MAP NUMBER – SEE KEY OVERLEAF FOR PAGE NUMBER)

See 'Exmoor & North Devon Coast Path SWCP-1' guidebook

See 'Dorset & South Devon Coast Path SWCP-3' guidebook

CORNWALL COAST PATH

ATLANTIC OCEAN

ENGLISH CHANNEL

DARTMOOR

DEVON

CORNWALL

★ Trailblazer

0   30 miles

0   50km

START Bude

FINISH Plymouth

Ferry to the